P9-DJL-641

AMERICA

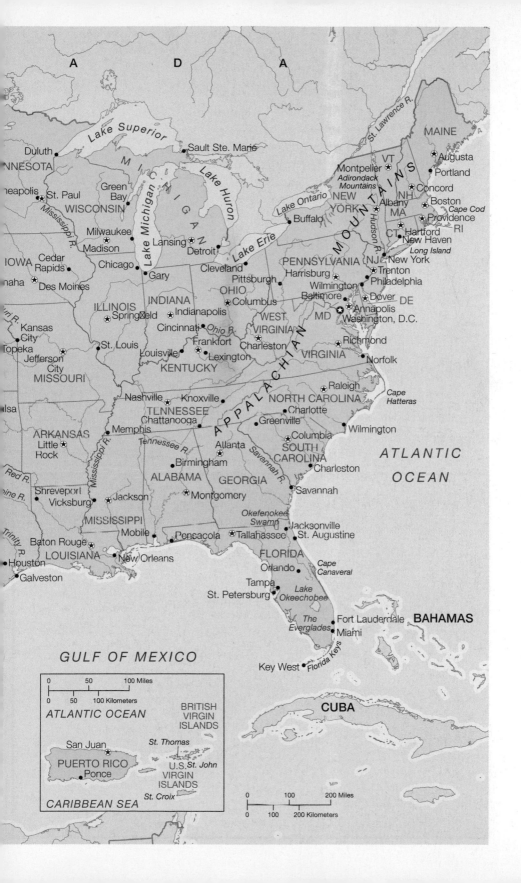

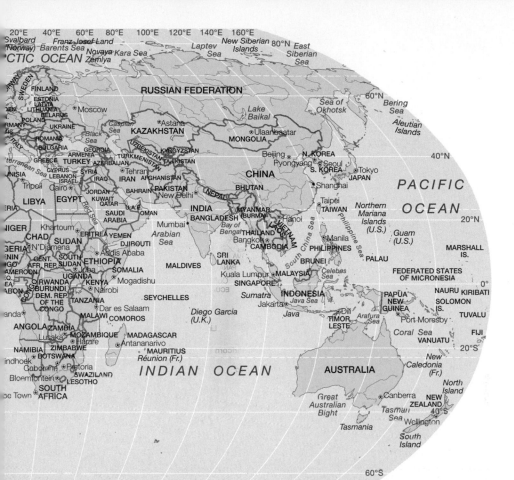

brief tenth edition
VOLUME 1

AMERICA

A Narrative History

David Emory Shi

George Brown Tindall

W. W. NORTON & COMPANY, INC.

New York • London

W. W. Norton & Company has been independent since its founding in 1923, when William Warder Norton and Mary D. Herter Norton first published lectures delivered at the People's Institute, the adult education division of New York City's Cooper Union. The firm soon expanded its program beyond the Institute, publishing books by celebrated academics from America and abroad. By midcentury, the two major pillars of Norton's publishing program—trade books and college texts—were firmly established. In the 1950s, the Norton family transferred control of the company to its employees, and today—with a staff of four hundred and a comparable number of trade, college, and professional titles published each year—W. W. Norton & Company stands as the largest and oldest publishing house owned wholly by its employees.

Copyright © 2016, 2013, 2010, 2007, 2004, 1999, 1996, 1992, 1988, 1984 by W. W. Norton & Company, Inc.

All rights reserved
Printed in the United States of America

Editor: Jon Durbin
Associate Editors: Justin Cahill and Scott Sugarman
Project Editors: Melissa Atkin and Linda Feldman
Editorial Assistant: Travis Carr
Managing Editor, College: Marian Johnson
Managing Editor, College Digital Media: Kim Yi
Production Manager: Ashley Horna
Media Editor: Laura Wilk
Media Project Editor: Penelope Lin
Media Editorial Assistant: Chris Hillyer
Marketing Manager, History: Sarah England
Design Director: Hope Goodell-Miller
Photo Editor: Stephanie Romeo
Permissions Manager: Megan Jackson
Composition: Jouve North America
Manufacturing: Quad Graphics Taunton

Permission to use copyrighted material is included on page A147.

The Library of Congress has cataloged the full edition as follows:

Shi, David E. Tindall, George Brown.
  America: a narrative history / David Emory Shi, George Brown Tindall.
Tenth edition. New York: W.W. Norton & Company, 2016.
  Includes index.
LCCN 2015036484
  ISBN 9780393265934 (hardcover)
LCSH: United States—History—Textbooks.
LCC E178.1 .T55 2017 DDC 973—dc23 LC record available at http://lccn.loc.gov/2015036484

This edition: 9780393265972 (pbk.)

W. W. Norton & Company, Inc., 500 Fifth Avenue, New York, NY 10110-0017
wwnorton.com
W. W. Norton & Company Ltd., 15 Carlisle Street, London W1D 3BS

4 5 6 7 8 9 0

FOR
MY WIFE,
ANGELA HALFACRE SHI

DAVID E. SHI is a professor of history and the president emeritus of Furman University. He is the author of several books on American cultural history, including the award-winning *The Simple Life: Plain Living and High Thinking in American Culture* and *Facing Facts: Realism in American Thought and Culture, 1850–1920*.

GEORGE B. TINDALL, recently of the University of North Carolina, Chapel Hill, was an award-winning historian of the South with a number of major books to his credit, including *The Emergence of the New South, 1913–1945* and *The Disruption of the Solid South*.

CONTENTS

15 The War of the Union, 1861–1865 530

16 The Era of Reconstruction, 1865–1877 578

Glossary A1

Appendix A67

Further Readings

Credits

Index

MAPS

PREFACE

This Tenth Edition of *America: A Narrative History* seeks to improve upon a textbook grounded in a compelling narrative history of the American experience. From the start of our collaboration in 1984, George Tindall and I strove to write an engaging book focused on political and economic developments but animated by colorful characters, informed by balanced analysis and social texture, and guided by the unfolding of key events. Those classic principles, combined with a handy format and low price, have helped make *America: A Narrative History* one of the most popular and well-respected American history textbooks. This brief edition, which I have crafted by streamlining the narrative by nearly 20 percent, remains the most coherent and lively of its kind.

This Tenth Brief Edition of *America* features a number of important changes designed to make the text more teachable and classroom-friendly. Chief among them are major structural changes, including the joining of several chapters to reduce the overall number from thirty-four to thirty-two as well as the resequencing of several chapters to make the narrative flow more smoothly for students. Major organizational changes include:

- New Chapter 6, *Strengthening the New Nation*, combines *Shaping a Federal Union* and *The Federalist Era* from previous editions to better integrate the events after the Revolution.
- New Chapter 19, *Political Stalemate and Rural Revolt, 1865–1900* combines *The Emergence of Urban America* and *Gilded Age Politics and Agrarian Revolt* from previous editions to connect the clash of urban and rural cultures.

In terms of content changes, the overarching theme of the new edition is the importance of the culture of everyday life in understanding American history. While an introductory textbook must necessarily focus on major political, constitutional, diplomatic, economic, and social changes, it is also important to understand how ordinary people managed everyday concerns: housing, jobs, food, recreation, religion, and entertainment.

I have looked to broaden the political narrative by incorporating more social and cultural history into the text, primarily using the refreshed and expanded coverage of the culture of everyday life as the main vehicle for doing so. Key new discussions include:

- Chapter 1, *The Collision of Cultures*, features new material about Native American religious beliefs and practices as well as aspects of everyday life.
- Chapter 2, *England's Colonies*, provides additional insights into the status of indentured servants and slavery in the colonies.
- Chapter 3, *Colonial Ways of Life,* includes a new portrait of Antonio, an enslaved African brutalized by his Dutch owner in Maryland in the mid-seventeenth century. There is also new material about colonial houses, taverns, diets, and the competition among American colonists for British luxury goods in the 1760s and 1770s.
- Chapter 4, *From Colonies to States,* has more material on the nonimportation efforts (boycotts of British goods imported into America) led by ordinary Americans. It also includes new material about the conversion of farmers into soldiers after the shooting at Lexington and Concord.
- Chapter 5, *The American Revolution, 1776–1783*, includes more material about slaves who took advantage of the war to escape or join the British forces, and about the ways in which women, Native Americans, and slaves became engaged in the war effort.
- Chapter 6, *Strengthening the New Nation,* includes more about Shays's Rebellion and other expressions of agrarian discontent across the nation that occurred after the Revolution, and more on how women, Native Americans, and slaves figured into the thinking of the Founding Fathers during the Constitutional Convention in 1787.
- Chapter 7, *The Early Republic, 1800–1815*, has new material on the way in which the War of 1812 affected slavery/blacks.
- Chapter 8, *The Emergence of a Market Economy, 1815–1850*, includes new discussions of the emergence of the cotton culture in the South, the nature of farming, canals, boats, and steamship travel, and the plight of the Irish fleeing the famine at home and heading to America.
- Chapter 9, *Nationalism and Sectionalism, 1815–1828*, more fully fleshes out the role of labor advocates and unions in helping to forge what would become the Jacksonian movement.
- Chapter 10, *The Jacksonian Era, 1828–1840*, describes the effects of the Panic of 1837 and the ensuing depression on the working poor.

- Chapter 11, *The South, Slavery, and King Cotton, 1800–1860*, has substantial new material related to slavery, cotton, and everyday life within African American society. There is also a new discussion of a New Orleans slave uprising led by Charles Deslondes in 1811, the largest slave revolt in American history.
- Chapter 12, *Religion, Romanticism, and Reform, 1800–1860*, includes enriched treatment of the revivalism of the Second Great Awakening, a rewritten discussion of Mormonism, and a new section on Sylvester Graham and his health reform movement (Grahamism).
- Chapter 13, *Western Expansion, 1830-1848,* is enlivened by textured portraits of John Fremont and Sam Houston and a much fuller profile of James K. Polk.
- Chapter 15, *The War of the Union, 1861–1865*, includes new material about the social history of the Civil War, including more material on the everyday life of common soldiers, rioting in opposition to the military draft, and backwoods violence rarely included in discussions of the war, such as the summary of the execution of thirteen Unionists in Madison County, North Carolina.
- Chapter 16, *The Era of Reconstruction, 1865–1877,* has more material about former slaves—from their perspective. It also includes new examples of the ways in which the Freedmen's Bureau helped negotiate labor contracts between white planters and freedmen.
- Chapter 17, *Business and Labor in the Industrial Era, 1860–1900*, discusses the emergence of a new middle class during the Gilded Age, and includes substantially revised material on women's and labor history.
- Chapter 18, *The New South and the New West, 1865–1900,* includes a rewritten section on the emergence of new racial segregation in the South, and also new material about the everyday realities of Western expansion.
- Chapter 21, *The Progressive Era, 1890–1920*, includes new sections on the attitudes of Theodore Roosevelt and Woodrow Wilson concerning race.
- Chapter 22, *America and the Great War, 1914–1920*, now discusses the war's social effects in the United States, with special attention to women, blacks, and Mexican Americans. There is also new material about the grim nature of trench warfare.
- Chapter 23, *A Clash of Cultures, 1920–1929*, includes new material on the consumer culture, women's history, and revised material on the Harlem Renaissance with a new profile of Zora Neale Hurston. There are also fresh treatments of the impact of the radio, automobiles, cinema, and airplanes.

- Chapter 26, *The Second World War, 1933–1945*, includes new material about the social effects of the war at home, including the wartime experience of Mexican Americans.
- Chapter 27, *The Cold War and the Fair Deal, 1945–1952*, includes new coverage of George Kennan's role in inspiring the containment doctrine, women industrial workers, and also the efforts of Latinos to gain equal rights in the aftermath of World War II.
- Chapter 28, *Cold War America, 1950-1959*, features enhanced treatments of the emerging civil rights movement.
- Chapter 29, *A New Frontier and a Great Society, 1960–1968*, includes a new portrait of Fannie Lou Hamer, a black Mississippi activist, in the section on the early civil rights movements.
- Chapter 30, *Rebellion and Reaction, 1960s and 1970s*, includes new material on the women's movement, Mexican Americans, and Native Americans.
- Chapter 32, *Twenty-First-Century America, 1993–Present*, features developments in the twenty-first century—the presidency of Barack Obama , the killing of al-Qaida leader Osama bin Laden, the emergence of the Tea Party and the Occupy Wall Street movements—as well as the stagnant economy in the aftermath of the Great Recession.

In addition, I have incorporated throughout this edition fresh insights from important new scholarly works dealing with many significant topics. Whether you consider yourself a political, social, cultural, or economic historian, you'll find new material to consider and share with your students.

As part of making the new editions even more teachable and classroom friendly, the new Tenth Brief Edition of *America: A Narrative History* also makes history an immersive experience through its innovative pedagogy and digital resources. Norton InQuizitive for History—Norton's groundbreaking, formative, and adaptive new learning program—enables both students and instructors to assess learning progress at the individual and classroom level. The Norton Coursepack provides an array of support materials—free to instructors—who adopt the text for integration into their local learning-management system. The Norton Coursepack includes valuable assessment and skill-building activities like new primary source exercises, guided reading exercises, review quizzes, and interactive map resources. In addition, we've created new Office Hours videos that help students understand the Focus Questions and make history relevant for them (see pages xxiii–xxv for information about student and instructor resources).

MEDIA RESOURCES FOR INSTRUCTORS AND STUDENTS

America's new student resources are designed to make them better readers, guiding them through the narrative while at the same time developing their critical thinking and history skills.

The comprehensive ancillary package features a groundbreaking new formative and adaptive system, as well as innovative interactive resources, including maps and primary sources, to help students master the Focus Questions in each chapter and continue to strengthen the skills they need to do the work of historians. Norton is unique in partnering exclusively with subject-matter experts who teach the course to author these resources. As a result, instructors have all of the course materials they need to successfully manage their U.S. history survey course, whether they are teaching face-to-face, online, or in a hybrid setting.

INSTRUCTOR RESOURCES

LEARNING MANAGEMENT SYSTEM COURSEPACKS: STRONG ASSESSMENT AND LECTURE TOOLS

- **New! Office Hour Videos:** These segments feature David Shi speaking for 90 seconds on the Focus Questions of each chapter. There are over 100 of these new video segments.
- **New! Primary Source Exercises:** These activities feature several primary sources with multiple-choice and short essay questions to encourage close reading and analysis.
- **Guided Reading Exercises:** These exercises are designed by P. Scott Corbett (Ventura College) to help students learn how to read a textbook and, more important, comprehend what they are reading. The reading exercises instill a three-step Note-Summarize-Assess pedagogy. Exercises are based on actual passages from the textbook, and sample feedback is provided to model responses.
- **Interactive iMaps:** These interactive tools challenge students to better understand the nature of change over time by allowing them to explore the different layers of the maps from the book. Follow-up map worksheets help build geography skills by allowing students to test their knowledge by labeling.
- **Review Quizzes:** Multiple-choice, true/false, and chronological-sequence questions allow students to test their knowledge of the chapter content

and identify where they need to focus their attention to better understand difficult concepts.

- **Primary Sources:** Over 400 primary source documents and images are available on the Student Site that accompanies *America: A Narrative History*, Tenth Edition. Instructors and students can use these resources for assignments and further research on each chapter.
- **Norton American History Digital Archive:** The Digital Archive offers roughly 2,000 images and audio and video files spanning American history. The comprehensive collection provides endless opportunities to enhance lecture presentations, build new assignments, and expand your students' comprehension through visual history and artifacts. From government documents, to personal artifacts, this collection enhances students' understanding of history.

INSTRUCTOR'S MANUAL

The Instructor's Manual for *America: A Narrative History*, Tenth Brief Edition, is designed to help instructors prepare lectures and exams. The Instructor's Manual contains detailed chapter outlines, lecture ideas, in-class activities, discussion questions, as well as chapter concept maps.

TEST BANK

The Test Bank contains over 2,000 multiple-choice, true/false, and essay questions. This edition of the Test Bank has been completely revised for content and accuracy. All test questions are now aligned with Bloom's Taxonomy for greater ease of assessment.

LECTURE POWERPOINT SLIDES

These ready-made presentations provide comprehensive outlines of each chapter, as well as discussion prompts to encourage student comprehension and engagement.

STUDENT RESOURCES

NEW! NORTON INQUIZITIVE FOR HISTORY

This groundbreaking formative, adaptive learning tool improves student understanding of the Focus Questions in each chapter. Students receive personalized quiz questions on the topics with which they need the most help. Questions range from vocabulary and concepts to interactive maps and primary sources that challenge students to begin developing the skills necessary to do the work of a historian. Engaging game-like elements motivate students as they learn. As a result, students come to class better prepared to participate in discussions and activities.

NEW! STUDENT SITE

wwnorton.com/college/history/America10

Free and open to all students, Norton Student Site includes additional resources and tools to ensure they come to class prepared and ready to actively participate.

- **Office Hour Videos:** These segments feature David Shi speaking for 90 seconds on the Focus Questions of each chapter. There are over 100 of these new video segments.
- **iMaps:** Interactive maps challenge students to explore change over time by navigating the different layers of the maps from the book. Practice worksheets help students build their geography skills by labeling the locations.
- **Online Reader:** The online reader offers a diverse collection of primary source readings for use in assignments and activities.

PRIMARY SOURCE READERS TO ACCOMPANY *AMERICA: A NARRATIVE HISTORY*

- **New** sixth edition of *For the Record: A Documentary History of America*, by David E. Shi and Holly A. Mayer (Duquesne University), is the perfect companion reader for *America: A Narrative History*. *For the Record* now has 250 primary-source readings from diaries, journals, newspaper articles, speeches, government documents, and novels, including a number of readings that highlight the substantially updated theme of African American history in this new edition of *America*. If you haven't scanned *For the Record* in a while, now would be a good time to take a look.
- **New Norton Mix: American History** enables instructors to build their own custom reader from a database of nearly 300 primary- and secondary-source selections. The custom readings can be packaged as a standalone reader or integrated with chapters from *America* into a custom textbook.

ACKNOWLEDGMENTS

This Tenth Brief Edition of *America: A Narrative History* has been a team effort. Several professors who have become specialists in teaching the introductory survey course helped create the test bank, interactive media, and primary source exercises:

Erik Anderson, San Antonio College
Melissa Weinbrenner, Northeast Texas College
Mark Goldman, Tallahassee Community College
Brian McKnight, University of Virginia at Wise
Laura Farkas, Ivy Tech College–West Lafayette
Jon Lee, San Antonio College

The quality and range of reviews on this project were truly exceptional. The book and its accompanying media components were greatly influenced by the thoughts and ideas of numerous instructors.

Milan Andrejevich, Ivy Tech College–South Bend
Evan Bennett, Florida Atlantic University
Laura Bergstrom, Ivy Tech College–Sellersburg
Keith Berry, Hillsborough Community College
Albert Broussard, Texas A&M, College Station
Blanche Brick, Blinn College
Cory Burger, Ivy Tech College–Terre Haute
Brian Cervantez, Tarrant County College–Northwest Campus

Michael L. Collins, Midwestern State University
Lee Cowan, Tarrant County College
Thomas A. DeBlack, Arkansas Tech University
Scott Derr, Ivy Tech College–Bloomington
S. Matthew DeSpain, Rose State College
Michael Downs, Tarrant County College–Northeast Campus
Shannon Duffy, Southwest Texas State University
Karen Dunn-Haley, University of California, Davis
Stephen D. Engle, Florida Atlantic University
Laura Farkas, Ivy Tech College–West Lafayette
David Haney, Austin Community College
Andrew Hollinger, Tarrant County College–Southeast Campus
Frances Jacobson, Tidewater Community College
Robert MacDonald, Ivy Tech College–Lafayette
Richard McCaslin, University of North Texas–Denton
Suzanne McFadden, Austin Community College
Joel McMahon, Kennesaw State University
Greg Miller, Hillsborough Community College
Catherine Parzynski, Montgomery County Community College
R. Lynn Rainard, Tidewater Community College
Hazel Ramos, Glendale Community College
Nicole Ribianszky, Georgia Gwinnett College
Allen Smith, Ivy Tech College–Indianapolis
Bruce Solheim, Citrus College
Mark Stanley, University of North Texas–Denton
Melissa Weinbrenner, Northeast Texas College

As always, my colleagues at W. W. Norton shared with me their dedicated expertise and their poise amid tight deadlines, especially Jon Durbin, Justin Cahill, Melissa Atkin, Linda Feldman, Travis Carr, Ashley Horna, Laura Wilk, Chris Hillyer, Sarah England, Hope Goodell Miller, Stephanie Romeo, Marne Evans, John Gould, Heather Laskey, and Donna Ranieri.

In addition, Jim Stewart, a patient friend and consummate editor, helped winnow my wordiness.

Finally, I have dedicated this Tenth Brief Edition of *America* to Angela Halfacre Shi, my radiant wife who makes the present as fascinating as the past.

AMERICA

part one

A NOT-SO- "NEW" WORLD

History is filled with ironies. Luck and accidents—the unexpected and unplanned happenings of life—often shape events more than intentions. Long before Christopher Columbus lucked upon the Caribbean Sea in his effort to find a westward passage to the Indies (east Asia), the native peoples he mislabeled "Indians" had occupied and transformed the lands of the Western Hemisphere (also called the Americas—North, Central, and South). The "New World" he found was *new* only to the Europeans who began exploring, conquering, and exploiting the region at the end of the fifteenth century.

1

Over thousands of years, Native American peoples had developed highly sophisticated societies. Some were rooted in agriculture; others focused on trade or the conquest of others. Many Native Americans were healthier, better fed, and lived longer than many Europeans, but they and their cultures were almost destroyed by the arrival of Europeans and Africans. As the two different societies—European and Native American—collided, Indian peoples were exploited, infected, enslaved, displaced, and exterminated.

Yet the conventional story of invasion and occupation oversimplifies the complex process by which Indians, Europeans, and Africans interacted in the colonial period. The Native Americans, also called First Peoples, were more than passive victims of European power; they were trading partners and military allies of the transatlantic newcomers. They became neighbors and advisers, religious converts and loving spouses. As such, they participated actively in the creation of the new society known as America.

The Europeans who risked their lives to settle in the Western Hemisphere were themselves a diverse lot. Young and old, men and women, they came from Spain, Portugal, France, the British Isles, the Netherlands (Holland), Scandinavia, Italy, and the German states (Germany would not become a united nation until the mid–nineteenth century). Some were fortune seekers lusting for gold, silver, and spices. Others were passionate Christians eager to create kingdoms of God in the New World. Still others were adventurers, convicts, debtors, servants, landless peasants, and political or religious exiles. Many were simply seeking opportunities for a better way of life. A settler in Pennsylvania noted that "poor people of all kinds can here get three times the wages for their labor than they can in England."

Yet such wages never attracted sufficient numbers of workers to keep up with the rapidly expanding colonial economies, so Europeans early in the seventeenth century turned to Africa for their labor needs. In 1619, a Dutch warship brought the first twenty Africans to the English settlement at Jamestown, near the coast of Virginia, and exchanged that human cargo for food and supplies. This first of many transactions involving enslaved people in British America would transform American society in ways that no one at the time envisioned.

The intermingling of people, cultures, plants, animals, germs, and diseases from the continents of Africa, Europe, and the Western Hemisphere gave colonial American society its distinctive vitality and variety. In turn, the diversity of the environment and the varying climate spawned different economies and patterns of living in the various regions of North America.

At the same time, bitter rivalries among the Spanish, French, English, and Dutch triggered costly wars in Europe and around the world. The monarchs of Europe struggled to manage often-unruly colonists, many of whom displayed a feisty independence. A British official in North Carolina reported that the colonists were "without any Law or Order. Impudence is so very high, as to be past bearing." The Americans and their British rulers maintained an uneasy partnership throughout the seventeenth century. But as the royal authorities tightened their control during the mid–eighteenth century, they met resistance from colonists, which exploded into revolution.

1

The Collision
of Cultures

De Soto and the Incas This 1596 color engraving shows Spanish conquistador
Hernando de Soto's first encounter with King Atahualpa of the Inca Empire. Although
artist Theodor de Bry never set foot in North America, his engravings helped shape
European Spanish perceptions of Native Americans in the sixteenth century.

D ebate still rages about when and how humans first arrived in North America. Until recently, archaeologists and anthropologists had assumed that ancient peoples, risk-takers from northeast Asia, clothed in animal hides and furs, began following big game animals across the Bering Strait, a sixty-mile-wide waterway that now connects the Arctic and Pacific Oceans. During the Ice Age, however, the Bering Strait was dry—a vast, treeless, windswept landmass (Beringia) that served as a wide, inviting bridge connecting eastern Siberia with Alaska. The oldest place in the Bering region with traces of early human activity is Broken Mammoth, a 14,000-year-old site in central Alaska. More recently, archaeologists in central Texas unearthed evidence of people dating back almost 16,000 years.

Over hundreds of years, small hunting groups crossed into Alaska and then fanned out southward across the entire Western Hemisphere, from the Arctic Circle to the tip of South America. Some of them may also have traveled by boats hugging the coast. One major land pathway followed the Pacific coast, while the other used an open land corridor between two ice sheets east of the Rocky Mountains.

These settlers were skilled hunters and gatherers in search of large grazing mammals, rabbits, whales, seals, fish, and wild plants, berries, roots, and seeds. They also frequently killed each other. As they moved southward toward warmer weather, they trekked across prairies and plains, encountering massive animals unlike any found there today: mastodons, giant sloths, camels, bison (buffalos), lions, saber-toothed tigers, cheetahs, and giant wolves, beavers, and bears.

Recent archaeological discoveries in Pennsylvania, Virginia, and Chile, however, suggest that prehistoric humans may have arrived much earlier

focus questions

1. Why were there so many diverse societies in the Americas before Europeans arrived?

2. What were the major developments in Europe that enabled the Age of Exploration?

3. How were the Spanish able to conquer and colonize the Americas?

4. How did the Columbian Exchange between the "Old" and "New" Worlds affect both societies?

5. In what ways did the Spanish form of colonization shape North American history?

from various parts of Asia—and some may even have crossed the Atlantic Ocean from southwestern Europe. Regardless of when humans first set foot in North America, the continent eventually became a crossroads for various peoples from around the world: Europeans, Africans, Asians, and others, all bringing with them distinctive backgrounds, cultures, technologies, religions, and motivations that helped form the multicultural society known as America.

EARLY CULTURES IN AMERICA

Archaeologists have labeled the earliest humans in North America the *Clovis* peoples, named after a site in New Mexico where ancient hunters around 9500 B.C.E. (before the Common Era) killed tusked woolly mammoths using distinctive "Clovis" stone spearheads. Over many centuries, as the climate warmed, days grew hotter, and many of the largest mammals—mammoths, mastodons, giant bison, and single-hump camels—became extinct.

Over time, the ancient Indians adapted to their diverse environments— coastal forests, grassy plains, southwestern deserts, eastern woodlands. Some continued to hunt large animals; others fished and trapped small game. Some gathered wild plants and herbs and collected acorns and seeds; others farmed. They mastered the use of fire, improved technology such as spear points, basketry, and pottery, and developed their own nature-centered religions.

By about 5000 B.C.E., Native Americans had transformed themselves into farming societies. Agriculture provided reliable, nutritious food, which accelerated population growth and enabled a once nomadic (wandering) people to settle down in villages and become expert at growing the plants that would become the primary food crops of the entire hemisphere, chiefly **maize** (corn), beans, squash, chili peppers, avocados, and pumpkins. Many also grew cotton. The cultivation of such crops enabled Indian societies to grow larger and more complex, with their own distinctive social, economic, and political institutions.

THE MAYAS, INCAS, AND MEXICA

Around 1500 B.C.E., farming towns first appeared in Mexico. Agriculture supported the development of sophisticated communities complete with gigantic temple-topped pyramids, palaces, and bridges in Middle America (*Mesoamerica*, what is now Mexico and Central America, where North and

South America meet). The Mayas, who dominated Central America for more than 600 years, developed a rich written language, and elaborate works of art. They also used sophisticated mathematics and astronomy to create a yearly calendar more accurate than the one the Europeans were using at the time of Columbus.

THE INCAS Much farther south, as many as 12 million people speaking at least twenty different languages made up the sprawling Inca Empire. By the fifteenth century, the Incas' vast realm stretched some 2,500 miles along the Andes Mountains in the western part of South America. The Inca Empire featured irrigated farms, stone buildings, and interconnected networks of roads made of stone.

THE MEXICA (AZTECS) During the twelfth century, the **Mexica** (Me-SHEE-ka)—whom Europeans later called Aztecs ("People from Aztlán," the place they claimed as their original homeland)—began drifting southward from northwest Mexico. Disciplined, determined, and energetic, they eventually took control of the sweeping valley of central Mexico, where they started building the city of Tenochtitlán in 1325 on an island in Lake Tetzcoco, the site of present-day Mexico City. Tenochtitlán would become one of the largest cities in the world.

Warfare was a sacred ritual for the Mexica, but it was a peculiar sort of fighting. The Mexica fought with wooden swords intended to wound rather than kill, since they wanted captives to sacrifice to the gods and to work as slaves. Gradually, they conquered many of the neighboring societies, forcing them to pay tribute (taxes) in goods and services and developing a thriving trade in gold, silver, copper, and pearls, as well as agricultural products. Towering stone temples, broad paved avenues, thriving marketplaces, and some 70,000 adobe huts dominated the dazzling capital city of Tenochtitlán.

When the Spanish invaded Mexico in 1519, they found a vast **Aztec Empire** connected by a network of roads serving 371 city-states organized into thirty-eight provinces. As their empire expanded, the Aztecs had developed elaborate urban societies supported by detailed legal systems; efficient new farming techniques, including irrigated fields and engineering marvels); and a complicated political structure. Aztec rulers were invested with godlike qualities, and nobles, priests, and warrior-heroes dominated the social order.

Like most agricultural peoples, the Mexica were intensely spiritual. Their religious beliefs focused on the interconnection between nature and human life and the sacredness of natural elements—the sun, moon, stars, rain, mountains, rivers, and animals. To please the gods, especially Huitzilopochtli, the Lord of the Sun, and bring good harvests and victory in battle, the Mexica, like most Mesoamericans, regularly offered live human sacrifices in elaborate ceremonies. The constant need for more human sacrifices fed the Mexica's relentless warfare against other indigenous groups.

NORTH AMERICAN CIVILIZATIONS

Many indigenous societies existed north of Mexico, in the present-day United States. They shared several basic spiritual myths and social beliefs, including the sacredness of land and animals (animism); the necessity of communal living; and the importance of collective labor, communal food, and respect for elders. Native Americans did not worship a single god but believed in many "spirits." Many societies also believed in ghosts, the spirits of dead people who acted as bodyguards in battle.

In North America alone, there were probably 10 million native peoples organized into 240 different societies speaking many different languages when the Europeans arrived in the early sixteenth century. Native Americans had well-defined social roles. Men were hunters, warriors, and leaders. Women tended children, made clothes, blankets, jewelry, and pottery; dried animal skins, wove baskets; and gathered, grew, and cooked food. Extended family groups often lived together in a lodge or tipi (a Sioux word meaning "dwelling").

THE SOUTHWEST The dry Southwest (what is now Arizona, New Mexico, Nevada, and Utah) hosted corn-growing societies, elements of which exist today and heirs to which (the Hopis, Zunis, and others) still live in the multistory adobe (sunbaked mud) cliff-side villages (called *pueblos* by the Spanish) erected by their ancient ancestors.

The best known of the Southwest pueblo cultures were the Anasazi (Ancient Ones). They developed extensive settlements in the Four Corners region where the modern-day states of Arizona, New Mexico, Colorado, and Utah meet. Unlike the Aztecs and Incas, Anasazi society was remarkable for *not* having a rigid class structure. The religious leaders and warriors worked much as the rest of the people did, and the Anasazi engaged in warfare only as a means of self-defense. Toward the end of the thirteenth century, a lengthy drought and the aggressiveness of Indian peoples migrating from the north led to the disappearance of Anasazi society.

THE NORTHWEST Along the narrow coastal strip running up the heavily forested northwest Pacific coast, from northern California to Alaska, where shellfish, salmon, seals, whales, deer, and edible wild plants were abundant, there was little need for farming. Because of plentiful food and thriving trade networks, the Native American population was larger and more concentrated than in other regions. The social density enabled the Pacific coast peoples to develop intricate religious rituals and sophisticated woodworking skills, aspects embodied in the carved towering totem poles featuring decorative figures of animals and other symbolic characters. For shelter, they built large, earthen-floored, cedar-plank houses up to 100 feet long, where whole groups of families lived together. Socially, the Indian bands along the northwest Pacific coast were divided into slaves, commoners, and chiefs. Warfare usually was a means to acquire slaves.

THE GREAT PLAINS The many different peoples living on the Great Plains (Plains Indians), a vast, flat land of cold winters and hot summers west of the Mississippi River, and in the Great Basin (present-day Utah and Nevada) included the Arapaho, Blackfeet, Cheyenne, Comanche, Crow, Apache, and Sioux. As nomadic hunter-gatherers, they tracked enormous herds of bison, collecting seeds, nuts, roots, and berries as they roamed.

THE MISSISSIPPIANS East of the Great Plains, in the vast woodlands from the Mississippi River to the Atlantic Ocean, several "mound-building" cultures flourished as predominantly agricultural societies. Between 800 B.C.E. and 400 C.E., the Adena and later the Hopewell peoples developed communities along rivers in the Ohio Valley, where they focused on growing corn, squash, beans, and sunflowers, as well as tobacco for smoking. They left behind enormous earthworks and elaborate **burial mounds** shaped like great snakes, birds, and other animals. Some were nearly a quarter mile long. Artifacts buried in the mounds have revealed a complex social structure featuring a specialized division of labor, whereby different groups performed different tasks for the benefit of the society as a whole.

Like the Adena, the Hopewell developed an extensive trading network from the Gulf of Mexico to Canada, exchanging exquisite carvings, metalwork, pearls, seashells, copper ornaments, and jewelry. By the sixth century, however, the Hopewell culture disappeared, giving way to a new phase of Native American development east of the Mississippi River, the Mississippian

Great Serpent Mound At over 1,300 feet in length and three feet high, this snake-shaped burial mound in Adams County, Ohio, is the largest of its kind in the world.

culture, which flourished from 800 to 1500 c.e. The Mississippians, centered in the southern Mississippi Valley, grew corn, beans, squash, and sunflowers, and built substantial towns around central plazas and temples. Their ability to grow large amounts of corn in the fertile flood plains spurred rapid population growth around regional centers.

CAHOKIA The largest of these advanced regional centers, called *chiefdoms*, was **Cahokia** (1050–1250 c.e.), in southwest Illinois, just a few miles across the Mississippi River from what is now St. Louis, Missouri. There the Mississippians constructed an intricately planned farming settlement with monumental public buildings, spacious ceremonial plazas, and more than 100 flat-topped earthen pyramids with thatch-roofed temples on top. At the height of its influence, Cahokia hosted 15,000 people on some 3,200 acres, making it the largest city north of Mexico.

Cahokia, however, vanished after 1250. The overcutting of trees may have set in motion ecological changes that doomed the community when a massive earthquake struck around 1200 c.e. The loss of trees led to widespread flooding and the erosion of topsoil that finally forced people to seek better lands. As Cahokia disappeared, however, its former residents spread its advanced ways of life to other areas across the Midwest and into what is now the American South.

EASTERN WOODLANDS PEOPLES

After the collapse of Cahokia, the **Eastern Woodlands peoples** rose to dominance along the Atlantic seaboard from Maine to Florida and along the Gulf coast to Louisiana. They included three regional groups distinguished by their different languages: the Algonquian, the Iroquoian, and the Muskogean. These were the societies the Europeans would first encounter when they arrived in North America.

THE ALGONQUIANS The Algonquian-speaking peoples stretched from the New England seaboard to lands along the Great Lakes and into the Upper Midwest, and south to New Jersey, Virginia, and the Carolinas. They constructed no great mounds or temple-topped pyramids. Most Algonquians lived in small, round shelters called *wigwams* or multifamily longhouses. Their towns typically ranged in size from 500 to 2,000 people, but they often moved their villages with the seasons.

The Algonquians along the Atlantic coast were skilled at fishing and gathering shellfish; the inland Algonquians excelled at hunting deer, moose, elk, bears, bobcats, and mountain lions. They often traveled the region's waterways using canoes made of hollowed-out tree trunks (dugouts) or birch bark.

All of the Algonquians foraged for wild food (nuts, berries, and fruits) and practiced agriculture to some extent, regularly burning dense forests to improve soil fertility and provide grazing room for deer. To prepare their vegetable gardens, women broke up the ground with hoes tipped with clam shells or the shoulder blades from deer. In the spring, they planted corn, beans, and squash in mounds. As the cornstalks

Algonquian in war paint From the notebook of English settler John White, this sketch depicts a Native American chieftain.

rose, the tendrils from the climbing bean plants wrapped around them for support. Once the crops ripened, women made a nutritious mixed meal of *succotash*, combining corn, beans, and squash.

THE IROQUOIANS West and south of the Algonquians were the Iroquoian-speaking peoples (including the Seneca, Onondaga, Mohawk, Oneida, and Cayuga nations, as well as the Cherokee and Tuscarora), whose lands spread from upstate New York southward through Pennsylvania and into the upland regions of the Carolinas and Georgia. The Iroquois were farmers who lived in extended family groups (clans), sharing bark-covered *longhouses* in towns of 3,000 or more people. Villages were surrounded by *palisades*, tall fences made of trees intended to fend off attackers.

Unlike the Algonquian culture, in which men were dominant, women held the key leadership roles in the Iroquoian culture. As an Iroquois elder explained, "In our society, women are the center of all things. Nature, we believe, has given women the ability to create; therefore it is only natural that women be in positions of power to protect this function." The oldest woman in each longhouse served as the "clan mother" of the residents. No woman could be a chief; no man could head a clan. Women selected the chiefs, controlled the distribution of property, and planted and harvested the crops. After marriage, the man moved in with the wife's family. In part, the Iroquoian matriarchy reflected the frequent absence of Iroquois men, who as skilled hunters and traders traveled extensively for long periods.

War between rival groups of Native Americans, especially the Algonquians and Iroquois, was commonplace, and success in fighting was a warrior's highest honor. As a Cherokee explained in the eighteenth century, "We cannot live without war. Should we make peace with the Tuscaroras, we must immediately look out for some other nation with whom we can engage in our beloved occupation."

EASTERN WOODLANDS INDIANS The third major Native American group in the Eastern Woodlands included the southern peoples along the Gulf coast who spoke the Muskogean language: the Creeks, Chickasaws, and Choctaws. Like the Iroquois, they were often matrilineal societies, but they had a more rigid class structure. The Muskogeans lived in towns arranged around a central plaza. In the region along the coast of the Gulf of Mexico many of their thatch-roofed houses had no walls because of the hot, humid summers.

Over thousands of years, the native North Americans had displayed remarkable resilience, adapting to the uncertainties of frequent warfare, changing climate, and varying environments. They would display similar resilience in the face of the challenges created by the arrival of Europeans.

EUROPEAN VISIONS OF AMERICA

The European exploration of the Western Hemisphere resulted from several key developments during the fifteenth century. In Europe, dramatic intellectual changes and scientific discoveries transformed religion, warfare, family life, and the economy. In addition, the resurgence of old vices—greed, conquest, exploitation, oppression, racism, and slavery—would help fuel European expansion abroad.

A severe population decline caused by warfare, famine, and plagues (the Black Death) left once-great noble estates without enough workers to maintain them. By the end of the fifteenth century, medieval feudalism's static agrarian social system, in which serfs worked for local nobles in exchange for living on and farming the land, began to disintegrate, and a new "middle class" of profit-hungry bankers, merchants, and investors emerged.

A growing trade-based economy in Europe freed monarchs from their dependence on feudal nobles, enabling them to unify the scattered cities ruled by princes (principalities) into large kingdoms with stronger, more centralized governments. The rise of towns, cities, and a merchant class provided kings and queens with new tax revenues, and the once dominant nobility was gradually displaced by powerful new merchants, bankers, and monarchs.

THE RENAISSANCE At the same time, the rediscovery of ancient Greek and Roman writings about representative government (republics) spurred an intellectual revolution known as the *Renaissance* (rebirth). Educated people throughout Europe began to challenge prevailing beliefs as well as the absolute authority of rulers and churchmen. They discussed controversial new ideas about politics, religion, and science; engaged in scientific research; and unleashed their artistic creativity.

The Renaissance also brought the practical application of new ideas that sparked the Age of Exploration. New knowledge and new technologies made possible the construction of larger sailing ships capable of oceanic voyages. The development of more-accurate magnetic compasses, maps, and navigational instruments such as *astrolabes* and *quadrants* helped sailors determine their ship's location. The fifteenth and sixteenth centuries also brought the invention of gunpowder, cannons, and firearms—and the printing press.

THE RISE OF GLOBAL TRADE By 1500, trade between western European nations and the Middle East, Africa, and Asia was flourishing. The Portuguese, blessed with expert sailors and fast, three-masted ships called *caravels*, took the lead, roaming along the west coast of Africa. Eventually, these mariners continued all the way around Africa in search of the fabled Indies (India and Southeast Asia), then on to China and Japan, where they found what they had dreamed about: spices, silk cloth, and other exotic trade goods.

By the end of the fifteenth century, four powerful nations had emerged: England, France, Portugal, and Spain. The marriage of King Ferdinand of Aragon and Queen Isabella of Castile in 1469 led to the unification of their two kingdoms into a single new nation, Spain, and the king and queen were eager to spread the Catholic faith around the world. On January 1, 1492, after nearly eight centuries of religious warfare between Spanish Christians and Moorish Muslims, Ferdinand and Isabella declared victory for Catholicism at Granada, the last Muslim stronghold. The Christian monarchs gave the defeated Muslims, and soon thereafter, the Jews living in Spain and Portugal (called Sephardi), the same desperate choice: convert to Catholicism or leave.

The forced exile of Muslims and Jews was one factor that prompted Europe's involvement in global expansion. Other factors—urbanization, world trade, the rise of centralized nations, plus advances in knowledge, technology, and firepower—combined with natural human curiosity, greed, and religious zeal to spur the exploration and conquest of the Western Hemisphere. Beginning in the late fifteenth century, Europeans set in motion the events that, as one historian has observed, would bind together "four continents, three races, and a great diversity of regional parts."

THE VOYAGES OF COLUMBUS

Born in Genoa, Italy, in 1451, the son of a weaver, Christopher Columbus took to the sea at an early age, teaching himself geography, navigation, and Latin. By the 1480s, he was eager to win glory and riches and to spread Christianity across the globe. The tall, red-haired Columbus eventually persuaded Ferdinand and Isabella to finance his voyage. They agreed to award him a one-tenth share of any riches he gathered; they would keep the rest.

CROSSING THE ATLANTIC On August 3, 1492, Columbus and a crew of ninety men and boys set sail on three tiny ships, the *Santa María*, the *Pinta*, and the *Niña*. They traveled first to Lisbon, Portugal, and then headed west. For weeks they journeyed across the open sea, hoping to sight land, only to be disappointed. By early October, the worried sailors rebelled at the "madness" of sailing blindly and forced Columbus to promise that they would turn back if land were not sighted within three days.

Then, at dawn on October 12, a sailor named Rodrigo, on watch atop the masthead, yelled, "Tierra! Tierra!" ("Land! Land!"). He had spotted a small island in the Bahamas east of Florida that Columbus named San Salvador (Blessed Savior). Columbus mistakenly assumed that they must be near the Indies, so he called the island people "Indios." At every encounter with these peaceful native people, known as Tainos or Arawaks, his first question was whether they had any gold. If they did, the Spaniards seized it; if they did not, the Europeans forced them to search for it. Columbus described the Arawaks as "well-built, with good bodies, and handsome features. Their hair is short and coarse, almost like the hairs of a horse's tail." He marveled that they "would make fine servants," boasting that "with fifty men we could subjugate them all and make them do whatever we want." Thus began the typical European bias displayed toward the Indians: destroy or enslave them.

COLUMBUS'S VOYAGES

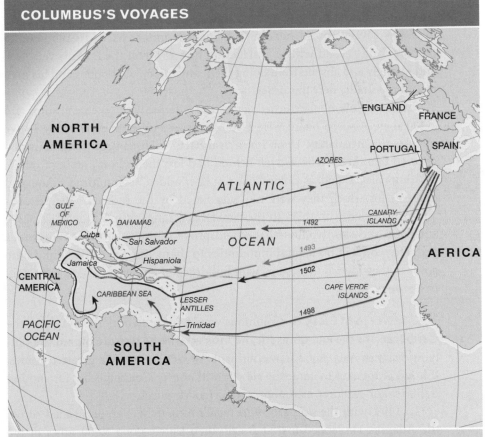

- How many voyages did Columbus make to the Americas?
- What is the origin of the name for the Caribbean Sea?
- What happened to the colony that Columbus left on Hispaniola in 1493?

EXPLORING THE CARIBBEAN After leaving San Salvador, Columbus continued to search for a passage to the Indies. He went ashore in Cuba, sword in one hand, cross in the other, exclaiming that this is the "most beautiful land human eyes have ever beheld." After a few weeks, he sailed eastward to the island he named Hispaniola (now Haiti and the Dominican Republic). There he found indigenous people who wore gold jewelry and introduced him to smoking tobacco.

At the end of 1492, Columbus, still convinced he had reached an outer island of Japan, sailed back to Spain after leaving about forty men on Hispaniola and capturing a dozen Arawaks to present as gifts to the Spanish king and queen. Upon reaching Spain, he received a hero's welcome. He promised Ferdinand and Isabella that his discoveries would provide them "as much gold as they need . . . and as many slaves as they ask."

Thanks to the newly invented printing press, news of Columbus's path-breaking voyage spread rapidly. The Spanish monarchs told Columbus to prepare for a second voyage, instructing him to "treat the Indians very well and lovingly and abstain from doing them any injury." Columbus and his men would repeatedly defy this order.

In 1493, Columbus returned across the Atlantic with seventeen ships and 1,400 men. Also on board were Catholic priests eager to convert the native peoples to Christianity. Upon his arrival back in Hispaniola, Columbus discovered that the men he had left behind had lost their senses, raping women, robbing villages, and, as Columbus's son later added, "committing a thousand excesses for which they were mortally hated by the Indians." The Europeans also carried with them to the Americas a range of infectious diseases—smallpox, measles, typhus—that would prove disastrous for the indigenous peoples, who had no natural immunities to them. The Spaniards found little gold, so they loaded their ships with hundreds of enslaved Indians to be sold in Europe.

NAMING AMERICA Columbus would make two more voyages to the Caribbean. To the end of his life, he insisted that he had discovered the outlying parts of Asia, not a new continent. By one of history's greatest ironies, this led Europeans to name the New World not for Columbus but for another Italian sailor-explorer, astronomer Amerigo Vespucci.

In 1499, with the support of Portugal's monarchy, Vespucci sailed across the Atlantic. He landed first at Brazil, then sailed along 3,000 miles of the South American coastline in hope of finding a passage to Asia. In the end, Vespucci reported that South America was so large that it must be a *new* continent rather than Asia. In 1507, a German mapmaker paid tribute to Vespucci's navigational skills by labeling the New World using a variant of his first name: America.

PROFESSIONAL EXPLORERS News of the remarkable voyages of Columbus and Vespucci stimulated other expeditions to the Western Hemisphere. Over the next two centuries, Spain, Portugal, France, Britain, the Netherlands, and Russia would dispatch ships and claim territory in the Americas by "right of discovery."

The first explorer to sight the North American continent was John Cabot, an Italian sponsored by King Henry VII of England. Cabot's landfall in 1497 at what the king called "the new founde lande," in present-day Canada, gave England the basis for a later claim to all of North America.

Lusting for gold and sudden riches, the Spanish still sought a passage from the Atlantic to the Pacific to reach Asia. In 1505, a Spanish ship unloaded pigs and goats in Puerto Rico, intending them to grow and multiply in anticipation of settling a colony there. Puerto Rico would be the first European settlement on what would become a territory of the United States of America.

In 1519, Ferdinand Magellan, a Portuguese sea captain hired by the Spanish, discovered the strait at the southern tip of South America that now bears his name. Magellan then kept sailing north and west across the Pacific Ocean, making landfall on the island of Guam and, eventually, the Philippines, where indigenous people killed him. Surviving crew members made their way back to Spain, and their dramatic accounts of the voyage around the world quickened Spanish interest in global exploration.

RELIGIOUS CONFLICT IN EUROPE

At the same time that explorers were crossing the Atlantic, powerful religious conflicts were tearing Europe apart in ways that would greatly influence settlement in the New World. The Protestant Reformation became one of the most powerful forces reshaping Europe—and its colonies.

MARTIN LUTHER The supremacy of the Roman Catholic Church in Europe began to crack in 1517 when Martin Luther (1483–1546), a German priest who taught at the University of Wittenburg, launched the **Protestant Reformation**.

Luther undermined the authority of the Catholic Church by calling the pope "the greatest thief and robber that has appeared or can appear on earth" and by criticizing the sale of *indulgences* (whereby priests would forgive sins in exchange for money or goods). God alone, through Christ, he insisted, offered people salvation; people could not earn it or buy it. As Luther exclaimed, "By faith alone are you saved!"

Luther tried to democratize Christianity by centering faith on the individual believer rather than in the authority of the church. He urged believers to read the Bible and not blindly follow the dictates of Catholic priests and the distant pope. The people, he claimed, represented a "priesthood of all believers," perhaps his most revolutionary idea.

Lutheranism exploded Catholic assumptions and certainties like a bomb. Angry Catholic officials lashed out against their critics, calling Luther a "wild boar" and "a leper with a brain of brass and a nose of iron." When the pope expelled Luther from the Catholic Church in 1521 and sentenced him to death, civil war erupted throughout the German principalities. Amid the fighting, a powerful German prince protected Luther from the Church's wrath.

What had begun as a fierce religious drama now became a political reformation, too. Luther was no longer simply an outspoken priest; he was a spiritual revolutionary, a folk hero, and a political prophet, encouraging German princes and dukes to separate themselves from the Italian papacy. A settlement between warring Lutherans and Catholics did not come until 1555, when each prince was allowed by the Treaty of Augsburg to determine the religion of his subjects.

JOHN CALVIN   Soon after Martin Luther began his revolt against Catholicism, Swiss Protestants also challenged papal authority. They were led by John Calvin (1509–1564), a brilliant French scholar who had fled Catholic France to more tolerant Geneva and brought the Swiss city under the sway of his powerful beliefs. In his great theological work, *The Institutes of the Christian Religion* (1536), Calvin taught that all Christians were damned by Adam's original sin, but Christ's sacrifice on the cross made possible the redemption of those whom God "elected" to be saved and thus had "predestined" to salvation.

Intoxicated by godliness, Calvin insisted that a true Christian practiced strict morality and hard work. Moreover, he taught that God valued all forms of work, even the most lowly. Calvin also permitted church members a share in governance through a body of elders and ministers called the presbytery. His doctrines formed the basis for the German Reformed Church, the Dutch Reformed Church, the Presbyterians in Scotland, some of the Puritans in England (and, eventually, in America), and the Huguenots in France.

John Calvin exerted a greater influence upon religious belief and practice in the English colonies than did any other leader of the Reformation. His insistence on the freedom of individual believers, as well as his recognition that monarchs and political officials were sinful like everyone else, helped contribute to the evolving ideas of representative democracy, whereby the people elected their rulers, and of the importance of separating church power from state (governmental) power.

THE PROTESTANT REVOLUTION

Even though the Catholic Church launched an aggressive Counter-Reformation, the Protestant revolt continued to spread rapidly. Most of northern Germany, along with Scandinavia, became Lutheran; the areas that did so often called themselves the "Protesting Estates," from which came the label "Protestants." Throughout the sixteenth and seventeenth centuries, Catholics and Protestants persecuted, imprisoned, tortured, and killed each other in large numbers in Europe—and in the Americas. Every major international conflict involved, to some extent, a religious holy war between Catholic and Protestant nations. The Protestant worldview, with its emphasis on the freedom of the individual conscience and personal Bible reading, would play a major role in the colonization of America.

THE REFORMATION IN ENGLAND In England, the Reformation followed a unique course, blending aspects of Protestantism with Catholicism. The Church of England, or the Anglican Church, emerged through a gradual process of integrating Calvinism with English Catholicism. In early modern England, the church and government were united and mutually supportive. The monarchy required people to attend religious services and to pay taxes to support the church. English rulers also supervised the church officials and often instructed religious leaders to preach sermons in support of particular government policies. As one English king explained, "People are governed by the pulpit more than the sword in time of peace."

KING HENRY VIII Purely political reasons initially led to the rejection of papal authority in England. Henry VIII, who ruled between 1509 and 1547, won from the pope the title Defender of the Faith for refuting Martin Luther's rebellious ideas. Henry's marriage to Catherine of Aragon, his brother's widow, had produced no male heir, however, and for him to marry again required that he convince the pope to annul, or cancel, his marriage. Catherine, however, was the aunt of Charles V, king of Spain and ruler of the Holy Roman Empire, whose support was vital to the Catholic Church. The pope refused to grant an annulment. Henry angrily responded by severing England's nearly 900-year-old connection with the Catholic Church. He then named a new archbishop of Canterbury, who granted the annulment, thus freeing Henry to marry his mistress, Anne Boleyn.

In one of history's greatest ironies, Anne Boleyn gave birth not to the male heir that Henry demanded but to a daughter named Elizabeth. The disappointed king took vengeance on his wife, accusing her of adultery, ordering her beheaded, and declaring the infant Elizabeth a bastard. Yet Elizabeth grew up to be quick-witted and nimble, cunning and courageous. After the bloody reigns of her Protestant half brother, Edward VI, and her Catholic half sister, Mary I, she ascended to the throne in 1558, at the age of twenty-five. Over the next forty-five years, Elizabeth proved to be the greatest female ruler in history. Her long reign was punctuated by political turmoil, religious strife, economic crises, and foreign wars. Yet Queen Elizabeth ruled confidently over England's golden age.

The Spanish Empire

During the sixteenth century, Spain was creating the world's most powerful empire at the same time it was trying to repress the Protestant Reformation. At its height, Spain controlled much of Europe, most of the Americas, parts of Africa, and various trading outposts in Asia.

But it was the gold and silver looted from the Americas that fueled Spain's "Golden Empire." By plundering, conquering, and colonizing the Americas and converting and enslaving its inhabitants, the Spanish planted Christianity in the Western Hemisphere and gained the resources to rule the world.

The Caribbean Sea served as the gateway through which Spanish power entered the Americas. After establishing colonies on Hispaniola, the Spanish proceeded eastward to Puerto Rico (1508) and westward to Cuba (1511–1514). Their motives, as one soldier explained, were "to serve God and the king, and also to get rich."

A Clash of Cultures

The often-violent relationship between the Spanish and Indians involved more than a clash between different peoples. It also involved contrasting forms of technological development. The Indians of Mexico used wooden canoes for transportation, while the Europeans crossed the ocean in heavily armed sailing vessels. Arrows and tomahawks were seldom a match for guns, cannons, and warhorses. A Spanish priest observed that gunpowder "frightens the most valiant and courageous Indian and renders him slave to the white man's command."

The Europeans enjoyed other cultural advantages. Before their arrival, for example, the only domesticated four-legged animals in North America were dogs and llamas. The Spanish brought with them strange beasts: horses, pigs, sheep, and cattle. Horses provided greater speed in battle and gave the Spanish a decided psychological advantage. "The most essential thing in new lands is horses," reported one Spanish soldier. "They instill the greatest fear in the enemy and make the Indians respect the leaders of the army." Even more feared among the Indians were the fighting dogs that the Spanish used to guard their camps.

CORTÉS'S CONQUEST The most dramatic European conquest on the North American mainland occurred in Mexico. On February 18, 1519, thirty-four-year-old Hernán Cortés, driven by dreams of gold and glory, set sail for Mexico from Cuba. His fleet of eleven ships carried nearly 600 soldiers and sailors. After landing on the coast of the Gulf of Mexico, Cortés convinced the Totomacs, a society conquered by the Mexica, to join his assault against the dominant Mexica, their hated rivals. To prevent his heavily armored soldiers, called *conquistadores* (conquerors), from retreating or deserting, Cortés had the ships dismantled. Conquistadores were widely recognized as the best soldiers in the world, loyal to the monarchy and the Catholic Church.

Cortés brashly set out to conquer the sprawling Mexica (Aztec) Empire, which extended from central Mexico to what is today Guatemala. The nearly 200-mile march through the mountains to the Mexica capital of Tenochtitlán (modern Mexico City) took nearly three months. Along the way, Cortés used treachery and terror to intimidate and then recruit the native peoples, most of whom had been conquered earlier by the Mexica. After entering the city of Cholula, he learned of a plot to ambush his army. He turned the tables on his hosts by inviting the local chieftains and nobles to the city's ceremonial plaza to talk and exchange gifts. When they arrived, the Spanish and their Indian allies, the Tlaxcalans, killed the leaders as well as thousands of other Cholulans.

SPANISH INVADERS As Cortés and his invading army continued their march across Mexico, they heard fabulous accounts of Tenochtitlán, the Aztec capital. With some 200,000 inhabitants, it was larger than most European cities. Graced by wide canals and bridges, stunning gardens, and formidable stone pyramids, the lake-encircled city and its stone buildings seemed impregnable. One Spanish conquistador described his first glimpse of the great capital city: "Gazing on such wonderful sights we did not know what to say or whether what appeared before us was real; for on the one hand there were great cities and in the lake ever so many more, and the lake itself was crowded with canoes, and in the causeway were many bridges at intervals, and in front of us stood the great City of Mexico, and we—we did not number even four hundred soldiers!"

Yet the Spanish made the most of their assets—their fighting experience, superior weapons, numerous Indian allies, and an aggressive sense of religious and racial superiority. Through a combination of threats and deceptions, the invaders entered Tenochtitlán peacefully and captured the emperor, Montezuma II. Cortés explained to the emperor why the invasion was necessary: "We Spaniards have a disease of the heart that only gold can cure." Montezuma submitted, in part because he mistook Cortés for a god.

After taking the Aztecs' gold and silver, sending 20 percent of it to the Spanish king (referred to as "the royal fifth"), and dividing the rest among themselves, the Spanish forced Montezuma to provide laborers to mine more of the precious metals. Then, in the spring of 1520, disgruntled Mexica decided that Montezuma was a traitor. They stoned him to death and attacked Cortés's forces. Forced to retreat, the Spaniards lost about a third of their men. Their 20,000 Indian allies remained loyal, however, and Cortés's forces gradually regrouped. They eventually surrounded the imperial city, cutting off its access

Cortés in Mexico Page from the *Lienzo de Tlaxcala*, a historical narrative from the sixteenth century. The scene, in which Cortés is shown seated on a throne, depicts the arrival of the Spanish in Tlaxcala.

to water and food and allowing a highly infectious smallpox epidemic to devastate the inhabitants. One of the Mexica reported that smallpox "spread over the people as great destruction. Some it covered on all parts—their faces, their heads, their breasts, and so on. There was great havoc. Very many died of it. . . . They could not move; they could not stir."

For three months, the Mexica bravely defended their capital, but the ravages of smallpox and the support of thousands of anti-Aztec Indians help explain how a small force of determined Spaniards was able to vanquish a proud nation of nearly 1 million people. After the Aztecs surrendered, a merciless Cortés ordered the leaders hanged and the priests devoured by dogs. He reported that, in the end, 117,000 Aztecs were killed. In two years, the Spanish and their Indian allies had conquered a fabled empire that had taken centuries to develop. The conquest of Mexico established the model for waves of plundering conquistadores to follow.

In 1531, Francisco Pizarro led a band of conquistadores down the Pacific coast of South America from Panama toward Peru, where they brutally subdued the huge Inca Empire. The Spanish invaders seized Inca palaces, took royal women as mistresses and wives, and looted the empire of its gold and silver. From Peru, Spain extended its control southward through Chile and north to present-day Colombia.

SPANISH EXPLORERS Throughout the sixteenth century, the Spanish expanded their control over much of North America, looting and destroying the native peoples, then forcing them to work the mines and plantations in return for learning the Spanish language and embracing the Catholic religion. Juan Ponce de León, then governor of Puerto Rico, made the earliest-known exploration of what the Spanish called La Florida—the Land of Flowers—in 1513.

Sixteenth-century knowledge of the North American interior came mostly from would-be conquistadores who plundered the region. The first, Pánfilo de Narváez, landed in 1528 at Tampa Bay, marched northward to Alabama, and then returned to the Gulf coast, where he and his crew built crude boats out of animal hides and headed for Mexico. High winds and heavy seas wrecked the vessels on the Texas coast. Some of the survivors worked their way overland. After *eight* years, including periods of captivity among the Indians, they wandered into a Spanish outpost in Mexico.

In 1539, Hernando de Soto, a conquistador who had helped conquer the Incas in Peru, explored Florida. He and his crew landed on Florida's west coast, traveled north as far as western North Carolina, and then moved westward, becoming the first Europeans to see the Mississippi River. Along the way, they looted and destroyed Native American villages and took enslaved Indians with

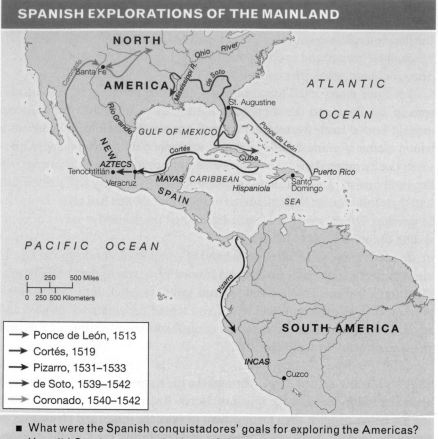

SPANISH EXPLORATIONS OF THE MAINLAND

→ Ponce de León, 1513
→ Cortés, 1519
→ Pizarro, 1531–1533
→ de Soto, 1539–1542
→ Coronado, 1540–1542

■ What were the Spanish conquistadores' goals for exploring the Americas?
■ How did Cortés conquer the Aztecs?
■ Why did the Spanish first explore North America, and why did they establish St. Augustine, the first European settlement in what would become the United States?

them in chains and iron collars. De Soto tried to impress the Indians by claiming to be "a son of the sun."

In the spring of 1542, having wandered America for three years, de Soto died near Natchez, Mississippi. The next year, the survivors among his party floated down the Mississippi River, and 311 of them found their way to Spanish Mexico. They left behind a trail of infectious diseases which continued to ravage the Indians for years.

NEW SPAIN The Spanish established provinces in North America not so much as commercial enterprises but as protective buffers to defend their empire in Mexico and South America. They were concerned about French traders infiltrating from Louisiana, English settlers crossing into Florida, and Russian seal hunters wandering down the California coast.

As the sixteenth century unfolded, the Spanish shifted from looting the native peoples to enslaving them. To reward the crusading conquistadores, Spain transferred to America a medieval socioeconomic system known as the *encomienda*, whereby favored army officers were given huge parcels of land. They were to provide the Indians with protection in exchange for "tribute"—goods and labor, tending farms or mining for gold and silver. New Spain therefore developed a society of extremes: wealthy *encomenderos* and powerful priests at one end of the spectrum, and Indians held in poverty at the other. The Spaniards used brute force to ensure that Indians accepted their new role as servants.

A CATHOLIC EMPIRE The Spanish (and later the French) launched a massive effort to convert the Indians (deeming them "heathens") into Catholic servants. Many of the Catholic missionaries believed that the Indians of Mexico could be converted only by force. "Though they seem to be a simple people," a Spanish priest declared in 1562, "they are up to all sorts of mischief, and are obstinately attached to the rituals and ceremonies of their forefathers. The whole land is certainly damned, and without compulsion, they will never speak the [religious] truth." By the end of the sixteenth century, there were more than 300 monasteries or missions in New Spain, and Catholicism had become a major instrument of Spanish imperialism.

Some Spanish officials criticized the abuse of Indians. In 1514, the Catholic priest Bartolomé de Las Casas (1474–1566) began urging the Spanish to change their approach: "Everything done to the Indians thus far," he claimed, "was unjust and tyrannical."

Las Casas spent the next fifty years advocating better treatment for indigenous people. He was officially named "Protector of the Indians." Las Casas insisted that the Indians should be converted to Catholicism only through "peaceful and reasonable" means. His courageous efforts aroused furious opposition, however. Most colonizers believed, as a Spanish bishop in Mexico declared in 1585, that the Indians must be "ruled, governed, and guided" to Christianity "by fear more than by love."

A leading Spanish scholar, Juan Ginés de Sepúlveda, claimed that the Indians were as inferior "as children are to adults, as women are to men, as different from Spaniards as cruel people are from mild people." Over time, however, Las Casas convinced the monarchy and the Catholic Church to issue new rules calling for better treatment of the Indians in New Spain. At Las Casas's urging, Pope Paul III declared that Indians were human beings deserving of respect

Missionaries in the "New World" A Spanish mission in New Mexico, established to spread the Catholic faith among the indigenous peoples.

and Christian salvation. Still, the use of "fire and the sword" continued. On returning to Spain, Las Casas said, "I left Christ in the Indies not once, but a thousand times beaten, afflicted, insulted and crucified by those Spaniards who destroy and ravage the Indians."

THE COLUMBIAN EXCHANGE

The first European contacts with the Western Hemisphere began the **Columbian Exchange** (also called the Great Biological Exchange), a worldwide transfer of plants, animals, and diseases. Europeans had never seen iguanas, bison, cougars, armadillos, opossums, sloths, tapirs, anacondas, condors, or hummingbirds. Nor had Native Americans seen horses, cattle, pigs, sheep, goats, chickens, and rats, which soon flooded the Americas.

THE EXCHANGE OF PLANTS AND FOODS The exchange of plant life between the Western Hemisphere and Europe/Africa transformed the diets of both regions. Before Columbus's voyage, three foods were unknown in Europe: maize (corn), potatoes (sweet and white), and many kinds of beans (snap, kidney, lima, and others). Other Western Hemisphere food plants included peanuts, squash, peppers, tomatoes, pumpkins, pineapples, sassafras, papayas, guavas, avocados, cacao (the source of chocolate), and chicle (for chewing gum). Europeans in turn introduced rice, wheat, barley, oats, wine grapes, melons, coffee, olives, bananas, "Kentucky" bluegrass, daisies, and dandelions to the Americas.

This biological exchange was more complementary than competitive. Corn, it turned out, could flourish almost anywhere. The new food crops transferred from the Americas helped spur a dramatic increase in the European population that in turn helped provide the restless, adventurous young people who would colonize the New World.

AN EXCHANGE OF DISEASES The most significant aspect of the biological exchange, however, was not food crops but the transmission of **infectious diseases**. During the three centuries after Columbus's first voyage, Europeans and enslaved Africans brought with them deadly diseases that Native Americans had never encountered: smallpox, typhus, diphtheria, bubonic plague, malaria, yellow fever, and cholera.

The results were catastrophic. Far more Indians—tens of millions—died from infections than from combat. Smallpox was an especially ghastly killer. In central Mexico alone, some 8 million people, perhaps a third of the entire Indian population, died of smallpox within a decade of the arrival of the Spanish. A Spanish explorer noted that half the Indians died from smallpox and "blamed us." Often there were not enough survivors to bury the dead; Europeans arrived at villages to discover only rotting corpses strewn everywhere. Unable to explain or cure the diseases, Native American chieftains and religious leaders often lost their stature—and their lives, as they were usually the first to meet the Spanish and thus were the first infected. As a consequence of losing their leaders, the indigenous peoples were less capable of resisting the European invaders. Many Europeans, however, interpreted such epidemics as diseases sent by God to punish those who resisted conversion to Christianity.

THE SPANISH IN NORTH AMERICA

Throughout the sixteenth century, no European power other than Spain held more than a brief foothold in what would become the United States. By the time the English established Jamestown in Virginia in 1607, the Spanish had already explored the Smoky Mountains and the Great Plains, and established colonies in the Southwest and Florida.

ST. AUGUSTINE The first Spanish outpost in the continental United States emerged in response to French actions. In the 1560s, spirited French Protestants (called Huguenots) established France's first American colonies, one on the coast of what became South Carolina and the other in Florida. They did not last long.

In 1565, the Spanish founded St. Augustine on the Atlantic coast of Florida. It became the first European town in the present-day United States. It included a fort, church, hospital, fish market, and more than 100 shops and houses—all built decades before the first English settlements in America.

In September 1565, Spanish soldiers from St. Augustine assaulted Fort Caroline, the French Huguenot colony in northeastern Florida, and hanged all men over age fifteen. The Spanish commander notified his Catholic king that he had killed all the French he "had found [in Fort Caroline] because . . . they were scattering the odious Lutheran doctrine in these Provinces." Later, when survivors from a shipwrecked French fleet washed ashore on Florida beaches after a hurricane, the Spanish commander told them they must abandon Protestantism and swear their allegiance to Catholicism. When they refused, he killed 245 of them.

THE SPANISH SOUTHWEST

The Spanish eventually established other permanent settlements in what are now New Mexico, Texas, and California. From the outset, the Spanish settlements in America were sparsely populated, inadequately supplied, and dreadfully poor. These northernmost regions of New Spain were so far from the capital in Mexico City that they were regularly neglected.

NEW MEXICO The land that would later be called **New Mexico** was the first center of Catholic missionary activity in the American Southwest. In 1595, Juan de Oñate, whose wife was a descendant of both Cortés and Montezuma II, received a land grant for *El Norte*, the mostly desert territory north of Mexico above the Rio Grande. Over the next three years, he recruited an army of colonists willing to move north: soldier-settlers and hundreds of Mexican Indians and *mestizos* (the offspring of Spanish and indigenous parents).

In 1598, the caravan of colonists, including women, children, and 7,000 cattle, horses, goats, and sheep, began moving north from the mountains above Mexico City across the harsh desert landscape of parched mesas, plateaus, and canyons enlivened by lush river valleys. "O God! What a lonely land!" one of the footsore travelers wrote. Upon crossing the Rio Grande at what became El Paso, Texas, Oñate claimed the entire region for the Spanish monarchy. Indians who resisted were killed. A priest recorded that Oñate "had butchered many Indians, human blood has been shed, and he has committed thefts, sackings, and other atrocities."

After walking more than 800 miles in seven months along ancient Indian footpaths that the Spanish settlers called the *Camino Real* (royal road), they established the colony of New Mexico, the farthest outpost of New Spain. The Spanish called the local Indians "Pueblos" (a Spanish word meaning village) for the city-like aspect of their terraced, multistoried buildings, sometimes chiseled into the walls of cliffs. They also dug out underground chambers called *kivas*, where they held religious ceremonies and stored sacred objects such as prayer sticks and feathered masks.

The Pueblos (mostly Hopis and Zunis) were farmers who used irrigation to water their crops. They were also skilled at making clay pottery and woven baskets. Some of the Native Americans wore buffalo skins, most wore decorative cotton blankets. "Their corn and vegetables," Oñate reported, "are the best and largest to be found anywhere in the world." Most of their customs resembled those practiced by the Mexicans. "Their government," he noted, "is one of complete freedom, for although they have chieftains, they obey them badly and in few matters."

Unlike the later English colonists in America, Spanish officials did not view Native Americans as *racially* inferior. Instead, they believed that the Indians were "burdened" by *culturally* inferior ways of life. The Spanish government never intended to establish large colonies of Spanish immigrants in America but to force the Native Americans to adopt Spanish ways of life. Oñate, New Mexico's first governor, told the Pueblos that if they embraced Catholicism and followed his orders, they would receive "an eternal life of great bliss" instead of "cruel and everlasting torment."

Oñate soon discovered that there was no gold or silver in New Mexico. Nor was there enough corn and beans to feed the Spanish invaders, who had to be resupplied by expensive caravans traveling for months from Mexico City. Oñate eventually established a system that forced the Indians to pay annual tributes (taxes) to the Spanish authorities in the form of a yard of cloth and a bushel of corn.

CATHOLIC MISSIONS Once it became evident that New Mexico had little gold, the Spanish focused their attention on religious conversion. Priests established Catholic missions where Indians were forced to work the fields they had once owned and perform personal tasks for the priests and soldiers, cooking, cleaning, and even providing sexual favors. Soldiers and priests used whips to herd the Indians to church services and to punish them for not working hard enough. A French visitor to a mission reported that it "reminded us of a . . . West Indian [slave] colony."

Some Indian peoples welcomed the Spanish missionaries as "powerful witches" capable of easing their burdens. Others tried to use the European invaders as allies against rival Indian groups. Still others rebelled. Before the end of New Mexico's first year, in December 1598, the Acoma Pueblos revolted, killing eleven soldiers.

Oñate's response to the rebellion was brutal. Over three days, Spanish soldiers destroyed the entire pueblo, killing 500 Pueblo men and 300 women and children. Survivors were enslaved. Twenty-four Pueblo men had one foot cut off to frighten others and keep them from escaping or resisting. Children were taken from their parents into a Catholic mission, where, Oñate remarked, "they may attain the knowledge of God and the salvation of their souls."

THE MESTIZO FACTOR   Spanish women were prohibited from traveling to the New World unless they were married and accompanied by a husband. As a result, there were so few Spanish women in North America that soldiers and settlers often married Native Americans or otherwise fathered mestizos. By the eighteenth century, mestizos were a majority in Mexico and New Mexico. Such widespread intermarriage and interbreeding led the Spanish to adopt a more inclusive social outlook toward the Indians than the English later did in their colonies along the Atlantic coast. Once most colonial officials were mestizo themselves, they were less likely to belittle the Indians. At the same time, many Native Americans falsely claimed to be mestizo as a means of improving their status and avoiding having to pay annual tribute.

THE PUEBLO REVOLT   The Spanish presence in New Mexico expanded slowly. In 1608, the government decided to turn New Mexico into a royal province and moved its capital to Santa Fe ("Holy Faith" in Spanish), the first permanent seat of government in the present-day United States. By 1630, there were fifty Catholic churches and monasteries in New Mexico as well as some 3,000 Spaniards.

Resentment among the Indians increased as the Spanish stripped them of their ancestral ways of life and forced them to embrace Christianity. In 1680, a charismatic Indian spiritual leader named Popé (meaning "Ripe Plantings") organized a massive rebellion. The Spanish claimed that he had cast a magical spell over his people, making "them crazy." The Indians, painted for war, burned Catholic churches, tortured, mutilated, and executed priests, destroyed all relics of Christianity, and forced the 2,400 survivors to flee in humiliation. The entire province of New Mexico was again in Indian hands.

The Pueblo Revolt of 1680 was the greatest defeat that Indians ever inflicted on European efforts to conquer the New World. It took twelve years and four military assaults for the Spanish to reestablish control over New Mexico.

Plains Indians The horse-stealing raid depicted in this hide painting demonstrates the essential role horses played in Plains life.

HORSES AND THE GREAT PLAINS

Another major consequence of the Pueblo Revolt was the opportunity it gave Indian rebels to gain possession of thousands of Spanish horses. The Pueblos in turn established a thriving horse trade with the Navajos, Apaches, and others. Stealing horses became one of the most honored ways for warriors to prove their courage. Horses soon spread across the Great Plains, the vast rolling grasslands extending from the Missouri Valley in the east to the base of the Rocky Mountains in the west.

HORSES AND INDIAN CULTURE The introduction of the horse provided the Plains Indians with a new source of mobility and power. The vast grasslands of the Great Plains were the perfect environment for horses, since the prairies offered plenty of forage for grazing animals. Horses could also haul up to seven times as much weight as dogs, and their speed and endurance made the indigenous people much more effective hunters and warriors. On the Great Plains, an Indian family's status reflected the number of horses it owned.

By the late seventeenth century, Native American horsemen were fighting the Spaniards on more equal terms. This helps explain why the Indians of the Southwest and Texas, unlike the Indians in Mexico, were able to sustain their cultures for the next 300 years: on horseback, they were among the most fearsome fighters in the world.

BISON HUNTING   Horses transformed the economy and ecology of the Great Plains. The Arapaho, Cheyenne, Comanche, Kiowa, and Sioux reinvented themselves as horse-centered cultures. They left their traditional woodland villages on the fringes of the plains and became nomadic bison (buffalo) hunters.

Indians used virtually every part of the bison they killed: meat for food; hides for clothing, shoes, bedding, and shelter; muscles and tendons for thread and bowstrings; intestines for containers; bones for tools; horns for eating utensils; hair for headdresses; and dung for fuel. They used tongues for hair brushes and tails for fly swatters. One scholar has referred to the bison as the "tribal department store."

Horses eased some of the physical burdens on women, but also imposed new demands. Women and girls tended to the horses, butchered and dried the bison meat, and tanned the hides. As the value of the hides grew, Indian hunters began practicing polygamy, primarily for economic reasons: more wives could process more bison carcasses. The rising value of wives eventually led Plains Indians to raid other tribes in search of captive brides.

The introduction of horses into the Great Plains was a mixed blessing. The horse brought prosperity and mobility but also triggered more conflict. Over time, the Indians on horseback eventually killed more bison than the herds could replace. Further, horses competed with the bison for food, often depleting the prairie grass. And, as Indians on horses traveled greater distances and encountered more people, infectious diseases spread more widely.

HISPANIC AMERICA

Spain's colonial presence in the Americas lasted more than three centuries, much longer than either England's or France's. New Spain was centered in Mexico, but its borders extended from Florida to Alaska. Hispanic placenames—San Francisco, Santa Barbara, Los Angeles, San Diego, Tucson, Santa Fe, San Antonio, Pensacola, and St. Augustine—survive to this day, as do Hispanic influences in art, architecture, literature, music, law, and cuisine.

The Spanish encounters with Indians produced a two-way exchange by which the contrasting societies blended, coexisted, and interacted. Even when locked in mortal conflict and driven by hostility and mutual suspicion, the two cultures eventually developed a mutual accommodation that enabled their living traditions to persist side by side.

Challenges to the Spanish Empire

Catholic Spain's successful conquests in the Western Hemisphere spurred Portugal, France, England, and the Netherlands (Holland) to begin their own exploration and exploitation of the New World.

The French were the first to pose a serious threat. Spanish treasure ships sailing home from Mexico, Peru, and the Caribbean offered tempting targets for French pirates. In 1524, the French king sent Italian Giovanni da Verrazano westward across the Atlantic. Upon sighting land (probably at Cape Fear, North Carolina), Verrazano ranged along the coast as far north as Maine. On a second voyage, in 1528, he was killed by Carib Indians.

NEW FRANCE The three voyages of Jacques Cartier, beginning in the next decade, led to the first French effort at colonization in North America. Cartier explored the Gulf of St. Lawrence and ventured up the St. Lawrence River, now the boundary between Canada and New York. But France after midcentury plunged into religious civil wars, and the colonization of Canada had to await the coming of Samuel de Champlain, "the Father of New France," after 1600. Champlain would lead twenty-seven expeditions from France to Canada during a thirty-seven-year period.

THE DUTCH REVOLT From the mid-1500s, greater threats to Spanish power in the New World arose from the Dutch and the English. In 1566, the Netherlands included seventeen provinces. The fragmented nation had passed by inheritance to the Spanish king in 1555, but the Dutch spurned Catholicism and had become largely Protestant (mostly Calvinists making up what was called the Dutch Reformed Church). During the second half of the sixteenth century, the Dutch began a series of sporadic rebellions against Spanish Catholic rule. During the long, bloody struggle for political independence and religious freedom, Protestant England aided the Dutch. The Dutch revolt was not a single cohesive event but a series of uprisings in different provinces at different times. Each province had its own institutions, laws, and rights. Although seven provinces joined together to form the Dutch Republic, the Spanish did not officially recognize the independence of the entire Netherlands until 1648.

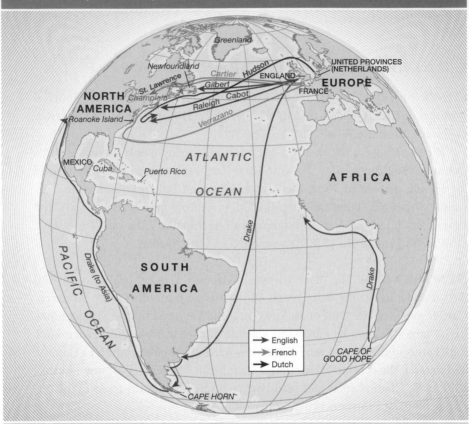

ENGLISH, FRENCH, AND DUTCH EXPLORATIONS

- Who were the first European explorers to rival Spanish dominance in the New World, and why did they cross the Atlantic?
- Why was the defeat of the Spanish Armada important to the history of English exploration?
- What was the significance of the voyages of Gilbert and Raleigh?

THE DEFEAT OF THE ARMADA Almost from the beginning of the Protestant revolt in the Netherlands, the Dutch captured Spanish treasure ships in the Atlantic and carried on illegal trade with Spain's colonies. While England's Queen Elizabeth worked to avoid open war with Spain, she encouraged both Dutch and English privateers to attack Spanish ships and their colonies in America.

The English raids on Spanish ships continued for some twenty years before open war erupted between the nations. Determined to conquer England, Philip II, the king of Spain who was Queen Elizabeth's brother-in-law and fiercest opponent, assembled the massive **Spanish Armada**: 132 warships, 8,000 sailors, and 18,000 soldiers. On May 28, 1588, the Armada sailed for England. The English navy was waiting for them.

As the two fleets positioned themselves for the battle, Queen Elizabeth donned a silver breastplate and told the English forces, "I know I have the body of a weak and feeble woman, but I have the heart and stomach of a king, and a King of England too." As the battle unfolded, the heavy Spanish galleons could not compete with the speed and agility of the English warships. The English fleet chased the Spanish ships through the English Channel.

Caught in a powerful "Protestant wind" from the south, the Spanish fleet was swept into the North Sea. The decimated armada limped home, scattering wreckage on the shores of Scotland and Ireland.

The stunning defeat of Spain's fearsome Armada greatly strengthened the Protestant cause across Europe. Queen Elizabeth commissioned a special medallion to commemorate the victory. The citation read, "God blew and they were dispersed." Spain's King Philip seemed to agree. Upon learning of the catastrophic defeat, he sighed, "I sent the Armada against men, not God's winds and waves."

The defeat of the Spanish Armada confirmed England's naval supremacy, cleared the way for its colonization of America, and established Queen Elizabeth's stature as a great ruler. Although she had many suitors eager to marry her, she refused to divide her power. She would have "but one mistress [England] and no master." Eager to live and die a virgin, she married herself to the fate of England. By the end of the sixteenth century, Elizabethan England had begun an epic transformation from a poor, humiliated, and isolated nation into a mighty global empire.

ENGLISH EXPLORATION OF AMERICA

English efforts to colonize America began a few years before the great battle with the Spanish Armada. They were driven by a desire to weaken Spain's control over the Americas. In 1578, Queen Elizabeth had given Sir Humphrey Gilbert permission to establish a colony in the "remote heathen and barbarous lands" of America.

Gilbert's group set out in 1583, intending to settle near Narragansett Bay (in present-day Rhode Island). They instead landed in fogbound Newfoundland (Canada). With winter approaching and his largest vessels lost, Gilbert and the colonists returned home. While in transit, however, his ship vanished, and he was never seen again.

The English in Virginia The arrival of English explorers on the Outer Banks, with Roanoke Island at left.

The next year, Queen Elizabeth asked Sir Walter Raleigh, Gilbert's half-brother, to organize a colonizing mission. Raleigh's expedition discovered the Outer Banks of North Carolina and landed at Roanoke Island. Raleigh named the area Virginia in honor of Elizabeth, the presumably "Virgin Queen," as she once described herself.

After several false starts, Raleigh in 1587 sponsored another expedition of about 100 colonists, including 26 women and children, led by Governor John White. White spent a month on Roanoke Island and then returned to England for supplies, leaving behind his daughter Elinor and his granddaughter Virginia Dare, the first English child born in the New World. White's journey back to Virginia was delayed because of the naval war with Spain. When he finally returned, in 1590, the Roanoke outpost had been abandoned and pillaged. The rude cabins had been dismantled and removed, suggesting that the colonists had left intentionally. On a post at the entrance to the village, someone had carved the word "CROATOAN," leading White to conclude that the settlers had set out for the island of that name some 50 miles south, where friendly Indians lived.

The "lost colonists" were never found. They may have been killed by Indians or Spaniards, but recent evidence indicates that the "Lost Colony" suffered from a horrible drought that prevented the colonists from growing enough food to survive.

There were no English colonists in North America when Queen Elizabeth died in 1603. The Spanish controlled the only colonial outposts on the continent. But that was about to change. Inspired by the success of the Spanish in exploiting the New World, and emboldened by their defeat of the Spanish Armada in 1588, the English—as well as the French and Dutch—would soon develop American colonial empires of their own.

NEW SPAIN IN DECLINE

During the one and a half centuries after 1492, the Spanish developed the most extensive, rich, and envied empire the world had ever known. It spanned southern Europe and the Netherlands, much of the Western Hemisphere, and parts of Asia. While Spanish rulers financed their imperial ambitions with silver and gold looted from the Americas, they mobilized huge armies and the naval armada in an effort to conquer Protestant Europe. The widespread religious wars of the sixteenth and seventeenth centuries killed millions, created intense anti-Spanish feelings among the English and Dutch, and eventually helped bankrupt the Spanish government. At the same time, the Spanish Empire grew so vast that its sprawling size and complexity eventually led to its disintegration.

From the outset, the Spanish in the Americas behaved more like occupying rulers than permanent settlers, carefully regulating every detail of colonial administration and life. They were less interested in creating self-sustaining communities than in taking gold, silver, and copper while enslaving the indigenous peoples and converting them to Christianity. Spain never encouraged vast numbers of settlers to populate New Spain, and, with few exceptions, those who did travel to the New World rarely wanted to make a living off the land; they instead wanted to live off the labor of the native population.

For three centuries, Spanish explorers, conquistadores, and priests imposed Catholicism and a cruel system of economic exploitation and dependence in their New World colonies. Their system created terrible disparities in wealth, education, and opportunity that would trigger repeated revolts and political instability. As Bartolomé de Las Casas concluded, "The Spaniards have shown not the slightest consideration for these people, treating them . . . as piles of dung in the middle of the road. They have had as little concern for their souls as for their bodies."

CHAPTER REVIEW

SUMMARY

- **Native American Societies**   Hunter-gatherers came across the Bering Strait by foot and settled the length and breadth of the Americas. Global warming enabled an agricultural revolution that allowed former hunter-gather peoples to settle and build empires, such as that of the *Mexica*, whose *Aztec Empire* included subjugated peoples and a vast system of trade and tribute. Some North American peoples developed an elaborate continental trading network and impressive cities like *Cahokia*; their *burial mounds* reveal a complex and stratified social organization. The *Eastern Woodlands peoples* that the Europeans would first encounter included both patriarchal and matriarchal societies as well as extensive language-based alliances. The Algonquian, Iroquoian, and Muskogean were among the major Indian nations. Warfare was an important cultural component, leading to shifting rivalries and alliances among tribes and with European settlers.

- **Age of Exploration**   By the 1490s, warfare, plagues, and famine had begun to undermine the old agricultural feudal system in Europe, and in its place arose a middle class that monarchs could tax. Powerful new nations replaced the land estates and cities ruled by princes. Navies became the critical components of global trade and world power. When the Spanish began to colonize the New World, the conversion of Indians to Roman Catholicism was important, but the search for gold and silver was primary. The rivalries of the *Protestant Reformation* in Europe shaped the course of conquest in the Americas.

- **Conquering and Colonizing the Americas**   Spanish *conquistadores* such as Hernán Cortés exploited their advantages in military technology, including steel, gunpowder, and domesticated animals such as the horse, to conquer the powerful Aztec and Inca Empires. European diseases, first introduced by Columbus, did even more to ensure Spanish victories. The Spanish *encomienda* system demanded goods and labor from their new subjects. As the Indian population declined, the Spanish began to import enslaved Africans.

- **Columbian Exchange**   Contact between the Old World and the New resulted in the *Columbian Exchange*, sometimes called the Great Biological Exchange. Crops such as *maize*, beans, and potatoes became staples in the Old World. Native peoples incorporated into their culture such Eurasian animals as the horse and pig. But the invaders also carried *infectious diseases* that set off pandemics of smallpox, plague, and other illnesses to which Indians had no immunity. The Americas were depopulated and cultures destroyed.

- **Spanish Legacy**   Spain left a lasting legacy in the borderlands from California to Florida. Catholic missionaries contributed to the destruction of the old ways of life by exterminating "heathen" beliefs in the Southwest, a practice that led to open rebellion in *New Mexico* in 1598 and 1680. Spain's rival European nation-states also began competing for gold and glory in the New World. England's defeat of the *Spanish Armada* cleared the path for English dominance in North America.

CHRONOLOGY

by 12,000 B.C.E.	Humans have migrated to the Americas
5000 B.C.E.	Agricultural revolution begins in Mexico
1050–1250 C.E.	The city of Cahokia flourishes in North America
1325	Mexica (Aztec) Empire founded in Central Mexico
1492	Columbus makes his first voyage of discovery in the Americas
1517	Martin Luther launches the Protestant Reformation
1519	Cortés begins the Spanish conquest of Mexico
1531	Pizarro subdues the Inca Empire in South America for Spain
1565	Spaniards found St. Augustine, the first permanent European outpost in the present-day United States
1584–1587	Raleigh's Roanoke Island venture
1588	The English navy defeats the Spanish Armada
1680	Pueblo Revolt

KEY TERMS

maize p. 6

Mexica p. 7

Aztec Empire p. 7

burial mounds p. 9

Cahokia p. 10

Eastern Woodlands peoples p. 11

Protestant Reformation p. 17

conquistadores p. 21

encomienda p. 25

Columbian Exchange p. 26

infectious diseases p. 27

New Mexico p. 28

Spanish Armada p. 35

🐇 INQUIZITIVE

Go to InQuizitive to see what you've learned—and learn what you've missed—with personalized feedback along the way.

2 England's Colonies

"Ould Virginia" As one of the earliest explorers and settlers of the Jamestown colony, John Smith put his intimate knowledge of the region to use by creating this seventeenth-century map of Virginia. In the upper right hand corner is a warrior of the Susquehannock, whom Smith called a "G[i]ant-like people."

Over the centuries, the island nation of England developed political practices and governing principles quite different from those on the continent of Europe. England's parliamentary monarchy began with the Magna Carta (Great Charter) of 1215, a statement of fundamental rights and liberties. The Magna Carta established the basic principle that everyone was equal before the law and no person—not even a king or queen—was above the law.

Unlike the absolute monarchs of France and Spain, English rulers shared power with the nobility and a lesser aristocracy, known as the *gentry*, whose representatives formed the legislature known as Parliament, made up of the House of Lords and the House of Commons. The most important power allocated to Parliament was the authority to impose taxes. By controlling government tax revenue, Parliament exercised great leverage over the monarchy.

RELIGIOUS CONFLICT AND WAR

When Queen Elizabeth, who never married, died in 1603 without a child of her own to inherit the throne, James VI of Scotland, her distant cousin, became King James I of England. While Elizabeth had ruled through constitutional authority, James ominously claimed to govern by "divine right," which meant he answered only to God.

James I confronted a divided Church of England, with reform-minded **Puritans** in one camp and the Anglican establishment, headed by the arch-

focus questions

1. What motivated England to establish American colonies?

2. What were the characteristics of the English colonies in the Chesapeake region, the Carolinas, the middle colonies—Pennsylvania, New York, New Jersey, and Delaware—and New England prior to 1700?

3. In what ways did the English colonists and Native Americans adapt to each other's presence?

4. What role did indentured servants and the development of slavery play in colonial America?

5. How did the English colonies become the most populous and powerful region in North America by 1700?

bishop and bishops, in the other. The Puritans were dissenters who believed that the Church of England needed further "purifying." They demanded the elimination of all Roman Catholic rituals, such as the use of holy water, organ music, elegant robes, jeweled gold crosses, and worship of saints. The Puritans wanted to simplify religion to its basics: people worshipping God in plain, self-governing congregations without any formal trappings. They had hoped the new king would support their efforts, but James I instead sought to banish them from England.

Some Puritans eventually decided to create their own independent congregations, thus earning the name *Separatists*. Their rebelliousness infuriated the leaders of the Church of England, who required people by law to attend Anglican services. During the late sixteenth century, the Separatists (also called *Nonconformists*) were "hunted and persecuted on every side." English authorities imprisoned Separatist leaders, and in 1604, James I vowed to make Separatists "conform or I will hurry them out of the land or do worse." Many Separatists left England, and some, who would eventually be known as Pilgrims, decided to sail for America.

The Execution of Charles I Flemish artist John Weesop witnessed the king's execution and painted this gruesome scene from memory. He was so disgusted by "a country where they cut off their king's head" that he refused to visit England again.

James's son, Charles I, succeeded his father in 1625 and proved to be an even more stubborn defender of absolute royal power; he raised taxes without consulting the House of Commons and House of Lords, and took the shocking step of disbanding Parliament from 1629 to 1640.

The monarchy went too far, however, when it forced Anglican forms of worship on Presbyterian Scots. In 1638, Scotland rose in revolt, and in 1640, King Charles, desperate for money to fund his army and save his skin, revived Parliament and ordered its members to raise taxes for the defense of his kingdom. Parliament, led by militant Puritans, refused.

In 1642, when the king tried to arrest five members of Parliament, a bloody civil war erupted in England between Royalists and Parliamentarians, leading many New England Puritans to return home to fight against the

Royalist army. In 1646, parliamentary forces led by Oliver Cromwell captured Charles and, in an unprecedented public trial, convicted him of high treason and contempt of Parliament, labeling him a "tyrant, traitor, murderer, and public enemy." He was beheaded in 1649. As it turned out, however, the Puritans had killed a king, but they had not slain the monarchy.

Oliver Cromwell, the Puritan leader of the parliamentary coup, outlawed Roman Catholics and Anglicans, but his dictatorial style fed growing resentment. Many Royalists, called *Cavaliers*, escaped by sailing to Virginia. After Cromwell's death in 1658, the army allowed new elections for Parliament and in 1660 supported the Restoration of the monarchy under Charles II, eldest son of the executed king.

Unlike his father, Charles II agreed to rule jointly with Parliament. His younger brother, the Duke of York (who became James II in 1685), was more rigid. He embraced Catholicism in Protestant England, ordered political opponents murdered or imprisoned, and defied Parliament.

The English people tolerated James II's rule so long as they expected one of his Protestant daughters, Mary or Anne, to succeed him. In 1688, however, the birth of a royal son who would be raised as a Roman Catholic stirred a revolt. Determined to prevent a Catholic monarchy, political, religious, and military leaders invited the king's Protestant daughter, Mary Stuart, and her Protestant husband, the ruling Dutch prince William III of Orange, to assume the English throne as joint husband and wife monarchs.

When William landed in England with a Dutch army, James II fled to France. Amid this dramatic transfer of power, which soon became known as the Glorious Revolution, Parliament reasserted its right to counterbalance the authority of the monarchy. Kings and queens could no longer suspend Parliament, create armies, or impose taxes without Parliament's consent. The monarchy would henceforth derive its power not from God but from the people.

AMERICAN COLONIES

PEOPLE AND PROFITS   During these eventful years, all of England's North American colonies—except Georgia—were founded. From the outset, English colonization differed significantly from the Spanish pattern. Spanish settlements were royal expeditions; much of the wealth and lands the Spanish stole in the Americas became the property of the monarchs who funded the conquistadores. In contrast, English colonization in the Americas was led by two different groups that sometimes overlapped: those seeking freedom from religious persecution, both Protestants and Catholics, and those seeking land and wealth.

In addition, English colonies were private business ventures or collective religious experiments rather than government enterprises. And they were expensive. Few individuals were wealthy enough to finance a colony over a long period. Those Englishmen interested in colonization thus banded together to share the financial risks of starting colonies in the "American wilderness." Investors purchased shares of stock to form **joint-stock companies**. That way, large amounts of money could be raised and, if a colony failed, no single investor would suffer the full loss. If a colony succeeded, the investors would share in the profits.

Yet while English monarchs did not fund the colonial expeditions, they did grant the royal charters (legal authorization) needed to launch them. The joint-stock companies represented the most important organizational innovation of the Age of Exploration and provided the first instruments of English colonization in America.

SELF-SUSTAINING COLONIES The English settlements in America were much more compact than those in New Spain, and the native peoples along the Atlantic coast were less numerous and less wealthy than the Mexica and the Incas.

Most English settlers viewed the Indians as devilish threats to be removed as they created family-based agricultural and trading communities. England's colonies were also much more populous than the Spanish and French colonies. By 1750, English colonists (male and female) still outnumbered the French (mostly male) nearly 20 to 1 (1.3 million to 70,000), whereas in the northern areas of New Spain, the lands that became Texas, New Mexico, Arizona, Florida, and California, there were only 20,000 Spaniards.

The English government and individual investors had two primary goals for their American colonies: (1) to provide valuable raw materials such as timber for shipbuilding, tobacco for smoking, and fur pelts for hats and coats; and, (2) to develop a thriving consumer market for English manufactured goods. To populate the colonies, the English encouraged social rebels (including convicts), religious dissenters, and the homeless and landless to migrate to America.

By far, the most powerful enticement to colonists was to offer them land and the promise of a better way of life—what came to be called the American dream. Land, plentiful and cheap, was English America's miraculous treasure—once it was taken from the Native Americans. What virtually all of the diverse immigrants shared was the courage to risk all for a new life of adventure in America. In the process of discovering a New World of opportunities and dangers, they also discovered and recreated themselves as Americans.

THE LANDLESS ENGLISH   During the late sixteenth century, England experienced a population explosion that outstripped its economy's ability to support the country's surplus of landless workers. Many of those poor laborers would find their way to America. An additional social strain for the English poor was the *enclosure* of farmlands on which peasants had lived and worked for generations. As trade in woolen products grew, landlords decided to "enclose" farmlands and evict the farmworkers in favor of grazing sheep.

The enclosure movement, coupled with the rising population, generated a great number of beggars and vagrants and gained immortality in the line from the Mother Goose tale: "Hark, hark, the dogs do bark. The beggars have come to town." The problems created by this uprooted peasant population provided a compelling reason to send many of them abroad to colonies in America and the Caribbean.

VIRGINIA   In 1606, King James I chartered a joint-stock enterprise called the Virginia Company. It was owned by merchant investors seeking to profit from the gold and silver they hoped to find in America. King James also ordered the settlers to take the "Christian religion" to the Indians, who "live in darkness and miserable ignorance of the true knowledge and worship of God." As was true of many colonial ventures, however, such missionary activities were quickly abandoned in favor of making money.

In 1607, the Virginia Company sent to America three tiny ships carrying about 100 men and boys. In May, after five storm-tossed months at sea, they reached Chesapeake Bay, along the present-day states of Virginia and Maryland. To avoid Spanish raiders, the English chose to settle about forty miles inland along a large river with a northwest bend. They called the river the James, in honor of the English king, and named their first settlement James Fort, later renamed Jamestown.

On a low-lying island surrounded by marshes, fed by salty water, and swarming with malaria-infested mosquitoes, the colonists built a fort with thatched huts and a church. They had come to America overflowing with misperceptions. They expected to find gold, friendly Indians, and easy living. Instead they found disease, drought, starvation, violence, and death. Most of them were ill equipped for the task, as they were either poor townsmen unfamiliar with farming or "gentleman" adventurers who despised manual labor. "A more damned crew hell never vomited," said the president of the Virginia Company.

The leaders of the company expected the Native Americans to submit to the authority of the colonists. They were wrong. The 14,000 Indians living along the Virginia coast were dominated by the **Powhatan Confederacy**. Powhatan, as the English called him, was the supreme chief of several hundred villages (of about 100 people each) organized into thirty chiefdoms in eastern Virginia. At the time, the Powhatan Confederacy may have been the most powerful group of native peoples along the Atlantic coast. Chief Powhatan (his proper name was Wahunsenacawh) lived in an imposing lodge on the York River not far from Jamestown, where he was protected by forty bodyguards and supported by a hundred wives. Colonist John Smith reported that the chieftain "sat covered with a great robe, made of raccoon skins, and all the tails hanging by," flanked by "two rows of men, and behind them as many women, with all their heads and shoulders painted red."

Powhatan was as much an imperialist as the English or Spanish. He forced the chieftains of rival peoples he had conquered to give him corn. Upon learning of the English settlement at Jamestown, he planned to impose his will on the "Strangers" as well.. When Powhatans happened upon a group of Englishmen stealing their corn, they killed all seventeen of them, stuffing their mouths with ears of corn.

The inexperienced colonists found a match for Chief Powhatan in John Smith, a canny, iron-willed, twenty-seven-year-old mercenary (soldier for hire) who arrived the next year with more colonists. The Virginia Company, impressed by Smith's exploits in foreign wars, had appointed him a member of the council to manage the new colony.

It was a wise decision. Of the original 105 settlers, only 38 had survived the first nine months. At one point, said Smith, all their food was gone, "all help abandoned, each hour expecting the fury of the savages." Smith imposed strict military discipline in the colony and forced everyone to work long days in the fields. He also bargained effectively with the Indians. Through his dictatorial efforts, Jamestown survived. But it was not easy. As he explained, the quarreling colonists were a sorry lot, "ten times more fit to spoil a commonwealth than . . . to begin one."

When no gold or silver was discovered near Jamestown, the Virginia Company shifted its money-making efforts to the sale of land, which would rise in value as the colony grew in population. The company recruited hundreds of new investors and settlers with promises that Virginia would "make them rich."

The influx of settlers nearly overwhelmed the struggling colony. During the winter of 1609–1610, the colony's food supply again ran out, and many died of disease or starvation. Desperate settlers ate their horses, cats, and dogs, then rats and mice. A few even ate the leather from their shoes and boots and the starch in their shirt collars. One hungry man killed, salted, and ate his pregnant wife. Horrified by such cannibalism, his fellow colonists tortured and executed him. But the cannibalism continued as the starvation worsened. "So great was our famine," Smith wrote, "that a savage we slew and buried, the poorer sort [of colonists] took him up again and ate him."

In June 1610, as the surviving colonists prepared to abandon Jamestown and return to England, a new governor, Lord De La Warr, arrived with three ships and 150 men. They established a settlement upstream at Henrico (Richmond) and two more downstream, near the mouth of the James River.

Their arrival was a critical turning point for the colony. After Lord De La Warr returned to England in 1611, Sir Thomas Gates took charge of the Virginia settlements and imposed a strict system of laws. The penalties for running away included shooting, hanging, and burning. Gates also ordered the colonists to attend church services on Thursdays and Sundays. Religious uniformity became an essential instrument of public policy and civil duty in colonial Virginia.

Over the next several years, the Jamestown colony limped along until at last the settlers found a profitable crop: **tobacco**. The plant had been grown on Caribbean islands for years, and smoking had become popular in Europe. In 1612, settlers began growing Virginia tobacco for export to England. By 1620, the colony was shipping 50,000 pounds of tobacco to England each year; by 1670, Virginia and Maryland were exporting 15 million pounds annually.

As large-scale tobacco growing emerged, farmers needed additional cleared lands and more workers. If "all our riches for the present do consist in Tobacco," explained a Jamestown planter, then it followed that "our principal wealth . . . consisteth in servants." Another planter wanted "lusty laboring men . . . capable of hard labor, and that can bear and undergo heat and cold."

INDENTURED SERVANTS To support their deepening investment in tobacco lands, planters purchased **indentured servants** (colonists who exchanged several years of labor for the cost of passage to America and an eventual grant of land). Indentured servitude became the primary source of laborers in English America during the colonial period. Of the 500,000 English immigrants to America from 1610 to 1775, some 350,000 came as indentured servants, most of them poor young men and boys. Not all came voluntarily. Many homeless children in London were "kid-napped" and sold into servitude. In addition, Parliament in 1717 declared that convicts could avoid prison or the hangman by relocating to the colonies.

Servants were provided food and a bed, but life was harsh and their rights were limited. Marriage required the master's permission. Masters could whip servants and extend their length of service as penalty for bad behavior. It was almost like being a slave, but servanthood, unlike slavery, did not last a life-time. When the indenture ended, usually after four to seven years, the servant could claim the "freedom dues" set by custom and law: tools, clothing, food, and, on occasion, small tracts of land. Some servants did very well. In 1629, seven members of the Virginia legislature were former indentured servants. Such opportunities were much less common in England or Europe, giving people even more reasons to travel to America.

POCAHONTAS   One of the most remarkable Powhatans was Pocahontas, the favorite daughter of Chief Powhatan. In 1607, then only eleven years old, she figured in perhaps the best-known story of the settlement—her plea for the life of John Smith, who had gotten into trouble by trespassing on Powhatan's territory. As the Indians prepared to execute him, according to Smith, Poca-hontas made a dramatic appeal for his life, convincing her father to release him in exchange for muskets, hatchets, beads, and trinkets.

Schoolchildren still learn the story of Pocahontas and John Smith, but through the years the story's facts have become distorted or even falsified. Poca-hontas and John Smith were friends, not Disney lovers. Moreover, the Indian prin-cess saved Smith on more than one occasion, before she herself was kidnapped by English settlers in an effort to blackmail Powhatan, her powerful father.

Pocahontas, however, surprised her English captors by choosing to join them. She embraced Christianity, was baptized and renamed Rebecca, and fell in love with John Rolfe, a twenty-eight-year-old widower who introduced tobacco to Jamestown. After their marriage, they moved in 1616 with their infant son, Thomas, to London. There the young princess drew excited atten-tion, but a few months after arriving, Rebecca, only twenty years old, con-tracted a lung disease and died.

THE VIRGINIA COMPANY PROSPERS   In 1618, Sir Edwin San-dys, a prominent member of Parliament, became head of the Virginia Com-pany and created a new policy to attract more colonists: the **headright** (land grant) program: any male English colonist who bought a share in the company and could pay for passage to Virginia could have fifty acres upon arrival, and fifty more for each servant he brought along.

The Virginia Company also promised that the settlers would have all the "rights of Englishmen," including an elected legislature to advise the colonial governor, arguing that "every man will more willingly obey laws to which he has yielded his consent." This was a crucial development, for the English had long enjoyed the broadest civil liberties and the least intrusive government in Europe. Now the colonists in Virginia were to have the same rights.

By 1619, the settlement had out-grown James Fort and was formally renamed Jamestown. The same year, a ship with ninety young women aboard arrived. Men rushed to claim them as wives by providing 125 pounds of tobacco to cover the cost of each trans-atlantic passage. In addition, a Dutch ship called the *White Lion* stopped at Jamestown and unloaded "20 Negars," the first enslaved Africans known to have reached English America. Thus began an inhumane system that would grow rapidly while spurring dramatic economic growth, sowing moral cor-ruption, and generating horrific suffer-ing for African Americans.

By 1624, some 14,000 English men, women, and children had migrated to Jamestown, although only 1,132 had survived or stayed. In that year, an English court dissolved the struggling Virginia Company, and "weak and miserable" Virginia became a royal colony. The settlers were now free to own property and start businesses. Their governors, however, would thereafter be appointed by the king. Sir William Berkeley, who arrived as the royal governor in 1642, presided over the colony's rapid growth for most of the next thirty-five years. Tobacco prices surged, and wealthy planters began to dominate social and political life.

STRANGE NEWS

FROM

VIRGINIA;

Being a full and true

ACCOUNT

OF THE

LIFE and DEATH

OF

Nathanael Bacon Esquire,

Who was the only Cause and Original of all the late Troubles in that COUNTRY.

With a full Relation of all the Accidents which have happened in the late War there between the Christians and Indians.

LONDON,

Printed for *William Harris,* next door to the Turn-Stile without *Moor-gate.* 1677.

News of the rebellion A pamphlet printed in London provided details about Bacon's Rebellion.

BACON'S REBELLION The relentless stream of settlers into Virginia exerted constant pressure on Indian lands and created growing social tensions among whites. The largest planters in the colony sought to live like the wealthy "English gentlemen" who owned huge estates in the British countryside. In Virginia, these men acquired the most fertile land along the coast and rivers, compelling freed servants to become farmworkers or forcing them inland in order to gain their own farms. In either case, the poorest Virginians found themselves at a disadvantage. By 1676, one fourth of the free white men were landless. They roamed the countryside, squatting on private property, working at odd jobs, poaching game, and struggling to survive.

The simmering tensions among the landless colonists contributed to the tangled events that came to be called **Bacon's Rebellion**. The discontent erupted when a squabble between a white planter and Native Americans on the Potomac River led to the murder of the planter's herdsman and, in turn, to retaliation by frontier vigilantes, who killed some two dozen Indians. When five native chieftains were later murdered, enraged Indians took revenge on frontier settlements.

Scattered attacks continued southward to the James River, where Nathaniel Bacon's overseer was killed. In 1676, when Governor Berkeley refused to take action against the Indian raiders, Bacon assumed command of a rebel group of more than 1,000 men determined to terrorize the "protected and darling Indians." Bacon said he would kill all the Indians in Virginia and promised to free any servants and slaves who joined him.

The rebellion quickly became a battle of landless servants, small farmers, and even some slaves against Virginia's wealthiest planters and political leaders. Bacon's ruthless assaults against peaceful Indians and his greed for power and land (rather than any commitment to democratic principles) sparked his conflict with the governing authorities and the planter elite.

For his part, Governor Berkeley didn't want warfare to disrupt the profitable deerskin trade the colonists enjoyed with the Native Americans. Bacon, whose ragtag "army" had now dwindled to a few hundred, issued a "Declaration of the People of Virginia" accusing Berkeley of corruption and attempted to take the governor into custody. Berkeley's forces resisted—feebly—and Bacon's men burned Jamestown in frustration. Bacon, however, could not celebrate the victory long; he fell ill and died a month later. With Bacon dead, the rebellion gradually disintegrated. Governor Berkeley had twenty-three of the rebels hanged. For such severity, the king denounced Berkeley as a "fool" and recalled him to England, where he died within a year.

MARYLAND   In 1634, ten years after Virginia became a royal colony, a neighboring settlement appeared on the northern shore of Chesapeake Bay. Named Maryland in honor of English queen Henrietta Maria, its 12 million acres were granted to Sir George Calvert, Lord Baltimore, by King Charles I. It became the first *proprietary* colony—that is, it was owned by an individual, not by a joint-stock company.

Calvert had long been one of the king's favorites. In 1619, he was appointed one of two royal secretaries of state for the nation. Forced to resign after a squabble with the king's powerful advisers, Calvert used the occasion of his resignation to announce that he had converted from Anglicanism to Catholicism.

Thereafter, Calvert persistently asked the new king, James II, to grant him a charter for an American colony to the north of Virginia. However, Calvert died before the king could act, so the charter was awarded to his son, Cecilius Calvert, the second Lord Baltimore, who actually founded the colony. Calvert wanted Maryland to be a refuge for English Catholics, yet he also wanted the colony to be profitable and to avoid antagonizing Protestants. He instructed his brother, Leonard, the colony's first proprietary governor, to ensure that Catholic colonists would worship in private and remain "silent upon all occasions of discourse concerning matters of religion."

EARLY MARYLAND AND VIRGINIA

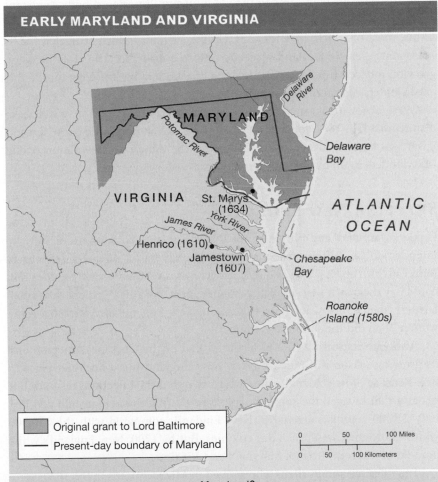

Original grant to Lord Baltimore
Present-day boundary of Maryland

- Why did Lord Baltimore create Maryland?
- How was Maryland different from Virginia?
- What were the main characteristics of Maryland's 1632 charter?

In 1634, the Calverts planted the first settlement in coastal Maryland at St. Marys. They sought to learn from the mistakes made at Jamestown. First, they recruited a more committed group of colonists—families intending to stay in the colony rather than single men seeking quick profits. Second, they wanted to create fortified towns, carefully designed to promote social interaction. Third, they wanted to avoid extremes of wealth and poverty by ensuring that the government would "do justice to every man."

The charter from the king gave the Calverts power to make laws with the consent of the *freemen* (all property holders). Yet they could not attract enough Roman Catholics to develop a self-sustaining economy. The majority of the servants who came to the colony were Protestants, both Anglicans and Puritans. To recruit servants and settlers, the Calverts offered them small farms, most of which grew tobacco. Unlike Virginia, which struggled for its first twenty years, Maryland succeeded more quickly because of its focus on growing tobacco from the start. Its long coastline along the Chesapeake Bay gave planters easy access to shipping.

Were it not for its success in growing tobacco, Maryland may well have disintegrated. In 1692, following the Glorious Revolution in England, Catholicism was banned in Maryland. Only after the American Revolution would Marylanders again be guaranteed religious freedom.

SETTLING NEW ENGLAND

Unlike Maryland and Virginia, the New England colonies were initially intended to be self-governing religious utopias based on the teachings of John Calvin. The New England settlers were mostly middle-class families that could pay their own way across the Atlantic, and most male settlers were small farmers, merchants, seamen, or fishermen. New England also attracted more women than did the southern colonies.

Although its soil was not as fertile as that of the Chesapeake region and its growing season was much shorter, New England was a healthier place to live. Because of its colder climate, settlers avoided the infectious diseases like malaria that ravaged the southern colonies. During the seventeenth century, only 21,000 colonists arrived in New England, compared with the 120,000 who went to the Chesapeake Bay colonies. But by 1700, New England's white population exceeded that of Maryland and Virginia.

The Pilgrims and Puritans who arrived in Massachusetts in the 1620s were on a divine mission to create a model Christian society. These self-described "saints" intended to purify their churches of all Catholic and Anglican rituals and enact a code of laws and a government structure based upon biblical principles. Unlike the Anglican Church, which allowed anyone, including sinners, to join, the Puritans would limit membership in their churches to saints—those who had been chosen by God for salvation. They also sought to stamp out gambling, swearing, and Sabbath breaking. Such holy settlements, they hoped, would provide a beacon of righteousness for a wicked England to emulate.

PLYMOUTH   The first permanent English settlement in New England was established by Separatists who were forced to leave England because of their refusal to worship in Anglican churches. The Separatist saints demanded that each congregation govern itself rather than be ruled by a bureaucracy of bishops and archbishops.

In September 1620, about 100 women, men, and children, some of whom were called "Strangers" rather than Separatists because they were not part of the religious group, crammed aboard the *Mayflower*, a leaky vessel only 100 feet long, and headed across the Atlantic bound for the Virginia colony, where they had obtained permission to settle. Storms, however, blew the ship off course to Cape Cod, just south of what became Boston, Massachusetts. Since they were outside the jurisdiction of any organized government, the forty-one Separatists on board signed the **Mayflower Compact**, a covenant (group contract) to form a church. The civil government grew out of the church government, and the members of each were identical. The signers of the Mayflower Compact at first met as the General Court of Plymouth Plantation, like a town meeting, which chose the governor and his assistants (or council). Other property owners were later admitted as members, or "freemen," but only church members were eligible to join the General Court. Eventually, as the colony grew, the General Court became a legislative body of elected representatives from the various towns.

The Plymouth colonists settled in a deserted Wampanoag Indian village that had been devastated by smallpox. They named their hillside colony Plymouth, after the English port from which they had embarked. They, too, experienced a "starving time" as had the early Jamestown colonists. During their first winter, half of the Pilgrims died, including thirteen of the eighteen married women. Only the discovery of stored Indian corn buried underground enabled the colony to survive.

MASSACHUSETTS BAY   The Plymouth colony was soon overshadowed by its much larger neighbor, the Massachusetts Bay Colony, which was also intended to be a holy Protestant commonwealth. The Massachusetts Bay Puritans, however, differed from the Pilgrims and Anglicans in important ways. They wanted to purify the Church of England from within, not separate from it. They were called *Congregationalists* because their churches were self-governing rather than ruled by an Anglican bishop in England. Their congregations limited membership to "visible saints"—those who could demonstrate receipt of the gift of God's grace.

EARLY NEW ENGLAND SETTLEMENTS

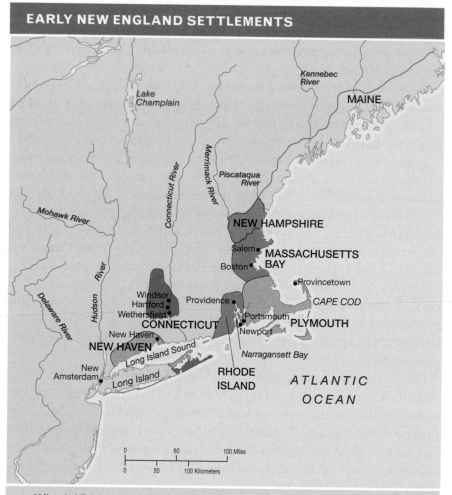

- Why did Pilgrims found the Plymouth colony?
- How were the settlers of the Massachusetts Bay Colony different from those of Plymouth?
- What was the origin of the Rhode Island colony?

In 1629, King Charles I gave a royal charter to the Massachusetts Bay Company, a joint-stock company which was planted in New England the following year. It consisted of a group of Calvinist Puritans led by John Winthrop, a prosperous lawyer with intense religious convictions. Winthrop wanted the colony to be a haven for Puritans and a model Christian community—"a city upon a hill," as he declared. To that end, he shrewdly took advantage of an oversight in the company charter: it did not require that the joint-stock company maintain its home office in England. Winthrop's group took the royal charter with them, thereby transferring government authority from London to Massachusetts, where they hoped to govern themselves.

Winthrop was a strong leader, virtually a dictator, who believed that the role of government should be to enforce religious beliefs and ensure social stability. Catholics, Anglicans, Quakers, and Baptists were imprisoned, banished, and sometimes executed. Quakers were especially hated. So that they could be more readily recognized, they were defaced by the authorities. Their nostrils were slit, their ears were severed, or their foreheads were branded with the letter H, for "heretic."

Even Puritans who spoke out against religious or political policies were quickly condemned. For example, Anne Hutchinson, the strong-willed, intelligent wife of a prominent merchant, raised thirteen children and hosted meetings in her Boston home to discuss sermons. Soon, however, the discussions turned into large gatherings at which Hutchinson shared her feelings about religious matters. According to one participant, she "preaches better Gospel than any of your black coats [male ministers]." Blessed with vast biblical knowledge and a quick wit, Hutchinson claimed to know which of her neighbors had truly been saved and which were damned, including ministers. She quickly was viewed as a "dangerous" woman.

A pregnant Hutchinson was hauled before the all-male General Court in 1637 for trying to "undermine the Kingdom of Christ," and for two days she sparred on equal terms with the Puritan leaders. Her ability to cite

John Winthrop The first governor of the Massachusetts Bay Colony, in whose vision the colony would be as "a city upon a hill."

The Trial of Anne Hutchinson In this nineteenth-century wood engraving, Anne Hutchinson stands her ground against charges of heresy from the all-male leaders of Puritan Boston.

chapter-and-verse biblical defenses of her actions led an exasperated Governor Winthrop to explode: "We are your judges, and not you ours. . . . We do not mean to discourse [debate] with those of your sex." He told Hutchinson that she had "stepped out of your place" as a woman in a man's world. As the trial continued, an overwrought Hutchinson was eventually lured into convicting herself by claiming direct revelations from God—blasphemy in the eyes of Puritans.

In 1638, Winthrop and the General Court banished the pregnant Hutchinson as a "leper" not fit for "our society." She initially settled with her family and about sixty followers on an island south of Providence, Rhode Island. The hard journey took its toll, however. Hutchinson grew sick, and her baby was stillborn, leading her critics in Massachusetts Bay to claim that the "monstrous birth" was God's way of punishing her. Hutchinson's spirits never recovered. After her husband's death, in 1642, she moved near New Amsterdam (New York City), which was then under Dutch control. The following year, she and six of her children were massacred by Indians. Her murder, wrote a spiteful John Winthrop, was "a special manifestation of divine justice."

REPRESENTATIVE GOVERNMENT The transfer of the Massachusetts Bay Colony's royal charter, whereby an English trading company evolved into a provincial government, was a unique venture in colonization. Unlike "Old" England, New England had no powerful lords or bishops, kings or queens. The Massachusetts General Court, wherein power rested under the royal charter, consisted of all the shareholders (property owners who were also called freemen). At first, the freemen had no power except to choose "assistants," who in turn elected the governor and deputy governor. In 1634, however, the freemen turned themselves into the General Court, with two or three deputies representing each town. A final stage in the democratization of the Massachusetts Bay government came in 1644, when the General Court organized itself like the English Parliament, with a House of Assistants corresponding roughly to the House of Lords, and a House of Deputies corresponding to the House of Commons. All decisions had to be ratified by a majority in each house.

The Puritans, who had fled religious persecution and political repression, ensured that their liberties in New England were spelled out and protected. Over time, membership in a Puritan church replaced the purchase of stock as the means of becoming a freeman, or voter, in Massachusetts Bay.

RHODE ISLAND   More by accident than design, the Massachusetts Bay Colony became the staging area for other New England colonies created by people dissatisfied with Puritan control. Roger Williams (1603–1683), who had arrived from England in 1631, was among the first to cause problems, precisely because he was the purest of Puritans—a Separatist. He criticized Puritans for not completely cutting ties to the "whorish" Church of England. Where John Winthrop cherished strict governmental and clerical authority, Williams championed individual liberty and criticized the way the Indians were being shoved aside. The combative Williams posed a radical question: If one's salvation depends solely upon God's grace, as John Calvin had argued, why bother to have churches at all? Why not give individuals the right to worship God in their own way?

In Williams's view, true *puritanism* required complete separation of church and state and freedom from all coercion in matters of faith. "Forced worship," he declared, "stinks in God's nostrils."

Such radical views led Governor Winthrop and the General Court to banish Williams to England. Before authorities could ship him back, however, he slipped away and found shelter among the Narragansett Indians. In 1636, he bought land from the Indians and established the town of Providence at the head of Narragansett Bay, the first permanent settlement in Rhode Island and the first in America to allow complete freedom of religion.

From the beginning, Rhode Island was the most democratic of the colonies, governed by the heads of households rather than by church members. Newcomers could be admitted to full citizenship by a majority vote, and the colony welcomed all who fled religious persecution in Massachusetts Bay. For their part, Puritans in Boston came to view Rhode Island as a refuge for rogues. A Dutch visitor reported that the new colony was "the sewer of New England. All the cranks of New England retire there."

CONNECTICUT, NEW HAMPSHIRE, AND MAINE In 1636, the Reverend Thomas Hooker led three church congregations from Massachusetts Bay to Connecticut, where they organized a self-governing colony. In 1639, the Connecticut General Court adopted the Fundamental Orders, a series of laws that provided for a "Christian Commonwealth" like that of Massachusetts, except that voting was not limited to church members. The Connecticut constitution specified that Congregational churches would be the colony's official religion. The governor was commanded to rule according to "the word of God."

To the north, most of what are now New Hampshire and Maine was granted in 1622 to Sir Ferdinando Gorges and Captain John Mason. In 1629, Mason and Gorges divided their territory, with Mason taking the southern part, which he named the Province of New Hampshire, and Gorges taking the northern part, which became the Province of Maine. During the early 1640s, Massachusetts took over New Hampshire, and in the 1650s it extended its authority to the scattered settlements in Maine. This led to lawsuits, and in 1678 English judges decided against Massachusetts in both cases. In 1679, New Hampshire became a royal colony, but Massachusetts continued to control Maine. A new Massachusetts charter in 1691 finally incorporated Maine into Massachusetts.

THE ENGLISH CIVIL WAR IN AMERICA

By 1640, English settlers in New England and around Chesapeake Bay had established two great beachheads on the Atlantic coast, with the Dutch colony of New Netherland in between. After 1640, however, the struggle between king and Parliament in England diverted attention from colonization, and migration to America dwindled for more than twenty years. During the English Civil War (1642–1646) and Oliver Cromwell's Puritan dictatorship (1653–1658), the struggling colonies were left pretty much alone by the mother country.

In 1643, Massachusetts Bay, Plymouth, Connecticut, and New Haven formed the New England Confederation to provide joint defense against the Dutch, French, and Indians. In some ways, the confederation behaved like a nation unto itself. It made treaties, and in 1653 it declared war against the Dutch, who were accused of inciting the Indians to attack Connecticut. Massachusetts, far from the scene of trouble, failed to cooperate, thus greatly weakening the confederation.

Virginia and Maryland also defied Cromwell's dictatorship. Virginia burgesses (legislators) in 1649 denounced the Puritans' execution of King Charles and claimed that his son, Charles II, was the lawful king. The colony grew rapidly during its years of independent government before reverting to royal control when William Berkeley returned as governor in 1660 after the monarchy was restored in England.

Cromwell allowed the colonies great flexibility but was not indifferent to Britain's North American empire. He fought trade wars with the Dutch, and his navy harassed England's traditional enemy, Catholic Spain, in the Caribbean. In 1655, a British force wrested Jamaica from Spanish control.

The Restoration of King Charles II in 1660 led to an equally painless reinstatement of previous governments in the colonies. Agents hastily dispatched by the colonies won reconfirmation of the Massachusetts charter in 1662 and the very first royal charters for Connecticut and Rhode Island in 1662 and 1663. All three remained self-governing corporations. Plymouth still had no charter, but it went unmolested. New Haven, however, was absorbed into the colony of Connecticut.

The Restoration in the Colonies

The Restoration of Charles II to the British throne revived interest among the English in colonial expansion. Within twelve years, the English would conquer New Netherland, and settle Carolina. In the middle region, formerly claimed by the Dutch, four new colonies emerged: New York, New Jersey, Pennsylvania, and Delaware. The new colonies were awarded by the king to men (proprietors) who had remained loyal to the monarchy during the civil war. In 1663, for example, Charles II granted Carolina to eight prominent supporters, who became lords proprietor (owners) of the region.

THE CAROLINAS From the start, the southernmost mainland colony in the seventeenth century consisted of two widely separated areas that eventually became two Carolina colonies, North and South. The northernmost part, long called Albemarle, had been settled in the 1650s by colonists from Virginia. For half a century, Albemarle remained an isolated cluster of farms along the shores of Albemarle Sound.

The eight lords proprietor focused on more-promising sites in southern Carolina. To speed their efforts to generate profits, they recruited experienced English planters from the Caribbean island of Barbados, the oldest, richest, and most heavily populated colony in English America. The English in Barbados had developed a hugely profitable sugar plantation system based on the hard labor of enslaved Africans. The island colony was dominated by a few

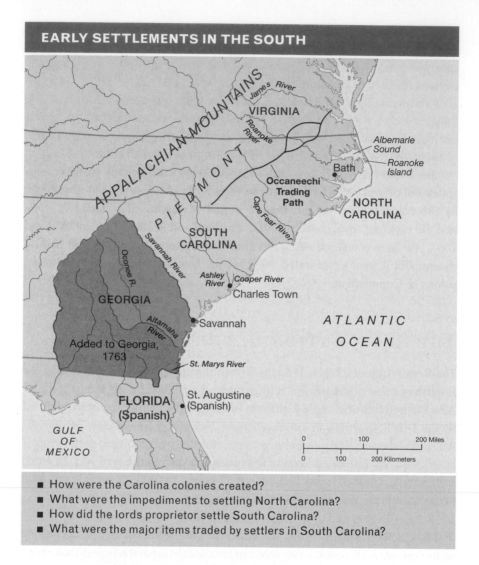

EARLY SETTLEMENTS IN THE SOUTH

- How were the Carolina colonies created?
- What were the impediments to settling North Carolina?
- How did the lords proprietor settle South Carolina?
- What were the major items traded by settlers in South Carolina?

wealthy planters who exercised powerful influence in the mother country. The renowned philosopher John Locke reported that the Barbadian English planters "endeavored to rule all." They also worked their slaves to death; the mortality rate for both slaves and whites in Barbados was twice that in Virginia—forcing English planters on the island to buy huge numbers of slaves each year as replacements. By 1670, however, all available land on Barbados had been claimed, and the sons and grandsons of the planter elite were forced to look elsewhere to find estates of their own. They seized the chance to settle South Carolina and bring the Barbadian plantation system to the new colony.

The first English colonists arrived in South Carolina in 1669 at Charles Town (later named Charleston). Over the next twenty years, half the South Carolina colonists came from Barbados and other island colonies in the Caribbean, such as Nevis, St. Kitts, and Jamaica. In a reference to Barbados and the other Caribbean colonies, John Yeamans, an Englishman in Carolina, explained in 1666 that "these settlements have been made and upheld by Negroes and without constant supplies of them cannot subsist."

From the start, South Carolina was a slave-based colony. Planters brought in enormous numbers of enslaved Africans to clear land, plant crops, and herd cattle. Carolina, a Swiss immigrant said, "looks more like a negro country than like a country settled by white people."

The government of Carolina grew out of a unique document, the Fundamental Constitutions of Carolina, drawn up by one of the eight proprietors, Lord Anthony Ashley Cooper, with the help of his secretary, John Locke. Its provisions for a formal titled nobility encouraged the awarding of large land grants to prominent Englishmen. From the beginning, however, headrights were given to every immigrant who could pay for passage across the Atlantic. The Fundamental Constitutions granted religious toleration, which gave Carolina a greater degree of religious freedom (extending to Jews and "heathens") than England or any other colony except Rhode Island.

In 1712, the Carolina colony was formally divided in two: North and South. After rebelling against the lords proprietor, South Carolina became a royal colony in 1719. North Carolina remained under the proprietors' rule until 1729, when it, too, became a royal colony.

Rice became the dominant commercial crop in coastal South Carolina. Because rice, like sugarcane and tobacco, was a labor-intensive crop, planters preferred enslaved Africans to work their plantations, in part because west Africans had been growing rice for generations. Both Carolinas also had huge forests of yellow pine trees that provided lumber and other key materials for shipbuilding. The sticky resin from pine trees could be boiled to make tar, which was needed to waterproof the seams of wooden ships (which is why North Carolinians came to be called Tar Heels).

ENSLAVING INDIANS   One of the quickest ways to make money in the early years of Carolina's development was through trade with local Indians. In the late seventeenth century, English merchants began traveling southward from Virginia into the Piedmont region of Carolina, where they developed a prosperous commerce in deerskins with the Catawbas.

The growing trade in deerskins entwined the Indians in a dependent relationship with Europeans that would prove disastrous to their traditional ways of life. English traders quickly became interested in buying enslaved Indians as well as deerskins. They gave Indians goods, firearms, and rum as payment for their capturing rivals to be sold as slaves.

The profitability of captive Indian workers prompted a frenzy of slaving activity among English settlers. As many as 50,000 Indians, mostly women and children, were sold as slaves in Charles Town between 1670 and 1715. More enslaved Indians were exported during that period than Africans were imported, and thousands of others were sold to "slavers" who took them to islands in the West Indies through New England ports.

The growing trade in enslaved Native Americans ignited unprecedented colonial violence. In 1712, the Tuscaroras of North Carolina attacked German and English colonists who had encroached upon their land. North Carolina authorities appealed to South Carolina for aid, and the colony, eager for more slaves, dispatched two expeditions made up mostly of Indian allies—Yamasees, Cherokees, Creeks, and Catawbas. They destroyed a Tuscarora town, executed 162 male warriors, and took 392 women and children captive for sale in Charles Town. The surviving Tuscaroras fled north, where they joined the Iroquois.

The Tuscarora War in North Carolina sparked more conflict in South Carolina. The Yamasees felt betrayed when white traders paid them less for their Tuscarora captives than they wanted. What made this shortfall so acute was that the Yamasees owed debts to traders totaling 100,000 deerskins. To recover their

The Broiling of Their Fish over the Flame In this drawing by John White, Algonquian men in North Carolina broil fish, a dietary staple of coastal societies.

debts, white traders cheated Yamasees, confiscated their lands, and began enslaving their women and children. In April 1715, the Yamasees attacked coastal plantations and killed more than 100 whites. Their assaults continued for months, aided by Creeks. Carolina colonists panicked, and hundreds fled to Charles Town.

The governor mobilized all white and black men to defend the colony, and other colonies supplied weapons. But it wasn't until the governor bribed the Cherokees to join them that the Yamasee War ended—in 1717. The Yamasees fled to Spanish-controlled Florida. To prevent another conflict, the colonial government outlawed all private trading with Indians. The end of the Yamasee War did not stop infighting among the Indians, however. For the next ten years or so, the Creeks and Cherokees engaged in a blood feud, much to the delight of the English. One Carolinian explained that their challenge was to figure out "how to hold both [tribes] as our friends, for some time, and assist them in cutting one another's throats without offending either. This is the game we intend to play if possible." Between 1700 and 1730, the indigenous population in the Carolinas dwindled from 15,000 to just 4,000.

THE MIDDLE COLONIES AND GEORGIA

The area between New England and the Chesapeake (Maryland and Virginia) included the "middle colonies" of New York, New Jersey, Delaware, and Pennsylvania that were initially controlled by the Netherlands. By 1670, the mostly Protestant Dutch had the largest merchant fleet in the world and the highest standard of living. They controlled northern European commerce and had become one of the most diverse and tolerant societies in Europe—and England's most ferocious competitor in international commerce.

NEW NETHERLAND BECOMES NEW YORK In London, King Charles II decided to pluck out that old Dutch thorn in the side of the English colonies in America: New Netherland. The Dutch colony was older than New England. The Dutch East India Company (organized in 1602) had hired an English sea captain, Henry Hudson, to explore America in hopes of finding a northwest passage to the spice-rich Indies. Sailing along the coast of North America in 1609, Hudson crossed Delaware Bay and then sailed up the river eventually named for him in what is now New York State.

Like Virginia and Massachusetts, New Netherland was created as a profit-making enterprise. And like the French, the Dutch were interested mainly in the fur trade. In 1610, they established fur-trading posts on Manhattan Island and upriver at Fort Orange (later called Albany).

In 1626, the Dutch governor purchased Manhattan (an Indian word meaning "island of many hills") from the Indians for 60 gilders, or about $1,000 in current values. The Dutch then built a fort and a fur-trading post at the lower end of the island. The village of New Amsterdam (eventually New York City), which grew up around the fort and expanded north to Wall Street, where the Dutch built a defensive wall, became the capital of New Netherland.

New Netherland was a corporate colony governed by the newly organized Dutch West India Company. All commerce with the Netherlands had to be carried in the company's ships, and the company controlled the beaver trade with the Indians.

Unlike most of the other European colonies in the Americas, the Dutch embraced ethnic and religious diversity. In 1579, the treaty creating the Dutch Republic declared that "everyone shall remain free in religion and . . . no one may be persecuted or investigated because of religion." Both the Dutch Republic and New Netherland welcomed exiles from the constant religious strife in Europe: Iberian and German Jews, French Protestants (Huguenots), English Puritans, and Catholics. There were even Muslims in New Amsterdam, where eighteen different languages were spoken.

In September 1654, a French ship arrived in New Amsterdam harbor carrying twenty-three *Sephardim*, Jews of Spanish-Portuguese descent. They had come seeking refuge from Portuguese-controlled Brazil and were the first Jewish settlers to arrive in North America.

The anti-Semitic colonial governor, Peter Stuyvesant, refused to accept them, however. Dutch officials overruled him, pointing out that it would be "unreasonable and unfair" to refuse to provide Jews a safe haven. They reminded Stuyvesant that some of the West India Company shareholders in the Netherlands were Jews. They told him that they wanted to "allow everyone to have his own belief, as long as he behaves quietly and legally, gives no offense to his neighbor, and does not oppose the government."

It would not be until the late seventeenth century that Jews could worship in public, however. Such restrictions help explain why the American Jewish community grew so slowly. In 1773, more than 100 years after the first Jewish refugees arrived, Jews represented only one tenth of 1 percent of the entire colonial population. Not until the nineteenth century would the American Jewish community experience dramatic growth.

The Dutch West India Company tolerated Jews, but its priority was making profits. In 1626, the company began importing enslaved Africans to meet its labor shortage. By the 1650s, New Amsterdam had one of the largest slave markets in America, although most of the African slaves sold there were sent to Virginia and Maryland.

The extraordinary success of the Dutch economy also proved to be its downfall, however. Like imperial Spain, the Dutch Empire expanded too rapidly. Although the Dutch dominated European trade with China, India, Africa, Brazil, and the Caribbean, they could not control their far-flung possessions, and it did not take long for European rivals to exploit the sprawling empire's weak points. By the mid–seventeenth century, England and the Netherlands were locked in ferocious commercial warfare.

The New Netherland governors were mostly stubborn autocrats, and were especially clumsy at Indian relations. They depended upon a small army for defense, and the residents of Manhattan, many of whom were not Dutch, were often contemptuous of the government. In 1664, the diverse colonists showed almost total indifference when Governor Stuyvesant called them to defend the colony against a threatening English fleet. Stuyvesant finally surrendered the colony without firing a shot.

The English conquest of New Netherland had been led by James Stuart, Duke of York, who would become King James II. Upon the capture of New Amsterdam, his brother, King Charles II, granted the entire Dutch region to him. The Dutch, however, negotiated an unusual surrender agreement that allowed New Netherlanders to retain their property, churches, language, and local officials. The English renamed both New Netherland and the city of New Amsterdam as New York, in honor of James, the Duke of York.

NEW JERSEY Shortly after the conquest of New Netherland, the Duke of York granted the lands between the Hudson and Delaware Rivers to Sir George Carteret and Lord John Berkeley (brother of Virginia's governor) and named the territory for Carteret's native Jersey, an island in the English Channel. In 1676, by mutual agreement, the new colony was divided into East and West Jersey, with Carteret taking the east and Berkeley the west. Finally, in 1682, Carteret sold out to a group of investors.

New settlements gradually arose in East Jersey. Disaffected Puritans from New Haven founded Newark, Carteret's brother brought a group to found Elizabethtown (named for Queen Elizabeth), and a group of Scots founded Perth Amboy. In the west, a scattering of Swedes, Finns, and Dutch remained, but they were soon overwhelmed by swarms of English and Welsh Quakers, as well as German and Scots-Irish settlers. In 1702, East and West Jersey were united as the single royal colony of New Jersey.

PENNSYLVANIA The Quakers, as the Religious Society of Friends was called (because they were supposed to "quake" and "tremble at the word of the Lord"), became the most controversial of the radical religious groups that emerged from the English Civil War. Founded in England in 1647 by George Fox, a saintly roving preacher, the Quakers, like the Puritans, rebelled against *all* forms of political and religious authority, including salaried ministers, military service, and paying taxes. They insisted that everyone, not just a select few, could experience a personal revelation from God, what they called the "Inner Light" of the Holy Spirit.

Quakers held radical beliefs for the time: they believed that people were essentially good and could achieve salvation through a personal, emotional communion with God. They demanded complete religious freedom for everyone and promoted equality of the sexes, including the full participation of women in religious affairs. They discarded all formal religious rituals and embraced a fierce pacifism. Like Fox, some Quakers went barefoot, others wore rags, and a few went naked to demonstrate their "primitive" commitment to Christ.

The Quakers suffered often violent abuse because their beliefs were so threatening to the social and religious order. Authorities accused them of disrupting "peace and order" and undermining "religion, Church order, and the state." New England Puritans banned, tortured, and executed them.

The settling of English Quakers in West Jersey encouraged other Friends to migrate, especially to the Delaware River side of the colony, where William Penn's Quaker commonwealth, the colony of Pennsylvania, soon arose. Penn, the son of wealthy Admiral Sir William Penn, had attended Oxford University, from which he was expelled for criticizing the university's requirement that students attend daily chapel services. His furious father, who had captured Jamaica for England in 1655, banished his son from their home.

The younger Penn lived in France for two years, then studied law before moving to Ireland to manage several family estates. There the twenty-two-year-old Penn was arrested in 1666 for attending a Quaker meeting. Much to the chagrin of his parents, he became a Quaker and was arrested several times for his religious convictions.

Upon his father's death, Penn inherited a fortune, including a huge tract of land in America, which the king urged him to settle as a means of ridding England of Quakers. The land, which was larger than England itself, was named, at the king's insistence, for Penn's father—Pennsylvania (literally, "Penn's Woods").

Penn aggressively encouraged people of different religions and from different countries to settle in his new colony, for he hoped that people of all faiths and nations would live together in harmony. By the end of 1681, thousands of immigrants had responded to Penn's offer, and a bustling town was emerging at the junction of the Schuylkill and Delaware Rivers. Penn called it Philadelphia (meaning "City of Brotherly Love").

The relations between the Native Americans and the Pennsylvania Quakers were unusually good because of the Quakers' friendliness and Penn's policy of purchasing land titles from the Native Americans. For some fifty years the settlers and the Native Americans lived in peace.

The colony's government, which rested on three Frames of Government drafted by Penn, resembled that of other proprietary colonies except that the freemen (property owners) elected the council members as well as the assembly. The governor had no veto, although Penn, as proprietor, did. Penn hoped to show that a colonial government could operate in accordance with Quaker principles, that it could maintain peace and order, and that religion could flourish without government support and with absolute freedom of conscience. Over time, however, the Quakers struggled to forge a harmonious colony. In Pennsylvania's first ten years, it went through six governors. A disappointed Penn wrote from London: "Pray stop those scurvy quarrels that break out to the disgrace of the province."

Quaker meeting The presence of women at this Friends meeting is evidence of progressive Quaker views on gender equality.

DELAWARE   In 1682, the Duke of York granted Penn the area of Delaware, another part of the former Dutch territory (which had been New Sweden before being acquired by the Dutch in 1655). At first, Delaware—taking its name from the Delaware River, which had been named to honor Thomas West (Baron De La Warr), Virginia's first colonial governor—became part of Pennsylvania, but

THE MIDDLE COLONIES

- Why was New Jersey divided in half?
- Why did the Quakers settle in Pennsylvania?
- How did the relations with Indians in Pennsylvania compare with other colonies?

after 1704 it was granted the right to choose its own assembly. From then until the American Revolution, Delaware had a separate assembly but shared Pennsylvania's governor.

GEORGIA   Georgia was the last of the English colonies to be established. In 1732, King George II gave the land between the Savannah and Altamaha Rivers to twenty-one English trustees appointed to govern the Province of Georgia, named in honor of the king. In two respects, Georgia was unique among the colonies: it was to provide a military buffer against Spanish Florida and to serve as a social experiment bringing together settlers from different countries and religions, many of them refugees, debtors, or "miserable wretches" making up the "worthy poor." General James E. Oglethorpe, a prominent member of Parliament, was appointed to head the colony.

In 1733, colonists founded Savannah on the Atlantic coast near the mouth of the Savannah River. The town, designed by Oglethorpe, featured a grid of crisscrossing roads graced by numerous parks. Protestant refugees from Austria began to arrive in 1734, followed by Germans and German-speaking Moravians and Swiss. The addition of Welsh, Highland Scots, Sephardic Jews, and others gave the early colony a diverse character.

As a buffer against Spanish Florida, the Georgia colony succeeded, but as a social experiment creating a "common man's utopia," it failed. Initially, landholdings were limited to 500 acres to promote economic equality. Liquor was banned, as were lawyers, and the importation of slaves was forbidden. But the idealistic rules soon collapsed as the colony struggled to become self-sufficient. The regulations against rum and slavery were widely disregarded and finally abandoned.

In 1754, Georgia became a royal colony. It developed slowly over the next decade but grew rapidly after 1763. Georgians exported rice, lumber, beef, and pork, and carried on a profitable trade with the islands in the West Indies. Almost unintentionally, the colony became an economic success and a slave-centered society.

NATIVE PEOPLES AND ENGLISH SETTLERS

Most English colonists adopted a strategy for dealing with the Indians quite different from that of the French and Dutch. Merchants from France and the Netherlands focused on exploiting the fur trade. The thriving commerce in animal skins—especially beaver, otter, and deer—helped spur exploration of the vast American continent. It also both enriched and devastated the lives of Indians.

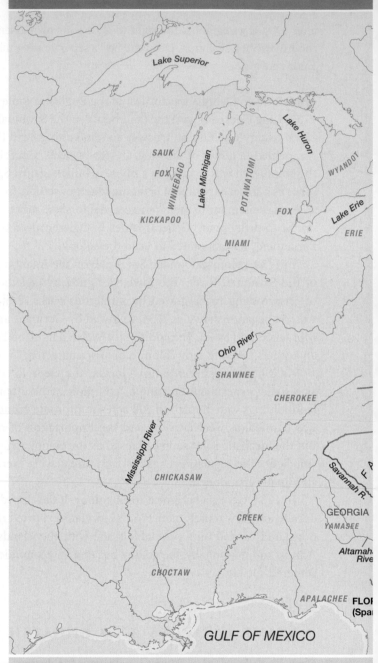

EUROPEAN SETTLEMENTS AND INDIAN

Lake Superior

Lake Huron

Lake Michigan

Lake Erie

SAUK

FOX

WINNEBAGO

POTAWATOMI

WYANDOT

FOX

ERIE

KICKAPOO

MIAMI

Ohio River

SHAWNEE

CHEROKEE

Mississippi River

CHICKASAW

Savannah R.

GEORGIA

CREEK

YAMASEE

Altamaha
River

CHOCTAW

APALACHEE FLOR
(Spar

GULF OF MEXICO

- Why did European settlement lead to the expansion of hostilities among the Indians?
- What were the consequences of the trade and commerce between the English settlers and the southern indigenous peoples?
- How were the relationships between the settlers and the members of the Iroquois League different from those between settlers and tribes in other regions?

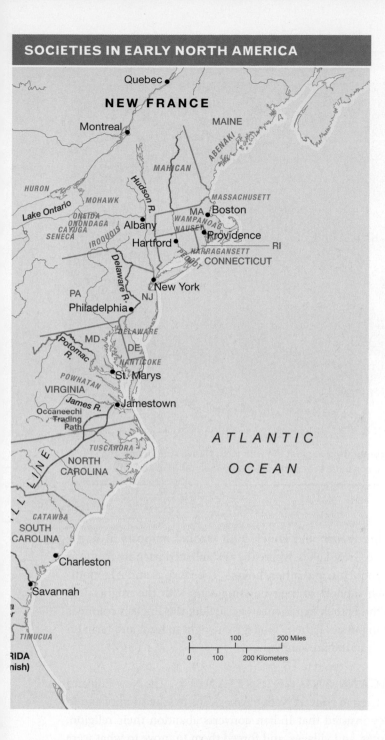

Quebec

NEW FRANCE

Montreal

MAINE

ABENAKI

MAHICAN

HURON

Hudson R.

MOHAWK

Lake Ontario

MASSACHUSETT

ONEIDA
ONONDAGA
CAYUGA
SENECA

MA · Boston

WAMPANOAG

Albany

NAUSET

IROQUOIS

Hartford

Providence

RI

Delaware R.

NARRAGANSETT

CONNECTICUT

PEQUOT

PA

New York

NJ

Philadelphia

DELAWARE

MD

DE

Potomac
R.

NANTICOKE

POWHATAN

St. Marys

VIRGINIA

James R.

Jamestown

Occaneechi
Trading
Path

ATLANTIC

TUSCARORA

OCEAN

FALL LINE

**NORTH
CAROLINA**

CATAWBA

**SOUTH
CAROLINA**

Charleston

Savannah

TIMUCUA

RIDA
(nish)

0   100   200 Miles

0   100   200 Kilometers

Algonquian ceremony celebrating harvest As with most Native Americans, the Algonquians' dependence on nature for survival shaped their religious beliefs.

To get fur pelts, the French and Dutch built trading outposts in upper New York and along the Great Lakes, where they established friendly relations with the Hurons, Algonquians, and other Indians. The Hurons and Algonquians also sought French support in their ongoing wars with the mighty Iroquois. In contrast to the French experience in Canada, the English colonists were more interested in pursuing their "God-given" right to hunt and farm on Indian lands and to fish in Indian waters.

NATIVE AMERICANS AND CHRISTIANITY The New England Puritans aggressively tried to convert Native Americans to Christianity and to "civilized" living. They insisted that Indian converts abandon their religion, language, clothes, names, and villages, and forced them to move to what were called "praying towns" to separate them from their "heathen" brethren.

THE PEQUOT WAR Indians who fought to keep their lands were forced out or killed. New England Puritans, like the colonists in Virginia, viewed

Indians as demonic savages, "barbarous creatures," "merciless and cruel heathens." As one colonist asserted, Indians had no place in a "new England."

In 1636, settlers in Massachusetts accused a Pequot of murdering a colonist; the English took revenge by burning a Pequot village. As the Indians fled, the Puritans killed them—men, women, and children. Sassacus, the Pequot chief, organized the survivors and counterattacked. During the ensuing Pequot War of 1637, the colonists and their Narragansett allies set fire to an Indian village near West Mystic, in the Connecticut Valley, and killed those who tried to escape. William Bradford, the governor of Plymouth, admitted that it was "a fearful sight" to see the Indians "frying in the fire and the streams of blood quenching" the flames, but "the victory seemed a sweet sacrifice" delivered by God. Under the terms of the Treaty of Hartford (1638), the Pequot Nation was dissolved.

KING PHILIP'S WAR   After the Pequot War, relations between colonists and Indians improved somewhat, but the continuing influx of English settlers and the decline of the beaver population eventually reduced the Native Americans to poverty. By 1675, the Indians and English settlers had come to fear each other deeply.

The era of peaceful coexistence came to a bloody end during the last quarter of the seventeenth century. Native American leaders, especially the chief of the Wampanoags, Metacomet (known to the colonists as King Philip), resented English efforts to convert Indians to Christianity. In the fall of 1674, John Sassamon, a Christian Indian who had graduated from Harvard College, warned the English that the Wampanoags were preparing for war.

A few months later, Sassamon was found dead in a frozen pond. Colonial authorities convicted three Wampanoags of murder and hanged them. Enraged Wampanoag warriors then burned Puritan farms on June 20, 1675. Three days later, an Englishman shot a Wampanoag; the Wampanoags retaliated by ambushing and beheading a group of Puritans.

The shocking violence soon spun out of control in what came to be called **King Philip's War**, or Metacomet's War. The brutal fighting resulted in more deaths and destruction in New England in proportion to the population than any American conflict since, including the Civil War. Vengeful bands of warriors destroyed twelve towns and attacked forty others.

Within a year, colonists conducted a surprise attack that killed 300 Narragansett warriors and 400 women and children. The Narragansetts retaliated by destroying Providence, Rhode Island, and threatening Boston itself, prompting a prominent minister to call it "the saddest time with New England that was ever known."

The situation grew so desperate that the colonies passed America's first conscription laws, drafting into the militia all males between the ages of sixteen and sixty. In the summer of 1676, Metacomet's wife and son were captured, leading the chieftain to cry: "My heart breaks; now I am ready to die."

In the end, staggering casualties and shortages of food and ammunition wore down the Naragansetts. Some surrendered; many succumbed to disease, and others fled to the west. Those who remained were forced into villages supervised by English officials. Metacomet initially escaped, only to be hunted down and killed. The victorious colonists marched his severed head to Plymouth, where it stayed atop a pole for twenty years. Metacomet's wife and son were sold into slavery in the Caribbean. By the end of King Philip's War, three quarters of the Indians in New England had been killed.

THE IROQUOIS LEAGUE The same combination of forces that wiped out the Indian populations of New England and the Carolinas affected the native peoples around New York City and the lower Hudson Valley. The inability of Indian groups to unite effectively against the Europeans, as well as their vulnerability to infectious diseases, doomed them to conquest and exploitation.

In the interior of New York, however, a different situation arose. There, sometime before 1600, the Iroquois nations—Seneca, Cayuga, Onondaga, Oneida, and Mohawk—had been convinced by Hiawatha, a Mohawk, to forge an alliance.

The **Iroquois League**, known to its members as the *Haudenosaunee*, or Great Peace, became so strong that the outnumbered Dutch and, later, English traders, were forced to work with them to acquire beaver pelts. By the early seventeenth century, a council of some fifty sachems (chieftains) oversaw the 12,000 members of the Iroquois League. Its capital was Onondaga, a bustling town a few miles south of what later became Syracuse, New York.

The League was governed by a remarkable constitution, called the Great Law of Peace, which had three main principles: peace, equity, and justice. Each person was a shareholder in the wealth of the nation. The constitution established a Great Council of fifty male *royaneh* (religious–political leaders), each representing one of the female-led clans of the Iroquois nations. The Great Law of Peace gave essential power to the people. It insisted that every time the royaneh dealt with "an especially important matter or a great emergency," they had to "submit the matter to the decision of their people," both men and women, for their consent.

The search for furs and captives led Iroquois war parties to range widely across what is today eastern North America. They gained control over a huge area from the St. Lawrence River to Tennessee and from Maine to Michigan. For more than twenty years, warfare raged across the Great Lakes region between the Iroquois (supported by Dutch and English fur traders) and the Algonquians and Hurons (and their French allies).

In the 1690s, the French and their Indian allies destroyed Iroquois crops and villages, infected them with smallpox, and reduced the male population by more than a third. Facing extermination, the Iroquois made peace with the French in 1701. During the first half of the eighteenth century, they stayed out of the almost constant wars between the two European powers, which enabled them to play the English off against the French while creating a thriving fur trade for themselves.

SLAVERY IN THE COLONIES

SLAVERY IN NORTH AMERICA By 1700, enslaved Africans made up 11 percent of the total population in the American colonies. (Slaves would comprise more than 20 percent by 1770.) But slavery differed greatly from region to region. Africans were a tiny minority in New England (about 2 percent). Because there were no large plantations in New England and fewer slaves were owned, "family slavery" prevailed, with masters and slaves usually living under the same roof.

Slavery was much more prevalent in the Chesapeake colonies and the Carolinas. By 1730, the black slave population in Virginia and Maryland had become the first in the Western Hemisphere to achieve a self-sustaining rate of population growth. By 1750, about 80 percent of the African American slaves in the Chesapeake Bay region, for example, had been born there.

SLAVERY'S AFRICAN ROOTS The transport of African captives across the Atlantic to the Americas was the largest forced migration in world history. More than 10 million people eventually made the terrifying journey, the vast majority of them going to Brazil or to Caribbean sugar islands such as Barbados and Jamaica.

Enslaved Africans spoke as many as fifty different languages and worshipped many different gods. Some had lived in large kingdoms and others in dispersed villages. In their homelands, Africans had preyed upon other Africans for centuries. Warfare was almost constant, as rival tribes conquered, kidnapped, enslaved, and sold one another.

Slavery in Africa, however, was less brutal than in the Americas. In Africa, slaves lived with their captors, and their children were not automatically enslaved. The involvement of Europeans in transatlantic slavery, whereby captives were sold and shipped to other nations, was much worse.

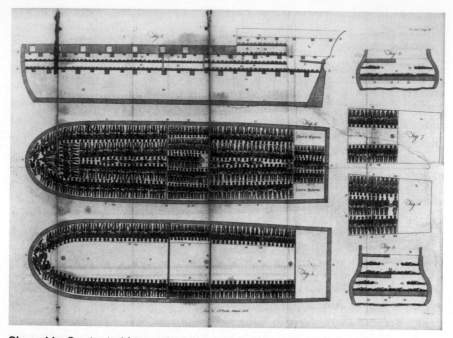

Slave ship One in six Africans died while crossing the Atlantic in ships like this one, from an American diagram ca. 1808.

During the seventeenth and eighteenth centuries, African slave traders brought captives to dozens of "slave forts" along the West African coast, where they were sold to European slave traders. Once purchased, the captives were branded on the back or buttocks with a company mark, chained, and loaded onto mostly British-owned slave ships. They were packed below deck and subjected to a four-week to six-month transatlantic voyage, known as the **Middle Passage** because it served as the middle leg of the so-called *triangular trade* in which British ships traveled on the first leg to West Africa, where they exchanged rum, clothing, and guns for slaves. The slaves then were taken on the second leg of the triangle to American ports, where the ships were loaded with commodities and timber before returning to Britain and Europe on the final of the three legs of the triangular trade.

One in six captives died en route, many by suicide, and almost one in every ten of the floating prisons experienced a revolt. Yet many whites engaged in slave trafficking considered their work highly respectable. "What a glorious and advantageous trade this is," wrote slave trader James Houston. "It is the hinge on which all the trade of this globe moves."

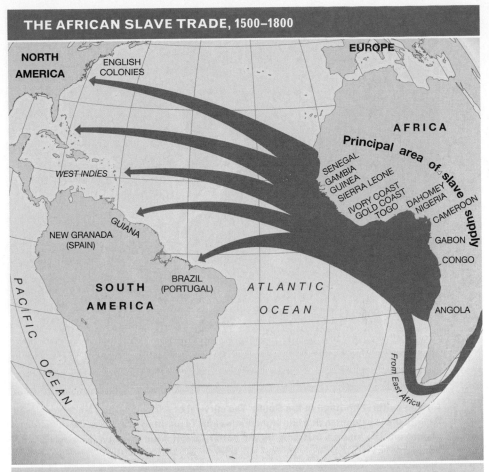

THE AFRICAN SLAVE TRADE, 1500–1800

NORTH AMERICA

ENGLISH COLONIES

EUROPE

WEST INDIES

AFRICA

Principal area of slave supply

SENEGAL
GAMBIA
GUINEA
SIERRA LEONE
IVORY COAST
GOLD COAST
TOGO
DAHOMEY
NIGERIA
CAMEROON

GUIANA

NEW GRANADA (SPAIN)

GABON

CONGO

PACIFIC OCEAN

SOUTH AMERICA

BRAZIL (PORTUGAL)

ATLANTIC OCEAN

ANGOLA

From East Africa

- How were Africans captured and enslaved?
- Describe how captive Africans were treated during the Middle Passage.
- How did enslaved African Americans create a new culture in the colonies?

The rapid growth of slavery in the Western Hemisphere was driven by high profits and justified by a widespread racism that viewed Africans as beasts of burden rather than human beings. Once in America, Africans were treated as property ("chattel"), herded in chains to public slave auctions, and sold to the highest bidder. On large southern plantations that grew tobacco, sugarcane, or rice, groups of slaves were organized into work gangs supervised by black "drivers" and white overseers. The slaves were often quartered in barracks, fed like livestock, and issued ill-fitting clothes and shoes so uncomfortable that many preferred to go barefoot. Colonial laws allowed whites to use brutal

African cultural heritage in the South The survival of African culture among enslaved Americans is evident in this late eighteenth-century painting of a South Carolina plantation. The musical instruments and pottery are of African origin (probably Yoruban).

means to discipline slaves. They were whipped, branded, shackled, castrated, or sold away, often to the Caribbean islands, where few survived the harsh conditions of harvesting sugarcane.

Enslaved Africans, however, found ingenious ways to cope. Some rebelled by resisting work orders, sabotaging crops and stealing tools, faking illness or injury, or running away. If caught, runaways faced terrible punishment. They also faced uncertain freedom. Where would they run *to* in a society ruled by whites and governed by racism?

SLAVE CULTURE In the process of being forced into lives of bondage in a new world, Africans from diverse homelands forged a new identity as African Americans. At the same time, they wove into American culture many strands of their heritage, including new words such as *tabby, tote, goober, yam,* and *banana*, as well as the names of the Coosaw, Pee Dee, and Wando Rivers. More significant were African influences upon American music, folklore, and religious practices. Slaves often used songs, stories, and religious preachings to circulate coded messages expressing their distaste for masters or overseers. The fundamental theme of slave religion, adapted from the Christianity that was forced upon them, was deliverance: God would eventually free them and open the gates to heaven's promised land.

THRIVING COLONIES

By the early eighteenth century, the English colonies in the New World had outstripped those of the French and Spanish. English America, both the mainland colonies and those in the Caribbean, had become the most populous, prosperous, and powerful of the European empires in the Americas. American colonists were better fed, clothed, and housed than their counterparts in Europe.

Yet the English colonization of North America included failures as well as successes. Many settlers found hard labor, desperation, and an early death in the New World. Others flourished only because they were able to exploit Indians, indentured servants, or Africans.

The English colonists enjoyed crucial advantages over their European rivals. While the tightly controlled colonial empires of Spain and France stifled innovation, the English colonies were organized as profit-making enterprises with a minimum of royal control. Where New Spain was dominated by wealthy men who controlled vast estates and often intended to return to Spain, many English colonists ventured to America because, for them, life in England had grown intolerable. The leaders of the Dutch and non-Puritan English colonies, unlike the Spanish and French, welcomed people from a variety of nationalities and religions who came in search of a new life. Perhaps most important, the English colonies enjoyed a greater degree of self-government, which made them more dynamic and creative than their French and Spanish counterparts.

Throughout the seventeenth century, geography reinforced England's emphasis on the concentrated settlements of its American colonies. The farthest western expansion of English settlement stopped at the eastern slopes of the Appalachian Mountains. To the east lay the wide expanse of ocean, which served as a highway for the transport of people, ideas, commerce, and ways of life from Europe to America. But the ocean also served as a barrier that separated old ideas from new, allowing the English colonies to evolve in a "new world"—while developing new ideas about economic freedom and political liberties that would flower later in the eighteenth century.

CHAPTER REVIEW

SUMMARY

- **English Background** England's colonization of North America differed from that of its European rivals. While chartered by the Crown, English colonization was funded by *joint-stock companies*, groups of investors eager for profits. Their colonial governments reflected the model of a two-house Parliament and long-cherished civil liberties. The colonization of the eastern seaboard of North America occurred at a time of religious and political turmoil in England, strongly affecting colonial culture and development.

- **English Settlers and Colonization** The early years of Jamestown and Plymouth were grim. In time, *tobacco* flourished, and its success paved the way for a slave-based economy in the South. Sugar and rice plantations developed in the proprietary Carolina colonies, which operated with minimal royal intrusion. Family farms and a mixed economy characterized the middle and New England colonies. Religion was the primary motivation for the founding of several colonies. *Puritans* drafted the *Mayflower Compact* and founded Massachusetts Bay Colony as a Christian commonwealth. Rhode Island was established by Roger Williams, a religious dissenter from Massachusetts. Maryland was founded as a refuge for English Catholics. William Penn, a Quaker, founded Pennsylvania and invited Europe's persecuted religious sects to his colony. The Dutch allowed members of all faiths to settle in New Netherland.

- **Indian Relations** Trade with the *Powhatan Confederacy* in Virginia enabled Jamestown to survive its early years, but brutal armed conflicts such as *Bacon's Rebellion* occurred as settlers invaded Indian lands. Puritans retaliated against Indian resistance in the Pequot War of 1637 and in *King Philip's War* from 1675 to 1676. Among the principal colonial leaders, only Roger Williams and William Penn treated Indians as equals. The powerful *Iroquois League* played the European powers against one another to control territories.

- **Indentured Servants and Slaves** The colonies increasingly relied on *indentured servants*, immigrants who signed contracts (indentures) that required them to work for several years upon arriving in America. By the end of the seventeenth century, enslaved Africans had become the primary form of labor in the Chesapeake. The demand for slaves in the sugar plantations of the West Indies drove European slave traders to organize the transport of Africans via the dreaded *Middle Passage* across the Atlantic. African cultures fused with others in the Americas to create a native-born African American culture.

- **Thriving English Colonies** By 1700, England had become a great trading empire. English America was the most populous and prosperous region of North America. Minimal royal interference in the proprietary for-profit colonies and widespread landownership encouraged settlers to put down roots. Religious diversity attracted a variety of investors and settlers.

CHRONOLOGY

1603	James I takes the throne of England
1607	The Virginia Company establishes Jamestown
1612	John Rolfe begins growing tobacco for export in Virginia
1619	First Africans arrive in English America
1620	Plymouth colony founded by Pilgrims; Mayflower Compact
1626	The Dutch purchase Manhattan from Indians
1630	Massachusetts Bay Colony is founded by Puritans
1634	Settlement of Maryland begins
1637	The Pequot War in New England
1642–1651	The English Civil War (Puritans versus Royalists)
1649	The Toleration Act in Maryland
1660	Restoration of English Monarchy
1664	English take control of New Amsterdam (New York City)
1669	Charles Town is founded in the Carolina colony
1675–1676	King Philip's War in New England
1676	Bacon's Rebellion in Virginia
1681	Pennsylvania is established
1733	Georgia is founded

KEY TERMS

Puritans p. 41

joint-stock companies p. 44

Powhatan Confederacy p. 45

tobacco p. 47

indentured servants p. 47

headright p. 48

Bacon's Rebellion p. 50

Mayflower Compact p. 53

King Philip's War p. 73

Iroquois League p. 74

Middle Passage p. 76

🐸 INQUIZITIVE

Go to InQuizitive to see what you've learned—and learn what you've missed—with personalized feedback along the way.

3 Colonial Ways of Life

The artisans of Boston (1766) While fishing, shipbuilding, and maritime trade dominated New England economies, many young men entered apprenticeships, learning a trade from a master craftsman in the hopes of becoming blacksmiths, carpenters, gunsmiths, printers, candlemakers, leather tanners, and more.

T he process of carving a new civilization out of an abundant "New World" involved often-violent encounters among European, African, and Indian cultures. War, duplicity, displacement, and enslavement were the tragic results. On another level, however, the process of transforming the American continent was a story of blending and accommodation, of diverse peoples and resilient cultures engaged in the everyday tasks of building homes, planting crops, trading goods, raising families, enforcing laws, and worshipping their gods. Those who colonized America during the seventeenth and eighteenth centuries were part of a massive social migration occurring throughout Europe and Africa. Everywhere, it seemed, people were in motion—moving from farms to villages, from villages to cities, and from homelands to colonies.

Most English and European settlers were responding to powerful social and economic forces. Rapid population growth and the rise of commercial agriculture squeezed poor farmworkers off the land and into cities like London, Edinburgh, Dublin, and Paris, where they struggled to survive. That most Europeans in the seventeenth and eighteenth centuries were desperately poor helps explain why so many were willing to risk their lives by migrating to the American colonies. Others sought political security or religious freedom. A tragic exception was the Africans, who were captured and transported to new lands against their will.

Those who initially settled in colonial America were mostly young (more than half were under twenty-five), male, and poor, and almost half were indentured servants or slaves. During the eighteenth century, England would transport some 50,000 convicts to the North American colonies to relieve

focus questions

1. What were the major factors that contributed to the demographic changes in the English colonies during the eighteenth century?

2. What roles did women play in the English colonies?

3. What were the differences and similarities between the societies and economies of the southern, middle, and New England colonies?

4. How did race-based slavery develop during the seventeenth century, and in what ways did this impact the social and economic development of colonial America?

5. In what ways did the Enlightenment and Great Awakening impact American thought?

overcrowded jails and provide needed workers. Once in America, many of the newcomers kept moving within and across colonies in search of better lands or new business opportunities. This extraordinary mosaic of adventurous people created America's enduring institutions and values, as well as its distinctive spirit and restless energy.

THE SHAPE OF EARLY AMERICA

Life in early America was hard and often short. Many in the first wave of American colonists died of disease or starvation; others were killed by Native Americans. The average **death rate** in the first years of settlement was 50 percent. Once colonial life became more settled and secure, however, the colonies grew rapidly. On average, the American population doubled every twenty-five years during the colonial period. By 1750, the number of colonists had passed 1 million; by 1775, it approached 2.5 million. By comparison, the combined population of England, Scotland, and Ireland in 1750 was 6.5 million.

POPULATION GROWTH Benjamin Franklin, a keen observer of life in the new country or said that the extraordinary growth in the colonial population came about because land was plentiful and cheap, and laborers were scarce and expensive. The opposite conditions prevailed in Europe. It suffered from overpopulation and expensive farmland. Once in the colonies, settlers tended to have large families, in part because farm children could lend a hand in the fields.

Colonists tended to marry and start families at an earlier age than in Europe. In England, the average age at marriage for women was twenty-five or twenty-six; in America, it dropped to twenty. Men in the colonies also married at a younger age. The **birth rate** rose accordingly, since women who married earlier had time for about two additional pregnancies during their childbearing years. On average, a married woman had a child every two

Colonial farm This plan of a newly cleared farm shows how trees were cut down and the stumps left to rot.

to three years before menopause, making for large families. Benjamin Franklin, for example, had sixteen brothers and sisters.

Birthing children, however, was also dangerous, since most babies were delivered at home in often unsanitary conditions and harsh weather. Miscarriages were common. Between 25 and 50 percent of women died during birthing or soon thereafter, and almost a quarter of all babies did not survive infancy, especially during the early stages of a colonial settlement. Each year, more deaths occurred among young children than any other age group.

Disease and epidemics were rampant in colonial America. In 1713, Boston minister Cotton Mather lost three of his children and his wife to a measles epidemic. (Mather lost eight of fifteen children in their first year of life.) Martha Custis, the Virginia widow who married George Washington, had four children during her first marriage, all of whom died young, at ages two, three, sixteen, and seventeen. Overall, however, mortality rates in the colonies were lower than in Europe. Because fertile land was plentiful, famine seldom occurred after the early years of settlement, and, although the winters were more severe than in England, firewood was abundant.

Americans, on the whole, were also less susceptible to disease than were Europeans. In part, this was because colonial settlements were more scattered and sparsely populated than those in Europe—and therefore colonists were less likely to be exposed to infectious diseases. That began to change, of course, as colonial cities grew larger and more congested, and trade and travel increased. By the mid–eighteenth century, the colonies were beginning to see levels of contagion much like those in the cities of Europe.

WOMEN IN THE COLONIES

In contrast to the colonies of New Spain and New France, English America had far more women, which largely explains the difference in population growth rates among the European empires competing in the Americas. More women did not mean more equality, however. Most colonists brought to America deeply rooted convictions about the inferiority of women. As one New England minister stressed, "the woman is a weak creature not endowed with [the] strength and constancy of mind [of men]."

Women, as had been true for centuries, were expected to focus their time and talents on what was then called the domestic sphere. They were to obey and serve their husbands, nurture their children, and maintain their households. Governor John Winthrop insisted that a "true wife" would find contentment only "in subjection to her husband's authority." The wife's role, said another Puritan, was "to guide the house etc. and not guide the husband."

Women in most colonies could not vote, hold office, attend schools or colleges, bring lawsuits, sign contracts, or become ministers. Divorces were usually granted only for desertion or "cruel and barbarous treatment," and no matter who was named the "guilty party," the father received custody of the children. A Pennsylvania court did see fit to send a man to prison for throwing a loaf of hard bread at his wife, "which occasioned her Death in a short Time."

"**WOMEN'S WORK**" Virtually every member of a household, regardless of age or gender, worked, and no one was expected to work harder than women. As John Cotton, a Boston minister, admitted in 1699, "women are creatures without which there is no Comfortable living for a man."

During the eighteenth century, **women's work** typically involved activities in the house, garden, and fields. Unmarried women often worked outside their home. Many moved into other households to help with children or to make clothes. Others stayed at home but took in children or spun thread into yarn to exchange for cloth. Still others hired themselves out as apprentices to learn a skilled trade or craft. Throughout colonial America, there were women silversmiths, blacksmiths, shoemakers, sailmakers, shopkeepers, and mill owners. Other women operated laundries or bakeries. Technically, any money earned by a married woman was the property of her husband.

Farm women usually rose and prepared breakfast by sunrise and went to bed soon after dark. They were responsible for building the fire and hauling water from a well or creek. They fed and watered the livestock, woke the children, churned butter, tended the garden, prepared lunch (the main meal of the day), played with the children, worked the garden again, prepared dinner, milked the cows, got the children ready for bed, and cleaned the kitchen before retiring. Women also combed, spun, spooled, wove, and bleached wool for clothing; knitted linen and cotton, hemmed sheets, pieced quilts; made candles and soap; chopped wood, hauled water, mopped floors, and washed clothes.

One of the most lucrative trades among colonial women was the oldest: prostitution. Many servants took up prostitution after their indenture was fulfilled, and the colonial port cities had thriving brothels. They catered to sailors and soldiers, but men from all walks of life, married and unmarried, frequented what were called "bawdy houses," or, in Puritan Boston, "disorderly houses." Virginia's William Byrd, perhaps the wealthiest man in the colony, complained in his diary that he had walked the streets of Williamsburg trying to "pick up a Whore, but could not find one." Local authorities frowned on such activities. In Massachusetts, convicted prostitutes were stripped to the waist, tied to the back of a cart, and whipped as it moved through the town.

In South Carolina, several elected public officials were dismissed because they were caught "lying with wenches."

On occasion, circumstances forced women to exercise leadership outside the domestic sphere. Such was the case with South Carolinian Elizabeth Lucas Pinckney (1722–1793). Born in the West Indies, raised on the island of Antigua, and educated in England, "Eliza" moved with her family to Charleston, South Carolina, at age fifteen, when her father, George Lucas, inherited three plantations. The following year, however, Lucas, a British army officer and colonial administrator, was called back to Antigua, leaving Eliza to care for her ailing mother and younger sister—and to manage three plantations worked by slaves. She wrote a friend in England, "I have the business of three plantations to transact, which requires much writing and more business and fatigue . . . [but] by rising early I find I can go through much business."

Eliza loved the "vegetable world," and experimented with several crops before focusing on *indigo*, a West Indian plant that produced a much-coveted blue dye for fabric, especially military uniforms. Indigo made her family a fortune, as it did for many other plantation owners on the Carolina coast. In 1744,

The First, Second, and Last Scene of Mortality Prudence Punderson's needlework (ca. 1776) shows the domestic path, from cradle to coffin, followed by most affluent colonial women.

she married Charles Pinckney, a widower twice her age, who was speaker of the South Carolina Assembly. She made him promise that she could continue to manage the plantation. As Eliza began raising a family, she "resolved to make a good wife to my dear husband . . . a good mother to my children . . . a good mistress to my servants [making] their lives as comfortable as I can."

WOMEN AND RELIGION During the colonial era, no denomination allowed women to be ordained as ministers. Only the Quakers let women hold church offices and preach (exhort) in public. Puritans cited biblical passages claiming that God required "virtuous" women to submit to male authority and remain "silent" in congregational matters.

Women who challenged ministerial authority were usually prosecuted and punished. Yet by the eighteenth century, as is true today, women made up the overwhelming majority of church members. Their disproportionate attendance at church services and revivals worried many ministers, since a feminized church was presumed to be a church in decline. In 1692, the influential Boston minister Cotton Mather observed that there "are far more Godly Women in the world than there are Godly Men." In explaining this phenomenon, Mather put a new twist on the old notion of women being the weaker sex. He argued that the pain associated with childbirth, which had long been interpreted as the penalty women paid for Eve's sinfulness, was in part what drove women "more frequently, & the more fervently" to commit their lives to Christ.

In colonial America, the religious roles of black women were quite different from those of their white counterparts. In most West African tribes, women were not subordinate to men and frequently served as priests and cult leaders. Although some enslaved Africans had been exposed to Christianity or Islam in Africa, most of them tried to sustain their traditional African religion once they arrived in the colonies. In America, black women (and men) were often excluded from church membership for fear that Christianized slaves might seek to gain their freedom. To clarify the situation, Virginia in 1667 passed a law specifying that children of slaves would be slaves even if they had been baptized as Christians.

SOCIETY AND ECONOMY IN THE SOUTHERN COLONIES

As the southern colonies matured, inequalities of wealth became more visible, and social life grew more divided. The use of enslaved Indians and Africans to grow and process the crops most in demand in Europe generated enormous wealth for a few large landowners and their families. Socially, the planters and merchants increasingly became a class apart from the "common folk." They dominated the legislatures, bought luxury goods from London and Paris, and built brick mansions with formal gardens—all the while looking down upon their social "inferiors," both white and black.

Warm weather and plentiful rainfall enabled the southern colonies to grow the **staple crops** (most profitable) valued by the mother country: tobacco, rice, sugarcane, and indigo. Virginia, as King Charles I put it, was "founded upon smoke." Tobacco production soared during the seventeenth century. "In Virginia and Maryland," wrote a royal official in 1629, "tobacco . . . is our All, and indeed leaves no room for anything else."

The same was true for rice cultivation in South Carolina and Georgia. Using only hand tools, slaves transformed the coastal landscapes, removing trees from swamps and wetlands infested with snakes, alligators, and mosquitos. They then created a system of floodgates to allow workers to drain or flood the fields as needed. Over time, the rice planters became the wealthiest group

Virginia plantation wharf Southern colonial plantations were often constructed along rivers, with easy access to oceangoing vessels, as shown on this 1730 tobacco label.

in the British colonies. As plantations grew in size, the demand for enslaved laborers, first Native Americans, and later Africans, rose dramatically.

The first English immigrants to Virginia and Maryland (the Chesapeake colonies) built primitive one-room huts with dirt floors and little privacy. They provided limited protection from the cold and wind and rotted quickly. A visitor to Virginia in 1622 reported that the colony's huts "were the worst I ever saw." Eventually, colonists built sparsely furnished cabins on stone or brick foundations roofed with thatched straw. The spaces between the log timbers were "chinked" with "wattle and daub"—a mix of mud, sand, straw, and wooden stakes that when dried formed a sturdy wall or seam. There were few furnishings in most colonial homes. Because most of the huts or cabins were too small for beds, residents slept on the floor and used blankets to keep warm. Rarely did they have glass to fill windows. Instead, they simply used wooden shutters to cover the openings.

SOCIETY AND ECONOMY IN NEW ENGLAND

Environmental, social, and economic factors contributed to the remarkable diversity among the early American colonies. New England was quite different from the southern and middle Atlantic regions: more-governed by religious concerns, less focused on commercial agriculture, more-engaged in trade, and much less involved with slavery.

TOWNSHIPS Whenever New England towns were founded, the first public structure built was usually a church. By law, every town had to collect taxes to support a church, and every resident—whether a church member or not—was required to attend midweek and Sunday religious services. The average New Englander heard 7,000 sermons in a lifetime.

The Puritans believed that God had created a *covenant*, or contract, in which people formed a congregation for common worship. This led to the idea of people joining together to form governments, but the principles of democracy were not part of Puritan political thought. Puritan leaders sought to do the will of God, not to follow the will of the people, and the ultimate source of authority was not majority rule but the Bible as interpreted by ministers and magistrates (political leaders).

Unlike the settlers in the southern colonies or in Dutch New York, few New England colonists received huge tracts of land. *Township grants* were usually awarded to organized groups of settlers, often already gathered into a church congregation. They would request from the General Court a "town" (what elsewhere was commonly called a township). They then divided the land according to a rough principle of equity. Those who invested more or had larger families or greater status might receive more land, while the town retained some pasture and woodland in common and held other tracts for later arrivals.

DWELLINGS AND DAILY LIFE The first colonists in New England initially lived in caves, tents, or cabins, but they soon built simple wood-frame houses. The roofs were steeply pitched to reduce the buildup of snow and were covered with thatched grasses or reeds. By the end of the seventeenth century, most New England homes were plain but sturdy dwellings centered on a fireplace. Some had glass windows brought from England. Interior walls were often plastered and whitewashed, but it was not until the eighteenth century that the exteriors of most houses were painted, usually a deep "Indian" red. The interiors were dark, illuminated by candles or oil lamps, both of which were expensive; out of practicality, most people usually went to sleep soon after sunset.

Family life revolved around the main room on the ground floor, called the hall, where meals were cooked in a large fireplace and where the family lived most of the time (hence, these areas came to be called *living* rooms). Food would be served at a table of rough-hewn planks, called the board. The father was sometimes referred to as the "chair man" because he sat in the only chair (the origin of the term *chairman of the board*). The rest of the family usually stood or sat on stools or benches and ate with their hands and wooden spoons. Forks were not introduced until the eighteenth century. A typical meal consisted of corn, boiled meat, and vegetables washed down with beer, cider, rum, or milk. Cornbread was a daily staple, as was cornmeal mush, known as hasty pudding.

THE NEW ENGLAND ECONOMY Early New England farmers and their families led hard lives. Clearing rocks from the glacier-scoured soil might require sixty days of hard labor per acre. The growing season was short, and no staple crops for sale in markets grew in the harsh climate. The crops and livestock were those familiar to the English countryside: wheat, barley, oats, some cattle, pigs, and sheep.

Many New Englanders turned to the sea for their livelihood. Codfish had been a regular element of the European diet for centuries, and the waters off the New England coast had the heaviest concentrations of cod in the world. Whales, too, abounded in New England waters. They supplied oil for lighting and lubrication, as well as ambergris, a waxy substance used in the manufacture of perfumes.

Profitable fisheries Catching, curing, and drying codfish in Newfoundland in the early 1700s. For centuries, the rich fishing grounds of the North Atlantic provided New Englanders with a prosperous industry.

New Englanders exported dried fish to Europe, with lesser grades going to the West Indies as food for slaves. The thriving fishing industry encouraged the development of shipbuilding, and the growing experience and expertise at seafaring spurred transatlantic commerce. Rising incomes and a booming trade with Britain and Europe soon brought a taste for luxury goods in New England that clashed with the Puritan ideal of plain living and high thinking. In 1714, a worried Puritan deplored the "great extravagance that people are fallen into, far beyond their circumstances, in their purchases, buildings, families, expenses, apparel, generally in the whole way of living."

SHIPBUILDING The abundant forests of New England represented a source of enormous wealth. Old-growth trees were especially prized for use as ships' masts and spars (on which sails were attached). Early on, the British government claimed the tallest and straightest American trees, mostly white pines and oaks, for use by the Royal Navy. At the same time, British officials encouraged the colonists to develop their own shipbuilding industry. American-built ships quickly became known for their quality and price. It was much less expensive to purchase ships built in America than to transport American timber to Britain for ship construction, especially since a large ship might require as many as 2,000 trees. Nearly a third of all British ships were made in the colonies.

TRADE By the end of the seventeenth century, the New England colonies had become part of a complex North Atlantic commercial network, trading not only with the British Isles and the British West Indies but also—often illegally—with Spain, France, Portugal, the Netherlands, and their colonies.

Trade in New England and the middle colonies differed from that in the South in two respects: their lack of staple crops to exchange for English goods was a relative disadvantage, but the success of shipping and commercial enterprises worked in their favor. After 1660, to protect its agriculture and fisheries, the English government placed prohibitive duties (taxes) on fish, flour, wheat, and meat, while leaving the door open to timber, furs, and whale oil, products

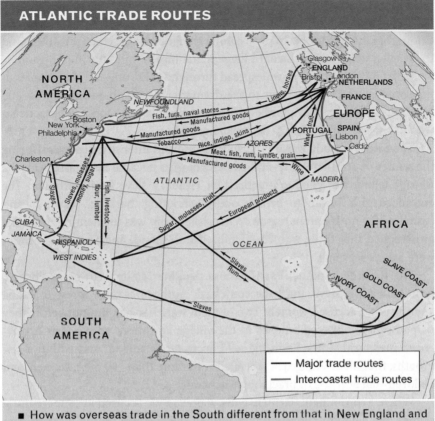

ATLANTIC TRADE ROUTES

- How was overseas trade in the South different from that in New England and the middle colonies?
- What was the "triangular trade"?
- What were North America's most important exports?

in great demand in the home country. Between 1698 and 1717, New England and New York bought more from England than they exported to it, creating an unfavorable trade balance, as more of their coins went out than came in.

These circumstances gave rise to the **triangular trade**, in which New Englanders, for example, shipped rum to the west coast of Africa, where it was exchanged for slaves; took the enslaved Africans to the West Indies to sell; and returned home with various West Indian commodities, including molasses, from which New Englanders then manufactured rum. In another version, they shipped provisions to the West Indies, carried sugar and molasses to England, and returned with goods manufactured in Europe.

THE DEVIL IN NEW ENGLAND The Puritans who settled New England were religious fundamentalists who looked to the Bible for authority and inspiration. They read the Bible daily and memorized much of it. Yet at times, religious zeal could get out of hand. The strains of Massachusetts's transition from Puritan utopia to royal colony reached a tragic climax in 1692 amid the witchcraft hysteria at Salem Village, some fifteen miles north of Boston.

Belief in witchcraft was widespread throughout Europe and the colonies in the seventeenth century. Prior to the dramatic episode in Salem, almost 300 New Englanders (mostly middle-aged women) had been accused of practicing witchcraft, and more than 30 had been hanged.

The Salem episode was unique in its scope and intensity, however. During the winter of 1691–1692, several adolescent girls became fascinated with the fortune telling and voodoo practiced by Tituba, a slave from Barbados. The entranced girls began to behave oddly—shouting, barking, crawling, and twitching for no apparent reason. When asked who was tormenting them, the girls replied that three women—Tituba, Sarah Good, and Sarah Osborne—were Satan's servants.

The Reverend Samuel Parris, whose daughter claimed to be bewitched, beat Tituba, his slave, until she confessed. Authorities then arrested Tituba and the other accused women. Two of them were hanged, but not before they named other supposed witches in the village and more young girls experienced inexplicable fits. Soon the wild accusations spread, and within a few months, the Salem Village jail was filled with more than 150 men, women, and children—all accused of practicing witchcraft.

When a prominent farmer, Giles Corey, was accused of supernatural crimes, his neighbors lowered him into an open grave, placed a board over his body, and began loading it with heavy boulders to force a confession. After three days of such abuse, the defiant old man finally succumbed, having muttered only two words: "more weight!" By denying guilt and choosing death, Corey ensured that his estate would go to his son rather than be confiscated by the government. That convicted witches forfeited their property, which was then put up for sale, revealed the practical benefits and self-interested motives behind some of the accusations.

As the allegations and executions multiplied, leaders of the Massachusetts Bay Colony began to worry that the witch hunts were out of control. The governor finally intervened when his own wife was accused of serving the devil. He disbanded the special court in Salem and ordered the remaining suspects released, including Tituba, who had languished in jail for thirteen months. By then, nineteen people (including some men married to women who had been convicted) had been hanged—all justified by the Biblical verse that tells believers not to "suffer a witch to live." A year after it had begun, the witchcraft frenzy was finally over.

What explains Salem's sudden eruption of religious fanaticism and mass hysteria? It may have represented nothing more than theatrical adolescents trying to enliven the dreary routine of everyday life. Some historians have stressed that most of the accused witches were women, many of whom had in some way defied the traditional roles assigned to females.

Still another interpretation suggests that the accusations may have reflected the panicky atmosphere caused by frequent Indian attacks occurring just north of Salem, along New England's northern frontier. Some of the accusing girls had seen their families killed by Indians.

Whatever its actual causes, the witchcraft controversy also reflected the peculiar social tensions and personal feuds in Salem Village. Late in 1692, as the hysteria subsided, several girls were traveling through nearby Ipswich when they encountered an old woman. "A witch!" they shouted and began writhing as if possessed. But the people of Ipswich showed no interest, and the "bewitched" girls picked themselves up and continued on their way.

SOCIETY AND ECONOMY IN THE MIDDLE COLONIES

Both geographically and culturally, the middle colonies (New York, New Jersey, Pennsylvania, Delaware, and Maryland) stood between New England and the South. They reflected the diversity of colonial life and foreshadowed the pluralism of the future nation.

AN ECONOMIC MIX The middle colonies produced surpluses of foodstuffs for export to the slave-based plantations of the South and the West Indies: wheat, barley, oats, and other grains, flour, and livestock. Three great rivers—the Hudson, the Delaware, and the Susquehanna—and their tributaries provided access to the backcountry of Pennsylvania and New York, which opened up a rich fur trade with Native Americans. The region's bustling commerce thus rivaled that of New England.

AN ETHNIC MIX In the makeup of their population, the middle colonies differed from both New England's Puritan settlements and the biracial plantation colonies to the south. In New York and New Jersey, Dutch culture and language lingered. Along the Delaware River near Philadelphia, the first settlers—Swedes and Finns—were overwhelmed by an influx of Europeans. By the mid–eighteenth century, the middle colonies were the fastest-growing region in North America.

The Germans came to America (primarily Pennsylvania) mainly from the Rhineland region of Europe, which had suffered from brutal religious wars that pitted Protestants against Catholics. William Penn's recruiting brochures in German translation circulated throughout central Europe, and his promise of religious freedom appealed to many persecuted sects, especially the Mennonites, German Baptists whose beliefs resembled those of the Quakers.

In 1683, a group of Mennonites founded Germantown, near Philadelphia. They represented the first wave of German migrants, a large proportion of whom paid their way as indentured servants, or "redemptioners." The large numbers of penniless German immigrants during the eighteenth century alarmed many English colonists. Benjamin Franklin worried that the Germans "will soon . . . outnumber us."

Throughout the eighteenth century, the Scots-Irish moved still farther out into the Pennsylvania backcountry. ("Scotch-Irish" is the more common but inaccurate name for the Scots-Irish, a mostly Presbyterian population transplanted from Scotland to northern Ireland by the English government a century earlier to give Catholic Ireland a more Protestant tone.)

Land was the great magnet attracting the poor Scots-Irish immigrants. They were, said a recruiting agent, "full of expectation to have land for nothing" and were "unwilling to be disappointed." In most cases, the lands they "squatted on" were claimed by Native Americans. In 1741, a group of Delaware Indians protested to Pennsylvania authorities that the Scots-Irish intruders were taking "our land" without giving "us anything for it." If the colonial government did not stop the flow of whites, the Delawares threatened, then they would "drive them off."

The Scots-Irish and the Germans became the largest non-English ethnic groups in the colonies. Other ethnic minorities also enriched the population in the middle colonies: Huguenots (French Protestants whose religious freedom had been revoked in 1685, forcing many to leave France), Irish, Welsh, Swiss, and Jews. New York had inherited from the Dutch a tradition of ethnic and religious tolerance, which had given the colony a diverse population before the English conquest: French-speaking Walloons (a Celtic people of southern Belgium), French, Germans, Danes, Portuguese, Spaniards, Italians, Bohemians, Poles, and others, including some New England Puritans.

THE BACKCOUNTRY Pennsylvania became the great distribution point for the different ethnic groups of European origin, just as the Chesapeake Bay region and Charleston, South Carolina, became the distribution points for African peoples. Before the mid–eighteenth century, settlers in the

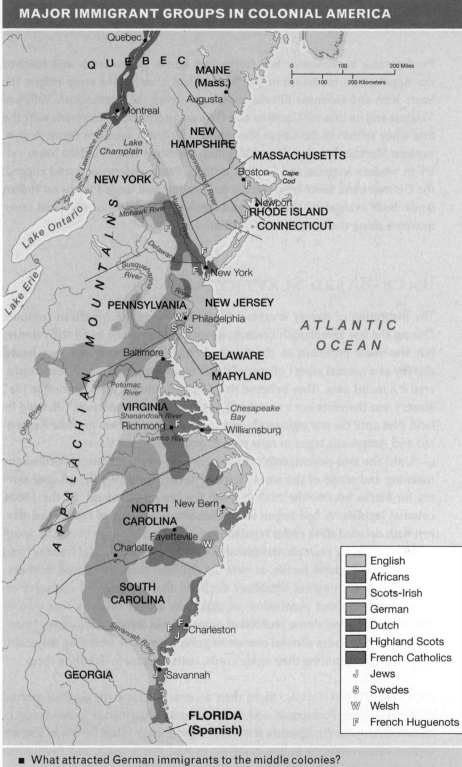

MAJOR IMMIGRANT GROUPS IN COLONIAL AMERICA

Quebec

QUEBEC

MAINE
(Mass.)

Augusta

Montreal

St. Lawrence River

Lake Champlain

NEW
HAMPSHIRE

NEW YORK

Connecticut River

MASSACHUSETTS

Boston   Cape
Cod

Lake Ontario

Mohawk River

Hudson River

Newport
RHODE ISLAND
CONNECTICUT

New York

Lake Erie

Delaware

Susquehanna
River

PENNSYLVANIA

Philadelphia

River

NEW JERSEY

ATLANTIC
OCEAN

Baltimore

DELAWARE

MARYLAND

Ohio River

Potomac
River

VIRGINIA

Shenandoah River

Richmond

James River

Chesapeake
Bay

Williamsburg

APPALACHIAN MOUNTAINS

NORTH
CAROLINA

New Bern

Fayetteville

Charlotte

SOUTH
CAROLINA

Savannah River

Charleston

GEORGIA

Savannah

FLORIDA
(Spanish)

	English
	Africans
	Scots-Irish
	German
	Dutch
	Highland Scots
	French Catholics
J	Jews
S	Swedes
W	Welsh
F	French Huguenots

0   100   200 Miles
0   100   200 Kilometers

- What attracted German immigrants to the middle colonies?
- Why did the Scots-Irish spread across the Appalachian backcountry?
- Where did the first Jews settle in America? How were they received?

Pennsylvania backcountry had trespassed across Indian lands and reached the Appalachian mountain range. Rather than crossing the steep ridges, the Scots-Irish and Germans filtered southward down the Shenandoah Valley of Virginia and on into the Carolina and Georgia backcountry. Germans were the first white settlers in the Upper Shenandoah Valley in southern Pennsylvania, western Maryland, and northern Virginia, and Scots-Irish filled the lower valley in western Virginia and North Carolina. Feisty, determined, and rugged, the Germans and Scots-Irish settlers built cabins and tended farms on Indian lands, built evangelical churches, and established contentious isolated communities along the frontier of settlement.

RACE-BASED SLAVERY

The institution of slavery is central to the history of the American colonies. During the late seventeenth century, slavery was legalized in all the colonies but was most prevalent in the South. White colonists viewed **race-based slavery** as a normal aspect of everyday life in an imperfect world; few considered it a moral issue. They believed that God determined one's "station in life." Slavery was therefore not a social evil but a "personal misfortune" dictated by God. Not until the late eighteenth century did large numbers of white Europeans and Americans begin to raise ethical questions about slavery.

Until the mid–seventeenth century, no laws in the colonies specified the meaning and scope of the word "slavery." Gradually, however, *life-long* slavery for blacks became the custom—and the law—of the land. By the 1660s, colonial legislatures had begun to legalize the institution of race-based slavery, with detailed **slave codes** regulating most aspects of their lives. The South Carolina code, for example, defined all "Negroes, Mulattoes, and Indians" sold into bondage as slaves for life, as were the children born of enslaved mothers.

In 1667, the Virginia legislature declared that slaves could not serve on juries, travel without permission, or gather in groups of more than two or three. Some colonies even prohibited owners from freeing their slaves (manumission). The codes allowed owners to punish slaves by whipping them, slitting their noses, cutting their ankle cords, castrating men, or killing them.

COLOR PREJUDICE More than a century before the English arrived in America, the Portuguese and Spanish had established a global trade in enslaved Africans (in Spanish, the word *negro* means "black"). While English settlers often enslaved Indian captives, as had the Spanish and Portuguese before them, the Europeans did not enslave other Europeans who were captured in warfare. Color was the crucial difference, or at least the crucial rationalization used to justify the institution of slavery and its hellish brutalities.

The English associated the color black with darkness and evil. To them, the different appearance, behavior, and customs of Africans and Native Americans represented savagery and heathenism. Colonial Virginians justified slavery by convincing themselves that blacks (and Indians) were naturally lazy, treacherous, and stupid, among other shortcomings.

COLONIAL SLAVERY During the seventeenth and eighteenth centuries, the profitable sugar-based economies of the French and British West Indies and Portuguese Brazil had the greatest demand for enslaved Africans, as sugar became valued almost as much as gold or silver. By 1675, the island colonies in the Caribbean had more than 100,000 slaves, while slaves in the American colonies numbered about 5,000. The profits generated by sugar colonies in the Caribbean were greater than all of the commerce in the American mainland colonies.

As tobacco, rice, and indigo crops became more established in Maryland, Virginia, and the Carolinas, however, the number of African slaves in those colonies grew enormously. At the same time, the flow of white indentured servants from Britain and Europe to America was slowing. Between 1700 and 1709, only 1,500 indentured servants arrived in the American colonies; 9,000 enslaved Africans arrived during the same period. Until the eighteenth century, English immigrants made up 90 percent of the American colonists. After 1700, the largest number of new arrivals were enslaved Africans who totaled more than all European immigrants combined.

The shifting popularity of black slaves over white servants reflected the growing industry of slave trading. In the late seventeenth century, the profitability of African slavery led dozens of new slave trading companies to emerge, both in Europe and America, thus expanding the availability of enslaved Africans and lowering the price. American colonists preferred slaves because they were officially viewed as property with no civil rights, and they (and their offspring) were servants for life, not for a fixed number of years. Africans were preferred over enslaved Indians because they could not escape easily in a land where they stood out because of their dark skin. In short, African slaves offered a better investment for colonial Americans.

THE MARKET IN SLAVES Once a slave ship arrived at an American port, Africans in chains, not knowing any English, would be auctioned to the highest bidder, who would cart them off to begin lifelong work for a complete stranger. They were usually forbidden to use their former languages, practice

African religions, or to sustain their native cultures. With only rare exceptions, slaves were allowed to own nothing.

Enslaved Africans were used in virtually all aspects of the expanding colonial economy. The vast majority worked on farms or plantations, often performing strenuous labor from dawn to dusk in oppressive heat and humidity. As Jedidiah Morse, a prominent Charleston minister, admitted in the late eighteenth century, "No white man, to speak generally, ever thinks of settling a farm, and improving it for himself, without negroes."

During the eighteenth century, the demand for slaves soared in the southern colonies. By 1750, there were almost 250,000 slaves in British America. The vast majority resided in Virginia and Maryland, about 150,000 compared with 60,000 in South Carolina and Georgia.

As the number of slaves grew, so, too, did the breadth of their talents and expertise. Over time, slaves became skilled artisans: blacksmiths, carpenters, bricklayers. Many enslaved women worked as household servants and midwives.

SLAVE ABUSE AND RESISTANCE Colonial laws allowed whites to use brutal means to discipline and control their slaves. They were whipped, branded, castrated, or sold away, often to the Caribbean islands, where working conditions were even worse. A 1669 Virginia law declared that accidentally killing a slave who was being whipped or beaten was not a serious crime. During a three-year period, a South Carolina overseer whipped five slaves to death. William Byrd II, a wealthy Virginia planter, confessed that the "unhappy effect of owning many Negroes is the necessity of being severe."

Colonial newspapers were sprinkled with notices about runaway slaves. A Georgia slave owner asked readers to be on the lookout for "a negro fellow named Mingo, about 40 years old, and his wife Quante, a sensible wench about 20 with her child, a boy about 3 years old, all this country born."

In a few cases, slaves organized armed rebellions in which they stole weapons, burned and looted plantations, and occasionally killed their captors. In the late summer of 1739, some twenty slaves attacked a store in Stono, South Carolina, south of Charleston. Led by a slave named Jemmy, they killed the owner, seized weapons, and headed south toward freedom in Spanish Florida, gathering more recruits along the way. Within a few days, the slaves had roamed over fifteen miles and killed twenty-five whites. The growing army of slaves marched in military formation, waving banners, beating drums, and freeing more slaves as they moved southward. Then the militia caught up with them. Most of the rebels were killed, and in the weeks that followed, sixty more were captured by enraged planters who "cut off their heads and set them up at every Mile Post."

Slavery in New Amsterdam (1642) The significance of African slaves to the colonial economy is the focus of this engraving of the Dutch colony New Amsterdam, later known as New York City.

The **Stono Rebellion** so frightened white planters that they convinced the colonial assembly to pass the so-called Negro Act of 1740, which called for more oversight of slave activities and harsher punishments for rebellious behavior. It also reduced the penalty for a white killing a slave to a minor offense and banned slaves from testifying in courts.

SLAVERY IN NEW YORK CITY In contrast to the experience of slaves in the southern colonies, most slaves in the northern colonies lived in towns or cities, and their urban environs gave them more opportunities to move about. New York City had more slaves than any other American city. By 1740, it was second only to Charleston in the percentage of slaves in its population.

As the number of slaves increased in the congested city, racial fears and tensions mounted—and occasionally exploded. In 1712, several dozen slaves revolted; they started fires and then used swords, axes, and guns to kill whites as they attempted to fight the fires. Called out to restore order, the militia captured twenty-seven slaves. Six committed suicide, and the rest were executed; some were burned alive. New York officials thereafter passed their own black code that strictly regulated slave behavior.

The harsh regulations did not prevent another major racial incident. In the bitterly cold March of 1741, city dwellers worried about a series of suspicious fires, including one at the governor's house. Their worst fear was that the fires were set by slaves. "The Negroes are rising!" shouted terrified whites.

The frantic city council launched an intense investigation to find the "villains." Mary Burton, a sixteen-year-old white indentured servant, told authorities that slaves and poor whites were plotting to "burn the whole town" and kill the white men. The plotters were supposedly led by John Hughson, a white trafficker in stolen goods who owned the tavern where Mary Burton worked. His wife, two slaves, and a prostitute were charged as co-conspirators. Despite their denials, all were convicted and hanged. Within weeks, more than half of the adult male slaves in the city were in jail. What came to be called the Conspiracy of 1741 finally ended after seventeen slaves and four whites were hanged; thirteen more blacks were burned at the stake, while many more were deported.

Such organized rebellions were rare, however, in large part because the likelihood of success was so small and the punishments so severe. Much more common were subtler forms of resistance and accommodation adopted by enslaved Africans—stealing food, breaking tools, destroying crops, feigning illness, etc.

COLONIAL CITIES

Throughout the seventeenth and eighteenth centuries, the American colonies were mostly populated by farmers or farmworkers. But a handful of cities blossomed into dynamic urban centers of political and social life. Economic opportunity drove most city dwellers. In New York City, for example, a visitor said the "art of getting money" dominated everything the residents did.

Colonial cities hugged the coastline or, like Philadelphia, sprang up on rivers large enough to handle oceangoing vessels. Never comprising more than 10 percent of the colonial population, the large coastal cities had a disproportionate influence on commerce, politics, society, and culture. By the end of the colonial period, Philadelphia, with some 30,000 people, was the largest city in the colonies, and New York City, with about 25,000, ranked second. Boston numbered 16,000; Charleston, South Carolina, 12,000; and Newport, Rhode Island, 11,000.

THE SOCIAL AND POLITICAL ORDER The urban social elite was dominated by wealthy merchants and property owners served by a middle class of shop owners, innkeepers, and skilled craftsmen. Almost two thirds of urban male workers were artisans—people who made their living at handicrafts. They included carpenters and coopers (barrel makers), shoemakers and tailors, silversmiths and blacksmiths, sailmakers, stonemasons, weavers, and potters. At the bottom of the social order were sailors, manual laborers, servants, and slaves.

Colonial cities were busy, crowded, and dangerous. Epidemics such as cholera, malaria, and yellow fever were common. The use of open fireplaces for heating caused frequent fires that in turn led to the development of fire companies. Rising crime and violence required increased policing of neighborhoods by sheriffs and local militias.

Colonists also were concerned about the poor and homeless. The number of Boston's poor receiving aid from colonial authorities rose from 500 in 1700 to 4,000 in 1736; in New York City, the number rose from 250 in 1698 to 5,000 in the 1770s. Those designated "helpless" among the destitute poor, especially the disabled, elderly, widows, and orphans, were often provided money, food, clothing, and fuel. In some towns, "poorhouses" were built to house the homeless poor and provide them with jobs.

THE URBAN WEB Overland travel in the colonies was initially by horse or by foot. Inns and taverns (also called public houses, or pubs) were especially important since travel at night was treacherous—and Americans loved to drink. (During the colonial period, it was said that when the Spanish settled an area, they would first build a church; the Dutch would first erect a fort; and the English would first construct a tavern.) In 1690, Boston alone had fifty-four taverns, half of them operated by women.

Colonial taverns and inns were places to eat, relax, read a newspaper, play cards, gossip, and conduct business. And, of course, they were the most popular places to drink alcoholic beverages: beer, hard cider, and rum, which became the favored drink. But ministers and magistrates began to worry that the pubs were promoting drunkenness and social rebelliousness. Not only were poor whites drinking heavily, but also Indians, which, one governor told the assembly, would have "fatal consequences to the Government."

Early in the eighteenth century, ministers succeeded in passing an anti-tavern law in Massachusetts Bay Colony. Called the Act against Intemperance,

Immorality, and Profaneness, it was directed at taverns that had become "nurseries of intemperance." It tightened the process of issuing licenses for the sale of liquor, eliminated fiddle-playing in pubs, called for the public posting of the names of "common drunkards," and banned the sale of rum and brandy, the most potent beverages.

After a few years, however, the law was rarely enforced, and the concerns about taverns and drinking continued. In 1726, a Bostonian declared that "the abuse of strong Drink is becoming Epidemical among us, and it is very justly Supposed . . . that the Multiplication of Taverns has contributed not a little to this Excess of Riot and Debauchery." The failed 1712 law was the last legislative effort to restrict alcohol consumption before the Revolution.

By the end of the seventeenth century, there were more taverns in America than any other business. Indeed, taverns became the most important social institution in the colonies—and the most democratic. They were places where rich and poor often intermingled, and by the mid–eighteenth century, they would become the gathering places for protests against British rule.

Long-distance communication was a more complicated matter. Postal service in the seventeenth century was almost nonexistent—people gave letters to travelers or sea captains in hopes they would be delivered. Under a parliamentary law of 1710, the postmaster of London named a deputy in charge of the colonies, and a postal system eventually encompassed most of the Atlan-

Taverns A tobacconist's business card from 1770 captures men talking in a Philadelphia tavern while they drink ale and smoke pipes.

tic Seaboard, providing the colonies with an effective means of communication that would prove crucial in the growing controversy with Great Britain.

More reliable mail delivery spurred the growing popularity of newspapers. Before 1745, twenty-two newspapers had been started: seven in New England, ten in the middle colonies, and five in the South. An important landmark in the development of freedom of the press was John Peter Zenger's 1735 trial for publishing criticisms of New York's royal governor in his newspaper, the *New-York Weekly Journal*. English common law held that one might be punished for libel, or criticism that fostered "an ill opinion of the government." Zenger's lawyer claimed that the editor had published the truth. The jury agreed and found the editor not guilty.

THE ENLIGHTENMENT IN AMERICA

The most significant of the new European ideas circulating in eighteenth-century America grew out of a burst of innovative intellectual activity known as the **Enlightenment**, a profound breakthrough in understanding human society and the natural world. The Enlightenment celebrated rational inquiry, scientific research, and individual freedom. Enlightened people were those who sought the truth, wherever it might lead, rather than remain content with believing ideas and dogmas passed down through the ages or taken from the Bible. Immanuel Kant, the eighteenth-century German philosopher, summed up the Enlightenment point of view by saying: "Dare to know! Have the courage to use your own understanding." He and others used the power of reason to analyze the workings of nature, and they employed new tools like microscopes and telescopes to engage in close observation, scientific experimentation, and precise mathematical calculation.

THE AGE OF REASON The Enlightenment, often called the Age of Reason, was triggered when the ancient view that the earth was at the center of the universe was challenged by the controversial, heliocentric (sun-centered) solar system described in 1533 by Nicolaus Copernicus, a Polish astronomer and Catholic priest. His theory that the earth orbits the sun was scorned by Catholic officials before it was confirmed by other scientists.

In 1687, Englishman Isaac Newton (1642–1727) announced his transformational theory of the earth's gravitational pull. Using both scientific experiments and mathematics, especially calculus, Newton challenged biblical notions of the world's workings by depicting a changing, dynamic universe moving in accordance with natural laws that could be grasped by human

Benjamin Franklin A champion of rational thinking and common sense behavior, Franklin was an inventor, philosopher, entrepreneur, and statesman.

reason and explained by mathematics. He implied that natural laws (rather than God) govern all things, from the orbits of the planets to the effects of gravity to the science of human relations: politics, economics, and society.

Some enlightened people, called **Deists**, carried Newton's scientific outlook to its logical conclusion, claiming that God created the world and designed its "natural laws," and that these laws governed the operation of the universe. In other words, Deists insisted that God planned the universe and set it in motion, but no longer interacted directly with the earth and its people. So the rational God of the Deists was nothing like the intervening (providential) God of the Christian tradition, to whom believers prayed for daily guidance and direct support.

Evil, according to the Deists, resulted not from humanity's inherent *sinfulness* as outlined in the Bible but from human *ignorance* of the rational laws of nature. Therefore, the best way to improve both society and human nature, according to Deists such as Thomas Jefferson and Benjamin Franklin, was by cultivating Reason, which was the highest Virtue. (Enlightenment thinkers often capitalized both words.) By using education, reason, and scientific analysis, societies were bound to improve their knowledge as well as their quality of life.

Faith in human progress was thus one of the most important beliefs of the Enlightenment. Equally important was the enlightened notion of political freedom. Both Jefferson and Franklin were intrigued by the English political philosopher John Locke (1632–1704), who maintained that "natural law" called for a government resting on the consent of the governed and respecting the "natural rights" of all. This idea would later influence colonial leaders' efforts to justify a revolution.

THE AMERICAN ENLIGHTENMENT Benjamin Franklin epitomized the Enlightenment. Born in Boston in 1706, Franklin left home at the age of seventeen, bound for Philadelphia. Six years later, he bought a print shop where he edited and published the *Pennsylvania Gazette*, one of the leading newspapers in the colonies. When he was twenty-six, he published *Poor Richard's Almanack*, a collection of seasonal weather forecasts, puzzles, household tips, and witty sayings. Before he retired from business at the age of forty-two, Franklin had founded a public library, started a fire company, helped create what became the University of Pennsylvania, and organized a debating club that grew into the American Philosophical Society.

Franklin was devoted to scientific investigation. Skeptical and curious, pragmatic and irreverent, he was an inventive genius. His wide-ranging experiments encompassed the fields of medicine, meteorology, geology, astronomy, and physics, among others. He developed the Franklin stove, the lightning rod, bifocal spectacles, and a glass harmonica.

Although raised as a Presbyterian, Franklin became a Deist who prized science and reason. He questioned the divinity of Jesus and the assumption that the Bible was truly the word of God. Like the European Deists, Franklin came to believe in a God that had created a universe directed by natural laws. For Franklin and others, to be "enlightened" meant developing the confidence and capacity to think for oneself, to think critically rather than simply accepting what tradition dictated as truth.

EDUCATION IN THE COLONIES White colonial Americans were among the most literate people in the world. Almost 90 percent of men (more than in England) could read. For the colonists at large, education in the traditional ideas and manners of society—even literacy itself—remained primarily the responsibility of family and church. The modern concept of free public education would not be fully embraced until the twentieth century. Yet colonists were concerned from the beginning that steps needed to be taken to educate their young.

The Puritan emphasis on reading Scripture, which all Protestants shared to some degree, led to the emphasis on literacy. In 1647, the Massachusetts Bay Colony required every town to set up a grammar school (a "Latin school" that could prepare a student for college).

The Dutch in New Netherland were as interested in education as the New England Puritans. In Pennsylvania, the Quakers established private schools. In the southern colonies, however, schools were rare. The wealthiest southern planters and merchants sent their children to England for schooling, or hired tutors.

THE GREAT AWAKENING

The growing popularity of Enlightenment rationalism posed a direct threat to traditional religious life in Europe and America. But Christianity has always shown remarkable resilience in the face of challenging new ideas. This was certainly true in the early eighteenth century, when the American colonies experienced a widespread revival of spiritual zeal designed to restore the primacy of emotion in the religious realm.

Between 1700 and 1750, when the controversial ideas of the Enlightenment were circulating among the best-educated colonists, hundreds of new Christian congregations were founded. Most Americans (85 percent) lived in colonies with an established church, meaning that the colonial government officially endorsed—and collected taxes to support—a single official denomination.

The Church of England, also known as Anglicanism, was the established church in Virginia, Maryland, Delaware, and the Carolinas. Puritan Congregationalism was the official faith in most of New England. In New York, Anglicanism vied with the Dutch Reformed Church for control. Pennsylvania had no single state-supported church, but Quakers dominated the legislative assembly. New Jersey and Rhode Island had no official denomination and hosted numerous Christian splinter groups.

Most colonies organized religious life on the basis of local parishes, which defined their theological boundaries and defended them against people who did not hold to the same faith. In colonies with official tax-supported religions, people of other faiths could not preach without the permission of the parish. In the 1730s and 1740s, the parish system was thrown into turmoil by the arrival of outspoken traveling evangelists, called *itinerants*, who claimed that most of the local parish ministers were incompetent. In their emotionally charged sermons, the itinerants, several of whom were white women and African Americans, insisted that Christians must be "reborn" in their convictions and behavior.

REVIVALISM During the early 1730s, worries about the erosion of religious fervor helped spark a series of emotional revivals known as the **Great Awakening**. The revivals quickly spread up and down the Atlantic coast. Every social class, ethnic group, and region that participated was swept up in the ecstasy of renewed spiritual passion. In the process, the revivals divided congregations, towns, and families, and fueled the growth of new denominations, especially the Baptists and Methodists. A skeptical Benjamin Franklin admitted that the Awakening was having a profound effect on social life: "Never did the people show so great a willingness to attend sermons. Religion is become the subject of most conversation."

JONATHAN EDWARDS In 1734–1735, a remarkable spiritual transformation occurred in the congregation of Jonathan Edwards, a prominent Congregationalist minister in the western Massachusetts town of Northampton. One of America's most brilliant philosophers and theologians, Edwards had entered Yale College in 1716, at age thirteen, and graduated at the top of his class four years later.

When Edwards arrived in Northampton in 1727, he was shocked by the town's lack of religious conviction. He claimed that the young people of Northampton were preoccupied with sinful pleasures; they indulged in "lewd practices" that "corrupted others." He warned that Christians had become dangerously obsessed with making and spending money, and that the new ideas associated with the Enlightenment were eroding the importance of religious life.

To counteract the secularizing forces of the Enlightenment, Edwards rushed to restore the emotional side of religion. "Our people," he said, "do not so much need to have their heads stored [with new scientific knowledge] as to have their hearts touched [with spiritual intensity]." Edwards was fiery and char-

Jonathan Edwards One of the foremost preachers of the Great Awakening, Edwards dramatically described the torments that awaited sinners in the afterlife.

ismatic, and his vivid descriptions of the sufferings of hell and the delights of heaven helped rekindle spiritual intensity among his congregants. By 1735, he could report that "the town seemed to be full of the presence of God; it never was so full of love, nor of joy." To judge the power of the religious awakening, he thought, one need only observe that "it was no longer the Tavern" that drew local crowds, "but the Minister's House."

In 1741, Edwards delivered his most famous sermon, "Sinners in the Hands of an Angry God." It was designed in part to frighten people into seeking salvation. Edwards reminded the congregation that hell is real and that God "holds you over the pit of hell, much as one holds a spider, or some loathsome insect, over the fire, abhors you, and is dreadfully provoked. . . . He looks upon you as worthy of nothing else, but to be cast into the fire." When he finished, he had to wait several minutes for the agitated congregants to quiet down before he led them in a closing hymn.

GEORGE WHITEFIELD The most celebrated promoter of the Great Awakening was a young English minister, George Whitefield, whose rep-

George Whitefield The English minister's dramatic eloquence roused Americans, inspiring many to experience a religious rebirth.

utation as a spellbinding evangelist preceded him to the colonies. Congregations were lifeless, he claimed, "because dead men preach to them." Too many ministers were "slothful shepherds and dumb dogs."

Whitefield set out to restore the fires of religious intensity in America. In the autumn of 1739, the twenty-five-year-old evangelist began a fourteen-month tour, preaching to huge crowds from Maine to Georgia. His critics were as fervent as his admirers. A disgusted Bostonian described a revival meeting's theatrics: "The meeting was carried on with . . . some screaming out in Distress and Anguish . . . some again jumping up and down . . . some lying along on the floor. . . . The whole with a very great Noise, to be heard at a Mile's Distance, and continued almost the whole night."

The short, thin, cross-eyed Whitefield enthralled audiences with his golden voice, flamboyant style, and unparalleled eloquence. His sermons produced electric effects. Even Benjamin Franklin, a confirmed rationalist who went to see Whitefield preach in Philadelphia, was so excited by the fiery sermon that he emptied his pockets into the collection plate.

Whitefield urged his listeners to experience a "new birth"—a sudden, emotional moment of conversion and salvation. By the end of his sermon, one listener reported, the entire congregation was "in utmost Confusion, some crying out, some laughing, and Bliss still roaring to them to come to Christ, as they answered, I will, I will, I'm coming, I'm coming."

RADICAL EVANGELISTS Edwards and Whitefield inspired many imitators, the most radical of whom carried emotional evangelism to extremes, stirring up women as well as those at the bottom of society—laborers, seamen, servants, slaves, and farm folk—and ordaining their own ministers.

William Tennent, an Irish-born Presbyterian revivalist, charged that many local ministers were "cold and sapless," afraid to "thrust the nail of terror into sleeping souls." Tennent's oldest son, Gilbert, also an evangelist, defended his aggressive tactics by explaining that he and other traveling preachers invaded parishes only when the local minister showed no interest in the "Getting of Grace and Growing in it."

The Tennents urged people to renounce their ministers and pursue salvation on their own. They also attacked the excesses of the wealthy and powerful. Worried members of the colonial elite charged that the radical revivalists were spreading "anarchy, levelling, and dissolution."

Equally unsettling to the elite was the Reverend James Davenport, the most radical of the revivalists, who urged Christians to renounce "rationalist" ministers and become the agents of their own salvation through a purely emotional conversion experience. A Connecticut minister warned that Davenport and other extremists were "frightening people out of their senses" rather than offering reasonable sermons. In 1743, in New London, Connecticut, Davenport attracted a huge crowd by building a bonfire and encouraging people to burn their fancy clothes and rationalist books. A few weeks later, the unstable Davenport reversed himself and called his rantings "enthusiastical and delusive."

WOMEN AND REVIVALS The Great Awakening's most controversial element was the emergence of women who defied the biblical injunction against women speaking in religious services. Scores of women served as lay exhorters, including Sarah Haggar Osborne, a Rhode Island schoolteacher who organized prayer meetings that eventually included men and women, black and white. When concerned ministers told her to stop, she refused to "shut my mouth and doors and creep into obscurity." Similarly, in western Massachusetts, Bathsheba Kingsley stole her husband's horse to spread the gospel among her rural neighbors because she had received "immediate revelations from heaven." When her husband tried to intervene, she pummeled him with "hard words and blows," praying loudly that he "go quick to hell." Jonathan Edwards denounced Kingsley as a "brawling woman" who should "keep chiefly at home." But for all of the turbulence created by the revivals, churches remained male bastions of political authority.

A CHANGING RELIGIOUS LANDSCAPE The Great Awakening made religion intensely personal by creating both a deep sense of spiritual guilt and an intense yearning for redemption. Yet it also undermined many of the established churches by emphasizing that all individuals, regardless of wealth or social status, could receive God's grace without the guidance of ministers. Denominations became bitterly divided as "Old Light" conservatives criticized disruptive and democratic revivalism and sparred with "New Light" evangelicals who delighted in provoking emotional outbursts among their listeners and celebrating individual freedom in matters of faith.

New England religious life would never be the same, as Puritanism disintegrated amid the intense warfare over the revivals of the Great Awakening. The Puritan ideal of religious uniformity was shattered. The crusty Connecticut Old Light minister, Isaac Stiles, denounced the "intrusion of choice into spiritual matters" and charged that the "multitudes were seriously, soberly, and solemnly out of their wits" in their embrace of ultra-emotional religion. John Henry Goetschius, a Dutch Reformed evangelist, shot back that Stiles and other Old Lights were simply determined to "impose on many people, against their will, their old, rotten, and stinking routine religion."

In Anglican Virginia, some fifty Baptist evangelists were jailed for disturbing the peace during the Great Awakening. New England subsequently attracted more and more Baptists, Presbyterians, Anglicans, and other denominations, while the revival frenzy scored its most lasting victories along the frontiers of the middle and southern colonies.

In the more sedate churches of Boston, the principle of rational or enlightened religion gained the upper hand in a reaction against the excesses of revivalistic emotion. Boston ministers such as Charles Chauncey and Jonathan Mayhew found Puritan theology too cold and forbidding. To them, the Calvinist concept that people could be forever damned by predestination was irrational. They embraced many insights drawn from Enlightenment rationalism, arguing that God created laws of nature which people could discover and exploit.

THE HEART VERSUS THE HEAD Like a ferocious fire that burned intensely before dying out, the Great Awakening subsided by 1750. The emotional Awakening, like its counterpart, the rational Enlightenment, influenced the forces leading to the revolution against Great Britain and set in motion powerful currents that still flow in American life.

Ministers could no longer control the direction of religious life, as more and more people took charge of their own spirituality and new denominations sprouted like mushrooms. The Awakening implanted in American culture the evangelical impulse and the emotional appeal of revivalism, weakened the status of the old-fashioned clergy and state-supported churches, and encouraged believers to exercise their own individual judgment. By encouraging the proliferation of denominations, it heightened the need for toleration of dissent.

In some respects, however, the warring Awakening and the Enlightenment, one stressing the urgings of the spirit and the other celebrating the cold logic of reason, led by different roads to similar ends. Both movements cut across

the mainland colonies and thereby helped bind them together. Both emphasized the power and right of individual decision making, and both aroused
hopes that America would become the promised land in which people might
attain the perfection of piety or reason, if not both.

By urging believers to exercise their own spiritual judgment, revivals
weakened the authority of the established churches and their ministers, just
as colonial resentment of British economic regulations would later weaken the
colonists' loyalty to the king. As such, the Great Awakening and the Enlightenment helped nurture a growing commitment to individual freedom and resistance to authority that would play a key role in the rebellion against British
"tyranny" in 1776.

CHAPTER REVIEW

SUMMARY

- **Colonial Demographics** Cheap land lured poor immigrants to America. The initial shortage of women eventually gave way to a more equal gender ratio and a tendency to earlier marriage than in Europe, leading to higher *birth rates* and larger families. People also lived longer on average in the colonies than in Europe. The lower *death rates* led to rapid population growth in the colonies.

- **Women in the Colonies** English colonists brought their traditional beliefs and prejudices with them to America, including convictions about the inferiority of women. Colonial women remained largely confined to *women's work* in the house, yard, and field. Over time, though, necessity created new opportunities for women outside their traditional roles.

- **Colonial Differences** A thriving colonial trading economy sent raw materials such as fish, timber, and furs to England in return for manufactured goods. The expanding economy created new wealth and a rise in the consumption of European goods, and it fostered the expansion of slavery. Agriculture diversified: tobacco was the *staple crop* in Virginia, rice in the Carolinas. Plantation agriculture based on slavery became entrenched in the South. New England's prosperous shipping industry created a profitable *triangular trade* among Africa, America, and England. By 1790, German, Scots-Irish, Welsh, and Irish immigrants, as well as other European ethnic groups, had settled in the middle colonies, along with Quakers, Jews, Huguenots, and Mennonites.

- **Race-Based Slavery** Deep-rooted prejudice led to *race-based slavery*. Africans were considered "heathens" whose supposed inferiority entitled white Americans to use them for slaves. Africans brought diverse skills to help build America's economy. The use of African slaves was concentrated in the South, where landowners used them to produce lucrative staple crops, such as tobacco, rice, and indigo. But slaves lived in cities, too, especially New York. As the slave population increased, race relations grew more tense, and *slave codes* were created to regulate the movement of enslaved people. Sporadic slave uprisings, such as the *Stono Rebellion*, occurred in both the North and South.

- **The Enlightenment and the Great Awakening** Printing presses, education, and city life created a flow of new ideas that circulated via long-distance travel, tavern life, the postal service, and newspapers. The attitudes of the *Enlightenment* were transported along international trade routes. Sir Isaac Newton's scientific discoveries culminated in the belief that Reason could improve society. Benjamin Franklin, who believed that people could shape their own destinies, became the face of the Enlightenment in America. *Deism* expressed the religious views of the Age of Reason. By the 1730s, a revival of faith, the *Great Awakening*, swept through the colonies. New congregations formed as evangelists insisted that Christians be "reborn." Individualism, not orthodoxy, was stressed in this first popular religious movement in America's history.

CHRONOLOGY

1619	First Africans arrive at Jamestown
1636	Harvard College is established
1667	Virginia enacts slave code declaring that enslaved children who were baptized as Christians remained slaves
1692	Salem witchcraft trials
1730s–1740s	Great Awakening
1735	John Peter Zenger is tried for seditious libel
1739	Stono Rebellion
	George Whitefield preaches his first sermon in America, in Philadelphia
1741	Jonathan Edwards preaches "Sinners in the Hands of an Angry God"

KEY TERMS

death rate p. 84

birth rate p. 84

women's work p. 86

staple crops p. 89

triangular trade p. 93

race-based slavery p. 98

slave codes p. 98

Stono Rebellion p. 101

Enlightenment p. 105

Deists p. 106

Great Awakening p. 108

🐰 INQUIZITIVE

Go to InQuizitive to see what you've learned—and learn what you've missed—with personalized feedback along the way.

4 From Colonies to States

Boston Tea Party Disguised as Native Americans, a swarm of Patriots boarded three British ships and dumped more than 300 chests of East India Company tea into Boston Harbor.

Four great European naval powers—Spain, France, England, and the Netherlands (Holland)—created colonies in North America during the sixteenth and seventeenth centuries as part of their larger fight for global supremacy. Throughout the eighteenth century, wars raged across Europe, mostly pitting the Catholic nations of France and Spain against Protestant Great Britain and the Netherlands. The conflicts increasingly spread to the Americas, and by the middle of the eighteenth century, North America had become a primary battleground, involving both colonists and Native Americans allied with different European powers.

Spain's sparsely populated settlements in the borderlands north of Mexico were small and weak compared to those in the British colonies. The Spanish failed to create colonies with robust economies. Instead, Spain emphasized the conversion of native peoples to Catholicism, prohibited manufacturing within its colonies, strictly limited trade with the Native Americans, and searched—in vain—for gold.

The French and British colonies developed a thriving trade with Native Americans at the same time that their fierce rivalry gradually shifted the balance of power in Europe. By the end of the eighteenth century, Spain and the Netherlands would be in decline, leaving France and Great Britain to fight for dominance. The nearly constant warfare led Great Britain to tighten its control over the American colonies to help raise the funds needed to combat France and Spain. Tensions over the British effort to preserve its empire at the expense of American freedoms would lead first to rebellion and eventually to revolution.

focus questions

1. What were the similarities and differences in the way that the British and French empires administered their colonies before 1763?

2. What were some of the effects of the French and Indian War? How did it change relations among the European powers in North America?

3. In what ways did the British try to strengthen their control over the colonies after the French and Indian War? How did the colonies respond?

4. What were the underlying factors in the events of the 1770s that led the colonies to declare their independence from Britain?

COMPETING NEIGHBORS

The French established colonies in North America at the same time as the English. The bitter rivalry between France and Great Britain fed France's desire to challenge the English presence in the Americas by establishing Catholic settlements in the Caribbean, Canada, and the region west of the Appalachian Mountains. Yet France never invested the people or resources in North America that England did. During the 1660s, the population of New France was less than that of the tiny English colony of Rhode Island. By the mid–eighteenth century, the residents of New France numbered less than 5 percent of British Americans.

NEW FRANCE

The actual settlement of New France began in 1605, when soldier-explorer Samuel de Champlain founded Port-Royal in Acadia, along the eastern Canadian coast. Three years later, Champlain established Quebec to the west, along the St. Lawrence River. (*Quebec* is an Algonquian word meaning "where the river narrows.") Champlain was the first European to explore and map the Great Lakes.

Until his death in 1635, Champlain governed New France on behalf of trading companies exploiting the fur trade with the Indians. The trading companies sponsored Champlain's voyages in hopes of creating a prosperous commercial colony. In 1627, however, the French government ordered that only Catholics could live in New France. This restriction stunted its growth—as did the harsh winter climate. As a consequence, the number of French who colonized Canada was *much* smaller than the number of British, Dutch, and Spanish colonists in other North American colonies.

Champlain knew that the outnumbered French could survive only by befriending the native peoples. To that end, he dispatched young trappers and traders to live with the indigenous peoples, learn their languages and customs, marry native women, and serve as ambassadors of New France. Many of these hardy woodsmen were *coureurs des bois* (runners of the woods), who pushed into the forested regions around the Great Lakes and developed a thriving fur trade.

In 1663, French King Louis XIV changed New France into a royal colony led by a governor-general who modeled his rule after that of the absolute royal monarchy. New France was fully subject to the French king. The colonists had no political rights or elected legislature, and public meetings could not be held without official permission.

Champlain in New France Samuel de Champlain firing at a group of Iroquois, killing two chieftains (1609).

To solidify New France, the king dispatched soldiers and settlers during the 1660s, including shiploads of young women, known as the King's Daughters, to be wives for the mostly male colonists. Louis also awarded large grants of land, called *seigneuries*, to lure aristocratic settlers. The poorest farmers usually rented land from the *seigneur*.

Yet none of these efforts transformed New France from being essentially a fur-trading outpost. Only about 40,000 French immigrants came to the Western Hemisphere during the seventeenth and eighteenth centuries, even though the population of France was three times that of Spain. By 1750, when the British colonists in North America numbered about 1.5 million, the total French population was 70,000.

From their Canadian outposts along the Great Lakes, French explorers in the early 1670s moved southward down the Mississippi River to the Gulf of Mexico. Louis Jolliet, a fur trader born in Quebec, teamed with Father Jacques Marquette, a Jesuit priest, to explore the Wisconsin River south to the Mississippi River. Traveling in canoes, they paddled to within 400 miles of the Gulf of Mexico, where they turned back for fear of encountering Spanish soldiers.

In 1682, René-Robert Cavelier, sieur de La Salle, organized an expedition that started in Montreal, crossed the Great Lakes, and eventually traveled down the Mississippi River to the Gulf of Mexico, becoming the first European to do so. Near what is today Venice, Mississippi, he buried an engraved plate and erected a cross, claiming for France the vast Ohio and Mississippi Valleys—all the way to the Rocky Mountains. He named the entire region Louisiana, after King Louis XIV.

Settlement of the Louisiana Territory finally began in 1699, when the French established a colony near Biloxi, Mississippi. The main settlement then moved to Mobile Bay and, in 1710, to the present site of Mobile, Alabama.

New France had one important advantage over its British rival: access to the great inland rivers that led to the heartland of the continent and the pelts of fur-bearing animals: beaver, otter, and mink. In the Illinois region, French settlers began farming the fertile soil, while Jesuits established missions to convert the Indians at places such as Terre Haute ("High Land," in what is now Indiana) and Des Moines ("Of the Monks," in present-day Iowa—the name probably shortened from Rivière des Moines, or "River of the Monks").

THE BRITISH COLONIAL SYSTEM

The diverse British colonies in North America were quite different from those of New France. Colonial governments typically were headed by a royal governor or proprietor, who could appoint and remove officials, command the militia, and grant pardons to people convicted of crimes.

The British colonies, unlike those of the Spanish, French, or Dutch, had *elected* legislatures; the "lower" houses were chosen by popular vote. Like Parliament, the assemblies controlled the budget and could pass laws and regulations. Most colonial assemblies exercised influence over the royal governors by paying their salaries. Unlike in New France, self-government in British America was expected and cherished.

MERCANTILISM The English Civil War during the 1640s sharply reduced the flow of money and people to America and created great confusion regarding colonial policies. It also forced English Americans to take sides in the conflict between Royalists and Puritans.

The 1651 victory of Oliver Cromwell's Puritan army over the monarchy had direct effects in the colonies. As England's new ruler, Cromwell embraced **mercantilism**, a political and economic policy adopted by most European monarchs during the seventeenth century. In a mercantile system, the government controlled all economic activities in an effort to strengthen national power. Key industries were regulated, taxed, or "subsidized" (supported by payments from the government). People with specialized skills or knowledge of new industrial technologies, such as textile machinery, were not allowed to leave the country.

Mercantilism also supported the creation of global empires. Colonies, it was assumed, enriched the mother country in several ways: (1) by providing silver and gold as well as the raw materials (furs, fish, grains, timber, sugar, tobacco, indigo, tar, etc.) needed to supply food, build ships, and produce goods; (2) by creating a captive market of colonial consumers who would be forced to buy goods created in the home country; (3) by relieving social tensions and political unrest in the home country, because colonies could absorb the growing numbers of poor, unemployed, and imprisoned; and, (4) by not producing goods that would compete with those produced in the home country.

NAVIGATION ACTS Such mercantilist assumptions prompted Oliver Cromwell to adopt the first in a series of **Navigation Acts** intended to increase England's control over its colonial economies. The Navigation Act of 1651 required that all goods going to and from the colonies be carried *only* in English ships. The law was intended to hurt the Dutch, who had developed a flourishing business shipping goods between America and Europe. Dutch shippers charged much less to transport goods than did the English, and they actively encouraged smuggling in the American colonies as a means of defying the Navigation Acts. By 1652, England and the Netherlands were at war—the first of three naval conflicts they waged against each other between 1652 and 1674.

After the British monarchy was restored to power in 1660, the new Royalist Parliament passed the Navigation Act of 1660, which specified that certain colonial products such as tobacco were to be shipped *only* to England or its colonies. The Navigation Act of 1663, the Staples Act, required that *all* shipments of goods from Europe to America must first stop in England to be offloaded and taxed before being sent on to the colonies.

By 1700, the English had surpassed the Dutch as the world's leading maritime power, and most products sent to and from America via Europe and Africa were carried in English ships. What the English government did not predict or fully understand was that the mercantile system would arouse resentment in the colonies.

COLONIAL RESENTMENT Colonial merchants and shippers loudly complained about the Navigation Acts, but the English government refused to lift its restrictions. New England, which shipped 90 percent of all American exports, was particularly hard hit. In 1678, a defiant Massachusetts legislature declared that the Navigation Acts had no legal standing. In 1684, King Charles II tried to teach the rebellious colonists a lesson by revoking the royal charter for Massachusetts.

Boston from the southeast This view of eighteenth-century Boston shows the importance of shipping and its regulation in the colonies.

The following year, Charles II died and was succeeded by his brother, King James II, the first Catholic monarch in more than 100 years. To demonstrate his power over Americans, the new king reorganized the New England colonies into a single royal supercolony called the Dominion of New England.

In 1686, the newly appointed royal governor, Sir Edmund Andros, arrived in Boston to take control of the Dominion. Andros stripped New Englanders of their civil rights, imposed new taxes as well as the Anglican religion, ignored town governments, strictly enforced the Navigation Acts, and punished American smugglers who tried to avoid regulation altogether.

The Glorious Revolution

In 1688, the Dominion of New England added the former Dutch provinces of New York, East Jersey, and West Jersey to its control, just a few months before the **Glorious Revolution** erupted in England in December. The revolution was called "Glorious" because it took place with little bloodshed. James II was forced to flee to France and was replaced by the king's Protestant daughter Mary and her Protestant husband William III, the ruling Dutch Prince.

William and Mary would rule as constitutional monarchs, their powers limited by Parliament. They soon issued a religious Toleration Act and a Bill of

Rights assuring the people that there never again would be an absolute monarchy in England.

In 1689, Americans in Boston staged their own revolution upon learning of the transfer of power in London. A group of merchants, ministers, and militiamen (citizen-soldiers) arrested Governor Andros and his aides and removed Massachusetts Bay Colony from the new Dominion of New England. Within a few weeks, the other colonies that had been absorbed into the Dominion also restored their independence.

The new British monarchs also allowed all of the colonies to regain their former status except Massachusetts Bay and Plymouth, which after some delay were united under a new charter in 1691 as the royal colony of Massachusetts Bay.

William and Mary, however, were also determined to crack down on American smuggling and rebelliousness. They appointed new royal governors in Massachusetts, New York, and Maryland. In Massachusetts, the governor was given authority to veto acts of the colonial assembly, and he removed the requirement that only church members could vote in elections.

JOHN LOCKE ON REVOLUTION England's Glorious Revolution had significant long-term effects on American history in that the removal of King James II revealed that a monarch could be deposed according to constitutional principles. The long-standing geographical designation "Great Britain" for the united kingdoms of England, Scotland, and Wales would soon be revived as the nation's official name.

A powerful justification for revolution appeared in 1690 when the English philosopher John Locke published his *Two Treatises on Government*, which had an enormous impact on political thought in the colonies. Locke rejected the "divine" right of monarchs to govern with absolute power. He also insisted that people are endowed with **natural rights** to life, liberty, and property. Locke noted that it was the need to protect those "natural" rights that led people to establish governments in the first place. When rulers failed to protect the property and lives of their subjects, Locke argued, the people had the right—in extreme cases—to overthrow the monarch and change the government.

AN EMERGING COLONIAL SYSTEM

In early 1689, New Yorkers sent a message to King William thanking him for delivering England from "tyranny, popery, and slavery." Many colonists were disappointed, however, when the king cracked down on American smugglers.

The Act to Prevent Frauds and Abuses of 1696 required colonial royal governors to enforce the Navigation Acts, allowed customs officials in America to use "writs of assistance" (general search warrants that did not have to specify the place to be searched), and ordered that accused smugglers be tried in royal *admiralty* courts (because juries in colonial courts rarely convicted their peers). Admiralty cases were decided by judges appointed by the royal governors.

Soon, however, British enforcement of the Navigation Acts waned. King George I (who ruled from 1714–1727) and George II (r. 1727–1760), German princes who were descendants of James I, showed much less interest in enforcing colonial trade laws, and Robert Walpole, the long-serving prime minister (1721–1742) and lord of the treasury, decided that the American colonies should be left alone to export needed raw materials (timber, tobacco, rice, indigo) and to buy manufactured goods from the mother country.

Under Walpole, Britain followed a policy of "a wise and salutary neglect" of the Navigation Acts and gave the colonies greater freedom to pursue their economic interests. What Walpole did not realize was that **salutary neglect** would create among many colonists an independent attitude that would eventually blossom into revolution.

THE HABIT OF SELF-GOVERNMENT Government within the colonies evolved without plan during the eighteenth century as the colonial assemblies acquired powers, particularly with respect to government appointments, that Parliament had yet to exercise itself.

The English colonies in America, unlike New France and New Spain, benefited from elected legislative assemblies. Whether called the House of Burgesses (Virginia), Delegates (Maryland), Representatives (Massachusetts), or simply the assembly, the "lower" houses were chosen by popular vote. Only male property owners could vote, based upon the notion that only men who held a tangible "stake in society" could vote responsibly. Members of the colonial assemblies tended to be wealthy, prominent figures, but there were exceptions. One colonist observed in 1744 that the New Jersey Assembly "was chiefly composed of mechanicks and ignorant wretches; obstinate to the last degree."

The most profound political trend during the early eighteenth century was the growing power exercised by the colonial assemblies. Like Parliament, the assemblies controlled the budget through their votes on taxes and expenditures, and they held the power to initiate legislation. Most assemblies also exerted leverage on the royal governors by controlling their salaries.

Throughout the eighteenth century, the assemblies expanded their power and influence, sometimes in conflict with the governors, sometimes in harmony with them. Self-government in America became first a habit, then a "right." By the mid–eighteenth century, the American colonies had become largely self-governing.

WARFARE IN THE COLONIES

The Glorious Revolution of 1688 transformed relations among the great powers of Europe. Protestants William and Mary, for example, were passionate foes of Catholic France's Louis XIV. King William organized an alliance of European nations against the French in a transatlantic war known in the American colonies as King William's War (1689–1697).

It was the first of four major wars fought in Europe and the colonies over the next seventy-four years. In each case, Britain and its European allies fought against Catholic France or Spain and their allies. By the end of the eighteenth century, the struggle between the British and the French would shift the balance of power in Europe.

The wars also reshaped Britain's relationship with America. Great Britain emerged from the wars in 1763 as the most powerful nation in the world. Thereafter, international commerce became increasingly essential to the expanding British Empire, thus making the American colonies even more strategically significant.

THE FRENCH AND INDIAN WAR The most important conflict between Britain and France in North America was the **French and Indian War** (1754–1763), globally known as the **Seven Years' War**. Unlike the three earlier wars, the French and Indian War started in America and ended with a decisive victory. It was sparked by French and British competition for the ancestral Indian lands in the vast Ohio Valley, and the stakes were high. Whoever controlled the "Ohio Country" would control the entire continent because of the area's access to the Ohio and Mississippi Rivers.

To defend their interests in the Ohio Country, the French pushed south from Canada and built forts in the region. When Virginia's British governor learned of the forts, he sent an ambitious, twenty-two-year-old militia officer, Major George Washington, to warn the French to leave. Washington made his way more than 450 miles to Fort Le Boeuf (just south of Lake Erie, in northwest Pennsylvania) in late 1753, only to be rebuffed by the French.

A few months later, in the spring of 1754, Washington, now a lieutenant colonel, went back to the Ohio Country with 150 volunteer soldiers and Indian allies. Their plan was to build a fort where the Allegheny, Monongahela, and Ohio Rivers converged (where the city of Pittsburgh later developed). The so-called Forks of the Ohio was the key strategic gateway to the vast territory west of the Appalachian Mountains, and both sides were determined to control it.

After two months of difficult travel through densely forested, hilly terrain, Washington learned that French soldiers had beaten him to the site and built Fort Duquesne. Washington decided to camp about forty miles from the fort. The next day, the Virginians ambushed a French scouting party, killing ten soldiers, including the commander—the first fatalities in what would become the French and Indian War.

Washington and his troops, reinforced by more Virginians and British soldiers dispatched from South Carolina, hastily constructed a tiny circular stockade at Great Meadows in western Pennsylvania. They called it Fort Necessity. Washington remarked that the valley provided "a charming field for an encounter," but there was nothing charming about the battle that erupted on July 3, 1754.

After the day-long, lopsided Battle of Great Meadows, Washington surrendered, having seen a third of his 300 men killed or wounded. The French and their Indian allies lost only three men. The French commander forced Washington to surrender his French prisoners and admit that he had "assassinated" the French soldiers at the earlier encounter. On July 4, Washington and the defeated Virginians began trudging home. Most of them, he noted, "are almost naked, and scarcely a man has either shoes, stockings, or hat."

France was now in undisputed control of the Ohio Country. Washington's bungled expedition not only had failed to oust the French; it had triggered a massive world war. As a British politician exclaimed, "the volley fired by a young Virginian in the backwoods of America set the world on fire."

THE ALBANY PLAN British officials, worried about war with the French and their Indian allies, urgently called a meeting of delegates from the northern colonies as far south as Maryland. Twenty-one representatives from seven colonies gathered in Albany, New York. It was the first time that a large group of colonial delegates had met to take joint action.

At the urging of Pennsylvania's Benjamin Franklin, the Albany Congress (June 19–July 11, 1754) approved the **Albany Plan of Union**. It called for eleven colonies to band together, headed by a president appointed by the king. Each colonial assembly would send two to seven delegates to a "grand council," which would have legislative powers. The Union would have jurisdiction over Indian affairs.

The Albany Plan of Union was too radical for the time, however. British officials and the colonial legislatures, eager to maintain their powers, wanted simply a military alliance against Indian attacks, so they rejected the Albany Plan. Benjamin Franklin later maintained that the Albany Plan of Union, had it been adopted, may have postponed or eliminated the eventual need for a full-scale colonial revolution. Franklin's proposal, however, did have lasting significance in that it would be the model for the form of governance (Articles of Confederation) created by the new American nation in 1777.

WAR IN NORTH AMERICA With the failure of the Albany Plan, the British decided to force a showdown with the "presumptuous" French. In June 1755, a British fleet captured the French forts protecting Acadia, a colony of New France along the Atlantic coast of Canada. The British then expelled 11,500 Acadians. Hundreds uprooted by the "Great Expulsion" eventually found their way to French Louisiana, where they became known as Cajuns (the name derived from *Acadians*).

In 1755, the British government sent 1,000 soldiers to dislodge the French from the Ohio Country. The arrival of unprecedented numbers of "redcoat" soldiers would change the dynamics of British North America. Although the colonists endorsed the use of force against the French, they later would oppose the use of British soldiers to enforce colonial regulations.

BRADDOCK'S DEFEAT The British commander in chief in America, General Edward Braddock, was a stubborn, overconfident officer who refused to recruit large numbers of Indian allies. Braddock viewed Indians with contempt, telling those willing to fight with him that he would not reward them with land for doing so: "No savage should inherit the land." His dismissal of the Indians and his ignorance of unconventional warfare would prove fatal. Neither he nor his troops had any experience fighting in the wilderness.

With the addition of some American militiamen, including George Washington as a volunteer officer, Braddock's force left northern Virginia to confront the French, hacking a 125-mile-long road west through the rugged Allegheny Mountains toward Fort Duquesne.

On July 9, 1755, as the British neared the fort, they were ambushed by French soldiers, Canadian militiamen, and Indians. The British troops, dressed in impractical bright-red wool uniforms in the summer heat, suffered shocking losses. Braddock was mortally wounded and would die three days later. Washington, his coat riddled by four bullets, helped lead a hasty retreat.

The first American political cartoon Benjamin Franklin's plea to the colonies to unite against the French in 1754 would become popular again twenty years later, when the colonies faced a different threat.

What came to be called the Battle of Monongahela was one of the worst British defeats in history. The French and Indians killed 63 of 86 British officers and 914 of 1,373 soldiers, and captured the British cannons and supplies. Twelve wounded British soldiers left behind on the battlefield were stripped and burned alive by Indians. A devastated Washington wrote his brother that the British army had "been scandalously beaten by a trifling body of men."

A WORLD WAR While Braddock's stunning defeat sent shock waves through the colonies, Indians allied with the French began attacking American farms throughout western Pennsylvania, Maryland, and Virginia. Desperate to respond, the Pennsylvania provincial government offered 130 Spanish dollars for each male Indian scalp and 50 dollars for female scalps.

Indians and colonists killed each other mercilessly throughout 1755 and 1756 during the French and Indian War. It was not until May 1756, however, that Protestant Britain and Catholic France formally declared war in Europe. The first truly "world war," the Seven Years' War in Europe and the French and Indian War in North America would eventually be fought on four continents and three oceans. In the end, it would redraw the political map of the world.

The onset of war brought a new British government, with William Pitt as prime minister. His ability and self-assurance matched his towering ego. "I know that I can save England and no one else can," he announced. Pitt assembled a force of 45,000 British troops and American militiamen, and in August 1759 they captured French forts near the Canadian border at Ticonderoga, Crown Point, and Niagara.

THE BATTLE OF QUEBEC In 1759, the French and Indian War reached its climax with a series of British triumphs on land and at sea. The most decisive victory was at Quebec, the hilltop fortress city and the capital of French Canada. During the dark of night, some 4,500 British troops scaled the cliffs above the St. Lawrence River and at dawn surprised the French in a battle that lasted only ten minutes. The French retreated in chaos, only to surrender four days later.

The Battle of Quebec was the turning point in the war. Thereafter, the conflict in North America diminished, although the fighting dragged on until 1763. Meanwhile, the Seven Years' War played out around the globe. In Europe, huge armies ravaged each other. Hundreds of towns and cities were plundered and destroyed, and more than a million people were killed.

A NEW BRITISH KING On October 25, 1760, British King George II arose at 6 A.M., drank his morning chocolate milk, and, suddenly, died on his toilet as the result of a ruptured artery. His death shocked the nation and brought an untested new king to the throne. George II's successor was his twenty-two-year-old grandson, who was despised by his grandfather. Although initially shy and insecure, King George III, the first in his German royal family to be born and raised in England, was an unabashed patriot: "I glory in the name of Britain." He became a strong-willed leader who oversaw the military defeat of France and Spain in the Seven Years' War. The Treaty of Paris, which ended the war, made Great Britain the ruler of an

George III The young king of a victorious empire.

enormous world empire. The American colonists celebrated the great British victories with as much excitement and pride as did Londoners.

THE TREATY OF PARIS (1763) In the **Treaty of Paris**, signed in February 1763, Britain took control of many important French colonies around the world, including several incredibly profitable "sugar island" colonies in the West Indies, most of the French colonies in India, and all of France's North

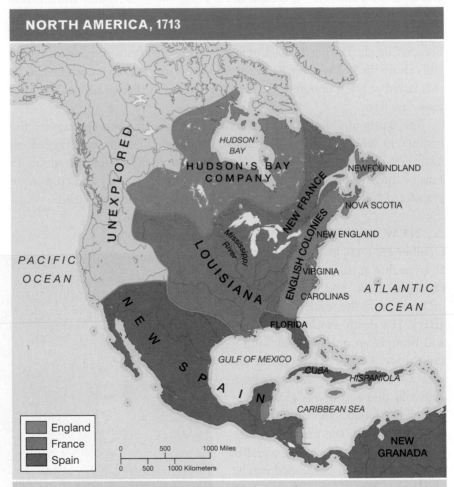

NORTH AMERICA, 1713

- What events led to the first clashes between the French and the British in the late seventeenth century?
- Why did New England suffer more than other regions of North America during the wars of the eighteenth century?
- What were the long-term financial, military, and political consequences of the wars between France and Britain?

American possessions east of the Mississippi River, including all of Canada and what was then called Spanish Florida (including much of present-day Alabama and Mississippi). As compensation, the treaty gave Spain control over the vast Louisiana Territory, including New Orleans and all French land west of the Mississippi River. The loss of Louisiana left France with no territory on the North American continent.

Britain's spectacular military success created massive challenges, however. The national debt doubled during the war, and the new cost of maintaining

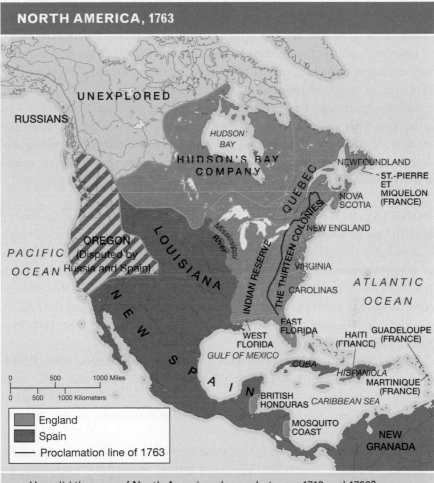

NORTH AMERICA, 1763

UNEXPLORED

RUSSIANS

HUDSON BAY

HUDSON'S BAY COMPANY

QUEBEC

NEWFOUNDLAND

ST.-PIERRE ET MIQUELON (FRANCE)

NOVA SCOTIA

NEW ENGLAND

Mississippi River

OREGON (Disputed by Russia and Spain)

PACIFIC OCEAN

LOUISIANA

INDIAN RESERVE

THE THIRTEEN COLONIES

VIRGINIA

CAROLINAS

ATLANTIC OCEAN

NEW SPAIN

EAST FLORIDA

WEST FLORIDA

GULF OF MEXICO

CUBA

HAITI (FRANCE)

GUADELOUPE (FRANCE)

HISPANIOLA

MARTINIQUE (FRANCE)

BRITISH HONDURAS

CARIBBEAN SEA

MOSQUITO COAST

NEW GRANADA

0   500   1000 Miles
0   500   1000 Kilometers

- ▓ England
- ▓ Spain
- — Proclamation line of 1763

- ■ How did the map of North America change between 1713 and 1763?
- ■ How did Spain win the Louisiana Territory?
- ■ What were the consequences of the British gaining all the land east of the Mississippi River?

the sprawling North American empire, including the permanent stationing of British soldiers in the colonies, was staggering. In winning a huge global empire, the British developed what one historian has called an "arrogant triumphalism," which led them to tighten—and ultimately lose—their control over the Indians and colonists in North America.

MANAGING A NEW EMPIRE No sooner was the Treaty of Paris signed than George III and his cabinet, working through Parliament, began strictly enforcing economic regulations on the American colonies to help reduce the crushing national debt caused by the war. During and after the war, the British government increased taxes in Britain to fund the military expenses. In 1763, the average British citizen paid twenty-six times as much in taxes each year as the average American colonist paid. With that in mind, British leaders thought it only fair that the Americans should pay more of the expenses for administering and defending the colonies.

Many Americans disagreed, however, arguing that the Navigation Acts restricting their economic activity were already a form of tax on them. The tension between the British need for greater revenue and the Americans' defense of their rights and liberties set in motion a chain of events that would lead to revolution and independence.

PONTIAC'S REBELLION After the war, colonists began squabbling over Indian-owned land west of the Appalachian Mountains that the French had ceded to the British in the Treaty of Paris. Native American leaders, none of whom attended the meetings leading to the treaty, were shocked to learn that the French had "given" their ancestral lands to the British. Ohio Indians complained to British army officers that "as soon as you conquered the French, you did not care how you treated us." One chieftain claimed that the British had treated them "like slaves."

The Indians fought back in the spring of 1763, capturing most of the British forts around the Great Lakes and in the Ohio Valley. "Never was panic more general," reported the *Pennsylvania Gazette*, "than that of the Back[woods] Inhabitants, whose terrors at this time exceed that followed on the defeat of General Braddock."

Native Americans also raided colonial settlements in Pennsylvania, Maryland, and Virginia, destroying farms and killing thousands. "Every day, for some time past," reported a Marylander, "has offered the melancholy scene of poor distressed families . . . who have deserted their plantations, for fear of falling into the cruel hands of our savage enemies." Refugees told of terrible massacres in which settlers "were most cruelly butchered; the woman was roasted . . . and several of the men had awls thrust in their eyes, and spears, arrows, pitchforks, etc., sticking in their bodies."

The Indian attacks came to be called **Pontiac's Rebellion** because of the prominent role played by the Ottawa chieftain who sought to unify several tribes in the effort to stop American expansion. Pontiac told a British official that the "French never conquered us, neither did they purchase a foot of our Country, nor have they a right to give it to you."

THE PROCLAMATION LINE To help keep peace with the Indians and to abide by the terms of an earlier agreement with the Delawares and Shawnees, called the Treaty of Easton (1758), King George III issued the **Royal Proclamation of 1763**, which drew an imaginary line along the crest of the Appalachian Mountains from Canada south to Georgia. White settlers ("our loving subjects") were forbidden to go west of the line to ensure that the Indians would not be "molested or disturbed" on their ancestral lands.

For the first time, American territorial expansion was to be controlled by royal officials. In practice, the proclamation line ended the activities of speculators buying huge tracts of Indian lands but did not keep land-hungry settlers from pushing across the Appalachian ridges into Indian country. By 1767, an Indian chief was complaining that whites were "making more encroachments on their Country than ever they had before."

REGULATING THE COLONIES

As Britain tightened its hold over the colonies after 1763, the colonists reminded Parliament that their original charters guaranteed that they should be treated as if they were English citizens, with all the rights and liberties protected by the nation's constitutional traditions. Such arguments, however, fell on deaf ears in Parliament. As one member explained, the British were determined "to make North America pay [for] its own army."

GRENVILLE'S COLONIAL POLICY Just as the Proclamation of 1763 was being drafted, a new British government led by George Grenville began to grapple with the huge debts the government had accumulated during the war—and with the added expenses of maintaining troops in America. Grenville insisted that the Americans, whom he called the "least taxed people in the world," must pay for the soldiers defending them. He also resented the large number of American merchants who engaged in smuggling to avoid paying British taxes on imported goods. Grenville ordered colonial officials to tighten enforcement of the Navigation Acts and sent warships to capture American smugglers.

THE SUGAR ACT   Grenville's effort to enforce the Navigation Acts posed a serious threat to New England's prosperity. Distilling rum out of molasses, a sweet syrup made from sugarcane, had become quite profitable, especially if the molasses could be smuggled in from Caribbean islands still controlled by the French.

To generate more money from the colonies, Grenville put through the American Revenue Act of 1764, commonly known as the Sugar Act, which cut the tax on molasses in half. Doing so, he believed, would reduce the temptation to smuggle French molasses or to bribe royal customs officers. But the Sugar Act also added new *duties* (taxes) on other goods (sugar, wines, coffee, spices) imported into America. The new revenues generated by the Sugar Act, Grenville estimated, would help pay for "the necessary expenses of defending, protecting, and securing, the said colonies."

With the Sugar Act, Parliament, for the first time, adopted a policy designed to raise *revenues* from the colonies and not merely to *regulate* trade with other nations. Colonists claimed that the Sugar Act taxed them without their consent, since they had no elected representatives in Parliament. British officials argued, however, that Parliament's power was absolute and indivisible. If the Americans accepted parliamentary authority in *any* area, they had to accept it in *every* area. In the end, however, the controversial new sugar tax did not produce more revenue for Great Britain; the cost of enforcing it was four times greater than the revenue it generated.

THE STAMP ACT   Prime Minister Grenville excelled at doing the wrong thing—repeatedly. In 1765, he persuaded Parliament to pass the Quartering Act, which required Americans to feed and house British troops. Most Americans saw no need for so many British soldiers in colonial cities. If the British were there to defend against Indians, why weren't they positioned closer to the Indians? Some colonists decided that the Quartering Act was actually an effort to use British soldiers to bully Americans.

Yet Grenville aggravated colonial concerns by pushing through an even more controversial measure. On February 13, 1765, Parliament passed the **Stamp Act**, which required colonists to purchase stamped paper for virtually every possible use: newspapers, pamphlets, bonds, leases, deeds, licenses, insurance policies, college diplomas, even playing cards. The requirement was to go into effect November 1. The Stamp Act was the first effort by Parliament to place a tax directly on American goods and services rather than levying an "external" tax on imports and exports. Not a single colony supported the new measure.

THE WHIG POINT OF VIEW In the late eighteenth century, Americans who opposed British policies began to call themselves Patriots, or *Whigs*, a name earlier applied to British critics of royal power. In turn, Whigs labeled the king and his "corrupt" government ministers and Parliamentary supporters as "*Tories*," a term of abuse meaning friends of the king.

In 1764 and 1765, Whigs felt that Grenville was violating their rights in several ways. A professional army was usually a weapon used by tyrants, and now, with the French defeated and Canada solidly under British control, thousands of British soldiers remained in America. Were the troops there to protect the colonists or to scare them into obedience?

Whigs also argued that British citizens had the right to be taxed only by their elected representatives in Parliament, but Americans had no such representatives. British leaders countered that the colonists enjoyed **virtual representation** in Parliament, whose members were sworn to represent not simply their own districts but Britons everywhere. William Pitt, a staunch supporter of American rights in Parliament, dismissed Grenville's concept of "virtual representation" as "the most contemptible idea that ever entered into the head of a man." Many others, in both Britain and America, agreed.

PROTESTS IN THE COLONIES The Stamp Act aroused fierce resentment and resistance. A New Yorker wrote that "this single stroke has lost Great Britain the affection of all her colonies." In a flood of pamphlets, speeches, resolutions, and street protests, critics repeated a slogan familiar to Americans: "No taxation without representation [in Parliament]."

Protesters, calling themselves **Sons of Liberty**, emerged in every colony, often meeting beneath "liberty trees"—in Boston a great elm, in Charleston, South Carolina, a live oak. In New York City, the Sons of Liberty erected "liberty poles" as symbols of their resistance. In Virginia, Patrick Henry convinced the assembly to pass the "Stamp Act Resolutions," which asserted yet again that the colonists could not be taxed without being first consulted by the British government or represented in Parliament by their own elected members.

THE NONIMPORTATION MOVEMENT Americans opposed to the Stamp Act knew that the most powerful form of leverage they had against the British was economic. To put pressure on the British government and show that they had not become "dependent" on Britain's "empire of goods," Patriots by the thousands signed what were called nonimportation agreements, pledging not to buy or consume any British goods.

The nonimportation movement of the 1760s and 1770s united Whigs from different communities and different colonies. It also enabled women to play a significant role in resisting Britain's colonial policies. Calling themselves **Daughters of Liberty**, many colonial women stopped buying imported British clothes. They also quit drinking British tea to "save this abused Country from Ruin and Slavery." Using herbs and flowers, they made "Liberty Tea" instead.

The Daughters of Liberty also participated in public "spinning bees," whereby they would gather to weave and spin yarn and wool into fabric, known as "homespun." In 1769, the *Boston Evening Post* reported that the "industry and frugality of American ladies" were enabling "the political salvation of a whole continent."

Patriots saw the effort to boycott British products as a way to restore their own virtue. A Rhode Islander declared that a primary cause of America's problems was the "luxury and extravagance" brought on by their freewheeling purchases of British goods. The nonimportation movement would help Americans restore "our frugality, industry, and simplicity of manners." A Boston minister claimed that those who could not do without British luxury goods and be satisfied with "plainness and simplicity" did not deserve to be American citizens.

COLONIAL UNITY The boycotts worked; imports of British goods fell by 40 percent. At the same time, the Virginia House of Burgesses struck the first official blow against the Stamp Act with the Virginia Resolves, a series of resolutions inspired by the fiery Patrick Henry. Virginians, Henry declared, were entitled to all the rights of Englishmen, and Englishmen could be taxed only by their own elected representatives. Because Virginians had no elected representatives in Parliament, they could only be taxed by the Virginia legislature. Newspapers spread the Virginia Resolves throughout the colonies, and other colonial assemblies hastened to follow Virginia's example. "No taxation without representation" became the rally cry for American Whigs.

In 1765, the Massachusetts House of Representatives invited the other colonial assemblies to send delegates to New York City to discuss their opposition to the Stamp Act. Nine responded, and from October 7–25, 1765, the Stamp Act Congress formulated a Declaration of the Rights and Grievances of the Colonies. The delegates insisted that they would accept no taxes being "imposed on them" without "their own consent, given personally, or by their representatives." Grenville responded by denouncing his colonial critics as "ungrateful" for all of the benefits provided them by the British government.

REPEAL OF THE STAMP ACT The storm over the Stamp Act had scarcely begun before Grenville was out of office. He had lost the confidence of the king, who replaced him with Lord Rockingham in July 1765. Then, in mid-August 1765, nearly three months before the Stamp Act was to take effect, a Boston mob plundered the homes of the royal lieutenant governor and the official in charge of enforcing the stamp tax. Thoroughly shaken, the stamp agent resigned. Other stamp agents throughout the colonies were also hounded out of office.

The growing violence in America and the success of the nonimportation movement convinced Rockingham that the Stamp Act was a mistake. In February 1766, a humiliated Parliament repealed it. To save face, Parliament passed the Declaratory Act, which asserted its power to govern the colonies "in all cases whatsoever."

THE TOWNSHEND ACTS In July 1766, King George III replaced Lord Rockingham with William Pitt, the former prime minister who had exercised heroic leadership during the Seven Years' War. For a time, the guiding force in the Pitt ministry was the witty but reckless Charles Townshend, the treasury

The Repeal, or The Funeral Procession of Miss Americ-Stamp This 1766 cartoon shows Grenville carrying the dead Stamp Act in its coffin. In the background, trade with America starts up again.

chief whose "abilities were superior to those of all men," said a colleague, "and his judgment [common sense] below that of any man."

In 1767, Townshend pushed through Parliament his ill-fated plan to generate more colonial revenue. A few months later, he died at age forty-two, leaving behind a bitter legacy: the **Townshend Acts**. The Revenue Act of 1767, which taxed colonial imports of glass, lead, paint, paper, and tea, was the most hated. It posed an even more severe threat than Grenville's taxes had, for Townshend planned to use the tax revenues to pay the salaries of the royal governors in the colonies. Until that point, the colonial assemblies paid the salaries, thus giving them leverage over the governors. John Adams observed that Townshend's plan would make the royal governor "independent of the people" and disrupt "that balance of power which is essential to all free governments." Writing in the *Boston Gazette*, Adams insisted that such "an INDEPENDENT ruler, [is] a MONSTER in a free state."

THE CRISIS GROWS

The Townshend Acts surprised and angered many colonists. As American rage bubbled over, firebrand Samuel Adams of Boston became convinced that a small group of determined Whigs could generate a mass movement. "It does not take a majority to prevail," Adams insisted, "but rather an irate, tireless minority, keen on setting brushfires of freedom in the minds of men."

Early in 1768, Adams and Boston attorney James Otis Jr. convinced the Massachusetts assembly to circulate a letter they had written to the other colonies. It restated the illegality of taxation without representation in Parliament and invited the support of other colonies. British officials ordered the Massachusetts assembly to withdraw the letter. The assembly refused, and the king ordered the assembly dissolved.

In response to an appeal by the royal governor of Massachusetts, 3,000 British troops were sent to Boston in October 1768 to maintain order. **Loyalists**, as the Americans who supported the king and Parliament were often called, welcomed the soldiers; **Patriots**, those rebelling against British authority, viewed the troops as an occupation force. Meanwhile, in London, the king appointed still another new chief minister, Frederick, Lord North, in January 1770.

THE FIRST BLOODSHED   In 1765, Benjamin Franklin had predicted that British soldiers sent to America would "not find a rebellion; they may indeed make one." The growing tensions between Americans and British troops triggered several violent incidents. The first, called the Battle at Golden

Hill, occurred in New York City, where "Liberty Boys" kept erecting "liberty poles," only to see British soldiers knock them down. The soldiers, called "lobsterbacks" or "redcoats" because of their bright red uniforms, also began posting signs declaring that the Sons of Liberty were "the real enemies of society."

On January, 18, 1770, a group of Patriots captured two British soldiers. Soon, an angry crowd formed around the twenty soldiers sent to rescue their comrades. The outnumbered soldiers retreated. When they reached Golden Hill, more soldiers arrived. At that point, the redcoats turned on the crowd pursuing them. An officer yelled: "Draw your bayonets and cut your way through them!" They attacked the crowd, and in the confusion, several people on both sides were seriously hurt.

The next day, more brawls erupted. Once the British soldiers left the scene, the Sons of Liberty erected another liberty pole which bore the inscription: "Liberty and Property." The first blood had been shed in the growing conflict over American liberties, and it was soon followed by more violence.

THE BOSTON MASSACRE Massachusetts had long been the center of resistance to British authority. In Boston, the presence of thousands of British soldiers had become a constant source of irritation. Crowds frequently heckled the soldiers, many of whom earned the abuse by harassing and intimidating Americans.

On the evening of March 5, 1770, two dozen Boston rowdies—teens, Irishmen, blacks, and sailors—began taunting Hugh White, a British soldier guarding the Custom House. Someone rang the town fire bell, drawing a larger crowd to the scene as the taunting continued: "Kill him, kill him, knock him down. Fire, damn you, fire, you dare not fire!"

A squad of soldiers arrived to help White, but the surly crowd surrounded them. When someone threw a club that knocked a soldier down, he arose and fired his musket. Others joined in. When the smoke cleared, five people lay dead or dying, and eight more were wounded. The first one killed, or so the story goes, was African American Crispus Attucks, a former slave who worked at the docks.

The so-called **Boston Massacre** sent shock waves throughout the colonies and all the way to London. Virtually the entire city of Boston attended the funerals for the deceased. Only the decision to postpone the trial of the British soldiers for six months allowed the tensions to subside. At the same time, the impact of the colonial boycott of British products persuaded Lord North to modify the Townshend Acts.

Late in April 1770, Parliament repealed all the Townshend duties except for the tea tax, which the king wanted to keep as a symbol of Parliament's authority. Colonial discontent subsided for two years thereafter. The redcoats

The Bloody Massacre Paul Revere's engraving of the Boston Massacre (1770).

left Boston but remained stationed nearby in Canada, and the British navy still patrolled the New England coast.

THE GASPÉE INCIDENT In June 1772, a naval incident further eroded the colonies' fragile relationship with the mother country. Near Warwick, Rhode Island, the HMS *Gaspée*, a British warship, ran aground while chasing suspected American smugglers. Its hungry crew seized local sheep, hogs, and chickens from local farms. An enraged crowd, some of them dressed as Mohawk Indians, boarded the ship, shot the captain, removed the crew, and burned the ship.

The *Gaspée* incident symbolized the intensity of anti-British feelings among growing numbers of Americans. When the British tried to take the suspects to London for trial, Patriots organized in protest. Thomas Jefferson said that it was the threat of transporting Americans for trials in Britain that reignited anti-British activities in Virginia.

In response to the *Gaspée* incident, Boston's Samuel Adams organized the **Committee of Correspondence**, which issued a statement of American rights and grievances and invited other towns to do the same. Similar committees sprang up across Massachusetts and in other colonies, forming a unified network of resistance. "The flame is kindled and like lightning it catches from soul to soul," reported Abigail Adams, the high-spirited wife of future president John Adams. By 1772, Thomas Hutchinson, the royal governor of Massachusetts, could tell the colonial assembly that the choice facing Americans was stark: they must choose between obeying "the supreme authority of Parliament" and "total independence."

THE BOSTON TEA PARTY The new British prime minister, Lord North, soon provided the colonists with the spark to transform resentment into rebellion. In 1773, he tried to bail out the struggling East India Company, which desperately needed to sell some 17 million pounds of tea before it rotted. Parliament passed the Tea Act of 1773 to allow the company to send its tea directly to America without paying any taxes. British tea merchants could thereby undercut the prices charged by their American competitors, most of whom were smugglers who bought tea from the Dutch. At the same time, King George III told Lord North to "compel obedience" in the colonies.

In Massachusetts, the Committees of Correspondence, backed by Boston merchants, advised colonists that the British government was trying to purchase colonial submission with cheap tea. The reduction in the price of tea was a clever trick to make colonists accept taxation without consent. In Boston, enraged Americans decided that their passion for liberty outweighed their love for tea. On December 16, 1773, scores of Patriots disguised as Indians boarded three British ships in Boston Harbor and dumped overboard 342 chests filled with 46 tons of East India Company tea.

The **Boston Tea Party** pushed British officials to the breaking point. The destruction of so much valuable tea convinced the king and his advisers that a forceful response was required.

THE COERCIVE ACTS In 1774, Lord North convinced Parliament to punish rebellious Boston by enacting a cluster of harsh laws called the **Coercive Acts** (Americans renamed them the "Intolerable" Acts). The Boston Port Act closed the Boston harbor until the city paid for the lost tea. A new Quartering Act ordered colonists to provide lodging for British soldiers. The Impartial Administration of Justice Act said that any royal official accused of a major crime would be tried in Great Britain rather than in the colony. Finally, the Massachusetts Government Act gave the royal governor the authority to appoint the colony's legislative council, which until then had been elected by the people, as well as judges and sheriffs. In May, Lieutenant-General Thomas Gage, commander in chief of British forces in North America, was named governor of Massachusetts and assumed command of the British soldiers who had returned to Boston.

The Intolerable Acts shocked the Massachusetts colonists. No one had expected such a severe reaction to the Boston Tea Party. Many towns held meetings in violation of the new laws, and voters elected their own unauthorized provincial legislative assembly—which ordered town governments to quit paying taxes to the royal governor. By August 1774, Patriots across Massachusetts had essentially taken control of local governments. They also began stockpiling weapons and gunpowder in anticipation of an eventual clash with British troops.

Elsewhere, colonists rallied to help Boston, raising money, sending supplies, and boycotting, as well as burning or dumping British tea. In Williamsburg, when the Virginia assembly met in May, a member of the Committee of Correspondence, Thomas Jefferson, suggested that June 1, the effective date of the Boston Port Act, become an official day of fasting and prayer in Virginia.

The royal governor responded by dissolving the assembly, whose members then retired to the Raleigh Tavern, where they decided to form a Continental Congress to represent all the colonies. As Samuel Savage, a Connecticut colonist, wrote in May 1774, the conflict had come down to a single question: "Whether we shall or shall not be governed by a British Parliament."

THE FIRST CONTINENTAL CONGRESS   On September 5, 1774, the fifty-five delegates making up the First Continental Congress assembled in Philadelphia. Over seven weeks, the Congress endorsed the Suffolk Resolves, which urged Massachusetts to resist British tyranny with force. The Congress then adopted a Declaration of American Rights, which proclaimed once again the rights of Americans as British citizens and denied Parliament's authority to regulate internal colonial affairs. "We demand no new rights," said the Congress. "We ask only for peace, liberty, and security."

Finally, the Congress adopted the Continental Association of 1774, which recommended that every colony organize committees to enforce a new and complete boycott of all imported British goods, a dramatic step that would be followed by a refusal to send American goods to Britain. If the ideal of republican virtue meant anything, it meant the sacrificing of self-interest for the public good. The Association was designed to show that Americans could deny themselves the "baubles of Britain" to demonstrate their commitment to colonial liberties and constitutional rights.

The county and city committees forming the Continental Association became the organizational network for the resistance movement. Seven thousand men across the colonies served on the local committees, and many more women helped put the boycotts into practice. The committees required colonists to sign an oath refusing to purchase British goods. Those who refused to sign were punished. In East Haddam, Connecticut, a Loyalist doctor was tarred, feathered, and rubbed with pig dung. Such violent incidents led Loyalists to claim that it was better to be a slave to the king than to a Patriot mob.

Thousands of ordinary men and women participated in the boycott of British goods, and their sacrifices on behalf of colonial liberties provided the momentum leading to revolution. It was common people who enforced the boycott, volunteered in Patriot militia units, attended town meetings, and ousted royal officials. The rebellion now extended well beyond simple grievances over taxation. Patriots decided that there was a *conspiracy* against their liberties at work in London. In Boston, an increasingly nervous General Gage requested more troops to suppress the growing rebellion. Mercy Otis Warren wrote that most Americans still balked "at the idea of drawing the sword against the nation from whence she [America] derived her origin." She feared, however, that Britain was poised "to plunge her dagger into the bosom of her affectionate offspring."

LAST-MINUTE COMPROMISE In London, King George fumed. He wrote Lord North that "blows must decide" whether the Americans "are to be subject to this country or independent." In early 1775, Parliament declared that Massachusetts was officially "in rebellion" and prohibited the New England colonies from trading with any nation outside the British Empire. On February 27, 1775, Lord North issued the Conciliatory Propositions, which offered to resolve the festering dispute by eliminating all taxes on any colony that voluntarily paid both its share for military defense and the salaries of the royal governors. In other words, North was asking the colonies to tax themselves. By the time the Conciliatory Propositions arrived in America, shooting had already started.

BOLD TALK OF WAR While most of the Patriots believed that Britain would back down, Patrick Henry of Virginia dramatically declared that war was unavoidable. The twenty-nine-year-old Henry, a farmer and storekeeper turned lawyer, claimed that the colonies "have done everything that could be done to avert the storm which is now coming on," but their efforts had been met only by "violence and insult." Freedom, the defiant Henry shouted, could be bought only with blood. If forced to choose, he supposedly shouted, "give me liberty"—then paused dramatically, clenched his fist as if it held a dagger, and plunged it into his chest—"or give me death."

As Henry had predicted, events quickly moved toward armed conflict. By mid-1775, the king and Parliament had effectively lost control; they could neither persuade nor force the Patriots to accept new regulations and revenue measures. In Boston, General Gage warned that armed conflict would unleash the "horrors of civil war." But Lord Sandwich, head of the British navy, dismissed the rebels as "raw, undisciplined, cowardly men" without an army or navy. Major John Pitcairn, a British army officer, agreed, writing that "one active campaign, a smart action, and burning two or three of their towns, will set everything to rights."

LEXINGTON AND CONCORD Major Pitcairn soon had his chance to quash the rebel resistance. On April 14, 1775, the British army in Boston received secret orders to stop the "open rebellion" in Massachusetts. General Gage had decided to arrest rebel leaders such as Samuel Adams and seize the militia's gunpowder stored at Concord, sixteen miles northwest of Boston. After dark on April 18, some 800 British soldiers secretly boarded boats and crossed the Charles River to Cambridge, then set out westward on foot to Lexington, a town about eleven miles away. When Patriots got wind of the plan, Paul Revere and William Dawes mounted their horses for their famous "midnight ride" to warn the rebel leaders that the British were coming.

In the gray dawn light of April 19, an advance unit of 238 redcoats found American Captain John Parker and about seventy "Minutemen" (Patriot militia who could assemble at a "minute's" notice) lined up on the Lexington town square, while dozens of villagers watched.

Parker and his men intended only a silent protest, but Major Pitcairn rode onto the Lexington Green, swinging his sword and yelling, "Disperse, you damned rebels! You dogs, run!" The outnumbered militiamen were backing away when someone, perhaps an onlooker, fired. The British soldiers immediately began shooting wildly at the Minutemen, then charged them with bayonets, leaving eight dead and ten wounded.

The British officers quickly brought their men under control and led them to Concord, where they destroyed hidden military supplies. While marching out of the town, they encountered American riflemen. Shots were fired, and a dozen or so British soldiers were killed or wounded. More important, the short skirmish and ringing church bells alerted rebel farmers, ministers, craftsmen, and merchants from nearby communities to grab their muskets. They were, as one of them said, determined to "be free or die."

By noon, the British began a ragged retreat back to Lexington. Less than a mile out of Concord, they suffered the first of many ambushes. The narrow

The Battle of Lexington Amos Doolittle's impression of the Battle of Lexington as shooting begins between the Royal Marines and the Minutemen.

road turned into a gauntlet of death as rebel marksmen fired on the British troops from behind stone walls, trees, barns, and houses. "It was a day full of horror," one of the soldiers recalled. "The Patriots seemed maddened."

By nightfall, the redcoat survivors were safely back in Boston, having suffered three times as many dead and wounded as the Americans. A British general reported that the colonists had earned his respect: "Whoever looks upon them as an irregular mob will find himself much mistaken."

Until the Battles of Lexington and Concord, both sides had mistakenly assumed that the other would back down when confronted with deadly force. Instead, the clash of arms turned a resistance movement into a war of rebellion. Masses of ordinary people were determined to fight for their freedoms against a British parliament and king bent on denying them their civil and legal rights. In Virginia, Thomas Jefferson reported that the news about Concord and Lexington had unleashed "a frenzy of revenge [against the British]" among "all ranks of people."

THE SPREADING CONFLICT

On June 15, 1775, the Second Continental Congress unanimously selected forty-three-year-old George Washington to lead a new national army. Washington's service in the French and Indian War had made him one of the few experienced American officers, and he was admired for his success as a planter, surveyor, and land speculator, as well as for his service in the Virginia legislature and the Continental Congress. Perhaps more important, he *looked* like a leader. Tall and strong, Washington was a superb horseman and fearless fighter.

Washington humbly accepted the responsibility of leading the American war effort, but refused to be paid. A few weeks later, Mercy Otis Warren wrote a friend in London that Washington was "a man whose military abilities & public & private virtue place him in the first class of the Good & the Brave."

THE BATTLE OF BUNKER HILL   On Saturday, June 17, the very day that George Washington was named commander in chief, Patriot militiamen engaged British forces in their first major clash, the Battle of Bunker Hill (adjoining Breed's Hill was the battle's actual location).

Some 2,400 British troops in Boston boarded boats and crossed over the Charles River to Charlestown, where they formed lines and advanced up Breed's Hill in tight formation as American defenders watched from behind their earthworks. The militiamen, mostly farmers, waited until the redcoats had come within thirty paces, then loosed a volley that shattered the front ranks. The British reformed and attacked again, but the Patriot riflemen forced them to retreat a second time. During the third British assault, the colonists ran out of gunpowder and retreated in panic. The British suffered 1,054 casualties, more than twice the American losses. "A dearly bought victory," reported British general Henry Clinton; "another such would have ruined us." There followed a nine-month stalemate around Boston, with each side hoping for a negotiated end to the crisis. Abigail Adams reported that the Patriots still living in Boston, where the British army governed by martial law, were being treated "like abject slaves under the most cruel and despotic of tyrants."

Three weeks after the Battle of Bunker Hill, in July 1775, the Continental Congress sent the king the Olive Branch Petition, urging him to negotiate with his rebellious colonies. When the petition reached London, however, King George refused to look at it. On August 22, he denounced the Americans as "open and avowed enemies." His arrogant dismissal of the Olive Branch Petition convinced Abigail Adams that war was now certain: "the die is cast . . . the sword is now our only, yet dreadful, alternative."

OUTRIGHT REBELLION   Resistance had grown into outright rebellion, but few Patriots in 1775 were ready to call for American independence. They still considered themselves British subjects, and when the Second Continental Congress convened at Philadelphia on May 10, 1775, most of the delegates still wanted Parliament to restore their rights so that they could resume being loyal British colonists.

Meanwhile, the British army in Boston was under siege by militia units and small groups of musket-toting men who had arrived from across New England to join the rebellion. They were still farmers, not trained soldiers, and the uprising was not yet an army; it lacked an organized command structure and effective support system. The Patriots also lacked training, discipline, and ammunition. What they did have was a growing sense of confidence and resolve. As a Massachusetts Patriot said, "Our all is at stake. Death and devastation are the instant consequences of delay. Every moment is infinitely precious."

With each passing day, war fever infected more and more colonists. "Oh that I were a soldier!" John Adams wrote home to Abigail from Philadelphia. "I will be. I am reading military books. Everybody must, and will, and shall be a soldier." On the very day that Congress met, the British Fort Ticonderoga, on Lake Champlain in upstate New York near the Canadian border, fell to a Patriot force of "Green Mountain Boys" led by Ethan Allen of Vermont and Massachusetts volunteers under Benedict Arnold. Two days later, the Patriots captured a smaller British fort at Crown Point, north of Ticonderoga.

INDEPENDENCE

The Revolutionary War was well under way in January 1776 when Thomas Paine, a recently arrived, thirty-nine-year-old English emigrant who found work as a radical journalist in Philadelphia, provided the Patriot cause with a stirring pamphlet titled **Common Sense**. Until it appeared, colonial grievances had been mainly directed at Parliament. Paine, however, directly attacked the British monarchy by openly appealing to the "passions and feelings of mankind."

The "common sense" of the matter, Paine stressed, was that King George III had caused the rebellion and ordered the savage and cruel denial of American rights. "Even brutes do not devour their young," he wrote, "nor savages make war upon their families." Yet Britain, the mother of America, was doing just that. Americans, Paine urged, should abandon the British monarchy: "The blood of the slain, the weeping voice of nature cries, 'tis time to part." Paine helped convince Americans that independence was inevitable. Only by declaring independence, he predicted, could the colonists gain the crucial support of France and Spain: "The cause of America is in great measure the cause of all mankind." The rest of the world would welcome and embrace an independent America; it would be the "glory of the earth." Paine concluded that the "sun had never shined on a cause of greater worth."

The coming revolution The Continental Congress votes for independence, July 2, 1776.

Within three months, more than 150,000 copies of Paine's stirring pamphlet were circulating throughout the colonies and around the world, an enormous number for the time. "*Common Sense* is working a powerful change in the minds of men," George Washington reported.

BREAKING THE BONDS OF EMPIRE *Common Sense* inspired the colonial population from Massachusetts to Georgia and helped convince British subjects still loyal to the king to embrace the radical notion of independence. "Without the pen of Paine," remembered John Adams, "the sword of Washington would have been wielded in vain." During the spring and summer of 1776, some ninety local governments, towns, and colonial legislatures issued declarations of independence from Great Britain.

Momentum for independence was building in the Continental Congress, too, but success was by no means assured. In Congress, John Dickinson of Pennsylvania urged delay. On June 1, he warned that independence was a dangerous step since America had no national government or European allies. But his was a lone voice of caution.

In June 1776, the colonies authorized their delegates in the Continental Congress to take the final step. On June 7, Richard Henry Lee of Virginia moved "that these United Colonies are, and of right ought to be, free and independent states." Lee's resolution passed on July 2, a date that John Adams predicted "will be the most memorable" in the history of America.

The more memorable date, however, became July 4, 1776, when the Congress formally adopted the **Declaration of Independence**. A few delegates refused to sign; others, said Adams, "signed with regret . . . and with many doubts." Most, however, signed wholeheartedly, knowing that by doing so they were likely to be hanged if captured by British troops. Benjamin Franklin acknowledged how high the stakes were: "Well, Gentlemen," he told the Congress, "we must now hang together, or we shall most assuredly hang separately."

JEFFERSON'S DECLARATION The Declaration of Independence was crucially important not simply because it marked the creation of a new nation but because of the ideals it expressed and the grievances it listed. It insisted that certain truths were self-evident, that "all men are created equal and independent" and have the right to create governments of their own choosing. Governments, in Thomas Jefferson's words, derive "their just powers from the consent of the people," who are entitled to "alter or abolish" those governments when rulers deny citizens their "unalienable rights" to "life, liberty, and the pursuit of happiness." Because King George III was trying to impose "an absolute tyranny over these states," the "Representatives of the United States of America" declared the thirteen "United Colonies" to be "Free and Independent States."

THE CONTRADICTIONS OF FREEDOM Once the Continental Congress chose independence, the members set about revising Thomas Jefferson's draft declaration before sending it to London. Southern representatives insisted on deleting the slave-owning Jefferson's section criticizing George III for perpetuating the African slave trade. In doing so, they revealed the major contradiction at work in the movement for independence: the rhetoric of freedom that animated the Revolution did not apply to America's original sin, the widespread system of slavery that fueled the southern economy. Slavery was the absence of liberty, yet few Americans confronted the inconsistency of their protests in defense of freedom—for whites.

In 1764, a group of slaves in Charleston watching a demonstration against British tyranny by white Sons of Liberty got caught up in the moment and began chanting "freedom, freedom, freedom." But that was not what southern planters wanted for African Americans. In 1774, when a group of slaves killed four whites in a desperate attempt to gain their freedom, Georgia planters responded by capturing the rebels and burning them alive.

Harvard-educated lawyer James Otis was one of the few Whigs who demanded freedom for blacks and women. In 1764, he had argued in a widely

The Declaration of Independence The Declaration in its most frequently reproduced form, an 1823 engraving by William J. Stone.

circulated pamphlet that "the colonists, black and white, born here, are free British subjects, and entitled to all the essential civil rights of such." He even went so far as to suggest that slavery itself should be ended, since "all men . . . white or black" were "by the law of nature freeborn."

Otis also asked, "Are not women born as free as men? Would it not be infamous to assert that the ladies are all slaves by nature?" His sister, Mercy Otis Warren, became a tireless advocate of American resistance to British "tyranny" through her poems, pamphlets, and plays. In a letter to a friend, she noted that British officials needed to realize that America's "daughters are politicians and patriots and will aid the good work [of resistance] with their female efforts."

In 1765, John Adams had snarled that he and other colonists angered by British actions would not "be their slaves." Actual slaves insisted on independence, too. In 1773, a group of enslaved African Americans in Boston appealed to the royal governor to free them just as white Americans were defending their freedoms against British tyranny. In many respects, the slaves argued, they had a more compelling case for liberty: "We have no property, We have no wives! No children! No city! No country!"

A few months later, four Boston slaves addressed a public letter to the town government in which they referred to the hypocrisy of slaveholders who protested against British regulations and taxes. "We expect great things from men who have made such a noble stand against the designs of their fellow-men to enslave them," they noted. But freedom was a celebration to which slaves were not invited. In 1775, South Carolinian William Henry Drayton expressed his horror that "impertinent" slaves were claiming "that the present contest [with Great Britain] was for obliging us to give them liberty."

I am very affectionately your Friend
Phillis Wheatley
Boston March 21. 1774.

Phillis Wheatley An autographed portrait of America's first African American poet.

George Washington himself acknowledged the contradictory aspects of the Revolutionary movement when he warned that the alternative to declaring independence was to become "tame and abject slaves, as the blacks we rule over with such arbitrary sway [absolute power]." Washington and other slaveholders at the head of the Revolutionary movement, such as Thomas Jefferson, were in part so resistant to "British tyranny" because they witnessed every day what actual slavery was like—for the blacks under their control.

A morally perplexed Jefferson admitted the hypocrisy of slave-owning revolutionaries. "Southerners," he wrote to a French friend, are "jealous of their own liberties but trampling on those of others." Such inconsistency was not lost on others. Phillis Wheatley, the first African American writer to see her poetry published in America, highlighted the "absurdity" of white colonists claiming their freedom while continuing to exercise "oppressive power" over enslaved Africans.

"**WE ALWAYS HAD GOVERNED OURSELVES**" Historians still debate the causes of the American Revolution. Americans in 1775–1776 were not desperately poor; overall, they probably enjoyed a higher standard of living than most societies and lived under the freest institutions in the world. Their diet was better than that of Europeans, as was their average life span. In addition, the percentage of free property owners in the thirteen American colonies was higher than in Britain or Europe. As Charlestonian Charles Pinckney remarked a few years later, Americans, by which he meant white Americans, were "more equal in their circumstances than the people of any other Country." At the same time, the new taxes forced on Americans after 1763 were not as great as those imposed on the British people. It is also important to remember that many American colonists, perhaps as many as half, were indifferent, hesitant, or actively opposed to rebellion.

So why did the Americans revolt? Historians have highlighted many factors: the clumsy British efforts to tighten their regulation of colonial trade, the restrictions on colonists eager to acquire western lands, the growing tax burden, the mounting debts to British merchants, the lack of American representation in Parliament, and the role of agitators such as Samuel Adams and Patrick Henry in stirring up anti-British feelings.

Yet colonists also sought liberty from British "tyranny" for reasons that were not so selfless or noble. Many of the New Englanders and New Yorkers most critical of tighter British regulations were smugglers. Boston merchant John Hancock, for example, embraced the Patriot cause in part because he was a smuggler. Paying more British taxes would have cost him a fortune. Likewise, South Carolina's Henry Laurens and Virginia's Landon Carter, both prosperous planters, worried that the British might abolish slavery.

Overall, however, what Americans most feared and resented were the British efforts to constrict their civil liberties, thereby denying their rights as British citizens. As Hugh Williamson, a Pennsylvania physician, explained, the Revolution resulted not from "trifling or imaginary" injustices but from "gross and palpable" violations of American rights that had thrown "the miserable colonists" into the "pit of despotism."

Yet how did the American colonies, the most diverse society in the world, develop such a unified resistance? Although most were of English heritage, many other peoples were represented: Scots, Irish, Scots-Irish, Welsh, Germans,

Dutch, Swedes, Finns, Swiss, French, and Jews, as well as growing numbers of Africans and diminishing numbers of Native Americans. In 1774, Thomas Hutchinson, the royal governor of Massachusetts, assured British officials that "a union of the Colonies was utterly impracticable" because the colonists "were greatly divided among themselves in every colony." He predicted that Americans would ultimately "*submit*, and that they *must*, and moreover would, *soon*."

Hutchinson was wrong, of course. What most Americans—regardless of their backgrounds—had come to share by 1775 was a defiant attachment to the civil rights and legal processes guaranteed by the English constitutional tradition. This new outlook, rooted in the defense of sacred constitutional principles, made the Revolution conceivable, armed resistance made it possible, and independence, ultimately, made it achievable.

The Revolutionary outlook was founded on the shared principle that all citizens were equal and independent, and that governmental authority had to be based on both the consent of those governed and longstanding constitutional principles. This "republican ideal" was the crucial force transforming a prolonged effort to preserve old rights and liberties enjoyed by British citizens into a movement to create an independent nation.

With their declaration of independence, the revolutionaries—men and women, farmers, artisans, mechanics, sailors, merchants, tavern owners, and shopkeepers—had at last become determined to develop their own society. Most Patriots still spoke the same language and worshipped the same God as the British, but they no longer thought the same way. Americans wanted to trade freely with the world and to expand what Jefferson called their "empire of liberty" westward, across the Appalachian Mountains.

Perhaps the last word on the complex causes of the Revolution should belong to Levi Preston, a Minuteman from Danvers, Massachusetts. Asked late in life about the British efforts to impose new taxes and regulations on the colonists, Preston responded by asking his young interviewer, "What were they? Oppressions? I didn't feel them." He was then asked, "What, were you not oppressed by the Stamp Act?" Preston replied that he "never saw one of those stamps . . . I am certain I never paid a penny for one of them." What about the tax on tea? "Tea-tax! I never drank a drop of the stuff; the boys threw it all overboard." His interviewer finally asked why he decided to fight for independence. "Young man," Preston explained, "what we meant in going for those redcoats was this: we always had governed ourselves, and we always meant to. They didn't mean we should."

CHAPTER REVIEW

SUMMARY

- **British and French Colonies**   New France followed the Spanish model of absolute power in governing its far-flung trading outposts. On the other hand, Great Britain's policy of *salutary neglect* allowed its colonies a large degree of self-government, until the British government's decision to rigidly enforce its policy of *mercantilism*, as seen in such measures as the *Navigation Acts*, became a means to enrich its global empire. The *Glorious Revolution* in Great Britain inspired new political philosophies that challenged the divine right of kings with the *natural rights* of free men.

- **The French and Indian War**   Four European wars affected America between 1689 and 1763 as the British and French, joined by their allies, fought throughout the world. Early in the French and Indian War, worried colonies created the *Albany Plan of Union*, which formed an early blueprint for an independent American government. *The Seven Years' War*, known as the *French and Indian War* (1754–1763) in the colonies, eventually was won by the British. In the *Treaty of Paris* in 1763, France lost all its North American possessions, Britain gained Canada and Florida, and Spain acquired the vast Louisiana Territory. The Indians fought to regain control of their ancestral lands in *Pontiac's Rebellion*, and Great Britain, weary of war, negotiated peace in the *Royal Proclamation of 1763*.

- **British Colonial Policy**   After the French and Indian War, the British government was saddled with an enormous debt. To reduce that burden, Prime Minister George Grenville implemented various taxes to compel colonists to pay for their own defense. Colonists resisted, claiming that they could not be taxed by Parliament because they were not represented in Parliament. British officials countered that the colonists had *virtual representation* in Parliament, since each member was supposed to represent his district as well as the Empire as a whole. Colonial reaction to the *Stamp Act* of 1765 was the first intimation of real trouble for British authorities. Conflicts between Whigs and Tories intensified when the *Townshend Acts* imposed additional taxes. The *Sons of Liberty* and the *Daughters of Liberty* mobilized resistance, particularly through boycotts of British.

- **Road to the American Revolution**   But the crisis worsened. Spontaneous resistance led to the *Boston Massacre*; organized protesters later staged the *Boston Tea Party*. The British response to the events in Boston, called the *Coercive Acts*, sparked further violence between *Patriots* and *Loyalists*. The First Continental Congress formed *Committees of Correspondence* to organize and spread resistance. Thomas Paine's pamphlet *Common Sense* helped kindle revolutionary fervor and plant the seed of independence, and the Continental Congress delivered its *Declaration of Independence*.

CHRONOLOGY

1651	First Navigation Act passed by Parliament
1688–1689	Glorious Revolution
1756–1763	French and Indian War
1763	Pontiac's Rebellion begins
	Treaty of Paris ends French and Indian War
	Royal Proclamation
1765	Stamp Act; Stamp Act Congress
1766	Repeal of the Stamp Act
1767	Townshend Acts
1770	Boston Massacre
1773	Tea Act; Boston Tea Party
1774	Coercive Acts
1775	Military conflict at Lexington and Concord
1776	Thomas Paine publishes *Common Sense*
	Continental Congress declares independence

KEY TERMS

mercantilism p. 120

Navigation Acts p. 121

Glorious Revolution p. 122

natural rights p. 123

salutary neglect p. 124

French and Indian War (Seven Years' War) p. 125

Albany Plan of Union p. 126

Treaty of Paris (1763) p. 130

Pontiac's Rebellion p. 133

Royal Proclamation of 1763 p. 133

Stamp Act p. 134

virtual representation p. 135

Sons of Liberty p. 135

Daughters of Liberty p. 136

Townshend Acts p. 138

Loyalists p. 138

Patriots p. 138

Boston Massacre p. 139

Committee of Correspondence p. 141

Boston Tea Party p. 141

Coercive Acts p. 141

Common Sense p. 147

Declaration of Independence p. 149

🔲 INQUIZITIVE

Go to InQuizitive to see what you've learned—and learn what you've missed—with personalized feedback along the way.

part two

BUILDING A NATION

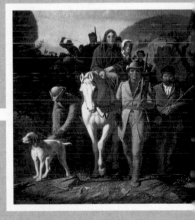

The signing of the Declaration of Independence in July 1776 thrilled the rebellious colonists and forced other Americans to make a hard choice: to remain loyal subjects of King George III and thus traitors to the new United States of America, or to embrace the rebellion and become traitors to Great Britain. It was one thing for Patriot leaders to declare independence and quite another to win it on the battlefield. The odds greatly favored the British; fewer than half of the colonists were Patriots who *actively* supported the Revolution, and many others—the

Loyalists—fought against it. The thirteen independent states had new, untested governments, and General George Washington found himself in charge of an inexperienced and poorly equipped army of amateurs facing the world's greatest military power.

Yet the Revolutionaries would persevere and prevail. As a military leader, Washington proved to be more dogged than brilliant, a general famous for his courage and composure—even in the face of adversity. He had extensive knowledge of the nation's geography and used it to his advantage against the British. Even more important to the Revolutionary cause was the decision by the French (and later the Spanish and Dutch) to join the war against Britain. The Franco-American military alliance, negotiated in 1778, was the decisive turning point in the war. In 1783, after eight years of sporadic fighting and heavy human and financial losses, the British gave up the fight and their American colonies.

While fighting the British, the Patriots also had to create new governments for themselves. Quite different colonies suddenly became coequal states. The deeply ingrained resentment of British imperial rule led Americans to give more power to the individual states than to the weak new national government, called the Confederation. As Thomas Jefferson declared, "Virginia is my country."

Such powerful local ties help explain why the Articles of Confederation, the original constitution organizing the thirteen states into a loose confederation, provided only minimal national authority when it was finally ratified (approved by the states) in 1781. Final power to make and execute laws remained with the states.

After the Revolutionary War, the flimsy political bonds authorized by the Articles of Confederation could not meet the needs of the new nation. This realization led to the Constitutional Convention of 1787. The process of drafting and approving the new constitution generated heated debate about the respective powers granted to the states and the national government, a debate that became the central theme of American political thought.

The Revolution also helped reshape American society. What would be the role of women, African Americans, and Native Americans in the new nation?

How would the different economies of the various regions of the United States be developed? Who would control access to the vast Native American ancestral lands to the west? How would the United States of America relate to the other nations of the world?

These questions gave birth to the first national political parties in the United States. During the 1790s, the Federalist party, led by George Washington, John Adams, and Alexander Hamilton, and the Democratic-Republican party, led by Thomas Jefferson and James Madison, furiously debated the political and economic future of the nation.

With Jefferson's election as president in 1800, the Republicans gained the upper hand in national politics and would remain dominant for the next quarter century. In the process, they presided over a maturing republic that aggressively expanded westward at the expense of the Native Americans, embraced industrial development, engaged in a second war with Great Britain, and witnessed growing tensions between North and South over slavery.

5 The American Revolution

1776–1783

The Death of General Mercer at the Battle of Princeton (ca. 1789–1831) After the American victory at Trenton, New Jersey, George Washington (center, on horseback) launched a surprise attack on the British at the Battle of Princeton. The Americans won the battle, but one of the casualties was Washington's close friend, General Hugh Mercer (bottom), whose death created a rallying symbol for the Revolution.

F ew Europeans thought the upstart American Revolutionaries could win a war against the world's richest and most powerful empire— and, indeed, the Americans did lose most of the battles in the Revolutionary War. But they outlasted the British, eventually forcing them to end the war and grant independence to the United States of America.

This stunning result reflected the tenacity of the Patriots as well as the difficulties the British faced in fighting a transatlantic war 3,000 miles from home. It took five to ten weeks for orders from the government in London to reach British commanders in America, and often they were out of date by the time they arrived. The British also had to adjust to the often unorthodox American ways of warfare. They discovered that Patriots were willing to fight at night, in the cold, in the woods, in the rain and snow.

What began as a war for independence became both a *civil war* between Americans (Patriots/Whigs versus Loyalists/Tories), joined by their Indian allies, and a *world war* involving numerous "allied" European nations. The crucial development was the ability of the United States to forge military alliances with France, Spain, and the Netherlands, all of which were eager to humble Great Britain and seize its colonies around the world. Those nations provided the Revolutionaries with desperately needed money, supplies, soldiers, and warships. The French and Spanish also sent a combined fleet of warships to the English Channel—forcing much of the Royal Navy to remain at home, thus weakening the British effort to blockade American ports.

America's war for independence also unleashed unexpected social and political changes, as it required "common people" to take a more active role in

focus questions

1. What challenges faced the British and American military leaders in fighting the Revolutionary War?

2. What were some of the key turning points in the Revolutionary War? How did they change the direction of the war?

3. In what ways did the American Revolution function as a civil war?

4. How was the Revolutionary War an "engine" for political and social change?

5. How did the Revolutionary War impact African Americans, women, and Native Americans?

governments at all levels—local, state, and national. After all, as the Declaration of Independence asserted, governments derive "their just powers from the consent of the governed." The common people readily took advantage of their new opportunities. In Virginia, voters in 1776 elected a new state legislature that, as an observer noted, "was composed of men not quite so well dressed, nor so politely educated, nor so highly born" as had been the case in the past.

MOBILIZING FOR WAR

The British Empire sent some 35,000 soldiers and half of its huge navy across the Atlantic to put down the American rebellion. The British also hired foreign soldiers (mercenaries), as almost 30,000 Germans served in the British armies in America. Most were from the German state of Hesse-Cassel—thus they became known to Americans as **Hessians**.

The British also recruited American Loyalists, Native Americans, and African Americans to fight on their behalf, but there were never as many willing to join them as they had hoped. Further, the British faced a formidable challenge in supplying their large army and navy in America. They initially assumed that there would be enough food for their troops and plenty of forage for their horses in America. As the war ground on, however, most of the supplies had to come from Britain. The war in America became terribly expensive, and eventually demoralizing to the British people and their leaders.

The British government under Lord North also never had a consistent war strategy. Initially, the British focused on blockading New England's seaports to try to strangle American trade. When that failed, British military leaders sought to destroy George Washington's Continental army in New York. Despite their initial success in driving the Americans out of the city, the British commanders failed to pursue and eliminate the retreating army. They next tried to drive a wedge between New England and New York, splitting the colonies in two. That too would fail, leading to the final British strategy: moving their main army into the southern colonies in hopes of rallying Loyalists in the region.

THE CONTINENTAL ARMY While the Patriots had the advantage of fighting on their home ground, they also had to create an army and navy from scratch, and with little money to do so. Recruiting, supplying, equipping, training, and paying soldiers and sailors were monumental challenges.

Before the war, **citizen-soldiers** (militiamen) were primarily civilians summoned from their farms and shops on short notice to defend their communities. Once the danger passed, the militiamen quickly dispersed and returned to their homes. Many militiamen were unreliable and ungovernable. They "come in, you cannot tell how," General Washington said in exasperation, "go, you cannot tell when, and act you cannot tell where, consume your provisions, exhaust your stores [supplies], and leave you at last at a critical moment."

Once the war started, Washington knew that militiamen alone could not win a war against veteran British and German soldiers. He needed a professional army, with full-time soldiers. While recruiting fighters, Washington was pleased to see that the men from different colonies were developing a national (or "continental") viewpoint, in which they thought of themselves as fighting for a new *nation*, not just protecting their particular communities like militiamen. Washington thus decided to call it the *Continental army*. About half of the 200,000 Americans

George Washington at Princeton Commissioned for Independence Hall in Philadelphia, this 1779 painting by Charles Willson Peale portrays Washington as the hero of the Battle of Princeton.

who served in the war were in the Continental army. They were mostly young, single, relatively poor farmers, laborers, or indentured servants.

What the Continental army needed most at the start of the war were capable officers, intensive training, modern weapons, and multiyear enlistment contracts. The Patriot soldiers also needed strict discipline, for they had no room for error against the British. As Washington began whipping the new army into shape, those who violated the rules were jailed, flogged, or sent packing. Some deserters were hanged.

Many Patriots who had not fought in the French and Indian War found army life unbearable and combat horrifying. As General Nathanael Greene, a Rhode Island Quaker who abandoned the pacifism of his religion for the war effort and became Washington's ablest commander, pointed out, few Patriots had ever engaged in mortal combat, and they were hard-pressed to "stand the shocking scenes of war, to march over dead men, to hear without concern the groans of the wounded." Desertions grew as the war dragged on. At times, Washington could put only a few thousand men in the field. Eventually, to recruit more soldiers, Congress was forced to provide more generous enticements, such as land grants and cash bonuses, in exchange for recruits agreeing to serve in the Continental army for the duration of the war.

PROBLEMS OF FINANCE AND SUPPLY   Financing the Revolution was much harder for the new nation than it was for Great Britain. Lacking the power to impose taxes, the Confederation Congress could only *ask* the states to provide funds for the national government. Yet the states rarely provided their expected share of the war's expenses, and the Continental Congress reluctantly had to allow the Patriot armies to take supplies directly from farmers in return for written promises of future payment.

In a predominantly agricultural society, like America, turning farmers into soldiers hurt the national economy. William Hooper, a North Carolinian who signed the Declaration of Independence, grumbled that "a soldier made is a farmer lost." Many states found a ready source of revenue in the sale of abandoned Loyalist homes, farms, and plantations. Nevertheless, Congress and the states still fell short of funding the war's cost and were forced to print more and more paper money. At the start of the fighting there were no uniforms for the soldiers and sailors, and soldiers' weapons were "as various as their costumes." Most weapons and ammunition were acquired either by capturing British weapons or by importing them from France, a government all too glad to help the Patriots fight its arch-enemy.

NATIVE AMERICANS AND THE REVOLUTION   Both the British and Americans recruited Indians to fight with them, but the British were far more successful, largely because they had longstanding relationships with chieftains and they promised to protect Indian lands. The peoples making up the Iroquois League split their allegiances, with most Mohawks, Onondagas, Cayugas, and Senecas, led by Mohawk Joseph Brant and Seneca Old Smoke, joining the British, and most Oneidas and Tuscaroras supporting the Patriots. The Cherokees also joined the British in hopes of driving out American settlers who had taken their lands.

Most Indians in New England tried to remain neutral or sided with the Patriots. The Stockbridge Indians in Massachusetts, mostly Mahicans, formed a company of Minutemen who fought alongside Patriot units. They pledged that "wherever your armies go, there we will go; you shall always find us by your side; and if providence calls us to sacrifice our lives in the field of battle, we will fall where you fall, and lay our bones by yours." Yet however much the British or Americans claimed Native Americans as allies, most Indians engaged in the war as a means of protecting themselves and their own interests.

DISASTER IN CANADA In July 1775, the Continental Congress authorized an ill-planned military expedition in Canada against Quebec in the vain hope of rallying support among the French Canadians. One Patriot detachment, under General Richard Montgomery, a former British army officer, headed toward Quebec by way of Lake Champlain along the New York–Canadian border; another, under General Benedict Arnold, struggled westward toward Quebec through the dense Maine woods.

The Americans arrived outside Quebec in September, tired, exhausted, and hungry. A silent killer then ambushed them: smallpox. As the deadly virus raced through the American camp, General Montgomery faced a brutal dilemma. Most of his soldiers had signed up for short tours of duty, and many were scheduled for discharge at the end of the year. Because of the impending departure of his men, Montgomery could not afford to wait until spring for the smallpox to subside. Seeing little choice but to fight, he ordered an attack on the British forces defending Quebec during a blizzard, on December 31, 1775.

The American assault was a disaster. Montgomery was killed early in the battle, and Benedict Arnold was seriously wounded. More than 400 Americans were taken prisoner. The rest of the Patriot force retreated to its camp outside the walled city and appealed to the Continental Congress for reinforcements. Smallpox spread throughout the American army, and Arnold warned George Washington in February 1776 that the runaway disease would soon bring "the entire ruin of the Army." The British, sensing weakness, attacked the American camp and sent the ragtag Patriots on a frantic retreat up the St. Lawrence River to the American-held city of Montreal, and eventually back to New York and New England.

By the summer of 1776, the American Revolutionaries had come to realize that their quest for independence would be neither short nor easy, for the king and Parliament were determined to smash the revolt and restore their empire.

WASHINGTON'S NARROW ESCAPE On July 2, 1776, the day the Continental Congress voted for independence, British redcoats landed on Staten Island, across New York City's harbor from Manhattan. They were the first wave in a major British assault intended to end the war quickly with a decisive victory.

For several weeks, while the British troops prepared for action, General Howe met with American leaders in an effort to negotiate a settlement of the revolution. After the negotiations failed, on August 22, 1776, a massive British fleet of 427 ships carrying 32,000 troops, including 8,000 hired German soldiers, began landing on Long Island near New York City. It was the largest seaborne military expedition in history to that point. "I could not believe my eyes," recalled a Pennsylvania militiaman. "I declare that I thought all London was afloat."

Meanwhile, George Washington, after ousting the British from Boston, had moved his forces to defensive positions around New York City in February 1776. He still struggled to raise an army powerful enough to match the British. During the winter and spring, he could gather only about 19,000 poorly trained militiamen and recruits. Although a veteran of frontier fighting, Washington had never commanded a large force or supervised artillery (cannon) units. As he confessed to the Continental Congress, he had no "experience to move [armies] on a large scale" and had only "limited . . . knowledge . . . in military matters." Washington was still learning the art of generalship, and the British invasion of New York taught him some costly and painful lessons.

The new American army suffered a humiliating defeat at the Battle of Long Island as the British invaders perfectly executed their assault. An American officer noted that the fighting on Long Island was nothing but "fright, disgrace, and confusion." As General Washington watched the British advance, he sighed: "Good God! What brave fellows I must this day lose." In the face of steadily advancing ranks of British soldiers with bayonet-tipped muskets, many of the untested American defenders and their officers panicked. The smoke and chaos of battle disoriented the Patriots. Over the next week of intense fighting, the confused, disorganized, undisciplined, and indecisive Americans steadily gave ground. Only a timely rainstorm and heroic efforts by experienced boatmen enabled the retreating Americans to cross the harbor from Brooklyn to Manhattan during the night of August 29.

Had Howe's British army moved more quickly in pursuing the retreating Patriots, it could have trapped Washington's entire force and ended the Revolution. But the British rested as the main American army, joined by Patriot civilians, made a miraculous escape from Manhattan over the next several weeks. They crossed the Hudson River, and retreated with furious urgency into New Jersey and then over the Delaware River into eastern Pennsylvania. A New Jersey resident reported that the retreating Americans "marched two abreast, looked ragged, some without a shoe to their feet, and most of them wrapped in blankets." Thousands had been captured during the New York campaign, and hundreds more deserted, eager to go home ahead of their British pursuers. George Washington assumed full responsibility for the setbacks in New York.

The situation was bleak in the fall of 1776. New York City became the headquarters of both the Royal Navy and the British army. Local Loyalists (Tories) in New York City and New Jersey excitedly welcomed the British occupation. "Hundreds in this colony are against us," a New York City Patriot wrote to John Adams. "Tories openly express their sentiments in favor of the enemy."

By December 1776, the American Revolution was near collapse. A British officer reported that many "rebels" were "without shoes or stockings, and several were observed to have only linen drawers . . . without any proper shirt. They must suffer extremely" in the winter weather. Indeed, Washington had only 3,000 men left. Unless a new army could be raised quickly, he warned, "I think the game is pretty near up."

Then, almost miraculously, help emerged from an unexpected source: Englishman Thomas Paine. Having opened the eventful year of 1776 with his inspiring pamphlet *Common Sense*, Paine now composed *The American Crisis*, in which he wrote these stirring lines:

> These are the times that try men's souls: The summer soldier and the sunshine patriot will, in this crisis, shrink from the service of his country; but he that stands it NOW deserves the love and thanks of man and woman. Tyranny, like Hell, is not easily conquered. Yet we have this consolation with us, that the harder the conflict, the more glorious the triumph.

Thomas Paine's *Common Sense* Thomas Paine's inspiring pamphlet was originally published anonymously because the British viewed it as treasonous.

Paine's rousing pamphlet boosted Patriot morale. Out of the disastrous defeat came major changes in the way the Continental Congress managed the war. On December 27, 1776, it gave General Washington "large powers" to strengthen the war effort, including the ability to offer army recruits cash, land, clothing, and blankets.

In December 1776, General William Howe, commander in chief of the British forces, decided that the war with America was all but won. He then casually settled down with his married Loyalist mistress (twenty-five-year-old Elizabeth Loring) to wait out the winter in New York City. (Eighteenth-century armies rarely fought during the winter months.) One American general concluded that Howe "shut his eyes, fought his battles, drank his bottle and had his little whore."

A DESPERATE GAMBLE   George Washington, however, was not ready to hibernate for the winter. The morale of his men and the hopes of the nation, he decided, required "some brilliant stroke" of good news after the devastating defeats around New York City. So he launched a desperate gamble to achieve a much-needed victory before more of his soldiers decided to leave the army and return home.

On Christmas night 1776, Washington led some 2,400 men, packed into forty-foot-long boats, from Pennsylvania across the icy Delaware River into New Jersey. Near dawn, at Trenton, the Americans surprised 1,500 sleeping Hessians, attacking them from three sides. An American sergeant said his "blood chill'd to see such horror and distress, blood mingling together, the dying groans. . . . The sight was too much to bear."

The **Battle of Trenton** was a total rout, from which only 500 Hessians escaped. Just two of Washington's men were killed. The American commander had been in the thick of the battle, urging his men forward: "Press on! Press on, boys!"

A week later, General Washington and the Americans again crossed the Delaware and won another battle in New Jersey, at Princeton, before taking shelter at Morristown, in the hills of northern New Jersey. A British officer muttered that the Americans had "become a formidable enemy."

The surprising victories at Princeton and Trenton saved the cause of independence and shifted the war's momentum, as a fresh wave of inspired Americans signed up to serve in Washington's army. A British officer recognized that the victories at Trenton and Princeton would "revive the dropping spirits of the rebels and increase their force." The military successes in New Jersey also revived Patriot confidence in George Washington's leadership. British war correspondents claimed that he was more talented than any of their own commanders. Yet although the "dark days" of the autumn of 1776 were over, unexpected challenges quickly chilled the Patriots' excitement.

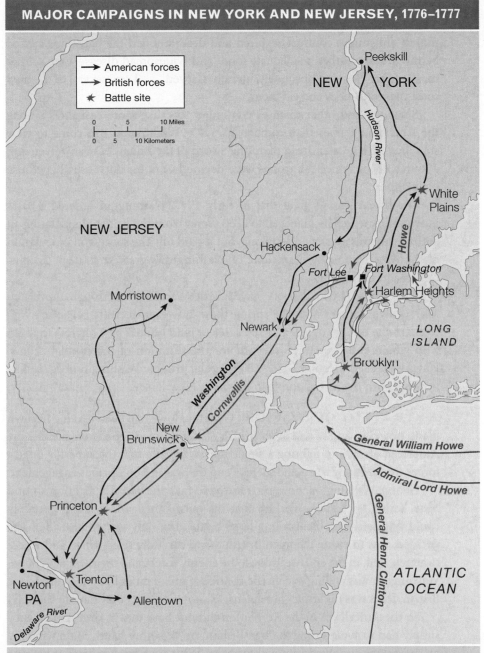

MAJOR CAMPAIGNS IN NEW YORK AND NEW JERSEY, 1776–1777

→ American forces
→ British forces
✳ Battle site

0   5   10 Miles
0   5   10 Kilometers

NEW   YORK

Peekskill

Hudson River

NEW JERSEY

Howe

White Plains

Hackensack

Fort Lee   Fort Washington

Harlem Heights

Morristown

Newark

LONG ISLAND

Washington

Cornwallis

Brooklyn

New Brunswick

General William Howe

Princeton

Admiral Lord Howe

General Henry Clinton

Newton

PA

Trenton

Allentown

Delaware River

ATLANTIC OCEAN

- Why did General Washington lead his army from Brooklyn to Manhattan and from there to New Jersey?
- How could the British army commander, General William Howe, have ended the rebellion in New York?
- What is the significance of the Battle of Trenton?

WINTER IN MORRISTOWN   During the record-cold winter in early 1777, George Washington's ragged army again nearly disintegrated as six-month enlistment contracts expired and deserters fled the hardships caused by the brutal weather, inadequate food, and widespread disease. One soldier recalled that "we were absolutely, literally starved. . . . I saw several of the men roast their old shoes and eat them."

Smallpox and other diseases continued to cause more casualties among the American armies than combat. By 1777, Washington had come to view smallpox with greater dread than "the Sword of the Enemy." On any given day, a fourth of the American troops were deemed unfit for duty, usually because of smallpox.

The threat was so great that in early 1777 Washington ordered a mass inoculation, which he managed to keep secret from the British. Inoculating an entire army was a risky undertaking, but it paid off. The successful inoculation of the American army marks one of Washington's greatest strategic accomplishments of the war.

Only about 1,000 Patriots stayed with Washington through the brutal Morristown winter. With the spring thaw, however, recruits began arriving to claim the bounty of $20 and 100 acres of land offered by Congress to those who would enlist for three years or for the duration of the conflict, if less. Having cobbled together some 9,000 regular troops, Washington began skirmishing with the British forces in northern New Jersey.

A STRATEGY OF EVASION   General Howe had been making his own plans, however, and so had other British officers. Howe hoped to maneuver the American army into fighting a single decisive battle that the superior British forces would surely win—and thereby end the war in one glorious engagement.

George Washington, however, refused to take the bait. The fighting around New York City had shown him that his outmanned army almost certainly could not defeat the British in a large battle. The only way to beat them, he decided, was to evade the main British army, carefully select when and where to attack, and, in the end, wear down the enemy forces and their will to fight on. Washington was willing to concede control of major cities like New York to the British, for it was his army, "not defenseless towns, [that] they have to subdue."

So the Americans in the Revolution did not have to win large battles; they simply had to avoid losing the war. Britain, on the other hand, could win only by destroying the American will to resist. With each passing year, it became more difficult—and expensive—for the British to supply their large army and navy in America. Over time, the British government and people would tire of the human and financial toll of conducting a prolonged war across the Atlantic.

AMERICAN SOCIETY AT WAR

The Revolution was as much a ruthless civil war among Americans (including the Native American peoples allied with both sides) as it was a prolonged struggle against Great Britain. The necessity of choosing sides divided families and friends, towns and cities.

Benjamin Franklin's illegitimate son, William, for example, was the royal governor of New Jersey. An ardent Loyalist, he sided with Great Britain in the war. His Patriot father later removed him from his will. Similarly, eighteen-year-old Bostonian Lucy Flucker defied her Loyalist father's wishes and married bookseller Henry Knox in 1774. (Knox would become an American general.) Lucy's estranged family fled with the British army when it left Boston in 1776, and she never saw them again. "I have lost my father, mother, brother, and sister, entirely lost them," she wrote.

The colonists were generally divided into three groups: Patriots, who formed the Continental army and fought in state militias; Loyalists, or Tories, as the Patriots mockingly called them; and a less committed middle group swayed by the better organized and more energetic Patriots. Loyalists may have represented 20 percent of the American population, but Patriots were the largest of the three groups. Some Americans (like Benedict Arnold) switched sides during the war. Both the Patriots and the British, once they took control of a city or community, would often require the residents to swear an oath of loyalty to their cause.

Where the Patriots rejected the monarchy, the Loyalists, whom George Washington called "abominable pests of society," viewed the Revolution as an act of treason. The British Empire, they felt, was much more likely than an independent America to protect them from foreign foes and enable them to prosper.

Loyalists were most numerous in the seaport cities, especially New York City and Philadelphia, as well as the Carolinas, but they came from all walks of life. Governors, judges, and other royal officials were almost all Loyalists; most Anglican ministers also preferred the mother country, as did many Anglican worshippers. In the backcountry of New York and across the Carolinas, many small farmers who had largely been unaffected by the controversies over British efforts to tighten colonial regulations rallied to the British side. More New York men joined Loyalist regiments than the Continental army. Many Loyalists calculated that the Revolution would fail or feared that it would result in mob rule. In few places, however, were there enough Loyalists to assume control without the support of British troops.

The Loyalists did not want to "dissolve the political bands" with Britain, as the Declaration of Independence demanded. Instead, as some 700 of them

Four Soldiers **(ca. 1781)** This illustration drawn by a French lieutenant captures the varied uniforms worn by Patriot forces in the war (left to right): a black soldier (freed for joining the 1st Rhode Island Regiment), a New England militiaman, a frontiersman, and a French soldier.

in New York City said in a petition to British officials, they "steadily and uniformly opposed" this "most unnatural, unprovoked Rebellion." The British were repeatedly frustrated by the failure of Loyalists to materialize in strength and the collapse of Loyalist militia units once British troops departed. Because Patriot militias quickly returned whenever the British left an area, Loyalists faced a difficult choice: either accompany the British and leave behind their property or stay and face the wrath of the Patriots. Even more disheartening was what one British officer called "the licentiousness of the [Loyalist] troops, who committed every species of rapine and plunder" and thereby converted potential friends to enemies.

The Patriots, both moderates and radicals, supported the war because they realized that the only way to protect their liberty was to separate themselves from British control. Patriots also wanted to establish an American republic, a unique form of government that would convert them from being *subjects* of a king to being *citizens* in a republic with the power to elect their own government and pursue their own economic interests. "We have it in our power," wrote Thomas Paine, "to begin the world over again. . . . The birthday of a new world is at hand."

Setbacks for the British (1777)

In 1777, a carefully conceived but poorly executed British plan to defeat the "American rebellion" involved a three-pronged assault on the state of New York. By gaining control of that important state, the British planned to split America in two, cutting off New England from the rest of the colonies.

The complicated plan called for a British army based in Canada and led by General John Burgoyne to advance southward from Quebec via Lake Champlain to the Hudson River. At the same time, another British force would move eastward from Oswego, in western New York. General William Howe, meanwhile, would lead a third British army up the Hudson River from New York City. All three advancing armies would eventually converge in central New York and wipe out any remaining Patriot resistance.

The three British armies, however, failed in their execution—and in their communications with one another. At the last minute, Howe changed his mind and decided to move his army south from New York City to attack the Patriot capital, Philadelphia. General Washington withdrew most of his men from New Jersey to meet the British threat in Pennsylvania while other American units banded together in upstate New York to deal with the British threat there.

On September 11, 1777, at Brandywine Creek, southwest of Philadelphia, the British overpowered Washington's army and occupied Philadelphia, then the largest and wealthiest American city. The members of the Continental Congress were forced to flee the city. Battered but still intact, Washington and his army withdrew to winter quarters twenty miles away at Valley Forge, while Howe and his men remained in the relative comfort of Philadelphia.

THE CAMPAIGN OF 1777 Meanwhile, in northern New York, a second British army had stumbled into an American trap. In June, an overconfident General Burgoyne (nicknamed "General Swagger") had led his mistress and 7,000 soldiers southward from Canada toward New York's Lake Champlain.

The American army commander in northern New York was General Horatio Gates. Thirty-two years earlier, in 1745, he and Burgoyne had served as officers in the same British regiment. Now they were commanding opposing armies. As Burgoyne's army pushed deeper into New York, it became harder to get food and supplies from Canada. Short of wagons and carts, the advance slowed to a snail's pace, thereby allowing the Americans to spring a trap.

The outnumbered but more mobile Patriots had the benefit of fighting in familiar territory. They inflicted two serious defeats on the British forces in

MAJOR CAMPAIGNS IN NEW YORK AND PENNSYLVANIA, 1777

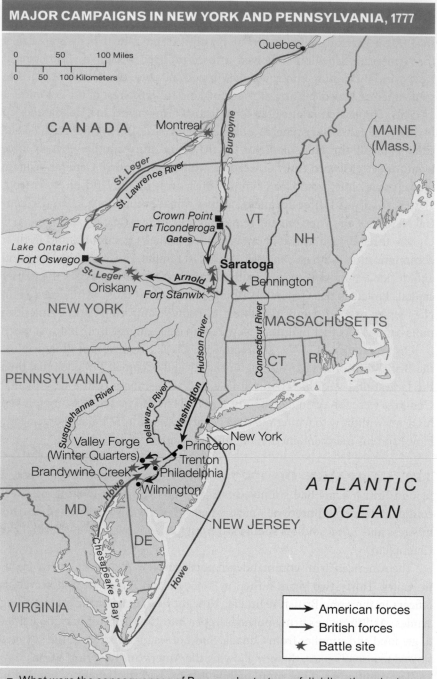

- What were the consequences of Burgoyne's strategy of dividing the colonies by invading upstate New York from Canada?
- How did life in the American winter camp at Valley Forge transform the army?
- Why were the Battles of Saratoga a turning point in the American Revolution?

August 1777. At Oriskany on August 6, Patriot militiamen, mostly local German American farmers and their Indian allies, withstood an ambush by Loyalists and Indians and gained time for Patriot reinforcements to arrive at nearby Fort Stanwix, which had been besieged by British soldiers. When the British demanded the fort's surrender, General Gates rejected the offer "with disdain," saying that the fort would be defended to the "last extremity." As the days passed, the Iroquois deserted the British army, leading the British commander to order a withdrawal. As a result, the strategic Mohawk Valley running across central New York was secured for the Patriot forces.

General John Burgoyne Commander of Britain's northern forces. Burgoyne and most of his troops surrendered to the Americans at Saratoga on October 17, 1777.

To the east, at Bennington, Vermont, on August 16, New England militiamen, led by Colonel John Stark, decimated a detachment of Hessians and Loyalists. Stark had pledged that morning, "We'll beat them before night, or Molly Stark will be a widow."

As Patriot militiamen converged from across central New York, Burgoyne pulled his dispirited forces back to the village of Saratoga, near the Hudson River. In the ensuing, three-week-long **Battles of Saratoga**, Gates's army surrounded the British forces, cutting off their supply lines. Desperate for food and ammunition, the British failed twice to break through the encircling Americans. "Thus ended all our hopes of victory," noted a British officer.

The trapped Burgoyne surrendered on October 17, 1777, turning over 5,800 troops, 7,000 muskets, and forty-two brass cannons to Gates. In London, King George fell "into agonies on hearing the account" of Burgoyne's defeat. William Pitt, the former British prime minister, made a shocking prediction to Parliament after the defeat: *"You cannot conquer America."*

ALLIANCE WITH FRANCE   The surprising American victory at Saratoga was a strategic turning point because it convinced the French, who had lost four wars to the British in the previous eighty years, to sign two crucial treaties that created an American **alliance with France**.

Under the Treaty of Amity and Commerce, France officially recognized the new United States and offered important trading privileges to American shipping. Under the Treaty of Alliance, both parties agreed, first, that if France entered the war, both countries would fight until American independence was won; second, that neither would conclude a "truce or peace" without "the formal consent of the other"; and third, that each would guarantee the other's possessions in America "from the present time and forever against all other powers." France further agreed not to seek Canada or other British possessions on the mainland of North America.

In the end, the intervention of the French army and navy determined the outcome of the war. The Americans would also form important alliances with the Spanish (1779) and the Dutch (1781), but neither provided as much support as the French.

After the British defeat at Saratoga and the news of the French alliance with the United States, Parliament tried to end the war by granting all the demands that the Americans had made before they declared independence. But the Continental Congress would not negotiate until Britain officially recognized American independence and withdrew its military forces. King George refused.

1778: BOTH SIDES REGROUP

VALLEY FORGE AND STALEMATE For George Washington's army at **Valley Forge**, near Philadelphia, the winter of 1777–1778 was a time of intense suffering and unrelenting cold, hunger, and disease. Some soldiers lacked shoes and blankets, and their makeshift log-and-mud huts offered little protection from the chilling winds. By February, 7,000 troops were too ill for duty. More than 2,500 soldiers died at Valley Forge; another 1,000 deserted. Fifty officers resigned on one December day, and several hundred more left before winter's end. Desperate for relief, Washington sent troops across New Jersey, Delaware, and the Eastern Shore of Maryland to confiscate horses, cattle, and hogs in exchange for "receipts" promising future payment.

By March 1778, the troops at Valley Forge saw their strength restored. Their improved health enabled Washington to begin a rigorous training program. Because few of the American officers had any formal military training, their troops lacked leadership, discipline, and skills. To remedy this defect, Washington turned to an energetic Prussian soldier of fortune, Friedrich Wilhelm, baron von Steuben, who used an interpreter and frequent profanity to instruct the troops in the fundamentals of close-order drill.

Steuben was one of several foreign volunteers who joined the American army at Valley Forge. Another was a nineteen-year-old, red-haired French orphan named Gilbert du Motier, Marquis de Lafayette. A wealthy idealist excited by the American cause ("I was crazy to wear a uniform," he said), Lafayette offered to serve in the Continental army for no pay in exchange for being named a general.

Washington was initially skeptical of the young French aristocrat, but Lafayette soon became the commander in chief's most trusted aide. Washington noted that Lafayette possessed "a large share of bravery and military ardor." The young French general also proved to be an able diplomat in helping to forge the military alliance with France.

The Continental army's morale rose when the Continental Congress promised extra pay and bonuses after the war, and it rose again with the news of the military alliance with France. In the spring of 1778, British forces withdrew from Pennsylvania to New York City, with the American army in hot pursuit. Once the British were back in Manhattan, Washington's army encamped at nearby White Plains, north of the city. From that time on, the combat in the north settled into a long stalemate.

WAR IN THE WEST The Revolution had created two wars. In addition to the main conflict between armies in the east, a frontier guerrilla war of terror and vengeance pitted Indians and Loyalists against isolated Patriot settlers along the northern and western frontiers. In the Ohio Valley, as well as western New York and Pennsylvania, the British urged frontier Loyalists and their Indian allies to raid farm settlements and offered to pay bounties for American scalps.

To end the English-led attacks, early in 1778 George Rogers Clark took 175 Patriot frontiersmen on flatboats down the Ohio River. On the evening of July 4, the Americans captured English-controlled Kaskaskia, in present-day Illinois. Then, without bloodshed, Clark took Cahokia (in Illinois across the Mississippi River from St. Louis) and Vincennes (in present-day Indiana).

After the British retook Vincennes, Clark led his men (almost half of them French volunteers) across icy rivers and flooded prairies, sometimes in water neck-deep, and prepared to attack the British garrison. Clark's rugged frontiersmen, called Rangers, captured five Indians carrying American scalps. Clark ordered his men to kill the Indians in sight of the fort. After watching the terrible executions, the British surrendered.

While Clark's Rangers were in the Indiana territory, a much larger U.S. military force moved against Iroquois strongholds in western New York, where Loyalists (Tories) and their Indian allies had been terrorizing frontier settlements. These Iroquois attacks, led by Mohawk chief Joseph Brant, had killed hundreds of militiamen.

In response, George Washington sent 4,000 men under General John Sullivan to crush "the hostile tribes" and "the most mischievous of the Tories." At Newton, New York, on August 29, 1779, Sullivan's soldiers destroyed about

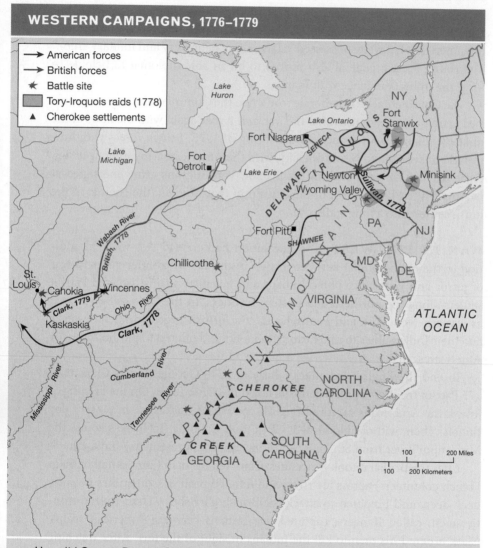

WESTERN CAMPAIGNS, 1776–1779

Legend:
- → American forces
- → British forces
- ✳ Battle site
- Tory-Iroquois raids (1778)
- ▲ Cherokee settlements

- How did George Rogers Clark secure Cahokia and Vincennes?
- Why did the American army destroy Iroquois villages in 1779?
- Why were the skirmishes between settlers and Indian tribes significant for the future of the trans-Appalachian frontier?

forty Seneca and Cayuga villages, which broke the power of the Iroquois Confederacy for all time.

In the Kentucky territory, the legendary frontiersman Daniel Boone and his small band of settlers repeatedly clashed with the Shawnees and their British and Loyalist allies. In 1778, Boone and some thirty men, aided by their wives and children, held off an assault by more than 400 Indians at Boonesborough. Later, Boone himself was twice shot and twice captured. Indians killed two of his sons, a brother, and two brothers-in-law. His daughter was captured, and another brother was wounded four times.

In early 1776, a delegation of northern Indians—Shawnees, Delawares, and Mohawks—had talked the Cherokees into attacking at frontier settlements in Virginia and the Carolinas. Swift retaliation had followed as Carolina militiamen led by Andrew Pickens burned dozens of Cherokee villages. By weakening the major Indian tribes along the frontier, the American Revolution cleared the way for white settlers to seize Indian lands after the war.

THE WAR MOVES SOUTH

In late 1778, the British launched their southern strategy, built on the assumption that large numbers of Loyalists in the Carolinas, Virginia, and Georgia would join the British cause. Once the British gained control of the southern colonies, they would have the shrinking United States pinched between Canada and a British-controlled South.

In December 1778, General Sir Henry Clinton, the new commander in chief of British forces in America, sent 3,000 redcoats, Hessians, and Loyalists to take the port city of Savannah, on the southeast Georgia coast, and roll northeast from there. The plan was to enlist support from local Loyalists and the Cherokees, led by Chief Dragging Canoe, who promised to leave the ground "dark and bloody."

BRITISH MOMENTUM Initially, Clinton's southern strategy worked. Within twenty months, the British and their allies had defeated three American armies; seized the strategic port cities of Savannah and Charleston, South Carolina; occupied Georgia and much of South Carolina; and killed, wounded, or captured some 7,000 American soldiers. The success of the "southern campaign" led Lord George Germain, the British official in London overseeing the war, to predict a "speedy and happy termination of the American war."

Germain's optimistic prediction, however, fell victim to three developments: first, the Loyalist strength in the South was weaker than estimated; second, the British effort to unleash Indian attacks convinced many undecided backcountry settlers to join the Patriot side; and, third, some British and Loy-alist soldiers behaved so harshly that they drove Loyalists to switch sides.

WAR IN THE CAROLINAS The Carolina campaign took a major turn when British forces, led brilliantly by Generals Clinton and Charles Cornwal-lis, bottled up an entire American army on the Charleston Peninsula. Benja-min Lincoln, the U.S. commander, begged local planters to arm their slaves and let them join the defense of the city, but the slaveholders refused. Prom-inent South Carolina leaders then used their control of local militia units to prevent Lincoln and his army from escaping the British invasion.

On May 12, 1780, General Lincoln surrendered Charleston and its 5,500 defenders. It was the single greatest Patriot loss of the war. Soon thereafter, General Cornwallis, in charge of the British troops in the South, defeated a much larger American force led by General Horatio Gates at Camden, South Carolina.

Cornwallis had Georgia and most of South Carolina under British control by 1780. Then he made a tactical blunder by sending lieutenants into the country-side to organize Loyalist fighters to root out Patriots. In doing so, they mercilessly burned homes and hacked to death surrendering rebels. Their behavior alienated many poor rural folk who had been neutral. Francis Kinlock, a Loyalist, warned that "the lower sort of people, who were in many parts . . . originally attached to the British government, have suffered so severely and been so frequently deceived, that Great Britain now has a hundred enemies where it had one before."

In mid-1780, small bands of Patriots based in the swamps and forests of South Carolina launched a successful series of hit-and-run raids. Led by col-orful fighters such as Francis Marion, "the Swamp Fox," and Thomas Sumter, "the Carolina Gamecock," the Patriot guerrillas gradually wore down British confidence and morale. By August 1780, the British commanders were forced to admit that South Carolina was "in an absolute state of rebellion."

Warfare in the Carolinas was especially brutal. Patriots fought Loyalists who were neighbors of each other. Both sides looted farms and plantations and tortured, scalped, and executed prisoners. Families were fractured by divided loyalties. Fathers fought sons and brothers killed brothers.

Edward Lacey, a young South Carolina Patriot who commanded a militia unit, had to tie his Tory father to a bedstead to prevent him from informing the British of his whereabouts. Chilling violence occurred on both sides. One Pennsylvania Loyalist, John Stevens, testified that Patriots dragged him "by a rope fixed about his neck" across the Susquehanna River. In Virginia, the planter Charles Lynch set up vigilante courts to punish Loyalists by "lynching" them—which in this case meant whipping them. Others were tarred and feathered.

In the Carolinas and Georgia, British army commanders encouraged their poorly disciplined Loyalist allies to wage a scorched-earth war of terror, arson, and intimidation. "In a civil war," the British general Charles Cornwallis declared, "there is no admitting of neutral characteristics." He urged his commanders to use the "most *vigorous* measures to *extinguish the rebellion.*"

THE BATTLE OF KINGS MOUNTAIN Cornwallis's two most cold-blooded cavalry officers, Sir Banastre Tarleton and Major Patrick Ferguson, who were in charge of training Loyalist militiamen, eventually overreached themselves. The British officers often let their men burn Patriot farms, liberate slaves, and destroy livestock. Major Ferguson sealed his doom when he threatened to march over the Blue Ridge Mountains, hang the mostly Scots-Irish Presbyterian frontier Patriot leaders ("backwater barbarians"), and destroy their frontier farms. Instead, the feisty "overmountain men" from southwestern Virginia and western North and South Carolina (including "Tennesseans"), all of them experienced hunters and riflemen, went hunting for Ferguson and his army of Carolina Loyalists in late September 1780.

On October 7, the two sides clashed near Kings Mountain, a heavily wooded ridge along the border between North Carolina and South Carolina. In a ferocious hour-long battle, Patriot sharpshooters, told by an officer to "shout like hell and fight like devils," devastated the Loyalist troops. Seven hundred Loyalists were captured, twenty-five of whom were later hanged. "The division among the people is much greater than I imagined," an American officer wrote to one of General Washington's aides. The Patriots and Loyalists, he said, "persecute each other with . . . savage fury."

As with so many confrontations during the war in the South, the Battle of Kings Mountain resembled an extended family feud. Seventy-four sets of brothers fought on opposite sides, and twenty-nine sets of fathers and sons.

After the battle, Patriot Captain James Withrow refused to help his Loyalist brother-in-law, who had been badly wounded, and left him to die on the battlefield. When Withrow's wife learned how her husband had treated her brother, she asked for a separation.

Five brothers in the Goforth family from Rutherford County, North Carolina, fought at Kings Mountain; three were Loyalists, two were Patriots. Only one of them survived. Two of the brothers, Preston and John Preston, fighting on opposite sides, recognized each other during the battle, took deadly aim as if in a duel, and fired simultaneously, killing each other.

The American victory in the Battle of Kings Mountain was crucial because it undermined the British strategy in the South. Thomas Jefferson later said that the battle was "the turn of the tide of success." After Kings Mountain, the

British forces under Cornwallis were forced to retreat to South Carolina and found it virtually impossible to recruit more Loyalists.

SOUTHERN RETREAT In late 1780, the Continental Congress chose a new commander for the American army in the South: General Nathanael Greene, "the fighting Quaker" of Rhode Island. A former blacksmith blessed with unflagging persistence, he was bold and daring, and well-suited to a drawn-out war.

Greene arrived in Charlotte, North Carolina, to find himself in charge of a "shadow army." The 2,200 troops lacked everything "necessary either for the Comfort or Convenience of Soldiers." Greene wrote General Washington that the situation was "dismal, and truly distressing." Yet he also knew that if he could not create a victorious army, the whole South would be "re-annexed" to Britain.

Like Washington, Greene adopted a hit-and-run strategy. From Charlotte, he moved his army eastward while sending General Daniel Morgan, one of the heroes of the Battles of Saratoga, a heavy-drinking, fist-fighting wagonmaster, with about 700 riflemen on a sweep to the west of Cornwallis's headquarters at Winnsboro, South Carolina.

On January 17, 1781, Morgan's force took up positions near Cowpens, an area of cattle pastures in northern South Carolina about twenty-five miles from Kings Mountain. There he lured Sir Banastre Tarleton's army into an elaborate trap. Tarleton, known for his bravery but hated for his brutality, rushed his men forward, "running at us as if they intended to eat us up," only to be ambushed by Morgan's cavalry. Tarleton escaped, but 110 British soldiers were killed and more than 700 were taken prisoner.

Cowpens was the most complete victory for the American side in the Revolution and was one of the few times that Patriots won a battle in which the two sides were evenly matched. When General Cornwallis learned of the American victory, he was so furiously disappointed that he snapped his ceremonial sword in two, saying that the news "broke my heart."

After the victory at Cowpens, Morgan's army moved into North Carolina and linked up with Greene's troops. Greene lured Cornwallis's starving British army north, then attacked the redcoats at Guilford Courthouse (near what became Greensboro, North Carolina) on March 15, 1781.

The Americans lost the Battle of Guilford Courthouse but inflicted such heavy losses that Cornwallis left behind his wounded and marched his weary men toward Wilmington, on the North Carolina coast, to lick their wounds and take on supplies from British ships. Greene then resolved to go back into South Carolina, hoping to lure Cornwallis after him or force the British to give up the state. Greene connected with local guerrilla bands led by Francis

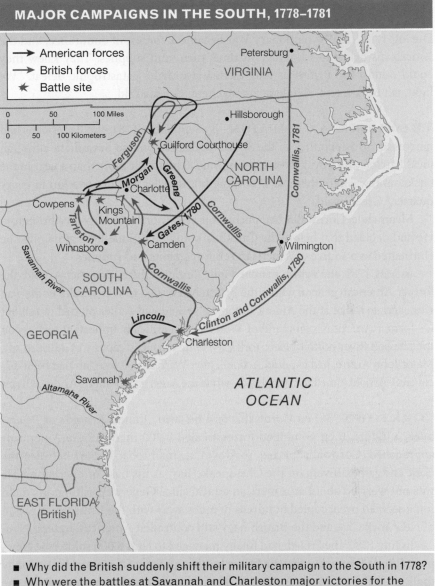

MAJOR CAMPAIGNS IN THE SOUTH, 1778–1781

American forces
British forces
⚹ Battle site

- Why did the British suddenly shift their military campaign to the South in 1778?
- Why were the battles at Savannah and Charleston major victories for the British?
- How did General Nathanael Greene undermine British control of the Lower South?

Marion, Andrew Pickens, and Thomas Sumter. By targeting outlying British units and picking them off one by one, the guerrillas eventually forced the British back into Charleston and Savannah. George Washington praised Greene for having done "great things with little means."

A WAR OF ENDURANCE

During 1780, the Revolutionary War became a contest of endurance, and the Americans held the advantage in time, men, and supplies. They knew they could outlast the British as long as they avoided a catastrophic defeat. "We fight, get beat, rise, and fight again," General Greene said.

THE VIRGINIA CAMPAIGN By September 1781, the Americans had narrowed British control in the South to Charleston and Savannah, although local Patriots and Loyalists would continue to battle for more than a year in the backcountry, where there was "nothing but murder and devastation in every quarter," Greene said.

Meanwhile, Cornwallis had pushed his army northward from Wilmington. He had decided that before the Carolinas could be subdued, Virginia must be eliminated as a source of American reinforcements and supplies.

In May 1781, the British marched into Virginia. There, Benedict Arnold, the former American general whom the British had bribed to switch sides in the war, was eager to strike at the American forces. Arnold had earlier plotted to sell out his former American command of West Point, a critically important fortress on the Hudson River north of New York City. Only the lucky capture of a British spy, Major John André, had exposed Arnold's plot. Warned that his plan had been discovered, Arnold joined the British side, while the Americans hanged André as a spy.

YORKTOWN When Cornwallis and his army joined Arnold's at Petersburg, Virginia, their combined forces totaled 7,200 men. As the Americans approached, Cornwallis picked Yorktown, a small tobacco port between the York and James Rivers on the Chesapeake Bay, as his base of operations. He was not worried about an American attack, since General Washington's main force seemed preoccupied hundreds of miles away with the British occupation of New York City, and the British navy still controlled American waters.

In July 1780, the French had finally managed to land 6,000 soldiers at Newport, Rhode Island, but they had been bottled up there for a year, blockaded by the British fleet. As long as the British navy maintained supremacy along the coast, the Americans could not hope to win the war.

In May 1781, however, the elements for a combined French-American action suddenly fell into place. As Cornwallis's army moved into Virginia, Washington persuaded the commander of the French army in Rhode Island to join in an attack on the British army in New York City.

Before they could strike, however, word came from the Caribbean that Admiral François-Joseph-Paul de Grasse was headed for the Chesapeake Bay with his large fleet of French warships and some 3,000 soldiers. The unexpected news led Washington to change his strategy. He immediately began moving his army south toward Yorktown. At the same time, French ships slipped out of the British blockade at Newport and also headed south. Somehow, in an age when communications were difficult, the French and Americans coordinated a complex plan to join naval and army forces and cut off and destroy the main British army. Success depended on the French fleet getting to the Chesapeake Bay off the coast of Virginia before the British navy did.

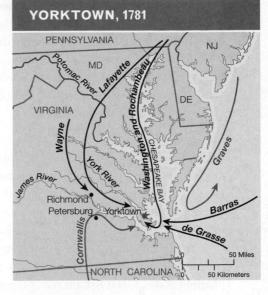

On August 30, Admiral de Grasse's twenty-four warships won the race to Yorktown, and French troops landed to join the Americans. On September 6, the day after a British fleet appeared, de Grasse attacked and forced the British navy to abandon Cornwallis's surrounded army, leaving him with no way to get fresh food and supplies. De Grasse then sent ships up the Chesapeake to ferry down the soldiers who were marching south from New York, bringing the combined American and French armies to 19,000 men—more than double the size of Cornwallis's army.

The **Battle of Yorktown** began on September 28. The American and French troops soon closed off Cornwallis's last escape route and began bombarding the British with artillery. The British held out for three grim weeks before running out of food and suffering from widespread disease.

On October 17, 1781, a glum Cornwallis surrendered. Two days later, the British forces marched out and laid down their weapons. Cornwallis himself claimed to be too ill to participate. His report to the British commander in chief in New York was painfully brief: "I have the mortification to inform your Excellency that I have been forced to surrender the troops under my command." Among Cornwallis's surrendered army were five of Thomas Jefferson's former slaves and two owned by George Washington.

THE TREATY OF PARIS (1783)

The war was not yet over. The British still controlled New York City, Charleston, and Savannah, and British ships still blockaded other American ports, but any lingering British hopes of a military victory vanished at Yorktown. In

London, Lord North reacted to the news as if he had "taken a ball [bullet] in the breast." The shaken prime minister exclaimed: "Oh God, it is all over."

In December 1781, King George decided against sending more troops to America. On February 27, 1782, Parliament voted to begin negotiations to end the war, and on March 20, Lord North resigned. In part, the British leaders chose peace in America so that they could concentrate on their continuing global war with France and Spain.

A NEGOTIATED PEACE Upon learning of the British decision to negotiate, the Continental Congress named a group of prominent Americans to go to Paris to discuss terms with the British. They included John Adams, who was then representing the United States in the Netherlands; John Jay, minister (ambassador) to Spain; and Benjamin Franklin, already in France.

The negotiations dragged on for months until, on September 3, 1783, the Treaty of Paris was finally signed. Its provisions were quite favorable to the United States. Great Britain recognized the independence of the thirteen former colonies and—surprisingly—agreed that the Mississippi River was America's western boundary, thereby more than doubling the territory of the new nation. The boundaries of the United States created by the treaty covered some 900,000 square miles, most of which were *west* of the Proclamation Line of 1763, a vast region long inhabited by Indians and often referred to as *trans-Appalachia*. Native Americans were given no role in the negotiations, and they were by far the biggest losers in the final treaty.

The treaty's unclear references to America's northern and southern borders would be a source of dispute for years. Florida, as it turned out, passed back to Spain from Britain. As for the prewar debts owed by Americans to British merchants, the U.S. negotiators promised that British merchants should "meet with no legal impediment" in seeking to collect money owed them.

WAR AS AN ENGINE OF CHANGE

Like all major wars, the American war for independence had unexpected effects on political, economic, and social life. The long war upset traditional social relationships and affected the lives of people who had long been discriminated against—African Americans, women, and Indians. In important ways, then, the Revolution was an engine for political experimentation and social change. It ignited a prolonged debate about what new forms of government would best serve the new American republic.

REPUBLICAN IDEOLOGY American Revolutionaries embraced a **republican ideology** instead of the aristocratic or monarchical outlook that had long dominated Europe. The new American republic was not a democracy in the purest sense of the word. In ancient Greece, the Athenians had practiced *direct democracy*, which meant that the men voted on all major decisions affecting them. The new United States, however, was technically a *representative*

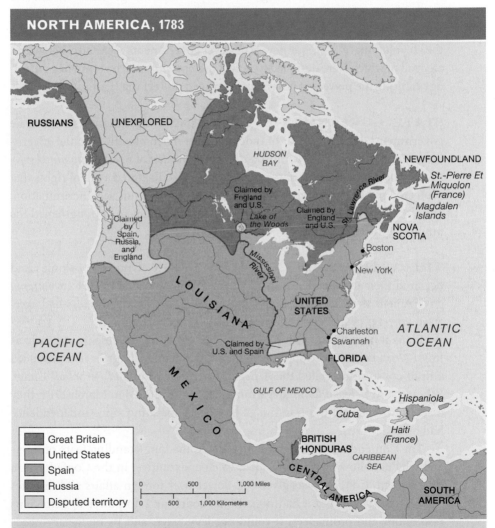

NORTH AMERICA, 1783

RUSSIANS

UNEXPLORED

HUDSON BAY

NEWFOUNDLAND

St.-Pierre Et Miquelon (France)

Magdalen Islands

Claimed by England and U.S.

Lake of the Woods

Claimed by England and U.S.

St. Lawrence River

NOVA SCOTIA

Claimed by Spain, Russia, and England

Mississippi River

Boston

New York

L O U I S I A N A

UNITED STATES

ATLANTIC OCEAN

PACIFIC OCEAN

Claimed by U.S. and Spain

Charleston

Savannah

FLORIDA

M E X I C O

GULF OF MEXICO

Hispaniola

Cuba

Haiti (France)

BRITISH HONDURAS

CARIBBEAN SEA

C E N T R A L A M E R I C A

SOUTH AMERICA

- Great Britain
- United States
- Spain
- Russia
- Disputed territory

0   500   1,000 Miles

0   500   1,000 Kilometers

- What were the terms of the Treaty of Paris?
- Why might the ambiguities in the treaty's language have led to conflicts among the Americans, the Spanish, and the British?

democracy, in which property-holding white men governed themselves through the concept of republicanism, whereby they elected representatives, or legislators, to make decisions on their behalf. As Thomas Paine observed, representative democracy had many advantages over monarchies, one of which was greater transparency: "Whatever are its excellencies and defects, they are visible to all."

To preserve the delicate balance between liberty and power in the new republic, Revolutionary leaders believed that they must protect the rights of individuals and states from being violated by the national government. The war for independence thus sparked a wave of new **state constitutions** that remains unique in history. Not only was a new nation coming into being as a result of the Revolutionary War, but new state-level governments were also being created, all of which were designed to reflect the principles of the republican ideology limiting the powers of government so as to protect the rights of the people.

STATE GOVERNMENTS The first state constitutions created state governments during the War of Independence much like the colonial governments, but with *elected* governors and senates instead of royally *appointed* governors and councils. Most of the constitutions also included a bill of rights that protected freedom of speech, trial by jury, freedom from self-incrimination, and the like. Most also limited the powers of governors and strengthened the powers of the legislatures.

THE ARTICLES OF CONFEDERATION Once the colonies had declared their independence in 1776, the Patriots needed to form a *national* government as well. Before March 1781, the Continental Congress had exercised emergency powers without any legal or official authority.

Plans for a permanent form of government emerged quickly. As early as July 1776, a committee appointed by the Continental Congress had produced a draft constitution called the *Articles of Confederation and Perpetual Union*. When the **Articles of Confederation** finally were ratified in March 1781, they essentially legalized the way things had been operating since independence had been declared.

The Confederation government reflected the long-standing fears of monarchy by not allowing for a president or chief executive. In the Confederation government, Congress was given full power over foreign affairs and disputes between the states. But it had no national courts and no power to enforce its resolutions and ordinances. It could not levy taxes, and its budgetary needs depended on requisitions from the states, which state legislatures often ignored. The states were in no mood to create a strong central government. The Confederation Congress, in fact, had less power than the colonists had once accepted in the British Parliament, because it could not regulate interstate and foreign commerce. For certain important acts, moreover, a "special majority" in the Confederation Congress was required. Nine states had to approve measures dealing with war, treaties, coinage, finances, and the army and navy. Unanimous approval from the states was needed both to impose tariffs (often called "duties," or taxes) on imports and to amend the Articles.

For all its weaknesses, however, the Confederation government represented the most practical structure for the new nation. After all, the Revolution on the battlefields had yet to be won, and an America besieged by British armies and warships could not risk divisive debates over the distribution of power. The new state governments were not willing in 1776 to create a strong national government that might threaten their liberties.

EXPANSION OF POLITICAL PARTICIPATION The new political opportunities afforded by the creation of state governments led more ordinary citizens to participate than ever before. Property qualifications for voting, which already allowed an overwhelming majority of white men to vote, were lowered after 1776 as a result of the Revolutionary fervor. In Pennsylvania, Delaware, North Carolina, and Georgia, any male taxpayer could vote, regardless of how much, if any, property they owned. Farmers, tradesmen, and shopkeepers were soon elected to state legislatures. In general, a higher percentage of American males could vote in the late eighteenth and early nineteenth century than could their counterparts in Great Britain.

THE SOCIAL REVOLUTION

What did the Revolution mean to the workers, servants, farmers, and freed slaves who participated? Many hoped that the Revolution would remove, not reinforce, the elite's traditional political and social advantages. Wealthy Patriots, on the other hand, would have been content to replace royal officials with the rich, the wellborn, and the able—and let it go at that.

In the end, the new republic's social fabric and political culture were visibly different after the war. The energy created by the concepts of liberty, equality, and democracy changed the dynamics of American social and political life in ways that people could not have imagined in 1776.

THE EXODUS OF LOYALISTS The Loyalists were hurt the most by the brutal civil war embedded within the Revolutionary War. They suffered greatly for their loyalty to King George III and for their refusal to pledge allegiance to the new United States. During and after the Revolution, their property was confiscated, and many were assaulted, brutalized, and executed by Patriots (and vice versa).

After the American victory at Yorktown, tens of thousands of panicked Loyalists made their way to seaports to board British ships and flee the United States. Thousands of African Americans, mostly runaway slaves, also flocked to New York City, Charleston, and Savannah, with many of their angry owners in hot pursuit.

General Guy Carleton, the commander of British forces in North America, organized the mass evacuation. He intentionally violated the provisions of the Treaty of Paris by refusing to return slaves to their owners, defiantly telling George Washington that his slaves had already escaped and boarded ships bound for Canada.

Some 80,000 desperate refugees—white Loyalists, free blacks, freed slaves, and Native Americans who had allied with the British—dispersed throughout the British Empire. Some 12,000 Georgia and South Carolina Loyalists, including thousands of their slaves (the British granted freedom only to the slaves of Patriots), went to British-controlled East Florida, only to see their new home handed over to Spain in 1783. Some of the doubly displaced Loyalists sneaked back into the United States, but most went to British islands in the Caribbean. The largest number of Loyalist exiles landed in Canada, where royal officials wanted them to displace the earlier French presence.

The departure of so many Loyalists from America was one of the most important social consequences of the Revolution. Their confiscated homes, land, and vacated jobs created new social, economic, and political opportunities for Patriots. In Paris, however, the Americans negotiating the peace treaty agreed that the Continental Congress would "earnestly recommend" to the states that the confiscated property be restored, although it rarely was.

FREEDOM OF RELIGION The Revolution also tested traditional religious loyalties and set in motion important changes in the relationship between church and government. Before the Revolution, Americans *tolerated* religious dissent; after the Revolution, Americans insisted on complete *freedom* of religion as embodied in the principle of separation of church and state.

The Anglican Church, established as the official religion in five colonies and parts of two others, was especially vulnerable to changes prompted by the war. Anglicans tended to be pro-British, and non-Anglicans, notably Baptists and Methodists, outnumbered Anglicans in all states except Virginia. All but Virginia eliminated tax support for the church before the fighting was over, and Virginia did so soon afterward. Although Anglicanism survived in the form of the new Episcopal Church, it never regained its pre-Revolutionary stature.

Religious development The Congregational Church developed a national presence in the early nineteenth century. Lemuel Haynes, depicted here, was its first African American minister.

In 1776, the Virginia Declaration of Rights guaranteed the free exercise of religion, and in 1786, the **Virginia Statute of Religious Freedom** (written by Thomas Jefferson) declared that "no man shall be compelled to frequent or support any religious worship, place or ministry whatsoever" and "that all men shall be free to profess, and by argument to maintain, their opinions in matters of religion." These statutes, and the Revolutionary ideology that justified them, helped shape the course that religious life would take in the new United States: diverse and voluntary rather than monolithic and enforced by the government.

SLAVES AND THE REVOLUTION

The sharpest irony of the American Revolution is that Great Britain offered enslaved blacks more opportunities for freedom than did the United States. In November 1775, the British royal governor of Virginia, John Murray (Lord Dunmore), himself a slave owner, announced that all slaves and indentured servants would gain their freedom if they joined the Loyalist cause. Within a month, the British had attracted more than 300 former servants and slaves to what came to be called the "Ethiopian Regiment." The number soon grew to almost 1,000 males and twice as many women and children. One former slave renamed himself "British Freedom."

Another runaway who joined the all-black Ethiopian Regiment was Harry Washington, one of George Washington's slaves. In his new role as soldier, he wore a uniform embroidered with the motto, "Liberty to Slaves." Washington's farm manager wrote the general that all his slaves "would leave us if they believed they could make their escape," for "liberty is sweet."

The British recruitment of slaves outraged George Washington, Thomas Jefferson, and other white plantation owners in Virginia, where 40 percent of the population was black. Washington predicted that if Dunmore's efforts were "not crushed" soon, the number of slaves joining the British army would "increase as a Snow ball by Rolling." Jefferson expressed the same concerns after twenty-three slaves escaped from his plantation outside Charlottesville. Jefferson eventually reclaimed six of them, only to sell them for their "disloyalty."

SOUTHERN BACKLASH   In the end, the British policy of recruiting slaves backfired. The "terrifying" prospect of British troops arming slaves persuaded many fence-straddling southerners to join the Patriot cause. Edward Rutledge of South Carolina said that the British decision to arm slaves did more to create "an eternal separation between Great Britain and the colonies than any other expedient." For Rutledge and many southern whites, the Revolution became primarily a war to defend slavery. In 1775, Thomas Jeremiah, a free black, was convicted and executed in Charleston, South Carolina, for telling slaves that British troops were coming "to help the poor Negroes."

In response to the British recruitment of enslaved African Americans, at the end of 1775 a desperate General Washington authorized the enlistment of free blacks—but not slaves—into the American army. In February 1776, however, southern representatives convinced the Continental Congress to instruct Washington to enlist no more African Americans, free or enslaved. Two states, South Carolina and Georgia, refused to allow any blacks to serve in the Patriot forces. As the war effort struggled, however, some states ignored southern wishes. Massachusetts organized two all-black army units, and Rhode Island organized one, which also included Native Americans. In all, about 5,000 African Americans fought on the Patriot side, most of them free blacks from northern states.

In the end, the British army, which liberated 20,000 enslaved blacks during the war, was a far greater instrument of emancipation than the American forces. Most of the newly freed blacks found their way to Canada or to British colonies on Caribbean islands.

While thousands of free blacks and runaway slaves fought in the war, the vast majority of African Americans did not choose sides so much as they chose freedom. Several hundred thousand enslaved blacks, mostly in the southern states, took advantage of the disruptions caused by the war to seize their freedom.

In the North, which had far fewer slaves than the South, the ideals of liberty and freedom led most states to end slavery, either during the war or shortly afterward. But those same ideals had little to no impact in the southern states. These contrasting attitudes toward slavery would continue to shape the political disputes of the young nation.

THE STATUS OF WOMEN   The ideal of liberty spawned by the Revolution applied to the status of women as much as to that of African Americans. The legal status of women was governed by British common law, which essentially treated them like children, limiting their roles to child rearing and maintaining the household. Women could not vote or hold office. Few had access to formal education. Boys were taught to read and write; girls were taught to read and sew. Most New England women in the eighteenth century could not write their own names. Until married, women were subject to the dictates of their fathers.

Once a woman married, she essentially became the property of her husband, and her property became his. A married woman had no right to buy, sell, or manage property. Technically, any wages a wife earned belonged to the husband. Women could not sign contracts, file lawsuits, or testify in court. A husband could beat and even rape his wife without fearing legal action. Divorces were extremely difficult to obtain.

Yet the Revolution offered women new opportunities for independence and public service. Women in many communities made clothing for soldiers and organized fund-raising efforts. Others became camp followers, traveling and camping with the soldiers, often with their children in tow. The women in the army camps cooked meals, washed clothes, nursed wounds, and, on occasion, took part in battle.

A few women disguised their gender and fought as ordinary soldiers. An exceptional case was Deborah Sampson, who joined a Massachusetts regiment as "Robert Shurtleff" and served from 1781 to 1783 by the "artful concealment" of her gender. She was wounded twice, leading Congress to declare after the war that she was the highest "example of female heroism, fidelity, and courage."

Perhaps the feistiest of the fighting women was Georgian Nancy Hart, a tall, red-haired cousin of American general Daniel Morgan and a skilled hunter (local Native Americans called her "War Woman"). When a group of Loyalists accused her of helping a Patriot escape, she didn't deny the charge. Instead, she shot two of them, then held the others at gunpoint until her husband arrived. Her husband, so the story goes, wanted to shoot the remaining Tories, but she insisted on hanging them instead.

WOMEN AND LIBERTY America's war against Great Britain led some women to demand their own independence. Early in the Revolutionary struggle, Abigail Adams, one of the most learned, spirited, and independent women of the time, wrote to her husband, John: "In the new Code of Laws which I suppose it will be necessary for you to make, I desire you would remember the Ladies. . . . Do not put such unlimited power into the hands of the Husbands." Since men were "Naturally Tyrannical," she wrote, "why then, not put it out of the power of the vicious and the Lawless to use us with cruelty and indignity with impunity." Otherwise, "if particular care and attention is not paid to the Ladies we are determined to foment a Rebellion, and will not hold ourselves bound by any Laws in which we have no voice, or Representation."

John Adams responded that he could not help but "laugh" at his wife's radical proposals for female equality. While surprised that women might be dissatisfied, he insisted on retaining the traditional privileges enjoyed by males. If women were to be granted equality, he warned, then "children and apprentices" and "Indians and Negroes" would also demand equal rights and freedoms.

Thomas Jefferson shared Adams's stance. In his view, there was no place in the new republic for female political participation. Women should not "wrinkle their foreheads with politics" but instead "soothe and calm the minds of their husbands." Improvements in the status of women would have to wait. New Yorker Margaret Livingston admitted as much in 1776 when she wrote that "our Sex are *doomed* to be obedient [to men] at every stage of life so that we shan't be great gainers by this contest [the Revolutionary War]."

NATIVE AMERICANS AND THE REVOLUTION Most Native Americans sought to remain neutral in the war, but both British and American agents urged the chiefs to fight on their side. The result was chaos. Indians on both sides attacked villages, burned crops, and killed civilians.

During and after the war, the new American government assured its Indian allies that it would respect their lands and their rights. But many white Americans used the disruptions of war to destroy and displace Native Americans. Once the war ended and independence was secured, there was no peace for the Indians. By the end of the eighteenth century, land-hungry Americans were again pushing into Indian territories on the western frontier.

THE EMERGENCE OF AN AMERICAN CULTURE

On July 2, 1776, when the Second Continental Congress had resolved "that these United Colonies are, and of right ought to be, free and independent states," John Adams had written Abigail that future generations would remember that date as their "day of deliverance." People, he predicted, would celebrate the occasion with "pomp and parade, with shows, games, sports, guns, bells, bonfires and illuminations [fireworks] from one end of this continent to the other, from this time forward, forever more." Adams got everything right but the date. As luck would have it, July 4, the date the Declaration of Independence was approved, became Independence Day rather than July 2, when independence was formally declared.

The celebration of Independence Day quickly became the most important public ritual in the United States. People from all walks of life suspended their normal routine to devote a day to parades, patriotic speeches, and fireworks displays. In the process, the infant republic began to create its own myth of national identity. "What a day!" exclaimed the editor of the *Southern Patriot* in 1815. "What happiness, what emotion, what virtuous triumph must fill the bosoms of Americans!"

American nationalism embodied a stirring idea. This new nation was not rooted in antiquity. Its people, except for the Native Americans, had not inhabited it over many centuries, nor was there any notion of a common ethnic descent. "The American national consciousness," one observer wrote, "is not a voice crying out of the depth of the dark past, but is proudly a product of the enlightened present, setting its face resolutely toward the future."

Many people, at least since the time of the Pilgrims, had thought of the "New World" as singled out for a special identity, a special mission assigned by God. John Adams proclaimed the opening of America "a grand scheme and design in Providence for the illumination and the emancipation of the slavish part of mankind all over the earth."

This sense of providential mission provided much of the energy for America's development. From the democratic rhetoric of Thomas Jefferson to the pragmatism of George Washington to heady toasts bellowed in South Carolina taverns, patriots everywhere claimed a special role for American leadership in history. The first mission was to gain independence. Now, people believed, God was guiding the United States to lead the world toward greater liberty and equality. Benjamin Rush, a Philadelphia doctor and scientist, issued a prophetic statement in 1787: "The American war is over: but this is far from being the case with the American Revolution. On the contrary, but the first act of the great drama is closed."

CHAPTER REVIEW

Summary

- **Military Challenges**   In 1776 the British had the mightiest army and navy in the world, and they supplemented their military might by hiring professional German soldiers called *Hessians* to help put down the American Revolution. The Americans had to create an army—the Continental army—from scratch. George Washington realized that the Americans had to turn unreliable *citizen-soldiers* into a disciplined fighting force and try to wage a long, costly war, staking that the British army was fighting thousands of miles from its home base and would eventually cut its losses and give up.

- **Turning Points**   After forcing the British to evacuate Boston, the American army suffered a string of defeats before George Washington surprised the Hessians at the *Battle of Trenton* at the end of 1776. The victory bolstered American morale and prompted more enlistments in the Continental Army. The French were likely allies for the colonies from the beginning of the conflict because they resented their losses to Britain in the Seven Years' War. After the British defeat at the *Battles of Saratoga*, the colonies brokered an *alliance with France*. Washington's ability to hold his ragged forces together, despite daily desertions and two especially difficult winters in Morristown and *Valley Forge*, was another major turning point. The British lost support on the frontier and in the southern colonies when terrorist tactics backfired. The Battle of Kings Mountain drove the British into retreat, and French supplies and the French fleet helped tip the balance and ensure the American victory at the *Battle of Yorktown*.

- **Civil War**   The American Revolution was also a civil war, dividing families and communities. There were at least 100,000 Loyalists in the colonies. They included royal officials, Anglican ministers, wealthy southern planters, and the elite in large seaport cities; they also included many humble people, especially recent immigrants. After the hostilities ended, many Loyalists, including slaves who had fled plantations to support the British cause, left for Canada, the West Indies, or England.

- **A Political and Social Revolution**   The American Revolution disrupted and transformed traditional class and social relationships. American Revolutionaries embraced a *republican ideology*, and more white men gained the right to vote as property requirements were removed. But fears of a monarchy being reestablished led colonists to vest power in the states rather than in a national government under the *Articles of Confederation*. New *state constitutions* instituted more elected positions, and most included bills of rights that protected individual liberties. The *Virginia Statute of Religious Freedom* led the way in guaranteeing the separation of church and state, and religious toleration was transformed into religious freedom.

- **African Americans, Women, and Native Americans**   Northern states began to free slaves, but southern states were reluctant. Although many women had undertaken nontraditional roles during the war, afterward they remained largely confined to the domestic sphere, with no changes to their legal or political status. The Revolution had catastrophic effects on Native Americans, regardless of which side they had allied with during the war. American settlers seized Native American land, often in violation of existing treaties.

CHRONOLOGY

1776	British forces seize New York City
	General Washington's troops defeat British forces at the Battle of Trenton
	States begin writing new constitutions
1777	American forces defeat British in a series of battles at Saratoga
1778	Americans and French form a military alliance
	George Rogers Clark's militia defeats British troops in Mississippi Valley
	American forces defeat the Iroquois Confederacy at Newtown, New York
1780	Patriots defeat Loyalists at the Battle of Kings Mountain
1781	British invasion of southern colonies turned back at the Battles of Cowpens and Guilford Courthouse
	American and French forces defeat British at Yorktown, Virginia
	Articles of Confederation are ratified
	Continental Congress becomes Confederation Congress
1783	Treaty of Paris is signed, formally ending Revolutionary War
1786	Virginia adopts the Statute of Religious Freedom

KEY TERMS

Hessians p. 162

citizen-soldiers p. 162

Battle of Trenton (1776) p. 168

Battles of Saratoga (1777) p. 175

alliance with France p. 175

Valley Forge (1777–1778) p. 176

Battle of Yorktown (1781) p. 185

republican ideology p. 187

state constitutions p. 188

Articles of Confederation p. 188

Virginia Statute of Religious Freedom (1786) p. 191

INQUIZITIVE

Go to InQuizitive to see what you've learned—and learn what you've missed—with personalized feedback along the way.

6

Strengthening the New Nation

Washington as a Statesman at the Constitutional Convention **(1856)** This painting
by Junius Brutus Stearns is one of the earliest depictions of the drafting of the
Constitution, capturing the moment after the convention members, including George
Washington (right), completed the final draft.

D uring the 1780s, the United States of America was rapidly emerging as the lone large republic in an unstable world dominated by monarchies. It was distinctive in that it was born out of a conflict over ideas, principles, and ideals rather than from centuries-old shared racial or ancestral bonds, as in Europe and elsewhere.

America was a democratic republic "brought forth" by self-evident political ideals—that people should govern themselves, that people should have an equal opportunity to prosper, and that governments exist to protect liberty and promote the public good. Those ideals were captured in phrases that still resonate: All men are created equal. Liberty and justice for all. *E pluribus unum* ("Out of many, one"—the phrase on the official seal of the United States). How Americans understood, applied, and violated these ideals shaped the new nation's development after 1783.

POWER TO THE PEOPLE

The American Revolution created not only an independent new republic but also a different conception of politics than prevailed in Europe. What Americans most feared in the late eighteenth century was governmental abuse of power. Memories of the tyranny of King George III, his prime ministers, and royal colonial governors were still raw. Freedom from such arbitrary power had been the ideal guiding the American Revolution, while freedom to "pursue happiness" became the ideal driving the new nation.

focus questions

1. What are the strengths and weaknesses of the Articles of Confederation? How did they contribute to the creation of a new U.S. constitution in 1787?

2. What political innovations did the 1787 Constitutional Convention develop for the new nation?

3. What were the debates surrounding the ratification of the Constitution? How were they resolved?

4. In what ways did the Federalists' vision for the United States differ from that of their Republican opponents during the 1790s?

5. How did the attitudes toward Great Britain and France shape American politics in the late eighteenth century?

To ensure their new freedoms, the Revolutionaries wrestled with a fundamental question: what is the proper role and scope of government? In answering that question, they eventually developed new ways to divide and balance power among the various branches of government so as to manage the tensions between ensuring liberty and maintaining order.

But even with victory in the war, America was a nation in name only. The quest for true nationhood after the Revolution was the most significant political transformation in modern history, for Americans would insist that sovereignty (ultimate power) resided not with a king or an aristocracy but with "the people," the mass of ordinary citizens.

FORGING A NEW NATION   The unlikely American victory in the Revolutionary War stunned the world, but the Patriots had little time to celebrate. As Alexander Hamilton, a brilliant young army officer turned congressman, noted in 1783, "We have now happily concluded the great work of independence, but much remains to be done to reach the fruits of it."

The transition from war to peace was neither simple nor easy. America was independent but not yet a self-sustaining nation. In fact, the Declaration of Independence never mentioned the word *nation*. Its official title was "the unanimous Declaration of the thirteen united States of America."

During the war, James Madison of Virginia predicted that the Confederation government would be only temporary. "The present Union will but little survive the present war," he wrote. The states must recognize, he continued, "the necessity of the Union during the war" and "its probable dissolution after it."

Forging a new *nation* out of a *confederation* of thirteen rebellious colonies-turned-"free-and-independent" states posed huge challenges, not the least of which was managing what George Washington called a "deranged" economy, suffocating in war-related debts. The accumulated war debt was $160 million, a huge amount at the time. Such financial stress made for trying times in the first years of the American republic.

The period from the drafting of the Declaration of Independence in 1776, through the creation of the new federal constitution in 1787, and ending with the election of Thomas Jefferson as president in 1800, was fraught with instability and tension. From the start, the new nation experienced growing political divisions, economic distress, and foreign troubles.

Three fundamental questions shaped political debate during the last quarter of the eighteenth century. Where would sovereignty reside in the new nation? What was the proper relationship of the states to each other and to the national government? And what was required for the new republic to flourish as an independent nation? The efforts to answer those questions created powerful tensions that continue to complicate American life.

THE CONFEDERATION GOVERNMENT

John Quincy Adams, a future president, called the years between 1783 and 1787 the "Critical Period" when American leaders developed sharp differences about economic policies, international relations, and the proper relationship of the states to the national government. Debates over those key issues unexpectedly gave birth to the nation's first political parties and, to this day, continue to influence the American experiment in **federalism** (the sharing of power among national, state, and local governments).

After the war, many Patriots who had feared government power and criticized British officials for abusing it now directed their attacks against the new state and national governments. In 1783, after Congress ran out of money, some army officers, upset at not being paid, had threatened to march on Congress and take over the government. Alexander Hamilton reported that the soldiers had become "a mob rather than an army, without clothing, without pay, without provisions [food], without morals, without discipline." Only George Washington's intervention stopped the rebellious officers from confronting Congress. At the same time, state legislatures, desperate for funds to pay off their war debts, sparked unrest and riots by raising taxes.

The often violent clashes between the working poor and the state governments were a great disappointment to Washington, John Adams and other Revolutionary leaders. For them and others disillusioned by the surge of "democratic" rebelliousness, the Critical Period was a time of hopes frustrated, a story shaded by regret at the absence of national loyalty and international respect. The weaknesses of the Articles of Confederation in dealing with the postwar turmoil led political leaders to design an entirely new national constitution and federal government.

A LOOSE ALLIANCE OF STATES The **Articles of Confederation**, formally approved in 1781, had created a loose alliance (confederation) of thirteen independent states. The states were united only in theory; in practice, each state government acted on its own. The first major provision of the Articles insisted that "each state retains its sovereignty, freedom, and independence."

The weak national government under the Articles had only one component, a one-house legislature. There was no national president, no executive branch, no separate national judiciary (court system). State legislatures, not voters, appointed the members of the Confederation Congress, in which each state, regardless of size or population, had one vote. This meant that Rhode Island, with 68,000 people, had the same power in the Confederation Congress as Virginia, the largest and most prosperous state, with more than 747,000 inhabitants.

George Washington called the Confederation "a half-starved, limping government." It could neither regulate trade nor create taxes to pay off the country's large war debts. It could approve treaties with other nations but had no power to enforce their terms. It could call for raising an army but could not force men to fill the ranks.

The Congress, in short, could not enforce its own laws, and its budget relied on undependable "voluntary" contributions from the states. In 1782, for example, the Confederation asked the states to provide $8 million for the national government; they sent $420,000. The lack of state support forced the Confederation Congress to print paper money, called Continentals, whose value plummeted to two cents on the dollar as more and more were printed, leading to the joking phrase, "Not worth a Continental." Virtually no gold and silver coins remained in circulation; they had all gone abroad to purchase items for the war.

The Confederation government ran up a budget deficit every year of its existence. It was even hard to find people to serve in such a feeble congress. And people only doubted the stability of the new American republic. As John Adams wrote to Thomas Jefferson, "The Union is still to me an Object of as much Anxiety as ever independence was."

Yet in spite of its limitations, the Confederation Congress survived the war years while laying important foundations for the new national government. The Articles of Confederation were crucially important in supporting the concept of *republicanism* (representative democracy), which meant that America would be governed not by kings or queens or nobles but "by the authority of the people" whose elected representatives would make decisions on their behalf. The Confederation Congress also created the national government's first executive departments and formulated the basic principles of land distribution and territorial government that would guide America's westward expansion.

LAND POLICY In ending the Revolutionary War and transferring Britain's North American colonies to America, the Treaty of Paris doubled the size of the United States, extending the nation's western boundary to the Mississippi River. Under the Articles of Confederation, land not included within the boundaries of the thirteen original states became *public domain*, owned and administered by the national government.

Between 1784 and 1787, the Confederation Congress created three major ordinances (policies) detailing how the government-owned lands in the West would be surveyed, sold, and developed. These ordinances rank among the

Confederation's greatest achievements—and among the most important in American history.

Thomas Jefferson drafted the Land Ordinance Act of 1784, which urged states to drop their competing claims to Indian-held territory west of the Appalachian Mountains so that the vast, unmapped area could be divided into as many as fourteen self-governing *territories* of equal size. In the new territories, all adult white males would be eligible to vote, hold office, and write constitutions for their territorial governments. When a territory's population equaled that of the smallest existing state (Rhode Island), it would be eligible for statehood.

Before Jefferson's plan could take effect, however, the Confederation Congress revised it through the Land Ordinance of 1785, which literally shaped the future of the nation. It outlined a plan of land surveys and sales for the Northwest Territory (the area that would become Ohio, Michigan, Indiana, Illinois, and Wisconsin), and later on, the Great Plains. Wherever Indian lands were purchased—or taken—they were divided into six-mile-square townships laid out along a grid of lines running east–west and north–south. Each township was in turn divided into thirty-six sections one mile square (640 acres), with each section divided into four farms. The 640-acre sections of "public lands" were to be sold at auctions, the proceeds of which went into the national treasury.

THE NORTHWEST ORDINANCE The third major land policy created by the Confederation Congress was the **Northwest Ordinance** of 1787. It set forth two key principles: the new western territories would eventually become states, and slavery was banned from the region north of the Ohio River (slaves already there would remain slaves, however). The Northwest Ordinance also included a promise, which would be repeatedly broken, that Indian lands "shall never be taken from them without their consent."

For a new territory to become a state, the Northwest Ordinance specified a three-stage process. First, Congress would appoint a territorial governor and other officials to create a legal code and administer justice. Second, when the population of adult males reached 5,000, they could elect a territorial legislature. Third, when a territory's population reached 60,000 "free inhabitants," it could draft a constitution and apply to Congress for statehood.

DIPLOMACY After the Revolutionary War, relations with Great Britain and Spain remained tense because both nations kept trading posts, forts, and soldiers on American soil, and both nations encouraged Indians to resist American efforts to settle on their tribal lands. The British refused to remove

Domestic industry American craftsmen, such as this cabinetmaker, favored tariffs on foreign goods that competed with their own products.

their troops south of the Canadian border in protest of the failure of Americans to pay their prewar debts to British merchants. Another major irritant in U.S.-British relations was the seizure of Loyalist property. During and after the war, Americans had confiscated Tory homes, businesses, farms, and slaves.

With Spain, the chief issues were the southern boundary of the United States and the right for Americans to send boats or barges down the Mississippi River, which Spain then controlled. After the Seven Years' War in 1763, Spain had acquired the vast Louisiana Territory, which included the valuable port of New Orleans, the Mississippi River, and all of the area west to the Rocky Mountains. After the Revolution, Spain closed the Mississippi River to American use, infuriating settlers in Kentucky and Tennessee. Spain also regained ownership of Florida, which then included southern Alabama. Thereafter, the Spanish governor in Florida provided firearms to Creek Indians, who resisted American encroachment on their lands in south Georgia.

TRADE AND THE ECONOMY   More troublesome than the behavior of the British and the Spanish was the fragile state of the American economy. Seven years of warfare had nearly bankrupted the new nation. The escape of some 60,000 slaves during and after the Revolution was a terrible blow to the southern economy. At the same time, many men who had served in the army had never been paid. Civilians who had loaned money, supplies, crops, and livestock to the war effort had also not been repaid.

After the war, the British treated the United States as an enemy nation, insisting that all Americans who had been born in England were still bound by allegiance to King George III. British warships began stopping American ships in the Atlantic, boarding them, kidnapping English-born American sailors, and "impressing" them into service in the Royal Navy.

The British also closed their island colonies in the Caribbean to American commerce. New England shipowners and southern planters were especially hard-hit, as exports of tobacco, rice, rum, and other commodities remained far below what they had been before the war. After 1783, merchant ships were allowed to deliver American products to England and return to the United States with English goods. But U.S. vessels could not carry British goods anywhere else in the world.

To punish Britain for banning U.S. trade with the British West Indies, many state governments imposed special taxes (called tonnage fees) on British vessels arriving in American ports and levied tariffs (taxes) on British goods brought to the United States. The British responded by sending their ships to ports in states whose tariff rates were lower.

By charging different tariffs on the same products, the states waged commercial war with each other. The result was economic chaos. By 1787, it was clear that the national government needed to regulate interstate trade and foreign relations, especially in regard to British and Spanish control of territories bordering the United States.

SCARCE MONEY Complex financial issues also hampered economic development during the Critical Period. There was no stable national currency, and the nation had only three banks, in Philadelphia, New York City, and Boston. Farmers who had profited during the war now found themselves squeezed by lower crop prices and mounting debts and taxes. The widespread shortage of "hard money" (gold and silver coins) led people to postpone paying their bills.

By 1785, indebted citizens urged states to print new paper currency. In a drama that would be replayed many times over the next century, debtors believed that printing paper money would ease their plight by increasing the money supply (inflation). In 1785–1786, seven states began issuing their own paper money to help indebted farmers and to pay the cash bonuses promised to military veterans.

THE "GATHERING CRISIS"

The economic difficulties weakening the Confederation were compounded by growing fears among wealthy "gentlemen" leaders ("natural aristocrats") that the democratic energies unleashed by the Revolution were undermining the authority of the traditional social and economic elite. Class distinctions were disappearing as many among the working poor and "middling classes" stopped deferring to their "betters."

The so-called better sort of people were appalled at the "leveling" behavior of the "antifederal peasants," "little folks," and "demagogues" who were challenging their leadership. A Virginia aristocrat grumbled that the "spirit of independency" that inspired the Revolution was being "converted into equality" after the war. The political culture was also changing; more men could now vote and hold office, as property-owning qualifications were reduced or eliminated in several states.

No sooner was the war over than Americans with large debts began to protest about taxes again. To begin paying down their war debts, most state legislatures had sharply increased taxes. In fact, during the 1780s, most Americans paid three times as much in taxes as they had under British "tyranny." Earlier, they had objected to taxation *without* representation; now, they objected to taxation *with* representation.

Some Patriots lost farms because of their inability to pay the new taxes; other debtors were imprisoned. In New Hampshire, in what was called the Exeter Riot, hard-pressed farmers surrounded the legislative building, demanding that the representatives print paper money to ease their plight. Similar appeals occurred in other states.

SHAYS'S REBELLION   Fears of a taxpayer "revolt from below" became all too real in western Massachusetts, when struggling farmers, many of them former soldiers, demanded that the state issue more paper money and give them more time to pay the "unjust" taxes owed on their land. Farmers also resented the new state constitution because it *raised* the property qualifications for voting and holding elected office, thus stripping poorer men of political power.

Shays's Rebellion Shays and his followers demanded that states issue paper currency to help ease the payment of debts and the right to postpone paying taxes until the postwar agricultural depression lifted.

When the merchant-dominated Massachusetts legislature refused to provide relief, however, three rural counties in the western part of the state revolted in 1786. One rebel farmer, Plough Jogger, expressed the fears of many when he charged that the "great men are going to get all we have, and I think it is time for us to rise and put a stop to it, and have no more courts, nor sheriffs, nor [tax] collectors, nor lawyers."

Armed groups of angry farmers, called Regulators, banded together to force judges and sheriffs to stop seizing the cattle and farms of those who could not pay their taxes. "Close down the courts," they shouted. A prominent Bostonian reported that Massachusetts was "in a state of Anarchy and Confusion bordering on Civil War."

The situation worsened when a ragtag "army" of unruly farmers, led by thirty-nine-year-old Daniel Shays, a war veteran, marched on the federal arsenal at Springfield in the winter of 1787. The state government responded by sending 4,400 militiamen, who scattered Shays's debtor army with a single cannon blast that left four farmers dead and many wounded. Shays fled to Vermont. Several rebels were arrested, two were hanged, and the rest were fined or whipped. The rebels nevertheless earned a victory of sorts, as the state legislature agreed to eliminate some of the taxes and fees on farmers.

News of **Shays's Rebellion** sent shock waves across the nation. In Massachusetts, Abigail Adams, the wife of future president John Adams, dismissed Shays and his followers as "ignorant, restless, desperadoes, without conscience or principles." In Virginia, George Washington was equally concerned. America, he said, needed a "government by which our lives, liberty, and properties will be secured." Unless an alternative could be found to the weak Confederation government, "anarchy and confusion will inevitably ensue."

CREATING THE CONSTITUTION

In the wake of Shays's Rebellion, a collective shiver passed through what wealthy New Yorker John Jay called "the better kind of people." Many among the "rich and well-born" agreed with George Washington that the nation was "tottering." The time had come to empower the national government to bring social order and economic stability.

THE "CRISIS IS ARRIVED"   During the 1780s, newspapers warned that the nation's situation had grown "critical and dangerous" and that its "vices" were threatening "national ruin." The states were behaving like thirteen ungovernable nations, pursuing their own trade regulations and foreign policies. "Our present federal government," said Henry Knox, a Boston bookseller who was a general during the Revolutionary War, "is a name, a shadow, without power, or effect."

Such concerns led political leaders to revise their assessment of the American republic. "We have, probably," concluded Washington in 1786, "had too good an opinion of human nature in forming our confederation." Fellow Virginian James Madison agreed, declaring in 1787 that the "crisis is arrived." It was time to create a new federal constitution that would repair the "vices of the political system" and "decide forever the fate of republican government." New Yorker Alexander Hamilton urged that a national gathering of delegates from each state be given "full powers" to revise the Articles of Confederation.

THE CONSTITUTIONAL CONVENTION In 1787, the Confederation Congress responded by calling for a special "federal" convention to gather in Philadelphia's Old State House (now known as Independence Hall) for the "purpose of revising the Articles of Confederation." Only Rhode Island refused to participate.

The delegates began work on May 25, 1787, meeting five hours a day, six days a week. After four months of secret deliberations, thirty-nine delegates signed the new federal constitution on September 17. Only three delegates refused to sign.

The durability of the Constitution reflects the thoughtful men who created it. The delegates were all white; their average age was forty-two, with the youngest being twenty-six. Most were members of the political and economic elite. Twenty-six were college graduates; two were college presidents, and thirty-four were lawyers. Others were planters, merchants, bankers, and clergymen.

Yet the "Founding Fathers" were also practical men of experience, tested in the fires of the Revolutionary War. Twenty-two had fought in the war; five were captured and imprisoned by the British. Seven had been state governors, and eight had helped write their state constitutions. Most had been members of the Continental or Confederation Congresses, and eight had signed the Declaration of Independence. Nearly all were considered "gentlemen," and more than half of them owned slaves.

DRAFTING THE CONSTITUTION The widely respected—even revered—George Washington served as presiding officer at the Federal Convention (later renamed the Constitutional Convention). He participated little in the debates, however, for fear that people would take his opinions too seriously. The governor of Pennsylvania, eighty-one-year-old Benjamin Franklin, the oldest delegate, was in such poor health that he had to be carried to the meetings in a special chair, borne aloft by inmates from the Philadelphia jail. Like Washington, Franklin said little from the floor but provided a wealth of experience, wit, and common sense behind the scenes.

Most active at the Convention was James Madison of Virginia, the ablest political theorist in the group. A thirty-six-year-old attorney who owned a huge tobacco plantation called Montpelier, not far from Jefferson's Monticello, Madison had arrived in Philadelphia with trunks full of books about governments and a head full of ideas about how best to strengthen the loose confederation of "independent and sovereign states."

Madison was an unlikely giant at constitution-making. Barely five feet tall and weighing only 120 pounds (a colleague said he was "no bigger than half a piece of soap"), he was too frail to serve in the Revolutionary army and suffered from epileptic seizures. "He speaks low, his person [body] is little and ordinary," and he was "too timid in his politics," remarked crusty Fisher Ames of Massachusetts.

Although painfully shy and soft-spoken, Madison had an agile mind, a huge appetite for learning, and a lifelong commitment to public service. He was determined to create a constitution that would ensure the "supremacy of national authority." The logic of his arguments—and his willingness to compromise on particular points—proved decisive in shaping the new constitution. "Every person seems to acknowledge his greatness," said a Georgia delegate.

Two interrelated assumptions guided the Constitutional Convention: that the national government must have direct authority over the citizenry rather than governing through the state governments, and that the national government must derive its legitimacy from the people rather than from the state legislatures.

James Madison This 1783 miniature shows Madison at thirty-two years old, just four years before he would assume a major role in drafting the Constitution.

The insistence on the sovereignty of "the people," that the voters were "the legitimate source of all authority," as James Wilson of Pennsylvania stressed, was the most important political innovation since the Declaration of Independence. By declaring the Constitution to be the voice of "the people," the founders authorized the federal government to limit the powers of the state governments.

The delegates realized, too, that an effective national government needed authority to collect taxes, borrow and issue money, regulate commerce, fund an army and navy, and make laws binding upon individual citizens. This meant that the states must be stripped of the power to print paper money, make treaties, wage war, and levy tariffs on imported goods. This concept of dividing authority between the national government and the states came to be called federalism.

THE VIRGINIA AND NEW JERSEY PLANS James Madison drafted the framework for the initial discussions at the Constitutional Convention.

His proposals, called the Virginia Plan, started with a radical suggestion: that the delegates scrap their original instructions to *revise* the Articles of Confederation and instead create an entirely *new* constitution.

The Virginia Plan called for a "*national* government [with] a *supreme* legislative, executive, and judiciary." It proposed a new Congress divided into two houses (bicameral): a lower House of Representatives chosen by the voters, and an upper house of senators elected by the state legislatures. The more-populous states would have more representatives in Congress than the smaller states. Madison also wanted to give Congress the power to veto state laws.

The Virginia Plan sparked furious disagreements. When asked why the small states were so suspicious of the plan, Gunning Bedford of Delaware replied: "I do not, gentlemen, trust you."

On June 15, Bedford and other delegates submitted an alternative called the New Jersey Plan, developed by William Paterson of New Jersey. It sought to keep the existing structure of equal representation of the states in a unicameral (one-house) national legislature. It also gave Congress the power to collect taxes and regulate commerce and the authority to name a chief executive as well as a supreme court, but not the right to veto state laws.

THE THREE BRANCHES OF GOVERNMENT

The intense debate over congressional representation was finally resolved in mid-July by the so-called Great Compromise, which used elements of both plans. The more populous states won apportionment (the allocation of delegates to each state) by population in the House of Representatives, while the delegates who sought to protect state power won equality of representation in the Senate, where each state would have two members, elected by the state legislatures rather than directly by the people.

THE LEGISLATURE The Great Compromise embedded the innovative concept of **separation of powers** in the new Congress. It would have two separate houses, each intended to counterbalance the other, with the House of Representatives representing the voters at large, and the Senate representing the state legislatures.

The "lower" house, the House of Representatives, was designed to be, as George Mason said, "the grand repository of the democratic principle of the Government." Its members would be elected by the voters every *two* years. (Under the Articles of Confederation, none of the members of Congress had been chosen by popular vote; all had been elected by state legislatures.) James Madison argued that allowing individual citizens to elect one part of the new legislature was "essential to every plan of free government."

The upper house, or Senate, was intended to be a more elite group, its members elected by state legislatures for *six*-year terms. It could use its power to overrule the House of Representatives or the president. Madison explained that the Senate would help "protect the minority of the opulent against the majority."

THE PRESIDENCY The Constitutional Convention struggled mightily over issues related to the executive branch. Some delegates wanted a powerful president who could veto acts of Congress. Others felt that the president should simply "execute" the laws as passed by Congress. Still others, like Benjamin Franklin, wanted a "plural executive" rather than a single man governing the nation.

The eventual decision to have a single chief executive caused many delegates "considerable pause," according to James Madison. George Mason of Virginia feared that a single president might start behaving like a king.

In the end, several compromises ensured that the president would be powerful enough to counterbalance the Congress. In some cases, the chief executive's powers actually exceeded those of the British king. The new president, to be elected for four-year terms, could veto acts of Congress, subject to being overridden by a two-thirds vote in each house; in Britain, the royal veto over parliamentary legislation had long since been abandoned. The president was to be the nation's chief diplomat and commander in chief of the armed forces, and was responsible for implementing the laws made by Congress.

Yet the powers of the president were also limited in key areas. The chief executive could neither declare war nor make peace; those powers were reserved for Congress. Unlike the British monarch, moreover, the president could be removed from office. The House of Representatives could impeach (bring to trial) the chief executive—and other civil officers—on charges of treason, bribery, or "other high crimes and misdemeanors." An impeached president could be removed from office if two-thirds of the Senate voted for conviction.

To preserve the separation of the three branches of the national government, the president would be elected not by Congress, but by a group of highly qualified "electors" chosen by "the people" in local elections. The number of electors for each state would depend upon the combined number of Congressional representatives and U.S. senators. This "Electoral College" was a compromise between those wanting the president elected by Congress and those preferring a direct popular vote.

THE JUDICIARY The third proposed branch of government, the judiciary, sparked little debate. The Constitution called for a supreme national court headed by a chief justice. The Supreme Court's role was not to make laws

Signing the Constitution, September 17, 1787 Thomas Pritchard Rossiter's painting shows George Washington presiding over what Thomas Jefferson called "an assembly of demi-gods" in Philadelphia.

(a power reserved to Congress) or to execute and enforce the laws (reserved to the presidency), but to *interpret* the laws and to ensure that every citizen received *equal justice* under the law.

The U.S. Supreme Court was given final authority in interpreting the Constitution and in settling constitutional disputes between states. Furthermore, Article VI of the Constitution declared that the Constitution, federal laws, and treaties would be "the supreme Law of the Land," state laws or constitutions "to the Contrary notwithstanding."

THE LIMITS OF THE CONSTITUTION

The men who drafted the new constitution claimed to be representing all Americans. To highlight that point, the Constitution begins with the words: "We the people of the United States, in order to form a more perfect Union . . . establish this Constitution for the United States of America." In fact, however, as Senator Stephen Douglas of Illinois noted seventy years later, the Constitution was "made by white men, for the benefit of white men and their posterity [descendants] forever."

Important groups of Americans were left out of the Constitution's protections. Native Americans, for example, were not considered federal or state citizens unless they paid taxes, which very few did. The Constitution declared that Native American "tribes" were not part of the United States but instead were separate "nations."

SLAVERY   Of all the issues that emerged during the Constitutional Convention, none was more explosive than slavery. When the Patriots declared independence in 1776, slavery existed in every state. By 1787, however, Massachusetts, Pennsylvania, Connecticut, and Rhode Island had abolished the practice.

Many of the framers viewed slavery as an embarrassing contradiction to the principles of liberty and equality embodied in the Declaration of Independence and the new Constitution. But most delegates from the southern states stoutly defended slavery. "Religion and humanity [have] nothing to do with this [slavery] question," declared John Rutledge of South Carolina. "Interest alone is the governing principle of nations."

Most southern delegates would have walked out had there been an attempt to abolish slavery. So the framers did not consider ending the cursed system, nor did they view the enslaved as human beings whose rights should be protected. Slaves were simply viewed as property, with a cash value. Those with qualms about slavery salved their consciences by assuming that the practice would eventually die out naturally.

If the slaves were not to be freed or their rights to be acknowledged, however, how were they to be counted? Since the size of state delegations in the proposed House of Representatives was to be based on population, southern delegates argued that slaves should be counted to help determine how many representatives from each state would serve in the new Congress. Northerners argued that it made no sense to count slaves for purposes of congressional representation when they were treated as property rather than as people.

The delegates finally agreed to a compromise in which three-fifths of "all other persons" (that is, the enslaved) would be included in population counts as a basis for apportioning a state's congressional representatives. In a constitution intended to "secure the blessings of liberty to ourselves and our posterity," the three-fifths clause was a glaring example of compromise being divorced from principle. The corrupt bargain over slavery would bedevil the nation for the next seventy-five years.

By design, the original Constitution never mentions the word *slavery.* Instead, it speaks of "free persons" and "all other persons," and of persons "held to service of labor." The word *slavery* would not appear in the Constitution until the Thirteenth Amendment (1865) abolished it.

The three-fifths clause gave southern states disproportionate power in Congress by increasing the number of southern votes in the House

Charles Calvert and His Slave
(1761) In military regalia, the five-year-old descendant of Lord Baltimore, founder of Maryland, towers over his slave, who is dressed as a drummer boy.

of Representatives. This, in turn, increased southern influence in the Electoral College, since the number of each state's electors was to be the total of its senators and representatives.

It was thus no accident that in the nation's first sixteen presidential elections, between 1788 and 1848, a southern slaveholder would be elected twelve times. The pro-slavery nature of the Constitution prompted abolitionist William Lloyd Garrison to declare in the 1830s that the framers of the document had forged a "covenant with death and an agreement with hell."

THE ABSENCE OF WOMEN

The delegates at the Constitutional Convention dismissed any discussion of political rights for women. Yet not all women were willing to maintain their traditional subordinate role. Just as the experiences of the Revolutionary War led many African Americans to seize their freedom, some brave women demanded political equality for themselves.

Eliza Yonge Wilkinson, born in 1757 to a wealthy plantation family living on an island south of Charleston, South Carolina, lost her husband early in the war. In June 1780, after Wilkinson was assaulted and robbed by "inhuman" British soldiers, she became a fiery Patriot who "hated Tyranny in every shape." She assured a friend that "We may be *led*, but we never will be *driven!*"

Likewise, Wilkinson expected greater freedom for women after the war. "The men say we have no business [with politics]," she wrote to a friend. "I won't have it thought that because we are the weaker sex as to bodily strength, my dear, we are capable of nothing more than minding the dairy, visiting the poultry-house, and all such domestic concerns." Wilkinson demanded more. "They won't even allow us the liberty of thought, and that is all I want."

Judith Sargent Murray, a Massachusetts essayist, playwright, and poet, argued that the rights and liberties fought for by Patriots belonged not just to men but to women, too. In "On the Equality of the Sexes," published in 1790, she challenged the prevailing view that men had greater intellectual capacities than women. She insisted that any differences resulted from prejudice and discrimination that prevented women from having access to formal education and worldly experience.

The arguments for gender equality, however, fell mostly on deaf ears. At the Constitutional Convention in Philadelphia, there was no formal discussion of women's rights, nor does the Constitution even include the word *women*. Writing from Paris, Thomas Jefferson expressed the hope that American "ladies" would be "contented to soothe and calm the minds of their husbands returning ruffled from political debate."

IMMIGRATION Although America was a nation of immigrants, the Constitution said little about immigration and naturalization (the process of gaining citizenship), and most of what it said was negative. In Article II, Section 1, it prohibits any future immigrant from becoming president, limiting the office to a "born Citizen." On defining citizenship, the Constitution gives Congress the authority "to establish a uniform Rule of Naturalization" but offers no further guidance. As a result, naturalization policy has changed repeatedly over the years in response to fluctuating social attitudes, economic needs, and political moods.

In 1790, the first Congress under the new constitution would pass a naturalization law that allowed "free white persons" who had been in the United States for as few as two years to be made naturalized citizens. This meant that persons of African descent were denied citizenship; it was left to individual states to determine whether free blacks were citizens. Because Indians were not "free white persons," they were also treated as aliens. Not until 1924 would Native Americans be granted citizenship—by an act of Congress rather than a constitutional amendment.

On September 17, 1787, the Federal Convention reported that it had completed the new constitution. "Gentlemen," announced Benjamin Franklin, "you have a republic, if you can keep it."

THE FIGHT FOR RATIFICATION

The final draft of the Constitution was submitted to thirteen special state conventions for approval (ratification) on September 28, 1787. Over the next ten months, people from all walks of life, in taverns and coffeehouses, on street corners, around dinner tables, and in the nation's ninety-two newspapers, discussed and debated the new constitution's merits. As Alexander Hamilton noted, the debate would reveal whether the people could establish good government "by reflection and choice" rather than by "accident and force."

The outcome was by no means certain, but Hamilton said that during the four-month Constitutional Convention, "there has been an astonishing revolution for the better in the minds of the people" about the new frame of government.

CHOOSING SIDES   Advocates for the Constitution assumed the name *Federalists*; opponents became **anti-Federalists**. The two sides formed the seeds for America's first two-party political system.

In the prolonged debate, the Federalists, led by James Madison and Alexander Hamilton, had several advantages. First, they had a concrete proposal, the proposed constitution itself; their opponents had nothing to offer instead but criticism. Second, the Federalist leaders were, on average, ten to twelve years younger and more energetic than the anti-Federalists; many of them had been members of the Constitutional Convention and were familiar with the disputed issues in the document. Third, the Federalists were more unified and better organized.

The anti-Federalist leaders—Virginians Patrick Henry, George Mason, Richard Henry Lee, and future president James Monroe; George Clinton of New York; Samuel Adams, Elbridge Gerry, and Mercy Otis Warren of Massachusetts; Luther Martin and Samuel Chase of Maryland—were a diverse group. Some wanted to reject the Constitution and retain the Confederation. Others wanted to convene another convention and start over. Still others wanted to revise the proposed constitution.

Most anti-Federalists worried that the new national government would eventually grow corrupt and tyrannical. Mercy Otis Warren of Massachusetts, the most prominent woman then writing regular political commentary, compared the constitution to "shackles on our own necks." A Philadelphia writer denounced those who drafted the Constitution, as representing "the Aristocratic Party" intent upon creating a "monarchical" national government.

The anti-Federalists especially criticized the absence of a "bill of rights" in the proposed constitution to protect individuals and states from the growing power of the national government. Other than the bill of rights, however, the anti-Federalists had no comprehensive alternative to the Constitution except the admittedly flawed Articles of Confederation.

THE FEDERALIST   Among the supreme legacies of the long debate over the Constitution is what came to be called *The Federalist Papers*, a collection of eighty-five essays published in New York newspapers between 1787 and 1788. Written by James Madison, Alexander Hamilton, and John Jay, the essays defended the concept of a strong national government and outlined the major principles and assumptions embodied in the Constitution. Thomas Jefferson called *The Federalist Papers* the "best commentary on the principles of government which ever was written."

In the most famous of the *Federalist* essays, Number 10, Madison turned the conventional wisdom about republics on its head. From ancient times, it had been assumed that self-governing republics survived only if they were small and homogeneous. Patrick Henry argued that a single national government "could not reign over so extensive a country as this is, without absolute despotism."

Madison, however, argued that small republics usually fell victim to warring factions—well-organized interest groups pursuing their self-interest at the expense of the whole. In the United States, he explained, the size and diversity of the expanding nation would make it impossible for any single faction to form a dangerous majority that could dominate the federal government—or society at large. The contending factions would, in essence, cancel each other out. In addition, he argued that it was the responsibility of the Congress to regulate "these various and interfering interests." Madison and the other framers created a legal and political system designed to protect minorities from a tyranny of the majority.

Given a new federal government in which power was checked and balanced among the three branches, a large republic could work better than a small one to prevent factional tyranny. "Extend the [geographic] sphere," Madison wrote, "and you take in a greater variety of parties and interests; you make it less probable that a majority of the whole will have a common motive to invade the rights of other citizens."

THE STATES DECIDE   Several of the smaller states—Delaware, New Jersey, and Georgia—were among the first to ratify the Constitution. Massachusetts, still sharply divided in the aftermath of Shays's Rebellion, was the first state in which the outcome was close, approving the Constitution by 187 to 168 on February 6, 1788.

On June 21, 1788, New Hampshire became the ninth state to ratify the Constitution, thereby reaching the minimum number of states needed for approval. The Constitution, however, could hardly succeed without the approval of Virginia, the largest, wealthiest, and most populous state, or New York, which had the third-highest population and occupied a key position geographically. Both states included strong opposition groups who were eventually won over by the same pledge as had been made in Massachusetts—the addition of a bill of rights.

Upon notification that New Hampshire had become the ninth state to ratify the Constitution, the Confederation Congress chose New York City as the initial national capital and called for the new government to assume power in 1789. The Constitution was adopted, but the spirited resistance to it convinced the new Congress to propose the first ten constitutional amendments now known as the Bill of Rights.

After attending a parade celebrating ratification, Benjamin Rush, a Philadelphia physician, noted with satisfaction that "It is done. We have become a nation." Other celebrants shared the hope that the new government would last. "Our Constitution is in actual operation," Benjamin Franklin wrote to a friend in 1789. "Everything appears to promise that it will last; but in this world nothing is certain but death and taxes." George Washington was even more uncertain about the future, predicting that the Constitution would not "last for more than twenty years."

The Constitution has lasted much longer, of course, and in the process its adaptability has provided a model of resilient republican government. The Constitution was by no means perfect (after all, it has been amended twenty-seven times); it was a bundle of messy compromises and concessions that left many issues, the most important of which was slavery, undecided or ignored. Few of the Constitution's supporters liked it in its entirety, but most believed that it was the best frame of government obtainable and that it would continue to evolve and improve over time.

The Constitution confirmed that the United States would be the first *democratic republic*. The founders believed that they were creating a unique political system based on a "new science of politics" combining the best aspects of democracies and republics. In a democracy, the people rule; in a republic, officials elected by the people rule. At the Constitutional Convention, the delegates combined aspects of both approaches so that they balanced and regu-

New beginnings An engraving from the title page of *The Universal Asylum and Columbian Magazine* (published in Philadelphia in 1790). America is represented as a woman laying down her shield to engage in education, art, commerce, and agriculture.

RATIFICATION OF THE CONSTITUTION

ORDER OF RATIFICATION	STATE	DATE OF RATIFICATION
1	Delaware	December 7, 1787
2	Pennsylvania	December 12, 1787
3	New Jersey	December 18, 1787
4	Georgia	January 2, 1788
5	Connecticut	January 9, 1788
6	Massachusetts	February 6, 1788
7	Maryland	April 28, 1788
8	South Carolina	May 23, 1788
9	New Hampshire	June 21, 1788
10	Virginia	June 25, 1788
11	New York	July 26, 1788
12	North Carolina	November 21, 1789
13	Rhode Island	May 29, 1790

lated each other, and ensured that personal freedoms and the public welfare were both protected in the process.

THE FEDERALIST ERA

The Constitution was ratified because it promised to create a more powerful national government better capable of managing a rapidly growing new republic. Yet it was one thing to ratify a new constitution and quite another to make the new government run smoothly.

With each passing year, the United States witnessed growing debate over how to interpret and apply the provisions of the new constitution. During the 1790s, a decade called the "age of passion," the federal government would confront rebellions, states threatening to secede, international tensions, and foreign wars, as well as something left unmentioned in the Constitution: the formation of fiercely competing political parties—Federalists and Democratic Republicans, more commonly known as **Jeffersonian Republicans**, or simply as Republicans.

The two political parties came to represent very different visions for America. The Democratic Republicans were mostly southerners, like Virginians Thomas Jefferson and James Madison, who wanted the country to remain a rural nation of small farmers dedicated to republican values. The Democratic Republicans distrusted the national government, defended states' rights, preferred a "strict" interpretation of the Constitution, and placed their trust in the masses. "The will of the majority, the natural law of every society," Jefferson insisted, "is the only sure guardian of the rights of men."

The Federalists, led by Alexander Hamilton and John Adams, were clustered in New York and New England and embraced urban culture, industrial development, and commercial growth. Federalists distrusted the "passions" of the common people and advocated a strong national government and a flexible interpretation of the Constitution. As Hamilton stressed, "the people are turbulent and changing; they seldom judge or determine right."

THE FIRST PRESIDENT On March 4, 1789, the new Congress convened in New York City. A few weeks later, the presiding officer of the Senate certified that George Washington, with 69 Electoral College votes, was the nation's first president. John Adams of Massachusetts, with 34 votes, the second-highest number, became vice president. (At this time there were no candidates for the vice presidency; the candidate who came in second, regardless of party affiliation, became vice president.)

George Washington was a reluctant first president. He would have preferred to stay at Mount Vernon, his Virginia plantation, but agreed to serve because he had been "summoned by my country." Some complained that Washington's personality was too cold and aloof. Others thought he was unsophisticated, since he had little formal education and had never visited Europe. The acidic John Adams groused that Washington was "too illiterate, unlearned, [and] unread" to be president.

Washington had virtues that Adams lacked, however. As a French diplomat said, President Washington had "the soul, look, and figure of a hero in action." He was a soldier who had married a wealthy young widow and become a prosperous tobacco planter and land speculator. He brought to the presidency both a detached dignity and a remarkable capacity for leadership that helped keep the young republic from disintegrating. Although capable of angry outbursts, Washington was honest, honorable, and remarkably self-disciplined; he had extraordinary stamina and patience, integrity and resolve, courage and resilience. And he exercised sound judgment. He usually asked people for their views, weighed his options, and made a decision. Most of all, he was fearless. Few doubted that he was the best person to lead the new nation.

In his inaugural address, Washington appealed for unity, pleading with the new Congress to abandon "local prejudices" and "party animosities" to create the "national" outlook necessary for the fledgling republic to thrive. Within a few months, he would see his hopes dashed. Personal rivalries, sectional tensions, and political infighting would dominate life in the 1790s.

WASHINGTON'S CABINET During the summer of 1789, Congress created executive departments corresponding to those formed under the Confederation. To head the Department of State, President Washington named Thomas Jefferson, recently back from diplomatic duties in France. To lead the Department of the Treasury, Washington appointed Alexander Hamilton, who was widely read in matters of government finance.

Washington selected John Jay as the first chief justice of the Supreme Court. After serving as president of the Continental Congress in 1778–1779, Jay became the American minister (ambassador) to Spain. While in Europe, he helped John Adams and Benjamin Franklin negotiate the Treaty of Paris in 1783. After the Revolution, Jay served as secretary of foreign affairs. He joined Hamilton and James Madison as co-author of *The Federalist Papers* and became one of the most effective champions of the Constitution.

President Washington routinely called his chief staff members together to discuss matters of policy. This was the origin of the president's *cabinet*, an advisory body for which the Constitution made no formal provision. The office of vice president also took on what would become its typical character: "The Vice-Presidency," John Adams wrote his wife, Abigail, is the most "insignificant office . . . ever . . . contrived."

THE BILL OF RIGHTS To address concerns raised by opponents of the new federal government, James Madison, now a congressman from Virginia, presented to Congress in May 1789 a set of constitutional amendments intended to protect individual rights from excessive government power. As Thomas Jefferson explained, such a "bill of rights is what the people are entitled to against every government on earth, general or particular, and what no just government should refuse." After considerable debate, Congress approved twelve amendments in September 1789. By the end of 1791, the necessary three-fourths of the states had approved *ten* of the twelve proposed amendments, now known as the **Bill of Rights**.

The Bill of Rights provided safeguards for individual rights of speech, assembly, and the press; the right to own firearms; the right to refuse to house soldiers; protection against unreasonable searches and seizures; the right to refuse to testify against oneself; the right to a speedy public trial, with an attorney present, before an impartial jury; and protection against "cruel and unusual" punishments. The Tenth Amendment addressed the widespread demand that powers not delegated to the national government "are reserved to the States respectively, or to the people."

The amendments were written in broad language that seemed to exclude no one. In fact, however, they technically applied only to property-owning white males. Native Americans were entirely outside the constitutional system, an "alien people" in their own land. And, like the Constitution itself, the Bill of Rights gave no protections to enslaved Americans. Instead, they were governed by state "slave codes." They had no access to the legal system; they could not go to court, make contracts, or own property. Similar restrictions applied to women, who could not vote in most state and national elections. Equally important, the Bill of Rights had a built-in flaw: it did not protect citizens from states violating their civil rights.

RELIGIOUS FREEDOM The debates over the Constitution and the Bill of Rights generated a religious revolution as well as a political revolution. Unlike the New England Puritans whose colonial governments enforced their particular religious beliefs, the Christian men who drafted and amended the Constitution made no direct mention of God. They were determined to protect religious life from government interference and coercion.

In contrast to the monarchies of Europe, the United States would keep the institutions of church and government separate and allow people to choose their own religions ("freedom of conscience"). To that end, the First Amendment declared that "Congress shall make no law respecting an establishment of religion or prohibiting the free exercise thereof." This statement has since become one of the most important—and controversial—principles of American government.

The United States was virtually alone among nations in not designating a single "established" national religion funded by the government. France, Spain, and Italy were officially Catholic nations; Great Britain was Anglican. In addition, when the Bill of Rights was ratified, all but two states—New York and Virginia—still supported an official religion or maintained a religious requirement for holding political office. Dissenters (the members of other churches or nonbelievers) were tolerated but prohibited from voting or holding political office.

The First Amendment was intended to create a framework within which people of all religious persuasions could flourish. It prohibited the federal government from endorsing or supporting any individual denomination or interfering with the religious choices that people make. As Thomas Jefferson later explained, the First Amendment erected a "wall of separation between church and State."

HAMILTON'S VISION OF A CAPITALIST AMERICA

In 1776, the same year that Americans were declaring their independence, Adam Smith, a Scottish philosopher, published a revolutionary book titled *An Inquiry into the Nature and Causes of the Wealth of Nations*. It provided the first full description of a modern *capitalist* economy and its social benefits.

Like the American Revolution, *The Wealth of Nations* was a declaration of independence from Great Britain's mercantilist system. Under *mercantilism*, national governments had exercised tight controls over economic life. Smith argued that instead of controlling economic activity, governments should allow individuals and businesses to compete freely for profits in the marketplace. Doing so would unleash the energies of the capitalist spirit.

Alexander Hamilton greatly admired *The Wealth of Nations*, and he eagerly took charge of managing the nation's complicated financial affairs. More than any other American, he grasped both the complex issues of government finance and envisioned what America would become: the world's most prosperous capitalist nation.

Alexander Hamilton The powerful Secretary of the Treasury from 1789 to 1795.

Hamilton was a self-made aristocrat. Born out of wedlock in the West Indies, in 1755, he was deserted by his Scottish father and left an orphan at thirteen by the death of his mother. With the help of friends and relatives, he found his way, at age fifteen, to New Jersey before moving a year later to New York City. There he entered King's College (now Columbia University).

When the war with Britain erupted, Hamilton joined the Continental army as a captain at the age of nineteen. After he distinguished himself in the battles of Trenton and Princeton, Hamilton became one of General Washington's favorite aides.

After the war, Hamilton established a thriving legal practice in New York City (a fellow lawyer said he "surpassed all of us in his abilities"), married into a prominent family, and served as a member of the Confederation Congress.

As Treasury secretary, Hamilton believed that the federal government should encourage the hustling, bustling, creative spirit that distinguished Americans from other peoples. He became the foremost advocate for an "energetic government" promoting capitalist development. In contrast to Jefferson, the southern planter, Hamilton, the urban capitalist, believed that the United States was too dependent on agriculture for its economic well-being. He championed trade, banking, finance, investment, and manufacturing, as well as the bustling commercial cities, as the most essential elements of America's future.

HAMILTON'S ECONOMIC REFORMS The United States was born in debt. To fight the war for independence, it had borrowed heavily from the Dutch and the French. Now, after the war, it had to find a way to pay off the debts. Yet there was no national bank, no national currency, and very few mills and factories. In essence, the American republic was bankrupt. It fell to Alexander Hamilton to determine how the debts should be repaid and how the new national government could balance its budget.

Governments have four basic ways to pay their bills: impose taxes or fees on individuals and businesses, levy tariffs (taxes on imported goods), borrow money by selling interest-paying government bonds to investors, and, last but not least, print money.

Under Hamilton's leadership, the United States did all of these things—and more. To raise funds, Congress, with Hamilton's support, enacted tariffs of 5 to 10 percent on a wide variety of imported items. Tariffs were hotly debated for two reasons: 1) they were the source of most of the federal government's annual revenue, and, 2) tariffs also "protected" American manufacturers by taxing their foreign competitors, especially those in Britain.

By discriminating against imported goods, tariffs enabled American manufacturers to charge higher prices for their products sold in the United States. This, penalized consumers, particularly those in the southern states that were most dependent upon imported goods. In essence, tariffs benefited the nation's young manufacturing sector, most of which was in New England, at the expense of the agricultural sector, since farm produce was rarely imported. Tariff policy soon became an explosive political issue.

DEALING WITH DEBTS The levying of tariffs marked but one element in Alexander Hamilton's ambitious plan to put the new republic on a sound financial footing. In a series of brilliant reports submitted to Congress between January 1790 and December 1791, Hamilton outlined his vision for the economic development of the United States.

The first of two "Reports on Public Credit" dealt with how the federal government should refinance the massive debt that the states and the Confederation government had accumulated during the war for independence. Hamilton insisted that the debts be repaid. After all, he explained, a capitalist economy depends upon its integrity and reliability: debts being paid, contracts being enforced, and private property being protected.

By selling government bonds to pay the interest due on the huge war-related debts, Hamilton argued, the U.S. government would also give investors ("the monied interest") a direct stake in the success of the new national government. A well-managed federal debt, he claimed, would become a "national blessing" by giving investors at home and abroad confidence in the national economy and the integrity of the government.

Hamilton also insisted that the federal government pay ("assume") the state debts from the Revolutionary War because they were in fact a *national* responsibility; all Americans had benefited from the war for independence. "The debt of the United States," he stressed, "was the price of liberty."

SECTIONAL DIFFERENCES Hamilton's complicated financial proposals created a storm of controversy, in part because many people, then and since, did not understand their complexities. James Madison, who had been Hamilton's close ally in the fight for the new constitution, broke with him over the federal government "assuming" the states' debts.

Madison, then the most powerful member of the new Congress, was troubled that northern states owed far more debt than southern states. Four states (Virginia, North Carolina, Georgia, and Maryland) had already paid off most of their war debts.

Madison's opposition to Hamilton's debt-assumption plan ignited a vigorous debate in Congress. In April 1790, the House of Representatives voted down Hamilton's "assumption" plan, 32–29. Hamilton did not give up, however. After failing to get members of Congress to switch their votes, he hatched an ingenious scheme. In June 1790, Hamilton invited Jefferson and Madison to join him for dinner in New York City.

By the end of the evening, the three had reached a famous compromise. First, they agreed that the national capital should move from New York City to Philadelphia for the next ten years. Then, the capital would move to a new city to be built in a "federal district" on the Potomac River between Maryland and Virginia. Hamilton agreed to find the votes in Congress to approve the move in exchange for Madison pledging to find the votes needed to pass the debt-assumption plan.

The votes in Congress went as planned, and the federal government moved in late 1790 to Philadelphia. Ten years later, the capital was moved to the new city of Washington, in the federal District of Columbia.

Hamilton's debt-funding scheme proved a success. The new bonds issued by the federal government in 1790 were quickly snatched up by eager investors, thereby providing money to begin paying off the war debts while covering its operating expenses. In addition, Hamilton obtained new loans from European governments.

To raise additional government revenue, Hamilton convinced Congress to create an array of *excise* taxes—taxes on particular products, such as carriages, sugar, and salt. A 25 percent excise tax on liquor in 1791 would prove to be the most controversial of all, but the excise taxes generated much-needed revenue.

By 1794, the nation had a higher financial credit rating than all of Europe. By making the new nation financially solvent, Hamilton set in motion the greatest economic success story in world history.

A NATIONAL BANK Part of the opposition to Hamilton's debt-financing scheme grew out of opposition to Hamilton himself. The brash young Treasury secretary viewed himself as President Washington's prime minister. That his Department of Treasury had *forty* staff members while Thomas Jefferson's State Department had *five* employees demonstrated the priority that President Washington gave to the nation's financial situation.

Hamilton was on a mission to develop an urban-centered economy anchored in finance and manufacturing. After securing Congressional approval of his debt-funding scheme, he called for a national bank modeled after the powerful Bank of England. Such a bank, Hamilton believed, would enable much greater "commerce among individuals" and provide a safe place for the federal government's cash.

By their nature, Hamilton explained, banks were essential to a new nation that was short on gold and silver. Banks would increase the nation's money supply by issuing currency in amounts greater than their actual "reserve"— gold and silver coins and government bonds—in their vaults. By issuing loans and thereby increasing the amount of money circulating through the economy, banks served as, according to Hamilton, the engines of prosperity: "industry is increased, commodities are multiplied, agriculture and manufactures flourish, and herein consist the true wealth and prosperity" of a "genuine nation."

Hamilton's idea of a powerful national bank generated intense criticism. Once again, Madison and Jefferson led the opposition, arguing that, since the Constitution said nothing about creating a national bank, the government could not start one. Jefferson also believed that Hamilton's proposed bank would not help most Americans. Instead, it would enrich only a small inner circle of self-serving financiers and investors who would, over time, exercise corrupt control over Congress.

Hamilton, however, had the better of the argument in Congress. Representatives from the northern states voted 33–1 in favor of the national bank; southern congressmen opposed the bank 19–6. The lopsided vote illustrated the growing political division between the North and South in the young nation.

Before signing the bank bill, President Washington sought the advice of his cabinet, where he found an equal division of opinion. The result was the first great debate on constitutional interpretation. Were the powers of Congress only those *explicitly* stated in the Constitution, or were other powers *implied*? The argument turned chiefly on Article I, Section 8, which authorized Congress to "make all Laws which shall be necessary and proper for carrying into Execution the foregoing Powers."

Such language left lots of room for disagreement about what was "necessary and proper" and led to a savage confrontation between Jefferson and Hamilton. The Treasury secretary had come to view Jefferson as a man of "profound ambition & violent passions" who was guided by an "unsound & dangerous" agrarian economic philosophy.

Secretary of State Jefferson, who despised banks almost as much as he hated the "monarchist" Hamilton, pointed to the Tenth Amendment of the Constitution, which reserves to the states and the people powers not explicitly delegated to Congress. Jefferson argued that a bank might be a convenient aid to Congress in collecting taxes and regulating the currency, but it was not *necessary*, as Article I, Section 8, specified.

In a lengthy 16,000 word report to the president, Hamilton countered that the power to charter corporations was an "implied" power of any government. As he pointed out, the three banks already in existence had been chartered by states, none of whose constitutions specifically mentioned the authority to incorporate banks.

Hamilton convinced Washington to sign the bank bill. In doing so, the president had, in Jefferson's words, opened up "a boundless field of power," which in coming years would lead to a further broadening of the president's implied powers, with the approval of the Supreme Court.

The new **Bank of the United States (B.U.S.)**, based in Philadelphia, had three primary responsibilities: (1) to hold the government's funds and pay its bills; (2) to provide loans to the federal government and to other banks to promote economic development; and (3) to manage the nation's money supply by regulating the power of state-chartered banks to issue paper currency (called banknotes). The B.U.S. could issue national banknotes as needed to address the chronic shortage of gold and silver coins. By 1800, the B.U.S. had branches in four cities, and four more were soon added. The American financial system was on the verge of becoming the most effective in the world.

ENCOURAGING MANUFACTURING Hamilton's bold economic vision for the new republic was not yet complete. In the last of his celebrated recommendations to Congress, the "Report on Manufactures," distributed in December 1791, he set in place the capstone of his design for a modern capitalist economy: the active governmental promotion of new manufacturing and industrial enterprises (mills, mines, and factories). Industrialization,

Thomas Jefferson A 1791 portrait by Charles Willson Peale.

Hamilton believed, would bring diversification to an American economy dominated by agriculture and dangerously dependent on imported British goods; improve productivity through greater use of machinery; provide work for those not ordinarily employed outside the home, such as women and children; and encourage immigration of skilled industrial workers from other nations.

To foster industrial development, Hamilton recommended that the federal government increase tariffs on imports, three quarters of which came from Britain, while providing financial incentives (called bounties) to key industries making especially needed products such as wool, cotton cloth, and window glass. Such government support, he claimed, was needed to enable new industries to compete "on equal terms" with longstanding European enterprises. Finally, Hamilton asked Congress to fund major transportation improvements, including the development of roads, canals, and harbors for commercial traffic.

Few of Hamilton's pro-industry ideas were enacted because of strong opposition from Jefferson, Madison and other southerners. They did not believe the federal government should support particular industries. Hamilton's proposals, however, provided an arsenal of arguments for the advocates of manufacturing and federally-funded transportation projects (called "internal improvements") in years to come.

HAMILTON'S VISIONARY ACHIEVEMENTS The economic impact of Hamilton's leadership was monumental. During the 1790s, as the Treasury Department began to pay off the Revolutionary War debts, foreign capitalists and banks invested heavily in the booming American economy, and European nations as well as China began a growing trade with the United States. Economic growth, so elusive in the 1780s, blossomed at the end of the century, as the number of new businesses soared. A Bostonian reported that the nation had never "had a brighter sunshine of prosperity. . . . Our agricultural interest smiles, our commerce is blessed, our manufactures flourish."

All was not well, however. By championing the values and institutions of a bustling new capitalist system and the big cities and industries that went along with it, Hamilton upset many, especially in the agricultural South and along the western frontier. Thomas Jefferson and James Madison had grown increasingly concerned that Hamilton's urban-industrial economic program and his political deal-making were threatening American liberties. Hamilton recognized that his successes had led Jefferson and Madison to form a party "hostile to me" and one intent on making Jefferson the next president.

The political competition between Jefferson and Hamilton boiled over into a nasty personal feud. Both men were visionaries, but their visions of America's future could not have been more different. Hamilton saw Britain as the model for the kind of economy and society he wanted America to develop; Jefferson preferred France. They also had markedly different hopes for the nation's economic development.

Jefferson told President Washington that Hamilton's efforts to create a capitalist economy would "undermine and demolish the republic" and create "the most corrupt government on earth." Hamilton, he added, was "really a colossus [giant] to the anti-republican party." In turn, Hamilton called the agrarian Jefferson an "intriguing incendiary" who had circulated "unkind whispers" about the Treasury secretary in an effort to "stab me in the dark." He accused Jefferson of being an agrarian romantic who failed to see that manufacturing, industry, and banking would drive the economic future of the United States.

Jefferson's spirited opposition to Hamilton's politics and policies fractured Washington's cabinet. Jefferson wrote that he and Hamilton "daily pitted in the cabinet like two cocks [roosters]." President Washington, who detested political squabbling, begged them to stop smearing each other with "wounding suspicions and irritating charges" and urged them to rise above their "dissensions." But it was too late: they had become mortal enemies—as well as the leaders of the first loosely organized political parties, the Federalists and the Democratic Republicans.

FEDERALISTS AND DEMOCRATIC REPUBLICANS

The Federalists were centered in New York and New England. Generally, they feared the excesses of democracy, distrusted the "common people," and wanted a strong central government committed to economic growth, social stability, and national defense. What most worried the Federalists, as Alexander Hamilton said, was the "poison" of "democracy." The people, he stressed, are "turbulent and changing; they seldom judge or determine right [wisely]." By contrast, the Democratic Republicans, led by Thomas Jefferson and James Madison, were most concerned about threats to individual freedoms and states' rights posed by a strong national government.

In July 1789, chaotic violence erupted in France when masses of the working poor, enraged over soaring prices for bread and in part inspired by the American Revolution, revolted against the absolute monarchy of Louis XVI, sending shock waves across the monarchies of Europe.

The **French Revolution** captured the imagination of many Americans, especially Jefferson and the Republicans, as royal tyranny was displaced by a democratic republic that gave voting rights to all adult men regardless of how much property they owned. Americans formed Democratic-Republican societies that hosted rallies on behalf of the French Revolution and in support of local Republican candidates. During the 1790s, James Madison assumed leadership of Hamilton's Republican opponents in Congress.

FOREIGN AND DOMESTIC CRISES

During the fragile infancy of the new nation, George Washington was the only man able to rise above party differences and hold things together. In 1792, he was unanimously reelected to a second term. And he quickly found himself embroiled in the cascading consequences of the French Revolution, which had started in 1789. The turmoil in France threatened to draw the United States into a European war. In 1791, the monarchies of Prussia and Austria had invaded France to stop the revolutionary movement from infecting their absolutist societies. The foreign invaders, however, only inspired the French revolutionaries to greater efforts to use force to spread their ideal of democracy.

By early 1793, the most radical of the French revolutionaries, called *Jacobins*, had executed the king and queen as well as hundreds of aristocrats and priests. The Jacobins not only promoted democracy, religious toleration, and human rights, but they went well beyond the ideals of the American Revolution in supporting social, racial, and sexual equality. Then, on February 1, 1793, the French revolutionary government declared war on Great Britain, beginning a conflict that would last twenty-two years.

As the French republic plunged into warfare, the Revolution entered its worst phase, the so-called Reign of Terror. In 1793–1794, thousands of "counterrevolutionary" political prisoners and priests were executed, along with many revolutionary leaders. Barbarism ruled the streets of Paris and other major cities.

Secretary of State Thomas Jefferson, who loved French culture and democratic ideals, wholeheartedly endorsed the revolution as "the most sacred cause that ever man engaged in." By contrast, Alexander Hamilton and Vice

President John Adams saw the French Revolution as vicious and godless. Such conflicting attitudes over events in Europe transformed the first decade of American politics into one of the most fractious periods in the nation's history.

The European war against revolutionary France tested the ability of the United States to remain neutral in world affairs. Both France and Britain purchased goods from America, and each sought to stop the other from trading with the United States, even if it meant attacking U.S. merchant ships.

Federalists and Jeffersonian Republicans alike agreed that a naval war with either European power would devastate the American economy. As President Washington began his second term in 1793, he faced an awkward decision. By the 1778 Treaty of Alliance, the United States was a *perpetual* ally of France. Americans, however, wanted no part of the European war. They were determined to maintain their profitable trade with both sides, although almost 90 percent of U.S. imports came from Britain.

Hamilton and Jefferson agreed that entering the European conflict would be foolish. Where they differed was in how best to stay out of the war. Hamilton had a simple answer: declare the military alliance formed with the French during the American Revolution invalid because it had been made with a monarchy that no longer existed. Jefferson preferred to delay, and to use the alliance with France as a bargaining point with the British.

In the end, President Washington took a wise middle course. On April 22, 1793, he issued a neutrality proclamation that declared the United States "friendly and impartial toward the belligerent powers" and warned U.S. citizens that they might be prosecuted for "aiding or abetting hostilities" or taking part in other un-neutral acts. Instead of settling matters in his cabinet, however, Washington's neutrality proclamation brought to a boil the ugly feud between Jefferson and Hamilton.

CITIZEN GENÊT At the same time that President Washington issued the neutrality proclamation, he accepted Secretary of State Jefferson's argument that the United States should officially recognize the new French revolutionary government (becoming the first nation to do so) and welcome its ambassador to the United States, the cocky, twenty-nine-year-old Edmond-Charles Genêt.

Early in 1793, Citizen Genêt, as he became known, landed at Charleston, South Carolina, to a hero's welcome. He then openly violated U.S. neutrality by recruiting four American privateers (privately owned warships) to capture English and Spanish merchant vessels.

After five weeks in South Carolina, Genêt sailed to Philadelphia, where his reckless efforts to draw America into the war on France's side embarrassed his friends in the Republican party. When Genêt threatened to go around President Washington and appeal directly to the American people, even Thomas

Jefferson disavowed "the French monkey." In August 1793, Washington, at Hamilton's urging, demanded that the French government replace Genêt.

The growing excesses of the radicals in France were fast cooling U.S. support for the Revolution. Jefferson, however, was so disgusted by his feud with Alexander Hamilton and by Washington's refusal to support the French Revolution that he resigned as secretary of state at the end of 1793 and returned to his Virginia home, eager to be rid of the "hated occupation of politics."

Vice President Adams greeted Jefferson's departure by saying "good riddance." President Washington felt the same way. He never forgave Jefferson and Madison for organizing Democratic-Republican societies to oppose his Federalist policies. After accepting Jefferson's resignation, Washington never spoke to him again.

JAY'S TREATY During 1794, tensions between the United States and Great Britain threatened to renew warfare between the old enemies. The Treaty of Paris (1783) that ended the Revolutionary War had left the western and southern boundaries of the United States in dispute. In addition, in late 1793, British warships violated international law by seizing U.S. merchant ships that carried French goods or were sailing for a French port. By early 1794, several hundred American ships had been confiscated, and their crews were given the terrible choice of joining the British navy, a process called "impressment," or being imprisoned. At the same time, British troops in the Ohio Valley gave weapons to Indians, who in turn attacked American settlers.

On April 16, 1794, President Washington sent Chief Justice John Jay to London to settle the major issues between the two nations. Jay agreed to the British demand that America not sell products to France for the construction of warships. Britain also gained trading advantages with the United States while refusing to stop intercepting American merchant ships and "impressing" their sailors. Finally, Jay conceded that the British need not compensate U.S. citizens for the enslaved African Americans who had escaped to the safety of British forces during the Revolutionary War.

In return, Jay won three important promises from the British: they would evacuate their six forts in northwest America by 1796, reimburse Americans for the seizures of ships and cargo in 1793–1794, and grant U.S. merchants the right to trade again with the British West Indies.

When the terms of **Jay's Treaty** were disclosed, however, many Americans, especially Republicans, were outraged. In Massachusetts, people shouted "Damn John Jay! Damn everyone who won't damn John Jay!" The uproar created the most serious crisis of Washington's presidency. Some called for his impeachment. Yet the president, while admitting that the proposed agreement was imperfect, decided that it was the only way to avoid a war with Britain that the United States was bound to lose (the U.S. Army then had only 672 men, and there was no navy).

In the end, with Washington's strong support, Jay's Treaty barely won the necessary two-thirds majority in the Senate. Some 80 percent of the votes *for* the treaty came from New England or the middle Atlantic states; 74 percent of those voting *against* the treaty were southerners, most of them Jeffersonian Republicans.

FRONTIER TENSIONS Meanwhile, new conflicts erupted in the Ohio Valley between American settlers and Native Americans. In the fall of 1793, Revolutionary War hero General "Mad" Anthony Wayne led a military expedition into the Northwest Territory's "Indian Country." They marched north from Cincinnati, built Fort Greenville, in western Ohio, and soon went on the offensive in what became known as the Northwest Indian War, a conflict that arose after the British transferred the Ohio Country to the United States. The Native Americans living in the region insisted that the British had no right to give away their ancestral lands. As pioneers moved into the Northwest Territory, the various Indian nations formed the Western Confederacy to resist American settlement.

In August 1794, the Western Confederacy of some 2,000 Shawnee, Ottawa, Chippewa, Delaware, and Potawatomi warriors, supported by the British and reinforced by Canadian militiamen, engaged General Wayne's troops and Indian allies in the Battle of Fallen Timbers, along the Michigan-Ohio border. The Americans decisively defeated the Indians, destroyed their crops and villages, and built a line of forts in northern Ohio and Indiana, one of which became the city of Fort Wayne, Indiana. The Indians finally agreed to the Treaty of Greenville, signed in August 1795, by which the United States bought most of the territory that would form the state of Ohio and the cities of Detroit and Chicago.

THE WHISKEY REBELLION Soon after the Battle of Fallen Timbers, the Washington administration displayed another show of strength in the backcountry, this time against the so-called **Whiskey Rebellion**. Alexander Hamilton's 1791 federal tax on "distilled spirits" had ignited resentment and resistance throughout the western frontier. Liquor made from grain or fruit was the rural region's most valuable product; it even was used as a form of currency. When protesters' efforts to repeal the tax failed, many turned to violence and intimidation. Beginning in September 1791, angry groups of farmers, hunters, militiamen, and laborers—attacked federal tax collectors and marshals.

In the summer of 1794, the discontent exploded into open rebellion in western Pennsylvania, home to a fourth of the nation's whiskey stills. The

Whiskey Rebellion George Washington as commander in chief reviews the troops mobilized to quell the Whiskey Rebellion in Pennsylvania in 1794.

rebels threatened to assault nearby Pittsburgh, loot the homes of the rich, and set the town ablaze. After negotiations failed, a U.S. Supreme Court justice declared on August 4, 1794, that western Pennsylvania was in a "state of rebellion." It was the first great domestic challenge to the federal government since the Constitution was ratified, and George Washington responded decisively.

At the urging of Alexander Hamilton, Washington ordered the whiskey rebels to disperse by September 1 or he would send in the militia. When the rebels failed to respond, some 12,500 militiamen from several states began marching to western Pennsylvania to suppress the rebellion. President Washington donned his military uniform and rode on horseback to greet the soldiers. It was the first and last time that a sitting president would lead troops in the field.

The huge army, commanded by Virginia's governor, Henry "Lighthorse Harry" Lee, quickly panicked the whiskey rebels, who vanished into the hills. Two dozen were charged with high treason; two were sentenced to hang, only to be pardoned by President Washington.

The new federal government had made its point and showed its strength. The show of force led the rebels and their sympathizers to change their tactics.

Rather than openly defying federal laws, they voted for Republicans, who won heavily in the next Pennsylvania elections.

PINCKNEY'S TREATY While the turbulent events were unfolding in Pennsylvania, the Spanish began negotiations over control of the Mississippi River as well as the disputed northern boundary of their Florida colony, which they had acquired from the British at the end of the Revolutionary War. U.S. negotiator Thomas Pinckney pulled off a diplomatic triumph in 1795 when he convinced the Spanish to accept a southern American boundary at the 31st parallel in west Florida, along the northern coast of the Gulf of Mexico (the current boundary between Florida and Georgia). The Spanish also agreed to allow Americans to ship goods, grains, and livestock down the Mississippi River to Spanish-controlled New Orleans. Senate ratification of Pinckney's Treaty (also called the Treaty of San Lorenzo) came quickly, for westerners were eager to transport their crops to New Orleans.

WESTERN SETTLEMENT

The treaties signed by John Jay and Thomas Pinckney spurred a new wave of settlers into the western territories. Their lust for land aroused a raging debate in Congress over what the federal government should do with the vast areas it had acquired (or taken) from the British, the Spanish, and from Native Americans.

LAND POLICY Federalists and Republicans differed sharply on federal land policy. Federalists wanted the government to charge high prices for western lands to keep the East from losing both political influence and a labor force important to the growth of manufactures. They also preferred that government-owned lands be sold in large parcels to speculators, rather than in small plots to settlers. Thomas Jefferson and James Madison were reluctantly prepared to go along with such land policies for the sake of reducing the national debt, but Jefferson preferred that government-owned land be sold to farmers.

For the time being, however, the Federalists prevailed. With the Land Act of 1796, Congress doubled the price of federal land (public domain) to $2 per acre. Half the townships would be sold in 640-acre sections, making the minimum cost $1,280, a price well beyond the means of ordinary settlers. By 1800, federal land offices had sold fewer than 50,000 acres. Criticism of the land policies led to the Land Act of 1800, which reduced the minimum parcel to 320 acres and spread payments over four years. Thus, with a down payment of $160, one could buy a farm.

THE WILDERNESS ROAD The lure of western lands led thousands of settlers to follow pathfinder Daniel Boone into the territory known as Kentucky, or Kaintuck, from the Cherokee name KEN-TA-KE (Great Meadow). In the late eighteenth century, the Indian-held lands in Kentucky were a farmer's dream and a hunter's paradise. The vast area boasted fertile soil; bluegrass meadows; abundant forests; and countless buffalo, deer, and wild turkeys.

Born on a small farm in 1734 in central Pennsylvania, Boone was a dead-eye marksman by the age of twelve who became an experienced farmer and an accomplished woodsman. After hearing numerous reports about the fertile lands over the Appalachian Mountains, he set out in 1769 to find a trail into Kentucky. He discovered what was called the Warriors' Path, a narrow foot trail along the steep ridges.

In 1773, Boone led a group of white settlers into Kentucky. Two years later, he and thirty woodsmen used axes to widen the 208-mile-long Warriors' Path into what became known as the Wilderness Road, a rough passageway that more than 300,000 settlers would use over the next twenty-five years. At a point where a branch of the Wilderness Road intersected with the Kentucky River, near what is now Lexington, Boone built the settlement of Boonesborough, one of the first American communities west of the Appalachian Mountains. In 1780, Kentucky was divided into three counties and integrated into the state of Virginia. In 1792, it became a separate state.

Daniel Boone Escorting Settlers through the Cumberland Gap Painting by George Caleb Bingham.

In the process of settling Kentucky, Boone became one of America's first folk heroes, a larger-than-life figure known as the "Columbus of the Woods." As he admitted, however, "many heroic actions and chivalrous adventures are related of me which exist only in the regions of fancy. With me the world has taken great liberties, and yet I have been but a common man."

A steady stream of settlers, mostly Scots-Irish migrants from Pennsylvania, Virginia, and North Carolina, poured into Kentucky during the last quarter of the eighteenth century. The pioneers came on foot or horseback, often leading a mule or a cow that carried their tools and other possessions. Near a creek or spring they would buy a parcel or stake out a claim and mark its boundaries by chopping notches into "witness trees." They would then build a lean-to for temporary shelter and clear the land for planting. The larger trees—those that could not be felled with an ax—were girdled: a cut would be made around the trunk, and the tree would be left to die. Because clearing trees often took years, a farmer had to hoe and plant a field filled with stumps.

The pioneers grew melons, beans, turnips, and other vegetables, but corn was the preferred crop because it kept well and had so many uses. Ears were roasted and eaten on the cob, and kernels were ground into meal for making mush, hominy grits, and hoecakes, or johnnycakes (dry flour cakes, suitable for travelers, that were originally called *journeycakes*). Pigs provided pork, and cows supplied milk, butter, and cheese. Many frontier families also built crude stills to manufacture a potent whiskey they called *corn likker.*

TRANSFER OF POWER

In 1796, President Washington decided that two terms in office were enough. Weary of the increasingly bitter criticism directed at him, he was eager to retire to his plantation at Mount Vernon. He would leave behind a formidable record of achievement: the organization of a new national government, a prosperous economy, the recovery of territory from Britain and Spain, a stable northwestern frontier, and the admission of three new states: Vermont (1791), Kentucky (1792), and Tennessee (1796).

WASHINGTON'S FAREWELL On September 17, 1796, Washington delivered a farewell address in which he criticized the rising spirit of political partisanship and the emergence of political parties. They endangered the republic, he felt, because they pursued the narrow interests of minorities rather than the good of the nation. In foreign relations, Washington advised, the United States should stay away from Europe's quarrels by avoiding "permanent alliances with any portion of the foreign world." His warning against permanent foreign entanglements would serve as a fundamental principle in U.S. foreign policy until the early twentieth century.

THE ELECTION OF 1796 With Washington out of the race, the United States had its first contested election for president. The Federalist "caucus," a group of leading congressmen, chose Vice President John Adams as their presidential candidate. Thomas Pinckney of South Carolina, fresh from his diplomatic triumph in Spain, also ran as a Federalist presidential candidate. As expected, the Republicans chose Thomas Jefferson. Aaron Burr, a young New York attorney and senator who was distrusted by many and disliked by most, also ran as a Republican.

The campaign of 1796 was mean and nasty. The Federalists were attacked for unpopular taxes, excessive spending, and abuses of power. Republicans called the pudgy John Adams "His Rotundity" and labeled him a monarchist because he loved the symbols of power and despised "the people." (Adams wanted people to refer to the president as "His Highness.") Federalists countered that Jefferson was a French-loving atheist eager for another war with Great Britain, and charged that he was not decisive enough to be president. Adams won the election with 71 electoral votes, but in an odd twist, Jefferson, who received 68 electoral votes, became vice president. The Federalists won control of both houses of Congress.

THE ADAMS ADMINISTRATION

Vain and prickly, opinionated and stubborn, John Adams had long lusted for the presidency, but he was a much better political theorist than he was a political leader. An independent thinker with a proud, combative spirit and volcanic temper, he fought as often with his fellow Federalists as he did with his Republican opponents. Benjamin Franklin said Adams was "always an honest man, often a wise one, but sometimes . . . absolutely out of his senses."

John Adams Political philosopher and politician, Adams was the first president to take up residence in the new White House, in the new national capital of Washington, D.C., in 1801.

Adams had crafted a distinguished career as a Massachusetts lawyer, and as a leader in the Revolutionary movement. Widely recognized as the hardest-working member of the Continental Congress, he had also authored the Massachusetts state constitution. During the Revolution, Adams had served as an exceptional diplomat in France, Holland, and Great Britain, and he had been George Washington's vice president.

In contrast to the tall, lanky Jefferson, the short, stocky Adams feared democracy and despised equality, both of which he believed, must be kept within bounds by wise leaders. He once referred to ordinary Americans as making up the "common herd of mankind." Adams was also haunted by a feeling that he was never properly appreciated—and he may have been right. Yet on the overriding issue of his presidency, war and peace, he kept his head when others about him were losing theirs—probably at the cost of his reelection.

THE WAR WITH FRANCE As America's second president, John Adams inherited a "Quasi War" with France, a by-product of the angry French reaction to Jay's Treaty between the United States and Great Britain. The navies of both nations were capturing U.S. ships headed for the other's ports. By the time of Adams's inauguration, in 1797, the French had plundered some 300 American vessels and broken diplomatic relations with the United States.

Adams sought to ease tensions by sending three prominent Americans to Paris to negotiate a settlement. When the U.S. diplomats arrived, however, they were accosted by three French officials (labeled X, Y, and Z by Adams in his report to Congress) who announced that negotiations could begin only if the United States paid a bribe of $250,000 and loaned France $12 million.

Conflict with France A cartoon indicating the anti-French sentiment generated by the XYZ Affair. The three American negotiators (at left) reject the Paris Monster's demand for bribery money before discussions could begin.

Such bribes were common in the eighteenth century, but the answer from the American side was "no, no, not a sixpence." When the so-called **XYZ Affair** became public, American hostility toward France soared. Many Republicans—with the exception of Vice President Thomas Jefferson—joined with Federalists in calling for war. Federalists in Congress voted to triple the size of the army and to construct warships. By the end of 1798, French and American ships were engaged in an undeclared naval war in the Caribbean Sea.

THE WAR AT HOME   The naval conflict with France sparked an intense debate between Federalists eager for a formal declaration of war and Republicans sympathetic to France. Amid the superheated emotions, Vice President Jefferson observed that a "wall of separation" had come to divide the nation's political leaders. He told a French official that President Adams was "a vain, irritable, stubborn" man.

For his part, Adams had tried to take the high ground. Soon after his election, he had invited Jefferson to join him in creating a bipartisan administration. Jefferson refused, saying that he would not be a part of the cabinet but instead would only preside over the Senate as vice president, as the Constitution specified. Within a year, he and Adams were at each other's throats. Adams regretted losing Jefferson as a friend but "felt obliged to look upon him as a man whose mind is warped by prejudice." Jefferson, he claimed, had become "a child and the dupe" of the Republican faction in Congress led by James Madison.

Jefferson and other Republicans were convinced that the real purpose of the French crisis was to provide Federalists with an excuse to quiet their American critics. The **Alien and Sedition Acts** (1798) seemed to confirm the Republicans' suspicions. These partisan acts, passed amid a wave of patriotic war fervor, gave the president extraordinary powers to violate civil liberties in an effort to stamp out criticism of the administration. They limited freedom of speech and of the press, as well as the liberty of "aliens" (immigrants who had not yet gained citizenship). Adams's support of the Alien and Sedition Acts ("war measures") would prove to be the greatest mistake of his presidency.

Three of the four Alien and Sedition Acts reflected hostility to French and Irish immigrants, many of whom had become militant Republicans in America. The Naturalization Act lengthened from five to fourteen years the residency requirement for U.S. citizenship. The Alien Act empowered the president to deport "dangerous" aliens, and the Alien Enemies Act authorized the president in wartime to expel or imprison enemy aliens at will. Finally, the

Sedition Act outlawed writing, publishing, or speaking anything of "a false, scandalous and malicious" nature against the government or any of its officers.

Of the ten people convicted under the Sedition Act, all were Republicans, including newspaper editors. To offset the "reign of witches" unleashed by the Alien and Sedition Acts, Jefferson and Madison drafted the Kentucky and Virginia Resolutions, passed by the legislatures of those two states in late 1798. The resolutions denounced the Alien and Sedition Acts as "alarming infractions" of constitutional rights and put forth the shocking idea that state legislatures should "nullify" (reject and ignore) acts of Congress that violated the constitutional guarantee of free speech. In attacking the Alien and Sedition Acts, Jefferson was suggesting something more dangerous: disunion.

While Adams and Jefferson were waging their war of words, the president was seeking peace with France. In 1799, he dispatched another team of diplomats to negotiate with a new French government under First Consul Napoléon Bonaparte, whose army had overthrown the republic. In a treaty called the Convention of 1800, the Americans won the best terms they could. They dropped their demands to be repaid for the ships taken by the French, and the French agreed to end the military alliance with the United States dating back to the Revolutionary War. The Senate quickly ratified the agreement, which became effective on December 21, 1801.

REPUBLICAN VICTORY IN 1800 The furor over the Alien and Sedition Acts influenced the pivotal presidential election of 1800. The Federalists nominated Adams, even though many of them continued to snipe at him and his policies, especially his refusal to declare war against France. Alexander Hamilton publicly questioned Adams's fitness to be president, citing his "disgusting egotism."

Thomas Jefferson and Aaron Burr, the Republican candidates, once again represented the alliance of the two most powerful states, Virginia and New York. The Federalists claimed that Jefferson's election would bring civil war and anarchy to America. His supporters portrayed him as a passionate idealist and optimist who was a friend of farmers and a courageous champion of states' rights, a limited federal government, and personal liberty.

In the important **election of 1800**, Jefferson and Burr, the two Republicans, emerged with 73 electoral votes each. Federalist John Adams received only 65. The tie vote in the Electoral College sent the election into the House of Representatives (a constitutional defect corrected in 1804 by the Twelfth Amendment). It took thirty-six ballots for the House of Representatives to choose Jefferson as the new president. The three months between the House vote for president and Thomas Jefferson's inauguration in March 1801 were so tense that people talked openly of civil war.

Before the Federalists turned over power on March 4, 1801, President Adams and Congress passed the Judiciary Act of 1801. It was intended to ensure Federalist control of the judicial system by creating sixteen federal circuit courts, with a new judge for each. It also reduced the number of Supreme Court justices from six to five in an effort to deprive the next president of appointing a new member. Before he left office, Adams appointed Federalists to all the new positions. The Federalists, quipped Jefferson, had "retired into the judiciary as a stronghold." They never again would exercise significant political power.

A NEW ERA   The election of 1800 did not resolve the fundamental political tensions that had emerged between ardent nationalists like Adams and Hamilton and those like Jefferson and Madison who clung to ideals of states' rights and an agriculture-based economy. In fact, the 1800 election further

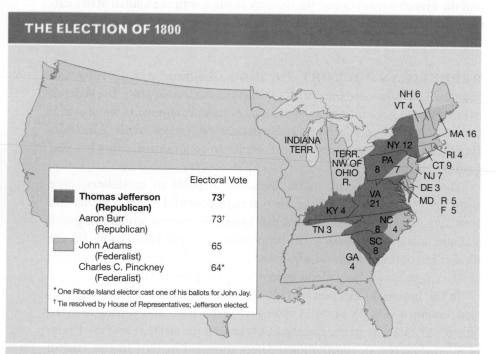

THE ELECTION OF 1800

Electoral Vote	
Thomas Jefferson (Republican)	73†
Aaron Burr (Republican)	73†
John Adams (Federalist)	65
Charles C. Pinckney (Federalist)	64*

*One Rhode Island elector cast one of his ballots for John Jay.

†Tie resolved by House of Representatives; Jefferson elected.

- Why was the election of 1800 a key event in American history?
- What voting patterns emerged in the election of 1800?
- How did Congress break the tie between Thomas Jefferson and Aaron Burr?

divided the young republic into warring political factions and marked a major turning point in the nation's history. It was the first time that one political party had relinquished presidential power to the opposition party, and it was the only election that pitted a sitting president (Adams) against his own vice president (Jefferson).

Jefferson's hard-fought victory signaled the emergence of a new, more democratic political culture dominated by bitterly divided parties and wider public participation. Before and immediately after independence, people took a keen interest in public affairs, but socially prominent families, the "rich, the able, and the wellborn," still dominated political life. However, the raging political battles of the late 1790s, culminating in 1800 with Jefferson's election, established the right of "common" men to play a more active role in governing the young republic. With the gradual elimination of the requirement that citizens must own property to vote, the electorate expanded enormously in the early nineteenth century.

Jefferson called his election the "Revolution of 1800," for it marked the triumph of the Republican party and the slaveholding South at the expense of the New England Federalists. Three Virginia Republican slaveholders—Jefferson, James Madison, and James Monroe—would hold the presidency for the next twenty-four years.

A bitter John Adams refused to participate in Jefferson's inauguration in the new federal capital in Washington, D.C. Instead, unnoticed and unappreciated, Adams boarded a stagecoach for the 500-mile trip to his home in Massachusetts. He and Jefferson would not communicate for the next twelve years. As Adams returned to work on his Massachusetts farm, he told his eldest son, John Quincy, who would become the nation's sixth president, that anyone governing the United States "has a hard, laborious, and unhappy life." The victorious Jefferson would soon feel the same way.

CHAPTER REVIEW

SUMMARY

- **Confederation Government**   Despite its many weaknesses, the government created by the *Articles of Confederation* managed to construct important alliances during the Revolutionary War, help win the War of Independence, and negotiate the Treaty of Paris (1783). It created executive departments and established, through the *Northwest Ordinance,* the process by which new western territories would be organized and governments formed before they applied for statehood. Yet the Articles of Confederation did not allow the national government to raise taxes to fund its debts. *Shays's Rebellion* made many Americans fear that such uprisings would eventually destroy the new republic unless the United States formed a stronger national government.

- **Constitutional Convention**   Delegates gathered at the convention in Philadelphia in 1787 to revise the existing government, but almost immediately they decided to scrap the Articles of Confederation and start over. An entirely new document emerged, which created a system called *federalism* in which a strong national government with clear *separation of powers* among executive, legislative, and judicial branches functioned alongside state governments with clearly designated responsibilities. Arguments about how best to ensure that the rights of individual states were protected and also that "the people" were represented in the new Congress were resolved by establishing a Senate, with equal representation for each state, and a House of Representatives, the number of whose delegates was determined by population counts.

- **Ratification of the Constitution**   Ratification of the Constitution was hotly contested. *Anti-Federalists,* such as Virginia's Patrick Henry, opposed the new structure of government because the absence of a bill of rights would lead to a loss of individual and states' rights. To sway New York State toward ratification, Alexander Hamilton, James Madison, and John Jay wrote *The Federalist Papers.* Ratification became possible only when Federalists promised to add a *Bill of Rights.*

- **Federalists versus Republicans**   Alexander Hamilton and the Federalists wanted to create a diverse economy in which agriculture was balanced by trade, finance, and manufacturing. Hamilton crafted a federal budget that funded the national debt through tariff and tax revenues, and he created a national bank, the first *Bank of the United States.* Thomas Jefferson and others, known as the *Jeffersonian Republicans,* worried that Hamilton's plans violated the Constitution and made the federal government too powerful. They envisioned a nation dominated by farmers and planters where the rights of states would be protected against federal power.

- **Trouble Abroad**   With the outbreak of war throughout much of Europe during the *French Revolution,* George Washington's policy of neutrality violated the terms of the 1778 treaty with France. At the same time, Americans sharply criticized *Jay's Treaty* with the British for giving too much away. French warships began seizing British and American ships and an undeclared war was under way. Federalists supported

Washington's approach, while Republicans were more supportive of France. During the presidency of John Adams, the United States fought an undeclared naval war with the French, which led to the controversial *Alien and Sedition Acts* of 1798.

CHRONOLOGY

1781	Articles of Confederation take effect
1783	Treaty of Paris ends the war for independence
1786–1787	Shays's Rebellion
1787	Northwest Ordinance
	The Constitutional Convention is held in Philadelphia
1787–1788	*The Federalist Papers* are published
1789	President George Washington is inaugurated
1791	Bill of Rights is ratified
	Bank of the United States is created
1793	Washington issues a proclamation of neutrality
1794	Jay's Treaty is negotiated with England
	Whiskey Rebellion in Pennsylvania
	U.S. Army defeats Indians in the Battle of Fallen Timbers
1795	Treaty of Greenville
	Pinckney's Treaty is negotiated with Spain
1796	John Adams is elected president
1798	Alien and Sedition Acts are passed
1800	Thomas Jefferson is elected president

KEY TERMS

federalism p. 201

Articles of Confederation p. 201

Northwest Ordinance (1787) p. 203

Shays's Rebellion (1786–1787) p. 207

separation of powers p. 210

anti-Federalists p. 216

The Federalist Papers p. 216

Jeffersonian Republicans p. 219

Bill of Rights (1791) p. 221

Bank of the United States (B.U.S.) (1791) p. 227

French Revolution p. 230

Jay's Treaty (1794) p. 232

Whiskey Rebellion p. 233

XYZ Affair p. 240

Alien and Sedition Acts (1798) p. 240

election of 1800 p. 241

INQUIZITIVE

Go to InQuizitive to see what you've learned—and learn what you've missed—with personalized feedback along the way.

7 The Early Republic

1800–1815

We Owe Allegiance to No Crown (ca. 1814) The War of 1812 generated a renewed spirit of nationalism, inspiring Philadelphia sign-painter John Archibald Woodside to create this patriotic painting.

W hen President Thomas Jefferson took office in early 1801, the United States and its western territories reached from the Atlantic Ocean to the Mississippi River. The nation remained primarily rural and agricultural. Nine of ten Americans lived or worked on the land, with most of them growing enough food and raising enough livestock to feed their families but rarely producing enough to sell outside the community, much less overseas.

That changed during the nineteenth century. With each passing year, more and more farmers began to produce surplus crops and livestock to sell in regional and world markets. Such *commercial agriculture* was especially evident in the South, where skyrocketing European demand for cotton caused prices to soar.

At the end of the Revolutionary War, George Washington predicted that Americans would move westward across the mountains into the Ohio Valley "faster than any other ever did, or any one would imagine." By 1840, more than 40 percent of the population lived west of the Appalachian Mountains, in eight new states. "The woods are full of new settlers," marveled a traveler in 1805. "Axes were resounding, and the trees literally were falling about us as we passed."

Thomas Jefferson described the United States in the early nineteenth century as an "empire of liberty" spreading westward. In 1800, people eager to own their own farms bought 67,000 acres of government-owned land; the next year they bought 498,000 acres. Native Americans fiercely resisted the invasion of their ancestral lands but ultimately succumbed to a federal government (and army) determined to relocate them.

Most whites, however, were less concerned about taking land owned by Indians and Hispanics than they were about seizing their own economic

focus questions

1. What were the major domestic political developments that took place during Thomas Jefferson's administration?

2. How did foreign events impact the United States during the Jefferson and Madison administrations?

3. What were the primary causes of the American decision to declare war on Great Britain in 1812?

4. What were the significant outcomes of the War of 1812 on the United States?

opportunities. Isaac Weld, a British visitor, remarked that the Americans were a "restless people, always on the lookout for something better or more profitable." Restless mobility and impatient striving soon came to define the American way of life.

JEFFERSONIAN REPUBLICANISM

On March 4, 1801, fifty-seven-year-old Thomas Jefferson was inaugurated without incident, leading some people to call his fiercely contested election "the peaceful revolution." It was the first democratic election in modern history that saw the orderly transfer of power from one political party to another.

Jefferson's installation marked a long period of domination of the nation's political life by Republicans—and Virginians. Virginia, the nation's most populous state, supplied a quarter of the Republican congressmen in the House of Representatives that convened in early 1801.

THE "PEOPLE'S PRESIDENT"   During his inauguration, Jefferson emphasized his connection to the "common" people. Instead of wearing a ceremonial sword and riding in an elegant horse-drawn carriage, as George Washington and John Adams had done at their inaugurations, Jefferson, a widower, walked to the Capitol building, escorted by members of Congress and Virginia militiamen. He read his inaugural address in a "femininely soft," high-pitched voice, then took the presidential oath administered by Chief Justice John Marshall, his Virginia cousin, with whom he shared a cordial hatred.

Jefferson's deliberate display of **republican simplicity** set the tone for his administration. He wanted Americans to notice the difference between the monarchical trappings of the Federalists and the down-to-earth simplicity and frugality of the Republicans. As president, he did not wear fancy clothes or host elegant parties. Jefferson often answered the door of the President's House himself, wearing a robe and slippers. (He did, however, order "a handsome chariot for both city and country use.")

In his eloquent inaugural address, Jefferson, his red hair now streaked with grey, imagined America as "a rising nation, spread over a wide and fruitful land, traversing all the seas with the productions of their industry, engaged in commerce with nations" across the globe. Although determined to overturn many Federalist policies and programs, he urged Americans to work together. "We are all Republicans—we are all Federalists," Jefferson stressed, noting that "every difference of opinion is not a difference of principle."

It was a splendid message, but Jefferson's appeal for a united nation proved illusory, in part because he retained his own fierce partisanship and bitter anti-

Federalist prejudices. In a letter to a British friend, Jefferson described the Federalists as "insane" men: "Their leaders are a hospital of incurables."

A MORE DEMOCRATIC AMERICA The inauguration of Thomas Jefferson ushered in a period in which intense party loyalties and broader participation made for a more democratic and often raucous political culture.

During and after the Revolutionary War, an increasing proportion of white males, especially small farmers and wage laborers, artisans, mechanics, and apprentices, gained the right to vote or hold office as states reduced or eliminated requirements that voters and candidates own a specified dollar amount of property. Benjamin Latrobe, Jefferson's favorite architect, observed that after the Constitution was ratified in 1788, "the extension of the right of suffrage [voting] in the States to a majority of all the adult male citizens, planted a germ which [has] gradually evolved and has spread actual and practical democracy and political equality over the whole union."

An enlarged and more engaged citizenry of white male voters, many of them landless and illiterate, however, was not universally welcomed. "Since the war," a Massachusetts Federalist complained, "blustering ignorant men . . . have been attempting to push themselves into office." A Virginian was greatly worried by the rising evidence of the "turbulence and follies of democracy." South Carolina steadfastly resisted efforts to shift political power away from the slaveholding planter elite to the working poor.

Many among the founding generation of political leaders, especially Federalists but some Republicans as well, became openly anti-democratic, worried that men of humble origins, some of whom were uneducated and illiterate, were replacing the social and political elite ("natural aristocracy") in the state legislatures.

As the nineteenth century unfolded, voters were not content to be governed solely by "their betters"; they wanted to do the governing themselves. George Cabot, a Boston Federalist, called unchecked democracy *the government of the worst.* He was convinced that Jefferson was going to unleash "the terrible evils of democracy." When the "pot boils," another Federalist noted, the "scum will rise." By 1806, Federalist former president John Adams so detested the democratic forces transforming politics and social life that he despaired for the nation's future: "Oh my Country," he moaned, "how I mourn over . . . thy contempt of Wisdom and Virtue and overweening admiration of fools and knaves! the never failing effects of *democracy!*"

A CONTRADICTORY GENIUS Thomas Jefferson, who owned hundreds of slaves, was a bundle of contradictions and inconsistencies. He mirrored the young republic's mix of virtues, flaws, failures, and compromises by being progressive and enlightened in some areas, self-serving and hypocritical in others.

The idealistic Jefferson, who had written in the Declaration of Independence that "all men are created equal," bought, bred, branded, whipped, and sold slaves while calling slavery "an abominable crime" and "unremitting despotism." Yet he never sought to free his slaves for the simple reason that he was too dependent on their forced labor. "We have the wolf by the ear," he confessed, "and we can neither hold him nor safely let him go."

Jefferson was also a man of expensive tastes who repeatedly condemned national indebtedness while deepening his own indebtedness. Although he celebrated the ideal of republican simplicity, he actually lived in an elegant Virginia mansion where he indulged expensive tastes in food, wine, books, artwork, silverware, and furnishings—all of which eventually bankrupted him.

As president, Jefferson, the foremost defender of states' rights and the greatest critic of executive power, would display his peculiarly divided nature by exercising extraordinary presidential authority in negotiating the Louisiana Purchase and in enforcing a nationwide embargo shutting off all trade with warring Europe. Such inconsistencies led Federalists in the Massachusetts legislature to put Jefferson on trial for hypocrisy in 1805.

JEFFERSON IN OFFICE In Jefferson's cabinet, the leading figures were his best friend, Virginia neighbor, and political ally, Secretary of State

The Capitol building This 1806 watercolor was painted by the building's architect, Benjamin Henry Latrobe, and inscribed to Thomas Jefferson. A prominent dome would be added later, after the building was damaged in the War of 1812.

James Madison, and Secretary of the Treasury Albert Gallatin, a Pennsylvania Republican congressman whose financial skills had won him the respect of Federalists and Republicans alike.

In filling lesser offices, however, Jefferson often succumbed to pressure from the Republicans to remove Federalists, only to discover that there were few qualified candidates to replace some of them. When Gallatin asked if he might appoint women to some posts, Jefferson revealed the limits of his liberalism: "The appointment of a woman to office is an innovation for which the public is not prepared, nor am I."

MARBURY V. MADISON In one area—the federal judiciary—the new president decided to remove most of the offices altogether, in part because the court system was the only branch of the government still controlled by Federalists. In 1802, at Jefferson's urging, the Republican-controlled Congress repealed the Judiciary Act of 1801, which the Federalists had passed just before the transfer of power to the Jeffersonian Republicans. The Judiciary Act was intended to ensure Federalist control of the judicial system by creating sixteen federal circuit courts and appointing—for life—a new Federalist judge for each. Jefferson's controversial effort to repeal the judgeships sparked the pathbreaking case of *Marbury v. Madison* (1803).

The case involved the appointment of Virginia Federalist William Marbury as a federal justice of the peace in the District of Columbia. Marbury's letter of appointment, or commission, signed by President Adams just two days before he left office, was still undelivered when Madison took office as secretary of state, and President Jefferson told him to withhold it. Marbury then filed suit to force Madison to deliver his commission.

The case went to the Supreme Court, which was presided over by Chief Justice John Marshall, a gifted Virginia Federalist. Blessed with a keen intellect and an analytical mind, Marshall was a fierce critic and lifelong enemy of Thomas Jefferson, whom he considered a war-shirking aristocrat posing as a democrat.

In the unanimous *Marbury v. Madison* ruling, Marshall and the Court held that Marbury deserved to be awarded his judgeship. Then, however, Marshall denied that the Court had jurisdiction in the case. The Federal Judiciary Act of 1789, which gave the Court authority in such proceedings, was unconstitutional, Marshall ruled, because the Constitution specified that the Court should have original jurisdiction only in cases involving foreign ambassadors or nations. The Court, therefore, could issue no order in the case.

With one bold stroke, Marshall had elevated the stature of the Court by reprimanding Jefferson while avoiding an awkward confrontation with an administration that might have defied his order. More important, the ruling subtly struck down a federal law, the Judiciary Act of 1789, on the grounds that it violated provisions of the Constitution, the "fundamental and paramount law of the nation." Marshall stressed that the Supreme Court was "emphatically" empowered "to say what the law is," even if it meant overruling both Congress and the president.

The *Marbury* decision granted to the Supreme Court a power not mentioned in the Constitution: the right of what came to be called *judicial review*, or deciding whether acts of Congress (and the presidency) are constitutional. Marshall established that the Supreme Court was the final authority in all constitutional interpretations.

President Jefferson fumed over what he called Marshall's "irregular" ruling. Giving judges "the right to decide which laws are constitutional, and what not," he wrote Abigail Adams, "would make the judiciary a despotic branch."

Jefferson, however, would lose that argument. Although the Court did not declare another federal law unconstitutional for fifty-four years, it has since struck down more than 150 acts of Congress and more than 1,100 "unconstitutional" acts of state legislatures, all in an effort to protect individual liberties and civil rights.

JEFFERSON'S ECONOMIC POLICIES   Although John Marshall got the better of Thomas Jefferson in court, the president's first term did include a series of triumphs. Surprisingly, he did not dismantle Alexander Hamilton's Federalist economic program, despite his harsh criticism of it. Instead, following the advice of Treasury secretary Albert Gallatin, Jefferson learned to accept the national bank as essential to economic growth. He did, however, reject Hamilton's argument that a federal debt was a national "blessing." If the debt were not eliminated, Jefferson told Gallatin, "we shall be committed to the English career of debt, corruption, and rottenness, closing with revolution."

To pay down the government debt, Jefferson slashed the federal budget. In his first message to Congress in 1801, he criticized the national government as being "too complicated, too expensive." He fired all federal tax collectors and cut the military budget in half, saying that state militias and small navy gunboats provided the nation with adequate protection against foreign enemies. Jefferson's was the first national government in history to *reduce* its own scope and power.

Jefferson also repealed the whiskey tax that Hamilton and George Washington had implemented in 1791. In doing so, he admitted that he had a peculiar affection for the "men from the Western side of the mountains"—grain farmers and backwoods distillers for whom whiskey was often the primary source of income. The prosperous economy helped the federal budget absorb the loss of the whiskey taxes. In addition, revenues from federal tariffs on imports rose with rising European trade, and the sale of government-owned western lands soared as Americans streamed westward. Ohio's admission to the Union in 1803 increased the number of states to seventeen.

ENDING THE SLAVE TRADE While shrinking the federal budget, Jefferson in 1807 signed a landmark bill that outlawed the importation of enslaved Africans, in part because southerners had come to believe that African-born slaves were more prone to revolt. The new law took effect on January 1, 1808, the earliest date possible under the Constitution. At the time, South Carolina was the only state that still permitted the purchase of enslaved Africans. For years to come, however, illegal traffic in African slaves would continue; as many as 300,000 were smuggled into the United States between 1808 and 1861.

THE BARBARY PIRATES Upon assuming the presidency, Jefferson promised "peace, commerce, and honest friendship with all nations," but some

Burning of the Frigate Philadelphia Lieutenant William Decatur set fire to the captured *Philadelphia* during the United States' standoff with Tripoli over the enslavement of American sailors in north Africa.

nations preferred war. On the Barbary Coast of North Africa, the Islamic rulers of Morocco, Algiers, Tunis, and Tripoli had for years engaged in piracy and extortion, preying upon unarmed European and American merchant ships. After the Revolution, they captured American vessels and enslaved the crews. The U.S. government made numerous blackmail payments to these **Barbary pirates** in exchange for captured American ships and crew.

In 1801, however, the ruler (pasha) of Tripoli upped his blackmail demands and declared war on the United States. Jefferson sent warships to blockade Tripoli. "Nothing will stop these pirates," he wrote, "but the presence of an armed force."

A sporadic naval war dragged on until 1805, punctuated in 1804 by the notable exploit of Lieutenant Stephen Decatur, who slipped into Tripoli Harbor by night and set fire to the frigate *Philadelphia,* which had been captured after it ran aground. The Tripoli ruler finally settled for a $60,000 ransom and released the *Philadelphia*'s crew. It was still blackmail (called "tribute" in the nineteenth century), but less than the $300,000 the pirates had demanded and much less than the cost of war.

WESTERN EXPANSION

Thomas Jefferson often looked to the West for inspiration. Only by expanding westward, he believed, could America avoid becoming overcrowded along the Atlantic coast. Westward expansion, however, meant invading areas long inhabited by Native Americans—and the Spanish and French.

THE LOUISIANA PURCHASE In 1801, American diplomats in Europe heard rumors that Spain had been forced to transfer its huge Louisiana province to its domineering ally, France, now led by the brilliant Napoléon Bonaparte. Short of stature but a giant on the battlefield, Napoléon was a war-loving military genius who had become the most feared ruler in the world, the conqueror of Egypt and Italy. After taking control of the French government, the ambitious Napoléon set out to restore his country's North American empire (Canada and Louisiana) that had been lost to Great Britain in 1763.

President Jefferson referred to Napoléon as "a gigantic force" threatening the future of the United States. A weak Spain in control of the territory west of the Mississippi River could have been tolerated, Jefferson explained, but Napoleonic France in control of the Mississippi Valley would lead to "eternal friction" and eventually war with the United States.

Concerned that France might seize control of the Mississippi River, Jefferson sent New Yorker Robert R. Livingston to Paris in 1801 as ambassador to

France. The president told Livingston that his primary objective should be to acquire the strategic city of New Orleans, which was situated along the banks of the Mississippi, the magisterial river that begins in northern Minnesota and flows 2,552 miles south to the Gulf of Mexico.

Jefferson told Livingston that purchasing New Orleans and West Florida (the territory along the Gulf coast from Pensacola to New Orleans) was of absolute importance, not only to control all the rivers flowing into the Gulf of Mexico but also to defend America from invasion. "The day that France takes possession of New Orleans . . . we must marry ourselves to the British fleet and nation" for protection. Louisiana under "the scoundrel" Napoléon's control, he warned, would become "a point of eternal friction with us."

In early 1803, Jefferson grew so concerned about the stalled negotiations over New Orleans that he sent James Monroe, his trusted friend and Virginia neighbor, to assist Livingston in Paris. No sooner had Monroe arrived than the French made a startling proposal: the United States could buy not just New Orleans but *all* of the immense Louisiana Territory, from the Mississippi River west to the Rocky Mountains and from the Canadian border south to the Gulf of Mexico.

The unpredictable Napoléon had decided to sell the Louisiana Territory because his army on the Caribbean island of Saint-Domingue (Haiti) had been decimated by epidemics of malaria and yellow fever and by a massive slave revolt led by Touissant L'Ouverture, who proclaimed the Republic of Haiti. It was the first successful slave rebellion in history, and it panicked slaveholders in the southern states who feared that news of the revolt would spread to America.

Napoléon had tried to regain control of Saint-Domingue because it was a phenomenally profitable source of coffee and sugar. He also had hoped to connect New Orleans and Haiti as a first step in expanding France's North American trading empire. But after losing more than 50,000 soldiers to disease and warfare, Napoléon decided to cut his losses by selling the Louisiana Territory to the United States and using the proceeds to finance his "inevitable" next war with Great Britain.

By the Treaty of Cession, dated May 2, 1803, the United States agreed to pay $15 million for the entire Louisiana Territory. When Livingston and Monroe asked Charles-Maurice de Talleyrand, Napoléon's negotiator, about the precise extent of the territory they were buying, the Frenchman replied: "I can give you no direction. You have made a noble bargain for yourselves. I suppose you will make the most of it." A delighted Livingston, the U.S. negotiator, said that "from this day the United States take their place among the powers of the first rank."

The arrival of the signed treaty in Washington, D.C., presented Jefferson, who for years had harshly criticized the Federalists for stretching the meaning of the Constitution, with a frustrating political dilemma. Nowhere did the Constitution mention the purchase of territory. Was such an action even legal? Jefferson admitted that the purchase was "not authorized by the Constitution," but in the end, his desire to double the size of the American republic trumped his concerns about an unconstitutional exercise of executive power.

Acquiring the Louisiana territory, the president explained, would serve "the immediate interests of our Western citizens" and promote "the peace and security of the nation in general" by removing French control and creating a protective buffer separating the United States from the rest of the world.

Jefferson also imagined that the region might be a place to relocate Indian nations or freed slaves, since he feared a multiracial society. Besides, Jefferson and his Republican supporters argued, if the nation waited to pass a constitutional amendment to enable the acquisition, Napoléon might change his mind.

New England Federalists opposed the purchase. They feared that adding a vast new empire in the West would weaken New England and the Federalist party, since the new states were likely to vote Republican. They also cringed at the prospect that the new territories would likely be settled by southern slaveholders who were Jeffersonian Republicans. As a newspaper editorialized, "Will [Jefferson and the] Republicans, who glory in their sacred regard to the rights of human nature, purchase an *immense wilderness* for the purpose of cultivating it with the labor of slaves?"

In a reversal of traditional stances, Federalists found themselves arguing for strict construction of the Constitution in opposing the Louisiana Purchase. In the end, Jefferson and the Republicans brushed aside Federalist criticism and their own constitutional reservations.

Eager to close the deal, Jefferson called a special session of Congress on October 17, 1803, at which the Senate ratified the treaty with the French by an overwhelming vote of 26–6. On December 20, 1803, U.S. officials took formal possession of the sprawling Louisiana Territory. The Indians living there were not consulted.

The purchase included 875,000 square miles of land (529,402,880 acres). Six states in their entirety, and most or part of nine more, would eventually be carved out of the **Louisiana Purchase**, from Louisiana north to Minnesota and west to Montana.

The Louisiana Purchase was the most significant event of Jefferson's presidency and one of the most important developments in American history. It spurred western exploration and expansion, and especially enticed cotton growers to settle in the Old Southwest—Alabama, Mississippi, and Louisiana. Andrew Jackson, a slaveholding planter in Tennessee, congratulated Jefferson on acquiring the Louisiana Territory: "Every face wears a smile, and every heart leaps with joy."

LEWIS AND CLARK To learn more about the Louisiana Territory's geography, plants, and animals, Jefferson appointed two army officers, Virginians Meriwether Lewis and William Clark, to lead what came to be known as the **Lewis and Clark expedition**. The twenty-nine-year-old Lewis was Jefferson's private secretary whom the president admired for his "boldness, enterprise, and discretion." Clark, it was said, was "a youth of solid and promising parts, and as brave as Caesar."

On a rainy May morning in 1804, Lewis and Clark's "Corps of Discovery," numbering nearly fifty men, set out from a small village near the former French town of St. Louis in several large canoes (called *pirogues*) and one large flat-bottomed keelboat filled with food, weapons, medicine, and gifts to share with Indians. They traveled up the Missouri River through some of the most rugged wilderness in North America. Six months later, near the Mandan Sioux villages in what would become North Dakota, the Corps of Discovery built Fort Mandan and wintered in relative comfort, sending downriver a barge loaded with maps, soil samples, and live creatures such as the prairie dog and the magpie, previously unknown in America.

In the spring of 1805, the Corps of Discovery added two guides: a French fur trader and his remarkable wife, a young Shoshone woman named Sacagawea. In appreciation for Lewis and Clark's help in delivering her baby, Sacagawea provided crucial assistance as a guide, translator, and negotiator as they explored the Upper Missouri and encountered various Native Americans, most of whom were "hospitable, honest, and sincere people."

The explorers crossed the Rocky Mountains on foot and on horseback and used canoes to descend the Snake and Columbia Rivers to the Pacific Ocean, where they arrived in November 1805. Near the future site of Astoria, Oregon, at the mouth of the Columbia River, they built Fort Clatsop, where they spent a cold, rainy winter. The following spring they headed back, having been forced to eat their dogs and horses, and having weathered blizzards, broiling sun, fierce rapids, raging grizzly bears, numerous injuries and illnesses, and swarms of mosquitoes.

The expedition returned to St. Louis in 1806, having been gone nearly 28 months and covered some 8,000 miles. Lewis and Clark brought back extensive journals describing their experiences and observations while

EXPLORATIONS OF THE LOUISIANA PURCHASE, 1804–1807

- How did the United States acquire the Louisiana Purchase?
- What was the mission of Lewis and Clark's expedition?
- What were the consequences of Lewis and Clark's widely circulated reports about the western territory?

detailing some 180 plants and 125 animals. Their maps attracted traders and trappers to the region and led the United States to claim the Oregon Country by right of discovery and exploration.

POLITICAL SCHEMES The Lewis and Clark expedition and the Louisiana Purchase strengthened Jefferson's already solid support in the South and West. In New England, however, Federalists panicked because they assumed that new states carved out of the Louisiana Territory would be dominated by

Jeffersonian Republicans. To protect their interests, Federalists hatched a complicated scheme to link New York politically to New England by trying to elect Vice President Aaron Burr, Jefferson's ambitious rival, as governor of New York. Burr chose to drop his Republican affiliation and run for governor as an independent candidate.

Several prominent Federalists opposed the scheme, however. Alexander Hamilton urged Federalists not to vote for Burr, calling him "a dangerous man, and one who ought not to be trusted with the reins of government."

Burr ended up losing the election to the Republican candidate, who had been endorsed by Jefferson. A furious Burr blamed Hamilton for his defeat and challenged him to a duel. At dawn on July 11, 1804, the two met near Weehawken, New Jersey. Hamilton fired first but intentionally missed as a demonstration of his religious and moral principles. Burr showed no such scruples. He shot Hamilton in the hip; the bullet ripped through his liver and lodged in his spine. He died the next day. Burr, who was still the vice president, was charged with murder by New Jersey authorities. He fled to South Carolina, where his daughter lived, hoping to ride out the storm.

Sacagawea Of the many memorials devoted to Sacagawea, this statue by artist Alice Cooper was unveiled at the 1905 Lewis and Clark Centennial Exposition.

JEFFERSON REELECTED   In the meantime, the presidential campaign of 1804 began. A congressional caucus of Republicans renominated Jefferson and chose George Clinton of New York as the vice presidential candidate. To avoid the problems associated with parties running multiple candidates for the presidency, in 1803 Congress had ratified the Twelfth Amendment to the

Constitution, stipulating that the members of the Electoral College must use separate ballots to vote for the president and vice president.

Given Jefferson's first-term achievements, the Federalist candidates, South Carolinian Charles C. Pinckney and New Yorker Rufus King, never had a chance, for Jefferson had accomplished much: the Louisiana Purchase, a prosperous economy, and a reduced federal government budget and national debt. Jefferson and Clinton won 162 of 176 electoral votes, carrying every state but Delaware and Connecticut.

DIVISIONS IN THE REPUBLICAN PARTY Jefferson's landslide victory, however, created problems within his own party. Freed from strong opposition—Federalists made up only a quarter of the new Congress in 1805—the Republican majority began to divide into two warring factions, one calling itself the Jeffersonian or Nationalist Republicans, and the other, the anti-Jeffersonian pro-British southern Republicans, choosing the name Old Republicans.

Fiery Virginian John Randolph was initially a loyal Jeffersonian, but over time he emerged as the most colorful of the radically conservative "Old Republicans"—a group formed mostly of southern agrarian political purists for whom protecting states' rights was more important than the need for a strong national government. As the imperious Randolph admitted, "I am an aristocrat. I love liberty. I hate equality." Old Republicans opposed any compromise with the Federalists, any expansion of federal authority at the expense of states' rights or a strict interpretation of the Constitution, any new taxes or tariffs, and any change in the nation's agrarian way of life.

The Jeffersonian Republicans, on the other hand, were more moderate, pragmatic, and nationalistic. They were willing to compromise their states' rights principles to maintain national tariffs on imports and preserve a national bank, and to stretch the "implied powers" of the Constitution to accommodate the Louisiana Purchase.

WAR IN EUROPE

In the spring of 1803, soon after completing the sale of Louisiana to America, Napoléon Bonaparte declared war on Great Britain. The massive conflict would last eleven years and eventually involve all of Europe. Most Americans wanted to remain neutral, but the British and French were determined to keep that from happening.

NAVAL HARASSMENT During 1805, the war in Europe reached a stalemate. The French army controlled most of Europe, and the British navy dominated the seas. In May 1806, Britain issued a series of declarations called Orders in Council, which imposed a naval blockade of the entire European coast to prevent merchant ships from other nations, including the United States, from making port in France.

Soon, British warships began seizing American merchant ships bound for France. An angry Congress responded by passing the Non-Importation Act, which banned the importation of British goods. In early 1807, Napoléon announced that French warships would blockade the ports of Great Britain. The British responded that they

Preparation for War to Defend Commerce Shipbuilders, like those pictured here constructing the *Philadelphia*, played an important role in America's early wars.

would no longer allow any foreign ships to trade with the French-controlled islands in the Caribbean. Soon thereafter, British warships appeared along the American coast, stopping and searching U.S. merchant vessels as they headed for the Caribbean or Europe.

The tense situation posed a terrible dilemma for American shippers. If they agreed to British demands to stop trading with the French, the French would retaliate by seizing U.S. vessels headed to and from Great Britain. If they agreed to French demands that they stop trading with the British, the British would seize American ships headed to and from France. Lured by high profits, many American merchants decided to risk becoming victims of the Anglo-French war. During 1807, hundreds of American ships and their cargoes were seized by British and French warships. For American sailors, the danger on the high seas was heightened by the practice of impressment, whereby British warships stopped U.S. vessels, boarded them, and kidnapped sailors they claimed were British citizens. Between 1803 and 1811, some 6,200 American sailors were "impressed" into the British navy.

THE *CHESAPEAKE* INCIDENT (1807) The crisis boiled over on June 22, 1807, when the British warship HMS *Leopard* stopped a smaller

U.S. vessel, the *Chesapeake*, eight miles off the Virginia coast. After the *Chesapeake*'s captain refused to allow the British to search his ship for English deserters, the *Leopard* opened fire without warning, killing three Americans and wounding eighteen. A British search party then boarded the *Chesapeake* and seized four men, one of whom, an English deserter, was hanged.

The attack on the *Chesapeake* was both an act of war and a national insult. The *Washington Federalist* screamed: "We have never, on any occasion, witnessed . . . such a thirst for revenge." In early July, Jefferson demanded an apology from Britain, banned all British warships from American waters, and called on state governors to mobilize their militias.

Like John Adams before him, however, Jefferson resisted war fever, in part because the undersized American army and navy were not prepared to fight. His caution infuriated his critics. Federalist congressman Josiah Quincy of Massachusetts called Jefferson a "dish of skim milk curdling at the head of our nation."

THE EMBARGO   President Jefferson decided on a strategy of "peaceable coercion" to force Britain and France to stop violating American rights. Late in 1807, he somehow convinced enough Republicans in Congress to cut off *all* American foreign trade. As Jefferson said, his choices were "war, embargo, or nothing."

The unprecedented **Embargo Act** (December 1807) stopped all exports of American goods—wheat, flour, pork, fish, and cattle, among other items—by prohibiting U.S. ships from sailing to foreign ports. Despite Treasury Secretary Albert Gallatin's strenuous objections, all trade with foreign nations was banned.

Jefferson and his secretary of state, James Madison, assumed that the embargo would quickly force the warring European nations to quit violating American rights. They were wrong. Neither Britain nor France yielded.

With each passing month, the embargo devastated the Republicans and the economy while reviving the political appeal of the Federalists, especially in New England, where merchants howled because the embargo cut off their primary industry: oceangoing commerce. The value of U.S. exports plummeted. Shipbuilding declined by two-thirds, and prices for exported farm crops were cut in half. New England's once-thriving port cities became ghost towns.

Americans raged at what critics called "Jefferson's embargo." A Bostonian accused the president of being "one of the greatest tyrants in the whole world." Another letter writer told the president that he had paid four friends "to shoot you if you don't take off the embargo."

The embargo turned American politics upside down. To enforce it, Jefferson, the nation's leading spokesman for *reducing* the power of the federal government, now found himself *expanding* federal power into every aspect of the nation's economic life. In effect, the United States used its own warships to blockade its own ports. Jefferson even activated the New York state militia in an effort to stop smuggling across the Canadian border.

Congress finally rebuked the president by voting 70–0 to end the ill-conceived embargo effective March 4, 1809, the day that the "splendid misery" of Jefferson's second presidential term ended. The dejected president left the White House and retired "to my family, my books, and my farms" in Virginia. No one, he said, could be more relieved "on shaking off the shackles of power."

Jefferson learned a hard lesson that many of his successors would also confront: a second term is rarely as successful as the first. As Jefferson admitted, "No man will ever carry out of that office [the presidency] the reputation which carried him into it."

In the election of 1808, the presidency passed to another prominent Virginian, Secretary of State James Madison. The Federalists, again backing Charles C. Pinckney of South Carolina and Rufus King of New York, won only 47 electoral votes to Madison's 122.

JAMES MADISON AND THE DRIFT TO WAR   In his inaugural address, President Madison confessed that he inherited a situation "full of difficulties." He soon made a bad situation worse. Although Madison had been a talented legislator and the "Father of the Constitution," he proved to be a weak, indecisive chief executive.

From the beginning, Madison's presidency was entangled in foreign affairs and crippled by his lack of executive experience. Like Jefferson, Madison and his advisers repeatedly overestimated the young republic's diplomatic leverage and military strength in shaping foreign policy. The result was international humiliation.

Madison insisted on upholding the principle of freedom of the seas for the United States and other neutral nations, but he was unwilling to create a navy strong enough to enforce it. He continued the policy of "peaceable coercion" against the European nations, which was as ineffective for Madison as it had been for Jefferson.

In place of the failed embargo, Congress passed the Non-Intercourse Act (1809), which reopened trade with all countries *except* France and Great Britain and their colonies. It also authorized the president to reopen trade with either France or Great Britain if it stopped violating American rights on the high seas.

In December 1810, France issued a vague promise to restore America's neutral rights, whereupon Madison gave Great Britain three months to do the same. The British refused, and the Royal Navy continued to seize American vessels and their cargoes and crews.

A reluctant Madison asked Congress to declare war against Great Britain on June 1, 1812. If the United States did not defend its rights as a neutral nation, he explained, then Americans were "not independent people, but colonists and vassals."

On June 5, the House of Representatives voted for war 79–49. Two weeks later, the Senate followed suit, 19–13. Every Federalist in Congress opposed what they called "Mr. Madison's War," while 80 percent of Republicans supported it. The southern and western states wanted war; the New England states opposed it.

By declaring war, Republicans hoped to unite the nation, discredit the Federalists, and put an end to British-led Indian attacks along the Great Lakes and in the Ohio Valley by conquering British Canada. To generate popular support, Thomas Jefferson advised Madison that he needed, above all, "to stop Indian barbarities. The conquest of Canada will do this." Jefferson presumed that the French Canadians were eager to rise up against their British rulers. With their help, the Republicans predicted, American invaders would easily conquer Britain's vast northern colony. It did not work out that way.

THE WAR OF 1812

The **War of 1812** marked the first time that Congress had declared war. Great Britain did not expect or want the war; it was preoccupied with defeating Napoléon in Europe. In fact, on June 16, 1812, the British government promised to quit interfering with American shipping. President Madison and the Republicans were not satisfied; only war, they believed, would put an end to the British practice of impressment and stop British-inspired Indian attacks along the western frontier.

SHIPPING RIGHTS AND NATIONAL HONOR Why the United States chose to declare war is a puzzle. One explanation is that many Americans in the South and West, especially Tennessee and Kentucky, believed the nation's *honor* was at stake.

Southerners often compared the British practice of impressing American sailors to slavery. John Campbell, a Virginia legislator, explained that "war has been declared to save the nation from slavery & disgrace & the sword of vengeance will now drink the blood of those who have been seeking our downfall."

NATIVE AMERICAN CONFLICTS Another factor leading to war was the growing number of Indian attacks, supported by the British, in the Ohio Valley. The story took a new turn with the rise of two remarkable

Shawnee leaders, Tecumseh and his brother, Tenskwatawa, who lived in a large Shawnee village called Prophetstown on the Tippecanoe River in northern Indiana.

Tecumseh ("Shooting Star") knew that the fate of the native peoples depended on their being unified. He hoped to create a single Indian nation powerful enough, with British assistance, to fend off further American expansion. His half brother Tenskwatawa (the "Open Door"), a one-eyed recovering alcoholic with a fierce temper who was known as "the Prophet," gained a large following among Native Americans for his predictions that white Americans ("children of the devil") were on the verge of collapse.

From Prophetstown, Tecumseh tried in 1811 to form alliances with a host of other Native American nations. "The whites have driven us from the sea to the lakes," he declared. "We can go no further." Tecumseh disavowed the many treaties in which indigenous peoples had "sold" ancient Indian lands.

Tecumseh The Shawnee leader, who tried to unite Native American peoples across the United States in defense of their lands, was later killed in 1813 at the Battle of the Thames.

"No tribe," he declared, "has the right to sell [land], even to each other, much less to strangers. . . . Sell a country!? Why not sell the air, the great sea, as well as the earth? Didn't the Great Spirit make them all for the use of his children?"

William Henry Harrison, governor of the Indiana Territory, learned of Tecumseh's bold plans, met with him twice, and described him as "one of those uncommon geniuses who spring up occasionally to produce revolutions and overturn the established order of things."

Yet Harrison vowed to eliminate Tecumseh. In the fall of 1811, he gathered 1,000 troops and advanced on Prophetstown while the Indian leader was away. Tenskwatawa was lured into making a foolish attack on Harrison's encampment. What became the Battle of Tippecanoe was a disastrous defeat for the Native Americans, as Harrison's troops burned the village and destroyed its supplies. **Tecumseh's Indian Confederacy** went up in smoke, and he fled to Canada.

THE LUST FOR CANADA AND FLORIDA Some Americans wanted war with Great Britain in 1812 because they wanted to seize control of Canada, not only as a means of expanding American territory and eliminating the British presence there, but also as a way to control the fur trade. That there were nearly 8 million Americans in 1812 and only 300,000 Canadians led many to believe that conquering Canada would be quick and easy.

The British were also vulnerable far to the south. East Florida, which the British had returned to Spain's control in 1783, posed a threat to the Americans because Spain was too weak (or unwilling) to prevent Indian attacks across the border with Georgia. Also, in the absence of a strong Spanish presence, British agents and traders remained in East Florida, smuggling goods and conspiring with Indians against Americans. Spanish Florida had also long been a haven for runaway slaves from Georgia and South Carolina. Many Americans living along the Florida-Georgia border hoped that war would enable them to oust the British and the Spanish from Florida.

WAR FEVER In the Congress that assembled in late 1811, new young representatives from southern and western districts shouted for war to defend "national honor" and rid the Northwest of the "Indian problem." Among the "war hawks" were Henry Clay of Kentucky and John C. Calhoun of South Carolina. Clay, the brash young Speaker of the House of Representatives, boasted that the Kentucky militia alone could conquer Canada, and his bravado inspired others. "I don't like Henry Clay," Calhoun said. "He is a bad man, an imposter, a creator of wicked schemes. I wouldn't speak to him, but, by God, I love him" for wanting war against Britain. When Calhoun learned that President Madison had finally decided on war, he threw his arms around Clay's neck and led his war-hawk colleagues in an Indian war dance.

In New England and much of New York, however, there was little enthusiasm for war. It threatened to cripple the region's dominant industry, shipping, since Great Britain remained the region's largest trading partner. Some Federalists tried to undermine the war effort. Both Massachusetts and Connecticut refused to send soldiers to fight in the war, and merchants openly sold supplies to British troops in Canada.

WAR PREPARATIONS As it turned out, the United States was woefully unprepared for war, both financially and militarily, and the short, soft-spoken James Madison lacked the leadership ability and physical stature to inspire public confidence and military resolve. He was no George Washington.

The national economy was weak, too. In 1811, Republicans had foolishly let the charter of the Bank of the United States expire. Many Republican congressmen owned shares in state banks and wanted the B.U.S. dissolved because it both competed with and regulated their local banks. Once the B.U.S. shut down, however, the number of unregulated state banks mushroomed, all with their own forms of currency, creating commercial chaos. Treasury Secretary Albert Gallatin was so upset that he wrote a scathing letter of resignation. President Madison begged him to reconsider, which he did, but the problems of waging a war with Britain without adequate financial resources did not go away.

Once war began, the British navy blockaded American ports, which caused federal tariff revenues to tumble. In March 1813, Gallatin warned Madison that the U.S. Treasury had "hardly enough money to last till the end of the month." Furthermore, Republicans in Congress were so afraid of public criticism that they delayed approving tax increases needed to finance the war.

The military situation was almost as bad. In 1812, the British had 250,000 professional soldiers and the most powerful navy in the world. By contrast, the U.S. Army numbered only 3,287 ill-trained and poorly equipped men, led by mostly incompetent officers with little combat experience. In January 1812, Congress authorized an army of 35,000 men, but a year later, just 18,500 had been recruited—many of them Irish American immigrants who hated the English and then only by enticing them with promises of land and cash bounties.

President Madison, who refused to allow free blacks or slaves to serve in the army, was forced to plead with the state governors to provide militiamen, only to have the Federalist governors in anti-war New England decline. The British, on the other hand, had thousands of soldiers stationed in Canada and the West Indies. The U.S. Navy was in better shape than the Army, with able officers and well-trained seamen, but it had only sixteen tiny gunboats compared to Britain's 600 warships. The lopsided military strength of the British led Madison to mutter that the United States was in "an embarrassing situation."

A CONTINENTAL WAR For these reasons and more, the War of 1812 was one of the strangest wars in history. In fact, it was really three different wars fought on three separate fronts. One theatre of conflict was the Chesapeake Bay along the coast of Maryland and Virginia, including Washington, D.C. The second theatre was in the South—Alabama, Mississippi, and West and East Florida—where American forces led by General Andrew Jackson invaded lands owned by the Creeks and the Spanish. The third front might be more accurately called the Canadian-American War. It began in what is now northern Indiana and Ohio, southeastern Michigan, and the contested border regions around the Great Lakes. The fighting raged back and forth as the United States repeatedly invaded British Canada, only to be embarrassingly repulsed.

THE WAR IN THE NORTH   Like the American Revolution, the War of 1812, often called America's second war for independence, was very much a civil war. The Canadians, thousands of whom were former American Loyalists who had fled north after the Revolutionary War, remained loyal to the British Empire, while the Americans and a few French Canadians and Irish Canadians sought to push Britain out and annex Canada.

Indians armed by the British dominated the heavily wooded borderlands around the Great Lakes. Michigan's governor recognized that the British and their Indian allies were dependent on each other: "The British cannot hold Upper Canada [Ontario] without the assistance of the Indians," but the "Indians cannot conduct a war without the assistance of a civilized nation [Great Britain]." So the American assault on Canada involved attacking Indians, Canadians, and British soldiers.

INVADING CANADA   President James Madison approved a three-pronged plan for the invasion of British Canada. It called for one army to move north through upstate New York, along Lake Champlain, to take Montreal, while another was to advance into Upper Canada by crossing the Niagara River between Lakes Ontario and Erie. The third attack would come from the west, with an American force moving east into Upper Canada from Detroit, Michigan. The plan was to have all three attacks begin at the same time to force the British troops in Canada to split up.

The complicated plan of invasion, however, was a disaster. The underfunded and undermanned Americans could barely field one army, let alone three, and communications among the separated commanders was spotty at best.

In July 1812, fifty-nine-year-old General William Hull, a Revolutionary War veteran and governor of the Michigan Territory, marched his disorganized and poorly supplied army across the Detroit River into Canada. He told the Canadians that he was there to free them from "tyranny and oppression." The Canadians, however, did not want to be liberated, and the Americans were soon pushed back to Detroit by British troops, Canadian militiamen, and their Indian allies.

As the British force lay siege to the Americans, Hull was tricked by the British commander's threats to unleash thousands of Indian warriors. Fearing a massacre by "savages," Hull did the unthinkable: he surrendered his entire force of 2,500 troops without firing a shot. His capitulation shocked the nation and opened the entire western frontier to raids by British troops and Canadian militiamen and their Indian allies.

President Madison and the Republicans felt humiliated. In Kentucky, a Republican said General Hull must be a "traitor" or "nearly an idiot" or "part

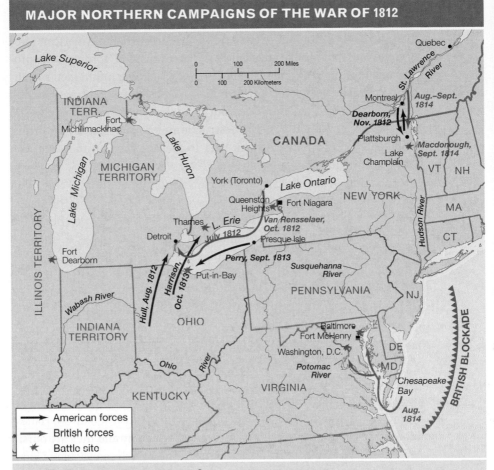

MAJOR NORTHERN CAMPAIGNS OF THE WAR OF 1812

Legend:
→ American forces
→ British forces
✶ Battle site

- How did the War of 1812 begin?
- What was the American strategy in regard to British Canada?
- Describe the battle that inspired Francis Scott Key to write "The Star-Spangled Banner."

of both." Hull was eventually put on trial and sentenced to death. Although he was pardoned by Madison, he was dismissed from the army for his cowardice.

The second prong of the American invasion plan, the assault on Montreal, never got off the ground. The third prong began at dawn on October 13, 1812, when U.S. troops led by General Stephen Van Rensselaer rowed across the Niagara River from Lewiston, New York, to the Canadian village of Queenston, where they suffered a crushing defeat in the Battle of Queenston Heights. The shameful defeats in Canada led many Americans to lose hope that they could win the war. In early 1813, a Kentuckian warned that any more military disasters would result in "disunion," and the "cause of Republicanism will be lost."

Then there was a glimmer of good news. In April 1813, an American force led by General Zebulon Pike attacked York (later renamed Toronto), the provincial capital of Upper Canada. The British and Canadian militiamen surrendered, and over the next several days, in part because Pike had been killed in the battle, the U.S. soldiers rampaged out of control, plundering the city and burning government buildings. The destruction of York outraged the British and Canadians and would lead them later to seek revenge on the American capital of Washington, D.C.

After the burning of York, the Americans sought to gain naval control of the Great Lakes and other inland waterways along the Canadian border. If they could break the British naval supply line and secure Lake Erie, they could divide the British from their Indian allies.

In 1813, at Presque Isle, Pennsylvania, near Erie, twenty-eight-year-old Oliver Hazard Perry supervised the construction of warships from timber cut in nearby forests. By the end of the summer, Commodore Perry's new warships set out in search of the British and some "warm fighting," finally finding them at Lake Erie's Put-in-Bay on September 10.

Two British warships used their superior weapons to pound the *Lawrence*, Perry's flagship. After four hours of intense shelling, none of the *Lawrence*'s guns was working, and most of the crew were dead or wounded. Perry refused to quit, however. He switched to another vessel, kept fighting, and, miraculously, ended up accepting the surrender of the entire British squadron. Hatless and bloodied, Perry reported that "we have met the enemy and they are ours."

American naval control of Lake Erie forced the British to evacuate Upper Canada. They gave up Detroit and were defeated at the Battle of the Thames in southern Canada on October 5, 1813. During the battle, the British fled, leaving the great chief Tecumseh and 500 warriors to face the wrath of the Americans. When Tecumseh was killed, the remaining Indians retreated.

Perry's victory and the defeat of Tecumseh enabled the Americans to recover control of most of Michigan and seize the Western District of Upper Canada. Thereafter, the war in the north lapsed into a military stalemate along the Canadian border, with neither side able to dislodge the other.

THE CREEK WAR In the South, too, the war flared up in 1813. The Creek Indians in western Georgia and Alabama had split into two factions: the Upper Creeks (called Red Sticks because of their bright-red war clubs), who opposed American expansion and sided with the British during the war, and the Lower Creeks, who wanted to remain on good terms with the Americans.

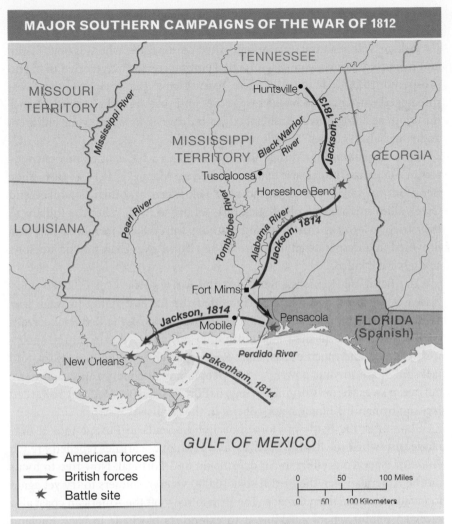

MAJOR SOUTHERN CAMPAIGNS OF THE WAR OF 1812

- Why did Andrew Jackson march his army into Florida on his way to New Orleans?
- What advantages did the American defenders have in the Battle of New Orleans?
- Why was the Battle of New Orleans important to the Treaty of Ghent?

On August 30, Red Sticks attacked Fort Mims on the Alabama River, thirty miles above the Gulf coast town of Mobile, and massacred 553 men, women, and children, scalping half of them.

Americans were incensed. Thirsting for revenge, Andrew Jackson, commanding general of the Army of West Tennessee, recruited about 2,500 volunteer militiamen and headed south. With him were David Crockett, a famous sharpshooter, and Sam Houston, a nineteen-year-old Virginia frontiersman who would later lead the Texas War for Independence against Mexico.

Jackson was a natural warrior and gifted commander who was both feared and respected. From a young age, he had embraced violence, gloried in it, and prospered from it. He told all "brave Tennesseans" that their "frontier [was] threatened with invasion by the savage foe" and that the Indians were advancing "with scalping knives unsheathed, to butcher your wives, your children, and your helpless babes. Time is not to be lost."

Jackson's volunteers crushed the Red Sticks in a series of bloody encounters in Alabama. The decisive battle occurred on March 27, 1814, at Horseshoe Bend on the Tallapoosa River. Jackson's volunteers and their Cherokee and Creek allies surrounded a Red Stick fort, set fire to it, and shot the Indians as they tried to escape. Nine hundred of them were killed, including 300 who drowned in a desperate effort to cross the river. Fewer than fifty of Jackson's soldiers were killed.

The Battle of Horseshoe Bend was the worst defeat ever inflicted upon Native Americans, and it effectively ended the Creeks' ability to wage war. With the Treaty of Fort Jackson, signed in August 1814, the Red Stick Creeks gave up two-thirds of their land—some 23 million acres—including southwest Georgia and much of Alabama. Red Eagle, chief of the Red Sticks, told Jackson: "I am in your power. . . . My people are all gone. I can do no more but weep over the misfortunes of my nation." President Madison rewarded Jackson by naming him a major general in the regular U.S. Army.

Soon after the Battle of Horseshoe Bend, events in Europe took a dramatic turn when the British, Spanish, and Portuguese armies repelled French emperor Napoléon's effort to conquer Spain and Portugal. Now free to focus on the American war, the British sent 16,000 veteran soldiers to try yet again to invade America from Canada. The British navy off the American coast also received reinforcement, enabling it to extend its blockade to New England ports and to bombard coastal towns from Delaware to Florida. The final piece of the British plan was to seize New Orleans and thereby sever American access to the Mississippi River, lifeline of the West.

FIGHTING ALONG THE CHESAPEAKE BAY Throughout the war, the pitifully small U.S. Navy was unable to protect the nation's long coastline. In February 1813, the British had more warships in the Chesapeake Bay than were in the entire American navy, and they frequently captured and burned American merchant vessels. The British fleet also launched numerous raids along the Virginia and Maryland shore, in effect mocking the Madison administration's ability to defend the nation. One British officer dismissed the United States as "a country of *Infants in War*."

The presence of British ships on the coast and inland rivers led many slaves to escape or revolt. As had happened during the Revolutionary War, British naval commanders promised freedom to slaves who aided or fought with them. More than 3,000 slaves in Maryland and Virginia stole boats or canoes that took them to the safety of British ships.

In September 1813, the British organized some 400 former slaves into an all-black military unit, called the Colonial Marines. The recruits were provided uniforms, meals, and $6 a month in wages. News of the all-black Colonial Marines panicked whites along the Chesapeake Bay who feared that the former slaves would "have no mercy on them." Virginia's John Randolph spoke for many when he insisted that the "question of slavery, as it is called, is to us a question of life and death."

THE BURNING OF WASHINGTON During the late summer of 1814, U.S. forces suffered their most humiliating experience of the war when British troops captured and burned Washington, D.C.

In August, 4,000 British soldiers landed at Benedict, Maryland, routed the American militia at Bladensburg, and headed for the nation's capital, only a few miles away. Thousands fled the city. President Madison frantically called out the poorly led and untrained militia, then left the White House to help rally the troops. His efforts failed, however, as the American defense disintegrated in the face of the British attack.

On August 24, British redcoats marched unopposed into the American capital. Madison and his wife, Dolley, had fled just in time ("Where I shall be tomorrow, I cannot tell!"), after first saving a portrait of George Washington and a copy of the Declaration of Independence. The vengeful British, aware that American troops had burned York, the Canadian capital, torched the White House, the Capitol, the Library of Congress, and other government buildings. A tornado the next day compounded the damage, but a violent thunderstorm dampened both the fires and the enthusiasm of the British forces, who headed north to assault Baltimore.

The destruction of Washington, D.C., shocked, embarrassed, and infuriated Americans. Even worse, people had lost confidence in the government and the military. David Campbell, a Virginia congressman, told his brother that America was "ruled by fools and the administration opposed by knaves." John Armstrong, the secretary of war, resigned because of the embarrassing sack of the nation's capital. Madison replaced him with James Monroe, who was also serving as secretary of state. A desperate Monroe soon proposed enlisting free blacks into the army. But many worried that such changes were too few and too late. A Virginia official noted that without a miracle, *This union is inevitably dissolved.*

President Madison was "heartbroken" by the turn of events. He called an emergency session of Congress and appealed to Americans to "expel the

The Burning of the Capitol This 1817 etching of the damaged Capitol shows shackled slaves (bottom right) and angels overhead. It appeared in a book arguing that the British effort to destroy "the temple of freedom" was a sign that God disapproved of slavery.

invaders." A Baltimore newspaper reported that the "spirit of the nation is roused." That determination showed itself when fifty British warships sailed into Baltimore Harbor on September 13 while 4,200 British soldiers, including the all-black Colonial Marines, assaulted the city by land. About 1,000 Americans held Fort McHenry on an island in the harbor.

During the night of September 13, the British unleashed a thunderous bombardment of Fort McHenry. "The portals of hell appeared to have been thrown open," a Baltimore resident reported. Yet the Americans refused to surrender. At daybreak on the 14th, the soldiers in the battered fort stood defiant, guns at the ready. The frustrated British fleet sailed away.

Francis Scott Key, a lawyer and occasional poet, watched the bombardment of Fort McHenry from a ship, having been sent to negotiate the release of a captured American. The sight of the U.S. flag still flying over the fort at dawn meant that the city had survived the onslaught. The dramatic scene inspired Key to scribble the verses of what came to be called "The Star-Spangled Banner," which began, "Oh, say can you see, by the dawn's early light?" Later revised and set to the tune of a popular English drinking song, it eventually became America's national anthem.

THE BATTLE OF LAKE CHAMPLAIN The British failure to conquer Baltimore nixed their hopes of a quick victory in the war while giving the Americans a desperately needed morale boost. More good news soon arrived from upstate New York, where the outnumbered Americans at Plattsburgh, along Lake Champlain, were saved by the superb ability of Commodore Thomas Macdonough, commander of the U.S. naval squadron.

On September 11, 1814, just days after the burning of Washington, D.C., British soldiers attacked at Plattsburgh while their navy engaged Macdonough's warships in a battle that ended with the entire British fleet either destroyed or captured.

The Battle of Lake Champlain (also called the Battle of Plattsburgh) forced the British to abandon the northern campaign—their main military push in the war—and retreat back into Canada. When the British officers came to surrender themselves and their swords, Macdonough said, "Gentlemen, return your swords to your scabbards; you are worthy of them."

In Florida in November, an army led by Andrew Jackson seized Spanish-controlled Pensacola, on the Gulf coast, thereby preventing another British army from landing and pushing northward into the southern states. The American victories in New York and Florida convinced Congress not to abandon Washington, D.C. Instead, the members voted to rebuild the Capitol and the White House.

The Aftermath of the War

While the fighting raged, U.S. diplomats had begun meetings in Ghent, near Brussels in present-day Belgium, to discuss ending the war. The negotiations were at a standstill when news arrived of the American victory at the Battle of Lake Champlain and the failure of the British invasion of Baltimore. The news made the British more flexible, but negotiations still dragged on for weeks. Finally, on Christmas Eve, 1814, the diplomats reached an agreement to stop the fighting.

THE TREATY OF GHENT The weary British decided to end the war in part because of military setbacks but also because London merchants were eager to renew trade with America. The British government had also concluded that the war was not worth the cost.

By the **Treaty of Ghent** (1814), the countries agreed to end the war, return each side's prisoners, and restore the previous boundaries. This was a godsend for the Americans, since British forces at the time still controlled eastern Maine, northern Michigan, a portion of western New York, and several islands off the coast of Georgia. The British also pledged to stop supporting Indian attacks along the Great Lakes.

What had begun as an American effort to protect its honor, end British impressment, and conquer Canada had turned into a second war of independence. Although the Americans lost the war for Canada and saw their national capital destroyed, they won the southern war to defeat the Indians and take their lands. More important, the treaty saved the fragile and splintered republic from possible civil war and financial ruin.

THE BATTLE OF NEW ORLEANS Because it took six weeks for news of the Treaty of Ghent to reach the United States, fighting continued in America at the end of 1814. On December 1, 1814, Andrew Jackson arrived in New Orleans to prepare for a British invasion of the strategic city. He announced that he "had come to protect the city" and "would drive the British into the sea, or perish in the effort." Jackson declared martial law, taking control of the governance of the city, which enabled him to transform New Orleans into a large armed camp.

On December 12, a British fleet with some 8,000 seasoned soldiers took up positions on the coast of Louisiana. The British hoped to capture New Orleans and thereby gain control of the Mississippi River. Federalists fed up with "Mr. Madison's War" predicted that New Orleans would be lost; some called for Madison's impeachment.

British general Sir Edward Pakenham's painfully careful preparation for an assault against the Americans gave Jackson time to organize hundreds of slaves "loaned" by planters to dig trenches, build ramparts, and stack cotton bales and barrels of sugar to protect the city from British fire.

The Americans built an almost-invulnerable position, but Pakenham, cocky and careless, rashly ordered a frontal assault at dawn on Sunday, January 8, 1815. His professional redcoats, including all-black units from the Caribbean islands, marched into a murderous hail of artillery shells and rifle fire. Line after line of advancing redcoats crumpled and fell, often on top of one another. When the smoke cleared, a Kentucky militiaman said that the battlefield looked first like "a sea of blood. It was not blood itself, but the red coats in which the British soldiers were dressed."

Before the devastated British withdrew, some 2,100 had been wounded or killed, including Pakenham, two other generals, and more than 80 officers. Only thirteen Americans had lost their lives. A British naval officer wrote that there "never was a more complete failure."

Although the **Battle of New Orleans** occurred after the Treaty of Ghent had been signed, it was still a vitally important psychological victory, as the treaty had yet to be officially ratified by either the United States or Great Britain. Jackson's lopsided victory ensured that both governments would act quickly to approve the treaty. The unexpected American triumph also generated a wave of patriotic nationalism that would later help transform Andrew Jackson into a dynamic president eager to move the nation into an era in which the "common man" would be celebrated. The rough-hewn Jackson, wrote a southerner in April 1815, "is everywhere hailed as the savior of the country. . . . He has been feasted, caressed, & I may say idolised."

THE HARTFORD CONVENTION Weeks before the Battle of New Orleans, many New England Federalists, frustrated by the rising expense of a war they had opposed, tried to take matters into their own hands at a meeting in Hartford, Connecticut. The **Hartford Convention** was the climax of New England's disgust with "Mr. Madison's War."

On December 15, 1814, the Hartford Convention assembled with delegates from Massachusetts, Rhode Island, Connecticut, Vermont, and New Hampshire. The convention proposed seven constitutional amendments designed to limit Republican (and southern) influence. The amendments included abolishing the counting of slaves in determining a state's representation in Congress, requiring a two-thirds supermajority rather than a simple majority vote to declare war or admit new states, prohibiting trade embargoes lasting more than sixty days, excluding immigrants from holding federal office, limiting the president to one term, and barring successive presidents from the same state (a provision clearly directed at Virginia).

Delegates at the Hartford Convention also discussed the possibility that some of the New England states might "secede" from the United States if their demands were dismissed. Yet the threat quickly evaporated. In February 1815, when messengers from the Hartford Convention reached Washington, D.C., they found the battered capital celebrating the good news from New Orleans. "Their position," according to a French diplomat, was "awkward, embarrassing, and lent itself to cruel ridicule."

Ignored by Congress and the president, the Hartford delegates turned tail for home. The whole sorry episode proved fatal to the Federalist party, which never recovered from the shame of disloyalty stamped on it by the Hartford Convention. The victory at New Orleans and the arrival of the peace treaty from Europe transformed the national mood. Almost overnight, President Madison went from being denounced and possibly impeached to being hailed a national hero.

THE WAR'S LEGACIES There was no clear military victor in the War of 1812, nor much clarification about the issues that had ignited the war. The Treaty of Ghent ended the fighting but failed to address the reasons why President Madison had declared war in the first place: the disputes about U.S. maritime rights and the British practice of impressment.

For all the clumsiness with which the war was managed, however, in the end it generated an intense patriotism across much of the nation and reaffirmed American independence. The young republic was at last secure from British or European threats. As James Monroe said, "we have acquired a character and a rank among the other nations, which we did not enjoy before."

Forgetting their many military disasters, Americans soon decided that the war was a glorious triumph for republican values. The people, observed Treasury Secretary Albert Gallatin, "are more American; they feel and act more as a nation; and I hope that the permanency of the Union is thereby better secured."

Soon after the Treaty of Ghent arrived in Washington, D.C., in mid-February 1815, Virginian William H. Cabell wrote his brother that the "glorious peace for America . . . has come exactly when we least expected but when we most wanted it." Another Virginian, Colonel John Taylor, recognized the happy outcome as largely resulting from "a succession of lucky accidents" that "enabled the administration to get the nation out of the war." Had the conflict dragged on, he predicted, "the Republican party and our form of government would have been blown up."

The war also propelled the United States toward economic independence, as the wartime interruption of trade with Europe forced America to expand its manufacturing sector and become more self-sufficient. The British blockade of the coast created a shortage of cotton cloth in the United States, leading to the creation of the nation's first cotton-manufacturing industry, in Waltham, Massachusetts.

By the end of the war, there were more than 100 cotton mills in New England and 64 more in Pennsylvania. Even Thomas Jefferson admitted in 1815 that his beloved agricultural republic had been transformed: "We must now place the manufacturer by the agriculturalist." After nearly forty years of independence, the new American republic was emerging as an agricultural, commercial, and industrial world power.

Perhaps the strangest result of the War of 1812 was the reversal of attitudes among the Republicans and the Federalists. The wartime experience taught James Madison and the Republicans some lessons in nationalism. First, the British invasion of Washington, D.C., impressed upon Madison the necessity of creating a strong army and navy. Second, the lack of a national bank had hurt the federal government's efforts to finance the war; state banks were so unstable that it was difficult to raise the funds needed to pay military expenses. In 1816, Madison, who had opposed a national bank, changed his mind and created the Second Bank of the United States. Third, the rise of new industries during the war prompted manufacturers to call for increased tariffs on imports to protect American companies from unfair foreign competition. Madison went along, despite his criticism of tariffs in the 1790s.

While Madison reversed himself by embracing nationalism and a broader interpretation of the Constitution, the Federalists similarly pivoted by embracing Madison's and Jefferson's earlier emphasis on states' rights and strict construction of the Constitution as they tried to defend the special economic interests of their regional stronghold, New England. It was the first great reversal of partisan political roles in constitutional interpretation. It would not be the last.

The War of 1812 proved devastating to all of the eastern Indian nations, most of which had fought with the British. The war accelerated westward settlement by Americans, and Native American resistance was greatly diminished after the death of Tecumseh and his Indian Confederacy. The British essentially abandoned their Indian allies. None of their former lands were returned to them, and the British vacated the frontier forts that had long served as supply centers for Indians.

Lakota chief Little Crow expressed the betrayal felt by Native Americans after the war when he rejected the consolation gifts from the local British commander: "After we have fought for you, endured many hardships, lost some of our people, and awakened the vengeance of our powerful neighbors, you make peace for yourselves. . . . You no longer need our service; you offer us these goods to pay us for [your] having deserted us. But no, we will not take them; we hold them and yourselves in equal contempt." In the years after the war, the United States negotiated more than 200 treaties with native peoples that transferred Indian lands to the federal government and created isolated reservations for them west of the Mississippi River.

As the Indians were pushed out, tens of thousands of Americans moved west into the Great Lakes region and southwest into Georgia, Alabama, and Mississippi, occupying more territory in a single generation than had been settled in the 150 years of colonial history. The federal government hastened western migration by providing war veterans with 160 acres of land between the Illinois and Mississippi Rivers.

The trans-Appalachian population soared from 300,000 to 2 million between 1800 and 1820. By 1840, more than 40 percent of Americans lived west of the Appalachians in eight new states. At the same time, the growing dispute over slavery and its controversial expansion into new western territories set in motion an explosive national debate that would test again the grand experiment in republican government.

CHAPTER REVIEW

SUMMARY

- **Jefferson's Administration**   The Jeffersonian Republicans did not dismantle much of Hamilton's economic program, but they did repeal the whiskey tax, cut government expenditures, and usher in a *republican simplicity* that championed the virtues of smaller government and plain living. While Republicans idealized the agricultural world that had existed prior to 1800, the first decades of the nineteenth century were a period of transformational economic and population growth in the United States. Commercial agriculture and exports to Europe flourished; Americans moved to the West in huge numbers. The *Louisiana Purchase*, which resulted from negotiations with French emperor Napoléon Bonaparte following French setbacks in Haiti, dramatically expanded the boundaries of the United States. Jefferson's *Lewis and Clark expedition* explored the new region and spurred interest in the Far West. In *Marbury v. Madison (1803)*, the Federalist chief justice of the Supreme Court, John Marshall, declared a federal act unconstitutional for the first time. With that decision, the Court assumed the right of judicial review over acts of Congress and established the constitutional supremacy of the federal government over state governments.

- **War in Europe**   Thomas Jefferson sent warships to subdue the *Barbary pirates* and negotiated with the Spanish and French to ensure that the Mississippi River remained open to American commerce. Renewal of war between Britain and France in 1803 complicated matters for American commerce. Neither country wanted its enemy to purchase U.S. goods, so both declared blockades. In retaliation, Jefferson convinced Congress to pass the *Embargo Act*, which prohibited all foreign trade.

- **Aftermath of the War of 1812**   The *Treaty of Ghent (1814)* ended the war by essentially declaring it a draw. A smashing American victory in January of 1815 at the *Battle of New Orleans* helped to ensure that the treaty would be ratified and enforced. The conflict established the economic independence of the United States, as many goods previously purchased from Britain were now manufactured at home. During and after the war, Federalists and Republicans seemed to exchange roles: delegates from the waning Federalist party met at the *Hartford Convention (1815)* to defend states' rights and threaten secession, while Republicans now promoted nationalism and a broad interpretation of the Constitution.

CHRONOLOGY

1800	U.S. population surpasses 5 million
1801	Thomas Jefferson inaugurated as president in Washington, D.C.
	Barbary pirates harass U.S. shipping
	The pasha of Tripoli declares war on the United States
1803	Supreme Court issues *Marbury v. Madison* decision
	Louisiana Purchase
1804–1806	Lewis and Clark expedition
1804	Jefferson overwhelmingly reelected
1807	British interference with U.S. shipping increases
1808	International slave trade ended in the United States
1811	Defeat of Tecumseh Indian Confederacy at the Battle of Tippecanoe
1812	Congress declares war on Britain
	U.S. invasion of Canada
1813–1814	"Creek War"
1814	British capture and burn Washington, D.C.
	Hartford Convention
1815	Battle of New Orleans
	News of the Treaty of Ghent reaches the United States

KEY TERMS

republican simplicity p. 248

Marbury v. Madison (1803) p. 251

Barbary pirates p. 254

Louisiana Purchase (1803) p. 256

Lewis and Clark expedition p. 257

Embargo Act (1807) p. 262

War of 1812 p. 264

Tecumseh's Indian Confederacy p. 265

Treaty of Ghent (1814) p. 275

Battle of New Orleans (1815) p. 276

Hartford Convention (1815) p. 277

🐰 INQUIZITIVE

Go to InQuizitive to see what you've learned—and learn what you've missed—with personalized feedback along the way.

part three

AN EXPANDING NATION

During the nineteenth century, the United States experienced a wrenching change from being a predominantly agrarian society to having a more diverse economy and urban society, with factories and cities emerging alongside farms and towns. The pace of life quickened with industrialization, and the possibilities for better living conditions rose. Between 1790 and 1820, the nation's boundaries expanded and its population—both white and black—soared, while the number of Native Americans continued its long decline. Immigrants from Ireland, Germany,

Scandinavia, and China thereafter poured into the United States seeking land, jobs, and freedom. By the early 1820s, the number of enslaved Americans was more than two and a half times greater than in 1790, and the number of free blacks doubled. The white population of the United States grew just as rapidly.

Accompanying the emergence of an industrial economy in the Northeast during the first half of the nineteenth century was the relentless expansion of the United States westward. Until the nineteenth century, most of the American population was clustered near the seacoast and along rivers flowing into the Atlantic Ocean or the Gulf of Mexico. That changed dramatically after 1800. The great theme of nineteenth-century American history was the migration of millions of people across the Allegheny and Appalachian Mountains into the Ohio Valley and the Middle West. Waves of adventurous Americans then crossed the Mississippi River and spread out across the Great Plains. By the 1840s, Americans had reached the Pacific Ocean.

These developments—the emergence of a market-based economy, the impact of industrial development, and dramatic territorial expansion—made the second quarter of the nineteenth century a time of restless optimism and rapid change. As a German visitor noted, "Ten years in America are like a century elsewhere."

Americans in the early Republic were nothing if not brash and self-assured. In 1845, an editorial in the *United States Journal* claimed that "we, the American people, are the most independent, intelligent, moral, and happy people on the face of the earth." The republic governed by highly educated "natural aristocrats" such as Thomas Jefferson, James Madison, James Monroe, and John Quincy Adams gave way to the frontier democracy promoted by Andrew Jackson and Henry Clay. Americans began to demand government of, by, and for the people.

During the first half of the nineteenth century, two very different societies—North and South—developed in the United States. The North, the more dynamic and faster-growing region, embraced industrial growth, large cities, foreign immigrants, and the ideal of "free labor" as opposed to the system of slavery in the southern states. The South remained rural, agricultural, and increasingly committed to enslaved labor as the backbone of its economy. Two great underlying fears worried southerners: the threat of mass slave uprisings and the possibility that a northern-controlled Congress might one day abolish slavery. The planter elite's aggressive efforts to pre-

serve and expand slavery stifled change and reform in the South and ignited a prolonged political controversy with the North that would eventually lead to civil war.

8

The Emergence of a Market Economy

1815–1850

Lackawanna Valley **(1855)** Often hailed as the father of American landscape painting, George Inness was commissioned by a railroad company to capture its trains coursing through the lush Lackawanna Valley in northeastern Pennsylvania. New inventions and industrial development would continue to invade and transform the rural landscape.

A mid the postwar celebrations in 1815, Americans set about transforming their victorious young nation. Soon after the war's end, prosperity returned as British and European markets again welcomed American ships and commerce. During the war, the loss of trade with Britain and Europe had forced the United States to develop more factories and mills of its own, spurring the development of the more diverse economy that Alexander Hamilton had envisioned in the 1790s.

Between 1815 and 1850, the United States also became a transcontinental power, expanding all the way to the Pacific coast. Hundreds of thousands of land-hungry people streamed westward toward the Mississippi River and beyond. In just six years following the end of the war, six states were added to the Union (Alabama, Illinois, Indiana, Mississippi, Missouri, and Maine).

Americans were a restless, ambitious people, seeking new ways to get ahead by using their ingenuity, skill, faith, and tenacity. The country's energy was dizzying. Everywhere, it seemed, people were moving to the next town, the next farm, the next opportunity. In many cities, half of the entire population moved every ten years. In 1826, the newspaper editor in Rochester, New York, reported that 120 people left every day, while 130 moved into the growing city. Frances Trollope, an English traveler, said that Americans were "a busy, bustling, industrious population, hacking and hewing their way" westward in the pursuit of happiness.

The lure of cheap land and plentiful jobs, as well as the promise of political and religious freedom, attracted millions of hardworking immigrants in the first half of the nineteenth century. This great wave of humanity was not always welcomed, however. Ethnic prejudices, anti-Catholicism, and language barriers made it difficult for many new immigrants, mostly from Ireland, Germany, and China, to be assimilated into American culture.

focus questions

1. How did changes in transportation and communication alter the economic landscape during the first half of the nineteenth century?

2. How did industrial development impact the way people worked and lived?

3. In what ways did immigration alter the nation's population and shape its politics?

4. How did the expanding "market-based economy" impact the lives of workers, professionals, and women?

In the Midwest, large-scale commercial agriculture emerged as big farms grew corn, wheat, pigs, and cattle to be sold in distant markets across the Atlantic. In the South, cotton became so profitable that it increasingly dominated the region's economy, luring farmers and planters (wealthy farmers with hundreds or even thousands of acres worked by large numbers of slaves) into the new states of Alabama, Mississippi, Louisiana, and Arkansas.

Cotton cloth was the first great consumer product of industrial capitalism; cotton from the American South provided most of the clothing for people around the world. As the cotton economy expanded, it required growing numbers of enslaved workers, many of whom were sold by professional slave traders and relocated from Virginia and the Carolinas to the Old Southwest—western Georgia and the Florida Panhandle, Alabama, Mississippi, and Louisiana, and Arkansas.

Meanwhile, the Northeast experienced a momentous surge of industrial development whose labor-saving machines and water- and steam-powered industries reshaped the region's economic and social life. Mills and factories began to dot the landscape and transform the ways people labored, dressed, ate, and lived. With the rise of the factory system, more and more economic activity in the northeastern states occurred outside the home and off the farm. "The transition from mother-daughter power [in the home] to water and steam power" in the mills and factories," said a farmer, was producing a "complete revolution in social life and domestic manners." An urban middle class began to emerge as Americans left farms and moved to towns and cities, drawn primarily by jobs in new mills, factories, and banks.

By 1850, the United States had become the world's fastest growing commercial, manufacturing, agricultural, and mining nation. The industrial economy also generated changes in other areas, from politics to the legal system, from the family to social values. These developments in turn helped expand prosperity and freedom for whites and free blacks.

They also sparked vigorous political debates over economic policies, transportation improvements, and the extension of slavery into the new territories. In the process, the nation began to divide into three powerful regional blocs— North, South, and West—whose shifting alliances and disputes would shape political life until the Civil War.

THE MARKET REVOLUTION

During the first half of the nineteenth century, a market revolution that had begun before the war of independence accelerated the transformation of the American economy into a global powerhouse. In the eighteenth century, most Americans were isolated farmers focused on a subsistence or household economy. They produced just enough food, livestock, and clothing for their own family's needs and perhaps a little more to barter (exchange) with their neighbors. Their lives revolved around a regular routine: feeding livestock and planting, cultivating, or harvesting crops in a daylong cycle punctuated by changing seasons and unpredictable weather.

As the nineteenth century unfolded, however, more and more farm families began engaging in *commercial* rather than *subsistence* agriculture, producing surplus crops and livestock to sell in distant regional and even international markets. In 1851, the president of the New York Agricultural Society noted that until the nineteenth century, "'production for consumption' was the leading purpose" of the farm economy. Now, however, "no farmer could find it profitable to do everything for himself. He now sells for money." With the cash they earned, farm families were able to buy more land, better farm equipment, and the latest manufactured household goods.

Such farming for sale rather than for consumption, often called a **market-based economy**, produced boom-and-bust cycles and was often built upon the backs of slave laborers, immigrant workers, and displaced Mexicans. But, overall, the standard of living rose, and Americans experienced unprecedented opportunities for economic gain and geographic mobility. The transition from a traditional household economy to a modern market economy involved massive changes in the way people lived, worked, traveled, and voted.

What the market economy most needed was what were then called "internal improvements"—deepened harbors, lighthouses, and a national network of canals, bridges, roads, and railroads—to improve the flow of goods by liberating people from the constraints of distance. In 1817, South Carolina congressman John C. Calhoun expressed his desire to "bind the Republic together with a perfect system of roads and canals." As the world's largest republic, the United States desperately needed a national transportation system. "Let us conquer space," he told the House of Representatives.

Calhoun's proposal sparked a fierce debate over how to fund the improvements: should it be the responsibility of the federal government, the individual states, or private corporations? Since the Constitution said nothing about the federal government's role in funding transportation improvements, many argued that such projects must be initiated by state and local governments. Others argued that the Constitution gave the federal government broad powers to promote the "general welfare," which included enhancing transportation and communication. The fierce debate over how best to fund internal improvements would continue throughout the nineteenth century.

TRANSPORTATION WEST, ABOUT 1840

~~~~ Canals   —— Roads
—— Navigable rivers

- Why were river towns important commercial centers?
- What was the economic impact of the steamboat and the flatboat in the West?
- How did the Erie Canal transform the economy of New York and the Great Lakes region?

BETTER ROADS Until the nineteenth century, travel in America had been slow, tedious, uncomfortable, and expensive. It took a stagecoach, for example, four days to go from New York City to Boston. Because of long travel times, many farm products could only be sold locally before they spoiled. That soon changed, as an array of innovations—larger horse-drawn wagons (called

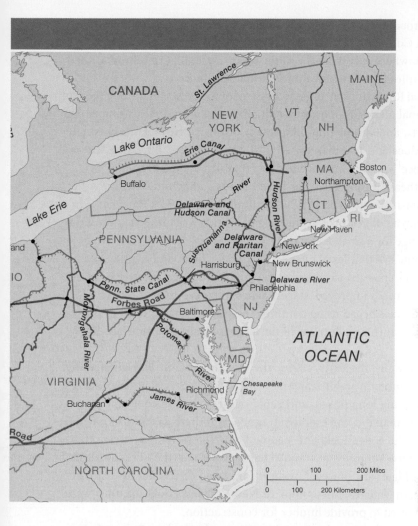

Conestogas), new roads, canals, steamboats, and railroads—knit together the expanding national market for goods and services and greatly accelerated the pace of life.

As more settlers moved west, people expressed a "passion for improving roads." In 1795, the Wilderness Road, along the trail first blazed by Daniel Boone, was opened to wagon and stagecoach traffic, thereby easing the over-the-mountains route from North Carolina into Kentucky and Tennessee.

In 1803, when Ohio became a state, Congress had ordered that 5 percent of the money from land sales in the state would go toward building a National Road from the Atlantic coast across Ohio and westward. Construction finally began in 1811. Originally called the Cumberland Road, it was the first interstate roadway financed by the federal government. By 1818, the road was open from Cumberland, Maryland, westward to Wheeling, Virginia (now West Virginia), where it crossed the Ohio River. By 1838, the National Road extended 600 miles farther westward to Vandalia, Illinois.

The National Road quickened the settlement of the West and the emergence of a truly national market economy by reducing transportation costs, opening up new markets, and stimulating the growth of towns. Farmers increasingly took their produce and livestock to sell in distant markets. But using federal money to finance "internal improvements" remained controversial.

To the northeast, a movement for paved roads gathered momentum after the Philadelphia-Lancaster Turnpike was completed in 1794. (The term *turnpike* derives from a pole, or pike, at the tollgate, which was turned to admit the traffic in exchange for a small fee or toll.)

By 1821, some 4,000 miles of turnpikes had been built, and stagecoach and freight companies emerged to move more people and cargo at lower rates. As the quality of the roads improved, stagecoaches increased their speed. In addition, stagecoach lines began using continual relays, or "stages," of fresh horses every 40 miles or so. This made travel faster, less expensive, and more accessible.

WATERWAYS By the early 1820s, the turnpike boom was giving way to dramatic advances in water transportation. Steamboats, flatboats (barges driven by men using long poles), and canal barges carried people and goods far more cheaply than did horse-drawn wagons. Hundreds of flatboats carried goods, farm produce, livestock, and people from Tennessee, Kentucky, Indiana, Ohio, western Pennsylvania, and other states down the Ohio and Mississippi Rivers. Flatboats, however, went in only one direction: downstream. Once unloaded in Natchez, Mississippi, or New Orleans, Louisiana, they were sold and dismantled to provide lumber for construction.

The difficulties of getting back upriver were solved when Robert Fulton and Robert R. Livingston sent the *Clermont*, the first commercial steamboat, up the Hudson River from New York City in 1807. Thereafter, the use of wood-fired **steamboats** spread rapidly, opening nearly half the continent to water traffic along the major rivers.

By bringing two-way travel to the Mississippi Valley, which included the areas drained by the Ohio and Missouri Rivers, steamboats created a transcontinental market and a commercial agricultural empire that produced much of the nation's timber, wheat, corn, cattle, and hogs. By 1836, there were 750 steamboats operating on American rivers. As steamboat use increased, the price for shipping goods plunged, thus increasing profits and stimulating demand.

The use of steamboats transformed St. Louis, Missouri, from a sleepy frontier village into a booming river port. New Orleans developed even faster. By 1840, it was perhaps the wealthiest American city, having developed a thriving trade with the Caribbean islands and the new Latin American republics that had overthrown Spanish rule. The annual amount of trade being shipped through the city doubled that of New York City by 1843, in large part because of the explosion in cotton production.

The wood-burning steamboats were crowded, dirty, and risky forms of transportation. Accidents, explosions, and fires were common, and sanitation was poor. Passengers crowded on board with pigs and cattle. There were no toilets on steamboats until the 1850s, and all passengers shared the same two washbasins and towels. For all of the inconveniences, however, steamboats became the fastest and most convenient form of transportation in the first half of the nineteenth century.

Canals also sped the market revolution. The **Erie Canal** connected the Great Lakes and the Midwest to the Hudson River and New York City. New York Governor DeWitt Clinton, vice president under James Madison, took the lead in promoting the risky engineering project, which Thomas Jefferson dismissed as "little short of madness." Clinton, however, boasted that his state had the opportunity to "create a new era in history, and to erect a work more stupendous, more magnificent, and more beneficial, than has hitherto been achieved by the human race."

It was not an idle boast. After the Erie Canal opened in 1825, it drew eastward much of the midwestern trade (furs, lumber, textiles) that earlier had been forced to go to Canada or to make the long journey down the Ohio and Mississippi Rivers to New Orleans and the Gulf of Mexico. Thanks to the Erie Canal, the backwoods village of Chicago developed into a bustling city because of its connection via the Great Lakes to New York City, and eventually across the Atlantic to Europe.

The Erie Canal was a triumph of engineering audacity. Forty feet wide and four feet deep, it was the longest canal in the world, extending 363 miles across New York from Albany in the east to Buffalo and Lake Erie in the west, and rising some 675 feet in elevation. Additional branches soon put most of the state within its reach.

The canal was built by tens of thousands of manual laborers, mostly German and Irish immigrants who were paid less than a dollar a day to drain swamps, clear forests, build stone bridges and aqueducts, and blast through solid rock. It brought a "river of gold" to New York City in the form of an unending stream of lumber, grain, flour, and other goods from western New York and the Midwest, and it unlocked the floodgates of western settlement. The canal also

The Erie Canal *Junction of the Erie and Northern Canals* (c. 1830–32), by John Hill.

reduced the cost of moving a ton of freight from $100 to $5. It was so profitable that it paid off its construction costs in just seven years.

The Erie Canal had enormous economic and political consequences, as it tied together the regional economies of the Midwest and the East while further isolating the Deep South. The Genesee Valley in western New York became one of the most productive grain-growing regions in the world, and Rochester became a boom town, processing wheat and corn into flour and meal. Syracuse, Albany, and Buffalo experienced similar growth because of the canal.

The success of the Erie Canal and the entire New York canal system inspired other states to build some 3,000 miles of waterways by 1837. By 1834, canals connected Pittsburgh to Philadelphia, a distance of 395 miles. Canals boosted the economy by enabling speedier and less expensive transport of goods and people. They also boosted real estate prices for the lands bordering them and transformed sleepy rural villages into booming cities.

RAILROADS For a brief period, canals were essential to the nation's economic growth. During the second quarter of the nineteenth century, however, a much less expensive but much more efficient, powerful and versatile form of transportation emerged: the railroad.

In 1825, the year the Erie Canal was completed, the world's first steam-powered railway began operating in England. Soon thereafter, a railroad-building "epidemic" infected the United States. In 1830, the nation had only

23 miles of railroad track. Over the next twenty years, railroad coverage grew to 30,626 miles.

The railroad was a truly transformational technology. It surpassed other forms of transportation because of its speed, carrying capacity, and reliability. **Railroads** could move more people and freight faster, farther, and cheaper than wagons or boats. The early trains averaged ten miles per hour, more than twice the speed of stagecoaches and four times that of boats and barges. That locomotives were able to operate year-round also gave rail travel a huge advantage over canals that froze in winter and dirt roads that became rivers of mud during rainstorms.

Railroads also provided indirect benefits by encouraging new western settlement and the expansion of commercial agriculture. The power of the railroad could be seen everywhere, from rural areas to big cities. A westerner reported that the opening of a new rail line resulted in three new villages emerging along the line, while "adding new life to the city." The depot, or rail station, became the central building in every town, a public place where people from all walks of life converged.

Building railroads stimulated the national economy not only by improving transportation but by creating a huge demand for iron, wooden crossties, bridges, locomotives, freight cars, and other equipment. Railroads also became the nation's largest corporations and employers. Perhaps most important, railroads enabled towns and cities not served by canals or turnpikes to compete economically. In other words, the railroads eventually changed what had once been a cluster of mostly local markets near rivers and the coast into an interconnected national marketplace for goods and services. Railroads expanded the geography of American capitalism, making possible larger industrial and commercial enterprises and shrinking distances for passengers.

But the railroad mania had negative effects as well. Its quick and shady profits frequently led to political corruption. Railroad titans often bribed legislators. By facilitating access to the trans-Appalachian West, railroads also accelerated the decline of Native American culture. In addition, they dramatically quickened the tempo, mobility, and noise of everyday life.

OCEAN TRANSPORTATION The year 1845 brought a great innovation in ocean transport with the launch of the first clipper ship, the *Rainbow*. Built for speed, the **clipper ships** were the nineteenth-century equivalent of the supersonic jetliner. They were twice as fast as the older merchant ships. Long and lean, with taller masts and larger sails than conventional ships, they cut dashing figures during their brief but colorful career, which lasted less than two decades. The American thirst for Chinese tea prompted the clipper boom. Asian tea leaves had to reach markets quickly after harvest, and the clipper ships made this possible.

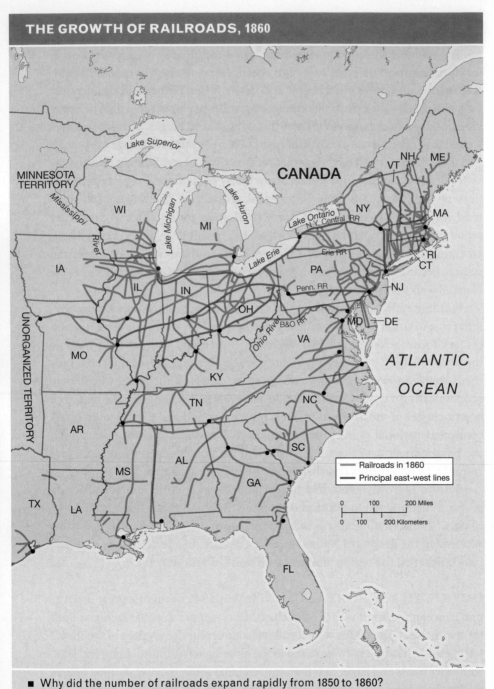

THE GROWTH OF RAILROADS, 1860

Railroads in 1860
Principal east-west lines

0 — 100 — 200 Miles
0 — 100 — 200 Kilometers

- Why did the number of railroads expand rapidly from 1850 to 1860?
- How did the growth of railroads impact national development?

Building a clipper ship This 1833 oil painting captures the Messrs. Smith & Co. Ship Yard in Manhattan, where shipbuilders are busy shaping timbers to construct a clipper ship.

The discovery of gold in California in 1848 lured thousands of prospectors and entrepreneurs. When the massive wave of would-be miners generated an urgent demand for goods on the West Coast, the clippers met it. But clippers, while fast, lacked space for cargo or passengers. After the Civil War, the clippers would give way to the steamship.

COMMUNICATIONS Innovations in transportation also helped spark improvements in communications, which knit the nation even closer together. At the beginning of the nineteenth century, traveling any distance was slow and difficult. It took days—often weeks—for news to travel along the Atlantic Seaboard. For example, after George Washington died in 1798 in Virginia, word of his death did not appear in New York City newspapers until a week later. By 1829, however, it was possible to deliver Andrew Jackson's inaugural address from Washington, D.C., to New York City by relay horse riders in less than twenty hours.

Mail deliveries also improved. The number of U.S. post offices soared from 75 in 1790 to 28,498 in 1860. In addition, new steam-powered printing presses provided for the mass production of newspapers and reduced their cost from six cents to a penny each, enabling virtually everyone to benefit from the news contained in the "penny press."

But the most important advance in communications was the national electromagnetic **telegraph system**, invented by Samuel F. B. Morse. In May 1844, Morse sent the first intercity telegraph message from Washington, D.C., to Baltimore, Maryland. It read: "What Hath God Wrought?"

By the end of the decade, most major cities were connected by telegraph lines that enabled people, companies, and governments to communicate faster and more easily. The electrical telegraph system also helped railroad operators schedule trains more precisely and thus avoid collisions. A New Orleans newspaper claimed that, with the invention of the telegraph, "scarcely anything now will appear to be impossible."

THE ROLE OF GOVERNMENT   Steamboats, canals, and railroads connected the western areas of the country with the East, boosted trade, helped open the Far West for settlement, and spurred dramatic growth in cities. Between 1800 and 1860, an undeveloped nation of scattered farms, primitive roads, and modest local markets was transformed into an engine of capitalist expansion, urban energy, and global reach.

The transportation improvements were financed by both state governments and private investors. Unlike in Europe, virtually all of the railroads in the United States were built by private companies and investors. But the federal government helped, despite intense political debates over whether it was constitutional to use federal funds to finance such "internal improvements." The national government also bought stock in turnpike and canal companies, and, after the success of the Erie Canal, awarded land grants to several western states to support canal and railroad projects.

INDUSTRIAL DEVELOPMENT

The concentration of huge numbers of people in commercial and factory cities, coupled with the transportation and communication revolutions, greatly increased the number of potential customers for given products. Such an expanding market demand in turn gave rise to a system of *mass production*, whereby companies used new technologies (labor-saving machines) to produce greater quantities of products that could be sold at lower prices to more people, thus generating higher profits.

The introduction of water-powered mills and coal-powered steam engines, as well as the application of new technologies to make manufacturing more efficient, sparked a wave of unrelenting **industrialization** in Europe and America from the mid-eighteenth century to the late nineteenth century.

Factories, mills, and mines emerged to supplement the agricultural economy. "It is an extraordinary era in which we live," reported Daniel Webster in 1847. "It is altogether new. The world has seen nothing like it before." New machines and improvements in agricultural and industrial efficiency led to a remarkable increase in productivity. By 1860, one farmer, miner, or mill worker could produce twice as much wheat, twice as much iron, and more than four times as much cotton cloth as in 1800.

AMERICAN TECHNOLOGY Such improvements in productivity were enabled by the "practical" inventiveness of Americans. Between 1790 and 1811, the U.S. Patent Office approved an annual average of 77 new patents certifying new inventions; by the 1850s, the Patent Office was approving more than 28,000 new inventions each year.

Many of the industrial inventions generated dramatic changes. In 1844, for example, Charles Goodyear patented a process for "vulcanizing" rubber, which made the product stronger, more elastic, waterproof, and winter-proof. Vulcanized rubber was soon being used for a variety of products, from shoes and boots to seals, gaskets, hoses and, eventually, tires.

In 1846, Elias Howe patented his design of the sewing machine. It was soon improved upon by Isaac Merritt Singer, who founded the Singer Sewing Machine Company, which initially produced only industrial sewing machines for use in textile mills but eventually offered machines for home use. The availability of sewing machines helped revolutionize "women's work" by dramatically reducing the time needed to make clothes at home, thus freeing up more leisure time for many women.

Technological advances improved living conditions; houses could be larger, better heated, and better illuminated. The first sewer systems helped clean up cities by ridding their streets of human and animal waste. Mechanization of factories meant that more goods could be produced faster and with less labor, and machines helped industries produce "standardized parts" that could be assembled by unskilled wage workers. Machine-made clothes using standardized forms fit better and were less expensive than those sewn by hand; machine-made newspapers and magazines were more abundant and affordable, as were clocks, watches, guns, and plows.

THE IMPACT OF THE COTTON GIN In 1792, Eli Whitney, a recent Yale graduate from New England, visited Mulberry Grove plantation on the Georgia coast, where he "heard much said of the difficulty of ginning cotton"—that is, separating the fibers from the seeds. Cotton had been used for clothing and bedding from ancient times, but until the nineteenth century,

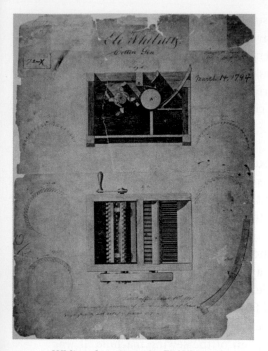

Whitney's cotton gin Eli Whitney's drawing, which accompanied his 1794 federal patent application, shows the side and top of the machine as well as the sawteeth that separated the seeds from the fiber.

cotton cloth was rare and expensive because it took so long to separate the lint (fibers) from tenacious cotton seeds.

At Mulberry Grove, Whitney learned that the person who could invent a "machine" to gin cotton would become wealthy overnight. Within a few days, he had devised a simple mechanism (he called it "an absurdly simple contrivance"), using nails attached to a roller, to remove the seeds from cotton bolls. The **cotton gin** (short for *engine*) proved to be fifty times more productive than a hand laborer. Almost overnight, it made cotton America's most profitable cash crop. In the process, it transformed southern agriculture, northern industry, race-based slavery, national politics, and international trade.

KING COTTON During the first half of the nineteenth century, southern-grown **cotton** became the dominant force driving both the national economy and the controversial efforts to expand slavery into the western territories. Cotton was called "white gold"; it brought enormous wealth to southern planters and merchants, as well as New England textile mill owners and New York shipowners.

By 1812, because of the widespread use of cotton gins, the cost of producing cotton yarn had plunged by 90 percent, and the recent spread of textile mills in Britain and Europe had created a rapidly growing global market for cotton. By the mid-nineteenth century, people worldwide were wearing more comfortable and easier-to-clean cotton clothing. When British textile manufacturers chose the less brittle American cotton over the varieties grown in the Caribbean, Brazil, and India, the demand for southern cotton skyrocketed, as did its price.

Cotton became America's largest export and the primary driver of the nation's economic growth. By 1860, British textile mills were processing a billion pounds of cotton a year, 92 percent of which came from the American South.

Cotton growing first engulfed the Piedmont region of the Carolinas and Georgia. After the War of 1812, it migrated into the contested Indian lands to the west—Tennessee, Alabama, Florida, Mississippi, Louisiana, Arkansas, and Texas. New Orleans became a bustling port—and active slave market— because of the cotton grown throughout the region and shipped down the Mississippi River. The South harvested raw cotton, and northern buyers and shipowners carried it to New England, Great Britain, and France, where textile mills spun the fiber into thread and fabric. Bankers in New York City and London financed the growth of cotton capitalism.

THE EXPANSION OF SLAVERY Because cotton was a labor-intensive crop, growers were convinced that only slaves could make their farms and plantations profitable. As a result, the price of slaves soared with the price of cotton. When farmland in Maryland and Virginia lost its fertility after years of relentless tobacco planting, which strips soil of its nutrients, many whites shifted to growing corn and wheat, since the climate in Maryland and Virginia was too cold for cotton. Many Virginia and Maryland planters sold their surplus slaves to work in the new cotton-growing areas in Georgia, Alabama, Mississippi, and Louisiana. Between 1790 and 1860, some 835,000 slaves were "sold south." In 1790, planters in Virginia and Maryland had owned 56 percent of all the slaves in the United States; by 1860, they owned only 15 percent.

Cotton created boom times in the Old Southwest. A cotton farmer in Mississippi urged a friend in Kentucky to sell his farm and join him: "If you could reconcile it to yourself to bring your negroes to the Mississippi Territory, they would certainly make you a handsome fortune in ten years by the cultivation of Cotton." Slaves became so valuable that stealing slaves became a common problem in the southern states, especially Alabama and Mississippi.

FARMING THE MIDWEST By 1860, more than half the nation's population lived west of the Appalachian Mountains. The flat, fertile farmlands in the Midwest—Ohio, Michigan, Indiana, Illinois, and Iowa—drew farmers from the rocky hillsides of New England and the exhausted soils of Virginia. People traveled on foot, on horseback, and in wagons in an effort to make a fresh start on their *own* land made available by the government.

The process of settling new lands followed the old pattern of clearing underbrush and felling trees, burning the debris, grubbing out the roots by hand and using horses and oxen to dislodge stumps, removing rocks and boulders, and then plowing and planting fields.

Corn was typically the first crop grown. Women and children often planted the seeds in small mounds about three feet apart. Once the corn sprouted, pumpkin, squash, or bean seeds would be planted around the seedlings. The strong corn stalk provided a pole for the bean vines to climb, the beans and squash or pumpkins added prized nitrogen to the soil, and the squash and pumpkin plants grew and spread over the ground, smothering weeds around the corn stalks. Once the corn was harvested, the kernels could be boiled to make porridge or ground up to make flour and cornmeal that was baked into a bread called johnnycake. Corn stalks were stored to provide winter feed for cattle and hogs.

Over time, technological advances led to greater agricultural productivity. The development of durable iron plows (replacing wooden ones) eased the backbreaking job of tilling the soil. In 1819, Jethro Wood of New York introduced an iron plow with separate parts that were easy to replace when needed. Further improvements would follow, including Vermonter John Deere's steel plow (1837), whose sharp edges could cut through the tough prairie grass in the Midwest and the Great Plains. By 1845, Massachusetts alone had seventy-three plants making more than 60,000 plows per year. Most were sold to farmers in the western states and territories, illustrating the emergence of a national marketplace for goods and services made possible by the transportation revolution.

Other technological improvements quickened the growth of commercial agriculture. By the 1840s, new mechanical seeders had replaced the process of sowing seed by hand. Even more important, in 1831, twenty-two-year-old Cyrus Hall McCormick invented a mechanical reaper to harvest wheat, a development as significant to the agricultural economy of the Midwest, Old Northwest, and Great Plains as the cotton gin was to the South.

In 1847, the **McCormick reapers** began selling so fast that McCormick moved to Chicago and built a manufacturing plant. Within a few years, he had sold thousands of the giant farm machines, transforming the scale of commercial agriculture. Using a handheld sickle, a farmer could harvest a half acre of wheat a day; with a McCormick reaper, two people could work twelve acres a day.

EARLY TEXTILE MANUFACTURERS   While technological breakthroughs such as the cotton gin, mechanical harvester, and railroads quickened agricultural development and created a national and international marketplace, other advances altered the economic landscape even more profoundly by giving rise to the factory system.

Mills and factories were initially powered by water wheels, then by coal-fired steam engines. The shift from water power to coal enabled the dramatic growth of the textile industry (and industries of all types) and launched an industrial era destined to end Britain's domination of the world economy.

In 1800, the output of America's mills and factories amounted to only one-sixth of Great Britain's production, and American textile production was slow and faltering until Thomas Jefferson's embargo in 1807 stimulated the domestic production of cloth. By 1815, hundreds of textile mills in New England, New York, and Pennsylvania were producing thread, cloth, and clothing. By 1860, the output of America's factories would be a third and by 1880 two thirds that of British industry.

After the War of 1812, however, British textile companies blunted America's industrial growth by flooding the United States with cheap cotton cloth in an effort to regain their customers who had been shut off by the war. Such postwar "dumping" nearly killed the infant American textile industry. A delegation of New England mill owners traveled to Washington, D.C., to demand a federal tariff (tax) on imported British cloth to make American textile mills more competitive. The efforts of the American mill owners to gain political assistance created a culture of industrial lobbying for congressional tariff protection against imported products that continues to this day.

What the mill owners neglected to admit was that import tariffs hurt consumers by forcing them to pay higher prices. Over time, as Scotsman Adam Smith explained in his book on capitalism, *The Wealth of Nations* (1776), consumers not only pay higher prices for foreign goods as a result of tariffs, but they also pay higher prices for domestic goods, since businesses invariably seize opportunities to raise the prices charged for their products.

Tariffs helped protect American industries from foreign competition, but competition is the engine of innovation and efficiency in a capitalist economy. New England shipping companies opposed higher tariffs because they would reduce the amount of goods being carried in their vessels across the Atlantic from Britain and Europe. Many southern planters opposed tariffs because of fears that Britain and France would retaliate by imposing tariffs on American cotton and tobacco shipped to their ports.

In the end, the New England mill owners won the tariff war. Congress passed the Tariff Bill of 1816, which

Mill girls Massachusetts mill workers of the mid-nineteenth century, photographed holding shuttles used in spinning thread and yarn.

placed a tax of twenty-five cents on every yard of imported cloth. Such tariffs were a major factor in promoting industrialization. By impeding foreign competition, they enabled American manufacturers to dominate the national marketplace.

THE LOWELL SYSTEM The factory system centered on wage-earning workers sprang full-blown upon the American scene at Waltham, Massachusetts, in 1813, when a group known as the Boston Associates constructed the first textile mill in which the mechanized processes of spinning yarn and weaving cloth were brought together under one roof.

In 1822, the Boston Associates, led by Francis Cabot Lowell, developed another cotton mill at a village along the Merrimack River twenty-eight miles north of Boston, which they renamed Lowell. The **Lowell system** soon became the model for mill towns throughout New England. The founders of the Lowell system sought not just to improve industrial efficiency, but to develop model

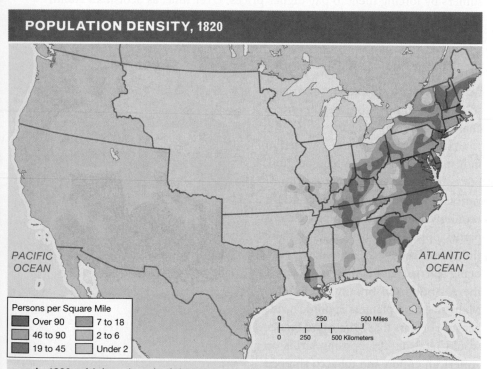

POPULATION DENSITY, 1820

PACIFIC OCEAN

ATLANTIC OCEAN

Persons per Square Mile
- Over 90
- 46 to 90
- 19 to 45
- 7 to 18
- 2 to 6
- Under 2

0   250   500 Miles
0   250   500 Kilometers

- In 1820, which regions had the greatest population density? Why?
- How did the changes in the 1820 land law encourage western expansion?
- What events caused the price of land to decrease between 1800 and 1841?

industrial communities. They located their four- and five-story brick-built mills along rivers in the countryside.

The mill owners at Waltham and Lowell hired mostly young women aged fifteen to thirty from farm families. The owners preferred women because of their skill in operating textile machines and their willingness to endure the mind-numbing boredom of operating spinning machines and looms for wages lower than those paid to men (even though their wages, $2.50 per week, were the highest in the world for women).

Moreover, by the 1820s New England had a surplus of women because so many men had migrated westward. In the early 1820s, a steady stream of single women began flocking toward Lowell. To reassure worried parents, mill owners promised to provide the "Lowell girls" with tolerable work, prepared meals, comfortable boardinghouses (four girls to a room), moral discipline, and educational and cultural opportunities.

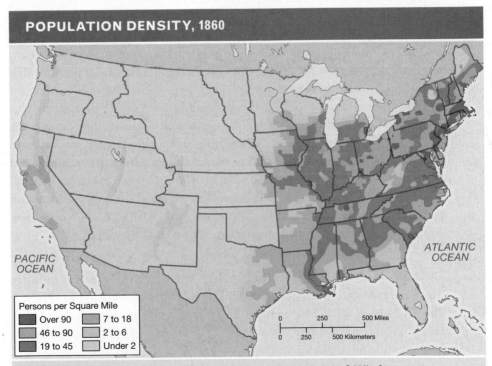

POPULATION DENSITY, 1860

Persons per Square Mile

- Over 90
- 46 to 90
- 19 to 45
- 7 to 18
- 2 to 6
- Under 2

PACIFIC OCEAN

ATLANTIC OCEAN

0   250   500 Miles
0   250   500 Kilometers

- In 1860, which regions had the greatest population density? Why?
- How did new technologies allow farmers to produce more crops on larger pieces of land?

Initially, the "Lowell idea" worked. Visitors commented on the well-designed red brick mills, with their lecture halls and libraries. The Lowell girls appeared "healthy and happy." They lived in cramped dormitories staffed by housemothers who enforced church attendance and evening curfews. Despite thirteen-hour work days and five-and-a-half day workweeks (longer hours than those of prison inmates), some of the women formed study groups, published a literary magazine, and attended lectures. By 1840, there were thirty-two mills and factories in Lowell.

As Lowell rapidly grew, however, the industrial village lost much of its innocence and became a grimy industrial city. Mill owners produced too much cloth, which depressed prices. To maintain profits, the owners cut wages and quickened the pace of work. As a worker said, "We go in at five o'clock [in the morning]; at seven we come out to breakfast; at half-past seven we return to our work, and stay until half past twelve. At one . . . we return to our work, and stay until seven at night."

In 1834, the unexpected happened when the Lowell women began going on strike to protest the deteriorating working and living conditions. The mill owners were not pleased. They labeled the 1,500 striking women "ungrateful" and "unfeminine"—and tried to get rid of the strike's leaders. One mill manager reported that "we have paid off several of these Amazons & presume that they will leave town on Monday."

The economic success of the New England textile mills raises an obvious question: why didn't the South build its own mills close to the cotton fields to keep its profits in the region? A few mills did appear in the Carolinas and Georgia, but they struggled to find workers because whites generally resisted factory work, and planters refused to allow slaves to leave the fields. African Americans, it was assumed, could not work efficiently indoors, and cotton planters considered textile mills an inefficient use of their labor resources. Agricultural slavery had made them rich. Why should they change?

INDUSTRIAL CITIES The rapid growth of commerce and industry drove the expansion of cities and mill villages. Lowell's population in 1820 was 200. By 1830, it was 6,500, and ten years later it had soared to 21,000. Other factory centers sprouted up across New England, displacing forests, farms, and villages while filling the air with smoke, noise, and stench.

Between 1820 and 1840, the number of Americans engaged in manufacturing increased 800 percent, and the number of city dwellers more than doubled. As Thomas Jefferson and other agrarians feared, the United States was rapidly becoming a global urban-industrial power, producing its own clothing and shoes, iron and engines.

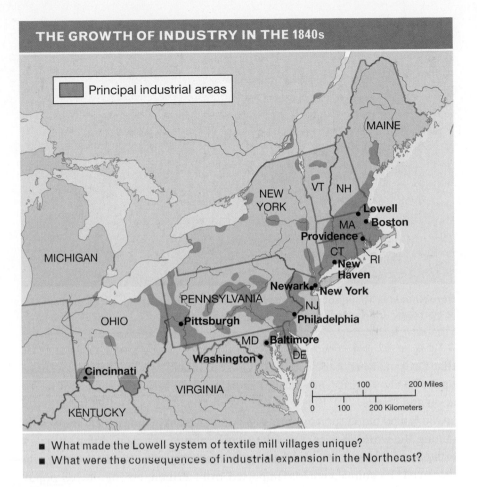

THE GROWTH OF INDUSTRY IN THE 1840s

Principal industrial areas

MAINE

NEW YORK

VT NH

Lowell

MA Boston

Providence

CT

New Haven RI

MICHIGAN

Newark New York

PENNSYLVANIA

NJ

OHIO

Pittsburgh

Philadelphia

MD Baltimore

Washington DE

Cincinnati

VIRGINIA

0   100   200 Miles

0   100   200 Kilometers

KENTUCKY

- What made the Lowell system of textile mill villages unique?
- What were the consequences of industrial expansion in the Northeast?

POPULAR CULTURE

During the colonial era, working-class Americans had little time for play or amusement. Most adults worked from dawn to dusk six days a week. In rural areas, free time was often spent in communal activities, such as barn raisings and corn-husking parties, shooting matches and footraces, while residents of the seacoast sailed and fished. In colonial cities, people attended dances, went on sleigh rides and picnics, and played "parlor games" such as billiards, cards, and chess. As people moved to cities in the first half of the nineteenth century, they developed a distinctive urban culture, and laborers and shopkeepers sought new forms of leisure and entertainment as diversions from their long workdays.

URBAN RECREATION Social drinking was pervasive during the first half of the nineteenth century. In 1829, the secretary of war estimated

Bare Knuckles Blood sports emerged as popular urban entertainment for men of all social classes, but especially among the working poor.

that three quarters of the nation's laborers drank at least four ounces of "hard liquor" daily. Taverns and social or sporting clubs served as centers of recreation and leisure.

So-called blood sports were also a popular form of amusement, especially among the working poor. For a time, cockfighting and dogfighting attracted excited crowds and frenzied betting, but prizefighting (boxing) eventually displaced the animal contests. Imported from Britain, boxing proved popular with all social classes. The early contestants tended to be Irish or English immigrants, often sponsored by a fire company, fraternal association, or street gang. In the antebellum era, boxers fought with bare knuckles, and the results were brutal. A match ended only when a contestant could not continue. A bout in 1842 lasted 119 rounds and ended when a fighter died in his corner. Such deaths prompted several cities to outlaw the practice, only to see it reappear as an underground activity.

THE PERFORMING ARTS Theaters became the most popular form of indoor entertainment. People from all walks of life flocked to opera houses, playhouses, and music halls to watch a wide spectrum of performances: Shakespeare's tragedies, "blood and thunder" melodramas, comedies, minstrel shows, operas, performances by acrobatic troupes, and local pageants. Audiences were predominantly men. "Respectable" women rarely attended; the

The Crow Quadrilles This sheet-music cover, printed in 1837, shows vignettes caricaturing African Americans. Minstrel shows enjoyed nationwide popularity while reinforcing racial stereotypes.

prevailing "cult of domesticity" kept women in the home. Audiences cheered the heroes and heroines and hissed at the villains. If an actor did not meet expectations, spectators hurled curses, nuts, eggs, fruit, shoes, or chairs.

The 1830s witnessed the emergence of the first uniquely American form of mass entertainment: blackface minstrel shows, featuring white performers made up as blacks. "Minstrelsy" drew upon African American folklore and reinforced racial stereotypes. It featured banjo and fiddle music, "shuffle" dances, and lowbrow humor. Between the 1830s and the 1870s, minstrel shows were immensely popular, especially among northern working-class ethnic groups and southern whites.

The most popular minstrel songs were written by a young white composer named Stephen Foster. In 1846 he composed "Oh! Susanna," which became a national favorite. Its popularity catapulted Foster into the limelight, and he responded with equally well-received tunes such as "Old Folks at Home" (popularly known as "Way Down upon the Swanee River"), "Massa's in de Cold, Cold Ground," "My Old Kentucky Home," and "Old Black Joe," all of which perpetuated the sentimental myth of contented slaves.

IMMIGRATION

More than ever before, the United States continued to be a nation of immigrants. During the forty years from the outbreak of the Revolutionary War to the end of the War of 1812, immigration had slowed to a trickle as European wars restricted travel. After 1815, new U.S. territories and states in the West actively recruited immigrants from Europe, often offering special incentives such as voting rights after only six-months' residency.

Why did people risk their lives and abandon their homelands to come to the United States? America offered jobs, higher wages, lower taxes, cheap and fertile land, no entrenched aristocracy, religious freedom, and voting rights.

After 1837, a worldwide financial panic and economic slump accelerated the pace of immigration to the United States. American employers aggressively recruited foreigners, in large part because they were often willing to work for lower wages than native-born Americans. The *Chicago Daily Tribune* observed that the tide of German immigrants was perfect for the "cheap and ingenious labor of the country." A German laborer was willing "to live as cheaply and work infinitely more intelligently than the negro."

The years from 1845 to 1854 marked the greatest proportional influx of immigrants in U.S. history, 2.4 million, or about 14.5 percent of the total population in 1845. By far, the largest number of immigrants between 1840 and 1860 came from Ireland and Germany.

THE IRISH No nation proportionately sent more of its people to America than Ireland. A prolonged agricultural crisis that brought immense social hardships caused many Irish to flee their homeland in the mid-nineteenth century. Irish farmers primarily grew potatoes; in fact, fully a third of them were dependent on the potato harvest for survival. The average adult male in Ireland ate five pounds of potatoes a day.

In 1845, a fungus destroyed the potato crop and triggered what came to be called the Irish Potato Famine. More than a million people died, and almost 2 million more left Ireland, a country whose total population was only 8 million. Most traveled to Canada and the United States. As one group of exiles explained, "All we want to do is get out of Ireland; we must be better anywhere but here." America, they knew, had plenty of paying jobs and "plenty to eat."

By the 1850s, the Irish made up more than half the population of Boston and New York City and were almost as dominant in Philadelphia. Most of them were crowded into filthy, poorly ventilated tenement houses in which "the low-paid and poverty-smitten . . . crowd by the dozens." Irish neighborhoods were plagued by high crime rates, deadly diseases, prostitution, and alcoholism. The archbishop of New York described the Irish as "the poorest and most wretched population that can be found in the world."

The Irish often took on the nation's hardest and most dangerous jobs. It was mostly Irish men who built the canals and railroads, and mostly Irish women who worked in the textile mills of New England and cleaned the houses of upper-middle-class Americans. One Irishman groaned that he worked like "a slave for the Americans."

Irish immigrants were stereotyped as filthy, bad-tempered, and heavy drinkers. They also encountered intense anti-Catholic prejudice among native-born Protestants. Many employers posted taunting signs reading "No Irish Need Apply."

Irish Americans, however, could be equally mean-spirited toward other groups, such as free African Americans, who competed with them for low-wage, mostly unskilled jobs. In 1850, the *New York Tribune* expressed concern that the Irish, having escaped from "a galling, degrading bondage" in their homeland, opposed equal rights for blacks and frequently arrived at the polls shouting, "Down with the Nagurs! Let them go back to Africa, where they belong." Irish freedom fighter Daniel O'Connell scolded the immigrants for their racism: "It was not in Ireland you learned this cruelty."

Many African Americans viewed the Irish with equal contempt. In 1850, a slave expressed a common sentiment when he noted that his "master" was "a great tyrant, he treats me badly as if I were a common Irishman."

Enterprising Irish immigrants did forge remarkable careers in America, however. Twenty years after arriving in New York, Alexander T. Stewart became the owner of the nation's largest department store and accumulated vast real estate holdings. Michael Cudahy, who began working at age fourteen in a Milwaukee meatpacking business, became head of the Cudahy Packing Company and developed a process for the curing of meats under refrigeration. Dublin-born Victor Herbert emerged as one of America's most revered composers, and Irish dancers and playwrights came to dominate the stage.

By the start of the Civil War, the Irish in America had energized trade unions, become the most important ethnic group supporting the Democratic party, and made the Roman Catholic Church the nation's largest religious denomination. Years of persecution had instilled in Irish Catholics a fierce loyalty to the church as "the supreme authority over all the affairs of the world." Such passion for Catholicism generated unity among Irish Americans—and fear among American Protestants.

The Irish loved to stick together. Most of them settled in Irish neighborhoods in the nation's largest cities and formed powerful Democratic political organizations, such as Tammany Hall in New York City, that would dominate political life during the second half of the nineteenth century.

THE GERMANS German immigrants were almost as numerous as the Irish. Unlike the Irish newcomers, however, the German arrivals included a large number of skilled craftsmen and well-educated professional people—doctors, lawyers, teachers, engineers—some of whom were refugees from the failed German revolution of 1848.

In addition to an array of political opinions, the Germans brought with them a variety of religious preferences. Most were Protestants (usually Lutherans), a third were Roman Catholics, and a significant number were Jews. Among the German immigrants who prospered in the New World were Heinrich Steinweg, a piano maker who in America changed his name to Steinway and became famous for the quality of his instruments, and Levi Strauss, a Jewish tailor who began making work pants, later dubbed "Levi's."

Germans settled more often in rural areas than in cities. Many were independent farmers, skilled workers, and shopkeepers who were able to establish themselves immediately. More so than the Irish, they migrated in families and groups. This clannish quality helped them better sustain elements of their language and culture in the United States. More of them also tended to return to their native country. About 14 percent of the Germans eventually went back to their homeland, compared with just 9 percent of the Irish.

THE BRITISH, SCANDINAVIANS, AND CHINESE Immigrants from Great Britain and Canada continued to arrive in large numbers during the first half of the nineteenth century. They included professionals, indepen-

A Know-Nothing cartoon This cartoon shows the Catholic Church supposedly attempting to control American religious and political life through Irish immigration.

dent farmers, and skilled workers. Two other large groups of immigrants were from Scandinavia and China. Norwegians and Swedes, mostly farmworkers, gravitated to Illinois, Wisconsin, and the Minnesota Territory, where the cold climate and dense forests reminded them of home. By the 1850s, the rapid development of California was attracting a growing number of Chinese, who, like the Irish in the East, did the heavy work, especially on railroads and bridges.

NATIVISM Not all Americans welcomed the flood of immigrants. A growing number of "nativists," people born in the United States who resented the newcomers, sought to restrict or stop immigration altogether. The flood of Irish and German Catholics especially aroused hostility among Protestants. A Boston minister described Catholicism as "the ally of tyranny, the opponent of material prosperity, the foe of thrift, the enemy of the railroad, the caucus, and the school."

Nativists eventually launched organized political efforts to stop the tide of immigrants. The Order of the Star-Spangled Banner, founded in New York City in 1849, grew into a powerful political group known as the American party. Members pledged never to vote for any foreign-born or Catholic candidates. When asked about the secretive organization, they were told to say, "I know nothing," a phrase which gave rise to the informal name for the party: the **Know-Nothings**.

For a while, the Know-Nothings appeared to be on the brink of major-party status, especially during the 1850s, when the number of immigrants was five times as large as it had been during the 1840s. In the state and local campaigns of 1854, they swept the Massachusetts legislature, winning all but two seats in the lower house, and that fall they elected more than forty congressmen. Forty percent of the Pennsylvania state legislators were Know-Nothings.

The Know-Nothings demanded that immigrants and Roman Catholics be excluded from public office and that the waiting period for naturalization (earning citizenship) be extended from five to twenty-one years. The party, however, was never strong enough to enact such legislation. Nor did Congress restrict immigration during that period. For a while, the Know-Nothings threatened to control New England, New York, and Maryland, but the anti-Catholic movement subsided when slavery became the focal issue of the 1850s.

ORGANIZED LABOR AND NEW PROFESSIONS

While most Americans continued to work as farmers during the nineteenth century, a growing number found employment in new or expanding enterprises: textile mills, shoe factories, banks, railroads, publishing, retail stores, teaching, preaching, medicine, law, construction, and engineering. Technological innovations (steam power, power tools, and new modes of transportation) and their social applications (mass communication, turnpikes, the postal service, banks, and corporations) fostered an array of new industries and businesses that transformed the nature of work for many Americans, both men and women.

EARLY UNIONS In 1800, only 12 percent of Americans worked for wages; by 1860, wage earners had grown to 40 percent of the nation's workforce. Proud apprentices, journeymen, and master craftsmen, who controlled their labor and invested their work with an emphasis on quality rather than quantity, resented the spread of mills and factories populated by "half-trained" workers dependent upon an hourly wage and subject to the fluctuations of the larger economy. Throughout the first half of the nineteenth century, the number of self-employed master craftsmen steadily declined as the number of factories and mills increased. Artisans who emphasized quality and craftsmanship in their custom-made products found it increasingly hard to compete

The shoe factory When Philadelphia shoemakers went on strike in 1806, a court found them guilty of a "conspiracy to raise wages." Here, shoemakers work at a Massachusetts shoe factory.

with the low prices for similar products made in much larger numbers in the factories and mass-production workshops.

The growing fear among artisans that they were losing status led many of them to become involved in politics and unions. Philadelphia furniture craftsmen, for example, called for a "union" to protect "their mutual independence." At first, these workers organized into interest groups representing their individual skills or trades. Such "trade associations" were the first type of labor unions. They pressured politicians for tariffs to protect their industries from foreign imports, provided insurance benefits, and drafted regulations to improve working conditions. In addition, they sought to control the number of tradesmen in their profession so as to maintain wage levels.

Early labor unions faced major legal obstacles—in fact, they were prosecuted as unlawful conspiracies. In 1806, for instance, Philadelphia shoemakers were found guilty of conspiring "to raise their wages." The court's decision broke the union. In 1842, though, the Massachusetts Supreme Judicial Court issued a landmark ruling in *Commonwealth v. Hunt* declaring that forming a trade union was not in itself illegal, nor was a demand that employers hire only members of the union. The court also said that union workers could strike if an employer hired laborers who refused to join the union.

Until the 1820s, labor organizations took the form of local trade unions, each confined to one city and one craft or skill. From 1827 to 1837, however, organization on a larger scale began to take hold. In 1834, the **National Trades' Union** was formed to organize local trade unions into a stronger national association. At the same time, shoemakers, printers, carpenters, and weavers established national craft unions representing their particular skills.

Women also formed trade unions. Sarah Monroe, who helped organize the New York Tailoresses' Society, explained that it was intended to defend "our rights." If it was "unfashionable for men to bear [workplace] oppression in silence, why should it not also become unfashionable with the women?" In 1831, the women tailors went out on strike demanding a "just price for labor."

Skilled workers also formed political organizations to represent their interests. A New York newspaper reported that people across the nation were organizing Workingmen's political parties to protect "those principles of liberty and equality unfolded in the Declaration of our

Symbols of organized labor
A pocket watch with an International Typographical Union insignia.

Independence." Workingmen's parties called for laws to regulate banks and abolish the common practice of imprisoning people who could not pay their debts.

THE RISE OF THE PROFESSIONS

The dramatic social changes opened up an array of new **professions**. Bustling new towns required new services—retail stores, printing shops, post offices, newspapers, schools, banks, law firms, medical practices. By definition, professional workers have specialized knowledge and training. In 1849, Henry Day delivered a lecture titled "The Professions" at the Western Reserve School of Medicine. He declared that the most important social functions in modern life were the professional skills and claimed that society had become utterly dependent upon "professional services."

TEACHING Teaching was one of the fastest-growing professions in the first half of the nineteenth century. Horace Mann of Massachusetts was instrumental in promoting the idea of free public education as the best way to transform children into disciplined, judicious citizens. Many states, especially in the North, agreed, and the number of schools exploded. New schools required teachers, and Mann helped create "normal schools" around the nation to train future teachers. Public schools initially preferred men as teachers, usually hiring them at age seventeen or eighteen. The pay was so low that few stayed in the profession their entire career, but for many educated, restless young adults, teaching offered independence and social status, as well as an alternative to the rural isolation of farming. Church groups and civic leaders started private academies, or seminaries, for girls.

LAW, MEDICINE, AND ENGINEERING Teaching was a common stepping-stone for men who became lawyers. In the decades after the American Revolution, young men would teach for a year or two before joining an experienced attorney as an apprentice (what today would be called an *intern*). They would learn the practice of law in exchange for their labors. (There were no law schools yet.)

Like attorneys, physicians in the early nineteenth century often had little formal academic training. Healers of every stripe assumed the title of *doctor* and established medical practices. Most were self-taught or had learned their profession by assisting a physician for several years, occasionally supplementing their internships with a few classes at the handful of medical schools. By 1860, there were 60,000 self-styled physicians, many of whom were "quacks," or frauds. As a result, the medical profession lost the public's confidence until the emergence of formal medical schools.

The industrial expansion of the United States also spurred the profession of engineering, a field that would eventually become the nation's largest professional occupation for men. Specialized expertise was required for the building of canals and railroads, the development of machine tools and steam engines, and the construction of roads, bridges, and factories.

"WOMEN'S WORK"   Meanwhile, most women still worked primarily in the home or on a farm. The only professions readily available to them were nursing (often midwifery, the delivery of babies) and teaching. Many middle-class women spent their time outside the home doing religious and social-service work. Then as now, women were the backbone of most churches.

A few women, however, courageously pursued careers in male-dominated professions. Elizabeth Blackwell of Ohio managed to gain admission to Geneva Medical College (now Hobart and William Smith College) in western New York despite the disapproval of the faculty. When she arrived at her first class, a hush fell upon the students "as if each member had been struck with paralysis." Blackwell had the last laugh when she finished first in her class in 1849, but thereafter the medical school refused to admit more women. The first American woman to earn a medical degree, Blackwell went on to start the New York Infirmary for Women and Children and later had a long career as a professor of gynecology at the London School of Medicine for Women.

EQUAL OPPORTUNITIES

The dynamic market-based economy that emerged during the first half of the nineteenth century helped spread the idea that individuals should have an equal opportunity to better themselves through their abilities and hard work. Equality of opportunity, however, did not assume equal outcomes. Americans wanted an equal chance to earn unequal amounts of wealth. In America, observed a journalist in 1844, "one has as good a chance as another according to his talents, prudence, and personal exertions."

The same ideals that prompted so many white immigrants to come to the United States, however, were equally appealing to African Americans and women. By the 1830s, they, too, began to demand their right to "life, liberty, and the pursuit of happiness." Such desires among "common people" would quickly spill over into the political arena. The great theme of American political life in the first half of the nineteenth century would be the continuing democratization of opportunities for white men, regardless of income or background, to vote and hold office.

CHAPTER REVIEW

SUMMARY

- **Transportation and Communication Revolutions**   Canals and other improvements in transportation, such as the *steamboat,* allowed goods to reach markets more quickly and cheaply and transformed the more isolated "household economy" of the eighteenth century into a *market-based economy* in which people bought and sold goods for profit in sometimes distant markets. *Clipper ships* shortened the amount of time to transport goods across the oceans. The *railroads* (which expanded rapidly during the 1850s) and the *telegraph system* diminished the isolation of the West and united the country economically and socially. The *Erie Canal* contributed to New York City's emerging status as the nation's economic center even as it promoted the growth of Chicago and other midwestern cities. Improvements in transportation and communication linked rural communities to a worldwide marketplace.

- **Industrialization**   Inventions in machine tools and technology as well as innovations in business organization spurred a wave of *industrialization* during the nineteenth century. The *cotton gin* dramatically increased cotton production, and a rapidly spreading *cotton* culture boomed in the South, with a resultant increase in slavery. Other inventions, such as John Deere's steel plow and the mechanized *McCormick reaper*, helped Americans, especially westerners, farm more efficiently and more profitably. In the North, mills and factories, powered first by water and eventually by coal-fired steam engines, spread rapidly. Mills produced textiles for clothing and bedding from southern cotton, as well as iron, shoes, and other products. The federal government's tariff policy encouraged the growth of domestic manufacturing, especially cotton textiles, by reducing imports of British cloth. Between 1820 and 1840, the number of Americans engaged in manufacturing increased 800 percent. Many mill workers, such as the women employed in the *Lowell system* of New England textile factory communities, worked long hours for low wages in unhealthy conditions. Industrialization, along with increased commerce, helped spur the growth of cities. By 1860, 16 percent of the population lived in an urban area.

- **Immigration**   The promise of cheap land and good wages drew millions of immigrants to America. By 1844, about 14.5 percent of the population was foreign-born. The devastating potato famine led to an influx of destitute Irish Catholic families. By the 1850s, they represented a significant portion of the urban population in the United States, constituting a majority in New York and Boston; German migrants, many of them Catholics and Jews, immigrated during this same time. Not all native-born Americans welcomed the immigrants. *Nativists* became a powerful political force in the 1850s, with the *Know-Nothing party* nearly achieving major-party status with its message of excluding immigrants and Catholics from the nation's political community.

- **Workers, Professionals, and Women**   Skilled workers (artisans) formed trade associations to protect their members and lobby for their interests. As the process of industrialization accelerated, some workers expanded these organizations nationally, forming the *National Trades' Union*. The growth of the market economy also expanded opportunities for those with formal education to serve in new or expanding *professions*. The number of physicians, teachers, engineers, and lawyers grew rapidly. By the mid-nineteenth century, women, African Americans, and immigrants began to agitate for equal social, economic, and political opportunities.

CHRONOLOGY

1793	Eli Whitney invents the cotton gin
1794	Philadelphia-Lancaster Turnpike is completed
1795	Wilderness Road opens
1807	Robert Fulton and Robert Livingston launch steamship transportation on the Hudson River near New York City
1825	Erie Canal opens in upstate New York
1831	Cyrus McCormick invents a mechanical reaper
1834	National Trades' Union is organized
1837	John Deere invents the steel plow
1842	Massachusetts Supreme Judicial Court issues *Commonwealth v. Hunt* decision
1845	Irish Potato Famine
1846	Elias Howe invents the sewing machine
1855	Know-Nothing party (American party) formed

KEY TERMS

market-based economy p. 289

steamboats p. 292

Erie Canal p. 293

railroads p. 295

clipper ships p. 295

telegraph system p. 298

industrialization p. 298

cotton gin p. 300

cotton p. 300

McCormick reapers p. 302

Lowell system p. 304

nativists p. 313

Know-Nothings p. 313

National Trades' Union p. 315

professions p. 316

🐾 INQUIZITIVE

Go to InQuizitive to see what you've learned—and learn what you've missed—with personalized feedback along the way.

9 Nationalism and Sectionalism

1815–1828

***Parade of the Victuallers* (1821)** On a beautiful day in March 1821, Philadelphia butcher William White organized a parade celebrating America's own high-quality meats. Many townspeople watched from their windows and balconies, while the spectators below could also enjoy the foods of various street vendors, such as the African American oyster peddler (bottom left). This watercolor by John Lewis Krimmel captures the vibrant nationalism that emerged in America after the War of 1812.

After the War of 1812, the British stopped interfering with American shipping. The United States could now develop new industries and exploit new markets around the globe. It was not simply Alexander Hamilton's financial initiatives and the capitalistic energies of wealthy investors and entrepreneurs that sparked America's dramatic economic growth in the early nineteenth century. Prosperity also resulted from the efforts of ordinary men and women who were willing to take risks, uproot families, use unstable paper money issued by unregulated local banks, and tinker with new machines, tools, and inventions.

By 1828, the young agrarian republic was poised to become a sprawling commercial nation connected by networks of roads and canals as well as regional economic relationships—all enlivened by a spirit of enterprise, experimentation, and expansion.

For all of the energy and optimism exhibited by Americans after the war, however, the fundamental tension between *nationalism* and *sectionalism* remained: how to balance the national interest with the particular economic and social needs of the nation's three growing regions—North, South, and West?

Americans who identified themselves as nationalists promoted the interests of the country as a whole. This required each region to recognize that no single section could get all it wanted without threatening the survival of the nation. Many sectionalists, however, were single-mindedly focused on promoting their region's priorities: shipping, manufacturing, and commerce

focus questions

1. How did the new spirit of nationalism that emerged after the War of 1812 affect economic and judicial policies?

2. What were the issues and ideas that promoted sectional conflict during this era?

3. How did the "Era of Good Feelings" emerge? What factors led to its demise?

4. What were the federal government's diplomatic accomplishments during this era? What was their impact?

5. What developments enabled Andrew Jackson to become president? How did he influence national politics in the 1820s?

in the Northeast; slave-based agriculture in the South; low land prices and transportation improvements in the West. Of all the issues dividing the young republic, the passions aroused by the expansion of slavery proved to be the most difficult to resolve.

A NEW NATIONALISM

After the War of 1812, Americans experienced a wave of patriotic excitement. They had won their independence from Britain for a second time, and a postwar surge of prosperity fed a widespread sense of optimism.

POSTWAR NATIONALISM In his first message to Congress in late 1815, President James Madison revealed how much the challenges of the war, especially the weaknesses of the armed forces and federal financing, had changed his attitudes toward the role of the federal government.

Now, Madison and other leading southern Republicans, such as South Carolina's John C. Calhoun, acted like nationalists rather than states' rights sectionalists. They abandoned many of Thomas Jefferson's presidential initiatives (for example, his efforts to reduce the armed forces and his opposition to the national bank) in favor of the *economic nationalism* developed by Federalists Alexander Hamilton and George Washington. Madison now supported a larger army and navy, a national bank, and tariffs to protect American manufacturers from foreign competition.

THE BANK OF THE UNITED STATES After President Madison and congressional Republicans allowed the charter for the First Bank of the United States to expire in 1811, the nation's finances fell into a muddle. States began chartering new local banks with little or no regulation, and their banknotes (paper money) flooded the economy with different currencies of uncertain value. Imagine trying to do business on a national basis when each state-chartered bank had its own currency, which often was not accepted by other banks or in other states.

In response to the growing financial turmoil, Madison urged Congress to establish the **Second Bank of the United States (B.U.S.)**. The B.U.S. was intended primarily to support a stable national currency that would promote economic growth. With the help of powerful congressmen Henry Clay and John C. Calhoun, Congress created the new B.U.S. in 1816, which, like its predecessor, was based in Philadelphia and was chartered for twenty years. In return for issuing national currency and opening branches in every state, the bank had to handle all of the federal government's funds without charge, lend the government up to $5 million upon demand, and pay the government a cash bonus of $1.5 million.

The bitter debate over the B.U.S., then and later, helped set the pattern of regional alignment for most other economic issues. Generally speaking, westerners opposed the national bank because it catered to eastern customers.

The controversy over the B.U.S. was also noteworthy because of the roles played by the era's greatest statesmen: Calhoun of South Carolina, Clay of Kentucky, and Daniel Webster of New Hampshire (and later Massachusetts). Calhoun, a war-hawk nationalist, introduced the banking bill and pushed it through, justifying its constitutionality by citing the congressional power to regulate the currency.

Clay, who had long opposed a national bank, now argued that new economic circumstances had made it indispensable. Webster led the opposition to the bank among the New England Federalists, who feared the growing financial power of Philadelphia. Later, Webster would return to Congress as the champion of a much stronger national government—at the same time that unexpected events would steer Calhoun away from economic nationalism and toward a defiant embrace of states' rights, slavery, and even secession.

A PROTECTIVE TARIFF The long controversy with Great Britain over shipping rights convinced most Americans of the need to develop their own manufacturing sector to end their dependence on imported British goods. Efforts to develop iron and textile industries, begun in New York and New England during the embargo of 1807, had accelerated during the War of 1812 when America did not have access to European goods.

After the war ended, however, the more-established British companies flooded U.S. markets with their less-expensive products, which undercut their American competitors. In response, northern manufacturers lobbied Congress for federal tariffs to protect their infant industries from what they called "unfair" British competition.

Congress responded by passing the **Tariff of 1816**, which placed a 20 to 25 percent tax on a long list of imported goods. Tariffs benefited some regions (the Northeast) more than others (the South), thus intensifying sectional tensions and grievances. The few southerners who voted for the tariff, led by Calhoun, did so because they hoped that the South might also become a manufacturing center over time. Within a few years, however, New England's manufacturing sector would roar ahead of the South, leading Calhoun to do an about-face and begin opposing tariffs.

INTERNAL IMPROVEMENTS The third major element of economic nationalism in the first half of the nineteenth century involved federal financing of "**internal improvements**"—the construction of roads, bridges, canals, and harbors. Most American rivers flowed from north to south, so the nation needed a network of roads running east to west.

In 1817, John C. Calhoun put through the House a bill to fund internal improvements. He believed that a federally-funded network of roads and canals in the West would help his native South by opening up trading relationships between the two regions. Support for federally-financed roads and canals came largely from the West, which badly needed transportation infrastructure. Opposition was centered in New England, which expected to gain the least from projects to spur western development.

POSTWAR NATIONALISM AND THE SUPREME COURT The postwar emphasis on economic nationalism also surfaced in the Supreme Court, where Chief Justice John Marshall strengthened the constitutional powers of the federal government at the expense of states' rights. In the path-breaking case of *Marbury v. Madison* (1803), the Court had, for the first time, declared a federal law unconstitutional. In the cases of *Martin v. Hunter's Lessee* (1816) and *Cohens v. Virginia* (1821), the Court ruled that the U.S. Constitution, as well as the nation's laws and treaties, could remain the supreme law of the land only if the Court could review and at times overturn the decisions of state courts.

PROTECTING CONTRACT RIGHTS The Supreme Court made two more major decisions in 1819 that strengthened the power of the federal government at the expense of the states: One, ***Dartmouth College v. Woodward***, involved the New Hampshire legislature's effort to change Dartmouth College's charter to stop the college's trustees from electing their own successors. In 1816, the state's legislature created a new board of trustees for the college. The original group of trustees sued to block the move. They lost in the state courts but won on appeal to the Supreme Court.

The college's original charter, wrote John Marshall in drafting the Court's opinion, was a valid contract that the state legislature had impaired, an act forbidden by the Constitution. This decision implied a new and enlarged definition of *contract* that seemed to put corporations beyond the reach of the states that had chartered them. Thereafter, states commonly wrote into the charters incorporating businesses and other organizations provisions making the charters subject to modification. Such provisions were then part of the "contract."

PROTECTING A NATIONAL CURRENCY The second major Supreme Court case of 1819 was Marshall's most significant interpretation of the constitutional system: ***McCulloch v. Maryland***. James McCulloch,

***Steamboat Travel on the Hudson River* (1811)** This watercolor of an early steamboat was painted by a Russian diplomat, Pavel Petrovich Svinin, who was fascinated by early technological innovations and the unique culture of America.

a B.U.S. clerk in the Baltimore office, had refused to pay state taxes on B.U.S. currency, as required by a Maryland law. The state indicted McCulloch. Acting on behalf of the national bank, he appealed to the Supreme Court, which ruled unanimously that Congress had the authority to charter the B.U.S. and that states had no right to tax the national bank.

Speaking for the Court, Chief Justice Marshall ruled that Congress had the right (that is, one of its "implied powers") to take any action not forbidden by the Constitution as long as the purpose of such laws was within the "scope of the Constitution." One great principle that "entirely pervades the Constitution," Marshall wrote, is "that the Constitution and the laws made in pursuance thereof are supreme: . . . They control the Constitution and laws of the respective states, and cannot be controlled by them."

REGULATING INTERSTATE COMMERCE John Marshall's last great judicial decision, ***Gibbons v. Ogden*** (1824), established the federal government's supremacy in regulating *interstate* commerce.

In 1808, the New York legislature granted Robert Fulton and Robert R. Livingston the exclusive right to operate steamboats on the state's rivers and lakes. Fulton and Livingston then gave Aaron Ogden the exclusive right to ferry people and goods up the Hudson River between New York and New Jersey. Thomas Gibbons, however, operated ships under a federal license that competed with Ogden. On behalf of a unanimous Court, Marshall ruled that the monopoly granted by the state to Ogden conflicted with the federal license issued to Gibbons.

DEBATES OVER THE AMERICAN SYSTEM

The major economic initiatives debated by Congress after the War of 1812— the national bank, federal tariffs, and federally-financed roads, bridges, ports, and canals—were interrelated pieces of a comprehensive economic plan called the **American System**.

The term was coined by Republican Henry Clay, the powerful congressional leader from Kentucky who would serve three terms as Speaker of the House before becoming a U.S. senator. Clay wanted to free America's economy from its dependence on Great Britain while tying together the diverse regions of the nation politically. He said, "I know of no South, no North, no East, no West to which I owe my allegiance. The Union is my country."

In promoting his American System, Clay sought to give each section of the country its top economic priority. He argued that high tariffs on imports were needed to block the sale of British products in the United States and thereby protect new industries in New England and New York from unfair foreign competition.

To convince the skeptical western states to support the tariffs, Clay first called for the federal government to use tariff revenues to build much-needed infrastructure—roads, bridges, canals, and other "internal improvements"— in the frontier West to enable speedier travel and faster shipment of goods to markets.

Second, Clay's American System would raise prices for federal lands sold to the public and distribute the additional revenue from the land sales to the states to help finance more roads, bridges, and canals. Third, Clay endorsed a strong national bank to create a single national currency and to regulate the often unstable state and local banks.

Clay was the consummate deal maker and economic nationalist. In many respects, he assumed responsibility for sustaining Alexander Hamilton's vision of a strong federal government nurturing a national economy that combined agriculture, industry, and commerce.

The success of Clay's program depended on each section's willingness to compromise. For a while, it worked.

Critics, however, argued that higher prices for federal lands would discourage western migration and that tariffs benefited the northern manufacturing sector at the expense of southern and western farmers and the "common" people, who had to pay higher prices for the goods produced by tariff-protected industries.

Many westerners and southerners also feared that the Second Bank of the United States would become so powerful and corrupt that it could dictate the nation's economic future at the expense of states' rights and the needs of particular regions. Missouri senator Thomas Hart Benton predicted that cash-strapped western towns would be at the mercy of the national bank in Philadelphia. Westerners, Benton worried, "are in the jaws of the monster! A lump of butter in the mouth of a dog! One gulp, one swallow, and all is gone!"

"An Era of Good Feelings"

As James Madison approached the end of his presidency, he turned to James Monroe, a fellow Virginian, to be his successor. In the 1816 election, Monroe overwhelmed his Federalist opponent, Rufus King of New York, by a 183–34 margin in the Electoral College. The "Virginia dynasty" of presidents continued. Monroe's presidency started with America at peace and its economy flourishing.

Soon after his inauguration, in early 1817, Monroe embarked on a goodwill tour of New England, the stronghold of the Federalist party. In Boston, a Federalist newspaper complimented the Republican president for making the effort to "harmonize feelings, annihilate dissentions, and make us one people." Those words were printed under the heading, "Era of Good Feelings," and the headline became a popular label for Monroe's administration.

James Monroe Portrayed as he began his presidency in 1817.

JAMES MONROE Like George Washington, Thomas Jefferson, and James Madison, Monroe was a slaveholding planter from Virginia. At the outbreak of the Revolutionary War, he dropped out of the College of William and Mary to join the army. He served under George Washington, who called him a "brave, active, and sensible army officer."

After studying law under Thomas Jefferson, Monroe served as a representative in the Virginia assembly, as governor, as a representative in the Confederation Congress, as a U.S. senator, and as U.S. minister (ambassador) to Paris, London, and Madrid. Under President Madison, he served as secretary of state and doubled as secretary of war during the War of 1812. John C. Calhoun, who would be Monroe's secretary of war, said that the new president was "among the wisest and most cautious men I have ever known." Jefferson noted that Monroe was "a man whose soul might be turned wrong side outwards without discovering a blemish to the world."

Although Monroe's presidency began peacefully enough, sectional loyalties eventually erupted at the expense of nationalist needs. Two major events signaled the end of the Era of Good Feelings and warned of stormy times ahead: the financial Panic of 1819 and the political conflict over statehood for Missouri.

THE PANIC OF 1819 The young republic experienced its first major economic depression when the **Panic of 1819** led to a prolonged financial slowdown. Like so many other economic collapses, it was fundamentally the result of too many people trying to get rich too quickly.

After the War of 1812, European demand for American products, especially cotton, tobacco, and flour, soared, leading farmers and planters to increase production. To fuel the roaring postwar economy, unsound local and state banks multiplied and made it easy—too easy—for people and businesses to get loans. The Bank of the United States (B.U.S.) aggravated the problem by issuing risky loans, too.

At the same time, the federal government aggressively sold vast tracts of public land, which spurred reckless real estate speculation by people buying large parcels with the intention of reselling them. On top of all that, good weather in Europe led to a spike in crop production there, thus reducing the need to buy American commodities. Prices for American farm products plunged.

The Panic of 1819 was ignited by the sudden collapse of cotton prices after British textile mills quit buying high-priced American cotton—the nation's leading export—in favor of cheaper cotton from other parts of the world. As the price of cotton fell and the flow of commerce slowed, banks began to fail, and unemployment spiked. The collapse of cotton prices was especially devastating for southern planters, but it also reduced the world demand for other American goods. Owners of new factories and mills, most of them in New

England, New York, and Pennsylvania, struggled to find markets for their goods and to fend off more-experienced foreign competitors.

The financial panic and the ensuing depression deepened tensions between northern and southern economic interests. It also spawned a widespread distrust of banks and bankers. Tennessee congressman David Crockett dismissed the "whole Banking system" as nothing more than "swindling on a large scale." Thomas Jefferson felt the same way. He wrote to John Adams that "the paper [money] bubble is then burst. This is what you and I, and every reasoning man . . . have long foreseen."

Other factors caused the financial panic to become a depression. Business owners, farmers, and land speculators had recklessly borrowed money to expand their business ventures or to purchase more land. With the collapse of crop prices and the decline of land values during and after 1819, both land speculators and settlers saw their income plummet.

The equally reckless lending practices of the numerous new state banks compounded the economic confusion. To generate more loans, the banks issued more paper money. Even the Second Bank of the United States, which was supposed to provide financial stability, was caught up in the easy-credit mania.

In 1819, newspapers revealed a case of extensive fraud and embezzlement in the Baltimore branch of the Bank of the United States. The scandal prompted the appointment of Langdon Cheves, a former South Carolina congressman, as the new president of the B.U.S. Cheves restored confidence in the national bank by forcing state banks to keep more gold coins in their vaults to back up the loans they were making. State banks in turn put pressure on their debtors, who found it harder to renew old loans or to get new ones. The economic depression lasted about three years, and many people blamed the B.U.S. After the panic subsided, many Americans, especially in the South and the West, remained critical of the national bank.

THE MISSOURI COMPROMISE As the financial panic deepened, another dark cloud appeared on the horizon: the onset of a fierce sectional controversy over expanding slavery into the western territories. The possibility of new western states becoming "slave states" created the greatest political debate of the nineteenth century. Thomas Jefferson admitted that the issue scared him "like a firebell in the night."

Jefferson realized that the United States was increasingly at risk of disintegrating over the future of slavery. By 1819, the country had an equal number of slave and free states—eleven of each. The Northwest Ordinance (1787) had banned slavery north of the Ohio River, and the Southwest Ordinance (1790) had authorized slavery south of the Ohio.

In the region west of the Mississippi River, however, slavery had existed since France and Spain first colonized the area. St. Louis became the crossroads through which southerners brought slaves into the Missouri Territory.

In 1819, residents in the Missouri Territory asked the House of Representatives to let them draft a constitution and apply for statehood, its population having passed the minimum of 60,000 white settlers (there were also some 10,000 slaves). It would be the first state west of the Mississippi River.

At that point, Representative James Tallmadge Jr., an obscure New York Republican, proposed a resolution to ban the transport of any more slaves into Missouri. Tallmadge's resolution enraged southern slave owners, many of whom had developed a profitable trade selling slaves to traders who took them to the western territories to be sold again. Any effort to restrict slavery in the western territories, southern congressmen threatened, could lead to "disunion" and civil war.

In addition, southerners worried that the addition of Missouri as a free state would tip the balance of power in the Senate against the slave states. Their fears were heightened when Congressman Timothy Fuller, an anti-slavery Republican from Massachusetts, declared that it was both "the right and duty of Congress" to stop the spread "of the intolerable evil and the crying enormity of slavery." After fiery debates, the House, with its northern majority, passed the Tallmadge Amendment on an almost strictly sectional vote. The Senate, however, rejected it, also along sectional lines.

At about the same time, Maine, which had been part of Massachusetts, applied for statehood. The Senate decided to link Maine's request for statehood with Missouri's, voting in 1820 to admit Maine as a free state and Missouri as a slave state, thus maintaining the political balance between free and slave states.

Illinois senator Jesse Thomas revised the so-called **Missouri Compromise** by introducing an amendment to exclude slavery in the rest of the Louisiana Purchase north of latitude 36°30′, Missouri's southern border. Slavery thus would continue in the Arkansas Territory and in the new state of Missouri but would be excluded from the remainder of the area west of the Mississippi River. By a narrow margin, the Thomas Amendment passed on March 2, 1820.

Then another issue arose. The pro-slavery faction in Missouri's constitutional convention inserted in the proposed state constitution a provision excluding free blacks and mulattoes (mixed-race people) from residing in the state. This violated the U.S. Constitution. Free blacks were already citizens of many states.

The dispute over the status of blacks threatened to unravel the deal until Speaker of the House Henry Clay fashioned a "second" Missouri Compromise whereby Missouri would be admitted as a state only if its legislature pledged

THE MISSOURI COMPROMISE, 1820

BRITISH POSSESSIONS

OREGON COUNTRY
Joint occupation by Britain and U.S.

UNORGANIZED TERRITORY

Mississippi River

MICHIGAN TERRITORY

MAINE 1820

VT

NH

NY

MA

RI

PA

CT

NJ

DE

IL   IN   OH

Ohio River

VA

MD

SPANISH POSSESSIONS

MISSOURI 1821

KY

ARKANSAS TERRITORY

TN

NC

SC

MS   AL   GA

LA

PACIFIC OCEAN

ATLANTIC OCEAN

FLORIDA TERRITORY

GULF OF MEXICO

BRITISH

SPANISH

Free states

Slave states

States and territories covered by the compromise

0   250   500 Miles

0   250   500 Kilometers

- What caused the sectional controversy over slavery in 1819?
- What were the terms of the Missouri Compromise?
- What was Henry Clay's solution to the Missouri constitution's ban on free blacks in that state?

never to deny free blacks their constitutional rights. The Missouri legislature approved Clay's suggestion but denied that it had any power to bind the state in the future. On August 10, 1821, Missouri became the twenty-fourth state, and the twelfth where slavery was allowed.

Nationalists praised the Missouri Compromise for deflecting the volatile issue of slavery. But the compromise settled little. In fact, it had the effect of hardening positions in both North and South.

NATIONALIST DIPLOMACY

The efforts of Henry Clay to promote economic nationalism and John Marshall to affirm judicial nationalism were reinforced by efforts to practice *diplomatic nationalism*. John Quincy Adams, secretary of state in the Monroe administration and the son of former president John Adams, aggressively exercised America's growing power to clarify and expand the nation's boundaries. He also wanted Europeans to recognize America's dominance in the Western Hemisphere.

RELATIONS WITH BRITAIN   The Treaty of Ghent (1814) had ended the War of 1812, but it left unsettled several disputes between the United States and Great Britain. Adams oversaw the negotiations of two important treaties, the Rush-Bagot Treaty of 1817 (named after the diplomats who arranged it) and the Convention of 1818, both of which eased tensions.

In the Rush-Bagot Treaty, the two nations agreed to limit the number of warships on the Great Lakes. The Convention of 1818 was even more important. It settled the disputed northern boundary of the Louisiana Purchase by extending it along the 49th parallel westward, from what would become Minnesota to the Rocky Mountains. West of the Rockies, the Oregon Country would be jointly occupied by the British and the Americans.

BOUNDARY TREATIES, 1818–1819

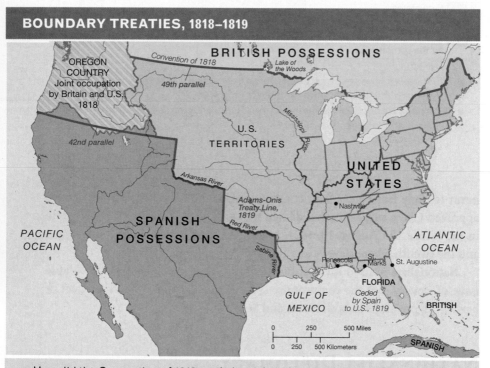

- How did the Convention of 1818 settle boundary disputes between Spain and the United States?
- How did Andrew Jackson's aggressive military actions in Florida help John Quincy Adams claim territory from Spain?

Massacre of the Whites by Indians and Blacks in Florida **(1836)** Published in a southerner's account of the Seminole War, this is one of the earliest known depictions of African Americans and Native Americans fighting as allies.

FLORIDA Still another disputed boundary involved western Florida. Spanish control over Florida during the early nineteenth century was more a technicality than an actuality. Spain was now a declining power, unable to enforce its obligations under Pinckney's Treaty of 1795 to keep Indians in the region from making raids into south Georgia.

In early 1818, Jackson's force of 2,000 federal soldiers, volunteer Tennessee militiamen, and Indian allies crossed into Spanish Florida from their encampment in south Georgia. In April, the Americans assaulted a Spanish fort at St. Marks and destroyed several Seminole villages along the Suwannee River, hanging two chiefs.

Jackson's soldiers also captured and court-martialed two British traders accused of provoking Indian attacks. When told that a military trial of the British citizens was illegal, Jackson gruffly replied that the laws of war did not "apply to conflicts with savages."

Jackson ordered the immediate execution of the British troublemakers, an illegal action that outraged the British government and alarmed President Monroe's cabinet. But the Tennessee general kept moving. In May, he captured Pensacola, the Spanish capital of West Florida, and established a provisional American government until Florida's future was decided.

While Jackson's conquests excited expansionists, they aroused anger in Spain and concern in Washington, D.C. Spain demanded that its territory be returned and that Jackson be punished for violating international law. Monroe's cabinet was at first prepared to disavow Jackson's illegal acts. Privately, Secretary of War Calhoun criticized Jackson for disobeying orders—a stand that would later cause bad blood between them.

Jackson, however, was a hero to most Americans. He also had an important friend in the cabinet—Secretary of State John Quincy Adams, who realized that Jackson's unauthorized conquest of Florida had strengthened his own hand in negotiating with the Spanish to purchase the territory. American forces withdrew from Florida, but negotiations resumed with the knowledge that the U.S. Army could retake Florida at any time.

In 1819, Adams convinced the Spanish to sign the **Transcontinental Treaty** (also called the Adams-Onís Treaty), which gave all of Florida to the United States for $5 million. In 1821, Florida became a U.S. territory; in 1845, it would become a state.

The treaty also clarified the western boundary separating the Louisiana Territory from New Spain. It would run from the Gulf of Mexico north along the Sabine River separating Louisiana from Texas and then, in stair-step fashion, up to the Red River, along the Red, and up to the Arkansas River. From the source of the Arkansas River, it would go north to the 42nd parallel and then west to the Pacific coast. The United States finally spanned the continent.

THE MONROE DOCTRINE The most important diplomatic policy crafted by President Monroe and Secretary of State Adams involved a determined effort to prevent any future European colonialism in the Western Hemisphere. The Spanish, British, French, Portuguese, Dutch, and Russians still controlled one or more colonies in the Americas.

One consequence of the Napoleonic Wars in Europe was the French occupation of Spain and Portugal. The turmoil in those two nations helped trigger independence movements among their colonies in the Americas. Within little more than a decade after the flag of rebellion was first raised in 1809 in Ecuador, Spain had lost almost its entire empire in the Americas; La Plata (later Argentina), Bolivia, Chile, Ecuador, Peru, Colombia, Mexico, Paraguay, Uruguay, and Venezuela had all proclaimed their independence, as had Portuguese Brazil. The only areas still under Spanish control were the islands of Cuba and Puerto Rico and the colony of Santo Domingo on the island of Hispaniola.

In 1823, rumors reached America that the monarchs of Europe were planning to help Spain recover its Latin American colonies. The British foreign minister, George Canning, told the United States that the two countries should jointly oppose any new incursions by European nations in the Western Hemisphere. Monroe initially agreed—if the London government would agree to recognize the independence of the new nations of Latin America. The British refused.

Adams, however, advised Monroe to go it alone in prohibiting further European involvement in the hemisphere. Adams stressed that "it would be more candid as well as more dignified" for America to ban further European intervention than to tag along with a British statement.

Monroe agreed. In his annual message to Congress in December 1823, the president outlined the four major points of what became known as the **Monroe Doctrine**: (1) that "the American continents . . . are henceforth not to be considered as subjects for future colonization by any European powers"; (2) that the United States would consider any attempt by a European nation to intervene "in this hemisphere as dangerous to our peace and safety"; (3) that the United States would not interfere with existing European-controlled colonies in the Americas; and (4) that the United States would keep out of the internal affairs of European nations.

Reaction to the Monroe Doctrine was mixed. In France, Marquis de Lafayette, the courageous, freedom-loving volunteer in the American Revolution, hailed the new policy "as the best little bit of paper that God had ever permitted any man to give to the world." Others were not as impressed by the "presumptuous" American declaration. No European nation recognized the Monroe Doctrine. In fact, the Russian ruler, Czar Alexander I, dismissed it with "profound contempt," since he knew that the tiny U.S. Navy could not protect its shores. At the time, the Russians controlled Alaska and claimed to own the Oregon Country as well.

To this day, the Monroe Doctrine has no official standing in international law. Symbolically, however, it has been an important statement of American intentions to prevent European involvement in the Western Hemisphere and an example of the young nation's determination to take its place among the world's great powers. Since it was announced, not a single Latin American nation has lost its independence to an outside invader.

THE RISE OF ANDREW JACKSON

After the War of 1812, the United States had essentially a one-party political system. The refusal of the Federalists to support the war had virtually killed the party. In 1820, President Monroe was reelected without opposition; the Federalists did not even nominate a candidate.

While the Republican party was dominant for the moment, however, it was about to follow the Federalists into oblivion. If Monroe's first term was the Era of Good Feelings, his second term became an Era of Bad Feelings, as sectional controversies erupted into disputes so violent that they gave birth to a new political party: the Democrats, led by Andrew Jackson.

ANDREW JACKSON   Born in 1767 along the border between the Carolinas, Andrew Jackson grew up in a struggling, single-parent household. His father was killed in a farm accident three weeks before Andrew was born, forcing his widowed mother Elizabeth to scratch out a living as a housekeeper while raising three sons.

During the Revolution, the Jackson boys joined in the fighting against the British. One of them, sixteen-year-old Hugh, died of heat exhaustion during a battle; another, Robert, died while trudging home from a prisoner-of-war camp.

In 1781, fourteen-year-old Andrew was captured. When a British officer demanded that the boy shine his muddy boots, Andrew refused, whereupon the angry officer slashed him with his sword, leaving ugly scars on Jackson's head and hand. Soon after her son was released, Elizabeth Jackson, who had helped nurse injured American soldiers, died of cholera. The orphaned Jackson thereafter despised the British, blaming them for the deaths of his brothers and mother.

After the Revolution, Jackson went to Charleston, South Carolina, where he learned to love racehorses, gambling, and fine clothes. He returned home and tried saddle making and teaching before moving to Salisbury, North Carolina, where he earned a license to practice law.

In 1788, at age twenty-one, Jackson moved to Nashville and became an attorney in backwoods Tennessee. He also fell in love with Rachel Donelson Robards, a beautiful married woman with whom he lived before she was legally divorced from her first husband. The Jacksons were passionately devoted to each other, but mean-spirited gossip about the origins of their relationship dogged them until Rachel's death in December 1828.

Jackson had a quick temper throughout his life. He loved a good fight. "When danger rears its head," he once told his wife, "I can never shrink from it." In 1806, he challenged Charles Dickinson to a duel for not pay a racing bet and then insulting his wife, Rachel. Although Dickinson was said to be the best shot in Tennessee, Jackson let him fire first. For his gallantry, the future president received a bullet in the chest that nearly killed him. He nevertheless straightened himself, patiently took aim, and coolly killed his foe. "I should have hit him," Jackson claimed, "if he had shot me through the brain."

In 1796, when Tennessee became a state, voters elected Jackson to the U.S. House and later to the Senate, where he served only a year before returning to Tennessee and becoming a judge. The ambitious Jackson made a lot of money, first as an attorney, then as a buyer and seller of horses, land, and slaves. He eventually owned 100 slaves on his large cotton plantation, called the Hermitage. He had no moral reservations about slavery and at times could be a cruel master. After one of his slaves escaped, Jackson offered a large reward for his recapture, and promised "ten dollars extra for every hundred lashes a person will give [him] to the amount of three hundred." When not farming or raising racehorses, Jackson served as the commander of the Tennessee militia.

Many American political leaders cringed at the thought of the rough-hewn, short-tempered Jackson, who had run roughshod over international law in his war against the British and Seminoles in Florida, presiding over the nation. "His passions are terrible," said Thomas Jefferson. John Quincy Adams scorned Jackson "as a barbarian and savage who could scarcely spell his name." Jackson dismissed such criticism as an example of the "Eastern elite" trying to maintain control of American politics. He responded to Adams's criticism of his literacy by commenting that he never trusted a man who could think of only one way to spell a word.

PRESIDENTIAL POLITICS No sooner had James Monroe started his second presidential term, in 1821, than leading Republicans began positioning themselves to be the next president, including three members of the president's cabinet: Secretary of War John C. Calhoun, Secretary of the Treasury William H. Crawford, and Secretary of State John Quincy Adams. The powerful speaker of the House, Henry Clay, also hungered for the presidency. And there was Andrew Jackson, who was elected to the Senate in 1823. The emergence of so many viable candidates revealed how fractured the Republican party had become.

In 1822, the Tennessee legislature named Jackson its long-shot choice to succeed Monroe. Two years later, Pennsylvania Republicans also endorsed Jackson for president and chose Calhoun for vice president. Meanwhile, the Kentucky legislature had nominated its favorite son, Clay, in 1822. The Massachusetts legislature nominated Adams in 1824. That same year, a group of Republican congressmen nominated Crawford, a cotton planter from Georgia.

Crawford's friends emphasized his devotion to states' rights and strict construction of the Constitution. Clay continued to promote the economic nationalism of his American System. Adams, the only non-slaveholder in the race, shared Clay's belief that the national government should finance internal improvements to stimulate economic development, but he was less strongly committed to tariffs.

Jackson declared himself the champion of the common people and the foe of the entrenched social and political elite. He claimed to represent the "old republicanism" of Thomas Jefferson. But Jefferson believed that Jackson lacked the education, polish, and prudence to be president. "He is," Jefferson told a friend, "one of the most unfit men I know," a "dangerous man." In 1824, Jefferson supported Crawford.

As a self-made military hero, Jackson was an attractive candidate, especially to voters of Irish background. The son of poor Scots-Irish colonists, he was beloved for having defeated the hated English in the Battle of New Orleans. In addition, his commitment to those he called the "common men" resonated with many Irish immigrants who associated aristocracy with centuries of English rule over Ireland.

THE "CORRUPT BARGAIN" The results of the 1824 election were inconclusive. Jackson won the popular vote and the Electoral College, where he had 99 votes, Adams 84, Crawford 41, and Clay 37. But Jackson did not have the necessary majority of electoral votes. In such a circumstance, as in the 1800 election, the Constitution specified that the House of Representatives would make the final decision from among the top three vote-getters. By the time the House could convene, however, Crawford had suffered a stroke and was ruled out for medical reasons. So the election came down to Adams and Jackson.

Clay's influence as Speaker of the House would be decisive. While Adams and Jackson courted Clay's support, he scorned them both, claiming they provided only a "choice of evils." But he regarded Jackson, his fierce western rival, as a "military chieftain," a frontier Napoléon unfit for the presidency. Jackson's election, Clay predicted, would "be the greatest misfortune that could befall the country."

Although Clay and Adams disliked each other, the nationalist Adams supported most of the policies that Clay wanted, particularly high tariffs, transportation improvements, and a strong national bank. Clay also expected Adams to name him secretary of state, the office that usually led to the White House. In the end, a deal between Clay and Adams broke the deadlock. Clay endorsed Adams, and the House of Representatives elected Adams with 13 state delegation votes to Jackson's 7 and Crawford's 4.

The controversial victory proved costly for Adams, however, as it united his foes and crippled his administration before it began. Jackson dismissed Clay as a "scoundrel," the "Judas of the West," who had entered into a self-serving **"corrupt bargain"** with Adams. Their "corruptions and intrigues," he charged, had "defeated the will of the People." American politics had entered an Era of Bad Feelings.

Almost immediately after the 1824 decision, Jackson's supporters launched a campaign to undermine the Adams administration and elect the military

John Quincy Adams A brilliant man but an ineffective leader, he appears here in his study in 1843. He was the first U.S. president to be photographed.

hero president in 1828. Crawford's supporters soon moved into the Jackson camp, as did the new vice president, John C. Calhoun, who quickly found himself at odds with the president.

JOHN QUINCY ADAMS John Quincy Adams of Massachusetts was one of the nation's hardest working presidents, yet he was also one of the most ineffective. Like his father, the stiff, formal Adams was a great and good man of colossal learning and steely ambition, but he lacked the common touch and the politician's gift for compromise. He worried, as had his father, that republicanism was rapidly turning into democracy and that government *of* the people was degenerating into government *by* the people, many of whom, in his view, were uneducated and incompetent.

Adams detested the democratic politicking that Andrew Jackson represented. He wanted politics to be a "sacred" arena for the "best men," a profession limited to the "most able and worthy" who were motivated by a sense of civic duty rather than a selfish quest for power and stature. The poet Walt Whitman wrote that although Adams was "a virtuous man—a learned man . . . he was not a man of the People."

Adams also suffered from bouts of depression and self-pity, qualities that did not endear him to fellow politicians or the public. In a fit of candor, he described himself as "a man of reserved, cold, austere, and forbidding manners." Yet after admitting the "defects" in his personality, Adams confessed that he could not change them.

Adams's first message to Congress, in December 1825, revealed his grand blueprint for national development. His vision of an energetic federal government funding an array of improvement projects outdid the plans of Alexander Hamilton, James Monroe, and Henry Clay.

The federal government, Adams stressed, should finance internal improvements (roads, canals, harbors, and bridges), create a great national university in Washington, D.C., support scientific explorations, build astronomical observatories, and establish a Department of the Interior to manage the vast federal lands. He challenged Congress to approve his proposals and not be paralyzed "by the will of our constituents." Adams believed that he knew what was best for the country, and he would not be stopped by the concerns of voters.

Reaction was overwhelmingly negative. Newspapers charged that Adams was behaving like an aristocratic tyrant, and Congress quickly revealed that it would approve none of his ambitious proposals. The disastrous start shattered Adams's confidence. He wrote in his diary that he was in a "protracted agony of character and reputation."

Adams's effort to expand the powers of the federal government was so divisive that the Republican party split in two, creating a new party system. Those who agreed with the economic nationalism of Adams and Clay began calling themselves National Republicans.

The opposition—made up of those who supported Andrew Jackson and states' rights—began calling themselves Democrats. They were strongest in the South and West, as well as among the working class in large eastern cities.

The Democrats were the first party to recruit professional state organizers, such as Martin Van Buren of New York, who developed sophisticated strategies for mobilizing voters and orchestrating grassroots campaigns featuring massive rallies, barbecues, and parades.

Perhaps most important, the Democrats convinced voters that their primary allegiance should be to their party rather than to a particular candidate. Party loyalty became the prized virtue among Democrats; it was the most powerful weapon they could muster against the "privileged aristocracy" running the state and federal governments.

Jackson claimed that Adams was behaving like a monarch rather than a president (a charge later applied to Jackson). If the president's schemes for expanding government power were not stopped "by the voice of the people," Jackson said, "it must end in consolidation & then in despotism."

Adams's opponents sought to use the always controversial tariff issue against him. In 1828, anti-Adams congressmen introduced a tariff bill designed to help elect Jackson. It placed duties on various imported raw materials such as wool, hemp, and iron that were also produced in key states where Jackson needed support: Pennsylvania, New York, Ohio, Kentucky, and Missouri.

The measure passed, only to be condemned as the "Tariff of Abominations" by the cotton states of the Deep South. In South Carolina, John C. Calhoun secretly wrote the *South Carolina Exposition and Protest* (1828), in which he ominously declared that a state could nullify an act of Congress that it found unconstitutional, such as the new tariff bill.

JACKSON'S ELECTION These maneuverings launched the savage **election of 1828** between John Quincy Adams and Andrew Jackson, the National Republicans versus the Jacksonian Democrats. Both sides engaged in vicious personal attacks. As a Jackson supporter observed, "The floodgates of falsehood, slander, and abuse have been hoisted" by the Adams campaign, "and the most nauseating filth is [being] poured" on Jackson's head.

Adams's supporters denounced Jackson as a hot-tempered, ignorant barbarian, a gambler and slave trader, a man who thrived on confrontation and violence and whose fame rested upon his reputation as a cold-blooded killer.

The most scurrilous attack on Jackson was that he had lived in adultery with his wife, Rachel. In fact, they had lived together as husband and wife for two years in the mistaken belief that the divorce from her first husband was final. As soon as the divorce was indeed official, Andrew and Rachel had remarried to end all doubts about their status. A furious Jackson blamed Henry Clay for the slurs against his wife, calling the Kentuckian "the basest, meanest scoundrel that ever disgraced the image of his god."

The Jacksonians, for their part, condemned Adams as an aristocrat and monarchist, a professional politician who had never had a real job. Newspapers claimed that the president had been corrupted by foreigners in the courts of Europe during his diplomatic career. The most outlandish charge was that Adams had allegedly delivered up an American girl to Czar Alexander I while serving as ambassador to Russia. Adams was left to gripe about the many "forgeries now swarming in the newspapers against me."

As a military hero and fabled Indian fighter, Jackson was beloved as the "people's champion" by farmers and working men. As a plantation owner, lawyer, and slaveholder, he had the trust of the southern political elite. Jackson was for a small federal government, individual liberty, an expanded military, and white supremacy. Above all, he was a nationalist committed to preserving the Union in the face of rising sectional tensions.

Candidate Jackson benefited from a growing spirit of democracy in which many viewed Adams as an elitist. Jackson insisted that the election came down to one question: "Shall the government or the people rule?" As president, Jackson promised, he would fight against the entrenched power of the wealthy and powerful.

When Adams's supporters began referring to Jackson as a "jackass," Old Hickory embraced the name, using the animal as a symbol for his "tough" campaign. The jackass eventually became the enduring symbol of the Democratic party.

THE "COMMON MAN" IN POLITICS Jackson's campaign explicitly appealed to the common voters, many of whom were able to vote in a presidential election for the first time as a result of the ongoing democratization of the political system. New Jersey in 1807 and Maryland and South Carolina in 1810 had abolished property and taxpaying requirements for voting, and after 1815 the new states of Indiana, Illinois, Alabama, and Mississippi gave voting rights (suffrage) to all white men regardless of how much property they owned. Other states followed, and by 1824, twenty-one of the twenty-four states had dropped property-owning requirements for voting. Only Virginia and the Carolinas, still dominated by the planter elite, continued to resist the democratizing trend.

The "democratization" of politics also affected many free black males in northern states, half of which allowed blacks to vote. Rufus King, the former presidential candidate, declared that in New York, "a citizen of color was entitled to all the privileges of a citizen . . . [and] entitled to vote."

The extension of voting rights to common men led to the election of politicians sprung from "the people" rather than from the social elite. Jackson, a frontiersman of humble origin and limited education, perfectly symbolized this emerging democratic ideal. "Adams can write," went one of the campaign slogans, "but Jackson can fight."

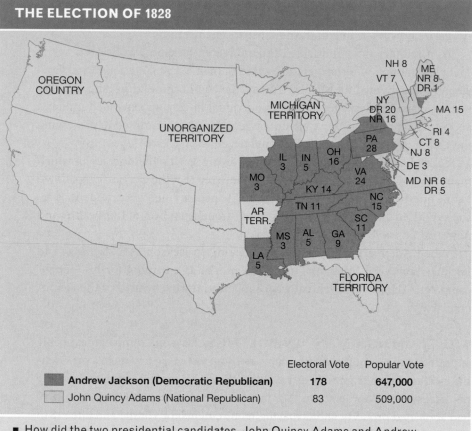

THE ELECTION OF 1828

	Electoral Vote	Popular Vote
Andrew Jackson (Democratic Republican)	178	647,000
John Quincy Adams (National Republican)	83	509,000

- How did the two presidential candidates, John Quincy Adams and Andrew Jackson, portray each other in the campaign?
- Why did Jackson seem to have the advantage in the election of 1828?
- How did the broadening of voting rights affect the presidential campaign?

LABOR POLITICS With the widespread removal of property qualifications for voting, the working class (laborers paid hourly wages) became an important political force in the form of the Working Men's parties. They were first organized in 1828 in Philadelphia, the nation's largest manufacturing center, with other parties following in New York City and Boston.

The Working Men's parties were devoted to promoting the interests of laborers, such as shorter working hours and allowing all males to vote regardless of the amount of property owned. But the overarching concern of the Working Men's parties was the widening inequality of wealth in American society.

The Working Men's parties faded quickly, however. The inexperience of labor politicians left them vulnerable to manipulation by political professionals. In addition, major national parties, especially the Jacksonian Democrats, co-opted many of their issues. Labor parties also proved vulnerable to charges of social radicalism, and the courts typically sided with management in dealing with strikes.

Yet the working-class parties succeeded in drawing attention to their demands. They promoted free public education for all children and the abolition of imprisonment for debt, causes that won widespread popular support. The labor parties and unions also called for a ten-hour workday to prevent employers from abusing workers. In large part because of Andrew Jackson's background as a "common man," union members loved him, and the new Democratic party proved adept at building a national coalition of working-class supporters.

PRESIDENT JACKSON When the 1828 election returns came in, Jackson had won the electoral vote by 178 to 83, and his 56 percent of the popular vote would be a margin unsurpassed during the nineteenth century. Equally important was the surge in voter turnout; more than twice as many men voted as in the 1824 election. Jackson won every state west and south of Pennsylvania.

As he prepared for his inauguration, the president-elect was still boiling with resentment at the way his opponents had besmirched the reputation of his wife, who had died in mid-December 1828, just a few days after learning of the political attacks on her and her "tarnished" marriage. Jackson became obsessed with punishing her persecutors, especially his archenemy, Henry Clay.

More important, Jackson wanted to launch a new democratic era that would silence his critics, restore government to "the people," and take power away from the Eastern "elite." He trusted the people because he was one of them. Now he would be the "people's president." As he headed for Washington, D.C., he was intent on transforming the nation's political landscape—for good and for ill, as it turned out.

CHAPTER REVIEW

SUMMARY

- **Nationalism**   After the War of 1812, the federal government pursued many policies to strengthen the *national* economy. The *Tariff of 1816* protected American manufacturing, and the *Second Bank of the United States* provided a stronger currency. Led by John Marshall, the Supreme Court limited the powers of states and strengthened the power of the federal government in *Dartmouth College v. Woodward* and *McCulloch v. Maryland*. The Marshall court interpreted the Constitution as giving Congress the right to take any action not forbidden by the Constitution as long as the purpose of such laws was within the "scope of the Constitution." In *Gibbons v. Ogden*, the Court protected contract rights against state action and established the federal government's supremacy over interstate commerce, thereby promoting growth of the national economy.

- **Sectionalism**   Henry Clay's *American System* supported economic nationalism by endorsing a national bank, a protective tariff, and federally-funded *internal improvements*, such as roads and canals. Many Americans, however, were more tied to the needs of their particular sections of the country. People in the different regions—North, South, and West—disagreed about which economic policies best served their interests. As settlers streamed west, the extension of slavery into the new territories became the predominant political concern, eventually requiring both sides to compromise repeatedly to avoid civil war.

- **Era of Good Feelings**   James Monroe's term in office began with peace and prosperity and was initially labeled the Era of Good Feelings. Two major events, however, ended the Era of Good Feelings: the financial *Panic of 1819* and the Missouri Compromise (1820). The explosive growth of the cotton culture transformed life in the South, in part by encouraging the expansion of slavery, which moved west with southern planters. But in 1819, the sudden collapse of world cotton prices devastated the southern economy and soon affected the national economy as well. The *Missouri Compromise*, a short-term solution to the issue of allowing slavery in the western territories, exposed the emotions and turmoil that the problem generated.

- **National Diplomacy**   The main diplomatic achievements of the period between the end of the War of 1812 and the coming Civil War concerned the extension of America's contested boundaries and the resumption of trade with its old enemy, Great Britain. The countries reached agreement on the northern U.S. borders, and to the south, the *Transcontinental Treaty (Adams-Onís Treaty)* with Spain extended the boundaries of the United States. The *Monroe Doctrine* expressed the idea that the Americas were no longer open to colonization and proclaimed American neutrality in European affairs.

- **The Election of 1828**   The demise of the Federalists left the Republicans as the only political party in the nation. The Republicans' seeming unity was shattered by the election of 1824, which Andrew Jackson lost as a result of what he believed was a *"corrupt bargain"* between John Quincy Adams and Henry Clay. Jackson won the presidency in the *election of 1828* by rallying southern and western voters with his appeal to the common man. His election opened a new era in national politics.

CHRONOLOGY

1816	Second Bank of the United States is established
	First protective tariff goes into effect
1817	Rush-Bagot Treaty between the United States and Great Britain
1818	The Convention of 1818 establishes the northern border of the Louisiana Purchase at the 49th parallel
1819	Panic of 1819
	Supreme Court issues *McCulloch v. Maryland* decision
	United States and Spain agree to the Transcontinental (Adams-Onís) Treaty
1820	Congress accepts the Missouri Compromise
1821	Maine and Missouri become states
	Florida becomes a territory
1823	President Monroe announces the Monroe Doctrine
1824	Supreme Court issues *Gibbons v. Ogden* decision
	John Quincy Adams wins the presidential election by what some claim is a "corrupt bargain" with Henry Clay
1828	Andrew Jackson wins the presidency

KEY TERMS

Second Bank of the United States (B.U.S.) p. 322

Tariff of 1816 p. 323

internal improvements p. 324

Dartmouth College v. Woodward p. 324

McCulloch v. Maryland p. 324

Gibbons v. Ogden p. 325

American System p. 326

Panic of 1819 p. 328

Missouri Compromise p. 330

Transcontinental Treaty (Adams-Onís Treaty) p. 334

Monroe Doctrine p. 335

"corrupt bargain" p. 338

election of 1828 p. 340

INQUIZITIVE

Go to InQuizitive to see what you've learned—and learn what you've missed—with personalized feedback along the way.

10 The Jacksonian Era

1828–1840

Hard times in the Jacksonian era Although Andrew Jackson championed the "poor and humble," his economic policies contributed to the Panic of 1837, a financial crisis that hit the working poor the hardest. This cartoon illustrates New York City during the seven-year depression: a frantic mob storms a bank, while in the foreground, a widow begs on the street with her child, surrounded by a banker or landlord and a barefoot sailor. At left, there is a drunken member of the Bowery Toughs gang and a down-on-his-luck militiaman. The cartoonist places the blame on Jackson, whose hat, glasses, and pipe overlook the scene. The white flag at left wryly states: "July 4, 1837, 61st Anniversary of Our Independence."

Andrew Jackson was a unique personality and a transformational leader. He was the first president from a western state (Tennessee), the first to have been born in a log cabin, the first *not* to have come from a prominent colonial family, the last to have participated in the Revolutionary War, and the first to carry two bullets in his body from a duel and a barroom brawl. Most important, Jackson was the plain-spoken, polarizing emblem of a new democratic era.

Born poor, orphaned early, and largely self-educated, Jackson never discarded his backwoods personality and rural ways. He was short-tempered and thin-skinned, proud and insecure, and he never hesitated to fight or get even if his honor was at stake. For Jackson, politics was personal and visceral, which helps explain why his actions and policies were at times contradictory.

Tall and lean, Jackson was an intimidating figure with his penetrating blue eyes, long nose, jutting chin, silver-gray hair, and intense, iron-willed personality. "Old Hickory," however, was not in good health as he assumed the presidency. He was plagued by blinding headaches and other ailments that led rival Henry Clay to describe him as "feeble in body and mind."

Despite his physical challenges, Jackson remained sharply focused and sure of himself. More than previous presidents, he loved the rough-and-tumble combat of the raucous new democratic political culture. "I was born for a storm," he once boasted. "A calm [life] does not suit me."

Jackson took the nation by storm. No political figure was so widely loved or more deeply despised. As a self-made soldier, lawyer, planter, and politician,

focus questions

1. What were Andrew Jackson's major beliefs regarding the common man, the presidency, and the proper role of government in the nation's economy?

2. What was Jackson's legacy regarding the status of Indians in American society?

3. How did Jackson respond to the nullification crisis?

4. What brought about the economic depression of the late 1830s and the emergence of the Whig party?

5. What were the strengths and weaknesses of Jackson's transformational presidency?

Jackson helped create and shape the Democratic party and helped introduce modern presidential campaigning to electoral politics. Jackson symbolized what he called the emergence of the "common man" in politics (by which he meant white men only), and he stamped his name and, more important, his ideas, personality, and values on an entire era of American history.

JACKSONIAN DEMOCRACY

Andrew Jackson's election marked the impact of thirty years of democratic innovations in politics. During the 1820s and 1830s, as America grew in population and people continued to move westward in ever larger numbers, most white men, whether they owned property or not, were allowed to vote and hold office. "The principle of universal suffrage," announced the *U.S. Magazine and Democratic Review*, "meant that white males of age constituted the political nation." Such a democratization of voting rights gave previously excluded white men equal status as citizens regardless of wealth or background. No longer was politics the arena for only the most prominent and wealthiest Americans.

Jackson was the most openly partisan and politically involved president in history to that point. Unlike previous presidents, who viewed campaigning as unseemly, he actively sought votes among the people, lobbied congressmen, and formed "Hickory Clubs" across the nation to campaign for him. Jackson also benefited from a powerful Democratic party "machine" run by his trusted secretary of state (later his vice president), Martin Van Buren, a wealthy New York lawyer with a shrewd political sense.

Democracy, of course, is a slippery and elastic concept, and Jacksonians rarely defined what they meant by the "rule of the people." Noah Webster, the Connecticut Federalist who produced the nation's first reliable dictionary, complained that "the men who have preached these doctrines [of democracy] have never defined what they mean by the *people*, or what they mean by *democracy*, nor how the *people* are to govern themselves." Jacksonian Democrats also showed little concern for *undemocratic* constraints on African Americans, Native Americans, and women, all of whom were denied basic political and civil rights.

ANTI-DEMOCRATIC FORCES Many southern slaveholders worried that the surge of democratic activism would threaten the slave system. Virginian Muscoe Garnett, a planter and attorney, declared that "democracy is indeed incompatible with slavery, and the whole system of Southern society." His fellow Virginian, George Fitzhugh, was more explicit in his disdain for democratic ideals. In every society, he asserted, "some were born with saddles on their backs, and others booted and spurred to ride them."

Still, in the face of such opposition, Jacksonian Democrats helped greatly expand economic opportunity and political participation for workingmen (white factory laborers, craftsmen and mechanics, small farmers, and land-hungry frontiersmen). Andrew Jackson promised to protect "the poor and humble" from the "tyranny of wealth and power." His goal was to elevate the "laboring classes" of white men who "love liberty and desire nothing but equal rights and equal laws."

DEMOCRACY UNLEASHED The rowdy inauguration of President Jackson symbolized the democratization of political life. Dressed in a black mourning suit in honor of his recently deceased wife, the self-described people's president stepped out of the U.S. Capitol at noon on March 4, 1829. Waiting for him in the cold were 15,000 people who collectively roared and waved their hats when they saw Jackson emerge. "I never saw anything like it before," marveled Daniel Webster, the great senator from Massachusetts.

Once the wild cheering finally subsided, Jackson delivered a brief speech in which he promised that his administration would be committed to "the

All Creation Going to the White House In this depiction of Andrew Jackson's inauguration party, satirist Robert Cruikshank draws a visual parallel to Noah's Ark, suggesting that people of all walks of life were now welcome in the White House.

task of reform" in the federal government, taking jobs out of "unfaithful or incompetent hands" and balancing states' rights with the exercise of national power. He also pledged to pursue the will of the people in exercising his new presidential powers.

After being sworn in by Chief Justice John Marshall, Jackson mounted his horse and rode down a muddy Pennsylvania Avenue to a reception at the White House, where his cherished democracy proceeded to lose control. The huge crowd of jubilant western Democrats partying in the White House and outside on the lawn quickly turned into a drunken mob as they consumed tubs of alcohol-laced punch. Dishes, glasses, and furniture were smashed, and muddy-booted revelers broke windows, ripped down draperies, and trampled on rugs.

Those already skeptical of Jackson's qualifications for office saw the boisterous inaugural party as a symbol of all that was wrong with the "democratic" movement. Supreme Court Justice Joseph Story said he had never seen such "a mixture" of rowdy people, from the "highest and most polished down to the most vulgar and gross in the nation." Here was Jacksonian democracy at work, he shuddered. "The reign of KING MOB seemed triumphant."

JACKSON AS PRESIDENT

Andrew Jackson sought to increase the powers of the presidency at the expense of the legislative and judicial branches. One of his opponents noted that previous presidents had assumed that Congress was the primary branch of government. Jackson, however, believed that the presidency was "superior." The ruling political and economic elite must be removed, he said, for "the people" are the government, and too many government officials had grown corrupt and self-serving at the expense of the public interest.

To dislodge the "corrupt" eastern political elite, Jackson launched a policy he called "rotation in office," whereby he replaced many federal officials with his own supporters. Government jobs—district attorneys, federal marshals, customs collectors—belonged to the people, not to career bureaucrats. Democracy, he believed, was best served when the winning party's "newly elected officials" appointed new government officials. Such partisan behavior came to be called "the spoils system," since, as a prominent New York Democrat declared, "to the victor belong the spoils."

Jackson also sought to cut spending to help pay off the federal debt (a "national curse"); he supported internal improvements that were national in scope, promoted a "judicious tariff," and called for the relocation of the "ill-fated race" of Indians still living in the East to new lands across the Mississippi

River so that they could be "protected" while their ancestral lands were confiscated, sold, and developed.

THE EATON AFFAIR Yet Jackson soon found himself preoccupied with squabbles within his own cabinet. From the outset, his administration was divided between supporters of Secretary of State Martin Van Buren and those allied with Vice President John C. Calhoun of South Carolina, both of whom wanted to succeed Jackson as president. Jackson did not trust Calhoun, a Yale graduate of towering intellect and fiery determination. Although earlier a nationalist, Calhoun now was focused on defending southern interests, especially the preservation of the slave-based cotton economy that had made him a wealthy planter.

In his rivalry with Calhoun, Van Buren took full advantage of a juicy social scandal known as the Peggy Eaton affair. Widower John Eaton, a former U.S. senator from Tennessee, was one of Jackson's closest friends. Eaton also had long been associated with Margaret "Peggy" O'Neale Timberlake, an outspoken Washington temptress married to John Timberlake, a naval officer frequently at sea.

The flirtatious Peggy Timberlake was devastatingly attractive to the men who kept her company while her husband was away. The ambitious daughter of an innkeeper, Peggy enjoyed "the attentions of men, young and old"; she took special delight in Senator John Eaton. In April 1828, John Timberlake died at sea. Although the official cause of death was respiratory failure, rumors swirled that he had committed suicide after learning of his wife's affair with Eaton.

Soon after the 1828 presidential election, Eaton had written President-elect Jackson to alert him of the spiteful gossip aimed at himself and Peggy Timberlake. Jackson responded quickly and firmly: "Marry her and you will be in a position to defend her." Eaton did so on January 1, 1829.

Eaton's enemies quickly criticized the "unseemly haste" of the marriage and continued to savage Peggy Eaton. Louis McLane, a U.S. senator from Delaware who would later serve in Jackson's cabinet, sneered that Eaton, soon to be named Jackson's secretary of war, "has just married his mistress, and the mistress of eleven dozen others." Floride Calhoun, the vice president's imperious wife, especially objected to Peggy Eaton's unsavory past. At Jackson's inaugural ball, she openly ignored her, as did the other cabinet-members' wives.

The constant gossip led Jackson to explode, shouting that "I did not come here [to Washington] to make a Cabinet for the Ladies of this place, but for the Nation." In his view, women had no right to mix politics with social life; their doing so was nothing more than vicious meddling. He demanded loyalty from his administrative team—and their wives. For his part, Calhoun acknowledged that his wife had a "suspicious and fault-finding temper" that caused "much vexation in the family."

King Andrew the First Opponents considered Jackson's veto of the Maysville Road Bill an abuse of power. This cartoon shows "King Andrew" trampling on the Constitution, internal improvements, and the Bank of the United States.

Peggy Eaton's plight reminded Jackson of the mean-spirited gossip that had plagued his own wife, Rachel. Intensely loyal to John Eaton, the president defended Peggy, insisting that she was as pure "as a virgin." His cabinet members, however, were unable to cure their wives of what Martin Van Buren dubbed "the Eaton Malaria."

Nor did Peggy Eaton help her own cause. She once said that "I never had a lover who was not a gentleman." Her social enemies, she explained, were so "very jealous of me" because "none of them had beauty, accomplishments or graces in society of any kind." The rumoring and sniping continued, month after month, and became a time-consuming distraction for the president.

Jackson blamed the Eaton scandal on his rivals Henry Clay and John C. Calhoun. The president assumed that Calhoun and his wife had targeted John Eaton because he did not support Calhoun's desire to be the next president. One of Calhoun's friends wrote in April 1829 that the United States was "governed by the President—the President by the Secretary of War—and the latter by his Wife." Jackson concluded that the scheming Calhoun was one of the "most dangerous men living—a man, devoid of principle" who "would sacrifice his friend, his country, and forsake his god, for selfish personal ambition."

THE MAYSVILLE ROAD VETO When Jackson was not dealing with the "Petticoat Affair," he decisively used his executive authority to limit the role of the federal government—while at the same time delivering additional blows to rivals John C. Calhoun and Henry Clay.

In 1830, Congress passed a bill pushed by Calhoun and Clay that authorized the use of federal monies to build a sixty-mile-long road across the state of Kentucky from the city of Maysville to Lexington, Clay's hometown. President Jackson, urged on by Martin Van Buren, vetoed the bill on the grounds that the proposed road was a "purely local matter," being solely in the state of Kentucky, and thus outside the domain of Congress because it was not an interstate project. Funding such local projects would require a constitutional amendment. Clay was stunned. "We are all shocked and mortified by the rejection of the Maysville road," he wrote a friend. But he had no luck convincing Congress to override the presidential veto.

THE EASTERN INDIANS

President Jackson's forcible removal of Indians from their ancestral lands was his highest priority and one of his lowest moments. Like most white frontiersmen, he saw Indians as barbarians who were to be treated as "subjects," not "nations." His National Republican opponent, Henry Clay, felt the same way, arguing that the Indians were "destined to extinction" and not "worth preserving."

After Jackson's election in 1828, he followed up on policies developed by previous presidents by urging that the Eastern Indians (east of the Mississippi River) be moved to reservations west of the Mississippi River, in what became Oklahoma. Jackson believed that moving the Indians would serve their best interests as well as the national interest, for the states in the Lower South, especially the Carolinas, Georgia, and Alabama, were aggressively restricting the rights of Indian nations and taking their land. President Jackson often told Indian leaders that he was their "Great Father" trying to protect them from the greedy state governments.

New state laws in Alabama, Georgia, and Mississippi abolished tribal units, stripped them of their civil rights, rejected ancestral Indian land claims, and denied Indians the right to vote or to testify in court. Jackson claimed that relocating the Eastern Indians was a "wise and humane policy" that would save them from "utter annihilation" if tribes tried to hold on to their lands in the face of state actions.

INDIAN REMOVAL In 1830, Jackson submitted to Congress the **Indian Removal Act**, which authorized him to ignore treaty commitments made by previous presidents and to convince the Indians remaining in the East and South to move to federal lands west of the Mississippi River. The federal government, the new program promised, would pay for the Indian exodus and give them initial support in their new lands in Oklahoma.

Jackson's proposal provoked heated opposition, not only among the Indian peoples but also among reformers who distrusted the president's motives and doubted the promised support from the federal government. Critics flooded Congress with petitions that criticized the removal policy and warned that

Jackson's plan would bring "enduring shame" on the nation. Indian leaders were skeptical from the start. As a federal agent reported, "They see that our professions are insincere, that our promises are broken, that the happiness of the Indian is a cheap sacrifice to the acquisition of new lands."

The proposal also sparked intense debate in Congress. Theodore Frelinghuysen, a New Jersey National Republican, gave a six-hour speech in the Sen-

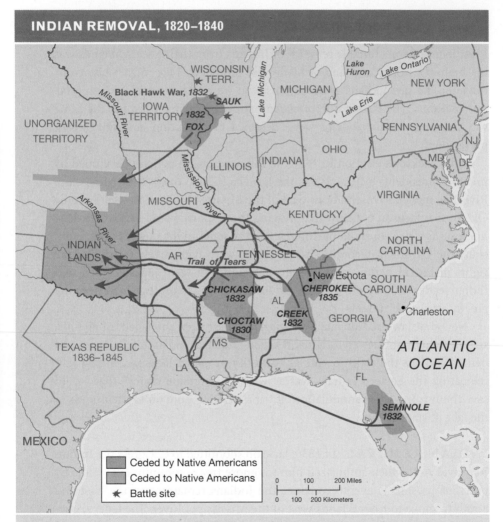

INDIAN REMOVAL, 1820–1840

- Why did Congress relocate the Choctaws, Chickasaws, Creeks, Seminoles, and Cherokees to territory west of Arkansas and Missouri?
- How far did the exiled Indians have to travel, and what were the conditions on the journey?
- Why were the Indians not forced to move before the 1830s?

ate during which he asked, "Do the obligations of justice change with the color of the skin? Is it one of the prerogatives of the white man, that he may disregard the dictates of moral principles, when an Indian shall be concerned?"

In the end, Congress answered yes. The House of Representatives and Senate both narrowly approved the Indian Removal Bill, with most southerners voting for it and northerners against it. Jackson signed the measure, and it became law on May 26, 1830. Federal agents thereafter bribed and bullied tribal chiefs to get their consent to relocate to the West. "Our doom is sealed," lamented a Choctaw warrior. "There is no other course for us but to turn our faces to our new homes toward the setting sun."

RESISTANCE   Most northern Indians gave in to federal threats and were relocated. In Illinois and the Wisconsin Territory, however, Sauk and Fox Indians fought to regain their ancestral lands. The Black Hawk War erupted in April 1832, when Chief Black Hawk led 1,000 Sauks—men, women, and children who had been relocated to the Iowa Territory—back across the Mississippi River to their homeland in Illinois, land shared with the Fox Nation. After several skirmishes, Indiana and Illinois militia chased the Sauk and Fox into the Wisconsin Territory and caught them on the eastern bank of the Mississippi River, a few miles downstream from the mouth of the Bad Axe River.

The soldiers misinterpreted the Indians' effort to surrender, and fighting erupted. In what became known as the Bad Axe Massacre, the militiamen murdered hundreds of women and children as they tried to escape. The soldiers then scalped the dead Indians and cut long strips of flesh from several of them for use as strops to sharpen razors. Six weeks later, the Sauk leader, Black Hawk, was captured and imprisoned.

In Florida, the Seminoles, led by Osceola (called by U.S. soldiers "the still unconquered red man") ferociously resisted the federal removal policy. For eight years, the Seminoles would fight a hit-and-run guerrilla war in the swamps of the Everglades—the longest, most costly, and deadliest war ever fought by Native Americans. Some 1,500 Americans were killed. At times, Seminole women killed their children rather than see them captured. But their heroic resistance waned after 1837, when Osceola was treacherously captured under a white flag of truce, imprisoned, and left to die of malaria at Fort Moultrie near Charleston, South Carolina. After 1842, only a few hundred Seminoles remained, hiding in the swamps. It was not until 1934 that the few surviving Seminoles in Florida became the last Native American tribe to end its war with the United States.

THE CHEROKEES   The Cherokee Nation also tried to defy the federal removal policy. A largely agricultural people, Cherokees had long occupied northwest Georgia and the mountainous areas of northern Alabama, eastern Tennessee, and western North Carolina. In 1827, relying upon their established treaty rights, the Cherokees adopted a constitution in which they declared that they were not subject to the laws or control of any state or federal government. Georgia officials had other ideas.

In 1828, shortly after Jackson's election, the Georgia government announced that after June 1, 1830, the authority of state law would extend to the Cherokees. They would no longer be a "nation within a nation." Under the new state laws, they would not be allowed to vote, own property, or testify against whites in court.

The discovery of gold in north Georgia in 1829 increased whites' lust for Cherokee land, attracted trespassing prospectors, and led to the new state law. It prohibited the Cherokees from digging for gold on their own lands. The Cherokees sought relief in the Supreme Court, arguing that "we wish to remain on the land of our fathers. We have a perfect and original right to remain without interruption or molestation."

In *Cherokee Nation v. Georgia* (1831), Chief Justice John Marshall ruled that the Cherokees had "an unquestionable right" to maintain control of their ancestral lands, but the Court could not render a verdict because of a technicality: the Cherokees had filed suit as a "foreign nation" when in Marshall's view they were "domestic dependent nations." If it were true that "wrongs have been inflicted," Marshall explained, "this is not the tribunal which can redress the past or prevent the future."

The following year, the Supreme Court *did* rule in favor of the Cherokees in *Worcester v. Georgia* (1832). The case arose when Georgia officials arrested a group of white Christian missionaries who were living among the Cherokees in violation of a state law forbidding such interaction. Two of the missionaries, Samuel Worcester and Elihu Butler, were sentenced to four years at hard labor. They appealed to the Supreme Court.

In the *Worcester* case, Marshall said that the missionaries must be released. The anti-Cherokee laws passed by the Georgia legislature, he declared, had violated "the Constitution, laws, and treaties of the United States." He added that the Cherokee Nation was "a distinct political community" within which Georgia law had no force.

Both Supreme Court decisions favored the Cherokee argument that their ancestral lands could not be taken from them, in part because they had earlier signed treaties with the state and federal governments confirming their rights to those lands. President Jackson, however, refused to enforce the Court's "wicked" decisions, claiming that he had no constitutional authority to intervene in Georgia. A New York newspaper editor reported that Jackson said, "John Marshall has made his decision, now let him enforce it."

Thereafter, Jackson gave the Cherokees and other Indian nations a terrible choice: either abide by the discriminatory new state laws or relocate to government-owned lands west of the Mississippi River, which would be theirs "forever." Jackson told the Creeks that they and whites could not live "in harmony and peace" if they remained on their ancestral lands and that told them that "a speedy removal" to the West was their only option. Soon, Georgia officials began selling Cherokee lands.

The irony of the new Georgia policy was that of all the southern tribes, the Cherokees had come closest to adopting the customs of white America. They had abandoned traditional hunting practices to develop farms, build roads, schools, and churches, and create trading posts and newspapers. Many Cherokees had married whites, adopted their clothing and food, and converted to Christianity. And the Cherokees owned some 2,000 enslaved African Americans.

THE TRAIL OF TEARS   The federal officials responsible for implementing the Indian Removal Act developed a strategy of divide and conquer with the Cherokees. In 1835, for example, a minority faction of the Cherokees signed the fraudulent Treaty of New Echota, which was rejected by 90 percent of the Cherokee people but readily accepted by the U.S. Senate and enforced by the U.S. Army.

Trail of Tears Thousands of Cherokees died on a nightmarish march from Georgia to Oklahoma after being forced from their native lands.

In 1838, after President Jackson had left office and Martin Van Buren was president, 17,000 Cherokees were evicted and moved West under military guard on the **Trail of Tears**, an 800-mile forced journey marked by the cruelty of soldiers and the neglect of irresponsible private contractors assigned to manage the process. Some 4,000 refugees died along the way.

The Trail of Tears was, according to a white Georgian, "the cruelest work I ever knew." A few Cherokees held out in the mountains of North Carolina; they became known as the "Eastern Band" of Cherokees. The Creeks and Chickasaws followed the Trail of Tears a few years later, after Alabama and Mississippi used the same techniques as the Georgia government to take control of their tribal lands.

Some 100,000 Eastern Indians were relocated to the West during the 1820s and 1830s, and the government sold some 100 million acres of Indian land, most of it in the prime cotton-growing areas of Georgia, Alabama, and Mississippi, known as the Old Southwest.

THE BANK WAR

Andrew Jackson showed the same principled stubbornness in dealing with the national bank as he did in removing the Indians. The First Bank of the United States (B.U.S.) had been renewed in 1816 as the **Second Bank of the United States**, which soon became the largest corporation in the nation and the only truly national business enterprise.

The second B.U.S. (the federal government owned only 20 percent of the bank's capital) was a private corporation with extensive public responsibilities—and powers. To benefit the government, the B.U.S. held all federal funds, including tax collections (mostly from land sales and tariff revenues), and disbursed federal payments for its obligations, all in exchange for an annual $1.5 million fee. The B.U.S., however, conducted other business like a commercial bank and was free to use the government deposits in its vaults as collateral for loans to businesses. Headquartered in Philadelphia and supported by twenty-nine branches around the nation, the B.U.S. competed with state-chartered banks for local business.

The B.U.S. helped accelerate business expansion by making loans to individuals, businesses, and state banks. It also helped promote a stable money supply and deter excessive lending by requiring the 464 state banks to keep enough gold and silver coins (called specie) in their vaults to back their own paper currency, which they in turn loaned to individuals and businesses. Prior to the B.U.S. being reestablished, the number of unstable and unregulated state banks had increased dramatically. Most of them issued their own paper money, and half of those created between 1810 and 1820 had gone bankrupt by 1825. The primary benefit of the B.U.S. was its ability to monitor and regulate many of the state banks.

With federal revenues soaring from land sales during the early 1830s, the B.U.S., led by Nicholas Biddle, had accumulated massive amounts of money—and economic power. Even though the B.U.S. benefited the national economy, state banks, especially in the South and West, feared its growing "monopolistic" power. Critics claimed that Biddle and the B.U.S. directors, most of whom lived in the Northeast, were so focused on their own profits that they were restricting lending by state banks and impeding businesses from borrowing as much as they wanted.

Andrew Jackson had always hated banks and bankers, whom he called "vipers and thieves." His prejudice grew out of his own experiences with banks in the 1790s, when he had suffered huge financial losses. Now, as a popularly elected president, he claimed to speak for ordinary Americans who felt that banks favored the "rich and powerful" in the East. Jackson also distrusted banks because they printed too much paper money, causing prices to rise (inflation). He wanted only gold and silver coins to be used for economic transactions. "I think it right to be perfectly frank with you," Jackson told Biddle in 1829. "I do not dislike your Bank any more than [I dislike] all banks."

Rechartering the Bank Jackson's effort to defeat the recharter of the B.U.S. is likened to fighting a hydra, a many-headed serpent from Greek mythology. Just as the hydra would sprout two heads when one was severed, for each B.U.S. supporter that Jackson subdued, even more supporters would emerge to take his place.

The national bank may have become too powerful, as Jackson charged, but the **Bank War** between Jackson and Biddle revealed that the president never truly understood the national bank's role or policies, and he continued to let personal animosity drive many of his policy decisions. The B.U.S. had provided a stable monetary system for the expanding economy, as well as a mechanism for controlling the pace and integrity of economic growth by regulating the ability of branch banks and state banks to issue paper currency.

THE RECHARTER EFFORT   Although the charter for the B.U.S. ran through 1836, Nicholas Biddle could not afford to wait until then for its renewal. Leaders of the National Republican party, especially Senators Henry Clay and Daniel Webster (who was a paid legal counsel to the B.U.S.), told Biddle that the charter needed to be renewed before the 1836 presidential election. They assured him that Congress would renew the charter, leading the impolitic Biddle to grow overconfident about the bank's future. Jackson, he said, "thinks because he has scalped Indians . . . he is to have his way with the Bank."

Biddle and his political allies, however, failed to appreciate Jackson's tenacity and the depth of his hatred for the B.U.S. And most voters were on Jackson's side. In the end, Biddle, Clay, and the National Republicans unintentionally handed Jackson a popular issue on the eve of the election. At their nominating convention in December 1831, the National Republicans endorsed Clay as their presidential candidate and approved the renewal of the B.U.S.

Early in the summer of 1832, both houses of Congress passed the bank recharter bill, in part because Biddle provided bribes to win votes. Upon learning of such shenanigans, Jackson's chief of staff concluded that the B.U.S. was "becoming desperate: *caught in its own net*."

Biddle, Webster, and Clay assumed that Jackson would not veto the recharter bill because doing so might cost him reelection. "Should Jackson veto the bill," Clay boasted, "I will veto him." On July 10, 1832, however, Jackson nixed the bill, sending it back to Congress with a blistering criticism of the bank's directors for making the "rich richer and the potent more powerful" while discriminating against "the humble members of society—the farmers, mechanics, and laborers."

Daniel Webster accused Jackson of using the bank issue "to stir up the poor against the rich." To Henry Clay, Jackson's veto represented another example of the president's desire to concentrate "all power in the hands of one man." Clay and Webster, however, could not convince the Senate to override the veto, thus setting the stage for a nationwide financial debate and a dramatic presidential campaign.

The overriding issue in the election was the future of the Bank of the United States. Let the people decide, Jackson argued. "I have now done my duty to the citizens of this country," he said in explaining his veto. "If sustained by my fellow-citizens [in the upcoming election], I shall be grateful and happy; if not, I shall find in the motives which impel me ample grounds for contentment and peace."

NULLIFICATION

Andrew Jackson eventually would veto twelve congressional bills, more than all previous presidents combined. Critics claimed that his behavior was "monarchical" in its frequent defiance of the will of Congress. Jackson, however, believed that the president represented *all* of the people, unlike congressmen who were elected locally. His commitment to nationalism over sectionalism was nowhere more evident than in his handling of the nullification crisis in South Carolina. In that volatile situation he would greatly expand the scope of presidential authority by forcing the nullifiers to back down.

CALHOUN AND THE TARIFF Vice President John C. Calhoun became President Jackson's fiercest critic because of changing economic conditions in Calhoun's home state of South Carolina. The financial panic of 1819 had sparked a nationwide depression. Through the 1820s, South Carolina continued to suffer from a collapse in cotton prices. The state lost almost 70,000 people during that ten-year period—the result of residents moving West in search of cheaper and more-fertile land for growing cotton. Twice as many would leave during the 1830s.

Most South Carolinians blamed their woes on the Tariff of 1828, which was labeled the **Tariff of Abominations**. By taxing British cloth coming into U.S. markets, the tariff hurt southern cotton growers by reducing British demand for raw cotton from America. It also hurt southerners by raising the prices they had to pay for imported products. The tariff debate revealed how the North and South had developed different economic interests and different ways of protecting those interests. Massachusetts was prospering while South Carolina was struggling.

In a lengthy pamphlet called the *South Carolina Exposition and Protest* (1828), Calhoun claimed that the Tariff of 1828 favored the interests of New England textile manufacturing over southern agriculture. Under such circumstances, he argued, a state could "nullify," or veto, a federal law it deemed unconstitutional.

Nullification was the ultimate weapon for those determined to protect states' rights against federal authority. As President Jackson and others pointed out, however, allowing states to pick and choose which federal laws they would follow would create national chaos, which he would not allow.

CLASH OF TITANS—WEBSTER–HAYNE DEBATE The controversy over the Tariff of 1828 simmered until 1830, when the Webster–Hayne debate in Congress sharpened the lines between states' rights and national authority. In a fiery speech, Senator Robert Y. Hayne of South Carolina argued that the anti-slavery Yankees were invading the South, "making war upon her citizens, and endeavoring to overthrow her principles and institutions." In Hayne's view, the Union was created by the states, and the states therefore had the right to nullify federal laws. The independence of the states was to him more important than the preservation of the Union.

Massachusetts senator Daniel Webster quickly challenged Hayne's arguments. Blessed with a thunderous voice and a theatrical flair, Webster was an unapologetic Unionist determined "to strengthen the ties that hold us together." He pointed out that the U.S. Constitution was created not by the states but by the American people. If states were allowed to nullify a federal law, the Union would be nothing but a "rope of sand." South Carolina's defiance of federal

Webster Replying to Senator Hayne (1848) The eloquent Massachusetts senator challenges the argument for nullification in the Webster–Hayne debate.

authority, he charged, "is nothing more than resistance by *force*—it is disunion by *force*—it is secession by *force*—it is civil war."

Webster's powerful closing statement—"Liberty and Union, now and forever, one and inseparable"—was printed in virtually every newspaper in the nation. Abraham Lincoln later called it "the very best speech ever delivered." Even Hayne was awestruck. He told Webster that "a man who can make such speeches as that ought never to die."

In the end, Webster had the better argument. Most political leaders agreed that the states could not act separately from the national government. As Jackson said, the Constitution and its laws remained "supreme."

CALHOUN VERSUS JACKSON That Jackson, like Calhoun, was a cotton-planting slaveholder led many southerners to assume that the president would support their resistance to the federal tariff. Jackson was sympathetic—until Calhoun and others in South Carolina threatened to "nullify" federal laws they did not like. He then turned on them with the same angry force he had directed toward the advancing British army at New Orleans in 1815.

On April 13, 1830, the Democratic party hosted scores of congressmen and political leaders at the first annual Jefferson Day dinner. When it was Jackson's turn to salute Jefferson's memory, he rose to his feet, raised his glass, and, while glaring at Calhoun, growled: "Our Union—It must be preserved!"

People gasped, knowing that the vice president, as if challenged to a duel, must reply to Jackson's threat to the southern weapon of nullification. Calhoun stood and, trembling with emotion, countered with a defiant toast to "the Union, next to our liberty the most dear!" In that dramatic exchange, Jackson and Calhoun laid bare the fundamental tension between federal authority and states' rights that has remained one of the animating themes of the American republic.

Soon thereafter, another incident deepened the hatred between the two men. On May 12, 1830, the president saw for the first time a letter from 1818 in which Calhoun, then secretary of war in the Monroe administration, had wanted to discipline Jackson for his unauthorized invasion of Spanish-held Florida. After exchanging heated letters about the incident with Calhoun, Jackson told a friend that he was finally through with the "double dealing of J.C.C."

The rift prompted Jackson to take a dramatic step suggested by Secretary of State Martin Van Buren, his closest and most cunning adviser. During one of their daily horseback rides together, Van Buren offered himself up as a sacrifice as a way to remove all Calhoun supporters from the cabinet and thereby end the ongoing Eaton affair that had fractured the administration.

As the first step in the planned cabinet coup, Van Buren convinced John Eaton to resign as secretary of war on April 4, 1831. Four days later, Van Buren resigned as secretary of state. "The long agony is over," crowed Samuel Ingham, the secretary of the Treasury, in a letter to Attorney General John Berrien. "Mr. V. B. and Major Eaton have resigned." What Ingham and Berrien did not realize was that a few days later, Jackson would force them—both Calhoun supporters—to resign as well. Jackson now had a clean slate on which to create another cabinet.

Never before had a president dismissed his entire cabinet. Critics saw through the secretary of state's scheme: "Mr. Van Buren may be called the 'Great Magician,'" wrote the *New York Courier*, "for he *raises his wand, and the whole Cabinet disappears.*" Others claimed that the cabinet purge showed that Jackson did not have the political skill to lead the nation. John Quincy Adams told his son that the purge had put all of Washington in a state of confusion: "people stare—and laugh—and say, what next?"

NEW CABINETS By the end of August 1831, Jackson had appointed a new cabinet, all of whom agreed to treat Peggy Eaton with respect. At the same time, Jackson increasingly relied upon the advice of Van Buren and others making up the president's so-called "kitchen cabinet," an informal group of close friends and supporters, many of them Democratic newspaper editors.

The kitchen cabinet soon convinced Jackson to drop his pledge to serve only one term. They explained that it would be hard for Van Buren, Jackson's chosen successor, to win the 1832 Democratic nomination because Calhoun would do everything in his power to stop him—and Calhoun might win the nomination himself. In early 1831, the *Washington Globe*, a Democratic newspaper, announced that Jackson would seek a second term. "The conquering Hero is again in the field, and it must now be seen who are his friends and who are his foes."

THE ANTI-MASONIC PARTY In 1832, for the first time in a presidential election, a third political party entered the field. The Anti-Masonic party grew out of popular hostility toward the Masonic fraternal order, a large, all-male social organization that originated in Great Britain early in the eighteenth century. The Masons often claimed to be the natural leaders of their communities, the "best men." By 1830, more than 2,000 Masonic "lodges" were scattered across the United States with about 100,000 members, including Andrew Jackson and Henry Clay.

The new anti-Masonic party owed its origins to a defrocked Mason, William Morgan, a fifty-two-year-old unemployed bricklayer in Batavia, New York. Morgan had been thrown out of the Masons because of his joblessness. Seeking revenge, he convinced a local printer to publish a widely circulated pamphlet revealing the secret rituals of the Masonic order. Masons then tried to burn down the print shop where the pamphlet had been published. They also had Morgan arrested on a trumped-up charge of indebtedness.

Soon thereafter, on September 12, 1826, someone paid for his release and spirited Morgan away in a waiting carriage. A year later, a man's decomposed body was found in Oak Orchard Creek, near Lake Ontario. Morgan's grieving wife confirmed that it was her husband. Governor Dewitt Clinton, himself a Mason, offered a reward for anyone who would identify the kidnappers.

The Morgan mystery became a major political issue. New York launched more than twenty investigations into Morgan's disappearance (and presumed murder) and conducted a dozen trials of several Masons but never gained a conviction. Each legal effort aroused more public indignation because most of the judges, lawyers, and jurors were Masons.

People began to fear that the Masons had become a self-appointed aristocracy lacking the education and character necessary for self-denying civic leadership. John Quincy Adams said that disbanding the "Masonic institution" was the most important issue facing "us and our posterity."

Suspicions of the Masonic order as a tyrannical secret brotherhood intent on subverting democracy gave rise to the grassroots political movement known as the Anti-Masonic party, whose purpose was to protect republican values from corruption by power hungry Masonic Insiders.

The new party drew most of its support from New Englanders and New Yorkers alienated by both the Democratic and National Republican parties. Anti-Masonic adherents tended to be rural evangelical Protestants, many of whom also opposed slavery.

Opposition to a fraternal organization was hardly the foundation upon which to build a lasting political coalition, but the Anti-Masonic party had three important "firsts" to its credit: in addition to being the first third party with a national base of support, it was the first political party to hold a national convention to nominate a presidential candidate, and the first to announce a formal platform of specific policy goals.

THE 1832 ELECTION   In preparing for the 1832 election, the Democrats and National Republicans followed the example of the Anti-Masonic party by holding presidential nominating conventions of their own. In December 1831, the National Republicans gathered to nominate Henry Clay.

Jackson endorsed the idea of a nominating convention for the Democratic party as well, because it gave the people a greater role in choosing nominees. The Democratic convention first adopted the two-thirds rule for nomination (which prevailed until 1936, when the requirement became a simple majority), and then named New Yorker Martin Van Buren as Jackson's vice presidential running mate. The Democrats, unlike the other two parties, adopted no formal platform and relied to a substantial degree upon the popularity of the president to carry their cause.

Nicholas Biddle invested the vast resources of the B.U.S. into the campaign against Jackson and paid for thousands of pamphlets promoting Clay. By the summer of 1832, Clay declared that "the campaign is over, and I think we have won the victory." He spoke too soon. His blinding ego prevented him from seeing the sources of Jackson's popularity. Where he dismissed Jackson as a power-hungry military chief, most Americans saw the president as someone fighting for their own causes.

Clay also failed to understand Jackson's effectiveness as a new type of engaged political candidate. The *National Intelligencer*, a newspaper that supported Clay, acknowledged that Jackson's eager participation in campaign events was "certainly a new mode of electioneering. We do not recollect before to have heard of a President of the United States descending in person into the political arena." Jackson gave stump speeches, dived into crowds to shake hands, and walked in parades or ate barbecue with loving supporters who cheered and mobbed him.

In the end, Jackson earned 219 electoral votes to Clay's 49, and enjoyed a solid victory in the popular vote: 688,000 to 530,000. William Wirt, the Anti-

The Verdict of the People George Caleb Bingham's painting depicts a socially diverse electorate, suggesting the increasingly democratic politics of the Jacksonian Era.

Masonic candidate, carried only Vermont, winning 7 electoral votes. Dazzled by the president's strong showing, Wirt observed that Jackson could "be President for life if he chooses."

THE NULLIFICATION CRISIS

In the fall of 1831, Jackson tried to defuse the confrontation with South Carolina by calling on Congress to reduce tariff rates. Congress responded with the Tariff of 1832, which lowered rates on some products but kept them high on British cotton fabric and clothing.

The new tariff disappointed Calhoun and others in his home state eager for the British to buy more southern cotton. South Carolinians seethed with resentment toward the federal government. Living in the only state where enslaved Africans were a majority of the population, they feared that if the northern representatives in Congress were powerful enough to create such high tariffs that proved so harmful to the South, they might eventually vote to end slavery itself. Calhoun declared that the "peculiar domestic institutions of the southern states" (by which he meant slavery) were at stake.

SOUTH CAROLINA NULLIFIERS In November 1832, just weeks after Jackson was reelected, a special convention in South Carolina passed an Ordinance of Nullification that disavowed the "unconstitutional" federal Tariffs of 1828 and 1832 (declaring them "null, void, and no law"). If federal authorities tried to use force to collect the tariffs on foreign goods unloaded in Charleston Harbor, South Carolina would secede from the Union. The state legislature then selected Senator Robert Hayne as governor and named Calhoun to replace him as U.S. senator. At the end of December, Calhoun resigned as vice president so that he could defend his nullification theory in Congress and oppose Jackson's "tyrannical" actions.

JACKSON SAYS NO TO NULLIFICATION President Jackson's public response was moderate. He promised to use "firmness and forbearance" but stressed that nullification "means insurrection and war; and the other states have a right to put it down."

In private, however, Jackson was furious. He asked how many soldiers it would take to go to South Carolina and "crush the monster [nullification] in its cradle." He also threatened to hang Calhoun and other "nullifiers" if there were any bloodshed. "Surely the president is exaggerating," Governor Hayne remarked to Senator Thomas Hart Benton of Missouri. Benton, who years before had been in a fistfight with Jackson, replied: "I have known General Jackson a great many years, and when he speaks of hanging, it is time to look for a rope."

During the fall of 1832, most northern state legislatures passed resolutions condemning the nullificationists. While slaveholder-dominated southern states expressed sympathy for South Carolina, none endorsed nullification. South Carolina was left standing alone against Jackson.

On December 10, 1832, the unyielding Jackson issued his official response to the people of South Carolina. In his blistering proclamation, he dismissed nullification as "an absurdity," a "mad project of disunion" that was "*incompatible with the existence of the Union, contradicted expressly by the letter of the Constitution, unauthorized by its spirit, inconsistent with every principle on which It was founded, and destructive of the great object for which it was formed.*" He warned that nullification would lead to secession (formal withdrawal of a state from the United States), and secession meant civil war. "Be not deceived by names. Disunion by armed force is TREASON. Are you really ready to incur its guilt?"

CLAY STEPS IN President Jackson then sent federal soldiers and a warship to Charleston to protect the federal customhouse where tariffs were applied to imported products arriving on ships from Europe. Governor Hayne responded by mobilizing the state militia, and the two sides edged toward a violent confrontation. A South Carolina Unionist reported to Jackson that many "reckless and dangerous men" were "looking for civil war and scenes of bloodshed." While taking forceful actions, Jackson still wanted "peaceably to nullify the nullifiers."

In early 1833, the president requested from Congress the authority to use the U.S. Army to "force" compliance with federal law in South Carolina. Calhoun exploded on the Senate floor, exclaiming that he and the others defending his state's constitutional rights were being threatened by what they called the **Force Bill** "to have our throats cut, and those of our wives and children." The greatest threat facing the nation, he argued, was not nullification but presidential despotism.

Calhoun and the nullifiers, however, soon backed down, and the South Carolina legislature postponed the implementation of the nullification ordinances in hopes that Congress would pass a more palatable tariff bill.

Passage of a compromise bill, however, depended upon the support of Senator Henry Clay, himself a slaveholding planter, who finally yielded to those urging him to step in and save the day for the Union. A fellow senator told Clay that these "South Carolinians are good fellows, and it would be a pity to see Jackson hang them."

Clay agreed. On February 12, 1833, he circulated a plan suggested by Jackson to reduce, gradually over several years, the federal tariff on key imported items. Clay urged Congress to treat South Carolina with respect and display "that great principle of compromise and concession which lies at the bottom of our institutions." The tariff reductions were less than South Carolina preferred, but Clay's compromise helped the nullifiers out of the dilemma they had created. Calhoun supported the compromise: "He who loves the Union must desire to see this agitating question [the tariff] brought to a termination."

On March 1, 1833, Jackson signed into law the compromise tariff and the Force Bill, the latter a symbolic statement of the primacy of the Union. Calhoun rushed home to convince the rebels in his state to back down. The South Carolina convention then met and rescinded its nullification of the tariff acts. In a face-saving gesture, the delegates nullified the Force Bill, which Jackson no longer needed.

Both sides felt they had won. Jackson had defended the supremacy of the Union without firing a shot, and South Carolina's persistence had brought tariff reductions. While the immediate crisis was defused, however, its underlying causes persisted. Southern slaveholders felt increasingly threatened by antislavery sentiment in the North. "There is no liberty—no security for the South," groused South Carolina radical Robert Barnwell Rhett. Others agreed. "The struggle, so far from being over," a defiant Calhoun wrote, "is not more than fairly commenced." Jackson concluded that the "tariff was only the pretext [for the nullification crisis], and disunion and southern confederacy the real object. The next pretext will be the negro, or slavery question." Two days after the nullification crisis was resolved, Jackson was sworn in for a second term as president.

WAR OVER THE B.U.S.

Jackson interpreted his lopsided reelection as a "decision of the people against the bank." Having vetoed the charter renewal of the B.U.S., Jackson ordered the Treasury Department to transfer federal monies from the national bank to twenty-three mostly western state banks—called "pet banks" by Jackson's critics because many were run by the president's friends and allies. When the Treasury secretary balked, Jackson fired him.

BIDDLE'S RESPONSE B.U.S. head Nicholas Biddle responded by ordering the bank to quit making loans and demanded that state banks exchange their paper currency for gold or silver coins as quickly as possible. Through such deflationary policies, the desperate Biddle was trying to bring the economy to a halt, create a depression, and thus reveal the importance of maintaining the national bank. An enraged Jackson said the B.U.S. under Biddle was "trying to kill me, *but I will kill it!*"

Biddle's plan to create a financial crisis worked. Northern Democrats worried that the president's "lawless and reckless" Bank War would ruin the party, but Jackson refused to flinch.

THE NEW WHIG PARTY The president's war on the bank led his opponents to create a new political party whose diverse members were unified by their
hatred of Jackson. His critics claimed that he was ruling like a monarch; they
dubbed him "King Andrew the First" and called his Democratic supporters Tories.
The new anti-Jackson coalition called themselves **Whigs**, a name that linked them
to the Patriots of the American Revolution (as well as to the parliamentary opponents of the *Tories* in Britain). Jackson preferred to call them Federalists.

The Whig party grew directly out of the National Republican party led by
John Quincy Adams, Henry Clay, and Daniel Webster. The Whigs also found
support among the Anti-Masons and some Democrats who resented Jackson's
war on the national bank. Of the forty-one Democrats in Congress who had
voted against Jackson on rechartering the national bank, twenty-eight had
joined the Whigs by 1836.

The Whigs, like the National Republicans they replaced, were economic
nationalists who wanted the federal government to promote manufacturing,
support a national bank, and finance a national road network. In the South,
the Whigs tended to be bankers and merchants. In the West, they were mostly
farmers who valued government-funded internal improvements. Unlike the
Democrats, who attracted Catholic voters from Germany and Ireland, Whigs
tended to be native-born Protestants—Congregationalists, Presbyterians,
Methodists, and Baptists—who advocated social reforms such as the abolition
of slavery and efforts to restrict alcoholic beverages.

For the next twenty years, the Whigs and the Democrats would be the
two major political parties. In 1834, the editor of the *Richmond Whig* newspaper gave a class-based explanation of the Whig opposition to Jacksonian
democracy. The Jacksonians, he wrote, have denounced "the rich and intelligent . . . as aristocrats. They have caressed, soothed, and flattered the heavy
[larger] class of the poor and ignorant, because they held the power which *they*
wanted." By appealing to the masses, Jacksonians had overturned the republican system created by the founding fathers: "*The Republic has degenerated
into a Democracy!*" In general, the Democrats, North and South, were solidly
in support of slavery, while the Whigs were increasingly divided on the issue.

KILLING THE B.U.S. In the end, the relentless Jackson won his battle
with Biddle's Bank. The B.U.S. would shut down completely by 1841, and the
United States would not have a central banking system until 1914. Jackson
exulted in his "glorious triumph." (Ironically, Jackson's picture has been on the
twenty-dollar bill since 1929.)

The destruction of the B.U.S. illustrated Jackson's strengths and weaknesses.
When challenged, he was a shrewd and ferocious fighter. Yet his determination
to humble Biddle and destroy the B.U.S. ended up hurting the national econ-

omy. The B.U.S. had performed a needed service. Without it, there was nothing to regulate the nation's money supply or its banks. The number of banks across the nation more than doubled between 1829 and 1837. Of even greater concern, however, was that the amount of loans made by these unregulated banks quadrupled, preparing the way for a financial panic and a terrible depression.

Jackson and the Democrats grew increasingly committed to the expansion of slavery westward into the Gulf coast states, driven by an unstable, unregulated banking system. "People here are run mad with [land] speculation," wrote a traveler through northern Mississippi. "They do business in a kind of frenzy." Gold was scarce but paper money was plentiful, and people rushed to buy lands freed up by the removal of Indians. In 1835, federal land offices in Mississippi sold more acres than had been sold across the entire nation just three years before. The South and West were being flooded by cotton, credit (paper money), and slaves, all of which combined to produce mountains of debt. People used paper money issued by reckless state banks to buy and sell land and slaves.

With the restraining effects of Biddle's national bank removed, scores of new state banks sprouted like mushrooms in the cotton belt, each irresponsibly printing its own paper currency that was often lent to land speculators and new businesses, especially in cotton-growing states like Mississippi and Louisiana.

The result was chaos. Too many banks emerged without adequate capital and with inadequate expertise and integrity. As Senator Thomas Hart Benton said in 1837, he had not helped his friend Jackson kill the B.U.S. to create a "wilderness of local banks. I did not join in putting down the paper currency of a national bank to put up a national paper currency of a thousand local banks." But that is what happened.

THE MONEY QUESTION During the 1830s, the federal government acquired huge amounts of money from the sale of government-owned lands. Initially, the Treasury Department used the annual surpluses from land sales to pay down the accumulated federal debt, which it eliminated completely in 1835—the first time any nation had done so. By 1836, the federal budget was generating an annual budget surplus, which led to intense discussions about what to do with the increasingly worthless paper money flowing into the Treasury's vaults.

The surge of unstable paper money peaked in 1836, when events combined to play havoc with the economy. Two key initiatives endorsed by the Jackson administration would devastate the nation's financial system and throw the economy into a sudden tailspin.

First, in June 1836, Congress approved the **Distribution Act**, initially proposed by Henry Clay and Daniel Webster, that required the federal government to "distribute" to the states surplus federal revenue from land sales. The federal surplus would be "deposited" the funds into eighty-one state banks in proportion to each state's representation in Congress. The state governments would then draw upon those deposits to fund roads, bridges, and other "internal" improvements.

Second, a month later, in July, Jackson issued the Specie Circular (1836), which announced that the federal government would accept only specie (gold or silver coins) in payment for land purchased by speculators. (Farmers could still pay with paper money.) Westerners were upset by the Specie Circular because most government land sales were occurring in their states. They helped convince Congress to pass an act overturning Jackson's policy. The president, however, vetoed it.

Once enacted, the Deposit and Distribution Act and the Specie Circular put added strains on the nation's already tight supplies of gold and silver. Eastern banks had to transfer much of their gold and silver reserves to western banks. As Eastern banks reduced their reserves of gold and silver coins, they had to reduce their lending. Soon, the once-bustling economy began to slow as the money supply contracted and it proved much more difficult for individuals and businesses to get loans. Nervous depositors rushed to their local banks to withdraw their money, only to learn that there was not enough specie in the vaults to redeem their deposits.

New Method of Assorting the Mail, As Practised by Southern-Slave Holders, Or Attack on the Post Office, Charleston S.C. (1835) On the wall of the post office a sign reads "$20,000 Reward for Tappan," referring to the bounty placed on the head of Arthur Tappan, founder and president of the American Anti-Slavery Society.

CENSORING THE MAIL While concerns about the strength of the economy grew, slavery emerged again as a flashpoint issue. In 1835, northern organizations pushing for the immediate abolition of slavery began mailing anti-slavery pamphlets and newspapers to prominent white southerners, hoping to convince them to end the "peculiar institution." They found little support. Francis Pickens of South Carolina urged southerners to stop the abolitionists from spreading their "lies." Angry pro-slavery South Carolinians in Charleston broke into the federal post office, stole bags of the abolitionist mailings, and ceremoniously burned them. Southern state legislatures passed laws banning such "dangerous" publications. Jackson asked Congress to pass a federal censorship law that would prohibit "incendiary" materials intended to incite "the slaves to insurrection."

Congress took action in 1836, but instead of banning abolitionist materials, a bipartisan group of Democrats and Whigs reaffirmed the sanctity of the federal mail. As a practical matter, however, southern post offices began censoring the mail anyway, arguing that federal authority ended when the mail arrived at the post office door. Jackson decided not to enforce the congressional action. His failure of leadership created what would become a growing split in the Democratic party over the future of slavery. Some Democrats decided that Jackson, for all of his celebrations of democracy and equality, was no different from John C. Calhoun and other southern white racists.

The controversy over the mails proved to be a victory for the growing abolitionist movement. One anti-slavery publisher said that instead of stifling their efforts, Jackson and the southern radicals "put us and our principles up before the world—just where we wanted to be." Abolitionist groups started mailing their pamphlets and petitions to members of Congress. James Hammond, a pro-slavery South Carolinian, called for Congress to ban such anti-slavery petitions. When that failed, Congress in 1836 adopted an informal solution suggested by Martin Van Buren: whenever a petition calling for the end of slavery was introduced, someone would immediately move that it be tabled rather than discussed. The plan, Van Buren claimed, would preserve the "harmony of our happy Union."

The supporters of this "gag rule" soon encountered a formidable obstacle in John Quincy Adams, the former president who now was a congressman from Massachusetts. He devised an array of procedures to get around the rule to squelch all anti-slavery discussion. Henry Wise, a Virginia opponent, called Adams "the acutest, the astutest, the archest enemy of southern slavery that ever existed." Jackson dismissed Adams as "the most reckless and depraved man living."

THE ELECTION OF 1836 In 1835, eighteen months before the presidential election, the Democrats nominated Jackson's handpicked successor,

Martin Van Buren Van Buren earned the nickname the "Little Magician," not only for his short stature but also his "magical" ability to exploit his political and social connections.

Vice President Martin Van Buren. The Whig coalition, united chiefly in its opposition to Jackson, adopted a strategy of multiple candidates, hoping to throw the election into the House of Representatives.

The Whigs put up three regional candidates: New Englander Daniel Webster, Hugh Lawson White of Tennessee, and William Henry Harrison of Indiana. But the multicandidate strategy failed. In the popular vote of 1836, Van Buren outdistanced the entire Whig field, winning 170 electoral votes while the others combined to collect only 113.

THE EIGHTH PRESIDENT

Martin Van Buren was a skillful politician whose ability to manipulate legislators had earned him the nickname "Little Magician." Elected governor of New York in 1828, he had resigned to join Andrew Jackson's cabinet as secretary of state, and then as vice president in 1833. Now, he was the first New Yorker to be elected president.

Van Buren had been Jackson's closest political adviser and most trusted ally, but many considered him too self-centered to do the work of the people. John Quincy Adams wrote that Van Buren was "by far the ablest" of the Jacksonians, but that he had wasted "most of his ability upon mere personal intrigues. His principles are all subordinate to his ambition." John C. Calhoun was even more cutting: "He is not of the race of the lion or the tiger." Rather, he "belongs to a lower order—the fox."

At his inauguration, Van Buren promised to follow "in the footsteps" of the enormously popular President Jackson. Before he could do so, however, the nation's financial sector began collapsing. On May 10, 1837, several large state banks in New York, running out of gold and silver, suddenly refused to convert customers' paper money into coins. Other banks across the nation quickly did the same, creating a panic among depositors across the nation. More than a third of the banks went under. This financial crisis would become known as the **Panic of 1837**. It would soon mushroom into the country's worst depression, lasting some seven years.

THE PANIC OF 1837   The causes of the financial crisis went back to the Jackson administration, but Van Buren got the blame. The problem actually started in Europe. During the mid-1830s, Great Britain, America's largest trading partner, experienced an acute financial crisis when the Bank of England, worried about a run on the gold and silver in its vaults, curtailed its loans. This forced most British companies to reduce their trade with America. As British demand for American cotton plummeted, so did the price paid for cotton. On top of everything else, in 1836 there had been a disastrous wheat crop. In the spring of 1836, *Niles' Weekly Register*, the nation's leading business journal, reported that the economy was "approaching a momentous crisis."

As creditors hastened to foreclose on businesses and farms unable to make their debt payments government spending plunged, and, in many cases, state governments could not repay their debts. In the crunch, 40 percent of the hundreds of recently created state banks failed. By early fall, 90 percent of the nation's factories had closed down.

Not surprisingly, the economic crisis frightened people. As a newspaper editorial complained in December 1836, the nation's economy "has been put into confusion and dismay by a well-meant, but *extremely mistaken*" pair of decisions by Congress and President Jackson: the Specie Circular and the elimination of the B.U.S. A functioning national bank could have served as a stabilizing force amid the financial panic. Instead, unregulated state banks around the country flooded the economy with worthless paper money that they printed without adequate backing in gold or silver.

Many deseperate southerners fled their debts altogether by moving to Texas, which was then a province of Mexico. Even the federal government itself, having put most of its gold and silver in state banks, was verging on bankruptcy. The *National Intelligencer* newspaper in Washington, D.C., reported in May that the federal Treasury "has not a dollar of gold or silver in the world!"

The poor were particularly hard hit. By the fall of 1837, one third of the nation's workers were jobless, and those still fortunate enough to be employed had their wages cut by 30 to 50 percent within two years. At the same time, prices for food and clothing soared. As the winter of 1837 approached, a New York City journalist reported that 200,000 people were "in utter and hopeless distress with no means of surviving the winter but those provided by charity." The nation had a "poverty-struck feeling."

POLITICS AMID THE DEPRESSION   The unprecedented economic calamity would last seven years and send shock waves through the political system. Critics among the Whigs called the president "Martin Van

Ruin" because he did not believe that he nor the federal government had any responsibility to rescue hard-pressed farmers, bankers, or businessmen, or to provide relief for the jobless and homeless. Any efforts to help people in distress must come from the states, not the national government.

How best to deal with the unprecedented depression clearly divided Democrats from Whigs. Unlike Van Buren, Whig Henry Clay insisted that suffering people were "entitled to the protecting care of a parental Government." To him, an enlarged role for the federal government was the price of a maturing, expanding republic in which elected officials had an obligation to promote the "safety, convenience, and prosperity" of the people. Clay, among others, savaged Van Buren for his "cold and heartless" attitude.

AN INDEPENDENT TREASURY   Van Buren believed that the federal government should stop risking its cash deposits in the insecure "pet" state banks that Jackson had selected. Instead, he wanted to establish an Independent Treasury system whereby the government would keep its funds in its own vaults and do business entirely in gold or silver, not paper currency. Van Buren wanted the federal government to regulate the nation's supply of gold and silver and let the marketplace regulate the supply of paper currency.

It took Van Buren more than three years to convince Congress to pass the **Independent Treasury Act** on July 4, 1840. Although it lasted little more than a year (the Whigs repealed it in 1841), it would be restored in 1846. Van Buren's Independent Treasury was a political disaster. Not surprisingly, the state banks that lost control of federal funds howled in protest. Moreover, it did nothing to end the widespread suffering caused by the deepening depression.

THE 1840 CAMPAIGN   By 1840, an election year, the Van Buren administration was in deep trouble. At their nominating convention, the Whigs passed over Henry Clay, Jackson's longtime foe, in favor of William Henry Harrison, whose credentials were impressive: victor at the Battle of Tippecanoe against Tecumseh's Shawnees in 1811, former governor of the Indiana Territory, and former congressman and senator from Ohio. To balance the ticket geographically, the Whigs nominated John Tyler of Virginia for vice president. Clay, who yearned to be president, was bitterly disappointed, complaining that "my friends are not worth the powder and shot it would take to kill them. I am the most unfortunate man in the history of parties."

The Whigs refused to take a stand on major issues. They did, however, seize upon a catchy campaign slogan: "Tippecanoe and Tyler Too." When a Democratic newspaper declared that General Harrison, at 67 the oldest candidate yet to seek the presidency, was the kind of man who would spend his retirement

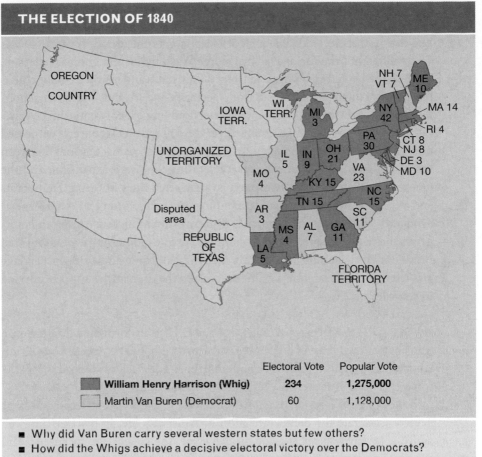

THE ELECTION OF 1840

	Electoral Vote	Popular Vote
■ William Henry Harrison (Whig)	234	1,275,000
☐ Martin Van Buren (Democrat)	60	1,128,000

■ Why did Van Buren carry several western states but few others?
■ How did the Whigs achieve a decisive electoral victory over the Democrats?
■ How was the Whig strategy in 1840 different from their campaign in 1836?

"in a log cabin [sipping apple cider] on the banks of the Ohio [River]," the Whigs chose the cider and log cabin symbols to depict Harrison as a simple man sprung from the people, in contrast to Van Buren's aristocratic lifestyle. (Harrison was actually from one of Virginia's wealthiest families.)

Harrison defeated Van Buren easily, winning 234 electoral votes to 60. The Whigs had promised a return to prosperity without explaining how it would happen. It was simply time for a change.

What was most remarkable about the election of 1840 was the turnout. More than 80 percent of white American men voted, many for the first time— the highest turnout before or since, as by this time almost every state had dropped property qualifications for voting.

Jackson's Legacy

The nation that elected William Henry Harrison to the presidency in 1840 was vastly different from the one led by George Washington and Thomas Jefferson. In 1828, the United States boasted twenty-four states and nearly 13 million people, many of them recent arrivals from Germany and Ireland. The national population was growing at a phenomenal rate, doubling every twenty-three years.

During the so-called Jacksonian era, the unregulated economy witnessed booming industrialization, rapidly growing cities, rising tensions between the North and South over slavery, accelerating westward expansion, and the emergence of the **second two-party system**, this time featuring Democrats and Whigs. A surge in foreign demand for southern cotton and other American goods, along with substantial British investment in new American enterprises, helped fuel an economic boom and a transportation revolution. That President-elect Jackson rode to his inauguration in a horse-drawn carriage and left eight years later on a train symbolized the dramatic changes occurring in American life.

A NEW POLITICAL LANDSCAPE   A transformational figure in a transformational era, Andrew Jackson helped reshape the American political landscape. Even his ferocious opponent, Henry Clay, acknowledged that Jackson had "swept over the Government . . . like a tropical tornado."

Like all great presidents, however, Jackson left a mixed legacy. Yes, he helped accelerate the democratization of American life. In his 1837 farewell address, he stressed his crusade on behalf of "the farmer, the mechanic, and the laboring classes of society—the bone and sinew of the country—men who love liberty and desire nothing but equal rights and equal laws."

Jackson championed opportunities for the "common man" to play a greater role in the political arena at the same time that working men were forming labor unions to increase their economic power and political clout. He helped establish the modern Democratic party and attracted to it the working poor and immigrants from eastern cities, as well as farmers from the South and East. Through a nimble combination of force and compromise, he saved the Union by suppressing the nullification crisis.

And, with great fanfare on January 1, 1835, Jackson announced that the government had paid off the national debt accumulated since the Revolutionary War, which he called a "national curse." It was the first time in history that a nation had eliminated a large debt. The *Washington Globe* celebrated the momentous occasion by noting that it coincided with the twentieth anniversary of the Battle of New Orleans, writing that "New Orleans and the National

Debt—the first of which paid off our scores to *our enemies*, whilst the latter paid off the last cent to *our friends.*"

Jackson's concept of "the people," however, was limited to a "white men's democracy," as it had been for all earlier presidents, and the phenomenon of Andrew Jackson, the heroic symbol of the common man and the democratic ideal, continues to spark historical debate, as it did during his own lifetime.

In 1828, William P. Anderson, a former army officer who had been one of Jackson's Tennessee horse-racing friends and political supporters but had turned into an outspoken opponent, wrote an open letter to the presidential candidate that was published in several newspapers. He attacked Jackson for having killed a man in a duel, then brutally outlined Old Hickory's faults: "Your besetting sins are ambition and the love of money. . . . You are naturally and constitutionally irritable, overbearing and tyrannical. . . . When you become the enemy of any man, you will put him down if you can, no matter by what means, fair or foul. . . . You are miserably deficient in principle, and have seldom or never had power without abusing it."

Although the criticism was too harsh, it contained more than a grain of truth. Jackson was so convinced of the rightness and righteousness of his ideals that he was selectively willing to defy constitutional limits on his authority when it suited his interests and satisfied his rage. He was both the instrument of democracy and its enemy, protecting "the humble people" and the Union by expanding presidential authority in ways that the founders had never envisioned, including removing federal money from the national bank, replacing government officials with party loyalists, censoring the mails, and ending nullification in South Carolina.

Jackson often declared that the only justification for using governmental power was to ensure equal treatment for everyone, the "high and the low, the rich and the poor." Yet his own use of government force was at times contradictory and even hypocritical. While threatening to "kill" the B.U.S. and hang John Calhoun and other South Carolina nullifiers, he refused to intervene when Georgia officials violated the legal rights of Cherokees. His aggressive use of presidential authority was less principled than it was political and personal. His inconsistent approach to executive power both symbolized and aggravated the perennial tension in the American republic between a commitment to democratic ideals and the exercise of presidential authority.

CHAPTER REVIEW

SUMMARY

- **Jackson's Views and Policies** The Jacksonians sought to democratize the political process and expand economic opportunity for the "common man" (that is, "poor and humble" white men). As the representative of "the people," Andrew Jackson expanded the role of the president in economic matters, reducing federal spending and eliminating the powerful *Second Bank of the United States*. His *Bank War* painted the national bank as full of "vipers and thieves" and was hugely popular, but Jackson did not understand its long-term economic consequences. In addition, his views on limited government were not always reflected in his policies. He left the high taxes from the *Tariff of Abominations (1828)* in place until opposition in the South created a national crisis.

- **Indian Removal Act of 1830** The *Indian Removal Act* of 1830 authorized the relocation of Eastern Indians to federal lands west of the Mississippi River. The Cherokees used the federal court system to try to block this relocation. Despite the Supreme Court's decisions in their favor, President Jackson forced them to move; the event and the route they took came to be known as the *Trail of Tears*. By 1840, only a few Seminoles and Cherokees remained in remote areas of the Southeast.

- **Nullification Controversy** The concept of *nullification*, developed by South Carolina's John C. Calhoun, enabled a state to disavow a federal law. When a South Carolina convention nullified the Tariffs of 1828 and 1832, Jackson requested that Congress pass a *Force Bill* authorizing the U.S. Army to compel compliance with the tariffs. After South Carolina, under the threat of federal military force, accepted a compromise tariff put forth by Henry Clay, the state convention nullified the Force Bill. The immediate crisis was over, with both sides claiming victory.

- **Democrats and Whigs** Jackson's arrogant behavior, especially his use of the veto, led many to regard him as "King Andrew the First." Groups who opposed him coalesced into a new party, known as the *Whigs*, thus producing the country's *second two-party system*. Two acts—the *Distribution Act* and the Specie Circular—ultimately destabilized the nation's economy. Jackson's ally and vice president, Martin Van Buren, succeeded him as president, but Jacksonian bank policies led to the financial *Panic of 1837* and an economic depression. Van Buren responded by establishing an *Independent Treasury* to safeguard the nation's economy but offered no help for individuals in distress. The economic calamity ensured a Whig victory in the election of 1840.

- **The Jackson Years** Andrew Jackson's America was very different from the America of 1776. Most white men had gained the vote, but political equality did not mean economic equality. Jacksonian Democrats wanted every American to have an equal chance to compete in the marketplace and in the political arena, but they never promoted equality of results. Inequality between rich and poor widened during the Jacksonian era.

CHRONOLOGY

1828	"Tariff of Abominations" goes into effect
1830	Congress passes the Indian Removal Act
	Andrew Jackson vetoes the Maysville Road Bill
1831	Supreme Court issues *Cherokee Nation v. Georgia* decision
1832	Supreme Court issues *Worcester v. Georgia* decision
	South Carolina passes Ordinance of Nullification
	Andrew Jackson vetoes the Bank Recharter Bill
1833	Congress passes the Force Bill, authorizing military force in South Carolina
	Congress passes Henry Clay's compromise tariff with Jackson's support
1836	Democratic candidate Martin Van Buren is elected president
1837	Financial panic deflates the economy
1837–1838	Eastern Indians are forced west on the Trail of Tears
1840	Independent Treasury established
	Whig candidate William Henry Harrison is elected president

KEY TERMS

Indian Removal Act (1830) p. 353

Trail of Tears (1838–1839) p. 358

Second Bank of the United States p. 358

Bank War p. 360

Tariff of Abominations (1828) p. 361

nullification p. 362

Force Bill (1833) p. 368

Whigs p. 370

Distribution Act (1836) p. 371

Panic of 1837 p. 374

Independent Treasury Act (1840) p. 376

second two-party system p. 378

🐸 INQUIZITIVE

Go to InQuizitive to see what you've learned—and learn what you've missed—with personalized feedback along the way.

11

The South, Slavery, and King Cotton

1800–1860

The Old South One of the enduring myths of the Old South is captured in this late nineteenth-century painting of a plantation on the Mississippi River: muscular slaves tending the lush cotton fields, a steamboat easing down the wide river, and the planter's family relaxing in the cool shade of their white-columned mansion. Novels and films like *Gone with the Wind* (1939) would perpetuate the notion of the Old South as a stable, paternalistic agrarian society led by white planters who were the "natural" aristocracy of virtue and talent within their communities.

Of all the regions of the United States during the first half of the nineteenth century, the pre–Civil War Old South was the most distinctive. What had once been a narrow band of settlements along the Atlantic coast dramatically expanded westward and southward to form a subcontinental empire rooted in cotton.

The southern states remained rural and agricultural long after the rest of the nation had embraced cities, immigrants, and factories. Yet the Old South was also instrumental in enabling the nation's capitalist development and its growing economic stature. After the War of 1812, southern-grown cotton became the key raw material driving industrial growth, feeding the textile mills of Great Britain and New England. The price of raw cotton doubled in the first year after the war, and the profits made by cotton producers flowed into the hands of northern and British bankers, merchants, and textile mill owners. Investors in Boston, New York City, and Philadelphia provided loans to southerners to buy more land and slaves. Northerners also provided the cotton industry with other essential needs: insurance, financing, and shipping.

The story of how southern cotton clothed the world, spurred the expansion of global capitalism, and transformed history was woven with threads of tragedy, however. The revolution spawned by the mass production of cotton was rooted in the explosive expansion of slavery across the South and into Texas, as Native Americans were pushed off their ancestral lands and relocated across the Mississippi River. A group of slaves in Virginia recognized the essential role they played in the surging economy when they asked, "Didn't we clear the

focus questions

1. What various factors made the South distinct from the rest of the United States during the early nineteenth century?

2. What role did cotton production and slavery play in the South's economic and social development?

3. What were the major social groups within southern white society? Why was each group committed to the continuation and expansion of slavery?

4. What was the impact of slavery on African Americans, both free and enslaved, throughout the South?

5. How did enslaved peoples respond to the inhumanity of their situation?

land, and raise the crops of corn, of tobacco, rice, of sugar, of everything? And then didn't the large cities in the North grow up on the cotton and the sugars and the rice that we made?"

THE DISTINCTIVENESS OF THE OLD SOUTH

People have long debated what set the Old South apart from the rest of the nation. Most arguments focus on the region's climate and geography in shaping its culture and economy. The South's warm, humid weather was ideal for cultivating profitable crops such as tobacco, cotton, rice, indigo, and sugarcane, which led to the plantation system of large commercial agriculture and its dependence upon enslaved labor.

Unlike the North, the South had few large cities, few banks, few railroads, few factories, and few schools. Most southern commerce was related to the storage, distribution, and sale of agricultural products, especially cotton. With the cotton economy booming, investors focused on buying land and slaves; there was little reason to create a robust industrial sector.

A BIRACIAL CULTURE What made the Old South most distinctive was not its climate or soil but its expanding system of race-based slavery. The majority of southern whites did not own slaves, but they supported what John C. Calhoun called the South's **"peculiar institution"** because slavery was so central to their society's way of life. Calhoun's carefully crafted phrase allowed southerners to avoid using the charged word *slavery*, while the adjective *peculiar* implied that slavery was *unique* to the South, as it essentially was.

The profitability and convenience of owning slaves created a sense of social unity among whites that bridged class differences. Poor whites who owned no slaves and resented the planters ("cotton snobs") could still claim racial superiority over enslaved blacks ("niggers"). Because of race-based slavery, explained Georgia attorney Thomas Reade Cobb, every white "feels that he belongs to an elevated class. It matters not that he is no slaveholder; he is not of the inferior race; he is a free-born citizen."

The Old South also differed from other sections of the country in its high proportion of native-born Americans. The region attracted few European immigrants after the Revolution, in part because of geography. The main shipping routes from Britain and Europe took immigrants to northern ports. Because most immigrants were penniless, they could not afford to travel to the South. Moreover, European immigrants, most of whom were manual laborers, could not compete with slave labor.

CONFLICTING MYTHS Southerners, a North Carolina editor wrote, are "a mythological people, created half out of dream and half out of slander, who live in a still legendary land." Myths are beliefs made up partly of truths and partly of lies, formed with accurate generalizations and willful distortions. During the nineteenth century, a powerful myth emerged among white southerners that the South was both different from *and* better than the North. This blended notion of distinctiveness and superiority became central to the self-image of many southerners. Even today, many southerners tenaciously cultivate a defiant pride and separate identity from the rest of the nation.

In defending the South and slavery from northern critics, southerners claimed that their region was morally superior. Kind planters, according to the prevailing myth, provided happy slaves with food, clothing, shelter, and security—in contrast to a North populated with greedy bankers and heartless factory owners who treated their wage laborers worse than slaves. John C. Calhoun insisted that in the northern states the quality of life for free people of color had "become worse" since slavery there had been banned, whereas in the South, the standard of living among enslaved African Americans had "improved greatly in every respect."

In this mythic version of the Old South, slavery was defended as beneficial to both slaves and owners. In *Aunt Phillis's Cabin; or, Southern Life As It Is* (1852), novelist Mary Henderson Eastman stressed "the necessity of the existence of slavery at present in our Southern States," and claimed "that, as a general thing, the slaves are comfortable and contented, and their owners humane and kind."

The agrarian ideal and the southern passion for guns, horsemanship, hunting, and the military completed this self-gratifying image of the Old South as a region of honest small farmers and aristocratic gentlemen, young belles and beautiful ladies who led leisurely lives of well-mannered graciousness, honor, and courage in a carefree, romantic world of white-columned mansions.

The contrasting myth of the Old South was much darker. Northern abolitionists (those who wanted an immediate end to slavery) pictured the region as being built on an immoral economic system dependent on the exploitation of blacks and the displacement of Native Americans. In this version of the southern myth, the white planters were rarely "natural aristocrats," like Thomas Jefferson, who were ambivalent about slavery. More often, planters were viewed as ambitious, self-made men who had seized opportunities to become rich by planting and selling cotton—and trading in slaves.

Northern abolitionists such as Harriet Beecher Stowe portrayed southern planters as cunning capitalists who raped enslaved women, brutalized slaves, and lorded over their communities with arrogant disdain. They treated slaves like cattle, broke up their families, and sold slaves "down the river" to toil in the Louisiana sugar mills and on rice plantations. An English woman traveling in the South in 1830 noted that what slaves in Virginia and Maryland feared most was being "sent to *the south* and sold. . . . The sugar plantations [in Louisiana] and, more than all, the rice grounds of Georgia and the Carolinas, are the terror of the American negroes."

MANY SOUTHS   The contradictory elements of these conflicting myths continue to fight for supremacy in the South, each pressing its claim to legitimacy, in part because the extreme descriptions are both built upon half-truths and fierce prejudices. The South has long been defined by two souls, two hearts, two minds competing for dominance. The paradoxes associated with southern mythmaking provided much of the region's variety, for the Old South, like the New South, was not a single culture but a diverse section with multiple interests and perspectives—and it was rapidly growing and changing.

The Old South included three distinct subsections with different patterns of economic development and diverging degrees of commitment to slavery. Throughout the first half of the nineteenth century, the seven states of the Lower South (South Carolina, Georgia, Florida, Alabama, Mississippi, Louisiana, and parts of Texas) grew increasingly dependent upon commercial cotton production supported by slave labor. A traveler in Mississippi observed in 1835 that ambitious whites wanted "to sell cotton in order to buy negroes—to make more cotton to buy negroes." By 1860, slaves represented nearly half the population of the Lower South, largely because they were the most efficient producers of cotton in the world.

The states of the Upper South (Virginia, North Carolina, Tennessee, and Arkansas) had more-varied agricultural economies—a mixture of large commercial plantations and small family farms (or "yeoman farms"), where crops were grown mostly for household use. Many southern states also had large areas without slavery, especially in the mountains of Virginia, the western Carolinas, eastern Tennessee, and northern Georgia, where the soil and climate were not suited to cotton or tobacco.

In the Border South (Delaware, Maryland, Kentucky, and Missouri), slavery was slowly disappearing because cotton could not thrive there. By 1860, approximately 90 percent of Delaware's black population and half of Maryland's were already free.

THE COTTON KINGDOM

After the Revolution, as the worn-out tobacco fields in Virginia and Maryland lost their fertility, tobacco farming spread into Kentucky and as far west as Missouri. Rice continued to be grown in the coastal areas ("low country") of the Carolinas and Georgia, where fields could easily be flooded and drained by tidal rivers flowing into the ocean. Sugarcane, like rice, was also an expensive crop to produce, requiring machinery to grind the cane to release the sugar syrup. During the early nineteenth century, only southern Louisiana focused on sugar production.

In addition to such "cash crops," the South led the nation in the production of livestock: hogs, horses, mules, and cattle. Southerners, both black and white, fed themselves largely on pork. It was the "king of the table." John S. Wilson, a Georgia doctor, called the region the "Republic of Porkdom." Southerners ate pork or bacon "morning, noon, and night." Corn was on southern plates as often as pork. During the early summer, corn was boiled on the cob; by late summer and fall it was ground into cornmeal, a coarse flour. Cornbread and hominy, as well as a "mush" or porridge made of whole-grain corn mixed with milk, were almost daily fare.

NEGRO VILLAGE ON A SOUTHERN PLANTATION.

"Negro Village on a Southern Plantation" This line drawing of slaves dancing after a day of work in the cotton fields is an example of the "happy slave" trope, wherein white Southerners glossed slavery as somehow cheerful and harmonious rather than oppressive. The drawing is from Mrs. Mary H. Eastman's *Aunt Phyllis's Cabin; or, Southern Life as It Is* — a pro-slavery novel published in 1853 in response to Harriet Beecher Stowe's anti-slavery novel *Uncle Tom's Cabin*.

KING COTTON During the first half of the nineteenth century, cotton surpassed rice as the most profitable cash crop in the South. Southern cotton (called "white gold") drove much of the national economy and the Industrial Revolution, feeding the mechanized textile mills in New England and Great Britain.

In fact, cotton became one of the transforming forces in nineteenth-century history. It shaped the lives of the enslaved who cultivated it, the planters who grew rich by it, the mill girls who sewed it, the merchants who sold it, the people who wore it, and the politicians who warred over it. "Cotton is King," exclaimed the *Southern Cultivator* in 1859, "and wields an astonishing influence over the world's commerce."

The Cotton Kingdom resulted largely from two crucial developments. Until the late eighteenth century, cotton fabric was a rarity produced by women in India using hand looms. Then British inventors developed machinery to convert raw cotton into thread and cloth in textile mills. The mechanical production of cotton made Great Britain the world's first industrial nation, and the number of British textile mills grew so fast that the owners could not get enough cotton fiber to meet their needs. American Eli Whitney solved the problem by constructing the first cotton gin, which mechanized the labor-intensive process of manually removing the sticky seeds from the bolls of what was called short-staple cotton.

Taken together, these two breakthroughs helped create the world's largest industry—and transformed the South in the process. By 1815, just months after Andrew Jackson's victory over British troops at New Orleans, some thirty British ships were docked at the city's wharves because, as an American merchant reported, "Europe must, and will have, cotton for her manufacturers." During that year alone, more than 65,000 bales of cotton were shipped down the Mississippi River to New Orleans. To be sure, other nations joined the global cotton-producing revolution—India, Egypt, Brazil, and China—but the American South was the driving force of cotton capitalism.

THE OLD SOUTHWEST Because of its warm climate and plentiful rainfall, the Lower South became the global leader in cotton production. The region's cheap, fertile land and the profits to be made in growing cotton generated a frenzied mobility in which people constantly searched for more opportunities and even better land. Henry Watson, a New Englander who moved to Alabama, complained in 1836 that "nobody seems to consider himself settled [here]; they remain one, two, three or four years & must move on to some other spot."

The cotton belt moved south and west during the first half of the nineteenth century, and hundreds of thousands of land-hungry southerners moved with it. As the oldest southern states—Virginia and the Carolinas—experienced soil exhaustion from the overplanting of tobacco and cotton, restless farmers moved to the **Old Southwest**—western Georgia, Alabama, Mississippi, Louisiana, Arkansas, and, eventually, Texas.

In 1820, the coastal states of Virginia, the Carolinas, and Georgia produced two thirds of the nation's cotton. By 1830, the Old Southwest states were producing two thirds of America's cotton. An acre of land in South Carolina produced about 300 pounds of cotton, while one acre in Alabama or in the Mississippi Delta, a 200-mile-wide strip of fertile soil between the Yazoo and Mississippi Rivers, could generate 800 pounds. It was the most profitable farmland in the world.

Such profits, however, required backbreaking labor, most of it performed by enslaved blacks. A white Virginian noted in 1807 that "there is a great aversion amongst our Negroes to be carried to distant parts, and particularly to our new countries [in the Old Southwest]." In marshy areas near the Gulf coast, slaves were put to work removing trees and stumps from the swampy muck. "None but men as hard as a Savage," said one worker, could survive such wearying conditions.

The formula for growing rich in the Lower South was simple: cheap land, cotton seed, and slaves. A North Carolinian reported that the "*Alabama Fever . . . has carried off* vast numbers of our citizens." Between 1810 and 1840, the combined population of Georgia, Alabama, and Mississippi increased from about 300,000 (252,000 of whom were in Georgia) to 1,657,799. Annual cotton production in the United States had grown from less than 150,000 bales (a bundle of cotton weighing 500 pounds) in 1814 to 4 *million* bales in 1860.

THE SOUTHERN FRONTIER   Farm families in the Old Southwest tended to be large. "There is not a cabin but has ten or twelve children in it," reported a traveling minister. "When the boys are eighteen and the girls are fourteen, they marry—so that in many cabins you will see . . . the mother looking as young as the daughter."

Women were a minority in the Old Southwest. Many resisted moving to what they had heard was a disease-ridden, male-dominated, violent, and primitive territory. Others feared that life on the southern frontier would produce a "dissipation" of morals. They heard wild stories of lawlessness, drunkenness, gambling, and whoring. A woman newly arrived in frontier Alabama wrote home that the farmers around her "live in a miserable manner. They think only of making money, and their houses are hardly fit to live in."

Enslaved blacks had many of the same reservations about relocating. Almost a million captive African Americans in Maryland, Virginia, and the Carolinas

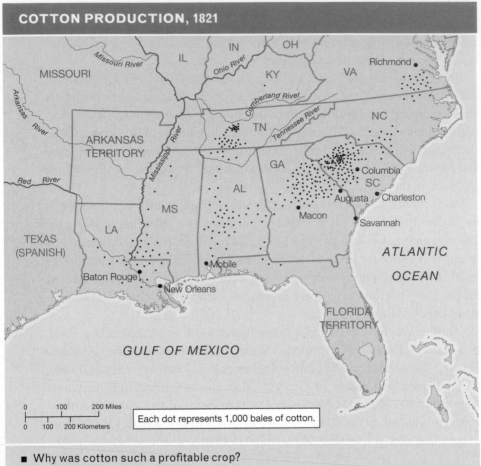

COTTON PRODUCTION, 1821

Each dot represents 1,000 bales of cotton.

- Why was cotton such a profitable crop?
- What regions produced the most cotton in 1821?
- What innovations enabled farmers to move inland and produce cotton more efficiently?

were forced to move to the Old Southwest during the first half of the nineteenth century. Herded onto steamboats or slave ships or forced to walk hundreds of miles manacled in iron collars and chains, they lived in "perpetual dread" of the region's harsh working conditions and its broiling summer heat and humidity.

The frontier environment in the Old Southwest was rude, rough, and lively. Men had a "hell of a lot of fun." They often drank, gambled, and fought. In 1834, a South Carolina migrant urged his brother to move west and join him because "you can live like a fighting cock with us." Most Old Southwest plantations had their own stills to manufacture whiskey, and alcoholism ravaged many frontier families.

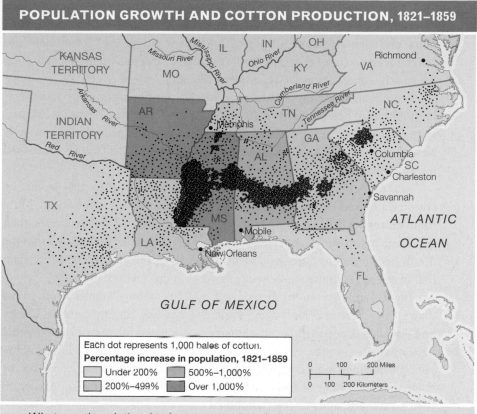

POPULATION GROWTH AND COTTON PRODUCTION, 1821–1859

Each dot represents 1,000 bales of cotton.

Percentage increase in population, 1821–1859

☐ Under 200%   ☐ 500%–1,000%
☐ 200%–499%   ☐ Over 1,000%

0   100   200 Miles
0   100   200 Kilometers

- What was the relationship between westward migration and the spread of cotton plantations?
- Why did cotton plantations cluster in certain regions of the South?
- What were the environmental and economic consequences of the South's emphasis on cotton?

Violence was commonplace, and the frequency of stabbings, shootings, and murders shocked visitors. Shocking, too, were the ways that white men abused women, both black and white. An Alabama woman was outraged by the "beastly passions" of the white men who fathered slave children and then sold them like livestock. She also recorded in her diary instances of men regularly beating their wives. Another woman wrote about a friend whose husband abused her, explaining that she had little choice but to suffer in silence, for she was "wholly dependent upon his care." The contrasting gender experiences in the Old Southwest were highlighted in a letter in which a woman reported: "All the men is very well pleased but the women is not very well satisfied."

THE SPREADING COTTON KINGDOM   By 1860, the center of the "**Cotton Kingdom**" stretched from eastern North Carolina, South Carolina, and Georgia through the fertile Alabama-Mississippi "black belt" (so called for the color of the fertile soil), through Louisiana, on to Texas, and up the Mississippi Valley as far as southern Illinois.

Steamboats made the Mississippi River the cotton highway by transporting millions of bales downriver from Kentucky, Tennessee, Arkansas, Mississippi, and Louisiana to New Orleans, where sailing ships took the cotton to New York, New England, Great Britain, and France. King Cotton accounted for more than half of all U.S. exports.

By 1860, Alabama, Mississippi, and Louisiana were the three top-producing cotton states, and two thirds of the richest Americans lived in the South. More millionaires per capita lived in Natchez, Mississippi, along the great river, than anywhere in the world. The rapid expansion of the cotton belt ensured that the South became even more dependent on enslaved black workers. More than half of the slaves in the South worked in cotton production.

The dynamic system of slavery was, as John Quincy Adams wrote in his diary, "the great and foul stain" upon the nation's commitment to liberty and equality. It persisted because it was such a powerful engine of economic development—and the most tangible sign of economic success. Enterprising young white men judged wealth and status by the number of slaves owned. By 1860, the dollar value of enslaved blacks outstripped the value of *all* American banks, railroads, and factories combined.

The soaring profitability of cotton fostered a false sense of security. In 1860, a Mississippi newspaper boasted that the South, "safely entrenched behind her cotton bags . . . can defy the world—for the civilized world depends on the cotton of the South." Cotton bred cockiness. In a speech to the U.S. Senate in 1858, South Carolina's former governor, James Henry Hammond, who owned a huge cotton plantation worked by more than 100 slaves, warned the critics of slavery in the North: "You dare not make war on cotton. No power on earth dares make war upon it. Cotton is King."

WHITES IN THE OLD SOUTH

The culture of cotton and slavery shaped the South's social structure and provided much of its political power. Unlike in the North and Midwest, southern society was dominated by an elite group of planters and merchants.

WHITE PLANTERS   Although there were only a few giant plantations in each southern state, their owners exercised overwhelming influence. As a

Virginian observed in the mid-1830s, "the old slaveholding families exerted a great deal of control . . . and they affected the manner and prejudices of the slaveholding part of the state."

The large planters behaved like an aristocracy, viewing their poor white neighbors with a contempt that was readily reciprocated. The richest planters and merchants were determined to retain control over southern society, in part because of self-interest and in part because they assumed they were the region's natural leaders. "Inequality is the fundamental law of the universe," declared one planter. James Henry Hammond was even more blunt, declaring that South Carolina planters are "essentially what the nobility are in other countries. They stand at the head of society and politics." Slavery, he argued, "does indeed create an aristocracy—an aristocracy of talents, of virtue, of generosity, and courage."

In addition to its size, what distinguished a plantation from a farm was the use of a large number of slaves supervised by drivers and overseers. Planters themselves rarely engaged in manual labor. They focused on managing the overseers and handling the marketing and sale of the cotton, tobacco, rice, or sugar.

Most planters had begun their careers as land traders, investors, cotton merchants (called "factors"), and farmers. Over time, they made enough money to acquire a plantation worked by slaves. Success required careful monitoring of the markets for cotton, land, and slaves, as well as careful management of workers and production.

When not working, planters enjoyed hunting, horse racing, and cards. As a plantation slave recalled, his master on Sundays liked to "gamble, run horses, or fight game-cocks, discuss politics, and drink whisky, and brandy and water all day long."

If, as historians have agreed, one had to own at least twenty slaves to be called a **planter**, only one out of thirty whites in the South in 1860 was a planter. The 10,000 most powerful planters, accounting for less than 3 percent of white men in the South, held more than half the slaves. Virginia's governor said that the wealthier planters had the leisure time to cultivate "morals, manners, philosophy, and politics."

Over time, planters and their wives (referred to as "mistresses") grew accustomed to being waited on by slaves, day and night. A Virginia planter told a British visitor that a slave girl slept in the master bedroom with him and his wife. When his guest asked why, he replied: "Good heaven! If I wanted a glass of water during the night, what would become of me?"

From colonial times, most southern white men embraced an unwritten social code centered on a prickly sense of personal honor in which they were expected to defend their reputations with words, fists, knives, or guns. Duels to the death (called "affairs of honor") were the ultimate expression of manly honor. Many prominent southern leaders—congressmen, senators, governors, editors, and planters—engaged in duels with pistols, although dueling was technically illegal in many states. The roster of participants included President Andrew Jackson of Tennessee and Senator Henry Clay of Kentucky. But men of all classes were ready to fight at the first sign of disrespect.

THE PLANTATION MISTRESS   The South, like the North, was a male-dominated society, only more so because of the slave system. A prominent Georgian, Christopher Memminger, explained that slavery heightened the need for a hierarchical social and family structure. White wives and children needed to be as subservient and compliant as slaves. "Each planter," he declared, "is in fact a Patriarch—his position compels him to be a ruler in his household," and he requires "obedience and subordination."

The **plantation mistress** supervised the domestic household in the same way as the planter took care of the cotton business. Overseeing the supply and preparation of food and linens, she also managed the housecleaning and care of the sick, the birthing of babies, and the operations of the dairy. A plantation slave remembered that her mistress "was with all the slave women every time a baby was born. Or, when a plague of misery hit the folks, she knew what to do and what kind of medicine to chase off the aches and pains."

Mary Boykin Chesnut, a plantation mistress in South Carolina, complained that "there is no slave, after all, like a wife." She admitted that she had few rights in the large household she managed, since her husband was the "master of the house." A wife was expected to love, honor, obey, and serve her husband. Virginian George Fitzhugh, a celebrated Virginia attorney and writer, spoke for most southern men when he said that a "man loves his children because they are weak, helpless, and dependent. He loves his wife for similar reasons."

Mary Boykin Chesnut Her diary describing life in the Confederacy during the Civil War was republished in 1981 and won the Pulitzer Prize.

White women living in a slaveholding culture confronted a double standard in terms of moral and sexual behavior. They were expected to be examples of Christian morality and sexual purity, even as their husbands, brothers, and sons often engaged in self-indulgent hedonism, gambling, drinking, carousing, and sexually assaulting enslaved women.

"Under slavery," Mary Chesnut wrote in her famous diary, "we live surrounded by prostitutes." Yet she did not blame enslaved women for playing that role. They were usually forced to do so. In fact, many planters justified their behavior by highlighting the additional money they were creating by impregnating enslaved women. "God forgive us," Chesnut added, "but ours is a monstrous system. Like the patriarchs of old, our men live all in one house with their wives and their [enslaved] concubines [lovers]; and the mulattoes [people of mixed races] one sees in every family partly resemble the white children. Any lady is ready to tell you who is the father of all the mulatto children in everybody's household but her own. Those, she seems to think, drop from the clouds."

Yet for all their private complaints and daily burdens, few plantation mistresses spoke out against the male-dominated social order and racist climate. They largely accepted the limited domestic role assigned them by men such as George Howe, a South Carolina religion professor. In 1850, he complimented southern women for understanding their subordinate place. "Born to lean upon others, rather than to stand independently by herself, and to confide in an arm stronger than hers," the southern woman had no desire for "power" outside the home, he said. The few women who were demanding equality were "unsexing" themselves and were "despised and detested" by their families and communities.

OVERSEERS AND DRIVERS On large plantations, *overseers* managed the slaves and were responsible for maintaining the buildings, fences, and grounds. They usually were white farmers or skilled workers, the sons of planters, or simply poor whites eager to rise in stature. Some were themselves slaveholders. The overseers moved often in search of better wages and cheaper land. A Mississippi planter described white overseers as "a worthless set of vagabonds." Likewise, Frederick Douglass, a mulatto who escaped from slavery in Maryland, said his overseer was "a miserable drunkard, a profane swearer, and a savage monster" always armed with a blood-stained bullwhip and a club that he used so cruelly that he even "enraged" the plantation owner. The overseer tolerated no excuses or explanations. "To be accused was to be convicted, and to be convicted was to be punished," Douglass said.

Usually, the highest managerial position a slave could hope for on a plantation was that of *driver*, a favored man whose job was to oversee a small group ("gang") of slaves, get them organized each morning by sunrise, and then direct their work until dark. Over the years, there were numerous examples of slaves murdering drivers for being too cruel.

There were a few black overseers. Francis Frederic, a slave in Kentucky, remembered that his grandmother's white master was a "hard one." He appointed her son, a slave, as the plantation's overseer. After the planter discovered that Frederic's grandmother had committed the crime of attending an outlawed prayer meeting, he ordered her son to give her "forty lashes with a thong of a raw cow's-hide, her master standing over her the whole time blaspheming and threatening what he would do if her son did not lay it on."

"PLAIN WHITE FOLK"   About half of white southerners were small farmers—**"plain white folk"** who were usually uneducated, often illiterate, and forced to scratch out hardscrabble lives of bare self-sufficiency. These small farmers (yeomen) typically lived with their families in simple two-room cabins on fifty acres or less. They raised a few pigs and chickens and grew enough corn and cotton to live on. They traded with neighbors more than they bought from stores. Women on these small farms worked in the fields during harvest time but spent most of their days doing household chores while raising lots of children. Farm children grew up fast. By age four they could carry a water bucket from the well to the house and collect eggs from the henhouse. Young boys could plant, weed, and harvest crops, feed livestock, and milk cows.

The average slaveholder was a small farmer working alongside five or six slaves. Such "middling" farmers usually lived in a log cabin rather than a columned mansion. In the backcountry and mountainous regions of the South, where slaves and plantations were scarce, small farmers dominated the social structure.

Southern farmers tended to be fiercely independent and suspicious of government authority, and they overwhelmingly identified with the Democratic party of Andrew Jackson. Although only a minority of middle-class white farmers owned slaves, most of them supported the slave system. They feared that slaves, if freed, would compete with them for land and jobs, and, although not wealthy, the farmers enjoyed the privileged social status that race-based slavery afforded them. As a white farmer told a northern traveler, "Now suppose they [slaves] was free. You see they'd all think themselves as good as we." James Henry Hammond and other rich white planters frequently reminded their white neighbors who owned no slaves that "in a slave country, every freeman is an aristocrat" because blacks are beneath them in the social order. Such racist sentiments pervaded the Lower South—and much of the rest of the nation—throughout the nineteenth century.

"POOR WHITES"   Visitors to the Old South often had trouble telling small farmers apart from the "poor whites," a category of desperately poor people who were relegated to the least desirable land and lived on the fringes of society. The "poor whites," often derided as "crackers," "hillbillies," or "trash," were usually day laborers or squatters who owned neither land nor slaves. Some 40 percent of white southerners worked as "tenants," renting land from others, or as farm laborers, toiling for others. They frequently took refuge in the pine barrens, mountain hollows, and swamps after having been pushed aside by the more enterprising and the more successful. They usually lived in log cabins or shacks and often made their own clothing, barely managing each year to keep their families clothed, dry, and fed.

BLACK SOCIETY IN THE SOUTH

Southern society was literally black and white. Whites had the power, and enslaved blacks were often treated as property rather than people. The system of slavery relied on overwhelming force and fear and was intentionally dehumanizing. "We believe the negro to belong to an inferior race," one planter declared. Southern apologists for slavery often stressed that African Americans were "inferior" beings incapable of living on their own. Thomas Reade Cobb proclaimed that they were better off "in a state of bondage."

Effective slave management therefore required teaching slaves to understand that they were supposed to be treated like animals. As Henry Garner, an escaped slave, explained, the aim of slaveholders was "to make you as much like brutes as possible." Others justified slavery as a form of benevolent paternalism. George Fitzhugh said that the enslaved black was "but a grown-up child, and must be governed as a child."

Such self-serving paternalism had one ultimate purpose: profits. Planters, explained a southerner, "care for nothing but to buy Negroes to raise cotton & raise cotton to buy Negroes." In 1818, James Steer in Louisiana predicted that enslaved blacks would be the best investment that southerners could make. Eleven years later, in 1829, the North Carolina Supreme Court declared that slavery existed to increase "the profit of the Master." The role of the slave was "to toil while another [the owners] reap the fruits."

Those in the business of buying and selling slaves reaped huge profits. One of them reported in the 1850s that "a nigger that wouldn't bring over $300, seven years ago, will fetch $1000, cash, quick, this year." Thomas Clemson of South Carolina, the son-in-law of John C. Calhoun, candidly explained that "my object is to get the most I can for the property [slaves]. . . . I care but little to whom and how they are sold, whether together [as families] or separated."

Owning, working, and selling slaves was the quickest way to wealth and social status in the South. The wife of a Louisiana planter complained in 1829 that white people talked constantly about how the profits generated by growing cotton enabled them to buy "plantations & negrows." In 1790, the United States had fewer than 700,000 enslaved African Americans. By 1830, it had more than 2 million, and by 1860, almost 4 million, virtually all of them in the South and border states.

THE SLAVE SYSTEM As the enslaved population grew, slaveholders developed an increasingly complex *system* of rules, regulations, and restrictions. Formal **slave codes** in each state regulated the treatment of slaves to deter runaways or rebellions. Slaves could not leave their owner's land or household without permission or stay out after dark without an identification pass. Some codes made it a crime for slaves to learn to read and write, for fear that they might pass notes to plan a revolt. Frederick Douglass said that slaveholders assumed that allowing slaves to learn to read and write "would spoil the best nigger in the world."

Slaves in most states could not testify in court, legally marry, own firearms, or hit a white man, even in self-defense. They could also be abused, tortured, and whipped. Despite such restrictions and brutalities, however, the enslaved managed to create their own communities and cultures within the confines of the slave system, forging bonds of care, solidarity, recreation, and religion.

Free blacks These badges, issued in Charleston, South Carolina, were worn by free black people so that they would not be mistaken for someone's "property."

"FREE PERSONS OF COLOR" African Americans who were not enslaved were called free persons of color. They occupied an uncertain and often vulnerable social status between bondage and freedom. Many lived in constant fear of being kidnapped into slavery.

To be sure, free blacks had more rights than slaves. They could enter into contracts, marry, own property (including slaves of their own), and pass on their property to their children. But they were not viewed or treated as equal to whites. In most states, they could not vote, own weapons, attend white church services, or testify against whites in court. In South Carolina, free people of color had to pay an annual tax and were not allowed to leave the state. After 1823, they were required to have a white "guardian" and an identity card.

Some slaves were able to purchase their freedom, and others were freed ("manumitted") by their owners. By 1860, approximately 250,000 free blacks lived in the slave states, most of them in coastal cities such as Baltimore, Charleston, Savannah, and New Orleans. Many were skilled workers. Some were tailors, shoemakers, or carpenters; others were painters, bricklayers, butchers, blacksmiths, or barbers. Still others worked on the docks or on steamships. Free black women usually worked as seamstresses, laundresses, or house servants.

Among the free black population were a large number of **mulattoes**, people of mixed racial ancestry. The census of 1860 reported 412,000 mulattoes in the United States, or about 10 percent of the black population—probably a drastic undercount. In cities such as Charleston, and especially New Orleans, "colored" society occupied a shifting status somewhere between that of blacks and that of whites.

Although most free people of color were poor, some mulattoes built substantial fortunes and even became slaveholders themselves. William Ellison was the richest freedman in the South. Liberated by his white father in 1816, he developed a thriving business in South Carolina making cotton gins while managing his own 900-acre plantation worked by more than sixty slaves. Ellison, like other wealthy mulattoes, came to view himself as a "brown aristocrat." He yearned to be accepted as an equal in white society; during the Civil War, he supported the Confederacy. In Louisiana, a mulatto, Cyprien Ricard, paid $250,000 for an estate that had ninety-one slaves. In Natchez, Mississippi, William Johnson, son of a white father and a mulatto mother, operated three barbershops, owned 1,500 acres of land, and held several slaves.

Black or mulatto slaveholders were few in number, however. The 1830 census reported that 3,775 free blacks, about 2 percent of the total free black population, owned 12,760 slaves. Many African American slaveholders were men who bought or inherited their own family members.

THE TRADE IN SLAVES   The rapid rise in the slave population during the early nineteenth century mainly occurred naturally, through slave births, especially after Congress and President Thomas Jefferson outlawed the African slave trade in 1808. By 1820, more than 80 percent of slaves were American born.

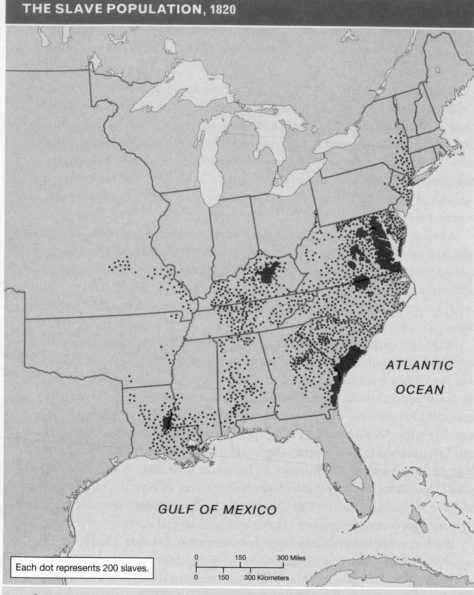

THE SLAVE POPULATION, 1820

ATLANTIC OCEAN

GULF OF MEXICO

Each dot represents 200 slaves.

0   150   300 Miles

0   150   300 Kilometers

- Consider where the largest populations of slaves were clustered in the South in 1820. Why were most slaves living in these regions and not in others?
- How was the experience of plantation slavery different for men and women?

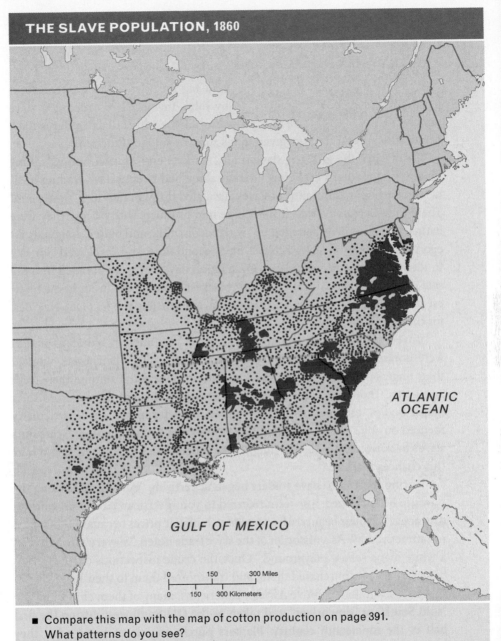

THE SLAVE POPULATION, 1860

ATLANTIC OCEAN

GULF OF MEXICO

| 0 | 150 | 300 Miles |
| 0 | 150 | 300 Kilometers |

- Compare this map with the map of cotton production on page 391. What patterns do you see?
- Why did many slaves resist migrating west?

Once the African slave trade was outlawed, the slave-trading network *within* the United States became much more important—and profitable. Between 1800 and 1860, the average price of slaves *quadrupled,* in large part because of the dramatic expansion of the cotton culture in the Old Southwest.

Breeding and selling slaves became a big business. Over a twenty-year period, a Virginia plantation owned by John Tayloe III recorded 252 slave births and 142 slave deaths, thus providing Tayloe with 110 extra slaves to be deployed on the plantation, given to his sons, or sold to traders.

To manage the growing slave trade, markets and auction houses sprang up in every southern city. New Orleans alone had twenty slave-trading businesses. Each year, thousands of slaves circulated through the city's "slave pens." There they were converted from people into products with prices. They were bathed and groomed; "fattened up" with bacon, milk, and butter; assigned categories such as Prime, No. 1, No. 2, and Second Rate; and "packaged" for sale in identical blue suits or dresses. On auction day, they were paraded into the sale room. The tallest, strongest, and "blackest" young men brought the highest prices. As a slaver stressed, "I must have if possible the *jet black* Negroes, for they stand the climate best."

Buyers physically inspected each slave on the "auction block" as if they were horses or cattle. They squeezed their muscles, felt their joints, worked their fingers back and forth, pried open their mouths to examine their teeth and gums. They then forced the slaves to strip and carefully inspected their naked bodies, looking for signs of disease or deformities. They particularly focused on any scars from whipping. As Solomon Northup noted, "scars on a slave's back were considered evidence of a rebellious or unruly spirit, and hurt [his chances for] sale."

During the 1830s, slave traders began advertising "fancy girls" among the slaves to be auctioned. The term referred to young African American women, distinctive for their beauty, who would fetch higher prices because of their sexual attractiveness. As a historian of the slave trade noted, "Slavery's frontier was a white man's sexual playground." Once the crude inspections ended, buyers bid on the slaves, purchased them, and transported them to their new homes.

Almost a million captive African Americans, many of them children, were "sold South" or "downriver" and taken to the Old Southwest during the first half of the nineteenth century. Planters purchasing slaves knew what they wanted. "It is better to buy *none in families,*" said a Mississippi buyer, "but to select *only choice, first rate, young hands from 16 to 25 years of age* (buying no children or aged negroes)."

The worst aspect of the domestic slave trade was the separation of children from parents and husbands from wives. Children were often taken from their parents and sold to new masters. In Missouri, one enslaved woman saw six of her seven children, ages one to eleven, sold to six different owners. Only Louisiana and Alabama (from 1852) prohibited separating a child younger than ten from his or her mother, and no state prevented the separation of a slave husband from his wife.

SLAVERY AS A WAY OF LIFE   The lives of slaves differed greatly from place to place, depending in part on the personality of their owner; in part on whether the enslaved were growing rice, sugar, tobacco, or cotton; and in part on whether they were on farms or in cities. Although many slaves were artisans or craftsmen (carpenters, blacksmiths, furniture makers, butchers, boatmen, house servants, cooks, nurses, maids, weavers, basket makers, etc.), the vast majority were **field hands** who were often organized into work gangs supervised by a black "driver" or white overseer. Some slaves were "hired out" to other planters or to merchants, churches, or businesses. Others worked on Sundays or holidays to earn cash of their own.

Plantation slaves were usually housed in one- or two-room wooden shacks with dirt floors. The wealthiest planters built slave cabins out of brick. Beds were a luxury, even though they were little more than boards covered with straw. Most slaves were expected to sleep on the cold, damp floor with only a cheap blanket for warmth. A set of inexpensive linen or cotton clothes was distributed twice a year, but shoes were generally provided only in winter. About half of all slave babies died in their first year, a rate more than twice that of whites. The weekly or monthly food allotment was cheap and monotonous: corn meal and pork, often served in bowls placed on the ground, as if the slaves were livestock.

Planters varied in their personalities and practices. Philip Jones, a Louisiana slave, observed that "many planters were humane and kind." Others were not. "Massa was purty good," one ex-slave recalled. "He treated us jus' 'bout like you would a good mule." Another said his master "fed us reg'lar on good, 'stantial food, jus' like you'd tend to your hoss [horse], if you had a real good one." A slave born in 1850 had a life expectancy of thirty-six years; the life expectancy of whites was forty years.

Solomon Northup, a freeborn African American from New York with a wife and three children, was kidnapped in 1845 by slave traders, taken first to Washington, D.C., and then to New Orleans, and eventually sold to a "repulsive and coarse" Louisiana cotton planter. More than a decade later, Northup was able to regain his freedom.

In *Twelve Years a Slave* (1853), Northup described his living and working conditions. His bed "was a plank twelve inches wide and ten feet long.

My pillow was a stick of wood. The bedding was a coarse blanket." The log cabin where he and others slept had a dirt floor and no windows. Each day, "an hour before daylight, the horn is blown. Then the slaves arouse, prepare their breakfast . . . and hurry to the field." If found in their "quarters after daybreak," they were flogged. "It was rarely that a day passed by without one or more whippings. . . . The crack of the lash, and the shrieking of the slaves, can be heard from dark till bed time."

Field hands worked from sunrise to sunset, six days a week. At times they worked at night as well, ginning cotton, milling sugarcane, grinding corn, or doing other indoor tasks. Women, remembered a slave, "had to work all day in de fields an' den come home an' do the housework at night." Sundays were precious days off. Slaves used the Sabbath to hunt, fish, dance to banjo and fiddle music, tell stories, and tend small gardens.

Beginning in August and lasting several months, the focus was on picking cotton. The productivity per slave increased dramatically during the first half of the nineteenth century, in large part because of the implementation of the "pushing system." During harvest season, each slave was assigned a daily quota of cotton to be picked, an amount that increased over the years.

Gangs of slaves, men and women, would sweep across a field, pull the bolls from the thorny pods, and stuff them in large sacks or baskets which they dragged behind them. All the while, they were watched and prodded by an overseer, bullwhip in hand, forcing them to keep up the pace. Solomon Northup remembered picking cotton until it was "too dark to see, and when the moon is full, they oftentimes labor till the middle of the night." Each evening, the baskets would be weighed and the number of pounds recorded on a slate board by each picker's name. Those who fell short of their quota were scolded and whipped.

THE VIOLENCE OF SLAVERY Although some owners and slaves developed close and even affectionate relationships, slavery on the whole was a system rooted in brutal force. The difference between a good owner and a bad one, according to one slave, was the difference between one "who did not whip you too much" and one who "whipped you till he'd bloodied you and blistered you."

Allen Sidney, a slave, recalled an incident on a Mississippi plantation that illustrated the ruthlessness of cotton production. A slave who fell behind while picking cotton resisted when a black driver started to "whip him up." Upon seeing the fracas, the white overseer, mounted on horseback, galloped over and shot the resisting slave, killing him. "None of the other slaves," Sidney noted, "said a word or turned their heads. They kept on hoeing as if nothing had happened."

At times, whites turned the punishment of slaves into spectacles to strike fear into anyone considering rebellion or escape. In Louisiana, whippings often followed a horrific procedure, as a visitor reported: "Three stakes is drove into the ground in a triangular manner, about six feet apart. The culprit [slave] is told to lie down . . . flat on his belly. The arms is extended out, sideways, and each hand tied to a stake hard and fast. The feet is both tied to the third stake, all stretched tight." The overseer would then step back "seven, eight or ten feet and with a rawhide whip about 7 feet long . . . lays on with great force and address across the Buttocks," cutting strips of flesh "7 or 8 inches long at every stroke."

URBAN SLAVERY   Slaves living in southern cities such as Richmond, Memphis, Atlanta, New Orleans, or Charleston had a much different experience from those on isolated farms and plantations. "A city slave is almost a freeman," claimed a Maryland slave.

Slaves in urban households tended to be better fed and clothed and had more privileges. They interacted not only with their white owners but with the extended interracial community—shopkeepers and police, neighbors and

Slave family in a Georgia cotton field The invention of the cotton gin sent cotton production soaring, deepening the South's dependence on slavery in the process.

strangers. Some were hired out to others and allowed to keep a portion of their wages. Generally speaking, slaves in cities enjoyed greater mobility and freedom than their counterparts in rural areas.

ENSLAVED WOMEN   Although enslaved men and women often performed similar chores, especially on farms, they did not experience slavery in the same way. Once slaveholders realized how profitable a fertile female slave could be by giving birth to babies that could later be sold, they "encouraged" female slaves to have as many children as possible. A South Carolina planter named William Johnson explained in 1815 that the "interest of the owner is to obtain from his slaves labor *and increase* [in their numbers]." Sometimes a woman would be locked in a cabin with a male slave whose task was to impregnate her. Pregnant slaves were given less work and more food. Some plantation owners rewarded new mothers with dresses and silver dollars.

But if motherhood provided enslaved women with greater stature and benefits, it also was exhausting. Within days after childbirth, mothers were put back to work spinning, weaving, or sewing. A few weeks thereafter, they were sent back to the fields; breast-feeding mothers were often forced to take their babies with them, strapped to their backs. Enslaved women were expected to do "man's work": cut trees, haul logs, spread fertilizer, plow fields, dig ditches, slaughter animals, hoe corn, and pick cotton.

Once women passed their childbearing years, their workload increased. Slaveholders put middle-aged women to work full-time in the fields or performing other outdoor labor. On large plantations, elderly women, called *grannies*, kept the children during the day, and slave women worked as cooks and seamstresses, midwives and nurses, healers and folk doctors.

Enslaved girls and women also faced the constant threat of sexual abuse. James Henry Hammond, the prominent South Carolina planter and former governor, confessed that he nurtured a "system of roguery" among his female slaves. He had a long affair with one of his young slaves, Sally Johnson, who bore several of his children. Later, to the horror of his long-suffering wife, Hammond began an affair with one of his and Sally's daughters, twelve-year-old Louisa, and fathered more children with her. (Hammond also had scandalous affairs with four "lovely and luscious" teen-aged nieces and two daughters of his sister-in-law.)

Forging a Slave Community

Despite being victims of terrible injustice and abuse, enslaved African Americans displayed endurance, resilience, and achievement. Wherever they could, they forged their own sense of community, asserted their individuality, and devised ingenious ways to resist their confinement. Many slaves, especially those on the largest plantations, would gather at secret "night meetings," usually after midnight, where they would drink stolen alcohol, dance, sing, and tell stories of resistance. Many of the stories were derived from African tales, such as that of "Brer [Brother] Rabbit," a smart little rabbit who used his wits to elude the larger animals stalking him by hiding in a patch of prickly briars. Such frequently told stories impressed upon slaves the importance of deceiving those with power over them.

Many religious **spirituals**, the predecessors to the blues, also contained double meanings, often expressing a longing to get to a "free country," what slaves called "Sweet Canaan" or the "promised land." The spiritual, "Wade in the Water," for example, contained underlying instructions to runaways about how to evade capture. Avoiding dry land and running in creek beds ("wading in the water") were common ways to throw off pursuing bloodhounds. Songs such as "The Gospel Train" and "Swing Low, Sweet Chariot" included disguised references to the Underground Railroad, the secret organization that helped slaves escape to the North.

Frederick Douglass recalled that the spirituals not only helped runaways but also were a form of protest. They "breathed the prayer and complaint of souls overflowing with the bitterest anguish. . . . The songs of the slave represent the sorrows of his heart, rather than his joys. Like tears, they were a relief to aching hearts."

THE SLAVE FAMILY   Although states did not recognize slave marriages, they did not prevent men and women from choosing life partners and forging families within the constraints of the slave system. Many slaveholders accepted unofficial marriages as a stabilizing influence; a black man who supported a family, they assumed, would be more reliable and obedient. Sometimes slaveholders performed "wedding" ceremonies in the slave quarters or had a minister conduct the service. Whatever the formalities, the norm for the slave community, as for the white, was the nuclear family, with the father as the head of the household.

A slave's childhood did not last long. At five or six years of age, children were put to work; they collected trash and firewood, picked cotton, scared away crows from planted fields, and ran errands. By age ten, they were full-time field hands.

Enslaved African Americans often extended the fellowship of family to those who worked with them, with older slave women being addressed as "granny," or coworkers as "sis" or "brother." Such efforts to create a sense of extended family resembled kinship practices in Africa. One white teacher visiting a slave community observed that they "all belonged to one immense family."

RELIGION IN THE OLD SOUTH

The Old South was made up of God-fearing people whose faith sustained them. Although there were pockets of Catholicism and Judaism in the large coastal cities—Baltimore, Richmond, Charleston, Savannah, and New Orleans—the vast majority of southerners, white and black, embraced evangelical Protestant denominations such as Baptists and Methodists, both of which wanted to create a Kingdom of God on earth before the millennium, when Jesus would return (the "second coming").

SLAVERY AND RELIGION   In the late eighteenth century, Baptists and Methodists had condemned slavery, welcomed blacks to their congregations, and given women important roles in their churches. Many slaveholders, led by George Washington and Thomas Jefferson, had agonized over the immorality of slavery.

By the 1830s, however, criticism of slavery in the southern states had virtually disappeared. Most preachers switched from attacking slavery to defending it as a divinely ordained, Bible-sanctioned social system that was a blessing to both master and slave. Alexander Glennie, a white minister, told slaves that their life of bondage was the "will of God." Most ministers who refused to promote slavery left the region.

***Plantation Burial* (1860)** The slaves of Mississippi governor Tilghman Tucker gather in the woods to bury and mourn for one of their own. The painter of this scene, Englishman John Antrobus, would serve in the Confederate army during the Civil War.

Frederick Douglass stressed that all of the men who owned him were Christians, but their faith never made a difference in how they treated their slaves. In 1832, Douglass's master experienced a powerful conversion to Christianity at a Methodist revival and became a religious "exhorter" himself. He prayed "morning, noon, and night," but his devotion to Christ had no effect on how he treated his slaves. In fact, he was even "more cruel and hateful," quoting a Bible verse as he whipped a lame young woman: "The servant that knoweth his master's will, and doeth it not, shall be beaten with many stripes."

AFRICAN AMERICAN RELIGION Among the most important elements of African American culture was its dynamic religion, a mixture of African, Caribbean, and Christian elements often practiced in secret because many slaveholders feared enslaved workers might use group religious services to organize rebellions. Religion provided slaves both relief for the soul and release for their emotions.

Most Africans brought with them to the Americas belief in a Creator, or Supreme God, whom they could recognize in the Christian God, and whom they might identify with Christ, the Holy Ghost, and the saints. But they also believed in spirits, magic, charms, and conjuring—the casting of spells. A conjurer, it was believed, was like a witch doctor or a voodoo priest who could suddenly make someone sick or heal the afflicted.

Whites usually tried to eliminate African religion and spirituality from the slave experience. Slaves responded by gathering secretly in what were called camp meetings, or bush meetings, to worship in their own way and share their joys, pains, and hopes.

By 1860, about 20 percent of adult slaves had joined Christian denominations. Many others practiced aspects of the Christian faith but were not considered Christians. As a white minister observed, some slaves had "heard of Jesus Christ, but who he is and what he has done for a ruined world, they cannot tell." But few whites fully understood the dynamics or mysteries of slave religion or its power.

Slaves found the Bible inspiring in its support for the poor and oppressed, and they embraced its promise of salvation through the sacrifice of Jesus. Likewise, the lyrics of religious spirituals helped slaves endure the strain of field labor and express their dreams of gaining freedom in "the promised land." Spirituals offered musical deliverance from worldly woes and strengthened solidarity among slaves. One popular spiritual, "Go Down, Moses," derived from the plight of the ancient Israelites held captive in Egypt, says: "We need not always weep and moan, / Let my people go. / And wear these slavery chains forlorn, / Let my people go." Another spiritual gave song to hope: "I do believe! / I do believe! / I will overcome some day.

Many white planters assumed that Christianized slaves would be more passive and obedient. A south Georgia planter declared that a Christian slave "is more profitable than an unfaithful one. He will do more and better work, be less troublesome, and [even] less liable to disease."

Planter James Henry Hammond despised the emotional singing, ecstatic shouting, raucous clapping, and energetic prayers that animated African American worship. He banned dancing and the beating of drums. Hammond, however, wanted his "heathen" slaves to become Christians. To do so, he hired itinerant white ministers ("plantation preachers") to conduct Christian services for them and constructed a Methodist church on his plantation. A white visitor who attended the church reported that there were no "religious excesses" or "hysteria" among the worshipping slaves. Hammond had forced them to display the religious passivity he desired.

SLAVE REBELLIONS

The greatest fear of whites in the Lower South was an organized slave revolt, as had occurred in 1791 in the French-controlled sugar colony of Saint-Domingue, which eventually became the independent Republic of Haiti. In a rebellion unprecedented in history, slaves rose up and burned plantations, destroyed cane fields, and killed white planters and their families.

The rebellion in Saint-Domingue, the world's richest colony and the leading source of sugar and coffee, was the first successful slave revolt in the Western Hemisphere. It sent shock waves across the United States. Many terrified whites who fled Haiti arrived in Charleston, where they told of the horrors they had experienced. Despite repeated attempts by both French and British armies to reconquer Haiti, the former slaves, led by Toussaint L'Ouverture, defeated them all.

The revolt in Haiti was the southern slaveholder's greatest nightmare. As a prominent Virginian explained, a slave uprising would "deluge the southern country with blood." Any sign of resistance or rebellion among the enslaved therefore risked a brutal and even gruesome response.

In 1811, for example, two of Thomas Jefferson's nephews, Lilburn and Isham Lewis, tied a seventeen-year-old slave named George to the floor of their Kentucky cabin and killed him with an axe in front of seven other slaves, all because George had run away several times. They then handed the axe to one of the slaves and forced him to dismember the body and put the pieces in the fireplace. The Lewises, who had been drinking heavily, wanted "to set an example for any other uppity slaves."

REVOLT IN LOUISIANA The overwhelming authority and firepower of southern whites made organized resistance risky. Nevertheless, in early 1811, the largest slave revolt in American history occurred just north of New Orleans, where powerful sugarcane planters had acquired one of the largest populations of slaves in North America. Many of those slaves were ripe for revolt. Sugarcane was known as a "killer crop" because working conditions were so harsh that many slaves died from laboring in the intense heat and humidity.

Late on January 8, a group of slaves led by Charles Deslondes, a trusted black overseer, broke into their owner's plantation house along the east bank of the Mississippi River. The planter was able to escape, but his son was hacked to death. Deslondes and his fellow rebels seized weapons, horses, and militia uniforms. Reinforced by more slaves and emboldened by liquor, the rebels headed toward New Orleans, some fifty miles away. Along the way, they burned houses, killed whites, and gathered more recruits. Over the next two days, their ranks swelled to more than 200.

Their success was short-lived, however. The territorial governor mobilized a group of angry whites—as well as several free blacks who were later praised for their "tireless zeal and dauntless courage"—to suppress the insurrection. U.S. Army units and militia joined in. Dozens of slaves were killed or wounded, and most of those who fled were soon captured. "We made considerable slaughter," reported one white planter.

Deslondes had his hands chopped off and was then shot in both thighs and his chest. As he was slowly bleeding to death, a bale of hay was scattered over him and ignited. As many as 100 slaves were tortured, killed, and beheaded, and the severed heads were placed on poles along the Mississippi River. A month after the rebellion was put down, a white resident noted that "all the negro difficulties have subsided and gentle peace prevails."

DENMARK VESEY The Denmark Vesey plot in Charleston, South Carolina, involved a similar effort to assault the white population. Vesey was a slave who, in 1799, purchased a lottery ticket and won $1,500, which he used to buy his freedom. He thereafter opened a carpentry shop in Charleston and organized a Bible study class in the African Methodist Episcopal (AME) Church.

In 1822, Vesey and several slaves developed a plan for a massive slave revolt. They would first capture the city's arsenal and distribute its hundreds of rifles to free and enslaved blacks. All whites in the city would then be killed, along with any blacks who refused to join the rebellion. Vesey then planned to burn the city, seize ships, and head for the black republic of Haiti.

The Vesey plot never got off the ground, however. A slave told his master about the plan, and soon Vesey and 100 other supposed rebels were captured and tried. The court found Vesey guilty of plotting to "trample on all laws, human and divine; to riot in blood, outrage, rapine . . . and conflagration, and to introduce anarchy and confusion in their most horrid forms." Vesey and thirty-four others were executed; three dozen more were transported to Spanish Cuba and sold. The AME church in Charleston was closed and demolished. When told that he would be hanged, Vesey replied that "the work of insurrection will go on."

Vesey's planned rebellion led South Carolina officials to place additional restrictions on the mobility of free blacks and black religious gatherings. It also influenced John C. Calhoun to abandon the nationalism of his early political career and become the South's most outspoken advocate for states' rights and slavery.

NAT TURNER'S REBELLION News of the Nat Turner insurrection of August 22, 1831, in Southampton County, Virginia, panicked whites throughout the South. Turner, a trusted black overseer, was also a preacher who believed God had instructed him to lead a slave rebellion. The revolt began when a small group of slaves joined Turner in methodically killing his owner's family. They then repeated the process at other farmhouses, where more slaves joined in. Before the revolt ended, fifty-seven whites had been killed, most of them women and children, including ten students at a school.

Federal troops, Virginia militiamen, and volunteers crushed the revolt, indiscriminately killing scores of slaves in the process. A newspaper described the behavior of the white vigilantes as comparable in "barbarity to the atrocities of the insurgents." Seventeen slaves were hanged; several were decapitated, and their severed heads were placed on poles along the road. Turner, called the "blood-stained monster," avoided capture for six weeks. He then was tried, found guilty, and hanged. His dead body was dismembered, with body parts given to the victims' families.

More than any other slave uprising, **Nat Turner's Rebellion** terrified whites by making real the lurking fear that enslaved blacks might launch organized revolts. A Virginia state legislator claimed that people suspected "that a Nat Turner might be in every family, that the same bloody deed could be acted over at any time."

The Virginia legislature responded by barring slaves from learning to read and write and from gathering for religious meetings. The city of Mobile, Alabama, prohibited gatherings of three or more slaves, and white ministers were dispatched to preach obedience to enslaved workers.

In addition, states created more armed patrols to track down runaways. A former slave highlighted the "thousand obstacles thrown in the way of the flying slave. Every white man's hand is raised against him—the patrollers are watching for him—the hounds are ready to follow on his track, and the nature of the country is such as renders it impossible to pass through it with any safety." Running away meant exposing oneself to flogging—or much worse.

THE LURE OF FREEDOM Yet stealthy and silent as fog, thousands of escaped slaves (called "fugitives") made it to freedom in spite of the obstacles facing them. The fugitive slaves were a powerful example of the enduring lure of freedom and the extraordinary courage of those who yearned for it. On average, some

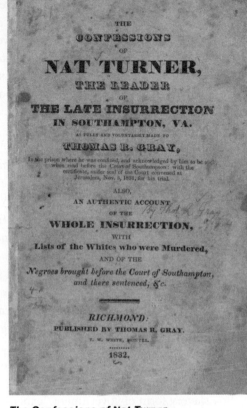

The Confessions of Nat Turner
Published account of Turner's rebellion, written by Turner's lawyer, Thomas Gray.

50,000 enslaved people tried to escape each year. Frederick Douglass decided that risking death was better than staying in bondage: "I had as well be killed running as die standing."

The odds were stacked against escape, in part because most slaves could not read, had no maps, and could not use public transportation such as stagecoaches, steamboats, and railroads. Blacks, whether free or enslaved, had to have an identity pass or official emancipation papers to go anywhere on their own. Runaways, the vast majority of whom were young males, often were forced to return when they ran out of food or lost their way. Others were tracked down by bloodhounds or bounty hunters. Only about 1,000 slaves each year safely made it to freedom.

Slaves who did not escape found other ways to resist. They often exasperated, enraged, and manipulated their owners. Some faked illness, stole or broke tools, destroyed crops, or secretly slaughtered and ate livestock. Others slacked off when unsupervised. As a slave song confessed, "You may think I'm working / But I ain't." Yet there were constraints on such rebellious behavior, for laborers would likely eat better on a prosperous plantation than on a struggling one. And the shrewdest slaveholders knew that offering rewards was more profitable than inflicting pain.

THE SOUTH—A REGION APART

The rapid settlement of the western territories during the first half of the nineteenth century set in motion a ferocious competition between North and South for political influence in the West. Would the new territories and states be "slave" or "free"? Congressmen from the newly admitted western states would tip the delicate political balance in Washington, D.C., one way or the other, slave or free.

The aggressive efforts to expand slavery westward in the face of growing criticism from the North ignited a prolonged political controversy that would end in civil war. As the 1832 nullification controversy in South Carolina had revealed, southerners despised being told what to do by outsiders, and they especially resented the growing demands for the abolition of slavery.

To cement the slave system in the culture of the South, many in the 1850s imagined every white family in the region owning slaves. "Ours is a pro-slavery form of government," explained a Georgia newspaper editor. "For our part, we would like to see every white man in the South the owner of a family of negroes."

The recurring theme of southern politics and culture from the 1830s to the outbreak of civil war in 1861 was the region's determination to remain a society dominated by whites who lorded over people of color. A South Carolinian asserted that "slavery with us is no abstraction—but a great and vital fact. Without it, our every comfort would be taken from us."

Protecting their right to own, transport, and sell slaves in the new western territories became the overriding focus of southern political leaders during the 1830s and after. Race-based slavery provided the South's prosperity as well as its growing sense of separateness—and defensiveness—from the rest of the nation.

Throughout the 1830s, southern state legislatures were "one and indivisible" in their efforts to preserve race-based slavery. They shouted defiance against northern abolitionists. Virginia's General Assembly, for example, declared that only the southern states had the right to control slavery and that such control must be "maintained at all hazards." The Georgia legislature agreed, announcing that "upon this point there can be no discussion—no compromise—no doubt."

With each passing year, the leaders of the Old South equated the survival of their distinctive region with the preservation of slavery. As the governor of Mississippi insisted in 1850, slavery "is entwined with our political system and cannot be separated from it." The increasingly militant efforts of northerners to restrict or abolish slavery helped reinforce southern unity while provoking an emotional defensiveness that would result in secession and war—and the unexpected end of slavery and the Cotton Kingdom it enabled.

CHAPTER REVIEW

SUMMARY

- **Southern Distinctiveness** The South remained rural and agricultural in the first half of the nineteenth century as the rest of the nation embraced urban industrial development. The region's climate favored the growth of cash crops such as tobacco, rice, indigo, and increasingly, cotton. These crops led to the spread of the plantation system of large commercial agriculture dependent on enslaved labor. The southern planter elite not only sought to preserve slavery but to expand it, despite growing criticism of the *"peculiar institution."*

- **A Cotton Economy** The Old South became increasingly committed to a cotton economy. Despite efforts to diversify the economic base, the wealth and status associated with cotton, as well as soil exhaustion and falling prices from Virginia to Georgia, prompted the westward expansion of the plantation culture to the *Old Southwest*. Slaves worked in harsh conditions as they prepared the terrain for cotton cultivation and experienced the breakup of their families. By 1860, the *Cotton Kingdom* stretched from the Carolinas and Georgia through eastern Texas and up the Mississippi River to Illinois. More than half of all slaves worked on cotton plantations. As long as cotton prices rose, southern planters searched for new land and invested in slaves to increase their cotton output.

- **Southern White Culture** White society was divided between the planter elite— those who owned twenty slaves or more—and all the rest. *Planters* represented only around 4 percent of the white population but they exercised a disproportionately powerful political and social influence. Other whites owned a few slaves, but most owned none. A majority of whites were *"plain white folk"*—simple farmers who raised corn, cotton, hogs, and chickens. Southern farmers were highly mobile and willing to move West. Southern white women spent most of their time on household chores. The *plantation mistress* supervised her home and household slaves. Most whites were fiercely loyal to the institution of slavery. Even those who owned no slaves feared the competition they believed they would face if slaves were freed, and they enjoyed the privileged status that race-based slavery gave them.

- **Southern Black Culture** As slavery spread and the southern economy became more dependent on slave labor, the enslaved faced more regulations and restrictions on their behavior. The vast majority of southern blacks served as *field hands*. They had few rights and could be bought and sold at any time. Their movements were severely limited and they had no ability to defend themselves. Any violations could result in severe punishments. Most southern blacks were slaves, but a small percentage were free. Many of the free blacks were *mulattoes*, having mixed-race parentage. Free blacks often worked for wages in towns and cities.

- **African American Resistance and Resilience**   Originally, slaves were treated more as indentured servants and were eligible for freedom after a specified number of years. But *slave codes* eventually codified the practice of treating slaves as property rather than as people. The enslaved responded in a variety of ways. Although many attempted to escape, only a few openly rebelled because the consequences were so harsh. Organized revolts such as *Nat Turner's Rebellion* in Virginia were rare. Most slaves survived by relying on their own communities, family ties, and Christian faith, and by developing their own culture, such as the singing of *spirituals* to express frustration, sorrow, and hope for their eventual deliverance.

CHRONOLOGY

1790	The enslaved population of the United States is almost 700,000
1791	Slave revolt in Saint-Domingue (Haiti)
1808	U.S. participation in the international slave trade is outlawed
1811	Charles Deslondes revolt in Louisiana
1814	Annual cotton production in the United States is 150,000 bales
1822	Denmark Vesey conspiracy is discovered in Charleston, South Carolina
1830	U.S. slave population exceeds 2 million
1831	Nat Turner leads slave insurrection in Virginia
1840	Population in the Old Southwest tops 1.5 million
1860	Annual cotton production in the United States reaches 4 million bales
	Slave population in the United States reaches 4 million

KEY TERMS

"peculiar institution" p. 384

Old Southwest p. 389

Cotton Kingdom p. 392

planters p. 393

plantation mistress p. 394

"plain white folk" p. 396

slave codes p. 398

mulattoes p. 399

field hands p. 403

spirituals p. 407

Nat Turner's Rebellion (1831) p. 412

🐦 INQUIZITIVE

Go to InQuizitive to see what you've learned—and learn what you've missed—with personalized feedback along the way.

12 Religion, Romanticism, and Reform

1800–1860

The Voyage of Life: Childhood **(1839–1840)** In his *Voyage of Life* series, Thomas Cole drew upon both the religious revivalism and Romantic ideals of the period to depict the four stages of a man's life: childhood (shown above), youth, manhood, and old age. In this painting, an infant drifts along the River of Life with his guardian angel into the fertile landscape from the dark cave, meant to be "emblematic of our earthly origin, and the mysterious Past."

During the first half of the nineteenth century, the United States was a nation of contrasts. Europeans traveling in America marveled at the nation's restless energy and expansive optimism, commitment to democratic ideals, and capitalist spirit. However, visitors also noticed that the dynamic young republic was experiencing growing pains as the market revolution continued to excite a lust for profits and to widen economic inequality. Sectional tensions over economic policies (such as tariffs and the regulation of banks) and increasingly heated debates over the morality and future of slavery made for a combative political scene.

Unlike the nations of Europe, which were steeped in history and romance, the United States was a young society whose founding leaders had embraced the central ideas of the Enlightenment—liberty, equality, and reason—which in turn led to the American ideals of representative government and the pursuit of happiness, most vividly set forth in Thomas Jefferson's Declaration of Independence.

During the first half of the nineteenth century, new, more-democratic ideals and expectations influenced religious life, literature, and the arts; social-reform movements grew in scope and significance as Americans sought to "perfect" their society. Politics was not the only battleground—religious and cultural life also experienced intense conflicts and radical new points of view.

After the Revolution, Americans were as interested in gaining religious salvation as they were in exercising political rights. A righteous army of Christian evangelists democratized the path to spiritual deliverance at the same time that states were democratizing the political process. So-called freewill ministers insisted that everyone, regardless of their wealth or circumstances, could

focus questions

1. What major changes took place in the practice of religion in America in the early nineteenth century? What impact did these have on American society?

2. How did transcendentalism emerge in the early nineteenth century?

3. What were the origins of the major social-reform movements in the early nineteenth century? How did they influence American society and politics?

4. How did the emergence of the anti-slavery movement impact American society and politics?

choose to be saved by embracing Jesus's promise of salvation—just as more men who owned no property were allowed to *choose* their elected officials.

Evangelicals assumed that the American republic had a God-mandated mission to provide a shining example of representative government, much as Puritan New England had once stood as an example of an ideal Christian community. The concept of America having a God-given *mission* to create an ideal society (often called "manifest destiny") still carried strong spiritual overtones.

The sense of America being on a God-directed mission also contained an element of perfectionism: people could become more and more perfect through a commitment to reforming themselves and society. Throughout the first half of the nineteenth century, reformers fanned out across the United States, and the combination of widespread religious energy and intense social activism brought major advances in human rights. It also at times triggered cynicism and disillusionment.

A More Democratic Religion

The energies of the rational Enlightenment and the spiritual Great Awakening flowed from the colonial period into the nineteenth century. In different ways, these two powerful modes of thought, one scientific and rational and the other religious and optimistic, eroded the old Calvinist view that people were innately sinful and that God had chosen only a select few for heavenly salvation (a doctrine referred to as "predestination").

During the nineteenth century, many Christians embraced a more democratic religious outlook. Just as Enlightenment rationalism stressed humanity's natural goodness and encouraged a belief in progress through democratic reforms and individual improvement, Protestant churches stressed that all people were capable of perfection through the guiding light of Christ and their own activism.

RATIONAL RELIGION Enlightenment ideas, including the religious concept of *Deism*, inspired prominent leaders such as Thomas Jefferson and Benjamin Franklin. Deists believed in a rational God—creator of the rational universe—and that all people were created as equals. They prized science and reason over traditional religion and blind faith.

Interest in Deism increased after the American Revolution. Through the use of reason and scientific research, Deists believed, people might grasp the natural laws governing the universe. Deists rejected the belief that every statement in the Bible was literally true and questioned the divinity of Jesus. They also defended free speech and opposed religious coercion.

UNITARIANISM AND UNIVERSALISM The same ideals of Enlightenment rationalism that excited Deists soon began to make deep inroads into American Protestantism. The old churches in and around Boston proved especially vulnerable to the appeal of anti-Puritan religious liberalism. By the end of the eighteenth century, well-educated New Englanders, most of them Congregationalists, were embracing Unitarianism, a "liberal" faith that emphasized the oneness ("unity") and compassion of a loving God, the natural goodness of humankind, the superiority of calm reason over emotional forms of worship, the rejection of the Calvinist belief in "predestination," and a general rather than literal reading of the Bible.

Unitarians abandoned the concept of the Trinity (God the Father, the Son, and the Holy Ghost) that had long been central to the Christian faith. Unitarians believed that God and Jesus are separate; Jesus was a saintly man (but not divine) who set a shining example of a good life. People are not inherently sinful, Unitarians stressed. By following the teachings of Jesus and trusting the guidance of their own consciences, *all* people are eligible for the gift of salvation from a God who is not angry and unforgiving but blessed with boundless love.

Boston became the center of the organized Unitarian movement, which initially emerged within Congregational churches. During the early nineteenth century, "liberal" churches adopted the name *Unitarian*. Many of its early supporters were among the best-educated and wealthiest New Englanders.

A parallel anti-Calvinist religious movement, Universalism, attracted a different—and much larger—social group: the working poor. In 1779, John Murray, a British clergyman, founded the first Universalist church, in Gloucester, Massachusetts. Like the Unitarians, **Universalists** proclaimed the dignity and worth of all people. They stressed that people must liberate themselves from the rule of priests and ministers and use their own capacity to reason to explore the mysteries of existence.

To Universalists and Unitarians, hell did not exist. Salvation was "universal," available to everyone through the sacrifice of Jesus. In essence, Universalists thought God was too good and caring to damn people to a place like hell, while Unitarians thought themselves too good to be damned. (The two denominations would combine in 1961, becoming the Unitarian Universalist faith.)

THE SECOND GREAT AWAKENING The rise of Universalism and Unitarianism did not mean that traditional religious beliefs were waning. In fact, evangelism was widespread. During the first Great Awakening in the early 1700s, traveling revivalists had promoted a more intense and personal relationship with God. In addition, Anglicanism suffered from being aligned with the Church of England; it lost its status as the official religion in most states after the American Revolution. To help erase their pro-British image, Virginia Anglicans renamed themselves *Episcopalians*.

But even the new name did not prevent the Episcopal Church from losing its leadership position in the South. Newer denominations, especially Baptists and Methodists, 20 percent of whom were African American, attracted masses of excited followers. These Christian sects were organized in accord with more-democratic principles; they allowed individual congregations to exercise more power on their own than did the Anglican Church.

In 1784, Methodists met in Baltimore and announced that they were abandoning Episcopalianism and forming a new denomination committed to the aggressive conversion of all people. The reform-minded Methodists, inspired by their founder, the English Anglican priest John Wesley, abandoned the gloomy predestination of Calvinism in favor of a life of "cheerful activism."

Around 1800, the United States experienced a huge wave of religious revivals called the **Second Great Awakening**. The nation's rampant materialism furnished evangelical ministers with plenty of ammunition, as did soaring crime rates. Without religion, revivalists warned, the American republic would give way to "unbridled appetites and lust."

While all denominations grew as a result of the Second Great Awakening, the evangelical sects—Baptists, Methodists, and Presbyterians—experienced explosive popularity. In 1780, the nation had only 50 Methodist churches; by 1860, there were 20,000, far more than any other denomination. The percentage of Americans who joined Protestant churches increased sixfold between 1800 and 1860.

The Second Great Awakening involved two different centers of activity. One developed among the elite New England colleges that were founded as religious centers of learning, then spread across western New York into Pennsylvania and Ohio, Indiana, and Illinois. The other emerged in the backwoods of Tennessee and Kentucky and spread in every direction across rural America. Both the urban and rural phases of Protestant revivalism shared a simple message: salvation is available to *anyone* who repents and embraces Christ.

FRONTIER REVIVALS   In its frontier phase, the Second Great Awakening, like the first, generated tremendous excitement and emotional excesses. It gave birth to two religious phenomena—the traveling backwoods evangelist and the frontier camp meeting—that helped keep the fires of revivalism and spiritual intensity burning.

People in the early nineteenth century readily believed in magic, dreams, visions, miraculous healings, and speaking in tongues (a spontaneous babbling precipitated by the workings of the Holy Spirit). Evangelists and "exhorters" (spiritual speakers who were not formal ministers) found ready audiences among lonely frontier folk hungry for spiritual intensity and a sense of community.

Mass revivals were family-oriented, community-building events; they bridged social, economic, political, and even racial divisions. Women, especially, flocked to the rural revivals and served as the backbone of religious life on the frontier.

At the end of the eighteenth century, ministers visiting the western territories reported that there were few frontier churches and few people attending them. To remedy the situation, traveling evangelists emerged.

The first large revivalist camp meeting occurred in August 1801 on a Kentucky hillside called Cane Ridge, east of Lexington. A Presbyterian minister named James McGready invited Protestants in the region to attend, and as many as 20,000 frontier folk came from miles around, camping in tents for nine days. White and black ministers, mostly Baptists and Methodists, preached day and night.

The **frontier revivals** generated intense emotions as people experienced on-the-spot conversions. One participant at Cane Ridge observed that "some of the people were singing, others praying, some crying for mercy." As news of the Cane Ridge gathering spread, Protestant evangelists, especially Methodists,

Religious revivalism Frontier revivals and prayer meetings ignited religious fervor within both ministers and participants. In this 1830s camp meeting, the women are so intensely moved by the sermon that they shed their bonnets and fell to their knees.

organized similar revivals in other states. One participant reported that the revivals created "such a gust of the power of God" that it seemed "the very gates of hell would give way."

The revivals were quite popular. "Hell is trembling, and Satan's kingdom falling," reported a South Carolinian in 1802. "The sacred flame" of religious revival is "extending far and wide." In 1776, about one in six Americans belonged to a church; by 1850, it was one in three. When asked to reflect on the social changes that had occurred during his life, William Grayson, a South Carolina planter, commented that "religion had revived. The churches were filled."

DENOMINATIONAL GROWTH Among the established denominations, Presbyterianism was entrenched among those with Scots-Irish backgrounds, from Pennsylvania to Georgia. Presbyterians gained further from the Plan of Union with the Congregationalists. Since the Presbyterians and the Congregationalists agreed on theology, they were able to form unified congregations and "call" (recruit) a minister from either denomination. The result through much of the Old Northwest (Ohio, Michigan, Indiana, and Illinois) was that New Englanders became Presbyterians by way of the "Presbygational" churches.

The frontier revivals were dominated by Baptist and Methodist factions. There were Primitive Baptists, Hardsell Baptists, Freewill Baptists and Methodists, Particular Baptists, and many others.

The Baptist theology was grounded in biblical fundamentalism—a certainty that every word and story in the Bible are divinely inspired and literally true. Unlike the earlier Puritans, however, the Baptists believed that *everyone* could gain salvation by choosing (via "free will") to receive God's grace and by being baptized as adults. The Baptists also stressed the social equality of all before God, regardless of wealth, status, or education.

The Methodists, who shared with Baptists the belief in free will, developed the most effective evangelical method: the "circuit rider," a traveling evangelist ("itinerant") on horseback who sought converts in remote frontier settlements. The itinerant system began with Francis Asbury, a tireless British-born revivalist who traveled across fifteen states and preached thousands of sermons.

After Asbury, Peter Cartwright emerged as the most successful circuit rider. Cartwright grew up in one of the most violent and lawless regions of frontier Kentucky. His brother was hanged as a murderer, and his sister was said to be a prostitute. Cartwright himself had been a hellion until, at age fifteen, he decided to attend a frontier revival meeting:

> In the midst of a solemn struggle of soul, an impression was made in my mind, as though a voice said to me, "Thy sins are all forgiven thee."

Divine light flashed all around me, unspeakable joy sprung up in my soul. I rose to my feet, opened my eyes, and it really seemed as if I was in heaven. . . . My mother raised the shout, my Christian friends crowded around me and joined me in praising God; and though I have been since then, in many instances, unfaithful, yet I have never for one moment, doubted that the Lord did, then and there, forgive my sins and give me religion.

The following year, Cartwright became a religious exhorter, preaching the faith even though he was not yet an ordained minister.

At age eighteen, Cartwright began roaming across Kentucky, Tennessee, Ohio, and Indiana as a Methodist circuit rider. For more than twenty years, Cartwright preached a sermon a day, three hours at a time. Crowds flocked to hear his simple message: salvation is free for all to embrace.

REVIVALISM AND AFRICAN AMERICANS The revivals broke down conventional social barriers. Free African Americans were especially attracted to the emotional energies of the Methodist and Baptist churches, in part because many white circuit riders were opposed to slavery. African

Black Methodists Holding a Prayer Meeting **(1811)** This caricature of an African American Methodist meeting in Philadelphia shows a preacher in the church doorway, while his congregation engages in exuberant prayer.

American Richard Allen, a freed slave in Philadelphia, said in 1787 that "there was no religious sect or denomination that would suit the capacity of the colored people as well as the Methodist." He decided that the "plain and simple gospel suits best for any people; for the unlearned can understand [it]."

Even more important, the Methodists actively recruited blacks. They were "the first people," Allen noted, "that brought glad tidings to the colored people." In 1816, Allen helped found the African Methodist Episcopal (AME) Church, the first black denomination in America.

CAMP MEETINGS AND WOMEN   The energies of the Great Revival, as the Second Great Awakening was called, spread through the western states and into more-settled regions back East. The fastest growth was along the frontier, where camp meetings were an expression of the frontier's democratic spirit. Revivals were typically held in late summer or fall, when farmwork eased.

Baptist, Methodist, and Presbyterian ministers often worked as a team, and crowds would frequently number in the thousands. Mass excitement swept up even the most skeptical onlookers, and infusions of the spirit sparked strange behavior. Some went into trances; others contracted the "jerks," babbled in unknown tongues, or got down on all fours and barked like dogs to "tree the devil."

The camp meetings also offered a social outlet to isolated rural folk, especially women, for whom the gatherings provided a welcome alternative to the rigors and loneliness of farm life. Evangelical ministers repeatedly applauded the spiritual energies of women and affirmed their right to give public witness to their faith and to play a leading role in efforts at social reform.

At a time when women were banned from preaching, Jarena Lee, a free black who lived in the Philadelphia area, was the first African American woman to become a minister in the African Methodist Episcopal Church (AME). As she wrote, "If the man may preach, because the Saviour died for him, why not the woman? Seeing [as] he died for her also." Lee became a tireless revivalist during the 1830s; according to her own records, she "traveled 2,325 miles and preached 178 sermons."

The organizational needs of large revivals offered ample opportunities for women. Phoebe Worrall Palmer, for example, hosted prayer meetings in her New York City home and eventually traveled across the country as a camp-meeting exhorter, assuring listeners that they could gain a life without sin.

Women like Palmer found public roles within evangelical denominations because of their emphasis on individual religious experiences rather than conventional, male-dominated church structures. Palmer claimed a woman's right to preach by citing the biblical emphasis on obeying God rather than man. "It is always right to obey the Holy Spirit's command," she stressed, "and if that is laid upon a woman to preach the Gospel, then it is right for her to do so; it is a duty she cannot neglect without falling into condemnation."

Such opportunities reinforced women's self-confidence, and their religious enthusiasm often inspired them to pursue social reforms for women, including greater educational opportunities and the right to vote.

RELIGION AND REFORM Regions roiled by revival fever were compared to forests devastated by fire. Western New York, in fact, experienced such fiery levels of evangelical activity that it was labeled the *burned-over district*. One reason the area was such a hotbed of evangelical activity was the Erie Canal, which opened in 1825. Both the construction of and traffic on the canal turned many towns into rollicking scenes of lawlessness: gambling, prostitution, public drunkenness, and crime. Such widespread sinfulness made the region ripe for revivalism.

CHARLES G. FINNEY The most successful evangelist in the burned-over district was a former attorney turned Presbyterian minister named Charles Grandison Finney. In the winter of 1830–1831, he theatrically preached with "a clear, shrill voice," pouring "out fire" for six months in Rochester, then in a canal boomtown in upstate New York. In the process, he generated some 100,000 conversions, became the most celebrated minister in the country, and perfected religious revivals as well-organized and orchestrated spectacles.

While rural camp-meeting revivals attracted farm families and other working-class groups, Finney's audiences in the Northeast attracted more-prosperous seekers. "The Lord," Finney declared, "was aiming at the conversion of the highest classes of society." In 1836, he built a huge church in New York City to accommodate his rapidly growing congregation.

Finney focused on the question that had preoccupied Protestantism for centuries: what role can the individual play in earning salvation? Finney and other freewill evangelists wanted to democratize the opportunity for salvation by insisting that everyone, rich or poor, black or white, could *choose* to be "saved" simply by embracing the promise of Jesus and rejecting the lure of sinfulness.

Finney's democratic gospel combined embracing faith and doing good works. For him, revivalism led first to personal reform and then to the improvement of society. By embracing Christ, a convert could thereafter be free of sin, but Christians also had an obligation to improve society by perfecting themselves.

The evangelical revivals provided much of the energy behind the sweeping reform impulse that characterized the age of Jacksonian democracy. Catharine Beecher, a leading advocate for evangelical religion and social reform, stressed that the success of American democracy "depends upon the intellectual and moral character of the mass of people. If they are intelligent and virtuous, democracy is a blessing; but if they are ignorant and wicked, it is only a curse."

THE MORMONS

The spiritual stirrings of the Second Great Awakening also spawned new religious groups. The burned-over district in New York gave rise to several religious movements, the most important of which was Mormonism. Its founder, Joseph Smith Jr., was the child of intensely religious Vermont farm folk who settled in the village of Palmyra, in western New York, amid the hyperemotional revivalism of the Second Great Awakening.

In 1823, the eighteen-year-old Smith reported that an angel named Moroni appeared by his bedside and announced that God needed Smith's help. Moroni had led him to a hillside near his father's farm, where he had unearthed a box containing golden plates on which was etched, in an ancient language, a lost "gospel" explaining the history of ancient America. It described a group of Israelites ("Nephites") who crossed the Atlantic on barges and settled America 2,100 years before Columbus.

Smith set about laboriously translating the "reformed Egyptian" inscriptions on the plates. Much of the language he transcribed was in fact drawn from the Bible. But that mattered not to his earnest followers. In 1830, Smith convinced a friend to mortgage his farm to pay for the publication of the first 5,000 copies of the 500-page text he called *The Book of Mormon: An Account Written by the Hand of Mormon upon Plates Taken from the Plates of Nephi*.

Young Smith began gathering thousands of converts ("saints"). Eventually, convinced that his authority came directly from God, he formed what he called the Church of Jesus Christ of Latter-day Saints, more popularly known as the **Mormons**. Smith maintained that God, angels, and people were all members of the same flesh-and-blood species.

In his self-appointed role as the Mormon Prophet, Smith criticized the sins of the rich, preached universal salvation, denied that there was a hell, urged his followers to practice a strict code of personal morality by avoiding liquor, tobacco, and caffeine, and asserted that the Second Coming of Christ was looming. He promised followers "a nation, a new Israel, a people bound as much by heritage and identity as by belief." Within a few years, Smith had gathered thousands of converts, most of them poor New England farmers who had migrated to western New York.

YEARS OF PERSECUTION From the outset, the Mormon "saints" upset both their "gentile" neighbors and the civil authorities. Mormons stood out with their secret rituals, their refusal to abide by local laws and conventions, and their clannishness. Smith denied the legitimacy of civil governments and the U.S. Constitution. As a result, no community wanted to host him and his "peculiar people," a term taken from the New Testament.

In their search for a refuge from persecution and for the "promised land," the ever-growing contingent of Mormons moved from western New York to Ohio, then to Missouri, where the governor called for them to be "exterminated or driven from the state." Forced out, Smith and the Mormons moved in 1839 to the half-built town of Commerce, Illinois, on the Mississippi River. They renamed the town Nauvoo (a crude translation of a Hebrew word meaning "beautiful land").

Within five years, Nauvoo had become the second largest city in the state, and Joseph Smith, "the Prophet," became Nauvoo's religious dictator. He owned the hotel and general store, published the newspaper, served as mayor, chief justice, and commander of the city's 2,000-strong army, and was the trustee of the Church. Smith's lust for power and for women grew as well. He began excommunicating dissidents, and in 1844 he announced his intention to become president of the United States.

Smith's remarkable sexual energy led him to practice "plural marriage" (polygamy); he accumulated more than two dozen wives, many of them already married to other men, and encouraged other Mormon leaders to do the same. In 1844, a crisis arose when Mormon dissenters, including Smith's first wife, Emma, denounced his polygamy. The result was not only a split in the church but also an attack on Nauvoo by non-Mormons.

When Smith ordered Mormons to destroy an opposition newspaper, he

Brigham Young Young was the president of the Mormons from 1847 to 1877.

and his brother Hyrum were arrested and charged with treason. On June 27, 1844, a mob stormed the jail and killed the Smith brothers. The *New York Herald* predicted that his death would kill Mormonism.

BRIGHAM YOUNG In Brigham Young, however, the Mormons found a new and, in many ways, better leader. Elected in 1844 to succeed Smith, Young would not only preserve the Mormon Church but create a new theocratic empire. Strong-minded, intelligent, authoritarian, and charismatic, Young was an early convert to Mormonism. Smith, he remembered, "took heaven . . . and brought it down to earth."

Because Nauvoo continued to arouse the suspicions of non-Mormons, Young began to look for another home for his flock. Their new destination turned out to be 1,300 miles away, near the Great Salt Lake in Utah, a vast,

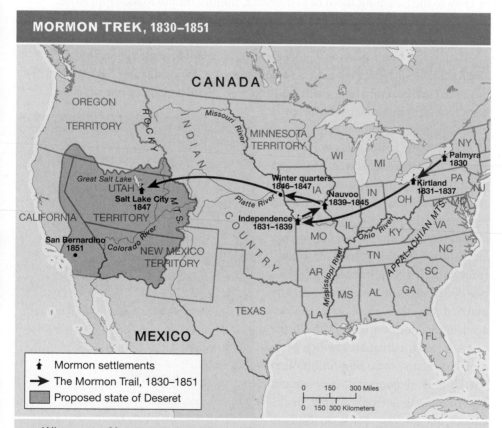

MORMON TREK, 1830–1851

Mormon settlements
The Mormon Trail, 1830–1851
Proposed state of Deseret

- Where were Mormon settlements established between 1830 and 1851?
- Why did Joseph Smith initially lead his congregation west?
- Why was the Utah Territory an ideal place for the Mormons to settle, at least initially?

sparsely populated area that was part of Mexico. The first to arrive at the Great Salt Lake in July 1847 found "a broad and barren plain hemmed in by the mountains . . . the paradise of the lizard, the cricket and the rattlesnake." But Young declared that "this is the place" to settle.

By the end of 1848, the Mormons had developed an efficient irrigation system for their farms, and over the next decade they brought about a spectacular greening of the desert. At first they organized their own state, named Deseret (meaning "Land of the Honeybee"), and elected Young governor.

Their independence was short-lived, however. In 1848, Mexico signed the Treaty of Guadalupe Hidalgo, transferring to the United States what is now California, Nevada, Utah, Texas, and parts of Arizona, New Mexico, Colorado, and Wyoming. Two years later, Congress incorporated the Utah Territory into the United States. Nevertheless, when Young was named the territorial governor, the new arrangement gave the Mormons virtual independence.

For more than twenty years, Young ruled with an iron hand, allowing no dissent and defying federal authority. Not until 1896, after the Mormons disavowed the practice of polygamy, was Utah admitted as a state. Out of its eerily secret beginnings and early struggles, Mormonism today is the fourth largest religious denomination in the world.

Romanticism in America

The revival of religious life during the early 1800s was one of many efforts throughout the United States and Europe to unleash the stirrings of the spirit. Another great cultural shift was the Romantic movement in thought, literature, and the arts.

The movement began in Europe, as young people rebelled against the well-ordered rational world promoted by the Enlightenment. Were there not, after all, more things in the world than reason, science, and logic could explain: spontaneous moods, impressions, and feelings; mysterious, unknown, and half-seen things?

In areas in which science could neither prove nor disprove concepts, the Romantics believed that people were justified in having faith. They preferred the stirrings of the heart over the calculations of the head, nonconformity over traditional behavior, and the mystical over the rational. Americans embraced the Romantics' emphasis on individualism and the virtues of common people.

TRANSCENDENTALISM The most intense American advocates of Romantic ideals were the transcendentalists of New England, the first group of rebellious intellectuals committed to reshaping the nation's cultural life.

The word *transcendentalism* came from an emphasis on thoughts and behaviors that *transcend* (or rise above) the limits of reason and logic. To transcendentalists, the inner life of the spirit took priority over science. Transcendentalism, said one of its champions, meant an interest in areas "a little beyond" the scope of reason.

Transcendentalism at times seemed irrational, rejecting both religious orthodoxy and the "corpse-cold" rationalism of Unitarianism. Transcendentalists believed that reality was not simply what you can touch and see; it included the innate promptings of the mind and the spiritual world. Above all, they believed in "self-reliance" and embraced a pure form of personal spirituality ("intuitions of the soul") uncorrupted by theological dogma. The miracles described in the Bible were much less important to transcendentalists than the evidence of an individual's own intuitive spirituality.

Transcendentalists wanted individuals to look *within* themselves for spiritual insights. Ralph Waldo Emerson, the movement's leader, stressed that its aim was to "purify one's own soul and live with full integrity, becoming a model, rather than a nagging goad, to others."

Transcendentalists also wanted to nurture a romantic spirituality in harmony with nature. Natural beauty, they believed, had the transcendent power to startle people into self-awareness. As Henry David Thoreau described his own nature-inspired spirituality, "I believe in the forest, and in the meadow, and in the night in which the corn grows." All people, transcendentalists believed, had the capacity for self-realization, enabling them to tap the divine "spark" present in all of God's creations.

In short, transcendentalists wanted everyone to summon the courage to think their *own* thoughts and develop their *own* beliefs. Self-discovery was the essential step in fulfilling potential. By the 1830s, New England transcendentalism had become the most influential force in American culture.

RALPH WALDO EMERSON More than anyone else, Ralph Waldo Emerson embodied the transcendentalist gospel, which rejected conventional religion in favor of individual spiritual growth and "self-culture." To Emerson, self-knowledge opened the doors to self-improvement and self-realization.

Emerson became the most popular speaker in the United States during the 1840s. "We have listened too long to the courtly muses of Europe," he said. "We will walk on our own feet; we will work with our own hands; we will speak with our own minds." He exhorted the young American republic to shed its cultural inferiority complex and create its own distinctive literature, art, and thought.

The son of a Unitarian preacher, Emerson graduated from Harvard College in 1821 and became a Unitarian parson in 1829, but three years later he turned

The Indian's Vespers (1847) Asher B. Durand's painting of a Native American saluting the sun captures the Romantic ideals of personal spirituality and the uncorrupted natural world that swept America during the early nineteenth century.

away from all organized religions because they stifled free thinking. He sought instead to cultivate a personal spirituality in communion with nature.

After traveling in Europe, where he met England's greatest Romantic writers, Emerson settled in Concord, Massachusetts, to take up the life of an essayist, poet, and lecturer ("preacher to the world"). He found God in nature and came to believe not in damnation but in human perfectibility. Impossibly optimistic, Emerson celebrated the virtues of self-reliance and the individual's unlimited potential. In 1836, he published the pathbreaking book *Nature*, which helped launch the transcendental movement. In it, he stressed that sensitive people could "transcend" the material world and discover the "spirit" animating the universe. Individuals, in other words, could exercise godlike powers.

The spirit of self-reliant individualism in Emerson's lectures and writings provided the energetic core of the transcendentalist outlook. "The American Scholar," a speech he delivered at Harvard in 1837, urged young Americans to put aside their reverence for European culture and explore the beauties and freedoms of their own world. Emerson's essay "Self-Reliance" (1841) expresses the distinctive transcendentalist outlook:

> Whoso would be a man, must be a nonconformist. . . . Nothing is at last sacred but the integrity of your own mind. . . . It is easy in the world to live after the world's opinion; it is easy in solitude to live after our own; but the great man is he who in the midst of a crowd keeps with perfect sweetness the independence of solitude. . . . A foolish consistency is the hobgoblin of little minds, adored by little statesmen and philosophers and divines. . . . Speak what you think now in hard words and tomorrow speak what tomorrow thinks in hard words again, though it contradict everything you said today. . . . To be great is to be misunderstood.

Emerson's belief that every man and woman possessed godlike virtues inspired generations. He championed a self-reliant individualism that reinforced the democratic energies inspiring Jacksonian America.

HENRY DAVID THOREAU Emerson's young friend and neighbor, Henry David Thoreau, practiced the thoughtful self-reliance and pursuit of perfection that Emerson preached. "I like people who can do things," Emerson said, and Thoreau, fourteen years his junior, could do many things: carpentry, masonry, painting, surveying, sailing, gardening. Thoreau displayed a powerful sense of uncompromising integrity and prickly individuality. "If a man does not keep pace with his companions," he wrote, "perhaps it is because he hears a different drummer."

Henry David Thoreau Thoreau was a social rebel, environmentalist, and lifelong abolitionist.

Thoreau described himself as "a mystic, a transcendentalist, and a natural philosopher" who questioned tradition and challenged authority. Emerson said his younger friend was "stubborn and implacable; always manly and wise, but rarely sweet." A neighbor was more blunt. "I love Henry," said Elizabeth Hoar, "but I do not like him."

Born in Concord in 1817, Thoreau attended Harvard, where he exhausted the library's resources. After a brief stint as a teacher, he worked with his father, a pencil maker. Like Emerson, however, Thoreau viewed "the indescribable innocence" of nature as a living bible; the earth to him was a form of poetry, full of hidden meanings and life-giving energies. Walks in the woods inspired him more than attending church. Christianity, he believed, was a dying institution. His priorities were inward. He once described himself as a "Realometer," working his feet "downward through the mud and slush of opinion, and prejudice and tradition, and delusion, and appearances . . . to a hard bottom."

Thoreau showed little interest in friends or marriage and no interest in wealth, which he believed corrupted the pursuit of happiness by making people slaves to materialism. "The mass of men," he wrote, "lead lives of quiet desperation" because they were preoccupied with making money. Thoreau yearned to experience the "extremities" of life and not be bound by stuffy tradition, unjust laws, "good behavior," or the opinions of his elders. He committed himself to leading what Emerson called a simple life centered on "plain living and high thinking." He loved to be alone, free to think for himself.

Thoreau rented a room at the Emersons' home, where he tended the family garden, worked as a handyman, and took long walks with his host. "I delight much in my young friend," Emerson wrote, "who seems to have as free and erect a mind as any I have ever met." In 1844, when Emerson bought fourteen acres along Walden Pond, Thoreau decided to embark upon an unusual experiment in self-reliance.

On July 4, 1845, at age twenty-seven, Thoreau took to the woods to live in a tiny, one-room cabin he had built for twenty-eight dollars at Walden Pond, just over a mile outside of Concord. His goal was to demonstrate that nature was sufficient for his needs. "I went to the woods because I wished to live deliberately," he wrote in *Walden, or Life in the Woods* (1854), ". . . and not, when I came to die, discover that I had not lived."

During Thoreau's two years at Walden Pond, the United States declared war against Mexico, largely to acquire Texas, then part of Mexico. He felt it was an unjust war pushed by southern cotton planters eager to add more slave territory. His disgust for the war led him to refuse to pay taxes, for which he was put in jail (for only one night; an aunt paid the tax).

This incident inspired Thoreau to write his now-classic essay, "Civil Disobedience" (1849), which would influence Martin Luther King Jr. in shaping the civil rights movement a hundred years later. "If the law is of such a nature that it requires you to be an agent of injustice to another," Thoreau wrote, "then, I say, break the law." Until his death in 1862, Thoreau attacked slavery and applauded those who worked to undermine it. The continuing influence of Thoreau's creed of taking individual action against injustice shows the impact that a thoughtful person can have on the world.

AN AMERICAN LITERATURE Although the transcendentalists attracted only a small following in their own time, they inspired a generation of writers that produced the first great age of American literature. The half decade of 1850 to 1855 witnessed an outpouring of extraordinary writing: *Representative Men* by Emerson; *Walden, or Life in the Woods* by Thoreau; *The Scarlet Letter* and *The House of the Seven Gables* by Nathaniel Hawthorne; *Moby-Dick* by Herman Melville; *Leaves of Grass* by Walt Whitman; and hundreds of poems by Emily Dickinson.

LITERARY GIANTS

NATHANIEL HAWTHORNE Nathaniel Hawthorne, the supreme writer of the New England group, never shared the sunny optimism of his neighbors or their perfectionist belief in reform. A native and longtime inhabitant of Salem, Massachusetts, he was haunted by the knowledge of evil bequeathed to him by his Puritan forebears, one of whom (John Hathorne) had been a judge at the Salem witchcraft trials. After college, Nathaniel Hawthorne worked in obscurity in Salem, gradually selling a few stories, and finally earning a degree of fame with *Twice-Told Tales* (1837). In these stories, as in most of his later work, his central themes examined sin and its consequences: pride and selfishness, secret guilt, and the impossibility of rooting sin out of the human soul.

EMILY DICKINSON Emily Dickinson, the most strikingly original of the New England poets, never married. In fact, as she wrote, she enjoyed the habit of "shunning Men and Women." From her birth in 1830 to her death in 1886, she lived with her parents and sister in Amherst, Massachusetts. There, in a Spartan corner bedroom on the second floor of the family house, the slim, red-haired poet found self-expression in poetry, ever grateful that "one is one's self & not somebody else."

Dickinson lived what her niece called a life of "exquisite self-containment." She often refused to meet visitors or even leave her room. Fired by "the light of insight and the fire of emotion," she wrote verse remarkable for its simplicity and brevity. Only a handful of her almost 1,800 poems were published before her death. As she famously wrote, "Success is counted sweetest / By those who ne'er succeed."

Whether her solitary existence was the result of severe eye trouble, aching despair generated by her love for a married minister, or fear of her possessive father, Dickinson's isolation and lifelong religious doubts led her, in the "solitude of space . . . that polar privacy," to probe the "white heat" of her heartbreak and disappointment in ways unusual for the time. Her often-abstract themes were elemental: life, death, fear, loneliness, nature, and above all, the withdrawal of God, "a distant, stately lover" who no longer could be found.

EDGAR ALLAN POE   Edgar Allan Poe was even more fascinated by the deepening menace of death. Born in Boston in 1809 and orphaned as a child, he was raised by foster parents (the Allans, who gave him his middle name) in Richmond, Virginia. Poe was a misfit who led a stormy life. Although a top student and popular storyteller at the University of Virginia, he left the school after ten months, having racked up excessive gambling debts. After a two-year stint in the army, he enrolled at the U.S. Military Academy at West Point, where in 1831 he was expelled for missing classes and disobedience.

After spending time in New York City and then in Baltimore, Poe relocated in 1835 to Richmond, where he became an assistant editor of the *Southern Literary Messenger*. He secretly married Virginia Clemm, his thirteen-year-old cousin, claiming that she was twenty-one. They moved to Philadelphia in 1837, where he edited magazines and wrote scathing reviews and terrifying mystery stories. As the creator of the detective story, his influence on literature has been enormous.

In 1844, Poe moved to New York City. The following year, he published "The Raven," a poem about a man who, "once upon a midnight dreary," having lost his lover, a "sainted maiden" named Lenore, responds to a rapping at his door, only to find "darkness there and nothing more." Scanning the darkness, "dreaming dreams no mortal ever dared to dream before," he confronts a silence punctuated only by his mumbled query, "Lenore?" The man closes the door, only to hear the strange knocking again. Both angered and perplexed, he flings open the door and, "with many a flirt and flutter," in flies a raven, that "grim, ungainly, ghastly, gaunt, and ominous bird of yore." The raven utters but one haunting word: "Nevermore."

"The Raven" was so popular that Poe became a household name across America, although he received only two dollars for publishing the poem. In 1847, however, tragedy struck when Poe's young wife died of tuberculosis. Thereafter, he was seduced as much by alcohol and drug abuse as by writing. He died at age forty of mysterious causes.

Poe left behind an extraordinary collection of "unworldly" tales and haunting poems. He used horror to explore the darkest corners of human psychology and to satisfy his lifelong obsession with death. To him, fear was the most powerful emotion, so he focused on making the grotesque and the supernatural seem disturbingly real. Anyone who has read "The Tell-Tale Heart" or "The Pit and the Pendulum" can testify to his success.

HERMAN MELVILLE   Herman Melville, the author of *Moby-Dick*, was a New Yorker who went to sea as a youth. After eighteen months aboard a whaler, he arrived in the Marquesas Islands, in the South Seas, and jumped ship with a companion. He spent several weeks with natives in "the valley of the Typees" before signing on with an Australian whaler. He joined a mutiny in Tahiti and finally returned home as a seaman aboard a U.S. Navy frigate. An account of his exotic adventures, *Typee* (1846), became an instant success, which he repeated in *Omoo* (1847).

In 1851, the thirty-two-year-old Melville produced *Moby-Dick*, one of the world's greatest novels. In the story of Captain Ahab's obsessive quest for an "accursed" white whale that had devoured his leg, Melville explored the darker recesses of the soul.

On one level, the book is a ripping good yarn of adventure on the high seas. On another level, however, it explores the unfathomable depths and darkness of human complexity, as the vengeful Ahab's crazed obsession with finding and killing the massive white whale turns the captain into a monster of destruction who sacrifices his ship, *The Pequod*, and his crew.

WALT WHITMAN   The most controversial writer during the nineteenth century was Walt Whitman, a New York journalist and poet. The swaggering Whitman was a self-promoting, robust personality. After meeting Whitman, Thoreau wrote that Whitman "was not only eager to talk about himself but reluctant to have the conversation stray from the subject for long." Unlike Thoreau, Whitman did not fear "the age of steam" and wrote excitedly about industrial development, urban life, working men, sailors, and "simple humanity."

Born in 1819 on a Long Island farm, Whitman moved with his family to Brooklyn, where he worked as a carpenter, teacher, Democratic party activist, and editor of the *Brooklyn Eagle*. He frequently took the ferry across the East River to bustling Manhattan, where he was fascinated by the city's restless energy.

By the time he met Ralph Waldo Emerson, Whitman had been "simmering, simmering," but Emerson "brought him to a boil" with his emphasis on defying tradition and celebrating the commonplaces of life, including sexuality and the body. All of these themes found their way into Whitman's controversial first book of unconventional, free-verse poems, *Leaves of Grass* (1855).

In its first year, it sold all of ten copies. One reviewer called it "an intensely vulgar, nay, absolutely *beastly* book." *Leaves of Grass*, however, became more influential with each passing year.

The brash Whitman introduced his book by declaring that "I celebrate myself, and sing myself." He was unapologetically "an American, one of the roughs . . . disorderly, fleshy, and sensual . . . eating, drinking, and breeding." Like Emerson, he was a self-proclaimed pioneer on behalf of "a new mightier world, a varied world," a bustling "world of labor" dignified by "common people." His poems were remarkable for their energy, exuberance, and intimacy, and were seasoned with frank sexuality and homoerotic overtones. They expressed the color and texture of American democracy, "immense in passion, pulse, and power." Thoreau, for one, viewed Whitman as a liberating force in American culture and described him as "the greatest democrat the world has seen."

Politics in an Oyster House **(1848)** Commissioned by social activist John H. B. Latrobe, this painting captures the public debates that were fueled by the proliferation of newspapers and magazines.

Although *Leaves of Grass* was banned in Boston because of its explicit sexuality, Emerson found it "the most extraordinary piece of wit and wisdom that America has yet contributed." More conventional literary critics, however, shuddered at the shocking "grossness" of Whitman's homosexual references ("manly love"; "the love of comrades"; "for the friend I love lay sleeping by my side").

NEWSPAPERS The flowering of American literature coincided with a massive expansion in newspaper readership sparked by rapid improvements in printing technology. The emerging availability of newspapers costing only a penny transformed daily reading into a form of popular entertainment. The "penny dailies," explained one editor, "are to be found in every street, lane, and alley; in every hotel, tavern, countinghouse, [and] shop."

By 1850, the United States had more newspapers than any nation in the world, and they forged a network of communications across the republic. As readership soared, the content of the papers expanded beyond political news and commentary to include society gossip, sports, and reports of sensational crimes and accidents. The proliferation of newspapers was largely a northern and western phenomenon, as literacy rates in the South lagged behind those of the rest of the country.

THE REFORM IMPULSE

In 1842, the United States was awash in reform movements led by dreamers and activists who saw social injustice or immorality and fought to correct it. Lyman Beecher, a champion of evangelical Christian revivalism (as well as the father of writer Harriet Beecher Stowe), stressed that the Second Great Awakening was not focused simply on promoting individual conversions; it was also intended to "reform human society."

While an impulse to "perfect" people and society helped excite the reform movements, social and economic changes invigorated many reformers, most of whom were women. The rise of an urban middle class enabled growing numbers of women to hire cooks and maids, thus freeing them to devote more time to societal concerns. Many women used their free time to join churches and charitable organizations, most of which were led by men.

Both women and men belonging to evangelical societies fanned out across America to organize Sunday schools, spread the gospel, and distribute Bibles to the children of the working poor. Other reformers tackled issues such as awful conditions in prisons and workplaces, care of the disabled, temperance (reducing the consumption of alcoholic beverages), women's rights, and the abolition of slavery. Transcendentalists broadened their initial emphasis on individual perfectionism to include reforms designed to improve the lot of the poor, the disenfranchised, and the enslaved.

That these earnest social reformers often met resistance, persecution, violence, and even death testified to the sincerity of their convictions and the power of their example. As Ralph Waldo Emerson said, "Never mind the ridicule, never mind the defeat, up again old heart!" For there is "victory yet for all justice."

TEMPERANCE The **temperance** crusade was the most widespread of the reform movements, in large part because many people argued that most social problems were rooted in alcohol abuse. In 1826, a group of ministers in Boston organized the American Society for the Promotion of Temperance, which sponsored lectures, press campaigns, and the formation of local and state societies. A favorite device was to ask each person who took the pledge to put by his or her signature a letter *T* for "total abstinence." With that a new word entered the language: *teetotaler*.

In 1833, the society held a national convention in Philadelphia, where the American Temperance Union was formed. Like nearly every reform movement of the day, temperance had a wing of absolutists. They would accept no compromise with Demon Rum and passed a resolution that liquor ought to be prohibited by law. The Temperance Union, at its spring convention in 1836, called for abstinence from all alcoholic beverages—which caused moderates to abstain from the movement.

PRISONS AND ASYLUMS   The Romantic impulse often included the liberal belief that people are innately good and capable of perfection. Such an optimistic view brought about major changes in the treatment of prisoners, the disabled, and dependent children. Before 1800, the insane were usually confined at home, with hired keepers, or in jails or almshouses, where homeless debtors were housed. In the years after 1815, however, asylums that separated the disturbed from the criminal began to appear.

The most important figure in boosting awareness of the plight of the mentally ill was Dorothea Lynde Dix. A pious Boston schoolteacher, she was asked to instruct a Sunday-school class at the East Cambridge House of Correction in 1841. There she found a roomful of insane people who had been completely neglected.

The scene so disturbed Dix that she began a two-year investigation of jails and almshouses in Massachusetts. In a report to the state legislature in 1843, she revealed that insane people were confined "in *cages, closets, cellars, stalls, pens! Chained, naked, beaten with rods,* and *lashed* into obedience." She won the support of leading reformers and proceeded to carry her campaign on behalf of "the miserable, the desolate, and the outcast" throughout the country and abroad. In the process, she helped to transform social attitudes toward mental illness.

WOMEN'S RIGHTS   While countless middle-class women devoted themselves to improving the quality of life in America, some argued that women should first focus on enhancing home life. In 1841, Harriet Beecher Stowe's sister, Catharine Beecher, a leader in the education movement, published *A Treatise on Domestic Economy*, which became the leading handbook promoting the **cult of domesticity**, a powerful ideology that called upon middle-class

Elizabeth Cady Stanton and Susan B. Anthony Stanton (left, in 1856) was a young mother who organized the Seneca Falls Convention, while Anthony (right, in 1848) started as an anti-slavery and temperance activist in her twenties. The two would meet in 1851 and form a lifelong partnership in the fight for women's suffrage.

women to accept and celebrate their role as manager of the household and the children, separate from the man's sphere of work outside the home.

While Beecher upheld high standards in women's education, she and many others argued that young women should be trained not for the workplace but in the domestic arts—managing a kitchen, running a household, and nurturing the children. Women, explained a Philadelphia doctor, were crucial to the future of the Republic because they instructed their children "in the principles of liberty and government."

The official status of women during the first half of the nineteenth century remained much as it had been in the colonial era. They were barred from the ministry and most other professions. Higher education was hardly an option. Women could not serve on juries, nor could they vote. A wife often had no control over her property or even her children. She could not make a will, sign a contract, or bring suit in court without her husband's permission. Her subordinate legal status was similar to that of a minor or a free black.

SENECA FALLS Gradually, however, women began to protest, and men began to listen. The organized movement for women's rights emerged in 1840, when the anti-slavery movement split over the question of women's right to participate. In 1848, two prominent advocates of women's rights, Lucretia Mott, a Philadelphia Quaker, and Elizabeth Cady Stanton, a New York abolitionist, called a convention of men and women to gather in Stanton's hometown of Seneca Falls, New York, a prosperous village along the Erie Canal, to discuss "the social, civil, and religious condition and rights of women."

On July 19, 1848, when the **Seneca Falls Convention** convened, revolution was in the air. In Italy, Germany, and other European states, militant nationalists, including many women, rebelled against monarchies and promoted unification. In France, the Society for the Emancipation for Women demanded that women receive equal political rights. In April, the French government abolished slavery in its Caribbean colonies, and in June, European feminists called for "the complete, radical abolition of all the privileges of sex, of birth, of race, of rank, and of fortune."

The activists at Seneca Falls did not go that far, but they did issue a clever paraphrase of the Declaration of Independence. The **Declaration of Rights and Sentiments** proclaimed that "all men and women are created equal." All laws that placed women "in a position inferior to that of men, are contrary to the great precept of nature, and therefore of no force or authority." Its most controversial demand was the right to vote.

Such ambitious goals and strong language were too radical for most of the 300 delegates, and only about a third of them signed the Declaration of Rights and Sentiments. One newspaper dismissed the convention as "the most shocking and unnatural incident ever recorded in the history of womanity." The *Philadelphia Public Ledger* sneeringly asked why women would want to climb down from their domestic pedestal and get involved with the dirty world of politics: "A woman is nothing. A wife is everything. A pretty girl is equal to ten thousand men, and a mother is, next to God, all powerful." Despite such opposition, however, the Seneca Falls gathering represented an important first step in the evolving campaign for women's rights.

SUSAN B. ANTHONY Although the movement for women's rights struggled in the face of meager funds and widespread anti-feminist sentiment, it was eventually successful because of the work of a few undaunted women. Susan B. Anthony, already active in temperance and anti-slavery groups, joined the crusade in the 1850s. Unlike Stanton and Mott, she was unmarried and therefore able to devote most of her attention to the women's crusade. As one observer put it, Stanton "forged the thunderbolts and Miss Anthony hurled them." Both lived into the twentieth century, focusing after the Civil War on demands for women's suffrage (the right to vote).

Women did not gain the vote in the nineteenth century, but they did make legal gains. In 1839, Mississippi became the first state to grant married women control over their property; by the 1860s, eleven more states had done so. Still, the only jobs open to educated women in any number were nursing and teaching. Both professions brought relatively lower status and pay than "men's work," despite the skills, training, and responsibilities involved.

EARLY PUBLIC SCHOOLS   Early America, like most rural societies, offered few educational opportunities for the masses. That changed in the first half of the nineteenth century as reformers lobbied for **public schools** to serve all children, rich or poor. The working poor wanted free schools to give their children an equal chance to pursue the American dream. Education, people argued, would improve manners while reducing crime and poverty.

A well-informed, well-trained citizenry was considered one of the basic premises of a republic. A Vermont newspaper editor stressed that educa-

The George Barrell Emerson School, Boston (ca. 1850) Although higher education for women initially met with some resistance, in the 1820s and 1830s, "seminaries" like this one were established to teach women mathematics, physics, and history, as well as music, art, and social graces.

tion was "the standing army of Republics." If political power resided with the people, as the Constitution asserted, then the citizenry needed to be well educated.

Horace Mann of Massachusetts, a state legislator and attorney, led the drive for statewide, tax-supported public school systems open to every child. He sponsored the creation of a state board of education, then served as its leader. Universal access to education, Mann argued, "was the great equalizer of the conditions of men—the balance-wheel of the social machinery."

Mann went on to promote the first state-supported "normal school" for the training of teachers, a state association of teachers, and a minimum school year of six months. He saw the public school system as a way not only to ensure that everyone had a basic level of knowledge and skills but also to reinforce values such as hard work and clean living. "If we do not prepare children to become good citizens, if we do not enrich their minds with knowledge," Mann warned, "then our republic must go down to destruction."

Such a holistic education, Mann argued, would enhance social stability and equal opportunity, as well as give women opportunities for rewarding work outside the home. Mann said they could become "mothers away from home" for the children they taught.

By the 1840s, most states in the North and Midwest had joined the public school movement. The initial conditions for public education, however, were seldom ideal. Funds for buildings, books, and equipment were limited; teachers were poorly paid and often poorly prepared. Most students going beyond the elementary grades attended private academies, often organized by churches. Public high schools became well established only after the Civil War.

By 1850, half of the nation's white children between ages five and nineteen were enrolled in schools, the highest percentage in the world. But few of those students were southerners. The South had some 500,000 illiterate whites, more than half the total in the country. The prolonged disparities between North and South in the number and quality of educational opportunities help explain the growing economic and cultural differences between the two regions. Then, as now, undereducated people were more likely to remain economically deprived, less healthy, and less engaged in political life.

UTOPIAN COMMUNITIES

Amid the pervasive climate of reform, the quest for utopia—communities with innovative social and economic relationships—flourished. Plans for ideal communities had long been an American passion, and more than 100 **utopian**

communities sprang up between 1800 and 1900. Many of them were *communitarian* experiments that emphasized the welfare of the entire community rather than individual freedom. Some experimented with "free love," socialism, and special diets.

THE SHAKERS Communities founded by the Shakers (officially the United Society of Believers in Christ's Second Appearing) proved to be long lasting. Ann Lee (known as Mother Ann Lee) arrived in New York from England with eight followers in 1774. Believing religious fervor to be a sign of inspiration from the Holy Ghost, Mother Ann and her followers saw visions and issued prophecies (predictions about the future). These manifestations later evolved into a ritual dance—hence the name "Shakers."

Shaker doctrine held God to be a dual personality. In Christ, the masculine side was revealed; in Mother Ann, the feminine element. Mother Ann preached celibacy to prepare Shakers for the perfection that was promised them in heaven.

After Mother Ann died in 1784, the group found new leaders, and the movement spread from New York into New England, Ohio, and Kentucky. By 1830, about twenty groups were flourishing. In these Shaker communities, all property was held in common. Shaker farms were among the nation's leading sources of garden seed and medicinal herbs, and many of their products, especially furniture, were prized for their simple beauty.

ONEIDA John Humphrey Noyes, founder of the Oneida Community, had a different vision of the ideal community. The son of a Vermont congressman, Noyes attended Dartmouth College and Yale Divinity School. But in 1834, he was expelled from Yale and his license to preach was revoked after he announced that he was "perfect" and free of all sin. In 1836, Noyes gathered a group of "Perfectionists" around his home in Putney, Vermont.

Ten years later, Noyes announced a new doctrine, "complex marriage," which meant that every man in the community was married to every woman, and vice versa. "In a holy community," he claimed, "there is no more reason why sexual intercourse should be restrained by law, than why eating and drinking should be." Authorities thought otherwise, and Noyes was charged with adultery for practicing his theology of "free love." (He coined the term.) He fled to New York and in 1848 established the Oneida Community, which had more than 200 members by 1851 and became famous for its production of fine silverware.

BROOK FARM Brook Farm in Massachusetts grew out of the transcendental movement. George Ripley, a Unitarian minister and transcendentalist, conceived of Brook Farm as a kind of early-day think tank, combining high philosophy, plain living, and manual labor. In 1841, he and several dozen like-minded utopians moved to the 175-acre farm eight miles southwest of Boston.

Brook Farm became America's first secular utopian community. One of its members, novelist Nathaniel Hawthorne, called it "our beautiful scheme of a noble and unselfish life." (He later would satirize the community in his novel *The Blithedale Romance*.) Its residents shared the tasks of maintaining the buildings, tending the fields, and preparing the meals. They also organized picnics, dances, lectures, and discussions. Emerson, Thoreau, and Margaret Fuller were among the visiting lecturers.

In 1846, however, Brook Farm's main building burned down, and the community spirit died in the ashes. In the end, utopian communities had little impact on the outside world, where reformers wrestled with the sins of the multitudes.

Among all the targets of the reformers' zeal, one great evil would take precedence over the others: human bondage. Transcendentalist reformer Theodore Parker declared that slavery was "the blight of this nation, the curse of the North and the curse of the South." The paradox of American freedom being coupled with American slavery, what novelist Herman Melville called "the world's fairest hope linked with man's foulest crime," would inspire the climactic crusade of the age, abolitionism, which would ultimately sweep the nation into an epic civil war.

THE ANTI-SLAVERY MOVEMENT

The men who drafted the U.S. Constitution in 1787 hoped to keep the new nation from splitting apart over the question of the slavery. To that end, they negotiated compromises that avoided dealing with the issue. But most of the founders knew that there eventually would be a day of reckoning. That day approached as the nineteenth century unfolded, and growing numbers of Americans decided that the daily horrors of slavery must come to an end.

EARLY OPPOSITION TO SLAVERY   The first organized emancipation movement appeared in 1816 with the formation of the **American Colonization Society (ACS)** in Washington, D.C., whose mission was to raise funds to "repatriate" free blacks back to Africa. Its supporters included James Madison, James Monroe, Andrew Jackson, Henry Clay, John Marshall, and Daniel Webster. Some supported the colonization movement because they opposed slavery; others saw it as a way to get rid of free blacks. "We must save the Negro," one missionary explained, "or the Negro will ruin us."

Leaders of the free black community denounced the colonization idea from the start. The United States, they stressed, was their native land, and they had as valid a claim on U.S. citizenship as anyone else.

Nevertheless, the ACS acquired land on the Ivory Coast of West Africa, and on February 6, 1820, the *Elizabeth* sailed from New York with the first eighty-eight emigrants who formed the nucleus of a new nation, the Republic of Liberia. Thereafter, however, the African colonization movement waned. During the 1830s, only 2,638 African Americans migrated to Liberia. In all, only about 15,000 resettled in Africa.

FROM GRADUALISM TO ABOLITIONISM   The fight against slavery started in Great Britain in the late eighteenth century, and the movement's success in ending British involvement in the African slave trade helped spur the anti-slavery cause in America. British abolitionists lectured across the northern United States and often bought freedom for runaway slaves. At the same time, most leading American abolitionists visited Great Britain and came away inspired by the breadth and depth of anti-slavery organizations there.

The British example helped convince black and white leaders of the cause in America to adopt an aggressive new strategy in the early 1830s. Equally important was the realization that slavery in the cotton states of the South

William Lloyd Garrison A militant abolitionist and a committed pacifist.

was not dying out; it was rapidly growing. This hard reality led to a change in tactics among anti-slavery organizations, many of which were energized by evangelical religions and the emerging social activism of transcendentalism. Their initial efforts to promote a *gradual* end to slavery by prohibiting it in the western territories and using moral persuasion to convince owners to free their slaves gradually gave way to demands for *immediate* **abolition** everywhere.

WILLIAM LLOYD GARRISON
A white Massachusetts activist named William Lloyd Garrison drove the movement. In 1831, free blacks helped

convince Garrison to launch an anti-slavery newspaper, the *Liberator*, which became the voice of the nation's first civil rights movement. In the Boston-based newspaper's first issue, Garrison condemned "the popular but pernicious doctrine of gradual emancipation." He dreamed of true equality in all spheres of American life, including the status of women. In pursuing that dream, he vowed to be "as harsh as truth, and as uncompromising as justice. . . . I am in earnest—I will not equivocate—I will not excuse—I will *not retreat a* single inch—AND I WILL BE HEARD."

Garrison's courage in denouncing slavery forced the issue onto the national agenda and outraged slaveholders in the South, as well as some whites in the North. In 1835, a mob of angry whites dragged him through the streets of Boston. The South Carolina and Georgia state legislatures promised a reward to anyone who kidnapped Garrison and brought him south for trial. A southern slaveholder warned him "to desist your infamous endeavors to instill into the minds of the negroes the idea that 'men must be free.'" The violence of the southern reaction wrecked the assumption of "Garrisonians" that moral righteousness would trump evil and that their fellow Americans would listen to reason.

Still, Garrison's unflagging efforts helped make the impossible—abolition—seem possible to more and more people. Two wealthy New York City evangelical merchants, Arthur and Lewis Tappan, provided financial support for Garrison and the *Liberator*. In 1833, they joined with Garrison and a group of Quaker reformers, free blacks, and evangelicals to organize the American Anti-Slavery Society (AASS).

That same year, Parliament freed some 800,000 enslaved colonial peoples throughout the British Empire by passing the Emancipation Act, whereby slaveholders were paid to give up their "human property." In 1835, the Tappans hired revivalist Charles G. Finney to head the anti-slavery faculty at Oberlin, a new college in northern Ohio that would be the first to admit black students.

The American Anti-Slavery Society, financed by the Tappans, created a national network of newspapers, offices, and 300 chapters, almost all of which were affiliated with a local Christian church. By 1840, some 160,000 people belonged to the AASS, which stressed that "slaveholding is a heinous crime in the sight of God, and that the duty, safety, and best interests of all concerned, require its *immediate abandonment*." The AASS even argued that blacks should have full social and civil rights.

In 1835, the group began flooding the South with anti-slavery pamphlets and newspapers. The anti-slavery materials so enraged southern slaveholders that a Louisiana community offered a $50,000 reward for the capture of the "notorious abolitionist, Arthur Tappan, of New York." Post offices throughout the South began destroying what was called "anti-slavery propaganda."

DAVID WALKER   The most radical figure among the largely white Garrisonians was David Walker, a free black man who owned a used clothing store in Boston. In 1829, he published his *Appeal to the Colored Citizens of the World*, a pamphlet that denounced the hypocrisy of Christians in the South for defending slavery and urged slaves to revolt against the planters. "The whites want slaves, and want us for their slaves," Walker warned, "but some of them will curse the day they ever saw us."

Copies of Walker's *Appeal* were secretly carried to the South by black sailors, but whites in major cities seized the "vile" pamphlet. In 1830, the state of Mississippi outlawed efforts to "print, write, circulate, or put forth . . . any book, paper, magazine, pamphlet, handbill or circular" intended to arouse the "colored population" by "exciting riots and rebellion."

A SPLIT IN THE MOVEMENT   As the abolitionist movement spread, debates over tactics intensified. The Garrisonians, for example, felt that slavery had corrupted virtually every aspect of American life. They therefore embraced every important reform movement of the day: abolition, temperance, pacifism, and women's rights. Garrison's unconventional religious ideas and social ideals led him to break with the established Protestant churches, which to his mind were in league with slavery; the federal government all the more so. The U.S. Constitution, he charged, was "a covenant with death and an agreement with hell."

Garrison was such a moral purist that he even refused to vote and encouraged others to do the same, arguing that the American republic could not continue to proclaim the ideal of liberty while tolerating the reality of slavery. He believed that the South could be shamed into ending slavery.

Other reformers were more practical and single-minded. They saw American society as fundamentally sound and concentrated on purging it of slavery. Garrison struck them as an unrealistic fanatic whose radicalism hurt the cause. Even Harriet Beecher Stowe, who would write *Uncle Tom's Cabin* (1852), called Garrisonians, most of whom were Unitarians, Quakers, or transcendentalists, "moral mono-maniacs." The powerful Tappan brothers broke with Garrison over religion. They argued that the anti-slavery movement should be led only by men of "evangelical piety," and they declared that the Unitarians and Universalists in New England failed to meet that standard.

THE GRIMKÉ SISTERS   A showdown between the rival anti-slavery camps erupted in 1840 over the issue of women's rights. Sarah and Angelina

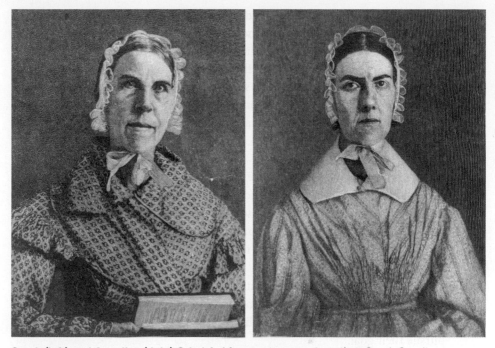

Sarah (left) and Angelina (right) Grimké After moving away from their South Carolina slaveholding family, the Grimké sisters devoted themselves to abolitionism and feminism.

Grimké, daughters of a wealthy South Carolina family, grew up being served by slaves. In 1821, soon after her father's death, Sarah moved from Charleston to Philadelphia, joined the Society of Friends (Quakers), and renounced slavery. Angelina soon joined her. In 1835, the sisters joined the abolitionist movement, speaking to northern women's groups in what were called "parlor meetings." After they appealed to southern Christian women to end slavery, the mayor of Charleston told their mother that they would be jailed if they ever returned home.

The Grimké sisters traveled widely, speaking first to audiences of women and eventually to groups of both sexes. Their unconventional ("promiscuous") behavior in speaking to mixed-gender audiences prompted sharp criticism from ministers in the anti-slavery movement. The chairman of the Connecticut Anti-Slavery Society declared that "no woman shall speak or vote. . . . It is enough for women to rule at home." Catharine Beecher reminded the Grimké sisters that women occupied "a subordinate relation in society to the other sex" and that they should limit their activities to the "domestic and social circle."

Angelina Grimké firmly rejected such arguments. For centuries, she noted, women had been raised to view themselves as "inferior creatures." Now, she insisted, "It is a woman's right to have a voice in all laws and regulations by which she is to be governed, whether in church or in state." Soon, she and her sister began linking their efforts to free the slaves with their desire to free women from centuries of male domination. "Men and women are CREATED EQUAL!" Sarah Grimké said. "Whatever is right for man to do is right for woman."

THE ROLE OF WOMEN The debate over the role of women in the anti-slavery movement finally exploded at the American Anti-Slavery Society's meeting in 1840, where the Garrisonians convinced a majority of delegates that women should participate equally in the organization. The Tappans and their supporters walked out and formed the American and Foreign Anti-Slavery Society.

A third faction of the American Anti-Slavery Society had grown skeptical that the nonviolent "moral suasion" promoted by Garrison would ever lead to abolition. They decided that political action was the most effective way to pursue their goal.

In 1840, activists formed the Liberty party in an effort to elect an American president who would abolish slavery. Their nominee, James Gillespie Birney, executive secretary of the American Anti-Slavery Society, was a former Alabama slaveholder turned abolitionist. His slogan was "vote as you pray, and pray as you vote." The platform called for an end to slavery in the western territories and the District of Columbia and a ban on intrastate slave trading.

Yet the Liberty party found few supporters. In the 1840 election, Birney polled only 7,000 votes. In 1844, however, he would win 60,000. From that time forward, an anti-slavery party contested every national election until the Thirteenth Amendment officially ended slavery in 1865.

BLACK ANTI-SLAVERY ACTIVITY

Although many whites worked courageously to end slavery, most of them, unlike Garrison, still insisted that blacks were socially inferior to whites. Freedom for slaves, in other words, did not mean social equality, and many white abolitionists expected free blacks to take a backseat in the movement.

WILLIAM WELLS BROWN Yet free African Americans were active in white anti-slavery societies. Former slaves such as Henry Bibb and William

Wells Brown, both escapees from Kentucky, and Frederick Douglass, who had escaped from Maryland, became the most effective critics of the South's "peculiar institution." Much of the energy and appeal of the abolitionist movement derived from the compelling testimonies provided by former slaves.

Brown was just twenty years old when he escaped from his owner, a steamboat pilot on the Ohio River. An Ohio Quaker named Wells Brown provided shelter to the runaway, and Brown adopted the man's name in the process of forging a new identity as a free man. He settled in Cleveland, Ohio, where he was a dockworker. He married, had three children, and helped runaway slaves cross the border into Canada. By 1842, he had learned to read and write, begun to publish columns in abolitionist newspapers, and was in great demand as a speaker at anti-slavery meetings. In 1847, Brown moved to Boston, where the Massachusetts Anti-Slavery Society hired him as a traveling lecturer.

That same year, the organization published Brown's autobiography, *Narrative of William W. Brown, A Former Slave, Written by Himself,* which became a best seller. Brown gave thousands of speeches in America and Europe calling for an end to slavery and equality for both blacks and women. He repeatedly stressed that African Americans were "endowed with those intellectual and amiable qualities which adorn and dignify human nature."

FREDERICK DOUGLASS Frederick Douglass was an even more effective spokesman for abolitionism. Having escaped from slavery in Baltimore, Maryland, Douglass made his way to Massachusetts, where he began speaking at anti-slavery meetings in black churches. Through his writings and dazzling presentations, he became the best-known black man in America. "I appear before the immense assembly this evening as a thief and a robber," he told a Massachusetts group in 1842. "I stole this head, these limbs, this body from my master, and ran off with them."

Fearful of capture after publishing his *Narrative of the Life of Frederick Douglass, An American Slave, Written by Himself* (1845), Douglass left for an extended lecture tour of the British Isles, returning two years later with enough money to purchase his official freedom. He then started an abolitionist newspaper for blacks, the *North Star*, in Rochester, New York. He named the newspaper after the star that runaway slaves used to guide them at night toward freedom.

SOJOURNER TRUTH The female counterpart to Frederick Douglass was Sojourner Truth. Born to enslaved parents in upstate New York in 1797,

Frederick Douglass (left) and Sojourner Truth (right) Both former slaves, Douglass and Truth were leading African American abolitionists and captivating orators.

she was given the name Isabella "Bell" Hardenbergh but renamed herself in 1843 after experiencing a conversation with God, who told her "to travel up and down the land" preaching against slavery. Having been a slave until she was freed in 1827, Sojourner Truth was able to speak with conviction and knowledge about the evils of the "peculiar institution" as well as the inequality of women.

Truth traveled and spoke throughout the North during the 1840s and 1850s. As she told the Ohio Women's Rights Convention in 1851, "I have plowed, and planted, and gathered into barns, and no man could head me— and ar'n't I a woman? I have borne thirteen children, and seen 'em mos' all sold off into slavery, and when I cried out with a mother's grief, none but Jesus heard—and ar'n't I a woman?"

Through such compelling testimony, Sojourner Truth demonstrated the powerful intersection of abolitionism and feminism. In the process, she tapped the distinctive energies that women brought to reformist causes. "If the first woman God ever made was strong enough to turn the world upside down all alone," she concluded in her address to the Ohio gathering, "these women together ought to be able to turn it back, and get it right side up again!"

THE UNDERGROUND RAILROAD While runaways often made it out of slavery on their own, many were aided by the **Underground Railroad**, a vast informal network of guides, secret routes, and "safe houses," where free blacks and white abolitionists (called "conductors") concealed runaway slaves in basements, attics, barns, and wagons before helping the fleeing "passengers" to the next "station" and eventually to freedom, often over the Canadian border.

In many northern cities, blacks and whites organized "vigilance committees" to thwart the slave catchers. In February 1851, Shadrach Minkins, a "stout, copper-colored man" who worked as a waiter at a Boston coffee house, was seized by U.S. marshals who claimed that he was a runaway slave from Virginia. During a court hearing, black and white members of the anti-slavery Boston Vigilance and Safety Committee active in the Underground Railroad rushed in, overcame armed guards, and snatched "the trembling prey of the slave hunters." An outraged President Millard Fillmore issued a proclamation demanding that citizens obey the law and that those responsible for "kidnapping" Minkins be prosecuted. None of the Bostonians charged in the case were convicted.

Between 1810 and 1850, tens of thousands of southern slaves fled north. Escaped slaves would make their way, usually at night, from one station to the next. The conductors included freeborn blacks, white abolitionists, former slaves, and Native Americans. Many were motivated by religious concerns. Quakers, Presbyterians, Methodists, and Baptists participated.

A few courageous runaway slaves returned to the South to organize more escapes. Harriet Tubman, the most celebrated member of the Underground Railroad, was born a slave in Maryland in 1820 but escaped to Philadelphia in 1849. She would return to the South nineteen times to help some 300 fugitive slaves, including her parents. She "never lost a passenger" during her legendary acts of bravery.

ELIJAH P. LOVEJOY Despite the growing efforts of anti-slavery organizations, racism remained widespread in the North, especially among the working poor. Abolitionist speakers confronted hostile white crowds who disliked blacks or found anti-slavery agitation bad for business. In 1837, a mob in Illinois killed Elijah P. Lovejoy, editor of an anti-slavery newspaper, giving the movement a martyr to the causes of both abolition and freedom of the press.

Lovejoy had begun his career as a Presbyterian minister in New England. After receiving a "sign by God" to focus his life on the "destruction of slavery," he moved to St. Louis, in slaveholding Missouri, where his newspaper denounced alcohol, Catholicism, and slavery. When a pro-slavery mob destroyed his printing office, he moved across the Mississippi River to a warehouse in Alton, Illinois, where he tried to start an anti-slavery society. There mobs twice more destroyed his printing press. When a new press arrived, Lovejoy and several supporters armed themselves and took up defensive positions.

On November 7, 1837, thugs began hurling stones and firing shots into the building. One of Lovejoy's allies fired back, killing a rioter. The mob then set fire to the warehouse, shouting, "Kill every damned abolitionist as he leaves." A shotgun blast killed Lovejoy, and his murder aroused a frenzy of indignation. At one of the hundreds of memorial services across the North, a grizzled John Brown rose, raised his right hand, and declared, "Here, before God, in the presence of these witnesses, from this time, I consecrate my life to the destruction of slavery!" Brown and other militants decided that only violence would dislodge the sin of slavery.

THE DEFENSE OF SLAVERY

During the 1830s and after, pro-slavery leaders worked out an elaborate rationale for what they considered the benefits of slavery. The Bible was frequently cited: had not the patriarchs of the Hebrew Bible held people in bondage? Had not Saint Paul advised servants to obey their masters and told a runaway servant to return to his master? And had not Jesus remained silent on the subject?

Soon, even bolder arguments emerged. In February 1837, South Carolina's John C. Calhoun, the most prominent southern political leader, told the Senate that slavery was "good—a great good," rooted in the Bible. He asserted that the "savage" Africans brought to America "had never existed in so comfortable, so respectable, or so civilized a condition, as that which is now enjoyed in the Southern states." If slavery were abolished, Calhoun warned, the principle of white racial supremacy would be compromised.

Calhoun and other defenders of slavery also claimed that blacks could not be expected to work under conditions of freedom. They were too shiftless, the argument went, and if freed, they would be a danger to themselves and to others. White workers, on the other hand, feared the competition for jobs if slaves were freed. Calhoun's strident defense of slavery led Henry Clay of Kentucky, himself a slaveholder, to describe Calhoun as "a rigid, fanatic, ambitious, selfishly partisan and sectional turncoat with too much genius and too little common sense, who will either die a traitor or a madman."

The increasingly heated debate over slavery drove a deep wedge between North and South. In 1831, William Lloyd Garrison predicted that an eventual "separation between the free and slave States" was "unavoidable." By midcentury, a large number of Americans had decided that southern slavery was an abomination that should not be allowed to expand into the western territories. The militant reformers who were determined to prevent slavery from expanding outside the South came to be called "free soilers." Their crusade would reach a fiery climax in the Civil War.

CHAPTER REVIEW

SUMMARY

- **Religious Developments** Starting in the late eighteenth century, *Unitarians* and *Universalists* in New England challenged the Christian notion of predestination and advocated that all humans (not just the select few) were capable of good deeds and could receive salvation. Echoing these ideas with their conception of salvation by free will, the preachers of the *Second Great Awakening* generated widespread interest among Protestants in *frontier revivals*. The more democratic sects, such as Baptists and Methodists, gained huge numbers of converts. Religion went hand in hand with reform in the "burned-over district" in western New York, which was also the birthplace of several religious movements, including the Church of Jesus Christ of Latter-day Saints (the *Mormons*).

- **Transcendentalists** A group of New England writers, ministers, and reformers who embraced a moral and spiritual idealism (Romanticism) in reaction to scientific rationalism and Christian orthodoxy. In their writings, they sought to "transcend" reason and the material world and encourage more-independent thought and reflection. At the same time, *transcendentalism* influenced the works of novelists, essayists, and poets, who created a uniquely "American" literature.

- **Social-Reform Movements** The *cult of domesticity* celebrated a "woman's sphere" in the home and argued that young women should be trained not for the workplace but in the domestic arts—managing a kitchen, running a household, and nurturing the children. However, the rise of an urban middle class offered growing numbers of women more time to devote to societal concerns. Social reformers—many of them women—sought to improve society and eradicate social evils. The most widespread movement was for *temperance*—the elimination of excessive drinking. Many activists focused on reforming prisons and asylums. With the *Seneca Falls Convention* of 1848, social reformers launched the women's rights movement with the *Declaration of Rights and Sentiments*. In many parts of the country, reformers called for greater access to education through *public schools*. Amid the pervasive climate of reform, more than 100 *utopian communities* were established, including the Shakers, Brook Farm, and the Oneida Community.

- **Anti-Slavery Movement** Northern opponents of slavery promoted several solutions, including the *American Colonization Society's* call for gradual emancipation and the deportation of African Americans to colonies in Africa. *Abolitionism* emerged in the 1830s, demanding an immediate end to slavery. Some abolitionists went even further, calling for full social and political equality among the races, although they disagreed over tactics. Abolitionist efforts in the North provoked fear and resentment among southern whites. Yet many northerners shared the belief in the racial inferiority of Africans and were hostile to the tactics and message of the abolitionists. African Americans in the North joined with abolitionists to create an *Underground Railroad*, a network of safe havens to help slaves escape bondage in the South.

CHRONOLOGY

1826	Ministers organize the American Society for the Promotion of Temperance
1830–1831	Charles G. Finney begins preaching in upstate New York
1830	Percentage of American churchgoers has doubled since 1800
	Joseph Smith publishes the *Book of Mormon*
1831	William Lloyd Garrison begins publishing the *Liberator*
1833	American Anti-Slavery Society is founded
1836	Transcendental Club holds its first meeting
1837	Abolitionist editor Elijah P. Lovejoy is murdered
1840	Abolitionists form the Liberty party
1840s	Methodists have become largest Protestant denomination in America
1845	*Narrative of the Life of Frederick Douglass* is published
1846–1847	Mormons, led by Brigham Young, make the difficult trek to Utah
1848	At the Seneca Falls Convention, feminists issue the Declaration of Rights and Sentiments
1851	Sojourner Truth delivers her famous speech "Ar'n't I a Woman?"
1854	Henry David Thoreau's *Walden, or Life in the Woods* is published

KEY TERMS

Unitarians p. 421

Universalists p. 421

Second Great Awakening p. 422

frontier revivals p. 423

Mormons p. 428

transcendentalism p. 432

temperance p. 440

cult of domesticity p. 441

Seneca Falls Convention (1848) p. 443

Declaration of Rights and Sentiments (1848) p. 443

public schools p. 444

utopian communities p. 445

American Colonization Society (ACS) p. 447

abolitionism p. 448

Underground Railroad p. 455

⟨⟩ INQUIZITIVE

Go to InQuizitive to see what you've learned—and learn what you've missed—with personalized feedback along the way.

part four

A HOUSE DIVIDED AND REBUILT

During the first half of the nineteenth century, Americans, restless and energetic, were optimistic about the future. The United States was the world's largest republic. Its population continued to grow rapidly, economic conditions were improving, and tensions with Great Britain had eased.

Above all, Americans continued to move westward, where vast expanses of cheap land lured farmers, ranchers, miners, and missionaries. By the end of the 1840s, the United States had again

dramatically expanded its territory, from Texas west to California and the Pacific Northwest. Americans had become a transcontinental nation from the Atlantic to the Pacific.

This extraordinary surge of territorial expansion was a mixed blessing, however. How to deal with slavery in the new western territories emerged as the nation's flashpoint issue as differences grew among America's three distinctive regions— North, South, and West.

A series of political compromises had glossed over the fundamental issue of slavery, but anti-slavery activists opposed efforts to extend slavery into the West, and an emerging generation of politicians proved less willing to compromise. The continuing debate over allowing slavery into new territories eventually led many Americans to decide that the nation could not survive half-slave and half-free. Something had to give.

In a last-ditch effort to preserve the institution of slavery, eleven southern states seceded from the Union and created a separate Confederate nation, prompting northerners such as Abraham Lincoln to risk a civil war to restore the Union.

No one realized in 1861 how costly the war would be: more than 700,000 soldiers and sailors would die in the struggle. Nor did anyone envision how sweeping the war's effects would be upon the nation's future. The northern victory in 1865 restored the Union and helped accelerate America's transformation into a modern nation-state. A national consciousness began to replace the sectional divisions of the prewar era, and a Republican-led Congress passed legislation to promote industrial and commercial development and western expansion.

Although the Civil War ended slavery, the status of the freed African Americans remained precarious. Former slaves found themselves legally free, but few had property, homes, education, or training. Although the Fourteenth Amendment (1868) guaranteed the civil rights of African Americans and the Fifteenth Amendment (1870) declared that black men could vote, southern officials often ignored the new laws (as did some in northern states as well).

The restoration of the former Confederate states to the Union did not come easily. Bitterness and resistance grew among the defeated southerners. Although Confederate leaders were stripped of voting rights, they continued to exercise considerable authority in political and economic matters. In 1877, when the last federal troops were removed from the South, former Confederates declared themselves "redeemed" from the stain of northern military occupation. By the end of the nineteenth century, most states of the former Confederacy had developed a system of legal discrimination against blacks that re-created many aspects of slavery.

13 Western Expansion

1830–1848

Emigrants Crossing the Plains, or the Oregon Trail (1869) German American painter Albert Bierstadt captures the majestic sights of the frontier, though the transcontinental trek was also often grueling and bleak.

I n the American experience, the westward march of settlement was always a source of energy, hope, and yearning. Henry David Thoreau exclaimed that Americans "go westward as into the future, with a spirit of enterprise and adventure"—and the hope of freedom.

The West—whether imagined as the enticing lands over the Allegheny Mountains that became Ohio and Kentucky, the "black belt" farmlands of the Old Southwest, the fertile prairies watered by the Mississippi River, or the spectacular area along the Pacific coast that became the states of California, Oregon, and Washington—served as a magnet for adventurous people dreaming of freedom, self-fulfillment, and economic gain. The Pacific Northwest teemed with fish, forests, and fur-bearing animals. Acquiring the ports along the Pacific coast would allow the United States to expand its trade with Asia.

During the 1840s and after, waves of people moved westward, seeking a better chance and more space. "If hell lay to the west," one pioneer declared, "Americans would cross heaven to get there." Millions endured unrelenting hardships to fulfill their "providential destiny" to subdue the entire continent, even if it meant displacing the Indians in the process. By 1860, some 4.3 million people had settled in the trans-Mississippi West.

Emigrants moved west largely for economic reasons. "To make money was their chief object," said a pioneer woman in Texas, "all things else were subsidiary to it." Waves of enterprising trappers and farmers, miners, merchants, clerks, hunters, ranchers, teachers, household servants, and prostitutes, among others, headed west to seek their fortunes. Others sought religious freedom or new converts to Christianity. Whatever the reason, the pioneers

focus questions

1. Why did Americans move west of the Mississippi River during the 1830s and 1840s? How did they accomplish this, and where did they move to?

2. How did Texas become part of the United States? Why was the process so complicated, and how did it impact national politics?

3. What were the similarities and differences in the process for how California and Texas were settled and how they became part of the United States?

4. How did the Mexican-American War impact national politics?

formed an unceasing migratory stream across the Great Plains and the Rocky Mountains.

Of course, the West was not empty land waiting to be developed. Others had been there long before the American migration. But the Indian and Hispanic inhabitants of the region soon found themselves swept aside by American settlers, all facilitated by U.S. presidents and congressmen who encouraged the nation's expansion.

Westward expansion was especially important to southerners, many of whom wanted cheap new lands to plant using slave labor. In addition, southerners had long enjoyed disproportionate political power because of the provision in the U.S. Constitution that counted slaves as part of the population in determining the number of congressional seats for each state. Thirteen of the first sixteen presidents were from the South, and most congressional leadership positions were held by southerners.

But southern political influence began dwindling as the industrializing Midwest and Northeast grew and increased their representation in Congress. Southerners wanted new western states to boost pro-southern representation and ensure that slavery was never threatened. As a Mississippi senator said, "I would spread the blessings of slavery . . . to the uttermost ends of the earth." Such motives made the addition of new western territory especially controversial. Would the territory be slave or free?

MOVING WEST

During the mid–nineteenth century, America remained a nation in motion. In 1845, New York newspaper editor and Democratic-party propagandist John L. O'Sullivan gave a catchy name to the nation's aggressive expansion. "Our **manifest destiny**," he wrote, "is to overspread and to possess the whole of the continent which Providence has given us for the free development of our yearly multiplying millions . . . [and for the] great experiment of liberty."

The concept of "manifest destiny" assumed that the United States had a God-given mission to extend its Christian republic and capitalist civilization from the Atlantic to the Pacific—and beyond. It also took for granted the superiority of American ideals and institutions, including the opportunity to bring liberty and prosperity to native peoples. This widely embraced notion of manifest ("self-evident") destiny offered a moral justification for territorial expansion and the expansion of slavery. But God was not driving American expansion; Americans were. However idealized, manifest destiny for many Americans was in essence a cluster of flimsy rationalizations and racist attitudes justifying the conquest of weaker peoples.

THE WESTERN FRONTIER Most western pioneers during the second quarter of the nineteenth century were American-born whites from the Upper South and the Midwest. Only a few free African Americans joined in the migration. What spurred the massive migration westward was the continuing population explosion in the United States and the desire for land and wealth.

Although some people traveled by sea to the Pacific coast, most went overland. Between 1841 and 1867, some 350,000 men, women, and children made the difficult trek to California or Oregon, while hundreds of thousands of others settled in such areas as Colorado, Texas, and Arkansas.

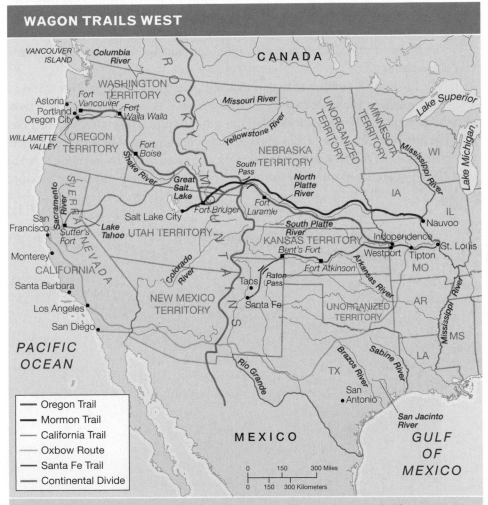

WAGON TRAILS WEST

- What did settlers migrating west of the Mississippi River hope to find?
- What were the perils of the Overland trails?
- Describe the experience of a typical settler traveling on the Overland Trails.

Most of the pioneers who made their way west on the **Overland Trails** traveled in family groups. By 1845, some 5,000 people were making the six-month journey annually. The discovery of gold in California in 1848 brought some 30,000 pioneers along the Oregon Trail in 1849. By 1850, the peak year of travel along the trail, the annual count had risen to 55,000.

PLAINS INDIANS More than 325,000 Indians inhabited the Southwest, the Great Plains, California, and the Pacific Northwest in 1840, when the great migration of white settlers into the region began. The Native Americans were divided into more than 200 nations, each with its own language, religion, cultural practices, and system of governance. Plains Indians included the Arapaho, Blackfoot, Cheyenne, Kiowa, and Sioux. Some were primarily farmers; others were nomadic, following buffalo herds across the prairie grasslands.

In the arid Southwest region that today includes Arizona, New Mexico, and southern Utah, the peaceful Pueblo nations—Acoma, Hopi, Laguna, Taos, Zia, Zuni—were sophisticated farmers who lived in adobe villages along rivers that irrigated their crops of corn, beans, and squash. Their rivals were the Apache and the Navajo, warlike hunters who roamed the countryside in small bands and preyed upon the Pueblos. They, in turn, were periodically harassed

Buffalo Hunt, Chasing Back (1860s) This painting by George Catlin shows a hunter outrunning a buffalo.

by the Comanche. Many Indian nations were hostile to each other, resulting in frequent wars and raids.

To the north in the Great Basin, Paiutes and Gosiutes struggled to survive in the harsh, arid region of what is today Nevada, Utah, and eastern California. They traveled in family groups and subsisted on berries, pine nuts, insects, and rodents. Along the California coast, Indians lived in small villages. They gathered wild plants and acorns and were experts at fishing.

The Native Americans in the Pacific Northwest—the Nisqually, Spokane, Yakama, Chinook, Klamath, and Nez Perce (Pierced Nose)—enjoyed the most abundant natural resources and the most temperate climate. The ocean and rivers provided whales, seals, salmon, and crabs, and lush inland forests harbored game, berries, and nuts. Majestic forests of fir, redwood, and cedar offered wood for cooking and shelter.

All these Indian societies eventually felt the unrelenting pressure of white expansion and conquest, and the influx of white settlers and hunters posed a direct threat to the Indians' cultural survival. When federal officials could not coerce, cajole, or confuse Indian leaders into selling the title to their tribal lands, fighting ensued. After the discovery of gold in California in early 1848, the tidal wave of white expansion flowed all the way to the west coast, violently engulfing Native Americans and Mexicans in its wake.

MEXICO AND THE SPANISH WEST As American settlers trespassed across Indian lands, they also encountered Spanish-speaking peoples. Many whites were as prejudiced toward Hispanics as they were toward Indians. Senator Lewis Cass from Michigan, who would be the Democratic candidate for president in 1848, expressed the common bias among white expansionists: "We do not want the people of Mexico, either as citizens or as subjects. All we want is their . . . territory."

The centuries-old Spanish efforts at colonization in the northernmost provinces of Mexico had been less successful in Arizona and Texas than in New Mexico and Florida. The Yumas and Apaches in Arizona and the Comanches and Apaches in Texas thwarted Spanish efforts to establish Catholic missions. By 1790, the Hispanic population in Texas numbered only 2,510, while in New Mexico it exceeded 20,000.

In 1807, French forces led by Napoléon had occupied Spain and imprisoned the king, creating confusion throughout Spain's colonial possessions in the Western Hemisphere, including Mexico. Miguel Hidalgo y Costilla, a creole priest (born in Mexico of European ancestry), took advantage of the fluid situation to convince Indians and Hispanics to revolt against Spanish rule in Mexico. But the poorly organized uprising failed miserably.

In 1820, Mexican creoles again tried to liberate themselves from Spanish authority. Facing a growing revolt, the last Spanish officials withdrew in 1821, and Mexico became independent. However, the infant republic struggled to develop a stable government and an effective economy. Americans eagerly took advantage of Mexico's instability, especially in its sparsely populated northern provinces—areas that included present-day Texas, New Mexico, Arizona, Nevada, California, and portions of Colorado, Oklahoma, Kansas, and Wyoming.

THE OVERLAND TRAILS During the early nineteenth century, the Far Northwest consisted of the Nebraska, Washington, and Oregon Territories. The Oregon Country included what became the states of Oregon, Idaho, and Washington, parts of Montana and Wyoming, and the Canadian province of British Columbia. It was an unsettled region claimed by both Great Britain and the United States. By the Convention of 1818, the two nations agreed to "joint occupation" of the Oregon Country, each drawn there initially by the profitable trade in fur pelts.

During the 1820s and 1830s, the fur trade inspired a reckless breed of "mountain men" to abandon civilization and embrace a primitive existence in the wilderness. The rugged trappers were the first whites to find their way around the Rocky Mountains, and they pioneered the trails that settlers would travel as they flooded the Oregon Country and headed across the border into California.

Fur Traders Descending the Missouri (1845) Originally titled "French-Trader, Half-Breed Son," this oil painting depicts a white settler sailing down the river with his half–Native American son—not an uncommon sight in western America.

THE GREAT MIGRATION Word of Oregon's fertile soil, plentiful rainfall, and magnificent forests gradually spread eastward. By 1840, a trickle of emigrants—farmers, missionaries, teachers, fur traders, and shopkeepers—was flowing along the Oregon Trail, a 2,000-mile footpath that formed the great highway connecting the Missouri River near St. Louis with Oregon.

Soon, "**Oregon fever**" swept the nation. To an Ohio woman, "going to the Far West seemed like the entrance to a new world, one of freedom, happiness, and prosperity." Some pioneers desperately sought to escape debts, or dull lives, or bad marriages. "We had nothing to lose," wrote one woman, "and we might gain a fortune." For whatever reason, tens of thousands of Americans began pulling up stakes and moving their families west.

In 1841 and 1842, the first sizable wagon trains made the long trip across half the continent, and in 1843 the movement became a mass migration. One pioneer said that the wagon trains, sometimes six miles long, were like mobile communities. "Everybody was supposed to rise at daylight, and while the women were preparing breakfast, the men rounded up the cattle, took down the tents, yoked the oxen to the wagons, and made everything ready to start."

The Oregon-bound wagon trains followed the trail west from Independence, Missouri, then along the winding North Platte River into what is now Wyoming, through South Pass down to Fort Bridger (abode of the celebrated mountain man Jim Bridger), then down the meandering Snake River through what is now Idaho to the salmon-filled Columbia River. From there they moved through the Cascade Mountains to their goal: Oregon's fertile Willamette Valley. They usually left Missouri in late spring, completing the grueling 2,000-mile trek in six months.

LIFE ON THE TRAIL Traveling in "prairie schooners," sturdy canvas-covered wagons pulled by teams of oxen, sunburned settlers bumped and jostled their way across the rugged trails, mountains, and plains blackened by vast herds of buffaloes. The long journey west was extraordinarily difficult because of the broiling summers, fierce thunderstorms, and bitterly cold, snowy winters. Wagons broke down, oxen died, and diseases like cholera and dysentery took their toll.

WOMEN PIONEERS The diary of Amelia Knight, who set out for Oregon in 1853 with her husband and seven children, reveals the mortal threats along the trail: "Chatfield quite sick with scarlet fever. A calf took sick and died before breakfast. Lost one of our oxen; he dropped dead in the yoke. I could hardly help shedding tears. Yesterday my eighth child was born."

Cholera claimed many lives because of tainted water and contaminated food. On average, there was one grave every eighty yards along the trail. Each step "of the slow, plodding cattle," wrote a woman emigrant, "carried us farther and farther from civilization into a desolate, barbarous country."

Initially, the western pioneers adopted the same division of labor used back East. Women cooked, washed, sewed, and monitored the children, while men drove the wagons, tended the horses and cattle, and did the heavy labor. But the unique demands of the western trails soon dissolved such neat distinctions. Women found themselves gathering buffalo dung for fuel, driving wagons, working to dislodge wagons mired in mud, helping to construct makeshift bridges, pitching tents, or participating in a variety of other "unladylike" tasks.

Southerner Lavinia Porter said that the trip along the California Trail was so difficult that it was still "a source of wonder to me how we [women] were able to endure it." Men on the plains, she observed, were not willing "to wait upon women as they were in more civilized communities." Through her hardships, she became convinced that the American woman was "endowed with the courage of her brave pioneer ancestors, and no matter what the environment she can adapt herself to all situations, even the perilous trip across the western half of this great continent."

THE SETTLEMENT OF CALIFORNIA California was also a powerful magnet for settlers and adventurers. It had first felt the influence of European culture in 1769, when Spain grew concerned about Russian seal traders moving south along the Pacific coast from Alaska. To thwart Russian intentions, Spain sent a naval expedition to settle the region. The Spanish discovered San Francisco Bay and constructed *presidios* (military garrisons) at San Diego and Monterey. Even more important, Franciscan friars, led by Junípero Serra, established a Catholic mission at San Diego. Over the next fifty years, Franciscans built twenty more missions spaced a day's journey apart along the coast from San Diego northward to San Francisco.

By the nineteenth century, Spanish Catholic missionaries, aided by Spanish soldiers, controlled most of the Indians living along the California coast. The friars (priests) enticed the Indians into "missions" by offering gifts or impressing them with their "magical" religious rituals. Once inside the missions, the Indians were baptized as Catholics, taught Spanish, and stripped of their cultural heritage.

CATHOLIC MISSIONS The California Catholic missions served as churches, villages, fortresses, homes, schools, shops, farms, and outposts of

Spanish rule. The missions also quickly became agricultural enterprises, producing crops, livestock, clothing, and household goods, both for profit and to supply the neighboring presidios. Indians provided most of the labor. The Franciscans viewed forced Indian labor as both a practical necessity and a morally enriching responsibility essential to transforming unproductive Indians into industrious Christians.

A mission's daily routine began at dawn with the ringing of a bell, which summoned the community to prayer. Work began an hour later and did not end until an hour before sunset. Most Indian men worked in the fields. Some were trained in special skills, such as masonry, carpentry, or leatherwork. Women handled domestic chores, but during harvest season, everyone was expected to help in the fields. Instead of wages, the Indians received clothing, food, housing, and religious instruction.

The Franciscans used force to control their captive laborers. Rebellious Indians were whipped or imprisoned, and mission Indians died at an alarming rate. One Franciscan friar reported that "of every four Indian children born, three die in their first or second year, while those who survive do not reach the age of twenty-five." Infectious disease was the primary threat, but the grueling labor regimen took a high toll as well. The Native American population along the California coast declined from 72,000 in 1769 to 18,000 by 1821. Saving souls cost many lives.

With Mexican independence in 1821, the Spanish missions slowly fell into disuse. By the time the first Americans began to trickle into California, they found a vast, beautiful province with only a small, scattered population of 6,000 Mexicans ruled by a few dominant *caballeros,* or *rancheros*—"gentlemen" who owned the largest ranches, much like the planters who lorded over the Lower South.

Hispanic Californians, called *Californios*, took comfort that Mexico City, the Mexican capital, was too far away to exercise effective control over them. Between 1821, when Mexico gained its independence, and 1841, Spanish-speaking Californians, as well as many recent American arrivals, staged ten revolts against Mexican governors.

Among the white immigrants in California in the mid–nineteenth century was John A. Sutter, a Swiss settler who had founded a colony of European emigrants. At the junction of the Sacramento and American Rivers (later the site of the city of Sacramento), Sutter built an enormous fort to protect the settlers and their shops.

New Helvetia (Americans called it Sutter's Fort), completed in 1843, stood at the end of what became the California Trail, which forked southward off the Oregon Trail and crossed the Sierra Nevada, a soaring mountain range running north/south along eastern California. By the start of 1846 there were perhaps 800 Americans in California, along with approximately 10,000 Californios.

THE PATHFINDER: JOHN FRÉMONT Despite the dangers of the overland crossing, the Far West proved an irresistible attraction for hundreds of thousands of pioneers. The most enthusiastic champion of American settlement in Mexican California and the Far West was John Charles Frémont, an impetuous junior army officer who became America's most famous celebrity— and a notorious troublemaker.

Born out of wedlock in Savannah, Georgia, Frémont developed a robust love of the outdoors. In 1838, after attending the College of Charleston, he was commissioned a second lieutenant in the U.S. Topographical Corps, an organization whose mission was to explore and map new western territories. Frémont soon excelled at surveying, mapmaking, and woodcraft while becoming versed in geology, botany, ornithology, and zoology.

In 1842, the fearless Frémont, who believed he was a man of destiny, set out from present-day Kansas City with two dozen soldiers to map the eastern half of the Oregon Trail. They spent five months collecting plant and animal specimens and drawing maps in uncharted territory.

With his wife's considerable help, Frémont published in newspapers across the nation excerpts from a rip-roaring account of his explorations titled *A Report on an Exploration of the Country Lying between the Missouri River and the Rocky Mountains on the Line of the Kansas and Great Platte Rivers.*

The popular stories of Frémont's adventures made him an instant celebrity and earned him the nickname, "the Pathfinder." The success of Frémont's first western explorations quickly led to another expedition, this time intended to map the second and more difficult half of the Oregon Trail. His group was the first to cross the snow- and ice-covered Sierra Nevada in the winter, a spectacular feat. His report of his expedition and the maps it generated spurred massive migrations to Utah, Oregon, and California, including the trek of the Mormons from Illinois to Salt Lake City, Utah.

Rarely one to follow orders, keep promises, or admit mistakes, the impulsive, iron-willed Frémont surprised his superior officers when he launched a "military" expedition on his own. In August 1845, Frémont, now a captain, and sixty-two heavily armed soldiers, sailors, scientists, hunters, and frontiersmen headed west from St. Louis on another mysterious expedition.

In December, Frémont's adventurers swept down the western slopes of the Sierra Nevada and headed southward through the Central Valley of Mexican-controlled California. Frémont told Mexican authorities that his mission was strictly scientific and that his men were civilians. In Monterey, in January 1846,

Frémont received secret instructions from President James K. Polk indicating that the United States intended to take control of California from Mexico. Frémont was ordered to encourage a "spontaneous" uprising among the Americans living there. Suspicious Mexican officials ordered Frémont to leave. He did so, leading his explorers into Oregon, attacking Indian villages along the way. But the Americans soon returned. To cover his efforts to spark a revolution among the English-speaking Californians, most of whom were Americans, Frémont officially submitted his resignation from the army so that he thereafter would be acting as a private citizen rather than as a member of the U.S. government.

Then Frémont and his band of soldiers and "rough, leather-jacketed frontiersmen" began stirring unrest. On June 14, 1846, American settlers captured Sonoma in northern California and proclaimed the Republic of California. They hoisted a linen flag featuring a grizzly bear and star, a version of which would later become the California state flag. On June 25, Frémont and his band marched into Sonoma. All of California was in American control when news arrived there of the outbreak of the Mexican-American War.

American pioneers This 1850 photograph captures some of the many pioneers who headed west for brighter futures.

AMERICAN SETTLEMENTS IN TEXAS The American passion for new western land focused largely on Texas, the closest of all the northern Mexican borderlands. During the 1820s, the United States had twice offered to buy Texas, but the Mexican government refused to sell. Mexicans were frightened and infuriated by the idea of Yankees acquiring their "sacred soil"—but that is what happened.

The leading promoter of American settlement in the coastal plain of Texas was Stephen Fuller Austin, a visionary land developer (*empresario*) who convinced the Mexican government that he could recruit 300 American families to settle between the Colorado and Brazo Rivers along the Gulf coast of Texas and create a "buffer" on the northern frontier between the feared Comanche Indians and the Mexican settlements to the south.

Americans eagerly settled in Austin's Anglo "colony" in east Texas. They each received 177 free acres and had access to thousands of acres of common pasture for ranching. (Austin received 65,000 acres for his efforts.) Most of the Anglos were ranchers or farmers drawn to the fertile, inexpensive lands in the river valleys. A few of the settlers were wealthy planters who brought large numbers of slaves with them at a time when Mexico was prohibiting the importation of slaves.

By 1830, coastal Texas had far more Americans living there than Hispanics (Tejanos) or Indians—about 20,000 white settlers (called Anglos or *Texians*), and 1,000 enslaved blacks, brought to grow and harvest cotton. By 1835, there were 35,000 Texians, 3,000 African American slaves, and a booming cotton economy. So many people in the Carolinas, Georgia, Alabama, Tennessee, and Missouri had migrated to Texas that the phrase "Gone to Texas"—or its initials, "GTT"—were often carved into the doors of cabins left behind.

The flood of Americans into Texas led to numerous clashes with Indians as well as Mexican officials, who began having second thoughts about their "tolerated guests." A Mexican congressman issued an accurate warning in 1830: "Mexicans! Watch closely, for you know all too well the Anglo-Saxon greed for territory. We have generously granted land to these Nordics; they have made their homes with us, but their hearts are with their native land. We are continually in civil wars and revolutions; we are weak, and know it—and they know it also. They may conspire with the United States to take Texas from us. From this time, be on your guard!"

THE TEXAS WAR FOR INDEPENDENCE Mexican officials were so worried about the behavior and intentions of Americans living in Texas that in April 1830 they suddenly outlawed further immigration from the United States. But Americans, who viewed the Mexicans, their army, and their incompetent government with contempt, kept coming. By 1835, the Texians and their enslaved blacks outnumbered the Tejanos (Spanish-speaking Texans) ten to one. In a letter to his cousin in 1835, Stephen F. Austin left no doubt about his plans: "It is very evident that Texas should be effectually, and fully, *Americanized*—that is—settled by a population that will harmonize with their neighbors on the *East*, in language, political principles, common origin, sympathy, and even interest. *Texas must be a slave country. It is no longer a matter of doubt*."

A changing political situation in Mexico aggravated the growing tensions. In 1834, General Antonio López de Santa Anna, the Mexican president, suspended the national congress and became a dictator, calling himself the "Napoleon of the West." Texans feared that Santa Anna planned to free "our slaves and to make slaves of us."

When Santa Anna imprisoned Austin in 1834, Texans decided that the Mexican ruler had to go. Upon his release from jail eighteen months later, Austin called for Texans to revolt: "War is our only resource. There is no other remedy. We must defend our rights, ourselves, and our country by force of arms." He urged that Texas become fully American, promote slavery, and join the United States.

In the fall of 1835, Texans followed Austin's lead and rebelled against Santa Anna's "despotism." A furious Santa Anna ordered all Americans expelled, all Texans disarmed, and all rebels arrested and executed as "pirates." As sporadic fighting erupted, hundreds of armed volunteers from southern states rushed to assist the 30,000 Texians and Tejanos fighting for their independence against a Mexican nation of 7 million people.

THE ALAMO At San Antonio, the provincial capital in southern Texas, General Santa Anna's 3,000-man army assaulted a group of fewer than 200 Texians, Tejanos, and members of the Texas volunteer army holed up in an abandoned Catholic mission called the Alamo.

The outnumbered and outgunned rebels were led by three colorful adventurers who symbolized the connection in the South between manly honor and violence: James "Jim" Bowie, William Barret Travis, and David Crockett. Bowie, born in Kentucky but raised in Louisiana, had become a ruthless slave trader and deceitful land speculator. He was most famous for the "bowie knife" he used to wound and kill men in numerous fights. Bowie claimed he had never started a fight nor lost one.

Bowie wore out his welcome in Louisiana and migrated to Texas in 1828, settled near San Antonio, and came to own about a million acres of Texas land. He married a prominent Mexican woman, became a Mexican citizen, and learned Spanish, but a cholera epidemic killed his wife and two children, as well as his in-laws.

The Alamo David Crockett, pictured fighting with his rifle over his head, joined the legendary effort to defend the Alamo against the Mexican army's repeated assaults.

Upon learning of the Texas Revolution, Bowie joined the volunteer army and fought in several battles before arriving in San Antonio in January 1836. Bowie, often "roaring drunk," commanded the Texas volunteers in the Alamo while William Travis, a hot-tempered, twenty-six-year-old lawyer and teacher, led the Texian "regular army" soldiers. Travis had come to Texas by way of Alabama, where he had left behind a failed marriage, a pregnant wife, a two-year-old son, considerable debts, and, rumors claimed, a man he had killed. Travis pledged that he would redeem his life by doing something great and honorable in Texas—or die trying. His determination to face an honorable death led him to refuse orders to retreat from the Alamo.

The most famous American at the Alamo was David Crockett, the Tennessee frontiersman, sharpshooter, bear hunter, and storyteller who had fought under Andrew Jackson and served in Congress as an anti-Jackson Whig. In his last speech before Congress after being defeated for reelection, Crockett, who was not called "Davy" until long after his death, told his colleagues that he "was done with politics for the present, and that they might go to hell, and I would go to Texas."

Soon after arriving in Texas with his trusty rifle "Old Betsy," Crockett, the "Lion of the West," was told he would receive 4,000 acres of land for his service as a fighter. He then was assigned to join the garrison at the Alamo. Full of bounce and brag, the forty-nine-year-old Crockett was thoroughly expert at killing. As he once told his men, "Pierce the heart of the enemy as you would a feller that spit in your face, knocked down your wife, burnt up your houses, and called your dog a skunk!"

What Crockett, Travis, and Bowie shared with the other defenders of the Alamo was a commitment to liberty in the face of Santa Anna's growing despotism. In late February 1836, Santa Anna demanded that the Alamo's defenders surrender. By then, Bowie had fallen seriously ill, was bedridden, and had turned over his command to Travis, who answered the Mexican ultimatum with cannon fire. He then sent urgent appeals to Texian towns for supplies and more men while promising that "*I shall never surrender or retreat. . . .* VICTORY OR DEATH!"

Help did not come, however, and Santa Anna launched a series of assaults against the outnumbered defenders. For twelve days, the Mexicans were thrown back and suffered heavy losses.

The furious fighting at the Alamo turned the rebellion into a war for Texan independence. On March 2, 1836, delegates from all fifty-nine Texas towns, most of them American immigrants, met at the tiny village of Washington-on-the-Brazos, some 150 miles northeast of San Antonio. There they signed a declaration of independence, and drafted a constitution for the new Republic of Texas. The delegates then named Sam Houston as commander of their disorganized but growing "army."

Four days later, the defenders of the Alamo were awakened at four o'clock in the morning by the sound of Mexican bugles playing the dreaded "Degüello" ("No Mercy to the Defenders"). Colonel Travis shouted: "The Mexicans are upon us—give 'em Hell!"

The climactic Battle of the Alamo was fought in the predawn dark. Wave after wave of Santa Anna's men attacked. They were twice forced back, but on the third try they broke through the battered north wall. Travis was killed by a bullet between the eyes. Some of the Texans took the fight outside the Alamo with tomahawks, knives, rifle butts, and fists, but in the end, virtually all of them were killed or wounded.

Seven Alamo defenders, perhaps including Crockett, survived and were captured. Santa Anna ordered them hacked to death with swords. A Mexican officer wrote that the captives "died without complaining and without humiliating themselves before their torturers."

By dawn, the battle was over. The only survivors were a handful of women and children, and Joe, Travis's slave. It was a costly victory, however, as more than 600 Mexicans died. The Battle of the Alamo also provided a rallying cry for vengeful Texians. While Santa Anna proclaimed a "glorious victory" and ordered the bodies of the revolutionaries burned, his aide wrote ominously in his diary, "One more such 'glorious victory' and we are finished."

GOLIAD Two weeks later, at the Battle of Coleto, a Mexican force again defeated a smaller Texian army, many of them recently arrived volunteers from southern states. The Mexicans marched the 465 captured Texians to a fort in the nearby town of Goliad. Despite pleas from his own men to show mercy, Santa Anna ordered the captives killed as "pirates and outlaws." On Palm Sunday, March 27, 1836, more than 300 Texians were murdered. The massacres at the Alamo and Goliad fueled a burning desire for revenge among the Texians.

SAM HOUSTON The fate of the **Texas Revolution** was now in the hands of Sam Houston, a hulking, hard-drinking frontiersman born in Virginia to Scots-Irish immigrants. At age fourteen, after his father died, Houston had moved with his mother and siblings to eastern Tennessee. Two years later, he ran away from home and lived among the Cherokees for a time. Like David Crockett, he had served under General Andrew Jackson during the War of 1812 before becoming an attorney, a U.S. congressman, and governor of Tennessee.

In 1829, Houston joined the Cherokee migration westward to the Arkansas Territory, where he married a Cherokee woman and was formally "adopted" by the Cherokee Nation. He also grew addicted to alcohol; the Cherokees called him "Big Drunk." In December 1832, he moved to Texas and joined the rebellion against Mexico. Houston was fearless, a quality sorely needed by the Texians as they struggled against the larger Mexican army.

THE BATTLE OF SAN JACINTO After learning of the massacre at the Alamo, Houston led his outnumbered troops on a long strategic retreat to buy time while hoping that Santa Anna's pursuing army would make a mistake. On April 21, 1836, the cocky Mexican general walked into Houston's trap, when his army of 900 fighters caught the 1,600 Mexicans napping near the San Jacinto River, about twenty-five miles southeast of the modern city of Houston. The Texians and Tejanos charged, yelling "Remember the Alamo." They overwhelmed the panic-stricken Mexicans, most of whom were sleeping.

The battle lasted only eighteen minutes, but Houston's troops spent the next two hours slaughtering fleeing Mexican soldiers. It was, said a Texian, a "frightful sight to behold." Some 630 Mexicans were killed and 700 captured. The Texians lost only nine men. Santa Anna was captured the next day but bought his freedom by signing a treaty recognizing the independence of the Republic of Texas, with the Rio Grande as its southern boundary with Mexico. The Texas Revolution had been accomplished in seven weeks.

THE LONE STAR REPUBLIC In 1836, the Lone Star Republic, as Texians called their new nation, legalized slavery, banned free blacks, elected Sam Houston as its first president, and voted overwhelmingly for annexation to the United States. No one expected the Republic of Texas, with only 40,000 people, to remain independent for long. But statehood for Texas soon became embroiled in the explosive sectional dispute over slavery.

John C. Calhoun told the Senate in 1836 that "there were powerful reasons why Texas should be part of this Union. The southern states, owning a slave population, were deeply interested in preventing that country from having the power to annoy them." Anti-slavery northerners disagreed. In 1837, the Vermont state legislature "solemnly protested" against the admission "of any state whose constitution tolerates domestic slavery."

The American president at the time was Houston's old friend and former commander, Andrew Jackson, who eagerly wanted Texas to join the Union. "Old Hickory," however, decided it was better to wait a few years. He knew that adding Texas as a slave state would ignite an explosive quarrel between North and South that would fracture the Democratic party and endanger the election of New Yorker Martin Van Buren, his handpicked successor. Worse, any effort to add Texas to the Union would likely mean a war with Mexico, which refused to recognize Texan independence.

So Jackson delayed official recognition of the Republic of Texas until his last day in office, early in 1837. Van Buren, Jackson's successor, did as predicted: he avoided all talk of Texas annexation during his single term as president.

WHIGS AND DEMOCRATS When William Henry Harrison succeeded Martin Van Buren as president in 1841, he was the oldest man (sixty-eight) and the first Whig to win the office. The Whigs, who now controlled both houses of Congress, had first emerged in opposition to Andrew Jackson and continued to promote strong federal government support for industrial development and economic growth: high tariffs to deter imports and federal funding for roads, bridges, and canals.

Yet Harrison was elected primarily on his prominence as a military hero. He had avoided taking public stances on controversial issues. In the end, it mattered little, as Harrison served the shortest term of any president. On April 4, 1841, exactly one month after his inauguration, he died of pneumonia, and vice president John Tyler became president.

The surprising turn of events pleased former president Jackson. "A kind and overruling providence had interfered," he wrote a friend, "to prolong our glorious Union and happy republican system which General Harrison and his cabinet was [sic] preparing to destroy under the dictation of that profligate demagogue, Henry Clay." Another former president, John Quincy Adams, had the opposite reaction. He dismissed new president Tyler as "a political sectarian, of the slave-driving, Virginian, Jeffersonian school" of politics, whose talents were barely "above mediocrity."

Upon learning of Harrison's death, Clay resolved to dominate the mild-mannered new president. Tyler "dares not resist," the imperious Clay threatened, or "I will drive him before me." Tyler, however, was not willing to be dominated.

JOHN TYLER The tall, thin, slave-owning Virginian was the youngest president to date—fifty-one, but he had lots of political experience, having served as a state legislator, governor, congressman, and senator. Most important, he was a man of stubborn independence and considerable charm. A political acquaintance said Tyler was "approachable, courteous, always willing to do a kindly action, or to speak a kindly word."

Originally a Democrat who had endorsed the Jeffersonian commitment to states' rights, strict construction of the Constitution, and opposition to national banks, Tyler had broken with the party and joined the Whigs over President Jackson's "condemnation" of South Carolina's attempt to nullify federal laws. Tyler believed that South Carolina had a constitutional right to secede from the nation. Yet he never truly embraced the Whigs. As president, Tyler opposed everything associated with Henry Clay's much-celebrated program of economic nationalism (the American System) that called for high tariffs, a national bank, and internal improvements.

When Congress met in a special session in 1841, Clay introduced a series of controversial resolutions. He called for the repeal of the Independent Treasury Act and the creation of another Bank of the United States, proposed to revive the distribution program whereby the money generated by federal land sales was given to the states, and urged that tariffs be raised on imported goods to hamper foreign competitors.

Although Tyler agreed to the repeal of the Independent Treasury Act and signed a higher tariff bill, he vetoed Clay's pet project: the new national bank. An incensed Clay responded by calling Tyler a traitor who had disgraced his party. He claimed that the president was left "solitary and alone, shivering by the pitiless storm" against his veto. The dispute was so heated that scuffles and fistfights between Whigs and Democrats broke out in Congress. Clay then convinced Tyler's entire cabinet to resign, with the exception of Secretary of State Daniel Webster. A three-year-long war between Clay and Tyler had begun.

Tyler replaced the defectors in his cabinet with anti-Jackson Democrats who, like him, had become Whigs. The Whigs then expelled Tyler from the party, calling him "His Accidency" and the "Executive Ass." Sixty Whig members of Congress signed a statement denouncing Tyler and declaring him no longer their representative. By 1842, Tyler had become a president without a party, shunned by both Whigs and Democrats.

The political turmoil coincided with the ongoing economic depression that had begun in the late 1830s. Bank failures mounted, businesses shut down, and unemployment soared. Yet Tyler refused to let either the sputtering economy or an international crisis with Great Britain deter him from annexing more territory into the United States.

TENSIONS WITH BRITAIN In late 1841, slaves being transported from Virginia to Louisiana on the American ship *Creole* revolted and took charge of the ship. They sailed into Nassau, in the Bahamas, where British authorities set 128 of them free. (Great Britain had abolished slavery throughout its empire in 1834.)

It was the most successful slave revolt in American history. Southerners were infuriated, and the incident mushroomed into an international crisis. Secretary of State Daniel Webster demanded that the slaves be returned as American property, but the British refused.

At this point, the British government decided to send Alexander Baring (Lord Ashburton), head of a major bank, to meet with Webster, who viewed good relations with Britain as essential for the American economy. The meetings concluded with the signing of the Webster-Ashburton Treaty (1842), which provided for joint naval patrols off Africa to police the outlawed slave trade. The treaty also resolved a long-standing dispute over the northeastern U.S. boundary with British Canada. But it did nothing about returning the freed slaves. (The dispute was not settled until 1853, when England paid $110,000 to the owners of the freed slaves.)

EFFORTS TO ANNEX TEXAS Texas leaders were frustrated that their newly won independence had not led to annexation, and Sam Houston threatened to expand the Republic of Texas to the Pacific. But with little money, a rising government debt, and continuing tensions with Mexico, which insisted that it remained at war with Texas, this was mostly talk.

The Lone Star Republic had no infrastructure—no banks, no schools, no industries. It remained largely a frontier community. Houston decided that the rickety republic had only two choices: annexation to the United States or closer economic ties to Great Britain, which extended formal diplomatic recognition to the republic and began buying cotton from Texas planters.

Meanwhile, thousands more Americans poured into Texas, enticed by the republic's offer of 1,280 acres of land to each white family. The population more than tripled between 1836 and 1845, from 40,000 to 150,000, and the enslaved black population grew even faster than the white population.

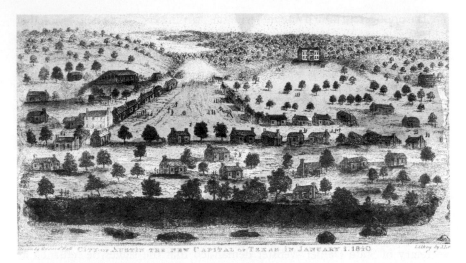

Austin, Texas, in 1840 A view of the capital of the newly formed Republic of Texas – the city's population at the time numbered less than a thousand.

A TRAGIC CRUISE In February 1844, President Tyler and a group of dignitaries boarded the U.S.S. *Princeton*, a new propeller-driven steam warship, for an excursion on the Potomac River. As sailors fired the ship's huge cannons, one of them, "the Peacemaker," exploded, killing eight people, including the secretary of state, the secretary of the navy, and a New York state legislator. More than a dozen others were seriously wounded.

Tyler seized the opportunity created by the tragic accident to reorganize his cabinet by naming southern Democrats to key positions. He appointed John C. Calhoun secretary of state, primarily because he wanted the South Carolinian to complete the annexation of Texas. Calhoun, however, stumbled by writing the British ambassador a letter in which he declared that blacks were inferior to whites and better off enslaved than free. Slavery, Calhoun insisted, was "essential to the peace, safety, and prosperity" of the South, and adding Texas as a state was necessary to keep the South in the Union. Outraged northerners in the Senate voted down Calhoun's annexation treaty 35 to 16.

THE ELECTION OF 1844 Thereafter, leaders in both political parties hoped to keep the divisive Texas issue out of the 1844 presidential campaign. Whig Henry Clay and Democrat Martin Van Buren, the leading candidates for each party's nomination, agreed that adding Texas to the Union would be a mistake.

For his part, Tyler, having alienated both parties, decided to run for reelection as an independent, using the slogan, "Tyler and Texas." Within a few weeks, however, he realized he had little support and dropped out of the race.

Van Buren's southern supporters, including Andrew Jackson, abandoned him because he opposed the annexation of Texas. They nominated James Knox Polk, former Speaker of the House and former governor of Tennessee. Like Tyler, Polk was an enthusiastic expansionist who wanted to make the United States a transcontinental global power. Unlike Tyler, Polk was a loyal Democrat who hated Whigs. On the ninth ballot, he became the first "dark horse" (unexpected) candidate to win a major-party nomination. The Democrats' platform called for the annexation of Texas and declared that the United States had a "clear and unquestionable claim" to all of the Oregon Country.

The 1844 presidential election proved to be one of the most significant in history. By promoting southern and western expansionism, the Democrats offered a winning strategy, one so popular it forced Clay, the Whig candidate, to alter his position on Texas at the last minute; he now claimed that he had "no personal objection to the annexation" if it could be achieved "without dishonor, without war, with the common consent of the Union, and upon just and fair terms."

Clay's waffling on Texas shifted more anti-slavery votes to the new Liberty party (the anti-slavery party formed in 1840), which increased its count in the presidential election from about 7,000 in 1840 to more than 62,000 in 1844. In the western counties of New York, the Liberty party drew enough votes away from Clay and the Whigs to give the crucial state to Polk.

Had Clay carried New York, he would have won the election by 7 electoral votes. Instead, Polk won a narrow national plurality of 38,000 popular votes (the first president since John Quincy Adams to win without a majority) but a clear majority of the electoral college, 170 to 105. Clay had lost his third and last effort to win the presidency. Clay could not understand how he lost to Polk, whom he considered a "third-rate" politician lacking leadership abilities.

JAMES K. POLK Yet Polk had been surprising people his whole career. Born near Charlotte, North Carolina, the oldest of ten children, he graduated first in his class at the University of North Carolina, then moved to Tennessee, where he became a successful lawyer and planter, entered politics, and served fourteen years in Congress (four as Speaker of the House) and two years as governor.

At age forty-nine, Polk was America's youngest president up to that time. Short, thin, and humorless, he was called "Young Hickory" because of his admiration for Andrew Jackson. And like Jackson, he believed that any effort by the federal government to promote economic growth necessarily helped some people and regions and hurt others. He was thus opposed to tariffs, a national bank, and federally funded roads.

Polk's greatest virtue was his relentless work ethic. "I am the hardest working man in this country," he declared. True to his word, he often worked from dawn to midnight and rarely took a vacation. Such unrelenting intensity eventually wore him out, however. Polk would die in 1849, at fifty-three years old, just three months after leaving office.

THE STATE OF TEXAS Texas, the hottest political potato, had been added as a new state just *before* Polk became president. In his final months in office, President John Tyler had taken an unusual step by asking Congress to annex Texas by joint resolution, which required only a simple majority in each house rather than the two-thirds Senate vote needed to ratify a *treaty* of annexation.

The resolution narrowly passed, with most Whigs opposed. On March 1, 1845, in his final presidential action, Tyler signed the resolution admitting Texas to the Union as the twenty-eighth state, and fifteenth slave state, on December 29, 1845. Six weeks later, on February 16, 1846, the Lone Star flag of the Republic of Texas was lowered, and the flag of the United States was raised over the largest state in the nation.

At the time, Texas had a population of 100,000 whites and 38,000 enslaved blacks. By 1850, the population—both white and black—had soared by almost 50 percent. (The census then did not include Native Americans.) By 1860, Texas had 600,000 people, most of them from southern states focused on growing cotton.

POLK'S GOALS Perhaps because he pledged to serve only one term, Polk was a president in a hurry. He focused on four major objectives, all of which he accomplished. He managed to (1) reduce tariffs on imports; (2) reestablish the Independent Treasury ("We need no national banks!"); (3) settle the Oregon boundary dispute with Britain; and (4) acquire California from Mexico. His top priority was territorial expansion. He wanted to add Oregon, California, and New Mexico to the Union to fill out the continent.

In keeping with long-standing Democratic beliefs, Polk wanted lower tariffs to allow more foreign goods to compete in the American marketplace and thereby help drive consumer prices down. Congress agreed by approving the Walker Tariff of 1846, named after Robert J. Walker, the secretary of the Treasury.

In the same year, Polk persuaded Congress to restore the Independent Treasury Act that Martin Van Buren had signed into law in 1840 and the Whig-dominated Congress had repealed the next year. The act established Independent Treasury deposit offices to receive all federal government funds. The system was intended to replace the Second Bank of the United States, which Jackson had "killed," so as to offset the chaotic growth of unregulated state banks whose reckless lending practices had helped cause the depression of the late 1830s.

The new Independent Treasury entrusted the federal government, rather than state banks, with the exclusive management of government funds and

Tariff of 1846 This political cartoon illustrates the public outcry—represented by a Quaker woman ready to whip Polk—against the Tariff of 1846, one of the lowest in the nation's history.

required that all disbursements be made in gold or silver, or paper currency backed by gold or silver.

Polk also twice vetoed Whig-passed bills for federally funded infrastructure projects. His efforts to reverse Whig economic policies satisfied the slaveholding South but angered northerners, who wanted higher tariffs to protect their industries from British competition, and westerners, who wanted federally financed roads and harbors.

OREGON Meanwhile, the dispute with Great Britain over the Oregon Country boundary heated up as expansionists insisted that Polk take the whole region rather than split it with the British. Polk was willing to go to the brink of war to achieve his goals. "If we do have war," the president blustered, "it will not be our fault."

Fortunately, neither Polk nor the British were willing to risk war. On June 15, 1846, James Buchanan, Polk's secretary of state, signed what was called the Buchanan-Pakenham Treaty, which extended the border between the United States and British Canada westward to the Pacific coast along the 49th parallel. Once the treaty was approved by both nations, the *New York Herald* announced that "Now, we can thrash Mexico into decency at our leisure."

THE MEXICAN-AMERICAN WAR

The settlement of the Oregon Country boundary dispute allowed the United States to turn its attention southward. On March 6, 1845, two days after James Polk took office, the Mexican government broke off relations with the United States to protest the annexation of Texas.

Polk was willing to wage war against Mexico to acquire California and New Mexico, but he did not want Americans to fire the first shot. So he ordered several thousand U.S. troops under General Zachary Taylor to take up positions around Corpus Christi, near the Rio Grande. The U.S. troops were knowingly in disputed territory, and Mexico viewed the arrival of U.S. troops as an act of war.

On the evening of May 9, 1845, Polk learned that Mexican troops had attacked U.S. soldiers north of the Rio Grande. Eleven Americans were killed, five wounded, and the remainder taken prisoner. "Hostilities may now be considered as commenced," Taylor reported.

Polk's scheme to provoke an attack had worked. To avoid the risk that Congress would vote down a declaration of war, Polk simply declared that the Mexicans had started a war that now needed to be funded. Mexico, he reported, "has invaded our territory, and shed American blood upon the American soil." Congress quickly authorized the recruitment of 50,000 soldiers.

Some congressmen, however, were skeptical of Polk's explanation. Whig Garret Davis of Kentucky asserted that the Rio Grande was part of Mexico, not Texas: "It is our own President who began this war." Even Democrats were concerned about the president's account. A New York senator, John Dix, said he would not be "surprised if the next accounts should show that there is no Mexican invasion of our soil." The war, he later added, "was begun in fraud . . . and I think will end in disgrace."

Polk steadfastly denied that the war had anything to do with the expansion of slavery. He argued that his efforts to extend the nation's boundaries were intended to replace sectional tensions with national unity. For Polk, the notion of manifest destiny was a means of promoting national unity. After all, he stressed, slavery could not flourish in places like New Mexico and California because cotton could not be grown there because of the climate.

With the outbreak of fighting, most Americans accepted the president's account of what happened along the Mexico-Texas border and rushed to support the military. "LET US GO TO WAR," screamed a New York newspaper. Another headline blared: "MEXICO OR DEATH!" The South was especially excited because of the possibility of acquiring more territory. So many southerners ("wild, reckless young fellows") rushed to volunteer that thousands had to be turned away.

Eventually, 112,000 whites served in the war (blacks were banned), including an array of young army officers who would later distinguish themselves as opposing leaders in the Civil War: Ulysses S. Grant, Thomas Jackson, James Longstreet, Robert E. Lee, George McClellan, George Meade, and William T. Sherman.

OPPOSITION TO THE WAR In New England and among northern abolitionists, there was much less enthusiasm for "Mr. Polk's War." Congressman John Quincy Adams called it "a most unrighteous war" designed to extend slavery into new territories. Many other New Englanders involved with the growing abolitionist movement denounced the war as the work of pro-slavery southerners eager for more land.

William Lloyd Garrison, the fiery Boston abolitionist, charged that the war was one of "aggression, of invasion, of conquest." A few miles away, in Concord, Henry David Thoreau spent a night in jail rather than pay taxes that might help fund the war. Thoreau's mentor, Ralph Waldo Emerson, predicted that the "United States will conquer Mexico, but it will be as the man who swallows arsenic, which brings him down in turn. Mexico will poison us."

Most northern Whigs, including a young Illinois congressman named Abraham Lincoln, opposed the war, arguing that Polk had maneuvered the Mexicans into attacking. The United States, they insisted, had no reason to place its army in the disputed border region between Texas and Mexico. Henry Clay called the war "unnatural" and "lamentable," while Daniel Webster charged that its origins were "unconstitutional." (Both Clay and Webster would lose sons in the war.)

PREPARING FOR BATTLE The United States was again ill prepared for a major war. At the outset, the regular army numbered barely more than 7,000, in contrast to the Mexican force of 32,000. Before the war ended, the U.S. military had grown to almost 79,000 troops, many of whom were frontier toughs who lacked uniforms, equipment, and discipline. Repeatedly, these soldiers engaged in plunder, rape, and murder. Yet they outfought the more numerous Mexican forces, which had their own problems with training, discipline, morale, supplies, and munitions.

The Mexican-American War would last two years, from March 1846 to April 1848, and would be fought on four fronts: southern Texas/northern Mexico, central Mexico, New Mexico, and California. Early in the fighting, General Zachary Taylor's army scored two victories north of the Rio Grande, at Palo Alto (May 8) and Resaca de la Palma (May 9). On May 18, the army crossed the Rio Grande and occupied Matamoros. These quick victories brought Taylor, a Whig, instant popularity, and Polk agreed to public demand that Taylor be made overall commander. It was an excellent choice, since Taylor, "Old Rough and Ready," had spent thirty-eight years in the army and had earned the respect and affection of his men.

THE ANNEXATION OF CALIFORNIA President Polk's foremost objective was not the defeat of Mexico but the acquisition of California. In particular, Polk feared that Great Britain or France would take control of California if the United States did not.

Polk had sent secret instructions to Commodore John D. Sloat, commander of the Pacific naval squadron, telling him that if war erupted with Mexico, he was to use his warships to gain control "of the port of San Francisco, and blockade or occupy such other ports as your force may permit."

In May 1846, Sloat, having heard of the outbreak of hostilities along the Rio Grande, set sail for California. In early July, U.S. sailors and troops went ashore in San Francisco, took down the flag of the Republic of California, raised the American flag, and claimed California as part of the United States. Soon thereafter, Sloat turned his command over to Commodore Robert F. Stockton, who sailed south to capture San Diego and Los Angeles. By mid-August, Mexican resistance had evaporated.

At the same time, another American military expedition headed for California. On August 18, General Stephen Kearny's army captured Santa Fe, the capital of New Mexico, then moved on to join Stockton's forces. They took control of Los Angeles on January 10, 1847, and the remaining Mexican forces surrendered three days later. Stockton and Kearny then quarreled over who was in command, since each had similar orders to conquer and govern California.

In the meantime, the unpredictable John C. Frémont arrived from Sonoma with 400 newly recruited troops and claimed that Stockton was in charge. Stockton responded by naming Frémont governor of California, and the power-hungry Frémont immediately set about giving orders, making proclamations, and appointing officials. This left Kearny in a bind; President Polk had ordered *him* to be the governor, but Frémont defied his orders.

In June, 1847, General Kearny, his mission complete, decided to return to Washington, D.C. Frémont went along. When they reached Fort Leavenworth, in Kansas, Kearny had Frémont arrested and charged with insubordination and mutiny. In Washington, D.C., Kearny was hailed as a hero while Frémont awaited trial.

In the most celebrated trial since that of Vice President Aaron Burr in 1807, Frémont was convicted and dismissed from the army. Polk, however, quickly reversed the sentence in light of Frémont's "meritorious and valuable services." He urged Frémont to "resume the sword," but "the Pathfinder" was so angered by the court's ruling that he resigned from the army and settled in California, where he would become the state's first U.S. senator.

WAR IN NORTHERN MEXICO Both California and New Mexico had been taken from Mexican control before General Zachary Taylor fought his first major battle in northern Mexico. In September 1846, Taylor's army assaulted the fortified city of Monterrey, which surrendered after a five-day siege. Then, General Antonio López de Santa Anna, who had been forced out of power in 1845, sent word to Polk from his exile in Cuba that he would end the war if he were allowed to return. Polk assured the exiled Mexican leader that the U.S. government would pay well for any territory taken from Mexico. In August 1846, on Polk's orders, Santa Anna was permitted to return to Mexico.

But the crafty Santa Anna had lied. Soon he was again president of Mexico and in command of the Mexican army. As it turned out, however, he was much more talented at raising armies than leading them in battle.

In October 1846, Santa Anna prepared to attack. When the Mexican general invited the outnumbered Americans to surrender, Taylor responded, "Tell him to go to hell." That launched the hard-fought Battle of Buena Vista (February 22–23, 1847), in northern Mexico. Both sides claimed victory, but the Mexicans suffered five times as many casualties as the Americans. Thereafter, the Mexicans continued to lose battles, but they refused to accept Polk's terms for surrender.

Frustrated by Taylor's inability to win a decisive victory, Polk authorized an American assault on Mexico City, the nation's capital. On March 9, 1847, a large American force led by Winfield Scott, the general-in-chief of the U.S. Army, landed on the beaches south of Veracruz. It was considered to be the strongest fortress in North America, with three forts guarding the approaches to the port city. The American assault on Veracruz was the largest amphibious operation ever attempted by U.S. military forces and was carried out without loss. The news of the American victory made General Scott a national hero. Veracruz surrendered on March 29. The American troops then rested, accumulating supplies and awaiting reinforcements.

In August, Scott's formidable army began marching toward the heavily defended Mexican capital, 200 miles away. After four brilliantly orchestrated battles in which they overwhelmed the Mexican defenders, U.S. forces arrived at the gates of Mexico City in early September 1847. The Duke of Wellington now changed his tune, calling Scott the world's "greatest living soldier." Ulysses S. Grant also applauded his commander, pointing out that with only half as many troops as the Mexicans, Scott had "won every battle, he captured the capital, and conquered the government."

THE TREATY OF GUADALUPE HIDALGO After the fall of Mexico City, Santa Anna resigned from office and fled the country. Peace talks began on January 2, 1848. When the **Treaty of Guadalupe Hidalgo** was signed on February 2, a humiliated Mexican government was forced to recognize the Rio Grande as the border with Texas and to transfer control of all or parts of the future states of California, New Mexico, Nevada, Utah, Arizona, Wyoming, and Colorado.

With the addition of territory in southern Arizona and New Mexico through the Gadsden Purchase of 1853, these annexations rounded out the continental United States, doubled its size, and provided routes for eventual transcontinental rail lines. In return for what Polk called "an immense empire" that encompassed more than half a million square miles, the United States agreed to pay $15 million. The Senate ratified the treaty on March 10, 1848. By the end of July, the last remaining U.S. soldiers had left Mexico.

THE WAR'S LEGACIES The Mexican-American War was America's first major military intervention outside the United States and the first time that U.S. military forces had conquered and occupied another country. More than 13,000 Americans died, 11,550 of them from disease, especially measles and dysentery. The war remains the deadliest in American history in terms of the percentage of soldiers lost. Out of every 1,000 soldiers in Mexico, some 110 died. The next highest death rate would be in the Civil War, with 65 dead out of every 1,000 participants.

The victory also helped end America's prolonged economic depression. As the years passed, however, the Mexican-American War was increasingly seen as a shameful war of conquest directed by a president bent on territorial expansion for the sake of slavery. Ulysses S. Grant later called it "one of the most unjust wars ever waged by a stronger against a weaker nation."

News of the victory over Mexico, however, thrilled American expansionists. The editor John O'Sullivan, who had coined the term *manifest destiny*, shouted, "More, More, More! Why not take all of Mexico?" Treasury secretary Robert Walker was equally giddy about the addition of California and the Oregon Country. "Asia has suddenly become our neighbor, . . . inviting our steamships upon the trade of a commerce greater than all of Europe combined."

The acquisition of the northern Mexican provinces made the United States a transcontinental nation and required a dramatic expansion of the federal government. In 1849, Congress created the Department of the Interior to supervise the distribution of land, the creation of new territories and states, and the "protection" of the Indians and their reservations. Americans now had their long coveted western empire. But what were they to do with it?

MAJOR CAMPAIGNS OF THE MEXICAN-AMERICAN WAR

- Why did John C. Frémont and his troops initially settle in the Salinas Valley before marching north, only to turn around and march south to San Francisco?

President Polk had naively assumed that the expansion of American territory to the Pacific would strengthen "the bonds of Union." He was wrong. No sooner was Texas annexed and gold discovered in California than a violent debate erupted over the extension of slavery into the territories acquired from Mexico. That debate would enflame sectional rivalries that would nearly destroy the Union.

CHAPTER REVIEW

SUMMARY

- **Westward Migration**   In the 1830s, Americans came to believe in *"manifest destiny"*—that the West was divinely ordained to be part of the United States. Although populated by Indians and Hispanics, the West was portrayed as an empty land. But a population explosion and the lure of cheap, fertile land prompted Americans to move along the *Overland Trails*, enduring great physical hardships, toward Oregon (*Oregon fever*) and California. Traders and trappers were the first Americans to move into California during the 1830s. The discovery of gold there in 1848 brought a flood of people from all over the world. Many southerners also moved to the Mexican province of Texas to grow cotton, taking their slaves with them. The Mexican government opposed slavery, however, and in 1830 forbade further immigration. Texians rebelled, winning their independence from Mexico in the *Texas Revolution*, but statehood would not come for another decade because political leaders were determined to avoid war with Mexico over the territory and the issue of adding another slave state to the Union.

- **Mexican-American War**   When the United States finally annexed Texas in 1845, Mexico was furious. The newly elected U.S. president, James K. Polk, sought to acquire California and New Mexico as well, but negotiations soon failed. When Mexican troops crossed the Rio Grande, Polk urged Congress to declare war. American forces eventually won, despite high casualties. In 1848, in the *Treaty of Guadalupe Hidalgo*, Mexico ceded California and New Mexico to the United States and gave up claims to land north of the Rio Grande. The vast acquisition did not strengthen the Union, however. Instead it ignited a fierce dispute over the role of slavery in the new territories.

CHRONOLOGY

1821	Mexico gains independence from Spain
1836	Americans are defeated at the Alamo
1841	John Tyler becomes president
1842	Americans and British agree to the Webster-Ashburton Treaty
1845	United States annexes Texas
1846	Mexican-American War begins
1848	Treaty of Guadalupe Hidalgo ends the Mexican-American War
1853	With the Gadsden Purchase, the United States acquires an additional 30,000 square miles from Mexico

Key Terms

🐰 InQuizitive

Go to InQuizitive to see what you've learned—and learn what you've missed—with personalized feedback along the way.

14 The Gathering Storm

1848–1860

"Bleeding Kansas" (1856) This engraving depicts the sack of Lawrence, Kansas, in May 1856 by pro-slavery "border ruffians." The violence sparked by these slave-holding Missourians proved to be a foreboding sign of the destruction that would engulf the nation in the coming decade.

A t midcentury, political storm clouds were forming over the fate of slavery. Without intending to, the United States had developed two quite different societies, one in the North and the other in the South, and the two sections increasingly disagreed over the nation's future. In 1833, Andrew Jackson had predicted that southerners "intend to blow up a storm on the slave question." He added that pro-slavery firebrands like John C. Calhoun "would do any act to destroy this union and form a southern confederacy bounded, north, by the Potomac River." By 1848, Jackson's prediction seemed close to reality.

The sectional tensions over slavery generated constant political conflict. The Compromise of 1850 provided a short-term resolution of some of the issues dividing North and South, but new controversies such as the fate of slavery in the Kansas Territory, the creation of the anti-slavery Republican party, and the growing militancy of abolitionists led more and more people to decide that the United States could not continue to be a nation "half slave and half free," as Abraham Lincoln insisted. The result was first the secession of eleven southern states and then a bloody civil war to force them back into the Union. In the process, the volatile issue of slavery was resolved by ending the "peculiar institution."

SLAVERY IN THE TERRITORIES

THE WILMOT PROVISO On August 8, 1846, soon after the Mexican-American War erupted, David Wilmot, an obscure Democratic congressman from Pennsylvania, delivered a speech to the House of Representatives in which he endorsed the annexation of Texas as a slave state. But if any *new* territory should be acquired as a result of the war with Mexico, he declared,

1. How did the federal government try to resolve the issue of slavery in the western territories during the 1850s?

2. What appealed to northern voters about the Republican party? How did this lead to Abraham Lincoln's victory in the 1860 presidential contest?

3. Why did seven southern states secede from the Union shortly after Lincoln's election in 1860?

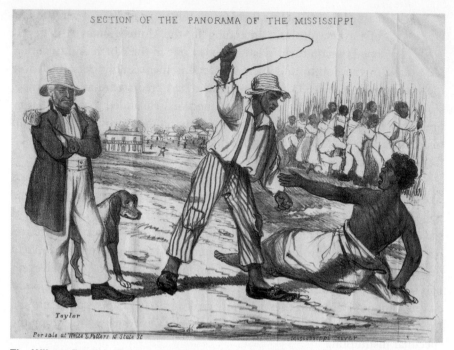

The Wilmot Proviso Taylor would refuse to veto the proviso as president, even though he was a slave owner. This political cartoon, "Old Zack at Home," highlights his seeming hypocrisy.

"God forbid" that slavery would be allowed there. He proposed a bill ("proviso") doing just that. In part, his opposition to slavery in Mexican territories reflected his desire to keep southern political power in Congress from expanding.

The proposed **Wilmot Proviso** reignited debate over the westward extension of slavery. The Missouri Compromise (1820) had provided a temporary solution by protecting slavery in states where it already existed but not allowing it in newly acquired territories. Now, with the possible addition of the territories taken from Mexico, the stage was set for an even more explosive debate.

The House of Representatives approved the Wilmot Proviso, but the Senate balked at the insistence of southern members. When Congress reconvened in December 1846, President Polk dismissed the proviso as "mischievous and foolish." He convinced Wilmot to withhold his amendment from any bill dealing with the annexation of Mexican territory. By then, however, others were ready to take up the cause. In one form or another, Wilmot's idea would continue to frame the debate in Congress for years thereafter.

POPULAR SOVEREIGNTY Senator Lewis Cass of Michigan, a Democrat, tried to remove the explosive controversy over slavery from national politics by giving the voters in each *territory* the right to "regulate their own internal concerns in their own way," like the citizens of a state.

Popular sovereignty, as Cass's idea was called, appealed to many because it seemed to be the most democratic solution. The moral defects of popular sovereignty, however, were obvious: it did not allow African Americans to vote on their fate, and it allowed a majority of whites to take away the most basic human right: freedom.

When Polk followed through on his promise to serve only one term and refused to run again in 1848, Cass won the Democrats' presidential nomination. But the party refused to endorse his "popular sovereignty" plan. Instead, it simply denied the power of Congress to interfere with slavery in the states and criticized all efforts by anti-slavery activists to bring the question of restricting or abolishing slavery before Congress.

The Whigs, as in 1840, again passed over their leader, Henry Clay, a three-time presidential loser. This time they nominated General Zachary Taylor, whose fame had grown during the Mexican-American War. Taylor, born in Virginia and raised in Kentucky, now owned a Louisiana plantation with more than 100 slaves. But he was also an ardent nationalist who vigorously opposed the extension of slavery into new western territories.

THE FREE-SOIL MOVEMENT As it had done in 1840, the Whig party offered no platform in the 1844 campaign in an effort to avoid the divisive issue of slavery. The anti-slavery crusade was not easily silenced, however. Americans who worried about the morality of slavery but could not endorse abolition could support banning slavery from the western territories. As a result, "free soil" in the new territories became the rallying cry for a new political organization: the Free-Soil party.

The **Free-Soil party** attracted three groups: northern Democrats opposed to slavery, anti-slavery northern Whigs, and members of the abolitionist Liberty party. In 1848, the Free-Soil party gathered to nominate former president Martin Van Buren as its candidate. The party's platform stressed that slavery would not be allowed in the western territories. The new party infuriated John C. Calhoun and other southern Democrats. Calhoun called Van Buren a "bold, unscrupulous and vindictive demagogue."

In the 1848 election, the Free-Soilers were spoilers: they split the Democratic vote enough to throw New York to the Whigs' Zachary Taylor, and they split the Whig vote enough to give Ohio to the Democrat Lewis Cass. But nationwide, Van Buren's 291,000 votes lagged well behind the totals of 1,361,000 for Taylor and 1,222,000 for Cass. Taylor won with 163 to 127 electoral votes.

THE CALIFORNIA GOLD RUSH Meanwhile, a new issue had emerged to complicate the growing debate over territorial expansion and slavery. On January 24, 1848, gold nuggets were discovered in a stream on the property of John A. Sutter along the south fork of the American River in the Mexican province of California, which nine days later would be transferred to the United States through the treaty ending the Mexican-American War.

News of the gold strike spread like wildfire, especially after President Polk announced to Congress that there was an "extraordinary abundance of gold" in California and other territories acquired from Mexico. Suddenly, a gold mania infected the nation. "We are on the brink of the Age of Gold," gushed Horace Greeley, editor of the *New York Tribune*.

In 1849, nearly 100,000 Americans, mostly men, set off for California, eager to find riches. Sailors jumped ship, soldiers deserted, and husbands abandoned their families to join the **California gold rush**. "Men are here nearly crazed with the riches forced suddenly into their pockets," a Tennessean wrote. By 1854, the number of newcomers would top 300,000, and the surge of interest in California's golden news added to the urgency of bringing the profitable new western territory into the Union.

The gold rush was the greatest mass migration in American history—and one of the most significant events in the first half of the nineteenth century. Between 1851 and 1855, California produced almost half of the world's output of gold. The infusion of California gold into the U.S. economy led to a prolonged national prosperity that eventually helped finance the Union military effort in the Civil War. In addition, it spurred the construction of railroads and telegraph lines, hastened the demise of the Indians, and excited dreams of an American economic empire based in the Pacific.

MINING LIFE The miners were mostly unmarried young men of varied ethnic and cultural backgrounds. Few were interested in staying in California; they wanted to strike it rich and return home. Mining camps thus sprang up like mushrooms and disappeared almost as rapidly. As soon as rumors of a new strike made the rounds, miners converged on the area; when no more gold could be found, they picked up and moved on.

Women were as rare in the mining camps as liquor and guns were abundant. In 1850, less than 8 percent of California's population was female. The few women who dared to live in the camps could demand a premium for their work as cooks, laundresses, entertainers, and prostitutes. In the mining camps,

Gold miners Chinese immigrants and white settlers mine for gold in the Auburn Ravine of California in 1856.

white miners often looked with disdain upon the Hispanics and Chinese, who were most often employed as wage laborers to help in the panning process, separating gold from sand and gravel. But the whites focused their contempt on the Indians: it was not considered a crime to kill Indians or work them to death.

THE COMPROMISE OF 1850 By late 1849, as confrontations over slavery mounted, each national political party was dividing into factions along North–South lines. Irate southern Whigs abandoned their party and joined the pro-slavery Democrats. Some threatened that their states would leave the Union if President Taylor followed through on his proposal to bring California and New Mexico directly into the Union as free states, skipping the territorial phase.

Jefferson Davis, Taylor's son-in-law, dismissed the president's plan as being anti-southern. Taylor responded by criticizing "intolerant and revolutionary southerners." Southerners—ministers, planters, and politicians—rushed to attack the president. "I avow before this House and country, and in the presence of the living God," shouted Robert Toombs, a Georgia congressman, "that if by your legislation you seek to drive us [slaveholders] from the territories of California and New Mexico . . . and to abolish slavery in this District [of Columbia] . . . *I am for disunion.*"

As the controversy unfolded, the spotlight fell on the Senate, where an all-star cast of outsized personalities with swollen egos resolved to find a way to preserve the Union. The "lions" of the Senate—Henry Clay, John C. Calhoun, and Daniel Webster (all of whom would die within two years)—took center stage, with William H. Seward, Stephen A. Douglas, and Jefferson Davis in supporting roles. Together, they staged one of the great dramas of American politics: the **Compromise of 1850**, a ten-month-long debate over a series of resolutions intended to reduce the crisis between North and South that had "unhinged" both political parties.

IN SEARCH OF COMPROMISE With southern extremists threatening secession, congressional leaders again turned to an aging Henry Clay, now seventy-two years old and struggling with tuberculosis. As Abraham Lincoln acknowledged, Clay was "regarded by all, as *the* man for the crisis." No man had amassed a more distinguished political career. Clay had gained every position he had sought except the presidency: senator, congressman, Speaker of the House, secretary of state.

Now, as his career was winding down, Clay hoped to save the Union by presenting his own plan to end another sectional crisis. On December 3, 1849, as the Thirty-First Congress assembled for what would become the longest session in its history, Clay strode into the Senate to waves of applause. He asked to be relieved of all committee responsibilities so that he could focus on the national crisis. Unless some compromise could be found, the slaveholding Clay warned, a "furious" civil war would fracture the Union.

The next day, in his annual message to Congress, President Taylor urged immediate statehood for California and the same as soon as possible for New Mexico. He then pleaded with Congress to avoid injecting slavery into the issue. It was too late, however. Admitting California as a free state would tip the political balance against slavery, with sixteen free states to fifteen slave states. The slaveholding states would become a permanent minority. As Jefferson Davis argued, the South could not allow that to happen.

Taylor hoped that his proposals would "create confidence and kind feeling" among the contending sections. But his speech only aggravated the seething tensions. It took weeks of combative debate before a Speaker of the House, Georgia slaveholder Howell Cobb, could be elected on the sixty-third ballot. "Madness rules the hour," wrote Philip Hone, a New York Whig, in his diary. For the first time in history, he noted, members of Congress were openly threatening to dissolve the Union.

Clay then stepped into the breach. On January 29, 1850, having gained the wholehearted support of Daniel Webster, the senior senator from Massachusetts whom he had known for thirty-six years, Clay presented to Congress his "amicable" plan for "compromise and harmony." Eager to see the Great Compromiser, people filled the Senate.

Using all of his charm and passion, Clay pleaded with the Senate to pass eight resolutions, six of which were paired as compromises between North and South, and all of which were designed to settle the "controversy between the free and slave states, growing out of the subject of slavery." He proposed (1) to admit California as a free state; (2) to organize the territories of New Mexico and Utah without restrictions on slavery, allowing the residents to decide the issue for themselves; (3) to deny Texas its extreme claim to much of New Mexico; (4) to compensate Texas by having the federal government pay the pre-annexation Texas debts; (5) to retain slavery in the District of Columbia, but (6) to abolish the sale of slaves in the nation's capital; (7) to adopt a more effective federal fugitive slave law ("the recapture of fugitives was not just a legal duty, but a *moral* one"); and (8) to deny congressional authority to interfere with the interstate slave trade.

Clay's cluster of proposals became in substance the Compromise of 1850, but only after seven months of negotiations punctuated by the greatest debates in congressional history. Clay's eloquence had won over the moderates but not those at the extremes: northern abolitionists or southern secessionists.

THE GREAT DEBATE On March 4, a feeble John C. Calhoun, desperately ill with tuberculosis, arrived in the Senate chamber. The uncompromising defender of slavery was so sick and shriveled that a colleague had to read his defiant speech. Calhoun urged that Clay's compromise be rejected. The "great questions" dividing the nation must be settled on southern terms. The South, he explained, needed Congress to protect the rights of slave owners to take their "property" into the new territories. Otherwise, Calhoun warned, the "cords which bind" the Union would be severed. If California were admitted as a free state, the South could no longer "remain honorably and safely in the Union." The southern states would leave the Union (secede) and form their own national government.

Three days later, Calhoun, who would die in three weeks, hobbled into the Senate to hear Daniel Webster speak. Webster was so famous for his theatrical speeches that they were major public events. The visitors' galleries were packed as he rose to address the Senate.

"I wish to speak today," Webster began, "not as a Massachusetts man, not as a Northern man, but as an American. . . . I speak today for the preservation of the Union." He blamed both northerners and southerners for the crisis but acknowledged that both regions had legitimate grievances: the South

Clay's compromise (1850) Warning against an impending sectional conflict, Henry Clay outlines his plan for "compromise and harmony" on the Senate floor.

understandably objected to the excesses of "infernal fanatics and abolitionists" in the North, and the North resented aggressive southern efforts to expand slavery into the new western territories. With respect to escaped slaves, Webster shocked his fellow New Englanders by declaring that "the South, in my judgment, is right, and the North is wrong." Fugitive slaves must be returned to their owners.

Webster had no patience, however, with the notion of secession. Leaving the Union would bring civil war. "Secession! Peaceable secession! Sir, your eyes and mine are never destined to see that miracle." Instead of looking into such "caverns of darkness," let "men enjoy the fresh air of liberty and union. Let them look to a more hopeful future." For almost four hours, he pleaded with his colleagues not to be uncompromising "pigmies" but compromising statesmen.

Webster's evenhanded speech angered both sides. No sooner had he finished than Calhoun stood to assert that the Union could indeed "be broken. Great moral causes will break it." At the same time, northern abolitionists savaged Webster for calling them fanatics.

On March 11, William Seward, a first-year Whig senator from New York, gave an intentionally provocative speech in which he opposed Clay's compromise, declaring that *any* compromise with slavery was "radically wrong and essentially vicious." There was, he said, "a *higher law* than the Constitution," and it demanded the abolition of slavery through acts of civil disobedience. He encouraged his fellow New Yorkers to defy the federal fugitive slave law by extending a "cordial welcome" to escaped slaves and defending them from all efforts to return them south. The southern supporters of slavery, he concluded, must give way to the inevitable "progress of emancipation."

Seward's inflammatory speech outraged southerners, who repudiated his "fanatical and wild notion" of there being a "higher law" than the Constitution and the implication that the godly abolitionists were somehow above the law. Clay felt compelled to dismiss Seward's "wild, reckless, and abominable theories." Seward, however, was unapologetic. He had sought to speak for the enslaved as well as all of humankind.

COMPROMISE EFFORTS On July 4, 1850, Congress took a break and celebrated Independence Day by gathering beneath a broiling summer sun at the base of the unfinished Washington Monument. President Taylor suffered a mild heatstroke while listening to three hours of patriotic speeches. He tried to recover by gorging himself on iced milk, cherries, and raw vegetables. That night, he suddenly developed a violent stomach disorder. He died five days later, the second president to die in office.

Taylor's shocking death actually bolstered the chances of a compromise in Congress, for his successor, Vice President Millard Fillmore, supported Clay's proposals. It was a striking reversal: Taylor, the Louisiana slaveholder, had been ready to make war on his native South to save the Union; Fillmore, whom southerners thought opposed slavery, was ready to make peace. The new president asserted his control by asking his entire cabinet to resign. He then appointed Webster as secretary of state, signaling that he also joined Webster in supporting compromise.

Fillmore was aided by Illinois senator Stephen A. Douglas, a rising young star in the Democratic party, who was friendly to the South. Douglas dramatically stepped up to rescue Clay's struggling plan. Brash and brilliant, short and stocky—he stood just five feet four—Douglas, the "Little Giant" who modeled himself after Andrew Jackson, cleverly suggested that the best way to salvage Clay's "comprehensive scheme" was to break it up into separate proposals and vote on them one at a time. Fillmore endorsed the idea.

The plan worked, in part because John C. Calhoun had died and was no longer in the Senate to obstruct efforts at conciliation. Each component of

Clay's compromise plan passed in the Senate and the House, several of them by the narrowest of margins. (Only five senators voted for all of the items making up the compromise.)

In its final version, the Compromise of 1850 included the following elements: (1) California entered the Union as a free state, ending forever the old balance of free and slave states; (2) the Texas–New Mexico Act made New Mexico a territory and set the Texas boundary at its present location. In return for giving up its claims, Texas was paid $10 million, which secured payment of the state's debt; (3) the Utah Act set up the Utah Territory and gave the territorial legislature authority over "all rightful subjects of legislation" (slavery); (4) a Fugitive Slave Act required the federal government and northern states to help capture and return runaway slaves; and (5) the public sale of slaves, but not slavery itself, was abolished in the District of Columbia.

By September 20, President Fillmore had signed the last of the measures into law, claiming that they represented a "final settlement" to the sectional tensions over slavery. "Let us cease agitating," Douglas urged, "stop the debate, and drop the subject" of slavery.

The so-called Compromise of 1850 defused an explosive situation and settled each of the major points at issue, but it was not so much an example of warring people making concessions as it was a temporary and imperfect truce. As Salmon P. Chase, an Ohio Free-Soiler, stressed, "the question of slavery in the territories has been avoided. It has not been settled." The Compromise of 1850 only postponed secession and civil war for ten years. It was a brilliant form of evading the fundamental issue dividing the nation. Soon, aspects of the compromise would reignite sectional tensions.

THE FUGITIVE SLAVE ACT People were naive to think that the Compromise of 1850 would eliminate discussions about the legitimacy of slavery. Within two months of the bill's passage, the squabbling between North and South resumed.

The **Fugitive Slave Act** was the most controversial element of the Compromise of 1850. It did more than strengthen the hand of slave catchers; it sought to recover slaves who had already escaped. The law also unwittingly enabled slave traders to kidnap free blacks in northern "free" states, claiming that they were runaway slaves. The law denied fugitives a jury trial. In addition, citizens under the new law were forced to help locate and capture runaways.

Abolitionists fumed. "This filthy enactment was made in the nineteenth century, by people who could read and write," Ralph Waldo Emerson marveled in his diary. He urged people to break the new law "on the earliest occasion."

In the eleven years of the Fugitive Slave Act, barely more than 300 escaped slaves were returned to bondage. The mere existence of the Fugitive Slave Act, however, infuriated northern abolitionists and prompted several to advocate violence. "The only way to make the Fugitive Slave Law a dead letter," Frederick Douglass threatened, "is to make half-a-dozen or more dead kidnappers." In Springfield, Massachusetts, a fiery abolitionist named John Brown formed an armed band of African Americans, called the League of Gileadites, to attack slave catchers.

UNCLE TOM'S CABIN During the 1850s, anti-slavery advocates gained a powerful new weapon in the form of Harriet Beecher Stowe's best-selling novel, *Uncle Tom's Cabin; or Life among the Lowly* (1852). The pious Stowe epitomized the powerful religious underpinnings of the abolitionist movement. While raising six children in Cincinnati, Ohio, during the 1830s and 1840s, she helped runaway slaves who had crossed the Ohio River from Kentucky.

Like many anti-slavery activists, Stowe was disgusted by the Fugitive Slave Act. In the spring of 1850, having moved to Maine, she began writing *Uncle Tom's Cabin.* "The time has come," she wrote, "when even a woman or a child who can speak a word for freedom and humanity is bound to speak."

Uncle Tom's Cabin was a smashing success. Within two days, the first printing had sold out, and by the end of its first year, it had sold 300,000 copies in the United States and more than a million in Great Britain. Soon there was a children's version and a traveling theater production. By 1855, it was called "the most popular novel of our day."

The novel revealed how the brutal realities of slavery harmed everyone associated with it. Abolitionist leader Frederick Douglass, a former slave himself, said that *Uncle Tom's Cabin* was like "a flash" that lit "a million camp fires in front of the embattled host of slavery." Slaveholders were

"The Greatest Book of the Age" *Uncle Tom's Cabin*, as this advertisement indicated, was an influential best seller.

incensed by the book, calling Stowe that "wretch in petticoats." One of them mailed her a parcel containing the severed ear of a disobedient slave.

THE ELECTION OF 1852 In 1852, it took the Democrats forty-nine ballots before they chose Franklin Pierce of New Hampshire as their presidential candidate. When Pierce heard the results, he was stunned: "You are looking at the most surprised man who ever lived!" When his wife Jane learned of the nomination, she fainted. Their concerns were well-founded.

The Democrats' platform endorsed the Compromise of 1850, including enforcement of the Fugitive Slave Act. For their part, the Whigs repudiated the lackluster Millard Fillmore, who had faithfully supported the Compromise of 1850, and chose General Winfield Scott, a hero of the Mexican-American War.

Scott, however, proved to be an inept campaigner. He carried only Tennessee, Kentucky, Massachusetts, and Vermont. The Whigs, now without their greatest leaders, Henry Clay and Daniel Webster, lost virtually all of their support in the Lower South. Pierce overwhelmed Scott in the electoral college, 254 to 42, although the popular vote was close: 1.6 million to 1.4 million. The third-party Free-Soilers mustered only 156,000 votes.

The 48-year-old Pierce, an undistinguished congressman and senator who had fought in the Mexican-American War, was, like James K. Polk, touted as another Andrew Jackson. Pierce eagerly promoted western expansion and the conversion of more territories into states, even if it meant adding more slave states to the Union, but he also acknowledged that the Compromise of 1850 had defused a "perilous crisis." He urged both North and South to avoid aggravating the other. As a Georgia editor noted, however, the feud between the two regions might be "smothered, but never overcome."

As president, Pierce proved unable to unite the warring factions of his own party. By the end of his first year in office, Democratic leaders had decided that he was a failure. James W. Forney, a political friend, confessed that the presidency "overshadows him. He is crushed by its great duties and seeks refuge in [alcohol]." By trying to be all things to all people, Pierce was labeled a "doughface": a "Northern man with Southern principles." His closest friend in the cabinet was Secretary of War Jefferson Davis, the future president of the Confederacy. Such friendships led Harriet Beecher Stowe to call Pierce an "arch-traitor."

THE KANSAS-NEBRASKA CRISIS During the mid–nineteenth century, Americans discovered the vast markets of Asia. As trade with China and Japan grew, merchants and manufacturers called for a transcontinental

railroad connecting the Eastern Seaboard with the Pacific coast to facilitate
both the flow of commerce with Asia
and the settlement of the western territories. Those promoting the railroad
did not realize that the issue would
renew sectional rivalries and reignite
the debate over the westward extension
of slavery.

In 1852 and 1853, Congress considered several proposals for a transcontinental rail line. Secretary of War
Jefferson Davis of Mississippi favored
a southern route across the territories
acquired from Mexico. Senator Stephen A. Douglas of Illinois insisted
that Chicago be the Midwest hub for
the new rail line and urged Congress to
pass the **Kansas-Nebraska Act** so that
the vast territory west of Missouri and
Iowa could be settled.

Stephen A. Douglas, ca. 1852 The
Illinois Democratic senator authored
the Kansas-Nebraska Act.

To win the support of southern legislators, Douglas championed "popular sovereignty," whereby voters in each new territory would decide whether
to allow slavery. It was a clever way to get around the 1820 Missouri Compromise, which excluded slaves north of the 36th parallel, where Kansas and
Nebraska were located.

Southerners demanded more, however, and Douglas reluctantly complied.
Although he knew it would "raise a hell of a storm" in the North, Douglas supported the South in recommending the formal repeal of the Missouri Compromise and the creation of *two* new territorial governments rather than one:
Kansas, west of Missouri, and Nebraska, west of Iowa and Minnesota. This
meant that millions of fertile acres would be opened to slaveholders. What
came to be called the Kansas-Nebraska Act "took us by surprise—astounded
us," recalled Abraham Lincoln.

In May 1854, Douglas masterfully assembled the votes for his Kansas-
Nebraska Act, recruiting both Democrats and southern Whigs. The measure
passed by a vote of 37 to 14 in the Senate and 113 to 100 in the House. The
anti-slavery faction in Congress, mostly Whigs, had been crushed, and the
national Whig party essentially died with them. Out of its ashes would arise a
new party: the Republicans.

THE EMERGENCE OF THE REPUBLICAN PARTY

The dispute over the Kansas-Nebraska Act led northern anti-slavery Whigs and some northern anti-slavery Democrats to gravitate toward two new parties. One was the American ("Know-Nothing") party, which had emerged in response to the surge of mostly Catholic immigrants from Ireland and Germany, nearly 3 million of whom arrived in the United States between 1845 and 1854. Many of the immigrants were poor and Catholic, which made them especially unwanted. The "Know-Nothings" embraced nativism (opposition to foreign immigrants) by denying citizenship to newcomers. Many also were opposed to the territorial expansion of slavery and the "fanaticism" of abolitionists.

The other new party, the Republicans, attracted even more northern Whigs. It was formed in February 1854 when the so-called "conscience Whigs" (those opposed to slavery) split from the southern pro-slavery "cotton Whigs." The conscience Whigs joined with anti-slavery Democrats and Free-Soilers to form a new party dedicated to the exclusion of slavery from the western territories.

"BLEEDING KANSAS" The passage of the Kansas-Nebraska Act soon placed Kansas at the center of the increasingly violent debate over slavery. While Nebraska would become a free state, Kansas was up for grabs. According to the Kansas-Nebraska Act, the residents of the Kansas Territory were "perfectly free to form and regulate their domestic institutions [slavery] in their own way." The law, however, said nothing about *when* Kansans could decide about slavery, so each side tried to gain political control of the vast territory. "Come on then, Gentlemen of the Slave States," New York senator William Seward taunted. "We will engage in competition for the virgin soil of Kansas, and God give the victory to the side which is stronger in numbers as it is in the right."

Groups for and against slavery recruited armed emigrants to move to Kansas. "Every slaveholding state," said an observer, "is furnishing men and money to fasten slavery upon this glorious land, by means no matter how foul." When Kansas's first federal governor arrived in 1854, he sent an urgent message to President Pierce, reporting that southerners were arriving with a "dogged determination to force slavery into this Territory" in advance of an election of a territorial legislature in March 1855.

On Election Day, thousands of heavily armed "border ruffians" from Missouri traveled into Kansas, illegally elected pro-slavery legislators, and vowed to kill every "God-damned abolitionist in the Territory." As soon as it convened, the territorial legislature expelled its few anti-slavery members and declared that the territory would be open to slavery. The governor then rushed to Washington, D.C., to plead with Pierce to intervene with federal troops. Pierce acknowledged that he was concerned about the situation, but his spineless solution was to replace the territorial governor with a man who would support the pro-slavery faction.

Outraged free-state advocates in Kansas, now a majority, spurned this "bogus" government and elected their own delegates to a constitutional convention which met in Topeka in 1855. They drafted a state constitution excluding slavery and applied for statehood. By 1856, a free-state "governor" and "legislature" were operating in Topeka. There were now two illegal govern-

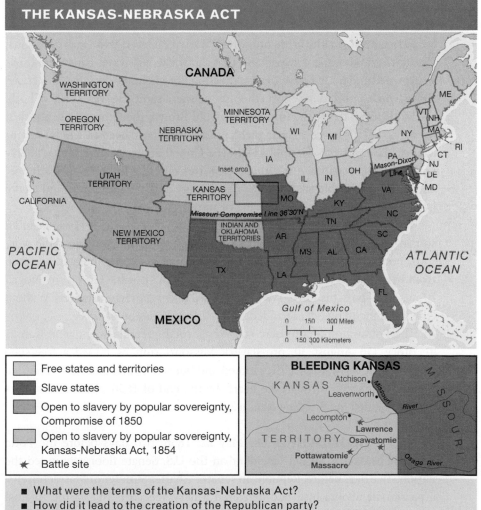

THE KANSAS-NEBRASKA ACT

Free states and territories
Slave states
Open to slavery by popular sovereignty, Compromise of 1850
Open to slavery by popular sovereignty, Kansas-Nebraska Act, 1854
★ Battle site

BLEEDING KANSAS

- What were the terms of the Kansas-Nebraska Act?
- How did it lead to the creation of the Republican party?
- What happened at Pottawatomie and Osawatomie?

ments claiming to rule the Kansas Territory. And soon there was a territorial civil war, which journalists called "**Bleeding Kansas**."

In May 1856, a pro-slavery force of more than 500 Missourians, Alabamans, and South Carolinians invaded the free-state town of Lawrence, Kansas, just twenty-five miles from the Missouri border. David Atchison, a former U.S. senator from Missouri, urged the southern raiders not "to slacken or stop until every spark of free-state, free-speech, free-niggers, or *free* in any shape is quenched out of Kansas." The mob rampaged through the town, destroying the newspaper printing presses, burning homes, and ransacking shops.

The "Sack of Lawrence" ignited the passions of abolitionist John Brown. The son of fervent Ohio Calvinists who taught their children that life was a crusade against sin, the grim, humorless Brown believed that Christians must "break the jaws of the wicked," and that the wickedest Americans were those who owned and traded slaves. Upon meeting Brown, many declared him crazy; those who supported his efforts thought he was a saint. He was a little of both.

By the mid-1850s, the fifty-five-year-old Brown, the father of twenty children, had left his home in Springfield, Massachusetts, to become a holy warrior against slavery. In his view, blacks in the United States deserved both liberty and full social equality. A newspaper reporter said that Brown was a "strange" and "iron-willed" old man with a "fiery nature and a cold temper, and a cool head—a volcano beneath a covering of snow."

Two days after the attack on Lawrence, Brown led four of his sons and a son-in-law to Pottawatomie, Kansas, a pro-slavery settlement near the Missouri border. On the night of May 24, Brown and his group dragged five men from their houses and hacked them to death with swords. "God is my judge," Brown told one of his sons. "We were justified under the circumstances." Without "the shedding of blood," he added, "there is no remission of sins."

The Pottawatomie Massacre started a brutal guerrilla war in the Kansas Territory. On August 30, pro-slavery Missouri ruffians raided a free-state settlement at Osawatomie. They looted and burned houses and shot Frederick Brown, John's son, through the heart. By the end of 1856, about 200 settlers had been killed in "Bleeding Kansas."

SENATE BLOODSHED On May 22, 1856, two days before the Pottawatomie Massacre, an ugly incident on the U.S. Senate floor astounded the nation. Two days before, Republican senator Charles Sumner of Massachusetts, a passionate abolitionist, had delivered a fiery speech ("The Crime Against Kansas") in which he showered slave owners with insults and charged them with unleashing thugs and assassins in Kansas. His most savage attack was directed at Andrew Pickens Butler, an elderly senator from South Carolina, a state that Sumner said displayed a "shameful imbecility" resulting from its passion for slavery. Butler, Sumner charged, was a fumbling old man who had "chosen a mistress . . . who . . . though polluted in the sight of the world, is chaste [pure] in his sight—I mean the harlot [prostitute], Slavery."

Sumner's speech enraged Butler's cousin Preston S. Brooks, a South Carolina congressman with a hair-trigger temper. On May 22, Brooks confronted Sumner as he sat at his Senate desk. Brooks shouted that Sumner had slandered Butler and the state of South Carolina, then began beating him about the head with a gold-knobbed walking stick until the cane splintered. Sumner, his head gushing blood, nearly died; he would not return to the Senate for almost four years.

In the South, Butler was celebrated as a hero. The *Richmond Enquirer* described his attack as "good in conception, better in execution, and best of all in consequences." Dozens of south-

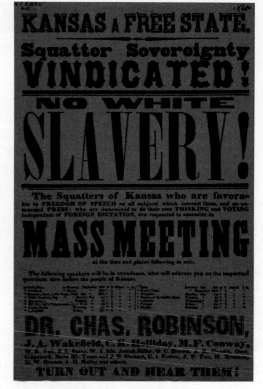

Kansas a Free State This broadside advertises a series of mass meetings in Kansas in support of the free-state cause, based on the principle of "squatter" or popular sovereignty, letting the residents decide the issue of slavery.

erners sent Butler new canes. In satisfying his rage, though, Brooks had created a martyr—"Bloodied Sumner"—for the anti-slavery cause. Sumner's empty Senate seat would serve as a solemn reminder of the violence done to him. His brutal beating also had an unintended political effect: it drove more northerners into the new Republican party.

SECTIONAL SQUABBLES The violence of "Bleeding Kansas" and "Bloodied Sumner" spilled over into the tone of the 1856 presidential election—one in which the major parties could no longer evade the slavery issue. At its first national convention, the Republicans fastened on the eccentric John C. Frémont, "the Pathfinder," who had led the conquest of Mexican California.

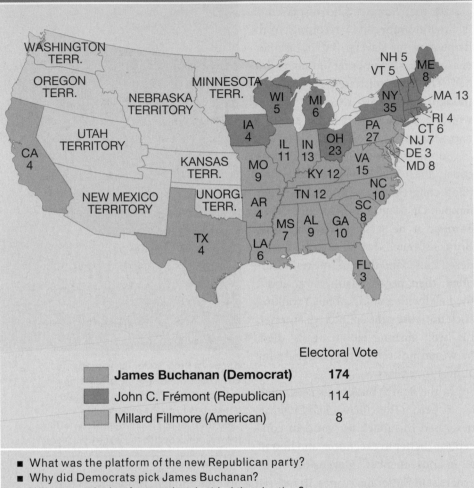

THE ELECTION OF 1856

WASHINGTON TERR.

OREGON TERR.

NEBRASKA TERRITORY

MINNESOTA TERR.

NH 5
VT 5
ME 8
NY 35
MA 13
RI 4
CT 6
PA 27
NJ 7
DE 3
MD 8

WI 5
MI 6

IA 4

UTAH TERRITORY

CA 4

KANSAS TERR.

IL 11
IN 13
OH 23

MO 9

KY 12
VA 15

NEW MEXICO TERRITORY

UNORG. TERR.

AR 4

TN 12

NC 10

SC 8

TX 4

LA 6

MS 7
AL 9
GA 10

FL 3

Electoral Vote

James Buchanan (Democrat)   174

John C. Frémont (Republican)   114

Millard Fillmore (American)   8

- What was the platform of the new Republican party?
- Why did Democrats pick James Buchanan?
- What were the key factors that decided the election?

The Republican platform borrowed heavily from the former Whigs. It endorsed federal funding for a transcontinental railroad and other transportation improvements. It denounced the repeal of the Missouri Compromise, the Democratic party's policy of territorial expansion, and the "barbarism" of slavery. For the first time, a major-party platform had taken a stand against slavery.

The southern-dominated Democrats dumped President Franklin Pierce, who remains the only elected president to be denied renomination by his party. Instead, they chose sixty-five-year-old James Buchanan of Pennsylvania, a former senator and secretary of state who had long sought the nomination.

The Democratic platform endorsed the Kansas-Nebraska Act, called for vigorous enforcement of the Fugitive Slave Act, and stressed that Congress should not interfere with slavery in states or territories.

In the campaign of 1856, the Republicans had very few southern supporters and only a handful in the border slave states of Delaware, Maryland, Kentucky, and Missouri. Frémont swept the northernmost states with 114 electoral votes, but Buchanan added five free states—Pennsylvania, New Jersey, Illinois, Indiana, and California—to his southern majority for a total of 174. The Democrats now would control the White House, the Congress, and the Supreme Court.

PRESIDENT BUCHANAN As Franklin Pierce prepared to leave the White House in March 1857, a friend asked what he was going to do. Pierce replied: "There's nothing left to do but get drunk."

James Buchanan also loved to drink, but he had different priorities. The president-elect had built his political career on his commitment to states' rights and his aggressive promotion of territorial expansion. Saving the Union, he believed, depended upon making concessions to the South. Republicans charged that he lacked the backbone to stand up to the southern slaveholders who dominated the Democratic majorities in Congress. His choice of four slave-state men and only three free-state men for his cabinet seemed another bad sign. It was.

Although Buchanan had vast experience, he had limited ability—and bad luck. During his first six months in office, two major events caused his undoing: (1) the Supreme Court decision in the *Dred Scott* case, and (2) new troubles in strife-torn Kansas.

The Financial Panic of 1857 only made a bad situation worse, for the new president and for the nation. By the summer of 1857, the economy was growing too fast. Too many railroads and factories were being built, and European demand for American corn and wheat was declining. The result was a financial panic triggered by the failure of the Ohio Life Insurance and Trust Company on August 24, 1857.

Upon hearing the news, worried customers began withdrawing their money from banks, which forced the banks to call in loans, causing many businesses to go bankrupt. By the fall, newspapers across the North highlighted the "hard times" that had befallen the nation. Jobless men roamed city streets demanding work or food or money. Federal troops had to be sent to disperse angry mobs in New York City.

Planters in the South, whose agricultural economy suffered the least during the panic, took great delight in the problems plaguing the northern economy.

Senator James Henry Hammond of South Carolina gave a speech in early 1858 in which he told northern businessmen

> Your slaves are white, of your own race; you are brothers of one blood. They are your equals in natural endowment of intellect, and they feel galled by your degradation. Our slaves do not vote. We give them no political power. Yours do vote, and being the majority, they are the depositories of all your political power.

Hammond suggested that the North adopt race-based slavery to prevent working-class whites from taking control of the social and political order. "Cotton is king," he triumphantly roared, and race-based slavery made it so.

THE *DRED SCOTT* CASE On March 6, 1857, two days after Buchanan's inauguration, the Supreme Court delivered a decision in the long-pending case of ***Dred Scott v. Sandford***. Scott, born a slave in Virginia, had been taken to St. Louis in 1830 and sold to an army surgeon, who took him to Illinois, then to the Wisconsin Territory (later Minnesota), and finally back to St. Louis in 1842. While in the Wisconsin Territory, Scott had married Harriet Robinson, and they eventually had two daughters.

In 1846, Scott filed suit in Missouri, claiming that his residence in Illinois and the Wisconsin Territory had made him free because slavery was outlawed in those areas. A jury decided in his favor, but the state supreme court ruled against him. When the case was appealed to the U.S. Supreme Court, the nation anxiously awaited its opinion on whether freedom once granted could be lost by returning to a slave state.

Seven of the nine justices were Democrats, and five were southerners. The vote was 7 to 2 against Scott. Seventy-nine-year-old Chief Justice Roger B. Taney of Maryland, a supporter of the South and of slavery, wrote the majority opinion. The chief justice ruled that Scott lacked legal standing because, like all former slaves, he was not a U.S. citizen. At the time the Constitution was adopted, Taney claimed, blacks "had for more than a century been regarded as . . . so far inferior, that they had no rights which the white man was bound to respect." On the issue of Scott's residency, Taney argued that the now-defunct Missouri Compromise of 1820 had deprived citizens of property by prohibiting slavery in selected states, an action "not warranted by the Constitution."

In the *Dred Scott* decision the Supreme Court had declared an act of Congress (the Missouri Compromise) unconstitutional for the first time since *Marbury v. Madison* (1803). Even more important, the decision now challenged the concept of popular sovereignty. If Congress itself could not exclude slavery from a territory, as Taney argued, then neither could a territorial government created by an act of Congress.

Yet instead of settling the issue of slavery in the territories, Taney's ruling fanned the flames. Pro-slavery advocates loved the Court's decision. Even President Buchanan approved. Republicans, on the other hand, protested the *Dred Scott* decision because it nullified their anti-slavery program.

THE LECOMPTON CONSTITUTION Meanwhile, in the Kansas Territory, the violent struggle over slavery continued. Just before James Buchanan's inauguration, in early 1857, the pro-slavery territorial legislature scheduled a constitutional convention. The governor vetoed the measure, but the legislature overrode his veto. The governor resigned in protest, and Buchanan replaced him with Robert J. Walker.

With Buchanan's approval, Governor Walker pledged to free-state Kansans (who made up an overwhelming majority of the residents) that the new constitution would be submitted to a fair vote. But when the pro-slavery constitutional convention, meeting at Lecompton, drafted a constitution under which Kansas would become a slave state, opponents of slavery boycotted the vote on the new constitution.

At that point, Buchanan took a critical step. Influenced by southern advisers and politically dependent upon southern congressmen, he endorsed the pro-slavery Lecompton convention. A new wave of outrage swept across the northern states. Stephen A. Douglas, the most prominent Midwestern Democrat, sided with anti-slavery Republicans because the majority of Kansas voters had been denied the right to decide the issue. Douglas told a newspaper reporter that "I made Mr. James Buchanan, and by God, sir, I will unmake him."

The rigged election in Kansas went as predicted: 6,226 for the constitution with slavery, 569 for the constitution without slavery. Meanwhile, a new acting governor had organized the anti-slavery legislature, which scheduled another election to decide the fate of the Lecompton Constitution up or down. Most of the pro-slavery settlers boycotted this election.

The result, on January 4, 1858, was decisive: 10,226 voted against the Lecompton Constitution, while only 138 voted for it. In April 1858, Congress ordered that Kansans vote again. On August 2, 1858, they rejected the constitution, 11,300 to 1,788. With that vote, Kansas cleared the way for its eventual admission as a free state.

DOUGLAS VERSUS LINCOLN The controversy over slavery in Kansas fractured the Democratic party. Stephen A. Douglas, one of the few remaining Democrats with support in both the North and the South, struggled to keep the party together. But first he had to secure his home base in Illinois, where in 1858 he faced reelection to the Senate.

To challenge Douglas, Illinois Republicans selected a respected lawyer from Springfield, Abraham Lincoln. Lincoln had served in the Illinois legislature and in 1846 had won a seat in the U.S. Congress. After a single unremarkable term, he returned to Springfield. In 1854, however, the Kansas-Nebraska Act drew Lincoln back into the political arena. Lincoln hated slavery but was no abolitionist. He did not believe that the nation should force the South to end "the monstrous injustice" but did insist that slavery not be expanded into new western territories.

In 1856, Lincoln joined the Republican party, and two years later he emerged as the obvious choice to oppose Douglas. Lincoln sought to raise his profile by challenging Douglas to a series of debates across the state. The seven **Lincoln-Douglas debates** took place from August 21 to October 15, 1858. They attracted tens of thousands of spectators and transformed the Illinois Senate race into a battle for the very future of the republic.

The basic difference between the two candidates, Lincoln insisted, lay in Douglas's indifference to the immorality of slavery. Douglas, he said, was preoccupied only with process ("popular sovereignty"); in contrast, Lincoln claimed to be focused on principle. "I have always hated slavery as much as any abolitionist," he stressed. The American government, he predicted, could not "endure, permanently half *slave* and half *free*. . . . It will become *all* one thing, or *all* the other." Douglas disagreed, asking what was to keep the United States from tolerating both slavery for blacks and freedom for whites? Douglas won the close election, but Lincoln's energetic underdog campaign made him a national figure. And across the northern states, the Republicans won so many congressional seats in 1858 that they seized control of the House of Representatives.

AN OUTNUMBERED SOUTH By the late 1850s, national politics was undergoing profound changes. In May 1858, the free state of Minnesota entered the Union; in February 1859, another non-slave territory, Oregon, gained statehood. The slave states of the South were quickly becoming a besieged minority, and their insecurity, even paranoia, deepened.

At the same time, political tensions over slavery were becoming more violent. In 1858, members of Congress engaged in the largest brawl ever staged on the floor of the House of Representatives. The fracas ended when John "Bowie Knife" Potter of Wisconsin yanked off the wig of a Mississippi congressman and claimed, "I've scalped him."

Like the scuffling congressmen, more and more Americans began to feel that compromise was impossible; slavery could be ended or defended only with violence. The editor of a pro-slavery Kansas newspaper wanted to kill abolitionists: "If I can't kill a man, I'll kill a woman; and if I can't kill a woman, I'll kill a child." Some southerners were already talking of secession. In 1858, former Alabama congressman William L. Yancey, the leader of a group of hot-tempered southern secessionists called "fire-eaters," said that it would be easy "to precipitate the Cotton States into a revolution."

JOHN BROWN'S RAID The gradual return of prosperity in 1859 offered hope that the sectional storms of the 1850s might pass, but the slavery issue continued to simmer. In October 1859, the militant abolitionist John Brown surfaced again, this time in the East. Since the Pottawatomie Massacre in Kansas in 1856, he had kept a low profile while acquiring money and weapons from New England sym-

John Brown On his way to the gallows, Brown predicted that slavery would end only "after much bloodshed."

pathizers. His heartfelt commitment to abolishing slavery and promoting racial equality had intensified because he saw slavery becoming more deeply entrenched, cemented by law, economics, and religious sanction.

Brown was convinced that he was carrying out a divine mission on behalf of a vengeful God. He struck fear into supporters and opponents alike, for he was a moral absolutist who disdained compromise. As one of the few whites willing to live among black people and die for them, he was a brilliant propagandist for the abolitionist cause.

In 1859, Brown hatched a plan to steal federal weapons and give them to rebellious slaves in western Virginia and Maryland, in the hope of triggering mass uprisings across the South. "I want to free all the negroes in this state," Brown said. "If the citizens interfere with me, I must burn the town and have blood."

On the cool, rainy night of October 16, 1859, Brown left a Maryland farm and crossed the Potomac River with about twenty men, including three of his sons and five African Americans. Under cover of darkness, they walked five miles to the federal rifle arsenal in Harpers Ferry, Virginia (now West Virginia). One of the raiders later said he "felt like they were marching to their own funeral." Brown and his soldiers took the sleeping town by surprise, cut the telegraph lines, and occupied the arsenal with its 100,000 rifles. He then dispatched several men to kidnap prominent slave owners and sound the alarm for local slaves to rise up and join the rebellion.

Only a few slaves heeded the call, however, and by dawn, armed townsmen had surrounded the raiders. Brown and a dozen of his men, along with eleven white hostages (including George Washington's great-grandnephew) and two of their slaves, holed up for thirty-two hours in a firehouse. Meanwhile, hundreds of armed whites poured into Harpers Ferry. Lieutenant Colonel Robert E. Lee also arrived with a force of U.S. Marines.

On the morning of October 18, a marine officer ordered the abolitionists to surrender. Brown replied that he preferred to die fighting, warning that he "would sell his life as dearly as possible." Twelve marines then broke open the doors and rushed in. Lieutenant Israel Green reported that he found himself face to face with "an old man kneeling with a carbine in his hand, with a long gray beard falling away from his face." Green would have killed Brown had his sword not bent back double when he plunged it into the abolitionist's chest. He then beat Brown until he passed out.

Brown's men had killed four townspeople and one marine while wounding another dozen. Of their own force, ten were killed (including two of Brown's sons) and five were captured; another five escaped.

A week later, Brown and his accomplices were tried and convicted of treason, murder, and "conspiring with Negroes to produce insurrection." At his sentencing, Brown delivered an eloquent speech in which he expressed pride in his effort to "mingle my blood further with the blood of my children and with the blood of millions in this slave country whose rights are disregarded by wicked, cruel, and unjust enactments."

On December 2, 1859, some 1,500 Virginia militiamen, including a young actor named John Wilkes Booth, who would later assassinate Abraham Lincoln, assembled for Brown's execution. Just before being placed atop his coffin in a wagon to take him to the scaffold, Brown wrote a final message, predicting that the "crimes of this *guilty* land will never be purged away, but with Blood." Although John Brown's Raid on Harpers Ferry failed to ignite a massive slave rebellion, it achieved two things: he became a martyr for the abolitionist cause, and he set off a hysterical panic throughout the slaveholding South.

Throughout the fall and winter of 1859–1860, wild rumors of abolitionist conspiracies and slave insurrections swept through the southern states, leading many to outlaw any anti-slavery activity. "We regard every man in our midst an enemy to the institutions of the South," said the *Atlanta Confederacy*, "who does not boldly declare that he believes African slavery to be a social, moral, and political blessing." Other newspapers claimed that Brown's raid had dramatically increased support for secession in the South. The *Richmond Whig* reported that thousands of Virginians had decided that the Union's "days are numbered, its glory perished" as a result of Brown's actions.

THE DEMOCRATS DIVIDE President Buchanan had chosen not to seek a second term, leaving Stephen A. Douglas as the frontrunner for the nomination. His northern supporters tried to straddle the slavery issue by promising to defend the institution in the South while assuring northerners that slavery would not spread to new states. Southern firebrands, however, demanded federal protection for slavery in the territories as well as the states. When the pro-slavery advocates lost, delegates from eight southern states walked out of the convention in Charleston, South Carolina.

The delegates then decided to leave Charleston. Douglas's supporters reassembled in Baltimore on June 18 and nominated him for president. Southern Democrats met first in Richmond and then in Baltimore, where they adopted the pro-slavery platform defeated in Charleston and named John C. Breckinridge, vice president under Buchanan, as their candidate because he promised to ensure that Congress would protect the right of emigrants to take their slaves to the western territories. Thus another cord of union had snapped: the last remaining national party had split into northern and southern factions. The fracturing of the Democratic party made a Republican victory in 1860 almost certain.

Abraham Lincoln A lanky and rawboned small-town lawyer, Lincoln won the presidential election in 1860.

LINCOLN'S ELECTION The Republican convention was held in May in the fast-growing city of Chicago, where everything came together for Abraham Lincoln. The uncommon common man won the nomination over New York senator William H. Seward, and the resulting cheer, wrote one journalist, was "like the rush of a great wind." The convention reaffirmed the party's opposition to the extension of slavery and, to gain broader support, endorsed a series of traditional Whig policies promoting national economic expansion: a higher protective tariff, free farms on federal lands out west, and federally financed internal improvements, including a transcontinental railroad.

The presidential nominating conventions revealed that opinions tended to be more radical in the Northeast and the Lower South. Attitude followed latitude. In the border states of Maryland, Delaware, Kentucky, and Mis-

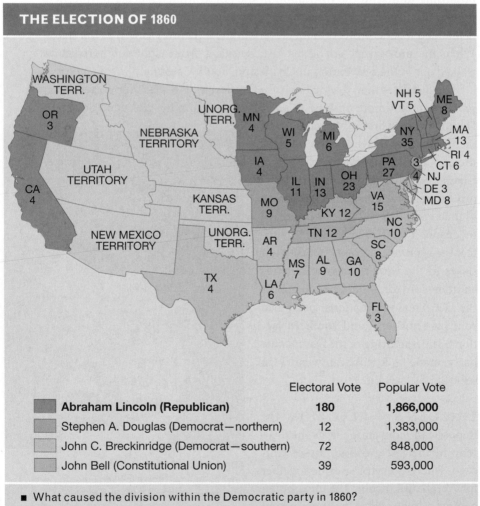

THE ELECTION OF 1860

	Electoral Vote	Popular Vote
Abraham Lincoln (Republican)	**180**	**1,866,000**
Stephen A. Douglas (Democrat—northern)	12	1,383,000
John C. Breckinridge (Democrat—southern)	72	848,000
John Bell (Constitutional Union)	39	593,000

- What caused the division within the Democratic party in 1860?
- What were the major factors that led to Lincoln's electoral victory?

souri, a sense of moderation aroused former Whigs to make one more try at reconciliation. Meeting in Baltimore a week before the Republicans met in Chicago, they reorganized themselves as the Constitutional Union party and nominated John Bell of Tennessee for president. Their platform centered on a vague statement promoting "the Constitution of the Country, the Union of the States, and the Enforcement of the Laws."

The bitterly contested campaign became a choice between Lincoln and Douglas in the North (Lincoln was not even on the ballot in the South), and Breckinridge and Bell in the South. Douglas, the only candidate to mount a nationwide campaign, promised that he would "make war boldly against Northern abolitionists and Southern disunionists." But his heroic effort did no good.

By midnight on November 6, Lincoln's victory was announced. He had won 39 percent of the popular vote, the smallest plurality ever, but garnered a clear majority (180 votes) in the electoral college. He carried all eighteen free states but none of the slave states.

THE RESPONSE IN THE SOUTH

Between November 8, 1860, when Lincoln was elected, and March 4, 1861, when he was inaugurated, the United States of America disintegrated. The election of Lincoln, an anti-slavery Midwesterner, panicked southerners who believed that the Republican party, as a Richmond, Virginia, newspaper asserted, was founded for one reason: "hatred of African slavery." Former president John Tyler wrote that with Lincoln's election the nation "had fallen on evil times" and that the "day of doom for the great model Republic is at hand."

False rumors that Lincoln planned to free the slaves raced across the South. One newspaper editorial called the president-elect a "bigoted, unscrupulous, and cold-blooded enemy of peace and equality of the slaveholding states." Lincoln responded that southern fears were misguided. He stressed in a letter to a Georgia congressman that he was not a radical abolitionist and his administration would not interfere with slavery, either "*directly or indirectly.*" Lincoln, however, refused to provide such assurances in public, in part because he misread the depth of southern anger and concern over his election.

SOUTH CAROLINA SECEDES Pro-slavery fire-eaters in South Carolina, which had long been the state most resistant to federal authority, viewed Lincoln's election as the final signal to abandon the Union. After Lincoln's victory, the state's entire congressional delegation resigned and left Washington, D.C. The state legislature then appointed a convention to decide whether it should remain in the Union.

South Carolina had a higher percentage of slaves in its population (60 percent) than any other state, and its political leadership was dominated by slave-owning hotheads. It had been a one-party state (Democratic) for decades, and it was the only state that did not allow its citizens to vote in presidential elections; the legislature, controlled by white planters, did the balloting.

Meeting in Charleston on December 20, 1860, the special convention unanimously voted to secede from the Union. David Jamison Rutledge, who presided over the convention, announced that "the Ordinance of Secession has been signed and ratified, and I proclaim the State of South Carolina an Independent Commonwealth." (Rutledge would have four sons killed in the Civil War and see his house burned to the ground.) James L. Petigru, one of the few Unionists in Charleston, quipped that his newly independent state was "too small to be a Republic and too large to be an insane asylum."

As the news of South Carolina's secession spread through Charleston, church bells rang, and shops closed. Cadets at the Citadel, the state military college, fired artillery salutes, new flags were unfurled, and volunteers donned militia uniforms. "THE UNION IS DISSOLVED!" screamed the *Charleston Mercury*. One Unionist in Charleston kept a copy of the newspaper, scribbling on the bottom of it: "You'll regret the day you ever done this. I preserve this to see how it ends."

PRESIDENT BUCHANAN BALKS The nation needed a decisive president, but James Buchanan was not up to the task. The president blamed the crisis on fanatical northern abolitionists, then declared that secession was illegal, only to claim that he lacked the constitutional authority to force a state to rejoin the Union. In the face of Buchanan's inaction, all the southerners in his cabinet resigned, and secessionists seized federal property, arsenals, and forts in the southern states. Among those federal facilities was Fort Sumter, nestled on a tiny island at the mouth of Charleston Harbor.

When South Carolina secessionists demanded that Major Robert Anderson, a Kentucky Unionist, surrender the undermanned fort, he refused. On January 5, 1861, Buchanan sent an unarmed ship, the *Star of the West*, to resupply Fort Sumter. As the ship approached Charleston Harbor on January 9, Confederate cannons opened fire and drove it away.

It was an act of war, but Buchanan chose to ignore the challenge and try to ride out the remaining weeks of his term, hoping against hope that a compromise would be reached to avoid war. Many southerners, however, were not in a compromising mood. The crisis, said a southern senator, could only be defused when "northern people" agreed "to review and reverse their whole policy upon the subject of slavery."

SECESSION OF THE LOWER SOUTH

By February 1, 1861, the states of the Lower South—South Carolina, Mississippi, Florida, Alabama, Georgia, Louisiana, and Texas—had seceded. Although their secession ordinances mentioned various grievances against the federal government, they made clear that their primary reason for leaving the Union was the preservation of slavery.

On February 4, 1861, representatives of the seceding states, 90 percent of whom were slave owners, met in Montgomery, Alabama, where they adopted a constitution for the Confederate States of America. The constitution mandated that "the institution of negro slavery, as it now exists in the Confederate States, shall be recognized and protected."

"The Union Is Dissolved!" An 1860 newspaper headline announcing South Carolina's secession from the Union.

Mississippi's Jefferson Davis, a West Point graduate who had served in the House of Representatives and the Senate, was elected president, with Alexander H. Stephens of Georgia as vice president. Stephens left no doubt about why the Confederacy was formed. "Our new government," he declared, "is founded upon . . . the great truth that the negro is not equal to the white man; that slavery, subordination to the superior [white] race, is his natural and normal condition."

In mid-February Davis traveled from Mississippi to Montgomery, Alabama, the Confederate capital, for his installation. On February 18, William

Yancey, an Alabama fire-eater, introduced Davis to the crowd by announcing that the "man and the hour have met." In his remarks, Davis ominously claimed that "the time for compromise is now passed."

FINAL EFFORTS AT COMPROMISE Members of Congress, however, desperately sought a compromise to avoid a civil war. On December 18, 1860, John J. Crittenden of Kentucky offered a series of resolutions that allowed for slavery in the new western territories *south* of the Missouri Compromise line (36°30′ parallel) and guaranteed the preservation of slavery where it already existed. Lincoln, however, opposed any plan that would expand slavery westward, and the Senate defeated the Crittenden Compromise, 25 to 23.

Several weeks later, in February 1861, twenty-one states sent delegates to a peace conference in Washington, D.C. Former president John Tyler presided, but the peace convention's proposal, substantially the same as the Crittenden Compromise, had little support in either house of Congress. (Tyler himself voted against it and urged Virginia to secede at once.) The only proposal that generated much interest was a constitutional amendment guaranteeing slavery where it existed. Many Republicans, including Lincoln, were prepared to go that far to save the Union, but no further.

As it happened, after passing the House, the slavery amendment passed the Senate 24 to 12 on the morning of March 4, 1861, Lincoln's inauguration day. It would have become the Thirteenth Amendment, and would have been the first time the word *slavery* had appeared in the Constitution, but the states never ratified it. When a Thirteenth Amendment was eventually ratified, in 1865, it did not protect slavery—it ended it.

LINCOLN'S INAUGURATION In mid-February 1861, Abraham Lincoln boarded a train in Springfield, Illinois, headed to Washington, D.C., for his inauguration. Along the way, he told the New Jersey legislature that he was "devoted to peace" but warned that "it may be necessary to put the foot down."

In his inaugural address on March 4, the fifty-two-year-old Lincoln repeated his pledge not "to interfere with the institution of slavery in the states where it exists." But the immediate question facing the nation had shifted from slavery to secession. Lincoln insisted that "the Union of these States is perpetual." No state, he stressed, "can lawfully get out of the Union." He pledged to defend "federal forts in the South," but beyond that "there will be no invasion, no using of force against or among the people anywhere." In closing, he appealed for the Union:

> We are not enemies, but friends. We must not be enemies. Though passion may have strained, it must not break our bonds of affection.

The mystic chords of memory, stretching from every battlefield and patriot grave to every living heart and hearthstone all over this broad land, will yet swell the chorus of the Union, when again touched, as surely they will be, by the better angels of our nature.

Southerners were not impressed. A North Carolina newspaper warned that Lincoln's speech made civil war "inevitable." On both sides, however, people assumed that any warfare would be over quickly and that their lives would then go on as usual.

THE END OF THE WAITING GAME On March 5, 1861, his first day in office, President Lincoln found on his desk a letter from Major Anderson at Fort Sumter. Time was running out for the Union soldiers. Anderson reported that his men had enough food for only a few weeks, and that the Confederates were encircling the fort with a "ring of fire." It would take thousands of federal soldiers to rescue them.

On April 4, 1861, Lincoln ordered that unarmed ships take food and supplies to the sixty-nine soldiers at Fort Sumter. Jefferson Davis was equally determined to stop any effort to supply the fort, even if it meant using military force. The secretary of state for the Confederacy, Richard Lathers, warned Davis that if the South fired first, it would unify northern opinion against the secessionists: "There will be no compromise with Secession if war is forced upon the north." Davis ignored the warning.

On April 11, Confederate general Pierre G. T. Beauregard, who had studied under Robert Anderson at West Point, urged his former professor to surrender Fort Sumter. Anderson refused. At 4:30 A.M. on April 12, Confederate cannons began firing on Fort Sumter. During some thirty-four hours of relentless bombardment, more than 5,000 shells were exchanged. Finally, Major Anderson, his ammunition gone and with no help in sight, lowered the "stars and stripes." A civil war of unimagined horrors had begun.

CHAPTER REVIEW

SUMMARY

- **Slavery in the Territories**   Representative David *Wilmot's Proviso*, although it never became law, declared that since Mexican territories acquired by the United States had been free, they should remain so. Like the Wilmot Proviso, the new *Free-Soil party* demanded that slavery not be expanded in the territories. But it was the discovery of gold in California and the ensuing *California gold rush* of 1849 that escalated tensions. Californians wanted to enter the Union as a free state. Southerners feared that they would lose federal protection of their "peculiar institution" if there were more free states than slave states. It had been agreed that *popular sovereignty* would settle the status of the territories, but when the territories applied for statehood, the debate over slavery was renewed. Through the wildly celebrated *Compromise of 1850*, California entered the Union as a free state; the territories of Texas, New Mexico, and Utah were established without direct reference to slavery; the slave trade (but not slavery) was banned in Washington, D.C.; and a new *Fugitive Slave Act* was passed. Tensions turned violent with the passage of the *Kansas-Nebraska Act*, which overturned the Missouri Compromise by allowing slavery in the territories where the institution had been banned by Congress in 1821.

- **The Republican Party's Appeal**   Pro-slavery advocates in the territory of Kansas and the mob violence that tried to force slavery on the state enraged northern opinion, even though anti-slavery settlers such as John Brown were equally violent in the events known as *Bleeding Kansas*. The Supreme Court's *Dred Scott v. Sandford* decision, which ruled that Congress could not interfere with slavery in the territories, further fueled sectional conflict. Northern voters gravitated toward the Republican party as events unfolded. Republicans also advocated raising protective tariffs and funding the development of the nation's infrastructure, which appealed to northern manufacturers and commercial farmers. Abraham Lincoln's narrow failure to unseat Democrat Stephen A. Douglas in the 1858 Illinois Senate election, which included the famous *Lincoln-Douglas debates*, revealed the Republican party's growing appeal. In 1860, Lincoln carried every free state and won a clear electoral college victory.

- **The Secession of the Lower South and Civil War**   Following Lincoln's election, South Carolina seceded. Six other Lower South states quickly followed. Together they formed the Confederate States of America, citing their belief that secession was necessary for the preservation of slavery. In his inaugural address, Lincoln made it clear that secession was unconstitutional but that the North would not invade the South. However, the Confederate states stood by their declarations of secession, and war came when South Carolinians fired on the "stars and stripes" at Fort Sumter.

CHRONOLOGY

1848	Free-Soil party is organized
1849	California gold rush begins
1854	Congress passes the Kansas-Nebraska Act
	The Republican party is founded
1856	A pro-slavery mob sacks Lawrence, Kansas; John Brown stages the Pottawatomie Massacre in retaliation
	Charles Sumner of Massachusetts is caned and seriously injured by a pro-slavery congressman in the U.S. Senate
1857	U.S. Supreme Court issues the *Dred Scott* decision
	Lecompton Constitution declares that slavery will be allowed in Kansas
1858	Abraham Lincoln debates Stephen A. Douglas during the 1858 Illinois Senate race
1859	John Brown and his followers stage a failed raid at Harpers Ferry, Virginia, in an attempt to incite a slave insurrection
1860–1861	South Carolina and six other southern states secede from the Union
	Crittenden Compromise is proposed but fails
March 4, 1861	Abraham Lincoln is inaugurated president
April 1861	Fort Sumter falls to Confederate forces, triggers Civil War

KEY TERMS

Wilmot Proviso (1846) p. 498

popular sovereignty p. 499

Free-Soil party p. 499

California gold rush (1849) p. 500

Compromise of 1850 p. 502

Fugitive Slave Act (1850) p. 506

Kansas-Nebraska Act (1854) p. 509

Bleeding Kansas (1856) p. 512

Dred Scott v. Sandford (1857) p. 516

Lincoln-Douglas debates (1858) p. 518

🐇 INQUIZITIVE

Go to InQuizitive to see what you've learned—and learn what you've missed—with personalized feedback along the way.

15 The War of the Union

1861–1865

***Lincoln's Drive through Richmond* (1866)** Shortly after the Confederate capital of
Richmond, Virginia, fell to Union forces in April 1865, President Abraham Lincoln
visited the war-torn city. His carriage was swarmed by enslaved blacks who were freed
by the war, as well as whites whose loyalties were with the Union.

The fall of Fort Sumter started the war of the Union and triggered a wave of patriotic bluster on both sides. A southern woman prayed that God would "give us strength to conquer them, to exterminate *them*, to lay waste every Northern city, town and village, to destroy them utterly." By contrast, Nathaniel Hawthorne reported from Massachusetts that his transcendentalist friend Ralph Waldo Emerson was "breathing slaughter" as the Union army prepared for its first battle.

Many southerners, then and since, argued that the Civil War was not about slavery but about the South's effort to defend states' rights. Confederate president Jefferson Davis, for example, owner of a huge Mississippi plantation with 113 slaves, claimed that the war was fought on behalf of the South's right to secede from the Union and its need to defend itself against a "tyrannical majority," meaning those who had elected President Abraham Lincoln, the anti-slavery Republican.

For his part, Lincoln stressed repeatedly that the "paramount object in this struggle *is* to save the Union, and is *not* either to save or to destroy slavery. If I could save the Union without freeing *any* slave I would do it, and if I could save it by freeing *all* the slaves I would do it; and if I could save it by freeing some and leaving others alone I would also do that." If the southern states returned to the Union, he promised, they could retain their slaves. None of the Confederate states accepted Lincoln's offer, in large part because most white southerners were convinced that he was lying.

However much Jefferson Davis and other southerners argued that secession and the war were about states' rights, the states of the Lower South seceded in 1860–1861 to protect slavery. The South Carolina Declaration on the

focus questions

1. What were the respective advantages of the North and South as the Civil War began? How did those advantages affect the military strategies of the Union and the Confederacy?

2. Why did Lincoln decide to issue the Emancipation Proclamation? How did it impact the war?

3. In what ways did the war affect social and economic life in the North and South?

4. What were the military turning points in 1863 and 1864 that ultimately led to the Confederacy's defeat?

5. How did the Civil War change the nation?

Immediate Causes of Secession was quite clear, highlighting the "increasing hostility on the part of the non-slaveholding states to the institution of slavery." Mississippi only mentioned one reason for seceding: preserving slavery. Georgian Alexander Stephens, the vice president of the Confederate States of America, was equally emphatic, saying that slavery was the "immediate cause" of secession and war. As Lincoln noted in his second inaugural address, everyone knew that slavery "was somehow the cause of the war."

On April 15, three days after the Confederate attack on Fort Sumter, Lincoln called upon the loyal states to supply 75,000 soldiers to suppress the rebellion. Senator Stephen Douglas insisted that "there are only two sides to the question [of civil war]. Every man must be for the United States or against it. There can be no neutrals in this war, only patriots—or traitors."

The Civil War would force everyone—men and women, white and black, immigrants and Native Americans, free and enslaved—to choose sides. Thousands of southerners fought for the Union; thousands of northerners fought for the Confederacy. Thousands of European volunteers fought on each side.

CHOOSING SIDES

The first seven states to secede were all from the Lower South—South Carolina, Mississippi, Florida, Alabama, Georgia, Louisiana, and Texas—where the cotton economy was strongest and slaves the most numerous. All the states in the Upper South, especially Tennessee and Virginia, had areas (mainly in the mountains) where whites were poor, slaves were scarce, and Union support was strong. Nevertheless, the outbreak of actual fighting led four more southern slave states to join the Confederacy: Virginia, Arkansas, Tennessee, and North Carolina.

On the eve of the Civil War, the U.S. Army had only 16,400 men, about 1,000 of whom were officers. Of them, about 25 percent, like future Confederate general Robert E. Lee, resigned to join the Confederate army. On the other hand, many southerners made great sacrifices to remain loyal to the Union. Some left their native region once the fighting began; others remained in the South but found ways to support the Union. Some 100,000 men from the southern states fought *against* the Confederacy.

REGIONAL ADVANTAGES Once battle lines were finally drawn, the Union held twenty-three states, including four states along the border between North and South, Missouri, Kentucky, Maryland, and Delaware. The Confederacy included eleven states. The population count was about 22 million in the

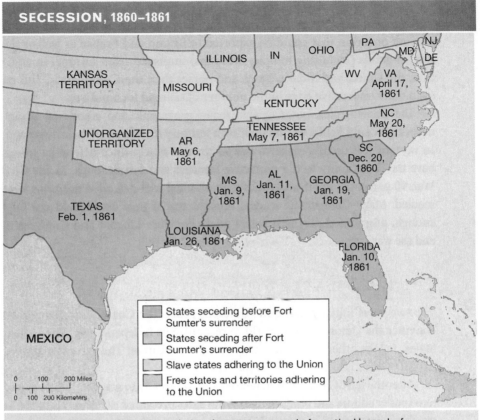

SECESSION, 1860–1861

- Why did South Carolina and six other states secede from the Union before the siege at Fort Sumter?
- Why did secession not win unanimous approval in Tennessee and Virginia?
- How did Lincoln keep Maryland in the Union?

Union (some 400,000 of whom were enslaved African Americans) to 9 million in the Confederacy (of whom about 3.5 million were enslaved). To help balance the odds, the Confederacy mobilized 80 percent of its military-age white men, a third of whom would die during the four-year war.

An even greater advantage for the North was its superior industrial development. The southern states produced just 7 percent of the nation's manufactured goods on the eve of the war. The Union states produced 97 percent of the firearms and 96 percent of the railroad equipment.

The North also had a huge advantage in transportation, particularly ships. At the start of the war, the Union had ninety warships; the South had no navy at all. Federal gunboats and transports played a direct role in securing the Union's control of the Mississippi River and its larger tributaries, which provided easy invasion routes into the center of the Confederacy. Early on, the Union navy's blockade of the major southern ports sharply reduced the amount of cotton that could be exported to Britain and France as well as the flow of goods (including military weapons) imported from Europe. In addition, the Union had more wagons and horses than the Confederacy, and an even more impressive edge in the number of railroad locomotives.

The Confederates, however, had major geographic and emotional advantages: they could fight a war on their own territory in defense of their homeland. In warfare, it is usually easier to defend than to attack, since defending troops have the opportunity to dig protective trenches and fortifications. In the Civil War, 90 percent of the time, armies that assaulted well-defended positions were mauled. Many Confederate leaders thought that if they could hold out long enough, disgruntled northern voters might convince Lincoln and Congress to end the war.

THE WAR'S EARLY STRATEGIES

The two sides initially had quite different goals. The Confederacy sought to convince the Union and the world to recognize its independence. The United States, on the other hand, fought to restore the Union. The future of slavery was not yet an issue.

After the fall of Fort Sumter, neither side was ready to wage war, but excited newspaper editors and politicians on both sides pressured the generals to strike quickly. "Forward to Richmond!" screamed a New York newspaper headline. In the summer of 1861, Jefferson Davis told General Pierre G. T. Beauregard to rush the main Confederate army to Manassas Junction, a railroad crossing in northern Virginia, about twenty-five miles southwest of Washington. President Lincoln hoped that the Union army (often called Federals), led by General Irvin McDowell, Beauregard's West Point classmate, would overrun the outnumbered Confederates (often called Rebels) and quickly push on to Richmond, only 107 miles to the south. "What a picnic," predicted a New York soldier, "to go down South for three months and clean up the whole business."

FIRST BULL RUN When word reached Washington, D.C., that the two armies were converging for battle, hundreds of civilians packed picnic lunches and rode out to watch the spectacle, assuming that the first clash would be short, glorious, and bloodless. It was a hot, dry Sunday on July 21, 1861, when 37,000 untested Union recruits breezily marched to battle, some of them breaking ranks to eat blackberries or drink water from streams along the way.

First Bull Run Moments before battle, a spectator in a top hat chats with Union soldiers (bottom right), while an artist sketches the passing troops breezily heading to war (at left).

Many of them died with the berry juice still staining their lips as they engaged the Confederates dug in behind a branch of the Potomac River called Bull Run, near the Manassas Junction railroad station. For most of the soldiers, the battle at Bull Run was their first taste of the chaos and confusion of combat. Many were disoriented by the smoke from gunpowder and saltpeter, the deafening roar of cannon fire, the screaming of fallen comrades, and the distinctive sound of bullets whizzing past. Because neither side yet wore standard-colored uniforms, the soldiers had trouble deciding friend from foe.

The Union troops almost won the battle early in the afternoon. But Confederate reinforcements poured in to tip the balance. Amid the furious fighting, a South Carolina officer rallied his troops by pointing to the courageous example of Thomas Jackson's men: "Look! There is General Jackson with his Virginians, standing like a stone wall!" Jackson ordered his men to charge the faltering Union ranks, urging them to "yell like furies!" From that day forward, "Stonewall" became Jackson's nickname, and he would be the most celebrated—and feared—Confederate commander.

The Union army's retreat from Bull Run turned into a panicked rout (the "great skedaddle") as fleeing soldiers and terrified civilians clogged the road to Washington, D.C. The victorious Confederates, however, were so disorganized and exhausted that they failed to give chase. As the armies moved on, they left behind a battlefield strewn with the dead and dying—mangled men and bloated horses and mules, all scattered among discarded equipment, rifles, wagons, and cannons. Stonewall Jackson sent his wife a letter reporting that "we fought a great battle and gained a great victory, for which all the glory is due to God alone." His Union counterpart, General William T. Sherman, admitted that the Federals had suffered a "terrible defeat" during which many inexperienced soldiers "degenerated into an armed mob."

The First Battle of Bull Run (or First Manassas)* was a sobering experience for both sides, each of which had miscalculated the other's strength and tenacity. Much of the romance of war—the colorful uniforms, bright flags, marching bands, and rousing songs—gave way to the agonizing realization that this would be a long, costly, grim struggle. *Harper's Weekly* bluntly warned: "From the fearful day at Bull Run dates war. Not polite war, not incredulous war, but war that breaks hearts and blights homes."

THE UNION'S "ANACONDA" PLAN   The Battle of Bull Run demonstrated that the war would not be decided with one sudden stroke. General Winfield Scott, the seventy-five-year-old commander of the Union war effort, devised a three-pronged strategy that called first for the Army of the Potomac, the main Union army, to defend Washington, D.C., and exert constant pressure on the Confederate capital at Richmond.

At the same time, the Federal navy's blockade of southern ports would cut off the Confederacy's access to foreign goods and weapons. The final component of the plan called for other Union armies to divide the Confederacy by pushing south along the crucial inland water routes: the Mississippi, Tennessee, and Cumberland Rivers. This so-called **Anaconda Plan** was intended to slowly trap and crush the southern resistance, like an anaconda snake strangling its prey.

CONFEDERATE STRATEGY   Confederate president Jefferson Davis was better prepared than Lincoln at the start of the war to guide military strategy. A graduate of the U.S. Military Academy at West Point, he had served with distinction both as an officer during the Mexican-American War and was U.S. secretary of war from 1853 to 1857. If the war could be prolonged, as Davis and others hoped, then the British or French, desperate for southern cotton, might be persuaded to join their cause. Or, perhaps a long war would influence public sentiment in the North and force Lincoln to seek a negotiated settle-

---

*The Federals most often named battles for natural features; the Confederates, for nearby towns—thus Bull Run (Manassas), Antietam (Sharpsburg), Stones River (Murfreesboro), and the like.

ment. So while armies were forming in the South, Confederate diplomats were seeking military and financial assistance in London and Paris, and Confederate sympathizers in the North and in Congress were urging an end to the Union's war effort.

The Confederate representatives in Paris won a promise from France to recognize the Confederacy as a new nation *if* Great Britain would do the same. But the British refused, partly in response to pressure from President Lincoln and partly out of Britain's desire to maintain trade with the United States. Confederate leaders had assumed that Britain would support the South to get its cotton. As it turned out, however, the British were able to import enough cotton from India to maintain production. In the end, Confederate diplomacy in Europe was more successful in getting military supplies than in gaining official recognition of the Confederacy as an independent nation.

FORMING ARMIES Once fighting began, President Lincoln called for 500,000 more men, a staggering number at the time and one that the Confederacy struggled to match. In Illinois, Ulysses S. Grant, a graduate of the U.S. Military Academy at West Point who had displayed courage and a knack for leadership in the Mexican-American War, rejoined the army in 1861, explaining that there "are but two parties now—traitors and patriots—and I want hereafter to be ranked with the latter."

Confederates were equally committed to their cause. Charleston, wrote Mary Chesnut, the literary wife of a prominent planter, was "crowded with soldiers" who feared "the war will be over before they get a sight of the fun." Tennessee's twenty-one-year-old Sam Watkins reported that everyone in his town "was eager for the war."

The basic unit of the nineteenth-century armies was the regiment, about 1,000 soldiers, and during the war most regiments were made up of friends, neighbors, and relatives from the same community. Ethnic groups also formed their own regiments. A quarter of the Union troops were foreign-born, many of whom did not speak English.

Immigrants were attracted to serve for many reasons: a strong belief in the Union cause, cash bonuses, regular pay, or the need for a steady job. Whatever the reason, the high proportion of immigrants in the Union army gave it an ethnic diversity absent in the Confederate ranks.

Because the Confederacy had a smaller male population than the North, Jefferson Davis was forced to enact a conscription law (mandatory military draft). On April 16, 1862, all white male citizens between eighteen and thirty-five were required to serve in the army for three years. "From this time until the end of the war," a Tennessee soldier wrote, "a soldier was simply a machine, a conscript. . . . All our pride and valor had gone, and we were sick of war and cursed the Southern Confederacy."

The Confederate conscription law included controversial loopholes. A draftee might avoid service either by paying a "substitute" who was not of draft age, or by paying $500 to the government. Elected officials and key civilian workers, as well as planters with twenty or more slaves, were exempted from military service. Many among the planter elite argued that if they left to fight, their slaves would escape or riot. Equally galling to many Confederate soldiers was the behavior of wealthy officers who brought their enslaved servants with them to army camps.

The Union waited nearly a year to force men into service. In 1863, with the war going badly for the Federal armies, the government began to draft men. As in the South, northerners found ways to avoid military service. Exemptions were granted to selected federal and state officeholders and to others on medical or compassionate grounds; or a draftee might pay $300 to avoid service. Such exemptions led to bitter complaints on both sides about the conflict being "a rich man's war and a poor man's fight."

The U.S. Army recruiting office in City Hall Park, New York City The sign advertises the money offered to those willing to serve: $677 to new recruits, $777 to veteran soldiers, and $15 to anyone who brought in a recruit.

THE LIFE OF A SOLDIER The average Civil War soldier or sailor was twenty-five years old, stood five feet eight inches, and weighed 143 pounds. A third of the southern soldiers could neither read nor write. One in nine would be killed or wounded. Half of the Union soldiers and two-thirds of the Confederates were farmers.

Soldiers spent far more time preparing for war than actually fighting. A Pennsylvania private wrote home that "the first thing in the morning is drill. Then drill, then drill again. Then drill, drill, a little more drill, then drill, lastly drill." When not training, soldiers spent time outdoors, in makeshift shelters or small tents—talking, reading books, newspapers, or letters; playing cards or checkers; singing, washing and mending clothes; and fighting swarms of lice, ticks, chiggers, and mosquitoes. Their diet was plain and dull: baked bread crackers (called hardtack), salted meat (pork or beef), and coffee.

MIXED MOTIVES Several million mostly young and inexperienced Americans fought in the Civil War. As in all great wars, their motives varied dramatically. Sullivan Ballou, a thirty-two-year-old Rhode Island lawyer and legislator who enlisted in the Union army, wrote his wife that he would have loved nothing more than to have stayed with his family and seen their sons grow to "honorable manhood," but his ultimate priority was serving his country. He felt a great debt to "those who went before us through the blood and sufferings of the Revolution." A week later, Ballou was killed in the first Battle of Bull Run. In his last letter to his wife, he had expressed a premonition of death: "do not mourn me dead . . . wait for me, for we shall meet again."

Southerners felt the same sense of patriotism and manly honor. An Alabama planter explained to his anxious wife why he had to fight. "My honor, my duty, your reputation & that of my darling little boy," he stressed, forced him to don a uniform "when our bleeding country needs the services of every man." But as the months passed and the suffering grew, many combatants saw their initial enthusiasm fade.

BLACKS IN THE SOUTH As had happened during the Revolutionary War and the War of 1812, enslaved African Americans took advantage of the confusion created by the war to run away, engage in sabotage, join the Union war effort, or pursue their own interests. A plantation owner in Tennessee was disgusted by the war's effect on his slaves, as he confessed in his diary: "My Negroes all at home, but working only as they see fit, doing little." Some slaves had reported that they would "serve the Federals rather than work on the farm." Later, he revealed that when Union armies arrived in the area, his slaves

Union soldiers Smoking their pipes, these soldiers share a moment of rest and a bottle of whiskey.

had "stampeded" to join the Yankees: "Many of my servants have run away and most of those left had [just] as well be gone, they being totally demoralized and ungovernable."

Fighting in the West

KANSAS The most intense fighting west of the Mississippi occurred along the Kansas-Missouri border, where the disputes that had developed between the pro-slavery and anti-slavery settlers in the 1850s turned into brutal guerrilla warfare. The most prominent pro-Confederate leader in the area was William Quantrill. He and his followers, mostly teenagers, fought under a black flag, meaning that they would kill anyone who surrendered. Their opponents, the Jayhawkers, responded in kind. They tortured and hanged pro-Confederate prisoners, burned houses, and destroyed livestock.

KENTUCKY AND TENNESSEE Little happened of military significance east of the Appalachian Mountains before May 1862. On the other hand, important battles occurred in the West (from the Appalachians to the Mississippi River). Early in 1862, General Ulysses S. Grant made the first Union thrust against the weak center of Johnston's overextended lines. Moving on boats out of Cairo, Illinois, and Paducah, Kentucky, the Union army steamed up the Tennessee River and captured Fort Henry in northern Tennessee on February 6. Grant then moved quickly overland to attack nearby Fort Donelson. This first major Union victory touched off wild celebrations throughout the North. President Lincoln's delight, however, was tempered by the death of his eleven-year-old son Willie, who succumbed to typhoid fever. The tragedy "overwhelmed" the president. A White House staff member said she had never seen "a man so bowed down in grief."

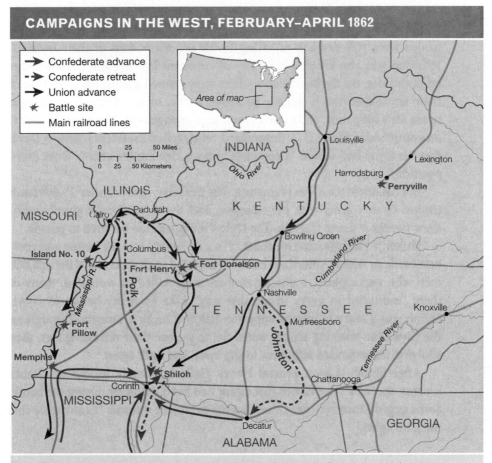

CAMPAIGNS IN THE WEST, FEBRUARY–APRIL 1862

- Why was General Grant's campaign in Kentucky a significant victory for the Union army?
- Describe the events at Shiloh. What were the costs to the Union as a result of the battle?

SHILOH After defeats in Kentucky and Tennessee, the Confederate forces in the West fled southward before regrouping under General Johnston at Corinth in northern Mississippi, near the Tennessee border. Their goal was to protect the Memphis and Charleston Railroad linking the lower Mississippi Valley and the Atlantic coast.

While planning his attack on Corinth, Grant made a costly mistake when he exposed his 42,000 troops on a rolling plateau between Lick and Snake Creeks flowing into the Tennessee River. Johnston recognized Grant's blunder, and at dawn on Sunday, April 6, he launched a surprise attack, urging his men to be "worthy of your race and lineage; worthy of the women of the South."

The 44,000 Confederates struck at Shiloh, a whitewashed Methodist chapel in the center of the Union camp in southwestern Tennessee. Most of Grant's troops were still sleeping or eating breakfast; many died in their bedrolls. Johnston was also killed. After a day of confused fighting and terrible losses on both sides, the fleeing Union soldiers were pinned against the river. One of them wrote that "this is going to be a great battle, such as I have been anxious to see for a long time, and I think I have seen *enough* of it." The new Confederate commander, Pierre G. T. Beauregard, telegraphed President Jefferson Davis that his army had scored "a complete victory, driving the enemy from every position."

But his celebration was premature. The next day, reinforced by 25,000 fresh troops, Grant's army took the offensive, and the Confederates glumly withdrew twenty miles to Corinth. The Union army was too battered to pursue.

Shiloh, a Hebrew word meaning "Place of Peace," was the largest and costliest battle in which Americans had ever engaged to that point. Of the 100,000 men who participated, a quarter of them were killed or wounded, many of them "mutilated in every imaginable way." Like so many battles to come, Shiloh was a story of missed opportunities and lucky accidents. Throughout the Civil War, winning armies would fail to pursue their retreating foes, thus allowing the wounded opponent to slip away and fight again.

After Shiloh, Union general Henry Halleck, already jealous of Grant's success, spread a false rumor that Grant had been drinking during the battle. Some urged Lincoln to fire Grant, but the president refused: "I can't spare this man; he fights."

NEW ORLEANS Just three weeks after the Battle of Shiloh, the Union won a great naval victory at New Orleans, as Admiral David G. Farragut's warships blasted their way past Confederate forts to take the largest city in the Confederacy. The loss of New Orleans was a devastating blow to the Confederate economy. The Union army gained control of 1,500 cotton plantations and 50,000 slaves in the Mississippi Valley and shut off the flow of goods, especially cotton, coming down the Mississippi River to the Gulf of Mexico. As a result, the slave system in Louisiana was "forever destroyed and worthless," reported a northern journalist.

Fighting in the East

The fighting in the East remained fairly quiet for nine months after the Battle of Bull Run. In the wake of the Union defeat, Lincoln had appointed General George B. McClellan as head of the Army of the Potomac. The thirty-four-year-old McClellan, who encouraged journalists to call him "Little Napoleon," set about building the Union's most powerful, best-trained army.

Yet for all of his boundless self-confidence and demonstrated organizational ability, McClellan's paralyzing cautiousness would prove crippling. Months passed while he remained in a state of perpetual preparation, building and training his massive army to meet the superior numbers of Confederates he mistakenly believed were facing him. "Tardy George" McClellan always found a reason to do something other than engage in battle. Lincoln finally lost his patience and ordered McClellan to attack.

MCCLELLAN'S PENINSULAR CAMPAIGN   In mid-March 1862, McClellan moved his huge army of 122,000 men on 400 ships and barges down the Potomac River and the Chesapeake Bay to the mouth of the James River at the tip of the Yorktown peninsula, within sixty miles of the Confederate capital of Richmond, Virginia. Thousands of residents fled the city in panic, but McClellan overestimated the number of Confederate defenders and waited too long to strike. A frustrated Lincoln told McClellan that the war could be won only by *engaging* the Rebel army. "Once more," Lincoln told his commanding general, "let me tell you, it is indispensable to *you* that you strike a blow."

On May 31, 1862, Confederate general Joseph E. Johnston struck at McClellan's army along the Chickahominy River, six miles east of Richmond. In the Battle of Seven Pines (Fair Oaks), only the arrival of Federal reinforcements, who somehow crossed the swollen river, prevented a disastrous Union defeat. Both sides took heavy casualties, and Johnston was severely wounded.

At this point, Robert E. Lee assumed command of the Confederates' main army, the Army of Northern Virginia, a development that changed the course of the war. The brilliant, dignified Lee had graduated second in his class at West Point, and during the Mexican-American War, he had impressed General Winfield Scott as the "very best soldier I ever saw in the field." In 1857, Scott

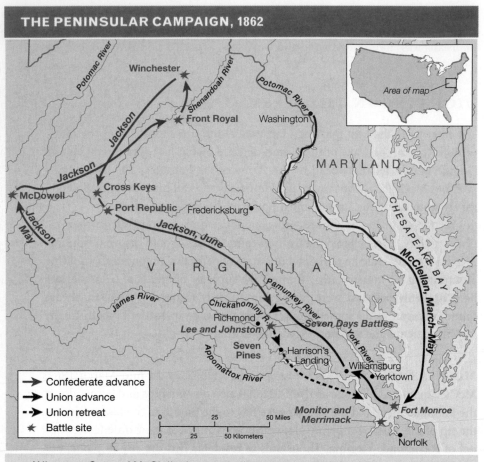

THE PENINSULAR CAMPAIGN, 1862

Area of map

Winchester

Potomac River
Shenandoah River
Front Royal   Washington
Potomac River

Jackson

MARYLAND

McDowell   Cross Keys
Port Republic   Fredericksburg
Jackson, May
Jackson, June

VIRGINIA

James River
Pamunkey River
Chickahominy R.
Richmond
Lee and Johnston   Seven Days Battles
Seven Pines   Harrison's Landing
Appomattox River   York River
Williamsburg
Yorktown
Monitor and Merrimack   Fort Monroe
Norfolk

CHESAPEAKE BAY
McClellan, March–May

→ Confederate advance
→ Union advance
--→ Union retreat
★ Battle site

0   25   50 Miles
0   25   50 Kilometers

- What was General McClellan's strategy for attacking Richmond?
- How did General Jackson divert the attention of the Union army?
- Why did President Lincoln demote McClellan after the Peninsular campaign?

predicted that Lee would become America's greatest military leader. Lee would prove to be a daring, even reckless, strategist who was as aggressive as McClellan was timid. "He is silent, inscrutable, strong, like a God," said a Confederate officer.

On July 9, when Lincoln visited McClellan's headquarters on the coast of Virginia, the general complained that the administration had failed to support him and lectured the president at length on military strategy. Such insubordination was ample reason to relieve McClellan of his overall command. After returning to Washington, Lincoln called Henry Halleck from the West to take charge.

SECOND BULL RUN Lincoln and Halleck ordered McClellan to move his Army of the Potomac back to Washington, D.C., and join with General John Pope, commander of the Union Army of Virginia, in a new assault on Richmond. Pope declared that his goal "was attack and not defense." In a letter to his wife, a jealous McClellan predicted—accurately—that "Pope will be thrashed and disposed of" by Lee's army. He also dismissed Lincoln "as an idiot." Lee moved northward to strike Pope's army before McClellan's troops could arrive. Lee knew that his only chance was to drive a wedge between the two larger Union armies so that he could deal with them one at a time.

Violating a basic rule of military strategy, Lee boldly divided his forces, sending Stonewall Jackson's "foot cavalry" around Pope's flank to attack his

Robert E. Lee Military adviser to President Jefferson Davis and later commander of the Army of Northern Virginia.

supply lines in the rear. At the Second Battle of Bull Run (or Manassas), fought on almost the same site as the earlier battle, a confused Pope assumed that he faced only Jackson, but Lee's main army by that time had joined in.

On August 30, 1862, a crushing attack drove the larger Union army from the field, giving the Confederates a sensational victory and leading one disheartened Union officer to confess from his deathbed that "General Pope had been outwitted. . . . Our generals have defeated us." In contrast, a Rebel soldier wrote home that "General Lee stands now above all generals in modern history. Our men will follow him to the end."

EMANCIPATION

The Confederate victories in 1862 devastated morale in the North and convinced Lincoln that he had to take bolder steps to win the war. Now the North had to assault slavery itself. When fighting began in 1861, the need to keep the border slave states (Delaware, Kentucky, Maryland, and Missouri) in the Union dictated caution on the volatile issue of emancipation. Beyond that, Lincoln had to contend with a deep-seated racial prejudice among most

Contrabands Former slaves on a farm in Cumberland Landing, Virginia, 1862.

northerners, who were willing to allow slavery to continue in the South as long as it was not allowed to expand into the West. Lincoln himself harbored doubts about his constitutional authority to end slavery, and he did not believe that blacks, if freed, could coexist with whites.

SLAVES IN THE WAR The expanding war forced the issue. As Federal forces pushed into the Confederacy, fugitive slaves began to turn up in Union army camps, and the commanders did not know whether to declare them free. One general designated them as "contraband of war," and thereafter the slaves who sought protection and freedom with Union forces were known as **contrabands**. Some Union officers put the refugee slaves to work digging trenches, building fortifications, and burying the dead; others simply set them free.

Lincoln, meanwhile, began to edge toward ending slavery. On April 16, 1862, he signed an act that abolished slavery in the District of Columbia; on June 19, he signed another bill that excluded slavery from the western territories. Still, he insisted that the war was about restoring the Union and ending secession, not ending slavery.

But the course of the war changed Lincoln's outlook. In the summer of 1862, he decided that emancipation of slaves in the Confederate states was necessary to win the war. Many of the more than 3 million enslaved laborers in the Confederacy were being forced to aid the Rebel war effort—digging trenches, hauling supplies, cooking meals for the armies, and working as servants for Confederate officers.

In July 1862, Lincoln confided to his cabinet that "decisive and extreme measures [to win the war] must be adopted." Emancipation, he said, had become "a military necessity, absolutely necessary to the preservation of the Union. We must free the slaves or be ourselves subdued." Secretary of State William H. Seward agreed, but advised Lincoln to delay the announcement until after a Union battlefield victory, to avoid being viewed as desperate.

ANTIETAM: A TURNING POINT Robert E. Lee made his own momentous decision in the summer of 1862: he would invade Maryland and thereby force the Army of the Potomac and its "timid" commander McClellan to leave northern Virginia and relieve the pressure on Richmond, the Confederate capital. Lee also hoped to influence the upcoming elections in the North; he wanted to gain official British and French recognition of the Confederacy, which would bring his troops desperately needed military supplies. In addition, Lee and Jefferson Davis planned to capture Maryland, with its many Confederate supporters, and separate it from the Union. For those reasons and others, in September 1862, Lee and his ragged band of 40,000 troops pushed north into western Maryland.

On September 17, 1862, the Union and Confederate armies clashed in the furious **Battle of Antietam** (Sharpsburg). Had Union soldiers not discovered Lee's detailed battle plans wrapped around three cigars that a messenger had carelessly dropped on the ground, the Confederates might have won. Moreover, McClellan, had he moved his 100,000 men more quickly, could have destroyed Lee's Army of Northern Virginia while it was scattered and on the move. As always, however, McClellan moved slowly, enabling Lee and his troops to regroup at Sharpsburg, between Antietam Creek and the Potomac River.

There, over the course of fourteen hours, the poorly coordinated Union army launched repeated attacks. The fighting was savage; a Union officer counted "hundreds of dead bodies lying in rows and in piles." The scene after "five hours of continuous slaughter" was "sickening, harrowing, horrible. O what a terrible sight!"

The next day, Lee braced for another Union attack, but it never came. That night, cloaked by fog and drizzling rain, the battered Confederates slipped south back across the Potomac River to the safety of Virginia. "The 'barefoot boys' have done some terrible fighting," a Georgian wrote his parents. "We are a dirty, ragged set [of soldiers], mother, but courage & heroism find many a true disciple among us."

Although the battle was technically a draw, Lee's northern invasion had failed. Both sides displayed heroic courage and reckless bravery in what one Rebel general called the "hardest fought battle of the war." McClellan, never known for his modesty, claimed that he "had fought the battle splendidly" against great odds. To him, the Battle of Antietam was "the most terrible battle of the age." Indeed, it was the bloodiest single day in American military history. Some 6,400 soldiers on both sides were killed, twice as many as at Shiloh, and another 17,000 were wounded or listed as missing.

President Lincoln was pleased that Lee's army had been forced to retreat, but he was disgusted by McClellan's failure to attack the retreating Confederates and win the war. The president sent a sarcastic message to the general: "I have just read your dispatch about sore-tongued and fatigued horses. Will you pardon me for asking what the horses of your army have done . . . that fatigues anything?" Failing to receive a satisfactory answer, Lincoln sacked McClellan as commander of the Army of the Potomac and assigned him to recruiting duty in New Jersey. Never again would McClellan command troops, but he would challenge Lincoln for the presidency in 1864 as a Democrat.

The Battle of Antietam had several important results. It revived sagging northern morale, dashed the Confederacy's hopes of forging alliances with Great Britain and France, and convinced Lincoln to transform the war from an effort to restore the Union to a crusade to end slavery.

Union view of the Emancipation Proclamation A thoughtful Lincoln composes the proclamation with the Constitution and the Bible in his lap. The Scales of Justice hangs on the wall behind him.

EMANCIPATION PROCLAMATION On September 22, 1862, five days after the Battle of Antietam, Abraham Lincoln issued the preliminary **Emancipation Proclamation**, which warned the Confederacy that if it did not stop fighting, all slaves still under Rebel control were to be made "forever free" in exactly 100 days, on January 1, 1863.

The Emancipation Proclamation was not based on ideals of racial equality or human dignity. It was, according to Lincoln, a "military necessity." The proclamation freed only those slaves in areas still controlled by the Confederacy; it had no bearing on the slaves in the four border states, because they remained in the Union. Lincoln believed that the Constitution allowed each state to decide the fate of slavery, so his only legal avenue was to act as commander in chief of the armed forces rather than as president. He would declare the end of slavery as a "fit and necessary war measure" to save the federal Union.

When Lincoln officially signed the Emancipation Proclamation in January, however, he amended his original message, adding that the proclamation was "an act of justice" as well as a military necessity. Lincoln's constitutional concerns about abolishing slavery would lead him to promote the Thirteenth

Confederate view of the Emancipation Proclamation Surrounded by demonic faces hidden in his furnishings, Lincoln pens the proclamation with a foot trampling the Constitution. The devil holds the inkwell before him.

Amendment ending slavery across the nation. As Lincoln signed the Emancipation Proclamation, he said, "I never, in my life, felt more certain that I was doing the right thing than I do in signing this paper." Simply restoring the Union was no longer the purpose of the war; the transformation of the South and the slave system was now the goal.

REACTIONS TO EMANCIPATION Lincoln's threat to free slaves under Confederate control triggered emotional reactions. The *Illinois State Register* savaged the president for violating the Constitution and causing "the permanent disruption of the republic." Democrats exploded with rage, calling the president's decision dictatorial, unconstitutional, and catastrophic. "We Won't Fight to Free the Nigger," proclaimed one popular banner. Many voters felt likewise.

In the November 1862 congressional elections, Republicans lost almost two dozen seats. Illinois, Indiana, Pennsylvania, New York, and Ohio went Democratic, largely because of opposition to the Emancipation Proclamation. Even Lincoln's home district in Illinois elected a Democrat.

Although Lincoln's proclamation technically would free only the slaves where Confederates remained in control, many slaves in the northern border states and the South claimed their freedom anyway. As Lincoln had hoped, word spread rapidly among the slave community in the Confederacy, arousing hopes of freedom, creating general confusion in the cities, and encouraging hundreds of thousands to escape.

Confederate leaders were incensed by Lincoln's action, predicting it would ignite a race war in the South. By contrast, Frederick Douglass, the African American abolitionist leader, was overjoyed at the "righteous decree"; he knew that, despite its limitations, it would inspire abolitionists in the North and set in motion the eventual end of slavery.

As Lincoln had hoped, the Emancipation Proclamation did aid the Union war effort by undermining support for the Confederacy in Europe. The decision to end slavery in the Confederacy gave the Federal war effort greater moral legitimacy in the eyes of Europeans—and many Americans.

FREDERICKSBURG In selecting a new commanding general to lead the war effort, Lincoln made his poorest choice of all in the fall of 1862 when he turned to Ambrose E. Burnside, a tall, imposing man whose massive facial hair gave rise to the term "sideburns." Twice before, Burnside had turned down the job, saying he was not worthy of such responsibility. Now he accepted, although he still neither sought the command nor wanted it. He was right to be hesitant. Burnside was an eager fighter but a poor strategist who, according to

Fanny Seward, the secretary of state's daughter, had "ten times as much heart as he has head." The Union army soon paid for his mistakes.

On December 13, 1862, Burnside foolishly sent the 122,000 men in the Army of the Potomac west across the icy Rappahannock River to assault Lee's outnumbered forces, who were well entrenched on a line of ridges and behind stone walls at the base of Marye's Heights, west of Fredericksburg, Virginia, midway between Richmond and Washington, D.C. Confederate cannons and muskets chewed up the advancing Federal soldiers as they crossed half a mile of open land.

None of the Union soldiers made it to the Rebel lines. The awful scene of dead and dying Federals, some stacked three deep on the battlefield, led Lee to remark: "It is well that war is so terrible—we should grow too fond of it." After 12,600 Federals were killed or wounded, compared with fewer than 5,300 for the Confederates, a weeping Burnside told his men to withdraw. Abraham Lincoln was devastated by the news of the Union catastrophe. "We are now on the brink of destruction," he wrote. "It appears to me the Almighty is against us, and I can hardly see a ray of hope."

The year 1862 ended with a stalemate in the East and the Union thrust in the West mired down. Northern morale plummeted, and northern Democrats' victories in the fall congressional elections sharply reduced the Republican majorities in the House and the Senate. Many Democrats were calling for a negotiated peace, and Republicans—even Lincoln's own cabinet members— grew increasingly critical of the president's leadership. "If there is a worse place than hell," Lincoln sighed, "I am in it." Newspapers circulated rumors that the president was going to resign. General Burnside, too, was under fire, with some of his own officers eager to testify publicly to his shortcomings.

NEW YORK CITY DRAFT RIOTS Lincoln's proclamation freeing slaves in the Confederacy created anxiety and anger among many laborers in the North who feared that freed slaves would eventually migrate north and take their jobs. In New York City, such fears erupted into violence. In July 1863, a group of 500 wage workers, led by volunteer firemen, assaulted the army draft office, shattering its windows, then burning it down. When the city police superintendent arrived at the scene, he was beaten unconscious, and the outnumbered policemen were forced to retreat.

The rioters, now swollen by thousands of working-class whites, mostly Irishmen, were angry over the unfair military draft, ruthlessly taking out their frustrations on blacks. Mobs rampaged through the streets of Manhattan, randomly assaulting African Americans, beating them, dragging them through the streets, and lynching a disabled black man while chanting "Hurrah for Jeff Davis." Thugs also burned down more than fifty buildings, including

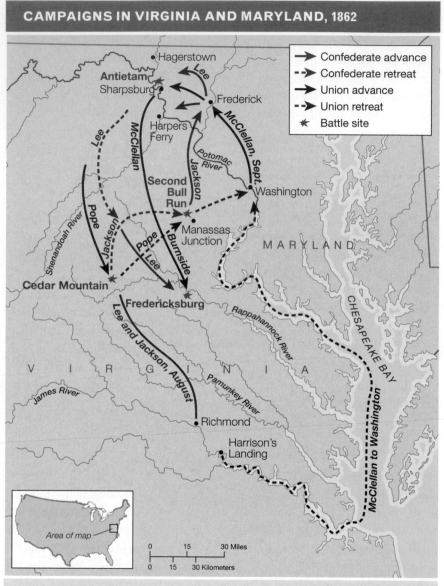

CAMPAIGNS IN VIRGINIA AND MARYLAND, 1862

- How did the Confederate army defeat General Pope at the Second Battle of Bull Run?
- Why was General Burnside's decision to attack at Fredericksburg a mistake?

the mayor's home, police stations, two Protestant churches, and the Colored Orphan Asylum, forcing 233 children to flee.

The raging violence went on for three days, killing 105 people and injuring thousands. Only the arrival of Federal soldiers put an end to the rioting. Thousands of terrified blacks thereafter moved out of the city for fear of continuing racial violence. Similar riots occurred in other northern cities, including Boston.

BLACKS SOLDIERS AND SAILORS In July 1862, in an effort to strengthen the Union war effort, the U.S. Congress had passed the **Militia Act**, which authorized the army to use freed slaves as laborers or soldiers. (They were already eligible to serve in the navy.) But Lincoln did not encourage the use of freed slaves as soldiers because he feared the reaction in the border states, where slavery remained in place. It was only after the formal signing of the Emancipation Proclamation in January 1863 that the Union army recruited blacks in large numbers.

On May 22, 1863, the U.S. War Department created the Bureau of Colored Troops to recruit free blacks and freed slaves. More than 180,000 blacks enlisted. Some 80 percent of them were from southern states, and 38,000 of them gave their lives. In the navy, African Americans accounted for about a fourth of all enlistments; of these, more than 2,800 died. Initially, blacks were not allowed in combat, but the need to win the prolonged war changed that. Once in battle, they fought tenaciously. A white Union army private reported in the spring of 1863 that the black troops "fight like the Devil."

Black Union army sergeant Wearing his uniform and sword, he poses with a copy of J. T. Headley's *The Great Rebellion* in his hand.

To be sure, racism in the North influenced the status of African Americans in the Union military. Many people who opposed slavery did not support racial equality. Black soldiers and sailors were placed in all-black units led by white officers. They were paid less than whites ($7 per month versus $16 for white recruits) and were ineligible for the enlistment bonus paid to whites. Still, as Frederick Douglass declared, "this is no time for hesitation. . . . This is our chance, and woe betide us if we fail to embrace it."

Service in the Union army or navy provided former slaves a unique opportunity to grow in confidence, awareness, and maturity. A northern social worker in the South Carolina Sea Islands was "astonished" at the positive effects of "soldiering" on ex-slaves: "Some who left here a month ago to join [the army were] cringing, dumpish, slow," but now they "are ready to look you in the eye—are wide awake and active." Commenting on Union victories at Port Hudson and Milliken's Bend, Louisiana, Lincoln reported that "some of our commanders . . . believe that . . . the use of colored troops constitutes the heaviest blow yet dealt to the rebels."

THE WAR BEHIND THE LINES

Feeding, clothing, and supplying the vast armies required tremendous sacrifices on both home fronts. Farms and villages were transformed into battlefields, churches became makeshift hospitals, civilian life was disrupted, and families grieved for soldiers who would not be coming home.

WOMEN AND THE WAR While breaking the bonds of slavery, the Civil War also loosened traditional restraints on female activity. "No conflict in history," a journalist wrote, "was such a woman's war as the Civil War." Women on both sides played prominent roles. They worked in mills and factories, sewed uniforms, composed patriotic poems and songs, and raised money and supplies. In Greenville, South Carolina, when T. G. Gower went off to fight, his wife Elizabeth took over the family business, converting production in their carriage factory to military wagons and ambulances. Other women, black and white, supported the freedmen's aid movement to help impoverished freed slaves.

In the North alone, some 20,000 women served as nurses and health-related volunteers. The most famous nurses were Clara Barton and Dorothea Lynde Dix. Barton explained that her place was "anywhere between the bullet and the battlefield." Dix declared that nurses should be "plain looking" women between the ages of thirty-five and fifty who could "bear the presence of suffering and exercise entire self-control." Barton, who later founded the American Red Cross, claimed that the war advanced by fifty years the progress of women in gaining social and economic equality.

In many southern towns and counties, the home front became a world of white women and children and African American slaves. Women suddenly found themselves full-time farmers or plantation managers, clerks, and schoolteachers. A few women disguised themselves as men and fought in the war, while dozens served as spies. Others traveled with the armies, cooking meals, writing letters, and assisting with amputations. In 1864, President Lincoln told a soldier that all the praise of women over the centuries did not do justice "for their conduct during the war."

Clara Barton She oversaw the distribution of medicines to Union troops and would later help found the American Red Cross.

WARTIME GOVERNMENT While freeing the slaves in the Confederacy was a transformational development, a political revolution began as a result of the shift in congressional power from the South to the North after secession.

In 1862, the Republican-dominated Congress sought to promote the "prosperity and happiness of the whole people" by passing a more comprehensive tariff bill (called the Morrill Tariff in honor of its sponsor, Vermont Republican congressman Justin Smith Morrill) to raise government revenue and "protect" America's manufactures, agriculture, mining, and fishing industries from foreign competition. For the rest of the nineteenth century, U.S. manufacturers were the most protected in the world in terms of high federal tariffs discouraging foreign imports.

The Republicans in Congress, with Lincoln's support, enacted legislation promoting economic development. To that end, Congress approved the Pacific Railway Act (1862), which provided federal funding and grants of land for construction of a 1,900 mile-long transcontinental railroad line from Omaha, Nebraska, to Sacramento, California. In addition, a **Homestead Act** (1862) granted 160 acres of public land to each settler who agreed

Susie King Taylor Born into slavery, she served as a nurse in Union-occupied Georgia and operated a school for freed slaves.

to work the land for five years. To help farmers become more productive, Congress created a new federal agency, the Department of Agriculture.

Two other key pieces of Republican legislation were the **Morrill Land Grant Act** (1862), which provided states with 30,000 acres of federal land to establish public universities that would teach "agriculture and mechanic arts," and the National Banking Act (1863), which created national banks that could issue paper money that would be accepted across the country. These wartime measures had long-term significance for the growth of the national economy—and the expansion of the federal government.

UNION FINANCES In December 1860, as southern states announced their plans to secede, the federal treasury was virtually empty. To meet the war's huge expenses, Congress needed money fast—and lots of it. It focused on three options: raising taxes, printing paper money, and selling government bonds to investors. The taxes came chiefly in the form of the Morrill Tariff on imports and a 3 percent tax on manufactures and most professions.

In 1862, Congress created the Internal Revenue Service to collect the first income tax on citizens and corporations. The tax rate was 3 percent on those with annual incomes more than $800. The tax rate went up to 5 percent on incomes of more than $10,000. Yet only 250,000 people out of a population of 39 million had income high enough to pay taxes.

Congressman Justin S. Morrill, who had authored the Land Grant Act and the Tariff Act of 1862, endorsed the concept of "progressive" taxation, in which tax *rates* rose with designated income levels. Taxation, he argued, "must be distributed equally, not upon each man an equal amount, but a tax [rate] proportionate to his ability to pay."

The new federal tax revenues, however, fell so short of what was needed—in the end they would meet only 21 percent of wartime expenditures—that Congress in 1862 resorted to printing paper money. With the Legal Tender

Act of 1862, Congress approved issuing $450 million in new paper currency, which soon were called *greenbacks* because of the color of the ink used to print the bills.

The federal government also relied upon the sale of bonds. A Philadelphia banker named Jay Cooke (the "Financier of the Civil War") mobilized a nationwide campaign to sell $2 billion in government bonds to private investors.

CONFEDERATE FINANCES In comparison to the Union, the Confederate efforts to finance the war were a disaster. Jefferson Davis had to create a treasury and a revenue-collecting system from scratch. Moreover, the South's agrarian economy was land-rich but cash-poor. While the Confederacy owned 30 percent of America's assets (businesses, land, slaves) in 1861, its currency in circulation was only 12 percent of that in the North. In its first year, the Confederacy created a property tax, which should have yielded a hefty amount of revenue. But collection of the taxes was left to the states, and the result was chaos. In 1863, the desperate Confederate Congress began taxing nearly everything, but enforcement was poor and evasion easy. Altogether, taxes covered no more than 5 percent of Confederate war costs, and bond issues accounted for less than 33 percent.

During the course of the war, the Confederacy issued more than $1 billion in paper money, which, along with a shortage of consumer goods, caused prices to soar. By 1864, a turkey sold in the Richmond market for $100, flour brought $425 a barrel, and bacon was $10 a pound. Such rampant inflation (price increases) caused great distress, and frustrations over the burdens of war increasingly erupted into rioting, looting, and mass protests.

UNION POLITICS The North had its share of dissension and factionalism. President Lincoln was forced to use all of his substantial political genius to fend off uprisings in Congress and conspiracies among cabinet members. He loved the jockeying of backroom politics, and he excelled at it. Throughout the war, the president faced a radical wing of Republicans composed mainly of militant abolitionists who criticized his leadership of the war effort. Led by Thaddeus Stevens in the House and Charles Sumner in the Senate, the so-called Radical Republicans in Congress wanted more than defeat of the Confederacy; they wanted to "reconstruct" it by allowing Union armies to seize southern plantations and give the land to the former slaves. The majority of Republicans, however, continued to back Lincoln's more cautious approach.

The Democratic party was devastated by the departure of its long-dominant southern wing and the death of its national spokesman, Stephen A. Douglas, in

June 1861. What were called Peace Democrats favored restoring the Union "as it was [before 1860] and the Constitution as it is." They reluctantly supported Lincoln's war policies but opposed Republican economic legislation. So-called war Democrats, such as Tennessee senator Andrew Johnson and Secretary of War Edwin M. Stanton, backed Lincoln's policies.

A few Peace Democrats verged on disloyalty to the Union cause. The **Copperhead Democrats** (poisonous snakes) were strongest in states such as Ohio, Indiana, and Illinois, that had substantial numbers of former southerners. The Copperheads openly sympathized with the Confederacy, savagely criticized Lincoln, and called for an end to the war.

CIVIL LIBERTIES Such support for the enemy led Lincoln to crack down hard. Like all wartime leaders, he faced the challenge of balancing the urgent needs of winning a war with the protection of civil liberties. Using his authority as commander in chief in wartime, Lincoln exercised emergency powers, including suspending the writ of *habeas corpus*, which guarantees arrested citizens a speedy hearing before a judge. The Constitution states that the right of habeas corpus may be suspended only in cases of rebellion or invasion, but Supreme Court justice Roger Taney and several congressional leaders argued that Congress alone had the authority to take such action.

By the Habeas Corpus Act of 1863, Congress allowed the president to order people arrested on the suspicion of treason. Thereafter, Union soldiers and local sheriffs arrested thousands of Confederate sympathizers in the northern states without using a writ of habeas corpus. Union general Henry Halleck jailed one Missourian for saying, "[I] wouldn't wipe my ass with the stars and stripes."

CONFEDERATE POLITICS AND STATES' RIGHTS Unlike Lincoln, Jefferson Davis never had to worry about reelection. He and his vice president, Alexander Stephens, were elected in 1861 for six-year terms. But discontent with their leadership grew

Jefferson Davis President of the Confederacy.

as the war dragged on. Poor white southerners expressed bitter resentment of the planter elite while food grew scarce and prices skyrocketed. A food riot erupted in Richmond on April 2, 1863, and ended only when Davis himself threatened to shoot the protesters.

Davis's greatest challenge came from the southern politicians who criticized the "tyrannical" powers of the Confederate government in Richmond. Critics asserted states' rights against the authority of the Confederate government, just as they had against the Union.

The Confederacy also suffered from Davis's difficult personality. Whereas Lincoln was a pragmatist, Davis was a brittle ideologue with a stinging temper. Once he made a decision, nothing could change his mind, and he could never admit a mistake. One southern politician said that Davis was "as stubborn as a mule." Such a dogmatic personality was ill suited to the chief executive of an infant—and fractious—nation. Cabinet members resigned almost as soon as they were appointed. During the four years of the Confederacy, there were three secretaries of state and six secretaries of war, and Vice President Stephens constantly warred against Davis's "military despotism."

THE FALTERING CONFEDERACY

The Confederate strategy of fighting largely a defensive war worked well at first. As the armies maneuvered for battle in the spring of 1863, however, President Lincoln found a commanding general in the West as capable as Robert E. Lee was in the East. Humble, unassuming, plain-spoken Ulysses S. Grant, five feet eight inches tall and weighing only 135 pounds, was blessed with an uncommonly ruthless determination to win on the battlefield—at all cost.

CHANCELLORSVILLE After the Union disaster at Fredericksburg at the end of 1862, President Lincoln turned to General Joseph Hooker, a hard-fighting, hard-drinking leader who had earned the nickname "Fighting Joe." With a force of 130,000 men, the largest Union army yet gathered, an overconfident Hooker failed his leadership test at Chancellorsville, in eastern Virginia, during the first week of May, 1863. "My plans are perfect. . . . May God have mercy on General Lee," Hooker boasted, "for I will have none."

Hooker spoke too soon. Robert E. Lee, with perhaps half as many troops, split his army in thirds and gave Hooker a lesson in the art of elusive mobility when Stonewall Jackson's 28,000 Confederates surprised the Union army by smashing into its exposed right flank. The attack sparked days of confusing and desperate fighting, ultimately forcing Hooker's army to retreat. "My God, my God," moaned Lincoln when he heard the news. "What will the country

Thomas "Stonewall" Jackson The celebrated Confederate commander, Jackson would later die of friendly fire in the Battle of Chancellorsville.

say?" Chancellorsville was the peak of Lee's military career, but it would also be his last significant victory.

VICKSBURG While Lee frustrated the Federals in the East, General Grant had been inching his army down the Mississippi River toward the Confederate stronghold of Vicksburg, Mississippi, a busy commercial town situated on high bluffs overlooking a sharp horseshoe bend in the river. Capturing the Rebel stronghold, Grant stressed, "was of the first importance," because Vicksburg was the only rail and river junction between Memphis, Tennessee, and New Orleans. President Lincoln said that Vicksburg held the "key" to a Union victory in the war, and Jefferson Davis agreed, saying that holding the Mississippi River open was "vital" to the Confederacy. "Vicksburg must not be lost!" If Union forces could gain control of the Mississippi River, they could split the Confederacy in two and prevent western food and livestock from reaching the Confederate armies.

While the Union warships sneaked past the Confederate cannons overlooking the river, Grant moved his army eastward on a campaign that Lincoln later called "one of the most brilliant in the world." Grant captured Jackson, Mississippi, before pinning the 31,000 Confederates inside Vicksburg so tightly that "not a cat could have crept out . . . without being discovered." The Union forces dug twelve miles of interconnected trenches, encircling the besieged city.

In the **Battle of Vicksburg**, Grant used constant bombardment and gradual starvation to wear down the Confederates trapped in the town. Many people were forced to live in cellars or caves dug to protect them from the incessant shelling. The Rebel soldiers and the city's residents were hopelessly trapped; they could neither escape nor be reinforced nor resupplied with food and ammunition. As the weeks passed, desperate Confederates ate their horses and mules, then dogs and cats, and, finally, rats, which sold for a dollar each.

General John C. Pemberton, the Confederate commander at Vicksburg, wrote Jefferson Davis that the situation was "hopeless." A group of soldiers pleaded with their commander: "If you can't feed us, you had better surrender us, horrible as that idea is."

GETTYSBURG Vicksburg's dilemma led Jefferson Davis to ask Robert E. Lee to send troops to break the siege. Lee, however, thought he had a better plan. He would make another daring strike into the North in hopes of forcing the Union army surrounding Vicksburg to retreat. He also wagered that a bold northern offensive would persuade peace-seeking northern Copperhead Democrats to end the war on terms favorable to the Confederacy. The stakes were high. A Confederate general said the invasion into Maryland and Pennsylvania would "either destroy the Yankees or bring them to terms." Or be a disaster for Lee.

In June 1863, the fabled Army of Northern Virginia, which Lee said was made up of "invincible troops" who would "go anywhere and do anything if properly led," again moved northward, taking thousands of animals and wagons as well as throngs of slaves for support. Once the Union commanders realized the Confederates were again moving north, they gave chase.

Neither side expected Gettysburg, a hilly crossroads farming town of 2,400 people in southeastern Pennsylvania, to be the site of the largest battle ever fought in North America. Both armies were caught by surprise when Confederate troops entered the town at dawn on June 30 and collided with Union cavalry units that had been tracking their movements.

The main forces of both sides—65,000 Confederates and 85,000 Federals—then raced to the scene, and on July 1, the armies began the **Battle of Gettysburg**, the most dramatic contest of the war. While preparing for battle, a Union cavalryman yelled at the soldiers from New York and Pennsylvania: "You stand alone, between the Rebel army and your homes. Fight like hell!"

Initially, the Confederates forced the Federals to retreat, but the Union troops regrouped to stronger positions on high ridges overlooking the town. The new Union commander, the cautious and conservative General George Meade, rushed reinforcements to his new lines along the heights.

On July 2, wave after wave of screaming Confederates assaulted Meade's army, pushing the Federal lines back but never breaking through. Some 16,000 were killed or wounded on both sides during the inconclusive second day of fighting. But worse was to come.

The next day, July 3, against the advice of his senior general, James Longstreet, Robert E. Lee risked all on a climactic assault against the well-defended

"A Harvest of Death" Timothy H. O'Sullivan's grim photograph of the dead at Gettysburg.

Union lines along Cemetery Ridge. For two hours, both sides bombarded the other, leading a Union soldier to write that it felt "as if the heavens and earth were crashing together." Deafening sounds "more terrible never greeted human ears."

Then, the cannons stopped firing. At about two o'clock on the broiling summer afternoon, three Confederate infantry divisions—about 12,500 men in all—emerged from the woods and prepared to attack. General George Pickett, commander of the lead division, told them to "Charge the enemy and remember Old Virginia!"

With drums pounding and bugles blaring, a gray wave of Rebels began a desperate, mile-long dash up a grassy slope. Awaiting them behind a low stone wall at the top of the ridge were 120 Union cannons and thousands of rifles. It was as hopeless a situation as the Union charge at Fredericksburg. A Union soldier said that the charging Confederates "came on in magnificent order with the step of men who believed themselves invincible."

When the Federals opened fire, the attacking Confederates were "enveloped in a dense cloud of dust. Arms, heads, blankets, guns, and knapsacks were tossed into the clear air." Only a few Rebels made it to the top of the ridge, where they fought bravely in hand-to-hand combat. A general leading the assault climbed atop the stone wall and shouted: "Come on, boys! Give them the cold steel! Who will follow me?" Two minutes later, he was dead—as was the Confederate attack—when Union soldiers held in reserve rushed to close the gap in their lines.

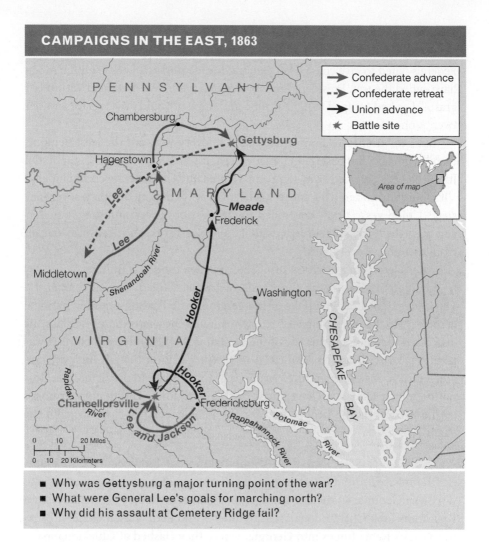

CAMPAIGNS IN THE EAST, 1863

- Why was Gettysburg a major turning point of the war?
- What were General Lee's goals for marching north?
- Why did his assault at Cemetery Ridge fail?

With stunning suddenness, the carnage was over. The surviving Confederates retreated to where they had started. The once roaring battlefield was now a deathly quiet field of horror punctuated by the "moanings and groanings" of thousands of wounded soldiers and horses.

What General Lee had called the "grand charge" was, in the end, a grand failure. As he watched the survivors straggling back across the bloody field, he muttered, "All this has been my fault." He then ordered General Pickett to prepare his battered division for another attack, only to have Pickett tartly reply: "General Lee, I have no division now."

LEE'S RETREAT Again, as after Antietam, Lee's mangled army was forced to retreat back to Virginia, this time in a driving rain—and again, the Federals failed to give chase. Had General Meade pursued Lee's army, he might have ended the war. President Lincoln was outraged: "We had them within our grasp!" Lee had escaped to fight again—and the war would grind on for another twenty-one months.

But Lee's desperate gamble had failed in every way, not the least being its inability to save the besieged Confederate army at Vicksburg, Mississippi. On July 4, as Lee's defeated army left Pennsylvania, the Confederate commander at Vicksburg surrendered his entire 30,000-man army, ending the forty-seven-day siege. Union vessels now controlled the Mississippi River, and the Confederacy was effectively split in two, with Louisiana, Texas, and Arkansas cut off from the other Rebel states.

After Gettysburg, a group of northern states funded a military cemetery in commemoration of the thousands of soldiers killed. On November 19, 1863, President Lincoln spoke at the ceremony dedicating the new national cemetery. In his brief remarks, known now as the Gettysburg Address, he expressed the pain and sorrow of the uncivil war. The prolonged conflict was testing whether a nation "dedicated to the proposition that all men are created equal . . . can long endure." In stirring words, Lincoln predicted that "this nation, under God, shall have a new birth of freedom—and that government of the people, by the people, and for the people, shall not perish from the earth."

CHATTANOOGA The third Union triumph of 1863 occurred in southern Tennessee around Chattanooga, the river port that served as a gateway to northern Georgia. In the late summer, a Union army led by General William Rosecrans took Chattanooga on September 9 and then chased General Braxton Bragg's Rebel forces into Georgia, where they clashed at Chickamauga (a Cherokee word meaning "river of death").

The Confederates, for once, had a numerical advantage, and the battered Union forces fell back into Chattanooga while the Confederates surrounded the city. Rosecrans reported that "we have met a serious disaster. Enemy overwhelmed us, drove our right, pierced our center, and scattered troops there." Lincoln urged him to persevere: "If we can hold Chattanooga, and East Tennessee, I think [the] rebellion must dwindle and die."

The Union command rushed in reinforcements, and on November 24 and 25, the Federal troops dislodged the Confederates from Lookout Mountain and Missionary Ridge, thereby gaining effective control of Tennessee. The South had lost the war in the West.

THE CONFEDERACY AT RISK The dramatic Union victories at Vicksburg, Gettysburg, and Chattanooga turned the tide against the Confederacy. During the summer and fall of 1863, however, Lincoln's generals in the East lost the momentum that Gettysburg had provided, thereby allowing the Army of Northern Virginia to nurse its wounds and continue fighting.

By 1864, Robert E. Lee was ready to renew the war. His men were "in fine spirits and anxious for a fight." Still, the tone had changed. Earlier, Confederate leaders assumed they could actually win the war. Now, they began to worry about defeat. A Confederate officer in Richmond, writing in his diary after the defeats at Gettysburg and Vicksburg, noted that "today absolute ruin seems to be our fortune. The Confederacy totters to its destruction."

A WARTIME ELECTION War or no war, 1864 was still a presidential election year, and by autumn the contest would become a referendum on the war itself. No president since Andrew Jackson had won reelection, and Lincoln became convinced that he would lose without a dramatic change in the course of the war. Radical Republicans, frustrated that the war had not been won, tried to prevent Lincoln's nomination for a second term, but he consistently outmaneuvered them. Once Lincoln was assured of the nomination, he selected Andrew Johnson, a War Democrat from Tennessee, as his running mate on the "National Union" ticket.

At their 1864 national convention in Chicago, the Democrats acknowledged that people were tired of the costly war and called for an immediate end to the fighting. They nominated General George B. McClellan, the former Union commander who had clashed with Lincoln, his commander in chief. McClellan pledged that if elected he would stop the war and, if the Rebels refused to return to the Union, he would allow the Confederacy to "go in peace."

Lincoln knew that the election would be decided on the battlefields. To save the Union before a new Democratic administration could stop the war and recognize the independence of the Confederacy, the president had brought his best general, Ulysses S. Grant, to Washington, D.C., in March 1864, and given him overall command of the war effort, promising him all the troops and supplies he needed. A New York newspaper reported that Lincoln's presidency was now "in the hands of General Grant, and the failure of the General will be the overthrow of the president."

GRANT'S STRATEGY The cigar-chewing Grant was a hard-nosed warrior with unflagging energy. He had a simple concept of war: "Find out where your enemy is, get to him as soon as you can, and strike him as hard as you can, and keep moving on"—regardless of the number of dead and wounded.

Ulysses S. Grant At his headquarters in City Point (now Hopewell), Virginia.

Grant dramatically changed the Union military strategy. He would focus on crippling Rebel armies rather than attacking particular cities, like Richmond. He planned for the three largest Union armies, one in Virginia, one in Tennessee, and one in Louisiana, to launch relentless offensives in the spring of 1864. No more short battles followed by long pauses. The Union armies would force the outnumbered Confederates to keep fighting, day after day, week after week, until they were worn out. "Grant is like a bulldog," Lincoln said. "Let him get his teeth in, and nothing can shake him loose."

Grant assigned his trusted friend, General William Tecumseh Sherman, a rail-thin, red-haired Ohioan, to lead the Union army in Tennessee southward and apply Grant's strategy of "complete conquest" to the heart of the Confederacy. Sherman, cool under pressure and obsessed with winning at all costs, owed much of his success to Grant's support. "He stood by me when I was crazy, and I stood by him when he was drunk," Sherman said.

CHASING LEE In May 1864, General Grant's massive Army of the Potomac, numbering about 115,000 to General Lee's 65,000, moved south across the Rappahannock and Rapidan Rivers in eastern Virginia. In the nightmarish Battle of the Wilderness (May 5–6), the armies clashed in dense woods, thickets and brambles, the horror and suffering of the scene heightened by crackling brushfires in which many wounded soldiers were burned to death.

Grant's men suffered more casualties than the Confederates, but the Rebels struggled to find replacements. Always before, when bloodied by Lee's troops, Union armies had quit fighting to rest and nurse their wounds, but now Grant refused to halt. Instead, he continued to push southward, forcing the Rebels to keep fighting.

The Union army engaged Lee's men again near Spotsylvania Court House, eleven miles southwest of Fredericksburg, on the road to Richmond. For twelve days in May, the two armies engaged in some of the fiercest combat of the war. Grant's troops kept the pressure on, pushing relentlessly toward Richmond.

In the first days of June, just as Republican party leaders were gathering to renominate Lincoln as their presidential candidate, Grant foolishly ordered a frontal attack on Lee's army. The Confederates were well-entrenched at Cold Harbor near the Chickahominy River, just ten miles east of Richmond. In twenty minutes, almost 4,000 Federals, caught in a blistering cross fire, were killed or wounded. A Confederate commander reported that "it was not war; it was murder."

The frightful losses nearly unhinged Grant, who later admitted that the botched attack was his greatest mistake as a commander. Critics, including Lincoln's wife Mary, called him "the Butcher" after Cold Harbor. In just two months, Grant's massive offensive across Virginia had cost some 60,000 killed and wounded soldiers, and criticism of the war in the North skyrocketed.

Yet Grant, for all of his mistakes, knew that his army could more easily replace its dead and wounded than could the Rebels. While the Confederates were winning battles, they were losing more and more men. In June 1864, Grant brilliantly maneuvered his battered forces around Lee's army and headed for Petersburg, a major supply center and transportation hub twenty-five miles south of Richmond. The opposing armies dug in along long lines of trenches above and below Petersburg.

For nine months, the two sides held each other in check around Petersburg. Grant's troops, twice as numerous as Lee's, were generously supplied by Union vessels moving up the James River, while the Confederates, hungry and cold, wasted away. Petersburg had become Lee's prison while disasters piled up for the Confederacy elsewhere. Lee admitted that it was "a mere question of time" before he would have to retreat or surrender.

SHERMAN PUSHES SOUTH Meanwhile, General Grant ordered William T. Sherman to drive through the heart of Dixie and "break it up," inflicting "all the damage you can." As Sherman moved his large army south from Chattanooga through the Georgia mountains toward the crucial railroad hub of Atlanta, he sent a warning to the city's residents: "prepare for my coming." By the middle of July, Sherman's troops had reached the outskirts of heavily-fortified Atlanta, trapping the 40,000 Confederate soldiers there. Jefferson Davis was so concerned about the situation that he made the hugely controversial decision to replace the Confederate commander, General Joseph Johnston, with General John Bell Hood, who had been Lee's most aggressive general after the death of Stonewall Jackson.

Hood, a Texan, was a reckless fighter. His arm had been shattered at Gettysburg, and he had lost a leg at Chickamauga. Strapped to his saddle, he refused simply to "defend" Atlanta; instead, he attacked Sherman's army, which

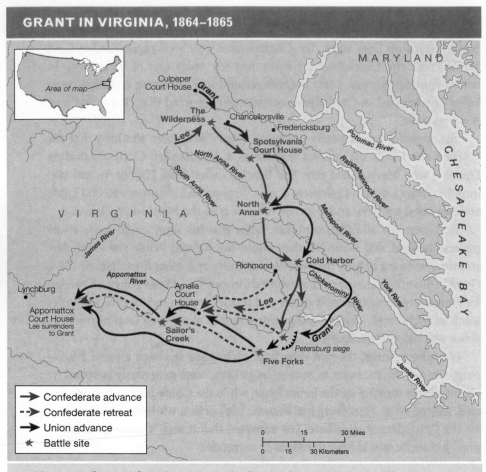

GRANT IN VIRGINIA, 1864–1865

Area of map

MARYLAND

Culpeper Court House • Grant

The Wilderness ✶

Chancellorsville

Fredericksburg •

Spotsylvania Court House

Potomac River

Rappahannock River

Lee

North Anna River

South Anna River

V I R G I N I A

North Anna ✶

Mattaponi River

CHESAPEAKE BAY

James River

Richmond •

Cold Harbor ✶

Chickahominy River

York River

Appomattox River

Amelia Court House

Lee

Lynchburg •

Appomattox Court House
Lee surrenders to Grant

Sailor's Creek ✶

Petersburg siege

Grant

James River

Five Forks ✶

➡ Confederate advance
--➤ Confederate retreat
➡ Union advance
✶ Battle site

| 0 | 15 | 30 Miles |
| 0 | 15 | 30 Kilometers |

- How were General Grant's tactics in the Battle of the Wilderness different from the Union's previous encounters with General Lee's army?
- Why did Grant have the advantage at Petersburg?

is exactly what Sherman, the Union commander, wanted him to do. Three times in eight days, the Confederates lashed out at the Union lines encircling the city. Each time, they were turned back, suffering *seven* times as many casualties as the Federals. The Battle of Atlanta left Hood's army shattered, surrounded, and outnumbered.

Finally, on September 1, the Confederates, desperately low on food and supplies, evacuated the city. Sherman then moved his troops into Atlanta. They stayed until November, resting and resupplying themselves. Sherman ordered the 20,000 residents to leave Atlanta. When city officials protested, the

Union commander replied: "War is cruelty." His men then set fire to the city's railroads, iron foundries, shops, mills, hotels, and businesses.

LINCOLN REELECTED William T. Sherman's conquest of Atlanta turned the tide of the **election of 1864**. As a Republican senator said, the Union victory in Georgia "created the most extraordinary change in public opinion here [in the North] that ever was known." The capture of Mobile, Alabama, by Union naval forces in August, and Confederate defeats in Virginia's Shenandoah Valley in October, also spurred the dramatic revival of Abraham Lincoln's political support in the North. The South's hope that northern discontent would lead to a negotiated peace vanished.

In the 1864 election, the Democratic candidate, General George McClellan, carried only New Jersey, Delaware, and Kentucky, with just 21 electoral votes to Lincoln's 212, and won only 1.8 million popular votes (45 percent) to Lincoln's 2.2 million (55 percent). Union soldiers and sailors voted in large numbers, and their choice was Lincoln.

SHERMAN'S "MARCH TO THE SEA" In November 1864, General Sherman led 60,000 soldiers out of burning Atlanta on their famous **"March to the Sea,"** advancing rapidly through Georgia toward the coast. Sherman planned to wage a modern war against soldiers and civilians. He pledged to "whip the rebels, to humble their pride, to follow them into their inmost recesses, and make them fear and dread us."

John Bell Hood's Confederate Army of Tennessee, meanwhile, tried a desperate gamble by heading in the opposite direction from the Union forces, pushing northward into Alabama and then Tennessee. Hood hoped to trick Sherman into chasing him. Sherman, however, refused to take the bait. He was determined to keep his main army moving southward to the Georgia coast and then into South Carolina, the seedbed of secession. But he did send General George Thomas and 30,000 soldiers north to shadow Hood's Confederates.

The two forces clashed in Tennessee. Hood was a ferocious fighter but a foolish commander. In the Battle of Franklin (November 30, 1864), near Nashville, he sent his 18,000 soldiers in a hopeless frontal assault against dug-in Union troops backed by cannons. In a few hours, Hood lost six generals and saw 6,252 of his men killed or wounded, a casualty figure higher than "Pickett's Charge" at Gettysburg. Two weeks later, in the Battle of Nashville, the Federals led by General Thomas scattered what was left of Hood's bloodied army. A few days later, a grieving Hood was relieved of his command.

William Tecumseh Sherman Sherman's campaign through Georgia developed into a war of maneuver as they raced to the coast, without the pitched battles of Grant's campaign in Virginia.

Meanwhile, Sherman's army pushed southward across Georgia, living off the land while destroying plantations, barns, crops, warehouses, bridges, and rail lines. "We are not only fighting hostile armies," Sherman explained, "but a hostile people" who must "feel the hard hand of war."

On December 24, 1864, Sherman sent a whimsical telegram to President Lincoln offering him the coastal city of Savannah as a Christmas present. By the time Sherman's army arrived in Savannah, it freed more than 40,000 slaves, burned scores of plantations, and destroyed the railroads. "God bless you, Yanks!" shouted a freed slave in Georgia. "Come at last! God knows how long I been waitin'."

SOUTH CAROLINA On February 1, 1865, Sherman's army headed north across the Savannah River into South Carolina, the "hell-hole of secession" in the eyes of Union troops. Sherman reported that his "whole army is burning with an insatiable desire to wreak vengeance upon South Carolina." General Joseph Johnston, who had been called out of retirement to take charge of the scattered remnants of the Rebel forces, knew that the war was all but over. All he could hope to do, he said, was "annoy" the advancing Federals.

South Carolina paid a high price. Sherman's army burned more than a dozen towns, including Barnwell, which they called "Burnwell." On February 17, 1865, Sherman's men captured the state capital of Columbia. Soon thereafter, Charleston surrendered, and the Union flag once again fluttered over Fort Sumter.

During the late winter and early spring of 1865, the Confederacy found itself besieged on all sides. Defeat was in the air. Jefferson Davis rejected any talk of surrender, however. If his armies should be defeated, he wanted the soldiers to scatter and fight an unending guerrilla war. "The war came and now it must go on," he stubbornly insisted, "till the last man of this generation falls in his tracks, and his children seize his musket and fight our battle."

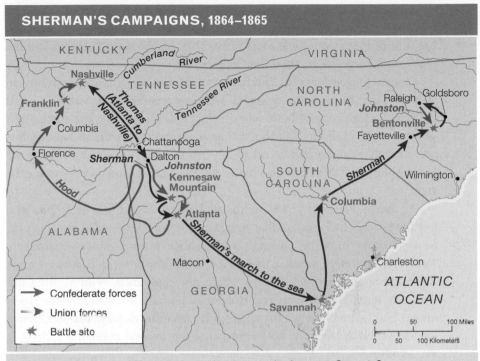

SHERMAN'S CAMPAIGNS, 1864–1865

- What was General Sherman's goal as he marched across Georgia?
- How much damage did Sherman do in Georgia and South Carolina?
- How did it affect the Confederate war effort?

A SECOND TERM While Confederate forces made their last stands, Abraham Lincoln prepared for his second term as president. The weary commander in chief had weathered constant criticism during his first term, but with the war nearing its end, Lincoln now garnered deserved praise. The *Chicago Tribune* observed that the president "has slowly and steadily risen in the respect, confidence, and admiration of the people."

On March 4, 1865, amid rumors of a Confederate attempt to abduct or assassinate the president, the six-foot-four-inch Lincoln, dressed in a black suit and stovepipe hat, his face weathered by prairie wind and political worry, delivered his second inaugural address on the East Portico of the Capitol. Not a hundred feet away, looking down on Lincoln from the Capitol porch, was a twenty-six-year-old actor named John Wilkes Booth, who five weeks later would kill the president in a desperate attempt to do something "heroic" for his beloved South.

Lincoln's second inaugural address was more a sermon than a speech. Slavery, he said, had "somehow" caused the war, and everyone bore some guilt for the national shame of racial injustice and the awful war to end it. Both sides had known before the fighting began that war was to be avoided at all costs, but "one of them would *make* war rather than let the nation survive; and the other would *accept* war rather than let it perish."

Lincoln longed for peace and reunion. "Fondly do we hope—fervently do we pray—that this mighty scourge of war may speedily pass away." He noted the paradoxical irony of both sides in the civil war reading the same Bible, praying to the same God, and appealing for divine support in its fight against the other. Now the president urged the Union forces "to finish the work we are in," bolstered with "firmness in the right insofar as God gives us to see the right."

As Lincoln looked ahead to the end of the fighting and a "just and lasting peace," he stressed that vengeance must be avoided at all costs. Reconciliation must be pursued "with malice toward none; with charity for all." Those eight words captured Lincoln's hopes for a restored Union. Redemption and reunion were his goals, not vengeance. With a loving tolerance of human complexity and sinfulness, Lincoln revealed how the rigors of war had helped him see the need for humility in victory. The abolitionist leader Frederick Douglass proclaimed Lincoln's second inaugural address "a sacred effort."

APPOMATTOX During the spring of 1865, General Grant's army kept pounding the Rebels defending Petersburg, Virginia. Lee was on the horns of a dilemma, and he knew it. He had no way to replace the men he was losing, and his dwindling army couldn't kill enough Yankees to make Grant quit. On April 2, 1865, Lee's exhausted army, now numbering fewer than 30,000 soldiers, tried to break out of Petersburg, but the Union army followed in hot pursuit. On April 7, Grant sent a note to Lee urging him to surrender. With his army virtually surrounded, Lee told General James Longstreet that "there is nothing left for me to do but go and see General Grant, and I would rather die a thousand deaths."

On April 9 (Palm Sunday), the dignified Lee, stiff and formal in his dress uniform, met the short, mud-spattered Grant in the village of **Appomattox Court House**. After discussing their service in the Mexican-American War, Lee asked what the terms of surrender would be. In keeping with Lincoln's desire for a gracious peace, Grant let the Confederates keep their pistols, horses, and mules, and he ensured that none of them would be tried for treason. Lee then confessed that his men were starving, and Grant ordered that they be provided rations. After signing the surrender documents in the parlor of a farmhouse, Lee mounted his horse and returned to his army.

The next day, as the gaunt Confederates formed ranks for the last time, Joshua Chamberlain, the Union general in charge of the surrender ceremony, ordered his men to salute the Rebel soldiers as they paraded past to give up their weapons. His Confederate counterpart signaled his men to do likewise. Chamberlain remembered that there was not a sound—no trumpets or drums, no cheers or jeers, simply an "awed stillness . . . as if it were the passing of the dead." The remaining Confederate forces surrendered in May. Jefferson Davis fled Richmond ahead of the advancing Federal troops, only to be captured in Georgia on May 10. He was eventually imprisoned in Virginia for two years.

The brutal war was at last over. Upon learning of the Union victory, John Wilkes Booth, a popular young actor in Washington, D.C., who hated Lincoln and the Union, wrote in his diary that "something *decisive* and great must be done" to avenge the Confederate defeat. He began plotting to kill President Lincoln and members of his cabinet.

A TRANSFORMING WAR

The Civil War was the most traumatic event in American history. "We have shared the incommunicable experience of war," reflected Oliver Wendell Holmes Jr., a twice-wounded Union officer who would one day become the nation's leading jurist. "We have felt, we still feel, the passion of life to its top. . . . In our youth, our hearts were touched by fire." In Virginia, elderly Edmund Ruffin, the arch secessionist planter who had been given the honor of firing the first shots at Fort Sumter, was so distraught by the Confederate surrender that he put his rifle barrel in his mouth and blew off the top of his head.

The long war changed the nation in profound ways. A *New York Times* editorial said that the war left "nothing as it found it. . . . It leaves us a different people in everything." The war destroyed the South's economy, many of its railroads and factories, much of its livestock, and several of its cities. In 1860, the northern and southern economies were essentially equal in size. By 1865, the southern economy's productivity had been cut in half. Many southern economic and political leaders had been killed during the war or had seen their plantations and businesses destroyed.

THE UNION PRESERVED The war ended the Confederacy and preserved the Union; shifted the political balance of power in Congress, the U.S. Supreme Court, and the presidency from South to North; and boosted the northern economy's industrial development, commercial agriculture, and western settlement. The Homestead Act (1862) made more than a billion acres in the West available to the landless. The power and scope of the federal government were expanded at the expense of states' rights. In 1860, the annual federal budget was $63 million; by 1865, it was more than $1 billion. In winning the war, the federal government had become the nation's largest employer.

By the end of the war, the Union was spending $2.5 million per day on the military effort, and whole new industries had been established to meet its needs for weapons, uniforms, food, equipment, and supplies. The massive amounts of preserved food required by the Union armies, for example, helped create the canning industry and transformed Chicago into the meatpacking capital of the world.

Federal contracts also provided the money needed to accelerate the growth of new industries such as the production of iron and steel, thus laying the groundwork for a postwar economic boom. Ohio senator John Sherman, in a letter to his brother, General William T. Sherman, said the war had dramatically expanded the vision "of leading capitalists" who now talk of earning "millions as confidently as formerly of thousands."

THE FIRST "MODERN" WAR In many respects, the Civil War was the first modern war. Its scope and scale were unprecedented, as it was fought across the entire continent. One of every twelve men on both sides served in the war, and few families were unaffected. More than 730,000 soldiers and sailors (37,000 of whom were blacks fighting for the Union) died, 50 percent more than the number who would die in the Second World War. The comparable number of deaths relative to today's population would be almost 7.5 million. Of the surviving combatants, 50,000 returned home with one or more limbs amputated. Disease, however, was the greatest threat to soldiers, killing twice as many as were lost in battle. Some 50,000 civilians were also killed during the war.

Unlike previous conflicts, much of the fighting in the Civil War was distant and impersonal, in part because of improvements in the effectiveness of muskets, rifles, and cannons. Men were killed at long distance, without knowing who had fired the shots that felled them. The opposing forces used an array of new weapons and instruments of war, such as cannons with "rifled," or grooved, barrels for greater accuracy; repeating rifles; ironclad ships; railroad artillery; the first military telegraph; observation balloons; and wire entanglements. The war was also modern because civilians could follow its activities by reading the newspapers that sent reporters to the front lines, or by visiting exhibitions of photographs taken at the battlefields and camps.

THIRTEENTH AMENDMENT The most important result of the war was the liberation of almost 4 million slaves. The Emancipation Proclamation had technically freed only those slaves in areas still controlled by the Confederacy. As the war entered its final months, however, freedom for all slaves emerged more fully as a legal reality as President Lincoln moved from viewing emancipation as a military weapon to seeing it as the mainspring of the conflict itself. Three major steps occurred in January 1865: Missouri and then Tennessee abolished slavery, and, at Lincoln's insistence, the U.S. House of Representatives passed an amendment to the Constitution that banned slavery everywhere. Upon ratification by three-fourths of the reunited states, the **Thirteenth Amendment** became law eight months after the war ended, on December 18, 1865. It removed any lingering doubts about the legality of emancipation. By then, slavery remained only in the border states of Kentucky and Delaware.

THE DEBATE CONTINUES Historians have provided conflicting assessments of the Union victory. Some have focused on the inherent weaknesses of the Confederacy: its lack of industry and railroads, the tensions between the states and the central government in Richmond, poor political leadership, faulty coordination and communication, the expense of preventing slave rebellions and runaways, and the advantages in population and resources enjoyed by the North. Still others have highlighted the erosion of Confederate morale in the face of terrible food shortages and unimaginable human losses.

The debate about why the North won and the South lost will probably never end, but as in other modern wars, disparities in resources were key factors. Robert E. Lee's own explanation remains accurate: "After four years of arduous service marked by unsurpassed courage and fortitude, the Army of Northern Virginia has been compelled to yield to overwhelming numbers and resources." Whatever the reasons, the North's victory resolved a key issue: no state could divorce itself from the Union. The Union, as Lincoln had always maintained, was indissoluble. At the same time, the war led to the Constitution being permanently amended to eliminate slavery. The terrible war thus served to clarify the meaning of the ideals ("All men are created equal") on which the United States had been established. The largest slaveholding nation in the world had at last chosen liberty—for all. In his first message to Congress in December 1861, Lincoln recognized early on what was at stake amid the onrush of civil war: "The struggle of today is not altogether for today; it is for a vast future also." So it was. The "fiery ordeal" of a war both "fundamental and astounding" produced, as Lincoln said, not just a preserved Union but "a new birth of freedom."

CHAPTER REVIEW

SUMMARY

- **Civil War Strategies**   When the war began, the Confederacy had a geographic advantage of fighting a defensive war on their own territory. The Union, however, held strong advantages in population and industrial development, particularly in the production of weapons, ships, and railroad equipment. After suffering a defeat at the First Battle of Bull Run, the Union military leaders adopted the "*Anaconda Plan*," imposing a naval blockade on southern ports and slowly crushing resistance on all fronts. The Union's industrial might was a deciding factor in the long war of attrition.

- **Emancipation Proclamation**   Initially, President Lincoln declared that the war's aim was to restore the Union and that slavery would be maintained where it existed. Gradually, Lincoln came to see that winning the war required ending slavery. He justified the *Emancipation Proclamation (1862)* as a military necessity because it would deprive the South of its captive labor force. After the Battle of *Antietam* in September 1862, he announced plans to free the slaves. He hoped that southern states would return to the Union before his deadline of January 1, 1863, when all slaves living in areas under Confederate control were declared free.

- **Wartime Home Fronts**   The federal government proved much more capable with finances than did the Confederacy. Through a series of tariffs, income taxes, bond issues, and banking reforms, the Union was better able to absorb the war's soaring costs. In the absence of the southern delegation in Congress, the Republican Congress approved a higher tariff, a transcontinental railroad, and a *Homestead Act*, all of which accelerated Union settlement of the West and the growth of a national economy. The *Morrill Land Grant Act* provided large land grants for the creation of state universities intended to promote economic development by turning out engineers and entrepreneurs. Both sides experienced pockets of opposition to the war efforts. In the North, *Copperhead Democrats* opposed the war and Lincoln's decision to end slavery.

- **The Winning Union Strategy**   The Union victories at the Battles of *Vicksburg* and *Gettysburg* in July 1863 turned the war in the Union's favor. With the capture of Vicksburg, the last Confederate-controlled city along the Mississippi River, Union forces cut the Confederacy in two, depriving armies in the East of supplies and manpower. In 1864, Lincoln placed General Ulysses S. Grant in charge of the Union's war efforts. For the next year, his forces constantly attacked Robert E. Lee's in Virginia while, farther south, General William T. Sherman's *"March to the Sea"* destroyed plantations, railroads, and morale in Georgia and South Carolina. His successes helped propel Lincoln to victory in the *election of 1864*. After that, southern resistance wilted. Lee surrendered his army to Grant at *Appomattox Court House* in April 1865.

- **The Significance of the Civil War**   The Civil War involved the largest number of casualties of any American war, and the Union's victory changed the course of the nation's development. Most important, the war ended slavery, embodied in the adoption of the *Thirteenth Amendment* to the U.S. Constitution in 1865. Not only did the power of the federal government increase, but the center of political and economic power shifted away from the South and the planter class. The Republican-controlled Congress enacted legislation during the war to raise tariffs, fund the first transcontinental railroad, and introduce many financial reforms that would drive the nation's economic development for the rest of the century.

CHRONOLOGY

April 1861	Virginia, North Carolina, Tennessee, and Arkansas join Confederacy; West Virginia splits from Virginia to stay with Union
July 1861	First Battle of Bull Run (Manassas)
April–September 1862	Battles of Shiloh, Second Bull Run, and Antietam
September 1862	Lincoln issues Emancipation Proclamation
January 1, 1863	Emancipation Proclamation takes effect
May–July 1863	New York City draft riots; siege of Vicksburg; Battle of Gettysburg
March 1864	Lincoln places General Ulysses S. Grant in charge of Union military operations
September 1864	General William T. Sherman seizes and burns Atlanta
November 1864	Lincoln is reelected
April 9, 1865	General Robert E. Lee surrenders at Appomattox Court House
1865	Thirteenth Amendment is ratified

KEY TERMS

Anaconda Plan p. 536

contrabands p. 546

Battle of Antietam (1862) p. 547

Emancipation Proclamation (1862) p. 549

Militia Act (1862) p. 553

Homestead Act (1862) p. 555

Morrill Land Grant Act (1862) p. 556

Copperhead Democrats p. 558

Battle of Vicksburg (1863) p. 560

Battle of Gettysburg (1863) p. 561

election of 1864 p. 569

"March to the Sea" p. 569

Appomattox Court House p. 572

Thirteenth Amendment (1865) p. 575

🐰 INQUIZITIVE

Go to InQuizitive to see what you've learned—and learn what you've missed—with personalized feedback along the way.

16 The Era of Reconstruction

1865–1877

***A Visit from the Old Mistress* (1876)** This powerful painting by Winslow Homer depicts a plantation mistress visiting her former slaves in the postwar South. Although their living conditions are humble, these freedwomen stand firmly and eye-to-eye with the woman who had kept them in bondage.

I n the spring of 1865, the Civil War was finally over. The war to restore the Union ended up transforming American life. The United States was a "new nation," said an Illinois congressman, because it was now "wholly free." At a cost of some 730,000 lives and the destruction of the southern economy, the Union had won the terrible war, and almost 4 million enslaved Americans had won their freedom. This was the most dramatic social change in the history of the nation, but the end of slavery did not bring the end of racism.

The Confederacy had its world turned upside down. The abolition of slavery, the war-related disruptions to the southern economy, and the horrifying human losses had destroyed the plantation system and upended racial relations in the South, which now had to come to terms with a new era and a new order as the United States government set about "reconstructing" the region—and policing defiant ex-Confederates. Diarist Mary Chesnut expressed the frustration felt by the defeated southern white elite when she wished that "they were *all* dead—all Yankees!"

Freed slaves felt just the opposite. Yankees were their saviors. No longer would enslaved workers be sold and separated from their families or prevented from learning to read and write or attending church. "I felt like a bird out of a cage," said former slave Houston Holloway of Georgia, who had been sold to three different owners during his first twenty years. "Amen. Amen. Amen. I could hardly ask to feel any better than I did that day."

Few owners, however, willingly freed their slaves until forced to by the arrival of Union soldiers. A North Carolina planter pledged that he and other whites "will never get along with the free negroes" because they were an "inferior race." Similarly, a Mississippi planter predicted that "these niggers will all be slaves again in twelve months."

focus questions

1. What major challenges faced the federal government in reconstructing the South after the Civil War during the period from 1865 to 1877?

2. How and why did Reconstruction policies change over time?

3. In what ways did white and black southerners react to Reconstruction?

4. What were the political and economic factors that helped lead to the end of Reconstruction in 1877?

5. What was the significance of Reconstruction for the nation's future?

At war's end in the spring of 1865, Henry Adams left the Louisiana plantation where he had been enslaved "to see whether I am free by going without a pass." A group of whites confronted him on the road, asked his owner's name, and beat him when he declared that "I now belong to no one." Some newly freed slaves rushed to give themselves new names to symbolize their changed status. Others left plantations and farms for towns and cities, where, as one of them said, "freedom was free-er."

The ratification of the Thirteenth Amendment to the U.S. Constitution in December 1865 was intended to end all doubt about the status of former slaves by abolishing slavery everywhere. Now the nation faced the huge task of "reconstructing" and reuniting a war-ravaged South while transforming ex-slaves into free workers and equal citizens.

It would not be easy. Freedom did not bring independence or self-reliance for millions of former slaves. At the same time, many white southerners resented and resisted efforts to "reconstruct" their region. As a South Carolina planter told a federal official in the fall of 1865, "The war is not over."

During the Reconstruction era, from 1865 to 1877, political leaders wrestled with how best to bring the Confederate states back into the Union and how best to help former slaves make the transition from bondage to citizenship. Those turbulent years witnessed a complex debate about the role of the federal government in ensuring civil rights.

Some northerners wanted the former Confederate states returned to the Union with little or no changes in their social, political, and economic life. Others called for former Confederate political and military leaders to be imprisoned or executed and the South rebuilt in the image of the rest of the nation. The editors of the nation's most popular magazine, *Harper's Weekly*, expressed this vengeful attitude when they declared that "the forgive-and-forget policy . . . is mere political insanity and suicide."

Although the Reconstruction era lasted only twelve years, it was one of the most significant periods in U.S. history. The decisions made and the policies enacted are still shaping American life nearly 150 years later.

THE WAR'S AFTERMATH IN THE SOUTH

The postwar South presented a sharp contrast to the victorious North, where the economy had been strengthened by the war efforts. Between 1860 and 1870, northern wealth grew by 50 percent while southern wealth dropped 60 percent. Along the path that General William Tecumseh Sherman's Union army had blazed across Georgia and the Carolinas, one observer reported in 1866, the countryside "looked for many miles like a broad black streak of ruin and desolation." Burned-out Columbia, South Carolina, said another witness, was "a wilderness of ruins"; Charleston, the birthplace of secession, had become a place of "vacant houses, of widowed women, of rotting wharves, of deserted warehouses, of weed-wild gardens, of miles of grass-grown streets, of acres of pitiful and voiceless barrenness."

Throughout the South, property values had collapsed. In the year after the war ended, eighty-one plantations in Mississippi were sold for less than a tenth of what they had been worth in 1860. Confederate bonds and paper money were worthless; personal savings had vanished.

Union soldiers who fanned out across the defeated South to impose order were cursed and spat upon. A Virginia woman expressed a spirited defiance common among her circle of friends: "Every day, every hour, that I live increases my hatred and detestation, and loathing of that race. They [Yankees] disgrace our common humanity. As a people I consider them vastly inferior to the better classes of our slaves." Fervent southern nationalists, both men and

Richmond after the Civil War Before evacuating the capital of the Confederacy, Richmond, Virginia, Rebels set fire to warehouses and factories to prevent their falling into Union hands. Pictured here is one of Richmond's burnt districts in April 1865. Women in mourning attire walk among the shambles.

women, implanted in their children a similar hatred of Yankees and a defiance of northern rule.

Many of the largest southern cities—Richmond, Atlanta, Charleston—were in ruins; most railroads were damaged or destroyed. Cotton that had not been destroyed by invading Union armies was seized by federal troops. Emancipation had eliminated $4 billion invested in slaves and left the agricultural economy in confusion. In 1860, just before the war began, the South generated 30 percent of the nation's wealth; in 1870, only ten years later, it produced but 12 percent.

Many southerners were homeless and hungry, emotionally exhausted and physically disabled. Countless families had lost sons and husbands, and many surviving war veterans returned home with one or more limbs missing. In 1866, the state of Mississippi spent a fifth of its annual budget on artificial limbs for Confederate soldiers.

Rebuilding the former Confederacy would not be easy, and the issues related to reconstruction were often complicated and controversial. For example, the process of forming new state governments first required determining the official status of the states that had seceded. Were they now conquered territories? If so, then the Constitution assigned Congress authority to re-create their state governments. But what if, as Abraham Lincoln had argued, the Confederate states had never officially left the Union because the act of secession was itself illegal? In that circumstance, the president would be responsible for re-forming state governments.

Whichever branch of government—Congress or the presidency—directed the reconstruction of the South, it would have to address the most difficult issue: What would be the political, social, and economic status of the freed slaves? Were they citizens? If not, what was their status as Americans? What the freed slaves wanted most was to become self-reliant as soon as possible. That meant being able to control their labor, reunite with their family members, gain education for their children, enjoy full participation in political life, and create their own community organizations and social life. Many whites were just as determined to prevent that from happening.

DEBATES OVER POLITICAL RECONSTRUCTION

The reconstruction of former Confederate states actually began during the war and went through several phases, the first of which was Presidential Reconstruction. In 1862, with Union forces advancing into the South, President Lincoln had named army generals to serve as temporary military governors for conquered Confederate areas. By the end of 1863, he had formulated a plan to reestablish governments in states liberated from Confederate rule.

LINCOLN'S PLAN In late 1863, President Lincoln issued a Proclamation of Amnesty and Reconstruction, under which any Confederate state could re-create a Union government once a number equal to 10 percent of those who had voted in 1860 swore allegiance to the Constitution and the Union. They also received a presidential pardon acquitting them of treason. Certain groups, however, were denied pardons: Confederate government officials; senior officers of the Confederate army and navy; judges, congressmen, and military officers of the United States who had left their posts to aid the rebellion; and those who had abused captured African American soldiers.

CONGRESSIONAL PLANS Northern politicians, however, disagreed over who had the authority to restore Rebel states to the Union. Many Republicans, especially the so-called Radicals, argued that Congress, not the president, should supervise Reconstruction. A few conservative and most moderate Republicans supported Lincoln's program that immediately restored pro-Union southern governments.

The **Radical Republicans**, however, favored a drastic transformation of southern society based upon granting freed slaves full citizenship rights. Many Radical Republican leaders, motivated primarily by religious values and moral ideals, believed that all people, regardless of race, were equal in God's eyes. They wanted no compromise with the "sin" of racism.

The Radicals also hoped to replace the white, Democratic planter elite with a new generation of small farmers, along with wage-earning and middle-class Republicans, both black and white. "The middling classes who own the soil, and work it with their own hands," explained Radical leader Thaddeus Stevens, "are the main support of every free government."

THE WADE-DAVIS BILL In 1864, with the war still raging, the Radical Republicans tried to take charge of Reconstruction by passing the Wade-Davis Bill, sponsored by Senator Benjamin Franklin Wade of Ohio and Representative Henry Winter Davis of Maryland. Unlike Lincoln's 10-percent plan, the Wade-Davis Bill required that a *majority* of white males swear their allegiance to the Union before a Confederate state could be readmitted.

But the Wade-Davis Bill never became law: Lincoln vetoed it as being too harsh. In retaliation, Republicans issued the Wade-Davis Manifesto, which accused Lincoln of exceeding his constitutional authority. Unfazed, Lincoln moved ahead with his efforts to restore the Confederate states to the Union. He also acted boldly to provide assistance to the freed slaves in the South.

THE FREEDMEN'S BUREAU In early 1865, Congress approved the Thirteenth Amendment to the Constitution, officially abolishing slavery in the United States. The amendment, and the war that enabled it, liberated almost 4 million slaves. Yet what did freedom mean for the former slaves, most of whom had no land, no home, no food, no jobs, and no education? Throughout the major northern cities, people had formed Freedmen's Aid Societies to raise funds and recruit volunteers to help the African Americans in the South. Many churches did the same. But the needs far exceeded such grassroots efforts.

It soon fell to the federal government to address the desperate plight of the former slaves. On March 3, 1865, Congress created the **Freedmen's Bureau** (within the War Department) to assist the "freedmen and their wives and children." It was the first federal experiment in providing assistance directly to people rather than to states.

In May 1865, General Oliver O. Howard, commissioner of the Freedmen's Bureau, declared that freed slaves "must be free to choose their own employers, and be paid for their labor." He sent agents to the South to negotiate labor contracts between blacks and white landowners, many of whom resisted. The Bureau provided former slaves with medical care and food and clothing, and also helped set up schools.

By 1870, the Bureau was supervising nearly 4,000 new schools serving almost 250,000 students, many of whose teachers were initially women volunteers from the North. The Freedmen's Bureau also helped former slaves reconnect with family members. Marriages that had been prohibited during slavery were now made legal.

FREED SLAVES AND LAND A few northerners argued that what ex-slaves needed most was their own land. A New Englander traveling in the postwar South noted that the "sole ambition of the freedman" was " . . . to become the owner of a little piece of land, there to erect a humble home, and to dwell in peace and security at his own free will and pleasure." In coastal South Carolina and in Mississippi, former slaves had been "given" land by Union armies that had taken control of Confederate areas during the war.

Even northern abolitionists balked at Radical proposals to confiscate white-owned land and distribute it to the freed slaves, however. Citizenship and legal rights were one thing, wholesale confiscation of property and land redistribution quite another. Nonetheless, the discussions fueled false rumors that freed slaves would get "forty acres and a mule," a slogan that swept across the South. Ulysses S. Grant, still general-in-chief of the U.S. Army, reported that the mistaken belief among the freed slaves that they would receive land was "seriously interfering" with their willingness to sign labor contracts agreeing to work as farmhands for pay.

In July 1865, hundreds of freed slaves gathered near an old church on St. Helena Island off the South Carolina coast. There, Virginia-born freeman Martin Delaney, the highest-ranking officer in the 104th U.S. Colored Troops, addressed them. Before the Civil War, he had been a prominent abolitionist in the North. Now, Major Delaney assured the gathering that slavery had been "absolutely abolished." But abolition, he stressed, was less the result of Abraham Lincoln's leadership than the outcome of former slaves and free blacks like him deciding to resist and undermine the Confederacy. Slavery was dead, and freedom was now in their hands. "Yes, yes, yes," his listeners shouted.

Delaney then noted that many white planters in the area claimed that the former slaves were lazy and "have not the intelligence to get on for yourselves without being guided and driven to the work by [white] overseers." Delaney dismissed such assumptions as lies intended to restore a system of forced labor for blacks. He told the freed slaves that their best hope was to become self-sustaining farmers: "Get a community and get all the lands you can—if you cannot get any singly." Then "grow as much vegetables etc., as you want for your families; on the other part of land, you cultivate rice and cotton." They must find ways to become economically self-reliant. Otherwise, he said, they would find themselves slaves again.

Several white planters attended Delaney's talk, and an army officer at the scene reported that they "listened with horror depicted in their faces" when Delaney urged the former slaves to become independent farmers. The planters predicted that such speeches would incite "open rebellion" among southern blacks.

DEATH OF A PRESIDENT The possibility of a lenient reconstruction of the Confederacy would die with Abraham Lincoln. The president offered his last view of Reconstruction in the final speech of his life. On April 11, 1865, he rejected calls by Radicals for a vengeful peace. He wanted "no persecution, no bloody work," no hangings of Confederate leaders, and no extreme efforts to restructure southern social and economic life. Three days later, on April 14, Lincoln and his wife Mary went to see a play at Ford's Theatre in Washington, D.C.

With his trusted bodyguard called away to Richmond, Lincoln was defenseless as John Wilkes Booth, a popular actor and a rabid Confederate, slipped into the unguarded presidential box and shot the president in the head. Lincoln, Booth claimed, was the cause of all the nation's "troubles," and God had directed him to kill the president. As the mortally wounded Lincoln slumped forward, Booth stabbed a military aide and jumped from the box to the stage, breaking his leg in the process. Booth limped out a stage door, mounted a waiting horse, and fled the city. Lincoln died nine hours later.

At the same time that Booth was shooting the president, other assassins were targeting Vice President Andrew Johnson and Secretary of State William H. Seward. Johnson escaped injury because his would-be assassin got cold feet and wound up tipsy in the barroom of the vice president's hotel. Seward and four others, including his son, suffered severe knife wounds when attacked at home.

The nation extracted a full measure of vengeance from the conspirators. After a desperate eleven-day manhunt, Booth was pursued into Virginia and killed in a burning barn. Three of his collaborators were convicted by a military court and hanged, as was Mary Surratt, who owned the Washington boardinghouse where the assassinations had been planned.

JOHNSON'S PLAN Lincoln's shocking death propelled into the White House Andrew Johnson of Tennessee, a pro-Union Democrat who had been added to the National Union ticket in 1864 solely to help Lincoln win reelection. Humorless and insecure, combative and obstinate, Johnson nursed fierce prejudices (he hated both the white southern elite and the idea of racial equality) and a weakness for liquor. At the inaugural ceremonies in early 1865, he had delivered his vice-presidential address in a state of slurring drunkenness.

Like Lincoln, Johnson was a self-made, self-taught man. Born in poverty in Raleigh, North Carolina, he never attended school. At age thirteen he relocated to Greeneville, in the mountains of east Tennessee, where he became a tailor and learned to read. Eventually, as the self-proclaimed friend of the "common man," he served as the mayor, a state legislator, governor, congressional representative, and U.S. senator.

Johnson's supporters were primarily small farmers and the working poor. He called himself a Jacksonian Democrat "in the strictest meaning of the term. I am for putting down the [Confederate] rebellion, because it is a war [of wealthy plantation owners] against democracy." Yet he also shared the racist attitudes of most southern whites. "Damn the negroes," he exclaimed to a friend during the war. "I am fighting those traitorous aristocrats, their masters." As a states' rights Democrat, he strongly opposed Republican economic policies designed to spur industrial development and insisted that the federal government should be as small and inactive as possible.

With Congress in recess, Johnson was temporarily in control of what he called the "restoration" of the Union. He needed to put his plan in place over the next seven months before the new Congress convened and the Republicans would take charge. In May 1865, he issued a new Proclamation of Amnesty that excluded not only those ex-Confederates whom Lincoln had barred from a presidential pardon but also anyone with property worth more than $20,000.

Johnson was determined to keep the wealthiest southerners from regaining political power. Surprisingly, however, he eventually pardoned most of the white "aristocrats" he claimed to despise. What brought about this change of heart? Johnson had decided that he could buy the political support of prominent southerners by pardoning them, improving his chances of reelection.

Johnson's Restoration Plan included the appointment of a Unionist as provisional governor in each southern state, a position with the authority to call a convention of men elected by "loyal" (that is, not Confederate) voters. His plan required that each state convention ratify the Thirteenth Amendment ending slavery before the state could be

Andrew Johnson A pro-Union Democrat from Tennessee.

readmitted to the Union. Johnson also encouraged the conventions to consider giving a few blacks voting rights, especially those with some education or with military service, so as to "disarm" the Republican "radicals who are wild upon" giving *all* African Americans the right to vote. Except for Mississippi, each state of the former Confederacy held a convention that met Johnson's requirements but ignored his suggestion about voting rights for blacks.

THE RADICALS REBEL Johnson's initial assault on the southern planter elite won him the support of the Radical Republicans, but not for long. Many Radicals who wanted "Reconstruction" to provide social and political equality for blacks were infuriated by Johnson's efforts to bring the South back into the Union as quickly as possible.

The leading Radical Republicans, such as Thaddeus Stevens of Pennsylvania and Charles Sumner of Massachusetts, wanted to deny former Confederates the right to vote to keep them from reelecting the old planter elite and to enable the Republican party to gain a foothold in the region. Stevens argued that the Civil War was intended to be a "*radical* revolution": the "whole fabric of southern society must be changed" to "revolutionize southern institutions, habits, and manners."

The iron-willed Stevens viewed the Confederate states as "conquered provinces" to be readmitted to the Union by the U.S. Congress, not the president.

President Johnson, however, balked at such an expansion of federal authority. He was committed to the states' rights to control their affairs. "White men alone must manage the South," Johnson told a visitor.

By the end of 1865, the Radical Republicans had gained a majority in Congress and were warring with Johnson over control of Reconstruction. On December 4, 1865, the president announced that the South had been restored to the Union. The final step in reconstruction, he added, would be for Congress to admit the newly elected southern representatives to their seats in the House and Senate.

Republicans, however, were not about to welcome back former Confederate leaders who had been elected to Congress. Georgia, for example, had elected Alexander Stephens, former vice president of the Confederacy. Across the South, four Confederate generals, eight colonels, six Confederate cabinet members, and fifty-eight Confederate legislators were elected. Outraged Republicans denied seats to all "Rebel" officials and appointed a congressional committee to develop a new plan to "reconstruct" the South.

JOHNSON VERSUS THE RADICALS   President Johnson started a war with Congress over reconstruction when he vetoed a bill that renewed funding for the Freedmen's Bureau and allowed the federal agency to begin providing homesteads and schools to former slaves in the South as well as the border states. Thaddeus Stevens and other Radicals realized that Johnson and the Democrats were trying to redefine the Civil War as a conflict between states' rights and federal power, not a struggle over slavery.

In mid-March 1866, the Radical-led Congress passed the pathbreaking Civil Rights Act, which announced that "all persons born in the United States" (except Indians) were citizens entitled to "full and equal benefit of all laws."

The new legislation enraged Johnson. Congress, he bristled, had no authority to grant citizenship to lazy former slaves who did not deserve it, and he argued that the Civil Rights Act discriminated against the "white race." So he vetoed both bills.

Now it was the Republicans' turn to be infuriated. In April 1866, Congress overrode Johnson's vetoes. From that point on, Johnson, a stubborn, uncompromising loner, steadily lost both public and political support.

Soon thereafter, in the spring and summer of 1866, rampaging white mobs in the South murdered and wounded hundreds of African Americans during race riots in Memphis and New Orleans. A Memphis newspaper glorified the killings: "The negroes now know, to their sorrow, that it is best not to arouse the fury of the white man." Northerners were incensed. The massacres, Radical Republicans argued, resulted from Andrew Johnson's lenient policy toward white supremacists. "Witness Memphis, witness New Orleans," Massachusetts senator Charles Sumner cried. "Who can doubt that the President is the author of these tragedies?" The mob attacks helped motivate Congress to pass the Fourteenth Amendment, extending federal civil rights protections to blacks.

BLACK CODES The violence was partly triggered by African American protests over restrictive laws passed by the new all-white southern state legislatures in 1865 and 1866. These "**black codes**," a white southerner explained, were intended to make sure "the ex-slave was not a free man; he was a free Negro." A northerner visiting the South said the black codes were intended to enforce a widespread insistence that "the blacks at large belong to the whites at large."

The black codes differed from state to state, but their purpose was clear: to restore white supremacy. While black marriages were recognized, African Americans could not vote, serve on juries, testify against whites, or attend public schools. They could not own farmland in Mississippi or city property in South Carolina. In Alabama, they could not own guns. In Mississippi, every black male over the age of eighteen had to be apprenticed to a white, preferably a former slave owner. Virtually all black codes required that adult freed slaves

sign annual labor contracts. Otherwise, they would be jailed as "vagrants." If they could not pay the vagrancy fine—and most could not—they were forced to work for whites as convict laborers.

The black codes disgusted Republicans. "We must see to it," Senator William Stewart of Nevada resolved, "that the man made free by the Constitution of the United States is a freeman indeed." And that is what they set out to do. A former slave who had served in the Union army shared the disbelief felt by most African Americans at the black codes: "If you call this Freedom, what do you call Slavery?"

"(?) Slavery Is Dead (?)" (1867)
Thomas Nast's cartoon argues that southern blacks were still being treated as slaves despite the passage of the Fourteenth Amendment. This detail illustrates a case in Raleigh, North Carolina: a black man was whipped for a crime despite federal orders specifically prohibiting such forms of punishment.

FOURTEENTH AMENDMENT To ensure the legality of the new federal Civil Rights Act, the Congressional Joint Committee on Reconstruction proposed in April 1866 a pathbreaking **Fourteenth Amendment** to the U.S. Constitution. It guaranteed citizenship to anyone born or naturalized in the United States, except Native Americans. It also prohibited any efforts to violate the civil rights of "citizens," black or white; to deprive any person "of life, liberty, or property, without due process of law"; or to "deny any person . . . the equal protection of the laws." With the Fourteenth Amendment, Congress gave the federal government responsibility for protecting (and enforcing) the civil rights of virtually all Americans. The amendment was approved by Congress on June 16, 1866. Not a single Democrat in the House or Senate voted for it. All states in the former Confederacy were required to ratify the amendment before they could be readmitted to the Union and to Congress.

Again, President Johnson fumed. "This is a country for white men," he insisted, "and, by God, as long as I am President, it shall be a government by white men." Johnson urged the southern states to refuse to ratify the amendment. He predicted that the Democrats would win the congressional elections in November and then nix the new amendment.

JOHNSON VERSUS RADICALS To win votes for Democratic candidates, Johnson went on a speaking tour of the Midwest during which he denounced Radical Republicans as traitors who should be hanged. Several of his speeches backfired, however. In Cleveland, Ohio, Johnson exchanged hot-tempered insults with a heckler. At another stop, while the president was speaking from the back of a railway car, the engineer mistakenly pulled the train out of the station, making the president appear quite the fool. Republicans charged that such unseemly incidents confirmed Johnson's image as a "ludicrous boor" and a "drunken imbecile."

In the end, the 1866 congressional elections were a devastating defeat for Johnson and the Democrats; in each house, Radical Republican candidates won more than a two-thirds majority, the margin required to override presidential vetoes. Congressional Republicans would now take over the process of reconstructing the former Confederacy.

CONGRESS TAKES CHARGE On March 2, 1867, the new Congress passed, over Johnson's vetoes, three crucial laws creating what came to be called **Congressional Reconstruction**: the Military Reconstruction Act, the Command of the Army Act, and the Tenure of Office Act.

The Military Reconstruction Act was the capstone of the Congressional Reconstruction plan. It abolished all new governments "in the rebel States" established under President Johnson's lenient reconstruction policies. In their place, Congress established military control over ten of the eleven former Confederate states. Tennessee was exempted because it had already ratified the Fourteenth Amendment. The other ten states were divided into five military districts, each commanded by a general who acted as governor.

The Military Reconstruction Act required each state to create a new constitution that guaranteed the right to vote for all adult males—black or white, rich or poor, landless or property owners. Women—black or white—did not yet have the vote and were not included in the discussions.

The Military Reconstruction Act also stipulated that the new state constitutions were to be drafted by conventions elected by male citizens "of whatever race, color, or previous condition." Each constitution had to guarantee African American males the right to vote. Once a constitution was ratified by a majority of voters and accepted by Congress, other criteria had to be met. The state legislature had to ratify the Fourteenth Amendment, and once the amendment became part of the Constitution, any given state would be entitled to representation in Congress. Several hundred African American delegates participated in the statewide constitutional conventions.

The Command of the Army Act required that the president issue all army orders through General in Chief Ulysses S. Grant. The Radical Republicans feared that President Johnson would appoint generals to head the military districts who would be too lenient. So they bypassed the president and entrusted Grant to enforce Congressional Reconstruction in the South.

The Tenure of Office Act required Senate permission for the president to remove any federal official whose appointment the Senate had confirmed. This act was intended to prevent Johnson from firing Secretary of War Edwin Stanton, the president's most outspoken critic in the cabinet.

Congressional Reconstruction embodied the most sweeping peacetime legislation in American history to that point. It sought to ensure that freed slaves could participate in the creation of new state governments in the former Confederacy. As Thaddeus Stevens explained, the Congressional Reconstruction plan was designed to create a "perfect republic" based on the principle of *equal rights* for all citizens. "This is the promise of America," he insisted. "No More. No Less."

IMPEACHING THE PRESIDENT The first two years of Congressional Reconstruction produced dramatic changes in the South, as new state legislatures rewrote their constitutions and ratified the Fourteenth Amendment. Radical Republicans now seemed fully in control of Reconstruction, but one person still stood in their way—Andrew Johnson. During 1867 and early 1868, more and more Radicals decided that the defiant Democratic president must be removed from office.

Johnson himself opened the door to impeachment (the formal process by which Congress charges the president with "high crimes and misdemeanors") when, in violation of the Tenure of Office Act, he fired Secretary of War Edwin Stanton, who had refused to resign from the cabinet despite his harsh criticism of the president's Reconstruction policy. Johnson, who considered the Tenure of Office Act an illegal restriction of presidential power, fired Stanton on August 12, 1867, and replaced him with Ulysses S. Grant.

The Radical Republicans now saw their chance. By removing Stanton without congressional approval, Johnson had violated the law. On February 24, 1868, the Republican-dominated House passed eleven articles of impeachment (that is, specific charges against the president), most of which dealt with Stanton's firing, and all of which were flimsy. In reality, the essential grievance against the president was that he had opposed the policies of the Radical Republicans.

The first Senate trial of a sitting president began on March 5, 1868 with Chief Justice Salmon P. Chase presiding. It was a dramatic spectacle before a packed gallery of journalists, foreign dignitaries, corporate executives, and political officials. As the trial began, Thaddeus Stevens, the Radical leader, warned the president: "Unfortunate, unhappy man, behold your doom!"

The five-week trial ended in stunning fashion, but not as the Radicals had hoped. The Senate voted 35 to 19 for conviction, only *one* vote short of the two-thirds needed for removal from office. Senator Edmund G. Ross, a young Radical from Kansas, cast the deciding vote in favor of acquittal, knowing that his vote would ruin his political career. "I almost literally looked down into my open grave," Ross explained afterward. "Friendships, position, fortune, everything that makes life desirable . . . were about to be swept away by the breath of my mouth." Ross was thereafter shunned by the Republicans. He lost his reelection campaign and died in near poverty.

The effort to remove Johnson was in the end a grave political mistake, for it weakened public support for Congressional Reconstruction. Nevertheless, the Radical cause did gain something: to avoid being convicted, Johnson had privately agreed to stop obstructing Congressional Reconstruction.

REPUBLICAN RULE IN THE SOUTH In June 1868, congressional Republicans announced that eight southern states were allowed again to send delegates to Congress. The remaining former Confederate states—Virginia, Mississippi, and Texas—were readmitted in 1870, with the added requirement that they ratify the **Fifteenth Amendment**, which gave voting rights to African American men. As black leader Frederick Douglass, himself a former slave, had declared in 1865, "slavery is not abolished until the black man has the ballot."

The Fifteenth Amendment prohibited states from denying any man the vote on grounds of "race, color, or previous condition of servitude." But Susan B. Anthony and Elizabeth Cady Stanton, seasoned leaders of the movement to secure an "honorable independence" and voting rights for women, demanded that the amendment be revised to include women. As Anthony stressed in a famous speech, the U.S. Constitution said: "we, the people; not we, the white male citizens; nor yet we, the male citizens; but we, the whole people, who formed the Union—women as well as men." Most men, however, remained unreconstructed when it came to voting rights for women. Radical Republicans tried to deflect the issue by declaring that it was the "Negro's hour." Women would have to wait—another fifty years, as it turned out.

BLACKS UNDER RECONSTRUCTION

When a federal official asked Garrison Frazier, a former slave in Georgia, if he and others wanted to live among whites, he said that they preferred "to live by ourselves, for there is a prejudice against us in the South that will take years to get over." In forging new lives, Frazier and many other former slaves set about creating their own social institutions.

FREED BUT NOT EQUAL White southerners used terror, intimidation, and violence to suppress black efforts to gain social and economic equality. In Texas, a white farmer told a former slave that his freedom would do him "damned little good . . . as I intend to shoot you"—and he did. In July 1866, a black woman in Clinch County, Georgia, was arrested and given sixty-five lashes for "using abusive language" during an encounter with a white woman. The Civil War had brought freedom to enslaved African Americans, but it did not bring them protection against exploitation or abuse.

Participation in the Union army or navy had provided many freedmen with training in leadership. Black military veterans would form the core of the first generation of African American political leaders in the postwar South. Military service gave many former slaves their first opportunities to learn to read and write, and army life alerted them to new opportunities for economic advancement, social respectability, and civic leadership. Fighting for the Union also instilled a fervent sense of nationalism. A Virginia freedman explained that the United States was "now *our* country—made emphatically so by the blood of our brethren."

BLACK CHURCHES AND SCHOOLS African American religious life in the South was transformed during and after the war. Many former slaves identified with the biblical Hebrews, who were led out of slavery into the "promised land." Emancipation demonstrated that God was on *their* side. Before the war, slaves who were allowed to attend white churches were forced to sit in the back. After the war, with the help of many northern Christian missionaries, both black and white, ex-slaves eagerly established their own African American churches.

The black churches were the first social institutions the former slaves could control and quickly became the crossroads for black community life. Black ministers emerged as social and political leaders as well as preachers. Many African Americans became Baptists or Methodists, in part because these were already the largest denominations in the South, and in part because they reached out to the working poor. In 1866 alone, the African Methodist Episcopal (AME) Church gained 50,000 members. By 1890, more than 1.3 million African Americans in the South had become Baptists, nearly three times as many as had joined any other denomination.

African American communities also rushed to establish schools. Education, said a freed slave in Mississippi, was "the next best thing to liberty." Most plantation owners had denied education to blacks in part because they feared that literate slaves would read abolitionist literature and organize uprisings. After the war, the white elite worried that formal education would encourage poor whites and poor blacks to leave the South in search of better social and economic opportunities.

White opposition made education all the more important to African Americans. South Carolina's Mary McLeod Bethune rejoiced in the opportunity: "The whole world opened to me when I learned to read." She earned a scholarship to college and went on to become the first black woman to found a school that became a four-year college: what is today known as Bethune-Cookman University, in Daytona Beach, Florida.

AFRICAN AMERICANS IN SOUTHERN POLITICS Groups encouraging freed slaves to embrace the Republican party were organized throughout the South. They were chiefly sponsored by the Union League, founded in Philadelphia in 1862. League recruiters enrolled African Americans and loyal whites, initiated them into the secrets and rituals of the order, and instructed them "in their rights and duties." The Union League was so

African American political figures of Reconstruction Blanche K. Bruce (left) and Hiram Revels (right) served in the U.S. Senate. Frederick Douglass (center) was a major figure in the abolitionist movement.

successful in recruiting African Americans that in 1867, it had eighty-eight chapters in South Carolina alone. The League claimed to have enrolled almost every adult black male in the state.

Of course, any African American participation in southern political life was a first. Some 600 blacks—most of them former slaves—served as state legislators under Congressional Reconstruction. In Louisiana, Pinckney Pinchback, a northern free black and former Union soldier, was elected lieutenant governor. Several other African Americans were elected lieutenant governor, state treasurer, or secretary of state. There were two black senators in Congress, Hiram Revels and Blanche K. Bruce, both Mississippi natives who had been educated in the North, as well as fourteen black members of the U.S. House of Representatives.

White southerners were appalled at the election of black politicians. Democrat extremists claimed that Radicals were trying to "organize a hell in the South" by putting "the Caucasian race" under the rule of "their own negroes." Southern whites complained that freed slaves were illiterate and had no civic experience or appreciation of political issues and processes. In this regard,

Freedmen voting in New Orleans The Fifteenth Amendment, ratified in 1870, guaranteed at the federal level the right of citizens to vote regardless of "race, color, or previous condition of servitude." But former slaves had been registering to vote—and voting in large numbers—in some state elections since 1867, as in this scene.

blacks were no different from millions of poor or immigrant white males who had been allowed to vote in many jurisdictions for years.

LAND, LABOR, AND DISAPPOINTMENT A few northerners argued that what the former slaves needed most was their own land, where they could gain economic self-sufficiency. Freed slaves felt the same way. Freedom, explained a black minister from Georgia, meant the freedom for blacks to "reap the fruit of our own labor, and take care of ourselves."

In several southern states, former slaves had been "given" land by Union armies after they had taken control of Confederate areas during the war. But transfers of white-owned property to former slaves were reversed during 1865 by President Andrew Johnson. In South Carolina, the Union general responsible for evicting former slaves urged them to "lay aside their bitter feelings, and become reconciled to their old masters." But the assembled freedmen shouted "No, never!" and "Can't do it!" They knew that ownership of land was the foundation of their freedom.

Tens of thousands of former slaves were forced to return their farms to the white owners. In addition, it was virtually impossible for former slaves to get loans to buy farmland because so few banks were willing to lend to blacks. Their sense of betrayal was profound. Reconstruction of the South would not include the redistribution of southern property.

What emerged was the labor system called **sharecropping**—where the landowner provided land, seed, and tools to a poor farmer in exchange for a *share* of the crop. Many freed blacks preferred sharecropping over working for wages, since it freed them from

Sharecroppers A family is shown outside their Virginia home in this 1899 photograph, taken by Frances Benjamin Johnston, one of the earliest American female photojournalists.

day-to-day supervision by white landowners. But over time, most sharecroppers, black and white, found themselves deep in debt to the landowner, with little choice but to remain tied to the same discouraging system of dependence that, over the years, felt much like slavery. As a former slave acknowledged, he and others had discovered that "freedom could make folks proud but it didn't make 'em rich."

TENSIONS AMONG SOUTHERN BLACKS African Americans in the postwar South were by no means a uniform community. They had their own differences and disputes, especially between the few who owned property and the many who did not.

Affluent northern blacks and the southern free black elite, most of whom were city dwellers and mulattos (people of mixed parentage), often opposed efforts to redistribute land to the freedmen, and many insisted that political equality did not mean social equality. In general, however, unity rather than dissension prevailed, and African Americans focused on common concerns, such as full equality under the law. "All we ask," said a black member of the state constitutional convention in Mississippi, "is justice, and to be treated like human beings."

With little or no training or political experience, many African Americans served in state governments with distinction. Nonetheless, the scornful label "black Reconstruction," used by critics then and since, distorts African

American political influence. Such criticism also overlooks the political clout of the large number of white Republicans, especially in the mountain areas of the Upper South, who favored the Radical plan for Reconstruction. Only South Carolina's Republican state convention had a black majority. Louisiana's was evenly divided racially, and in only two other state conventions were more than 20 percent of the members black: Florida and Virginia.

"CARPETBAGGERS" AND "SCALAWAGS" Most of the offices in the new southern state governments went to white Republicans, who were dismissed as "carpetbaggers" or "scalawags." Carpetbaggers, critics argued, were scheming northerners who rushed South with all their belongings in cheap suitcases made of carpeting ("carpetbags") to grab political power.

Some northerners were indeed corrupt opportunists. However, most were Union military veterans drawn to the South by the desire to rebuild the region's devastated economy. New Yorker George Spencer, for example, arrived in Alabama with the Union army during the war and decided to pursue his "chances of making a fortune" in selling cotton and building railroads. He eventually was elected to the U.S. Senate. Many other so-called carpetbaggers were teachers, social workers, or ministers motivated by a genuine desire to help the free blacks and poor whites improve the quality of their lives.

The scalawags, or white southern Republicans, were especially hated by southern Democrats, who considered them traitors. A Nashville newspaper editor called them the "merest trash."

Most scalawags had been Unionists opposed to secession. They were especially prominent in mountain counties as far south as Georgia and Alabama and especially in the hills of eastern Tennessee. Among the scalawags were several distinguished figures, including former Confederate general James Longstreet, who decided after Appomattox that the Old South must change its ways. He became a successful cotton broker in New Orleans, joined the Republican party, and supported the Radical Reconstruction program. Other scalawags were former Whigs attracted by the Republican party's economic program of industrial and commercial expansion. What the diverse "scalawags" had in common was a willingness to work with Republicans to rebuild the southern economy.

SOUTHERN RESISTANCE AND WHITE "REDEMPTION"
Most southern whites viewed secession not as a mistake but as a noble "lost cause." They used all means possible—legal and illegal—to "redeem" their beloved South from northern control, Republican rule, and black assertive-

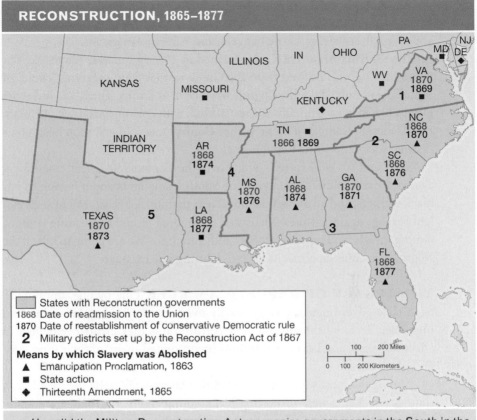

RECONSTRUCTION, 1865–1877

States with Reconstruction governments
1868 Date of readmission to the Union
1870 Date of reestablishment of conservative Democratic rule
2 Military districts set up by the Reconstruction Act of 1867

Means by which Slavery was Abolished
▲ Emancipation Proclamation, 1863
■ State action
◆ Thirteenth Amendment, 1865

- How did the Military Reconstruction Act reorganize governments in the South in the late 1860s and 1870s?
- What did the former Confederate states have to do to be readmitted to the Union?
- Why did "Conservative" white parties gradually regain control of the South from the Republicans in the 1870s?

ness. White southern ministers, for example, assured their congregations that God endorsed white supremacy.

The Civil War had brought freedom to enslaved African Americans, but it did not bring them protection against exploitation or abuse. The "black codes" created in 1865 and 1866 were the first of many continuing efforts to deny equality to African Americans. With each passing year, southern whites used terror, intimidation, and violence to prevent blacks from exercising their political rights, and resistance to Congressional Reconstruction and Radical Republican ("Radical") rule became more and more violent. Hundreds were killed and many more injured in systematic efforts to "keep blacks in their place." Several secret terrorist groups, including the Ku Klux Klan, the Knights of the White Camelia, and the White League, emerged to harass, intimidate, and even kill scalawags, carpetbaggers, and African Americans.

The **Ku Klux Klan (KKK)** was formed in 1866 in Pulaski, Tennessee. The name *Ku Klux* was derived from the Greek word *kuklos,* meaning "circle" or "band." *Klan* came from the English word *clan,* or family. The Klan, and other groups like it, began initially as a social club, with costumes and secret rituals. But its members, most of them former Confederate soldiers, soon began harrassing blacks and white Republicans.

Their motives were varied—anger over the Confederate defeat, resentment against federal soldiers occupying the South, complaints about having to pay black workers, and an almost paranoid fear that former slaves might seek violent revenge against whites. Klansmen rode about at night spreading rumors, issuing threats, and burning schools and churches. "We are going to kill all the Negroes," a white supremacist declared during one massacre.

THE LEGACY OF REPUBLICAN RULE One by one, the Republican state governments were gradually overturned. Yet they left behind an important accomplishment: the new constitutions they created remained in effect for years, and later constitutions incorporated many of their most progressive features.

Among the most significant innovations brought about by the Republican state governments were protecting black voting rights, restructuring legislatures to reflect shifting populations, and making more state offices elective to weaken the "good old boy" tradition of rewarding political supporters with state government jobs. In South Carolina, former Confederate leaders opposed the Republican state legislature not simply because of its black members but because poor whites were also enjoying political clout for the first time, thereby threatening the traditional power of wealthy white plantation owners and merchants.

Given the hostile circumstances under which Republican state governments operated in the South, their achievements were remarkable. They constructed an extensive railroad network and established public, though racially segregated, school systems funded by state governments and open to all children. Some 600,000 black pupils were enrolled in southern schools by 1877.

The Radicals also gave more attention to the poor and to orphanages, asylums, and institutions for the deaf and blind of both races. Public roads, bridges, and buildings were repaired or rebuilt. African Americans achieved rights and opportunities that would repeatedly be violated in coming decades but would never completely be taken away, at least in principle: equality before the law and the rights to own property, attend schools, learn to read and write, enter professions, and carry on business.

Yet several Republican state governments also engaged in corrupt practices. Bribes and kickbacks, whereby companies received government contracts in return for giving government officials cash or stock, were commonplace. In Louisiana, a twenty-six-year-old carpetbagger, Henry Clay Warmoth, a Union war veteran and an attorney, somehow turned an annual salary of $8,000 into a million-dollar fortune over four years as governor. (He was eventually impeached and removed from office.) "I don't pretend to be honest," he admitted. "I only pretend to be as honest as anybody in politics."

As was true in the North and the Midwest at the time, southern state governments awarded money to corporations, notably railroads, under conditions that invited shady dealings and outright corruption. In fact, some railroad officials received state funds but never built any railroads. Such corruption was not invented by the Radical Republican regimes, nor did it die with them. Governor Warmoth recognized as much: "Corruption is the fashion" in Louisiana, he explained.

The Grant Administration

Andrew Johnson's crippled presidency created an opportunity for Republicans to elect one of their own in 1868. Both parties wooed Ulysses S. Grant, the "Lion of Vicksburg" credited by most Americans with the Union victory in the Civil War. His falling-out with President Johnson, however, had pushed him toward the Republicans, who unanimously nominated him as their candidate.

THE ELECTION OF 1868 The Republican party platform endorsed Congressional Reconstruction. More important, however, were the public expectations driving the candidacy of Ulysses S. Grant, whose campaign slogan was "Let us have peace." Grant promised that, if elected, he would enforce the laws and promote prosperity for all.

The Democrats charged that the Radical Republicans were subjecting the South "to military despotism and Negro supremacy." They nominated Horatio Seymour, the wartime governor of New York and a passionate critic of Congressional Reconstruction. His running mate, Francis P. Blair Jr., a former Union general from Missouri who had served in Congress, appealed directly to white bigotry when he denounced Republicans for promoting equality for "a semi-barbarous race" of black men who sought to "subject the white women to their unbridled lust."

A Democrat later said that Blair's "stupid and indefensible" remarks cost Seymour a close election. Grant swept the electoral college, 214 to 80, but his popular majority was only 307,000 out of almost 6 million votes. More than 500,000 African American voters, mostly in the South, accounted for Grant's margin of victory. The efforts of Radical Republicans to ensure voting rights for southern blacks had paid off and would continue to do so throughout the nineteenth century. As Frederick Douglass, the revered black leader, explained, "the Republican party is the ship and all else is the sea" as far as black voters were concerned.

Grant, the youngest president ever (forty-six years old at the time of his inauguration), had proved himself a great military leader, but he was not a strong politician. He passively followed the lead of Congress and was often blind to the political forces and self-serving influence peddlers around him. Members of his own party would become his greatest disappointments and worst enemies. A failure as a storekeeper before the Civil War, Grant was awestruck by men of wealth who lavished gifts on him. He also showed poor judgment in his selection of cabinet members, often favoring friendship and loyalty over integrity and ability.

During Grant's two terms in office, his seven cabinet positions changed twenty-four times. Some of the men betrayed his trust and engaged in criminal behavior. His former comrade in arms, General William T. Sherman, said he felt sorry for Grant because so many supposedly "loyal" Republicans used the president for their own selfish gains. Carl Schurz, a Union war hero who became a Republican senator from Missouri, expressed frustration that Grant was misled by cunning advisers who "prostituted" his administration.

SCANDALS President Grant's administration was quickly mired in scandal. In the summer of 1869, two unprincipled financial schemers, Jay Gould and the colorful James Fisk Jr. (known as "Diamond Jim"), both infamous for bribing politicians and judges, plotted with Abel Corbin, the president's brother-in-law, to corner the gold market. They intended to create a public craze for gold by purchasing massive quantities of the precious metal to drive up its value. The only danger to the complicated scheme lay in the possibility that the federal Treasury would burst the bubble by selling large amounts of its gold supply, which would deflate the value of gold by putting more in circulation. When Grant was seen in public with Gould and Fisk, people assumed that he supported their scheme. As the false rumor spread in New York City's financial district that the president endorsed the run-up in gold, its value soared.

On September 24, 1869—soon to be remembered as "Black Friday"—the scheme to drive up the price of gold worked, at least at first. Starting at $150 an ounce, the bidding for gold started to rise, first to $160, then $165, leading more and more investors across the nation and around the world to join the stampede. Then, around noon, President Grant and his Treasury secretary realized what was happening and began selling huge amounts of government gold. Within fifteen minutes, the bubble created by Fisk and Gould burst, and the price of gold plummeted to $138. People who had bought gold in large amounts lost fortunes. Their agony, said a New Yorker, "made one feel as if the Battle of Gettysburg had been lost and the Rebels were marching down Broadway."

Soon, the turmoil spread to the entire stock market, claiming thousands of victims. As Fisk noted, "It was each man drag out his own corpse." For weeks after the gold bubble collapsed, financial markets were paralyzed and business confidence was shaken.

The plot to corner the gold market was only the first of several scandals that rocked the Grant administration. The secretary of war, it turned out, had accepted bribes from merchants who traded with Indians at army posts in the West. In St. Louis, whiskey distillers—dubbed the "whiskey ring" in the press—bribed federal agents in an effort to avoid taxes, bilking the government out of millions of dollars in revenue. Grant's personal secretary was enmeshed in the scheme.

Congressional committees investigated most of the scandals but uncovered no evidence that Grant himself was ever involved. His poor choice of associates, however, earned him widespread criticism. Democrats scolded Republicans for their "monstrous corruption and extravagance" and reinforced the public suspicion that elected officials were less servants of the people than they were self-serving bandits.

THE MONEY SUPPLY Complex financial issues—especially monetary policy—dominated Grant's presidency. Prior to the Civil War, the economy operated on a gold standard; state banks issued paper money that could be exchanged for an equal value of gold coins. So both gold coins and state bank notes circulated as currency. **Greenbacks** (so called because of the dye color used on the printed dollars) were issued during the Civil War to help pay for the war.

When a nation's supply of money grows faster than the economy itself, prices for goods and services increase (inflation). This happened when the greenbacks were issued. After the war, the U.S. Treasury assumed that the greenbacks would be recalled from circulation so that consumer prices would decline and the nation could return to a "hard-money" currency—gold, silver, and copper coins—which had always been viewed as more reliable in value than paper currency.

The most vocal supporters of a return to "hard money" were eastern creditors (mostly bankers and merchants) who did not want their debtors to pay them in paper currency. Critics of the gold standard tended to be farmers and other debtors. These so-called soft-money advocates opposed taking greenbacks out of circulation because shrinking the supply of money would bring lower prices (deflation) for their crops and livestock, thereby reducing their income and making it harder for them to pay their long-term debts. In 1868, congressional supporters of such a "soft-money" policy—mostly Democrats— forced the Treasury to stop withdrawing greenbacks from circulation.

President Grant sided with the "hard-money" camp. On March 18, 1869, he signed the Public Credit Act, which said that the investors who purchased government bonds to help finance the war effort must be paid back in gold. The Public Credit Act led to a decline in consumer prices that hurt debtors and helped creditors. It also ignited a ferocious political debate over the merits of "hard" and "soft" money that would last throughout the nineteenth century— and beyond.

FINANCIAL PANIC President Grant's effort to withdraw the greenbacks from circulation unintentionally helped cause a major economic collapse. During 1873, two dozen overextended railroads stopped paying their bills, forcing Jay Cooke and Company, the nation's leading business lender, to go bankrupt and close its headquarters on September 18, 1873. The shocking news created a snowball effect, as hard-pressed banks began shutting down. A Republican senator sent Grant an urgent telegram from New York City: "Results of today indicate imminent danger of general national bank panic."

The resulting **Panic of 1873** triggered a deep economic depression. Tens of thousands of businesses closed, millions of workers lost their jobs, and those with jobs saw their wages slashed. In the major cities, unemployed, homeless Americans formed long lines at charity soup kitchens.

The depression led the U.S. Treasury to reverse course and begin printing more greenbacks. For a time, the supporters of paper money celebrated, but in 1874, Grant, after a period of agonized reflection, overruled his cabinet and vetoed a bill to issue even more greenbacks. His decision pleased the financial community but also ignited a barrage of criticism. A prominent Republican, Edwards Pierrepont, telegraphed Grant that his veto represented "the bravest battle and biggest victory of your life." A Tennessee Republican congressman, however, called the veto of the currency bill "cold-blooded murder." In the end, Grant's decision only prolonged what was then the worst depression in the nation's history.

LIBERAL REPUBLICANS The sudden collapse of the economy in 1873 contributed to northerners' losing interest in Reconstruction and Republicans dividing into two factions: the Liberals (or Conscience Republicans) and the Capitalists (Stalwart Republicans). The Liberal Republicans, led by senators Charles Sumner and Carl Schurz, called for the "best elements" in both national parties to join together. Their goal was to oust the "tyrannical" Grant from the presidency, end federal Reconstruction efforts in the South, lower tariffs intended to line the pockets of big corporations, and promote "civil service reforms" to end the "partisan tyranny" of the "patronage system" whereby new presidents rewarded the "selfish greed" of political supporters with federal government jobs. The Liberal Republicans charged that Grant and his cronies were making decisions solely to benefit themselves, putting profits above principles.

In 1872, the breakaway Liberal Republicans, many of whom were newspaper editors suspicious of the "working classes," held their own national convention in Cincinnati, at which they accused the Grant administration of corruption, incompetence, and "despotism." They then committed political suicide by nominating an unlikely and ill-suited presidential candidate: Horace Greeley, editor of the *New York Tribune* and a longtime champion of a variety of causes: abolitionism, socialism, vegetarianism, and spiritualism. His image as an eccentric who repeatedly reversed his political positions was complemented by his record of hostility to the Democrats, whose support the Liberal Republicans needed if they were going to win the election.

The Democrats nevertheless gave their nomination to Greeley. Southern Democrats liked his criticism of federal reconstruction policies. His *New York Tribune*, for example, claimed that "ignorant, superstitious, semi-barbarian" former slaves were "extremely indolent, and will make no exertion beyond what is necessary to obtain food enough to satisfy their hunger." Moreover, Radical Republicans had given the vote to "ignorant" former slaves whose "Nigger Government" exercised "absolute political supremacy" in several states and was transferring the wealth from the "most intelligent" and "influential" southern whites to themselves.

Most northerners, however, were appalled at Greeley's candidacy. By nominating Greeley, said the *New York Times*, the Liberal Republicans and Democrats had killed any chance of electoral victory. Greeley carried only six southern states and none in the North. Grant won thirty-one states and car-

"Worse Than Slavery" This Thomas Nast cartoon condemns the Ku Klux Klan for promoting conditions "worse than slavery" for southern blacks after the Civil War.

ried the national election by 3,598,235 votes to 2,834,761. An exhausted Greeley confessed that he was "the worst beaten man who ever ran for high office." He died three weeks later. Grant was delighted that the "soreheads and thieves who had deserted the Republican party" were defeated, and he promised to be a better president by avoiding the "mistakes" he had made in his first term.

WHITE TERROR President Grant initially fought to enforce federal efforts to reconstruct the postwar South. But southern resistance to "Radical rule" increased and turned brutally violent. In Grayson County, Texas, a white man and two friends murdered three former slaves because they wanted to "thin the niggers out and drive them to their holes."

Klansmen focused their program of murder, violence, and intimidation on prominent Republicans, black and white—elected officials, teachers in black schools, state militias. They intentionally avoided clashes with federal troops. In Mississippi, they killed a black Republican leader in front of his family. Three white "scalawag" Republicans were murdered in Georgia in 1870. That same year, an armed mob of whites launched an attack at a Republican political rally in Alabama, killing four blacks and wounding fifty-four. An Alabama Republican pleaded with Grant to intervene. "Give us poor people some guarantee of our lives," G. T. F. Boulding wrote. "We are hunted and shot down as if we were wild beasts."

At the urging of President Grant, Republicans in Congress responded with three Enforcement Acts (1870–1871). The first of these measures imposed penalties on anyone who interfered with any citizen's right to vote. The second dispatched federal supervisors and marshals to monitor elections in southern districts where political terrorism flourished. The third, called the Ku Klux Klan Act, outlawed the main activities of the KKK—forming conspiracies, wearing disguises, resisting officers, and intimidating officials.

In general, however, the Enforcement Acts were not consistently enforced. As a result, the efforts of southern whites to use violence to thwart Reconstruction escalated. On Easter Sunday in 1873 in Colfax, Louisiana, a mob of white vigilantes, most of them ex-Confederate soldiers disappointed by local election results, used a cannon, rifles, and pistols to attack a group of black Republicans in the courthouse, slaughtering eighty-one and burning down the building. It was the bloodiest racial incident during the Reconstruction period.

SOUTHERN "REDEEMERS" The Ku Klux Klan's impact on southern politics varied from state to state. In the Upper South, it played only a modest role in helping Democrats win local elections. In the Lower South, however, Klan violence and intimidation had more serious effects. In overwhelmingly black Yazoo County, Mississippi, vengeful whites used terrorism to reverse the political balance of power. In the 1873 elections, for example, the Republicans cast 2,449 votes and the Democrats 638; two years later, the Democrats polled 4,049 votes, the Republicans 7.

Throughout the South, the activities of white supremacists disheartened black and white Republicans alike. "We are helpless and unable to organize," wrote a Mississippi scalawag. We "dare not attempt to canvass [campaign for candidates], or make public speeches." At the same time, northerners displayed a growing weariness with using federal troops to reconstruct the South. "The plain truth is," noted the *New York Herald*, "the North has got tired of the Negro."

President Grant, however, desperately wanted to use more federal force to preserve peace and asked Congress to pass new legislation that would "leave my duties perfectly clear." Congress responded with the Civil Rights Act of 1875, the most comprehensive guarantee of civil rights to that point. It said that people of all races must be granted equal access to hotels and restaurants, railroads and stagecoaches, theaters, and other places of public entertainment. Unfortunately for Grant, however, the new law provided little authority to enforce its provisions. Those who felt their rights were being violated had to file suit in court, and the penalties for violators were modest.

Public interest in protecting civil rights in the South continued to wane as other issues emerged to distract northerners. Western expansion, Indian wars, and economic issues surged to the forefront of voter concerns.

Republican political control in the South gradually loosened as all-white "Conservative" parties mobilized the anti-Reconstruction vote. White Democrats—the so-called **redeemers** who supposedly "saved" the South from Republican control and "black rule"—used the race issue to excite the white electorate and intimidate black voters. Where persuasion failed to work, Democrats used trickery. As one enthusiastic Democrat boasted, "The white and black Republicans may outvote us, but we can outcount them."

The Compromise of 1877 This illustration represents the compromise between Republicans and southern Democrats that elected Rutherford B. Hayes and ended Radical Reconstruction.

Republican political control ended in Virginia and Tennessee as early as 1869; in Georgia and North Carolina, it collapsed in 1870, although North Carolina had a Republican governor until 1876. Reconstruction lasted longest in the Lower South, where whites abandoned Klan robes for barefaced intimidation in paramilitary groups such as the Mississippi Rifle Club and the South Carolina Red Shirts. The last Radical Republican regimes collapsed, however, after the elections of 1876, and the return to power of the old white political elite in the South further undermined the country's commitment to Congressional Reconstruction.

THE CONTESTED ELECTION OF 1877 President Grant wanted to run for an unprecedented third term in 1876, but many Republicans had lost confidence in his leadership. In the summer of 1875, Grant acknowledged the inevitable, announced that he would retire, and admitted that he had entered the White House with "no political training" and had made "errors in judgment." James Gillespie Blaine of Maine, former Speaker of the House, was the likeliest Republican to succeed Grant, but his candidacy crumbled when it was revealed that he had promised political favors to railroad executives in exchange for shares of stock in the company.

The scandal led the Republican convention to pass over Blaine in favor of Ohio's favorite son, Rutherford B. Hayes. Elected governor of Ohio three times, most recently as a "hard money" gold advocate, Hayes also was a civil service reformer eager to reduce the number of federal jobs subject to political appointment. But his chief virtue was that he offended neither Radicals nor reformers. As a journalist put it, he was "obnoxious to no one."

The Democratic convention was uncharacteristically harmonious from the start. The nomination went to Samuel J. Tilden, a wealthy corporate lawyer and reform governor of New York.

The 1876 campaign avoided controversial issues. Both candidates favored relaxing federal military authority in the South. In the absence of strong ideological differences, Democrats highlighted the scandals embroiling the Republicans. In response, Republicans ignored the depression and repeatedly waved "the bloody shirt," linking the Democrats to secession, civil war, and the violence committed against Republicans in the South. As Robert G. Ingersoll, the most celebrated Republican public speaker of the time, insisted: "The man that assassinated Abraham Lincoln was a Democrat. . . . Soldiers, every scar you have on your heroic bodies was given you by a Democrat!"

Despite the lack of major issues, the 1876 election generated the most votes of any national election in U.S. history to that point. Early returns pointed to a victory for Tilden. Nationwide, he outpolled Hayes by almost 300,000 votes; by midnight following Election Day, Tilden had won 184 electoral votes, just one short of the total needed for victory. Overnight, however, Republican activists realized that the election hinged on 19 disputed electoral votes from Florida, Louisiana, and South Carolina.

The Democrats needed only one of the challenged votes to claim victory; the Republicans needed all nineteen. Republicans in those key states had engaged in election fraud, while Democrats had used physical intimidation to keep black voters at home. But all three states were governed by a Republican who appointed the election boards, each of which reported narrow victories for Hayes. The Democrats immediately challenged the results.

In all three states, rival election boards submitted conflicting vote counts. The nation watched and wondered as days, then weeks, passed with no solution. On January 29, 1877, Congress set up an electoral commission to settle the dispute. It met daily for weeks trying to verify the disputed vote counts.

Finally, on March 1, 1877, the commission voted 8 to 7 along party lines in favor of Hayes. The next day, the House of Representatives declared Hayes president by an electoral vote of 185 to 184. Tilden decided not to protest the decision. His campaign manager explained that they preferred "four years of Hayes's administration to four years of civil war."

Hayes's victory hinged on the defection of key southern Democrats, who, it turned out, had made a number of secret deals with the Republicans. On February 26, 1877, prominent Ohio Republicans and powerful southern Democrats struck a private bargain—the **Compromise of 1877**—at Wormley's Hotel in Washington, D.C. The Republicans promised that if Hayes were named president, he would remove the last federal troops from the South.

THE END OF RECONSTRUCTION In 1877, newly inaugurated President Hayes withdrew federal troops from Louisiana and South Carolina, whose Republican governments collapsed soon thereafter. Hayes insisted that it was not his fault: "The practical destruction of the Republican organization in the South was accomplished before my southern policy was announced."

Over the next thirty years, the protection of black civil rights in the South crumbled. As Henry Adams, a former Louisiana slave, observed in 1877, "The whole South—every state in the South—has got [back] into the hands of the very men that held us as slaves." New white state governments rewrote their constitutions, rid their administrations of "carpetbaggers, scalawags, and blacks," and cut spending. "The Yankees helped free us, so they say," a former North Carolina slave named Thomas Hall remembered, "but [in 1877] they let us be put back in slavery again."

RECONSTRUCTION'S SIGNIFICANCE

Congressional Reconstruction gave African Americans an opportunity to experience freedom—but not security or equality. As Thomas Hall noted in acknowledging the end of Reconstruction, African Americans were still dependent "on the southern white man for work, food, and clothing," and most southern whites remained hostile to the notion of civil rights and social equality. The collapse of Congressional Reconstruction in 1877 had tragic consequences, as the South aggressively renewed traditional patterns of discrimination against African Americans. Black activist W. E. B. DuBois called the effort to make slaves into citizens a "splendid failure."

Yet for all of the unfulfilled promises of Congressional Reconstruction, it left an enduring legacy—the Thirteenth, Fourteenth, and Fifteenth Amendments. If Reconstruction's experiment in interracial democracy did not provide true social equality or substantial economic opportunities for African Americans, it did create the essential constitutional foundation for future advances in the quest for equality and civil rights—and not just for African Americans, but for women and other minority groups. Until the pivotal Reconstruction era, the states were responsible for protecting citizens' rights. Thereafter, thanks to the Fourteenth and Fifteenth Amendments, blacks had gained equal rights (in theory), and the federal government had assumed responsibility for ensuring that states treated blacks equally. A hundred years later, the cause of civil rights would be embraced again by the federal government—this time permanently.

CHAPTER REVIEW

SUMMARY

- **Reconstruction Challenges**   With the defeat of the Confederacy and the passage of the Thirteenth Amendment, the federal government had to develop policies and procedures to address a number of vexing questions: What was the status of the defeated states and how would they be reintegrated into the nation's political life? What would be the political status of the former slaves and what would the federal government do to integrate them into the nation's social and economic fabric?

- **Reconstruction over Time**   Abraham Lincoln and his successor, southerner Andrew Johnson, wanted a lenient plan for Reconstruction. The *Freedmen's Bureau* helped to educate and aid freed slaves, negotiate labor contracts, and reunite families. Lincoln's assassination led many northerners to favor the *Radical Republicans*, who wanted to end the grasp of the old plantation elite on the South's society and economy. Whites resisted and established *black codes* to restrict the freedom of former slaves. *Congressional Reconstruction* responded by stipulating that to reenter the Union, former Confederate states had to ratify the *Fourteenth* and *Fifteenth Amendments* to the U.S. Constitution to protect the rights of African Americans. Congress also passed the Military Reconstruction Act, which used federal troops to enforce the voting and civil rights of African Americans.

- **Views of Reconstruction**   Many former slaves found comfort in their families and in the churches they established, but land ownership reverted to the old white elite, reducing newly freed blacks to *sharecropping*. African Americans enthusiastically participated in politics, with many serving as elected officials. Along with white southern Republicans (scalawags) and northern carpetbaggers, they worked to rebuild the southern economy. Many white southerners, however, supported the *Ku Klux Klan's* violent intimidation of the supporters of Reconstruction and pursued "redemption," or white Democratic control of southern state governments.

- **Political and Economic Developments and the End of Reconstruction**   Scandals during the Grant administration involved an attempt to corner the gold market, and the "whiskey ring's" plan to steal millions of dollars in tax revenue. In the face of these troubles and the economic downturn caused by both the *Panic of 1873* and disagreement over whether to continue the use of *greenbacks* or return to the gold standard, northern support for the status quo in government eroded and weakened Reconstruction. Southern white "*redeemers*" were elected in 1874, successfully reversing the political progress of Republicans and blacks. In the *Compromise of 1877*, Democrats agreed to the election of Republican Rutherford B. Hayes, who put an end to the Radical Republican administrations in the southern states.

- **The Significance of Reconstruction**   Southern state governments quickly renewed long-standing patterns of discrimination against African Americans, but the

Fourteenth and Fifteenth Amendments remained enshrined in the Constitution, creating the essential constitutional foundation for future advances in civil rights.

Chronology

1865	Congress sets up the Freedmen's Bureau
April 14, 1865	Lincoln assassinated
1865	Johnson issues Proclamation of Amnesty
	All-white southern state legislatures pass various "black codes"
1866	Ku Klux Klan organized
	Congress passes the Civil Rights Act
1867	Congress passes the Military Reconstruction Act
1868	Fourteenth Amendment is ratified
	The U.S. House of Representatives impeaches President Andrew Johnson; the Senate fails to convict him
	Grant elected president
	Eight former Confederate states readmitted to the Union
1869	Reestablishment of white conservative rule ("redeemers") in some former Confederate states.
1870	Fifteenth Amendment ratified
	First Enforcement Acts passed in response to white terror in the South
1872	Grant wins reelection
1873	Panic of 1873 triggers depression
1877	Compromise of 1877 ends Reconstruction; Hayes becomes president

Key Terms

Radical Republicans p. 583

Freedmen's Bureau p. 584

Johnson's Restoration Plan p. 587

black codes p. 589

Fourteenth Amendment (1866) p. 589

Congressional Reconstruction p. 590

Fifteenth Amendment (1870) p. 592

sharecropping p. 597

Ku Klux Klan (KKK) p. 600

greenbacks p. 603

Panic of 1873 p. 604

redeemers p. 607

Compromise of 1877 p. 610

🔍 INQUIZITIVE

Go to InQuizitive to see what you've learned—and learn what you've missed—with personalized feedback along the way.

GLOSSARY

1968 Chicago Democratic National Convention The meeting of Democratic delegates in Chicago to nominate a candidate for the 1968 presidential elections, which were marred by violent anti-war protests.

36°30' According to the Missouri Compromise, any part of the Louisiana Purchase north of this line (Missouri's southern border) was to be excluded from slavery.

abolition In the early 1830s, the anti-slavery movement shifted its goal from the gradual end of slavery to the immediate end or abolition of slavery.

abolitionism Movement that called for an immediate end to slavery throughout the United States.

Abigail Adams (1744–1818) As the wife of John Adams, she endured long periods of separation from him while he served in many political roles. During these times apart, she wrote often to her husband; their correspondence has provided a detailed portrait of life during the Revolutionary War.

John Adams (1735–1826) He was a signer of the Declaration of Independence and a delegate to the First and Second Continental Congresses. A member of the Federalist Party, he served as the first vice president of the United States and the second president. As president, he passed the Alien and Sedition Acts and endured a stormy relationship with France, which included the XYZ affair.

John Quincy Adams (1767–1848) As secretary of state, he urged President Monroe to issue the Monroe Doctrine, which incorporated his belief in an expanded use of federal powers. As the sixth president, Adams's nationalism and praise of European leaders caused a split in his party, causing some Republicans to leave and form the Democrat party.

Samuel Adams (1722–1803) A genius of revolutionary agitation, he believed that English Parliament had no right to legislate for the colonies. He organized the Sons of Liberty as well as protests in Boston against the British.

Jane Addams (1860–1935) She founded and ran of one of the best known settlement houses, the Hull House. Active in the peace and suffragist movements, she established child care for working mothers, health clinics, job training, and other social programs.

affirmative action Programs designed to give preferential treatment to women and minorities as compensation for past injustices.

Affordable Care Act (ACA), or Obamacare (2010) Vast health care reform initiative signed into law and championed by President Obama and widely criticized by Republicans that aims to make health insurance more affordable and make health-care accessible to everyone, regardless of income or prior medical conditions.

Agricultural Adjustment Act (1933) Legislation that paid farmers to produce less in order to raise crop prices for all; the act was later declared unconstitutional by the U.S. Supreme Court in the case of *United States v. Butler* (1936).

Emilio Aguinaldo (1869?–1964) He was a leader in Filipino struggle for independence. During the Spanish-American War (the War of 1898), Commodore George Dewey brought Aguinaldo back to the Philippines from exile to help fight the Spanish. However, after the Spanish surrendered to Americans, America annexed the Philippines and Aguinaldo fought against the American military until he was captured in 1901.

Alamo, Battle of the Siege in the Texas War for Independence of 1836, in which the San Antonio mission fell to the Mexicans. Davy Crockett and Jim Bowie were among the courageous defenders.

Albany Plan of Union A failed proposal by the seven northern colonies in anticipation of the French and Indian War, urging the unification of the colonies under one Crown-appointed president.

Alien and Sedition Acts of 1798 Four measures passed during the undeclared war with France that limited the freedoms of speech and press and restricted the liberty of non-citizens.

alliance with France Critical diplomatic, military, and economic alliance between France and the newly independent United States, codified by the Treaty of Amity and Commerce and the Treaty of Alliance (1778).

Allied Powers The nations fighting the Central Powers during the First World War, including France, Great Britain, and Russia; later joined by Italy and, after Russia quit the war in 1917, the United States.

American Anti-Imperialist League Coalition of anti-imperialist groups united in 1899 to protest American territorial expansion, especially in the Philippine Islands; its membership included prominent politicians, industrialists, labor leaders, and social reformers.

American Colonization Society (ACS) Established in 1817, an organization whose mission was to return freed slaves to Africa.

American Federation of Labor (AFL) Founded in 1881 as a national federation of trade unions made up of skilled workers.

American Indian Movement (AIM) Fed up with the poor conditions on Indian reservations and the federal government's unwillingness to help, Native Americans founded the American Indian Movement in 1963. In 1973, AIM led 200 Sioux in the occupation of Wounded Knee. After a ten-week standoff with the federal authorities, the government agreed to reexamine Indian treaty rights and the occupation ended.

American Recovery and Reinvestment Act Hoping to restart the weak economy, President Obama signed this $787 billion economic stimulus bill in February 2009. The bill included cash distributions to states, funds for food stamps, unemployment benefits, construction projects to renew the nation's infrastructure, funds for renewable-energy systems, and tax reductions.

American System Economic plan championed by Henry Clay of Kentucky that called for federal tariffs on imports, a strong national bank, and federally-financed internal improvements—roads, bridges, canals—all intended to strengthen the national economy and end American dependence on Great Britain.

American Tobacco Company Business founded in 1890 by North Carolina's James Buchanan Duke, who combined the major tobacco manufacturers of the time, ultimately controlling 90 percent of the country's cigarette production.

Anaconda Plan Union's primary war strategy calling for a naval blockade of major southern seaports and then dividing the Confederacy by gaining control of the Tennessee, Cumberland, and Mississippi Rivers.

Antietam, Battle of (1862) Turning-point battle near Sharpsburg, Maryland, leaving over 20,000 soldiers dead or wounded, in which Union forces halted a Confederate invasion of the North.

anti-Federalists Opponents of the Constitution as an infringement on individual and states' rights, whose criticism led to the addition of a Bill of Rights to the document. Many anti-Federalists later joined Thomas Jefferson's Democratic-Republican party.

Anti-Masonic party This party grew out of popular hostility toward the Masonic fraternal order and entered the presidential election of 1832 as a third party. It was the first party to run as a third party in a presidential election, as well as the first to hold a nomination convention and announce a party platform.

Appomattox Court House Virginia village where Confederate general Robert E. Lee surrendered to Union general Ulysses S. Grant on April 9, 1865.

Arab Awakening A wave of spontaneous democratic uprisings that spread throughout the Arab world beginning in 2011, in which long-oppressed peoples demanded basic liberties from generations-old authoritarian regimes.

Armory show A divisive and sensational art exhibition in 1913 which introduced European-inspired modernism to American audiences.

Benedict Arnold (1741–1801) A traitorous American commander who planned to sell out the American garrison at West Point to the British, but his plot was discovered before it could be executed and he joined the British army.

Articles of Confederation The first form of government for the United States, ratified by the original thirteen states in 1781; weak in central authority, it was replaced by the U.S. Constitution in 1789.

Atlanta Compromise (1895) A speech by Booker T. Washington that called for the black community to strive for economic prosperity before attempting political and social equality.

Atlantic Charter (1941) Joint statement crafted by Franklin D. Roosevelt and British prime minister Winston Churchill that listed the war goals of the Allied Powers.

Crispus Attucks (1723–1770) During the Boston Massacre, he was supposedly at the head of the crowd of hecklers who baited the British troops. He was killed when the British troops fired on the crowd.

Stephen F. Austin (1793–1836) He established the first colony of Americans in Texas, which eventually attracted 2,000 people.

"Axis" alliance Military alliance formed in 1937 by the three major fascist powers: Germany, Italy, and Japan.

Aztec Empire Mesoamerican people who were conquered by the Spanish under Hernando Cortés, 1519–1528.

baby boom Markedly high birth rate in the years following World War II, leading to the biggest demographic "bubble" in U.S. history.

Bacon's Rebellion Unsuccessful 1676 revolt led by planter Nathaniel Bacon against Virginia governor William Berkeley's administration, which, Bacon charged, had failed to protect settlers from Indian raids.

Bank of the United States (1791) National bank responsible for holding and transferring federal government funds, making business loans, and issuing a national currency.

Bank War Political struggle in the early 1830s between President Jackson and financier Nicholas Biddle over the renewing of the Second Bank's charter.

Barbary pirates North Africans who waged war (1801–1805) on the United States after President Thomas Jefferson refused to pay tribute (a bribe) to protect American ships.

Bay of Pigs Failed CIA operation that, in April 1961, deployed a band of Cuban rebels to overthrow Fidel Castro's Communist regime.

Bear Flag Republic On June 14, 1846, a group of Americans in California captured Sonoma from the Mexican army and declared it the Republic of California, whose flag featured a grizzly bear. In July, the commodore of the U.S. Pacific Fleet landed troops on California's shores and declared it part of the United States.

Beats Group of bohemian, downtown New York writers, artists, and musicians who flouted convention in favor of liberated forms of self-expression.

Berlin airlift (1948) Effort by the United States and Great Britain to deliver massive amounts of food and supplies flown in to West Berlin in response to the Soviet land blockade of the city.

Berlin Wall Twenty-seven-mile-long concrete wall constructed in 1961 by East German authorities to stop the flow of East Germans fleeing to West Berlin.

Bessemer converter Apparatus which blasts air through molten iron to produce steel in very large quantities.

Nicholas Biddle (1786–1844) He was the president of the second Bank of the United States. In response to President Andrew Jackson's attacks on the bank, Biddle curtailed the bank's loans and exchanged its paper currency for gold and silver. In response, state banks began printing paper without restraint and lent it to speculators, causing a binge in speculating and an enormous increase in debt.

Bill of Rights First ten amendments to the U.S. Constitution, adopted in 1791 to guarantee individual rights and to help secure ratification of the Constitution by the states.

Osama bin Laden (1957–2011) The Saudi-born leader of al Qaeda, whose members attacked America on September 11, 2001. Years before the attack, he had declared *jihad* (holy war) on the United States, Israel, and the Saudi monarchy. In Afghanistan, the Taliban leaders gave bin Laden a safe haven in exchange for aid in fighting the Northern Alliance, who were rebels opposed to the Taliban. Following the Taliban's refusal to turn over bin Laden to the United States, America and a multinational coalition invaded Afghanistan and overthrew the Taliban. In May 2011, bin Laden was shot and killed by American special forces during a covert operation in Pakistan.

birth rate Proportion of births per 1,000 of the total population.

black codes Laws passed in southern states to restrict the rights of former slaves; to combat the codes, Congress passed the Civil Rights Act of 1866 and the Fourteenth Amendment and set up military governments in southern states that refused to ratify the amendment.

black power movement Militant form of civil rights protest focused on urban communities in the North and led by Malcolm X that grew as a response to impatience with the nonviolent tactics of Martin Luther King Jr.

James Gillepsie Blaine (1830–1893) As a Republican congressman from Maine, he developed close ties with business leaders, which contributed to him losing the presidential election of 1884. He later opposed President Cleveland's efforts to reduce tariffs, which became a significant issue in the 1888 presidential election. Blaine served as secretary of state under President Benjamin Harrison.

Bleeding Kansas (1856) A series of violent conflicts in the Kansas territory between anti-slavery and pro-slavery factions over the status of slavery.

blitzkrieg (1940) The German "lightning war" strategy characterized by swift, well-organized attacks using infantry, tanks, and warplanes.

Bolsheviks Under the leadership of Vladimir Lenin, this Marxist party led the November 1917 revolution against the newly formed provisional government in Russia. After seizing control, the Bolsheviks negotiated a peace treaty with Germany, the Treaty of Brest-Litovsk, and ended their participation in World War I.

Bonus Expeditionary Force (1932) Protest march on Washington, D.C., by thousands of World War I veterans and their families, calling for immediate payment of their service bonuses certificates; violence ensued when President Herbert Hoover ordered their tent villages cleared.

boomtown Town, often in the West, that developed rapidly due to the sudden influx of wealth and work opportunities; often male-dominated with a substantial immigrant population.

Daniel Boone (1734–1820) He found and expanded a trail into Kentucky, which pioneers used to reach and settle the area.

John Wilkes Booth (1838?–1865) He assassinated President Abraham Lincoln at the Ford's Theater on April 14, 1865. He was pursued to Virginia and killed.

Boston Massacre Violent confrontation between British soldiers and a Boston mob on March 5, 1770, in which five colonists were killed.

Boston Tea Party Demonstration against the Tea Act of 1773 in which the Sons of Liberty, dressed as Indians, dumped hundreds of chests of British-owned tea into Boston Harbor.

bracero program System created in 1942 that permitted seasonal farm workers from Mexico to work in the United States on year-long contracts.

Joseph Brant (1742?–1807) He was the Mohawk leader who led the Iroquois against the Americans in the Revolutionary War.

brinkmanship Secretary of State John Foster Dulles believed that communism could be contained by bringing America to the brink of war with an aggressive communist nation. He believed that the aggressor would back down when confronted with the prospect of receiving a mass retaliation from a country with nuclear weapons.

John Brown (1800–1859) In response to a pro-slavery mob's sacking of a free-state town of Lawrence, Kansas, Brown went to the pro-slavery settlement of Pottawatomie, Kansas, which led to a guerrilla war in the Kansas territory. In 1859, he attempted to raid the federal arsenal at Harpers Ferry, hoping to use the stolen weapons to arm slaves, but he was captured and executed.

Brown v. Board of Education **(1954)** Landmark Supreme Court case that struck down racial segregation in public schools and declared "separate-but-equal" unconstitutional.

William Jennings Bryan (1860–1925) He delivered the pro-silver "cross of gold" speech at the 1896 Democratic Convention and won his party's nomination for president. Disappointed pro-gold Democrats chose to walk out of the convention and nominate their own candidate, which split the Democratic party and cost them the White House. Bryan's loss also crippled the Populist movement that had endorsed him.

"Bull Moose" Progressive party *See* Progressive party

Bull Run, Battles of (First and Second Manassas) First land engagement of the Civil War took place on July 21, 1861, at Manassas Junction, Virginia, at which surprised Union troops quickly retreated; one year later, on August 29–30, Confederates captured the federal supply depot and forced Union troops back to Washington.

Martin Van Buren (1782–1862) During President Jackson's first term, he served as secretary of state and minister to London. In 1836, Van Buren was elected president, and he inherited a financial crisis. He believed that the government should not continue to keep its deposits in state banks and set up an independent Treasury, which was approved by Congress after several years of political maneuvering.

General John Burgoyne (1722–1792) He was the commander of Britain's northern forces during the Revolutionary War. He and most of his troops surrendered to the Americans at the Battle of Saratoga.

burial mounds A funeral tradition, practiced in the Mississippi and Ohio Valleys by the Adena-Hopewell cultures, of erecting massive mounds of earth over graves, often in the designs of serpents and other animals.

burned-over district Area of western New York strongly influenced by the revivalist fervor of the Second Great Awakening. Disciples of Christ and Mormons are among the many sects that trace their roots to the phenomenon.

Aaron Burr (1756–1836) Even though he was Thomas Jefferson's vice president, he lost favor with Jefferson's supporters who were Republicans. He sought to work with the Federalists and run as their candidate for the governor of New York. Alexander Hamilton opposed Burr's candidacy and his stinging remarks on the subject led to Burr challenging him to duel in which Hamilton was killed.

George H. W. Bush (1924–) He had served as vice president during the Reagan administration and then won the presidential election of 1988. His presidency was marked by raised taxes in the face of the federal deficit, the creation of the Office of National Drug Control Policy, and military activity abroad, including the invasion of Panama and Operation Desert Storm in Kuwait. He lost the 1992 presidential election to Bill Clinton.

George W. Bush (1946–) In the 2000 presidential election, Texas governor George W. Bush won as the Republican nominee against Democratic nominee Vice President Al Gore. After the September 11 terrorist attacks, he launched his "war on terrorism." President Bush adopted the Bush Doctrine, and United States invaded Afghanistan and Iraq with unclear outcomes, leaving the countries divided. In September 2008, the nation's economy nosedived as a credit crunch spiraled into a global economic meltdown. Bush signed into law the bank bailout fund called Troubled Asset Relief Program (TARP), but the economy did not improve.

***Bush v. Gore* (2000)** The close 2000 presidential election came down to Florida's decisive twenty-five electoral votes. The final tally in Florida gave Bush a slight lead, but it was so small that a recount was required by state law. While the votes were being recounted, a legal battle was being waged to stop the recount. Finally, the case, *Bush v. Gore*, was present to the Supreme Court who ruled 5–4 to stop the recount and Bush was declared the winner.

Bush Doctrine National security policy launched in 2002 by which the Bush administration claimed the right to launch preemptive military attacks against perceived enemies, particularly outlaw nations or terrorist organizations believed to possess weapons of mass destruction.

buying (stock) on margin The investment practice of making a small down payment (the "margin") on a stock and borrowing the rest of the money needed for the purchase from a broker who held the stock as security against a down market. If the stock's value declined and the buyer failed to meet a margin call for more funds, the broker could sell the stock to cover his loan.

Cahokia The largest chiefdom and city of the Mississippian Indian culture located in present-day Illinois, and the site of a sophisticated farming settlement that supported up to 15,000 inhabitants.

John C. Calhoun (1782–1850) He served in both the House of Representatives and the Senate for South Carolina before becoming secretary of war under President Monroe and then John Quincy Adams's vice president. Though he started his political career as an advocate of a strong national government, he eventually believed that states' rights, limited central government, and the power of nullification were necessary to preserve the Union.

California gold rush (1849) A massive migration of gold hunters, mostly men, who transformed the economy of California after gold was discovered in the foothills of the Sierra Nevada mountains in the Sacramento River Valley in northern California.

Camp David Accords Peace agreement in 1978 between Prime Minister Menachem Begin of Israel and President Anwar Sadat of Egypt, the first Arab head of state to officially recognize the state of Israel.

"Scarface" Al Capone (1899–1947) He was the most successful gangster of the Prohibition era whose Chicago-based criminal empire included bootlegging, prostitution, and gambling.

Andrew Carnegie (1835–1919) He was a steel magnate who believed that the general public benefited from big business even if these companies employed harsh business practices. This philosophy became deeply ingrained in the conventional wisdom of some Americans. After retiring, he devoted himself to philanthropy in hopes of promoting social welfare and world peace.

Carnegie Steel Company Corporation under the leadership of Andrew Carnegie that came to dominate the American steel industry.

Carolina colonies English proprietary colonies comprised of North and South Carolina, whose semitropical climate made them profitable centers of rice, timber, and tar production.

carpetbaggers Northern emigrants who participated in the Republican governments of the reconstructed South.

Jimmy Carter (1924–) Elected president in 1976, Jimmy Carter was an outsider to Washington. He created the departments of Energy and Education and signed into law several environmental initiatives. In 1978, he successfully brokered a peace agreement between Israel and Egypt called the Camp David Accords. However, his unwillingness to make deals with legislators caused other bills to be either gutted or stalled in Congress. His administration was plagued with a series of crises: a recession and increased inflation, a fuel shortage, the Soviet invasion of Afghanistan, and the overthrow of the Shah of Iran, leading to the Iran Hostage Crisis Carter struggled to get the hostages released and was unable to do so until after he lost the 1980 election to

Ronald Reagan. He was awarded the Nobel Peace Prize in 2002 for his efforts to further peace and democratic elections around the world.

Jacques Cartier (1491–1557) He led the first French effort to colonize North America and explored the Gulf of St. Lawrence and reached as far as present day Montreal on the St. Lawrence River.

Fidel Castro (1926–) In 1959, his Communist regime came to power in Cuba after two years of guerrilla warfare against the dictator Fulgenico Batista. He enacted land redistribution programs and nationalized all foreign-owned property. The latter action as well as his political trials and summary executions damaged relations between Cuba and America. Castro was turned down when he asked for loans from the United States. However, he did receive aid from the Soviet Union.

Carrie Chapman Catt (1859–1947) She was a leader of a new generation of activists in the women's suffrage movement who carried on the work started by Elizabeth Cady Stanton and Susan B. Anthony.

Central Intelligence Agency (CIA) Intelligence-gathering government agency founded in 1947; under President Eisenhower's orders, secretly undermined elected governments deemed susceptible to communism.

Central Powers One of the two sides during the First World War, including Germany, Austria-Hungary, the Ottoman Empire (Turkey), and Bulgaria.

Cesar Chavez (1927–1993) He founded the United Farm Workers (UFW) in 1962 and worked to organize migrant farm workers. In 1965, the UFW joined Filipino farm workers striking against corporate grape farmers in California's San Joaquin Valley. In 1970, the strike and a consumer boycott on grapes compelled the farmers to formally recognize the UFW. As the result of Chavez's efforts, wages and working conditions improved for migrant workers. In 1975, the California state legislature passed a bill that required growers to bargain collectively with representatives of the farm workers.

child labor The practice of sending children to work in mines, mills, and factories, often in unsafe conditions; widespread among poor families in the late nineteenth century.

Chinese Exclusion Act (1882) Federal law that barred Chinese laborers from immigrating to America.

Church of Jesus Christ of Latter-day Saints Founded in 1830 by Joseph Smith, the sect was a product of the intense revivalism of the burned-over district of New York; Smith's successor Brigham Young led 15,000 followers to Utah in 1847 to escape persecution.

Winston Churchill (1874–1965) The British prime minister who led the country during the Second World War. Along with Roosevelt and Stalin, he helped shape the post-war world at the Yalta Conference. He also coined the term "iron curtain," which he used in his famous "The Sinews of Peace" speech.

citizen-soldiers Part-time nonprofessional soldiers, mostly poor farmers or recent immigrants who had been indentured servants, who played an important role in the Revolutionary War.

Civil Rights Act of 1957 First federal civil rights law since Reconstruction; established the Civil Rights Commission and the Civil Rights Division of the Department of Justice.

Civil Rights Act of 1964 Legislation that outlawed discrimination in public accommodations and employment, passed at the urging of President Lyndon B. Johnson.

civil service reform An extended effort led by political reformers to end the patronage system; led to the Pendleton Act (1883), which called for government positions to be awarded based on merit rather than party loyalty.

Henry Clay (1777–1852) In the first half of the nineteenth century, he was the foremost spokesman for the American system. As Speaker of the House in the 1820s, he promoted economic nationalism, "market revolution," and the rapid development of western states and territories. A broker of compromise, he formulated the "second" Missouri Compromise and the Compromise of 1850. In 1824, Clay supported John Quincy Adams, who won the presidency and appointed Clay to secretary of state. Andrew Jackson claimed that Clay had entered into a "corrupt bargain" with Adams for his own selfish gains.

Clayton Anti-Trust Act (1914) Legislation that served to enhance the Sherman Anti-Trust Act (1890) by clarifying what constituted "monopolistic" activities and declaring that labor unions were not to be viewed as "monopolies in restraint of trade."

Bill Clinton (1946–) The governor of Arkansas won the 1992 presidential election against President George H. W. Bush. In his first term, he pushed through Congress a tax increase, an economic stimulus package, the adoption of the North America Free Trade Agreement, welfare reform, a raise in the minimum wage, and improved public access to health insurance. His administration also negotiated the Oslo Accord and the Dayton Accords. After his reelection in 1996, he was involved in two high-profile scandals: his investment in the fraudulent Whitewater Development Corporation (but no evidence was found of him being involved in any wrongdoing) and his sexual affair with a White House intern. His attempt to cover up the affair led to a vote in Congress on whether or not to begin an impeachment inquiry. The House of Representatives voted to impeach Clinton, but the Senate found him not guilty.

Hillary Rodham Clinton (1947–) In the 2008 presidential election, Senator Hillary Clinton, the spouse of former President Bill Clinton, initially was the front-runner for the Democratic nomination, which made her the first woman with a serious chance to win the presidency. However, Senator Barack Obama's Internet-based and grassroots-orientated campaign garnered him enough delegates to win the nomination. After Obama became president, she was appointed secretary of state. Clinton stepped down from her Cabinet position in 2013 and, in 2015, announced her second presidential bid.

clipper ships Tall, slender, mid-nineteenth-century sailing ships that were favored over older merchant ships for their speed, but ultimately gave way to steamships because they lacked cargo space.

Coercive Acts Four parliamentary measures of 1774 that required the colonies to pay for the Boston Tea Party's damages, imposed a military government, disallowed colonial trials of British soldiers, and forced the quartering of troops in private homes.

Columbian Exchange The transfer of biological and social elements, such as plants, animals, people, diseases, and cultural practices, among Europe, the Americas, and Africa in the wake of Christopher Columbus's voyages to the "New World."

Christopher Columbus (1451–1506) The Italian sailor who persuaded King Ferdinand and Queen Isabella of Spain to fund his expedition across the Atlantic to discover a new trade route to Asia. Instead of arriving at China or Japan, he reached the Bahamas in 1492.

Committee of Correspondence Group organized by Samuel Adams in retaliation for the *Gaspée* incident to address American grievances, assert American rights, and form a network of rebellion.

Committee to Re-elect the President (CREEP) During Nixon's presidency, his administration engaged in a number of immoral acts, such as attempting to steal information and falsely accusing political appointments of sexual improprieties. These acts were funded by money illegally collected through CREEP.

Common Sense Popular pamphlet written by Thomas Paine attacking British principles of hereditary rule and monarchical government, and advocating a declaration of American independence.

Compromise of 1850 A package of five bills presented to the Congress by Henry Clay intended to avoid secession or civil war by reducing tensions between North and South over the status of slavery.

Compromise of 1877 Deal made by a special congressional commission on March 2, 1877, to resolve the disputed presidential election of 1876; Republican Rutherford B. Hayes, who had lost the popular vote, was declared the winner in exchange for the withdrawal of federal troops from the South, marking the end of Reconstruction.

Comstock Lode Mine in eastern Nevada acquired by Canadian fur trapper Henry Comstock that between 1860 and 1880 yielded almost $1 billion worth of gold and silver.

Conestoga wagons These large horse-drawn wagons were used to carry people or heavy freight long distances, including from the East to the western frontier settlements.

Congressional Reconstruction A more radical phase of Reconstruction, beginning in 1867, in which Congress, over President Johnson's objections, passed the Military Reconstruction Act that abolished the new Southern state governments in favor of federal military control. In addition, the Act required each state to draft a new constitution that guaranteed voting rights to all adult males regardless of race or economic status.

conquistadores Spanish term for "conquerors," applied to Spanish and Portuguese soldiers who conquered lands held by indigenous peoples in central and southern America as well as the current states of Texas, New Mexico, Arizona, and California.

consumer culture A society in which mass production and consumption of nationally advertised products comes to dictate much of social life and status.

containment U.S. cold war strategy that sought to prevent global Soviet expansion and influence through political, economic, and, if necessary, military pressure as a means of combating the spread of communism.

Continental army Army authorized by the Continental Congress (1775–1784) to fight the British; commanded by General George Washington.

contrabands Slaves who sought refuge in Union military camps or who lived in areas of the Confederacy under Union control.

Contract with America A list of conservatives' promises in response to the supposed liberalism of the Clinton administration, that was drafted by Speaker of the House Newt Gingrich and other congressional Republicans as the GOP platform for the 1994 midterm elections. More a campaign tactic than a practical program, few of its proposed items ever became law.

Contras The Reagan administration ordered the CIA to train and supply guerrilla bands of anti-Communist Nicaraguans called Contras. They were fighting the Sandinista government that had recently come to power in Nicaragua. The State Department believed that the Sandinista government was supplying the leftist Salvadoran rebels with Soviet and Cuban arms. A cease-fire agreement between the Contras and Sandinistas was signed in 1988.

Calvin "Silent Cal" Coolidge (1872–1933) After President Harding's death, his vice president, Calvin Coolidge, assumed the presidency. Coolidge believed that the nation's welfare was tied to the success of big business, and he worked to end government regulation of business and industry as well as reduce taxes. In particular, he focused on the nation's industrial development.

Copperhead Democrats Democrats in northern states who opposed the Civil War and argued for an immediate peace settlement with the Confederates; Republicans labeled them "Copperheads," likening them to venomous snakes.

General Charles Cornwallis (1738–1805) He was in charge of British troops in the South during the Revolutionary War. His surrendering to George Washington at the Battle of Yorktown ended the Revolutionary War.

Corps of Discovery Meriwether Lewis and William Clark led this group of men on an expedition of the newly purchased Louisiana territory, which took them from Missouri to Oregon. As they traveled, they kept detailed journals and drew maps of the previously unexplored territory. Their reports attracted traders and trappers to the region and gave the United States a claim to the Oregon country by right of discovery and exploration.

"corrupt bargain" Scandal in which presidential candidate and Speaker of the House Henry Clay secured John Quincy Adams's victory over Andrew Jackson in the 1824 election, supposedly in exchange for Clay being named secretary of state.

Hernán Cortés (1485–1547) The Spanish conquistador who conquered the Aztec Empire and set the precedent for other plundering conquistadores.

cotton White fibers harvested from cotton plants, spun into yarn, and woven into textiles that made comfortable, easy-to-clean products, especially clothing; the most valuable cash crop driving the economy in the United States and Great Britain during the nineteenth century.

cotton gin Hand-operated machine invented by Eli Whitney in the late eighteenth century that quickly removed seeds from cotton bolls, enabling the mass production of cotton in nineteenth-century America.

Cotton Kingdom Cotton-producing region, relying predominantly on slave labor, that spanned from North Carolina west to Louisiana and reached as far north as southern Illinois.

counterculture "Hippie" youth culture of the 1960s, which rejected the values of the dominant culture in favor of illicit drugs, communes, free sex, and rock music.

"Court-packing" scheme President Franklin D. Roosevelt's failed 1937 attempt to increase the number of U.S. Supreme Court justices from nine to fifteen in order to save his Second New Deal programs from constitutional challenges.

crop-lien system Credit system used by sharecroppers and share tenants who pledged a portion ("share") of their future crop to local merchants or land owners in exchange for farming supplies and food.

"cross of gold" speech In the 1896 election, the Democratic Party split over the issue of whether to use gold or silver to back American currency. Significant to this division was the pro-silver "cross of gold" speech that William Jennings Bryan delivered at the Democratic convention, which was so well received that Bryan won the nomination to be their presidential candidate. Disappointed pro-gold Democrats chose to walk out of the convention and nominate their own candidate.

Cuban missile crisis Thirteen-day U.S.-Soviet standoff in October 1962, sparked by the discovery of Soviet missile sites in Cuba; the crisis was the closest the world has come to nuclear war since 1945.

cult of domesticity A pervasive nineteenth-century ideology that urged women to celebrate their role as manager of the household and nurturer of the children.

George A. Custer (1839–1876) He was a reckless and glory-seeking lieutenant colonel of the U.S. Army who fought the Sioux Indians in the Great Sioux War. In 1876, he and his detachment of soldiers were entirely wiped out in the Battle of Little Bighorn.

***Dartmouth College v. Woodward* (1819)** Supreme Court ruling that enlarged the definition of *contract* to put corporations beyond the reach of the states that chartered them.

Daughters of Liberty Colonial women who protested the British government's tax policies by boycotting British products, such as clothing, and who wove their own fabric, or "homespun."

Dawes Severalty Act (1887) Federal legislation that divided ancestral Native American lands among the heads of each Indian family in an attempt to "Americanize" Indians by forcing them to become farmers working individual plots of land.

Jefferson Davis (1808–1889) He was the president of the Confederacy during the Civil War. When the Confederacy's defeat seemed inevitable in early 1865, he refused to surrender. Union forces captured him in May of that year.

death rate Proportion of deaths per 1,000 of the total population; also called *mortality rate*.

D-day June 6, 1944, when an Allied amphibious assault landed on the Normandy coast and established a foothold in Europe from which Hitler's defenses could not recover.

Eugene V. Debs (1855–1926) He founded the American Railway Union, which he organized against the Pullman Palace Car Company during the Pullman strike. Later he organized the Social Democratic party, which eventually became the Socialist Party of America. In the 1912 presidential election, he ran as the Socialist party's candidate and received more than 900,000 votes.

Declaration of Independence Formal statement, principally drafted by Thomas Jefferson and adopted by the Second Continental Congress on July 4, 1776, that officially announced the thirteen colonies' break with Great Britain.

Declaration of Rights and Sentiments Document based on the Declaration of Independence that called for gender equality, written primarily by Elizabeth Cady Stanton and signed by Seneca Falls Convention delegates in 1848.

Declaratory Act Following the repeal of the Stamp Act in 1766, Parliament passed this act that asserted Parliament's full power to make laws binding the colonies "in all cases whatsoever."

Deists Those who applied Enlightenment thought to religion, emphasizing reason, morality, and natural law rather than scriptural authority or an ever-present God intervening in human life.

détente Period of improving relations between the United States and Communist nations, particularly China and the Soviet Union, during the Nixon administration.

George Dewey (1837–1917) On April 30, 1898, Commodore George Dewey's small U.S. naval squadron defeated the Spanish warships in Manila Bay in the Philippines. This quick victory aroused expansionist fever in the United States.

John Dewey (1859–1952) He is an important philosopher of pragmatism. However, he preferred to use the term *instrumentalism*, because he saw ideas as instruments of action.

Dien Bien Phu Cluster of Vietnamese villages and site of a major Vietnamese victory over the French in the First Indochina War.

Ngo Dinh Diem (1901–1963) Following the Geneva Accords, the French, with the support of America, forced the Vietnamese emperor to accept Dinh Diem as the new premier of South Vietnam. President Eisenhower sent advisers to train Diem's police and army. In return, the United States expected Diem to enact democratic reforms and distribute land to the peasants. Instead, he suppressed his political opponents, did little or no land distribution, and let corruption grow. In 1956, he refused to participate in elections to reunify Vietnam. Eventually, he ousted the emperor and declared himself president.

Distribution Act (1836) Law requiring the distribution of the federal budget surplus to the states, creating chaos among state banks that had become dependent on such federal funds.

Dorothea Lynde Dix (1802–1887) She was an important figure in increasing the public's awareness of the plight of the mentally ill. After a two-year investigation of the treatment of the mentally ill in Massachusetts, she presented her findings and won the support of leading reformers. She eventually convinced twenty states to reform their treatment of the mentally ill.

Dixiecrats Breakaway faction of southern Democrats who defected from the national Democratic party in 1948 to protest the party's increased support for civil rights and to nominate their own segregationist candidates for elective office.

"dollar diplomacy" Practice advocated by President Theodore Roosevelt in which the U.S. government fostered American investments in less-developed nations and then used U.S. military force to protect those investments.

Donner party Forty-seven surviving members of a group of migrants to California were forced to resort to cannibalism to survive a brutal winter trapped in the Sierra Nevadas, 1846–1847; highest death toll of any group traveling the Overland Trail.

dot-coms In the late 1990s, the stock market soared to new heights and defied the predictions of experts that the economy could not sustain such a performance. Much of the economic success was based on dot-com enterprises, which were firms specializing in computers, software, telecommunications, and the Internet. However, many of the companies' stock market values were driven higher and higher by speculation instead of financial success. Eventually the stock market bubble burst.

Stephen A. Douglas (1812–1861) As a senator from Illinois, he authored the Kansas-Nebraska Act. Running for senatorial reelection in 1858, he engaged Abraham Lincoln in a series of public debates about slavery in the territories. Even though Douglas won the election, the debates gave Lincoln a national reputation.

Frederick Douglass (1818–1895) He escaped from slavery and become an eloquent speaker and writer against slavery. In 1845, he published his autobiography entitled *Narrative of the Life of Frederick Douglass* and two years later he founded an abolitionist newspaper for blacks called the *North Star*.

***Dred Scott v. Sandford* (1857)** U.S. Supreme Court ruling that slaves were not U.S. citizens and therefore could not sue for their freedom and that Congress could not prohibit slavery in the western territories.

W. E. B. Du Bois (1868–1963) He criticized Booker T. Washington's views on civil rights as being accommodationist. He advocated "ceaseless agitation" for civil rights and the immediate end to segregation and an enforcement of laws to protect civil rights and equality. He promoted an education for African Americans that would nurture bold leaders who were willing to challenge discrimination in politics.

John Foster Dulles (1888–1959) As President Eisenhower's secretary of state, he institutionalized the policy of containment and introduced the strategy of deterrence. He believed in using brinkmanship to halt the spread of communism. He attempted to employ it in Indochina, which led to the United States' involvement in Vietnam.

Dust Bowl Vast area of the Midwest where windstorms blew away millions of tons of topsoil from parched farmland after a long drought in the 1930s, causing great social distress and a massive migration of farm families.

Eastern Woodlands peoples Various Native American peoples, particularly the Algonquian, Iroquoian, and Muskogean regional groups, who once dominated the Atlantic seaboard from Maine to Louisiana.

Peggy Eaton (1796–1879) The wife of John Eaton, President Jackson's secretary of war, was the daughter of a tavern owner with an unsavory past. Supposedly her first husband had committed suicide after learning that she was having an affair with John Eaton. The wives of members of Jackson's cabinet snubbed her because of her lowly origins and past, resulting in a scandal known as the Eaton Affair.

Economic Opportunity Act (1964) Key legislation in President Johnson's "War on Poverty" which created the Office of Economic Opportunity and programs like Head Start and work-study.

Jonathan Edwards (1703–1758) New England Congregationalist minister, who began a religious revival in his Northampton church and was an important figure in the Great Awakening.

General Dwight D. Eisenhower (1890–1969) During the Second World War, he commanded the Allied Forces landing in Africa and was the supreme Allied commander as well as planner for Operation Overlord. In 1952, he was elected president on his popularity as a war hero and his promises to clean up Washington. His administration sought to cut the nation's domestic programs and budget, ended the fighting in Korea, and institutionalized the policies of containment and deterrence. He established the Eisenhower doctrine, which promised to aid any nation against aggression by a communist nation.

election of 1800 Presidential election between Thomas Jefferson and John Adams; resulted in the first Democratic-Republican victory after the Federalist administrations of George Washington and John Adams.

election of 1828 Highly contentious presidential election between Andrew Jackson and incumbent President John Quincy Adams; Jackson effectively campaigned as a war hero and champion of the "common man" to become the seventh president of the United States.

election of 1864 Abraham Lincoln's successful reelection campaign, capitalizing on Union military successes in Georgia, to defeat Democratic opponent, former general George B. McClellan, who ran on a peace platform.

election of 1912 The presidential election of 1912 featured four candidates: Wilson, Taft, Roosevelt, and Debs. Each candidate believed in the basic assumptions of progressive politics, but each had a different view on how progressive ideals should be implemented through policy. In the end, Taft and Roosevelt split the Republican party votes and Wilson emerged as the winner.

Queen Elizabeth I of England (1533–1603) The protestant daughter of Henry VIII, she was Queen of England from 1558–1603 and played a major role in the Protestant

Reformation. During her long reign, the doctrines and services of the Church of England were defined and the Spanish Armada was defeated.

Ellis Island Reception center in New York Harbor through which most European immigrants to America were processed from 1892 to 1954.

Emancipation Proclamation (1863) Military order issued by President Abraham Lincoln that freed slaves in areas still controlled by the Confederacy.

Embargo Act (1807) A law promoted by President Thomas Jefferson prohibiting American ships from leaving for foreign ports, in order to safeguard them from British and French attacks. This ban on American exports proved disastrous to the U.S. economy.

Ralph Waldo Emerson (1803–1882) As a leader of the transcendentalist movement, he wrote poems, essays, and speeches that discussed the sacredness of nature, optimism, self-reliance, and the unlimited potential of the individual. He wanted to transcend the limitations of inherited conventions and rationalism to reach the inner recesses of the self.

encomienda A land-grant system under which Spanish army officers (*conquistadores*) were awarded large parcels of land taken from Native Americans.

Enlightenment A revolution in thought begun in Europe in the seventeenth century that emphasized reason and science over the authority and myths of traditional religion.

Environmental Protection Agency (EPA) Federal environmental agency created in 1970 by Nixon to appease the demands of congressional Democrats for a federal environmental watchdog agency.

Erie Canal Most important and profitable of the many barge canals built in the early nineteenth century. It spanned 364 miles across New York state from west to east, connecting the Great Lakes to the Hudson River, and conveying so much cargo that it made New York City the nation's largest port.

ethnic cleansing The systematic removal of an ethnic group from a territory through violence or intimidation in order to create a homogenous society; the term was popularized by the Yugoslav policy brutally targeting Albanian Muslims in Kosovo.

Exodusters African Americans who migrated west from the South in search of a haven from racism and poverty after the collapse of Radical Republican rule.

Fair Deal (1949) President Truman's proposals to build upon the New Deal with national health insurance, the repeal of the Taft-Hartley Labor Act, new civil rights legislation, and other initiatives; most were rejected by the Republican-controlled Congress.

"falling domino" theory Theory that if one country fell to communism, its neighboring countries would follow suit.

Farmers' Alliances Like the Granger Movement, these organizations sought to address the issues of small farming communities; however Alliances emphasized more political action and called for the creation of a third party to advocate their concerns.

fascism A radical form of totalitarian government that emerged in Italy and Germany in the 1920s in which a dictator uses propaganda and brute force to seize control of all aspects of national life.

Federal-Aid Highway Act (1956) Largest federal project in U.S. history that created a national network of interstate highways and was the largest federal project in history.

Federal Deposit Insurance Corporation (FDIC) (1933) Independent government agency, established to prevent bank panics, that guarantees the safety of deposits in citizens' savings accounts.

Federal Reserve Act (1913) Legislation passed by Congress to create a new national banking system in order to regulate the nation's currency supply and ensure the stability and integrity of member banks who made up the Federal Reserve System across the nation.

Federal Trade Commission (FTC) (1914) Independent agency created by the Wilson administration that replaced the Bureau of Corporations as an even more powerful tool to combat unfair trade practices and monopolies.

Federal Writers' Project During the Great Depression, this project provided writers, such as Ralph Ellison, Richard Wright, and Saul Bellow, with work, which gave them a chance to develop as artists and be employed.

federalism Concept of dividing governmental authority between the national government and the states.

The Federalist Papers Collection of eighty-five essays, published widely in newspapers in 1787 and 1788, written by Alexander Hamilton, James Madison, and John Jay in support of adopting the proposed U.S. Constitution.

Federalists Proponents of a centralized federal system and the ratification of the Constitution. Most Federalists were relatively young, educated men who supported a broad interpretation of the Constitution whenever national interest dictated such flexibility. Notable Federalists included Alexander Hamilton and John Jay.

Geraldine Ferraro (1935–) In the 1984 presidential election, Democratic nominee Walter Mondale chose her as his running mate. As a member of the U.S. House of Representatives from New York, she was the first woman to be a vice-presidential nominee for a major political party. However, she was placed on the defensive because of her husband's complicated business dealings.

field hands Slaves who toiled in the cotton or cane fields in organized work gangs.

Fifteenth Amendment (1870) This amendment forbids states to deny any person the right to vote on grounds of "race, color or pervious condition of servitude." Former Confederate states were required to ratify this amendment before they could be readmitted to the Union.

"final solution" The Nazi party's systematic murder of some 6 million Jews along with more than a million other people including, but not limited to, gypsies, homosexuals, and handicap individuals.

First New Deal (1933–1935) Franklin D. Roosevelt's ambitious first-term cluster of economic and social programs designed to combat the Great Depression with a "new deal for the

American people;" the phrase became a catchword for his ambitious plan of economic programs.

First Red Scare (1919–1920) Outbreak of anti-Communist hysteria that included the arrest without warrants of thousands of suspected radicals, most of whom (mostly Russian immigrants) were deported.

flappers Young women of the 1920s whose rebellion against prewar standards of femininity included wearing shorter dresses, bobbing their hair, dancing to jazz music, driving cars, smoking cigarettes, and indulging in illegal drinking and gambling.

Food Administration After America's entry into World War I, the economy of the home front needed to be reorganized to provide the most efficient means of conducting the war. The Food Administration was a part of this effort. Under the leadership of Herbert Hoover, the organization sought to increase agricultural production while reducing civilian consumption of foodstuffs.

Force Bill (1833) Legislation, sparked by the nullification crisis in South Carolina, that authorized the president's use of the army to compel states to comply with federal law.

Gerald Ford (1913–2006) He was appointed to the vice presidency under President Nixon after the resignation of Spiro Agnew, and assumed the presidency after President Nixon's resignation. He resisted congressional pressure to both reduce taxes and increase federal spending, which sent the American economy into the deepest recession since the Great Depression. Ford retained Kissinger as his secretary of state and continued Nixon's foreign policy goals. He was heavily criticized following the collapse of South Vietnam.

Fort Laramie Treaty (1851) Restricted the Plains Indians from using the Overland Trail and permitted the building of government forts.

Fort Necessity After attacking a group of French soldiers, George Washington constructed and took shelter in this fort from vengeful French troops. Washington eventually surrendered to them after a day-long battle. This conflict was a significant event in igniting the French and Indian War.

Fort Sumter First battle of the Civil War, in which the federal fort in Charleston (South Carolina) Harbor was captured by the Confederates on April 14, 1861, after two days of shelling.

"forty-niners" Speculators who went to northern California following the discovery of gold in 1848; the first of several years of large-scale migration was 1849.

Fourteen Points (1918) President Woodrow Wilson's proposed plan for the peace agreement after the First World War that included the creation of a "league of nations" intended to keep the peace.

Fourteenth Amendment (1866) Guaranteed rights of citizenship to former slaves, in words similar to those of the Civil Rights Act of 1866.

Franciscan missions In 1769, Franciscan missionaries accompanied Spanish soldiers to California and over the next fifty years established a chain of missions from San Diego to San Francisco. At these missions, friars sought to convert Indians to Catholicism and make them members of the Spanish empire. The friars stripped the Indians of their native heritage and used soldiers to enforce their will.

Benjamin Franklin (1706–1790) A Boston-born American who epitomized the Enlightenment for many Americans and Europeans, Franklin's wide range of interests led him to become a publisher, inventor, and statesman. As the latter, he contributed to the writing of the Declaration of Independence, served as the minister to France during the Revolutionary War, and was a delegate to the Constitutional Convention.

Free-Soil party A political coalition created in 1848 that opposed the expansion of slavery into the new western territories.

Freedmen's Bureau Reconstruction agency established in 1865 to protect the legal rights of former slaves and to assist with their education, jobs, health care, and landowning.

Freedom Riders Activists who, beginning in 1961, traveled by bus through the South to test federal court rulings that banned segregation on buses and trains.

John C. Frémont, or "the Pathfinder" (1813–1890) He was an explorer and surveyor who helped inspire Americans living in California to rebel against the Mexican government and declare independence.

French and Indian War (Seven Years' War) The last—and most important—of four colonial wars fought between England and France for control of North America east of the Mississippi River.

French Revolution Revolutionary movement beginning in 1789 that overthrew the monarchy and transformed France into an unstable republic before Napoleon Bonaparte assumed power in 1799.

Sigmund Freud (1865–1939) He was the founder of psychoanalysis, which suggested that human behavior was motivated by unconscious and irrational forces. By the 1920s, his ideas were being discussed more openly in America.

frontier revivals Religious revival movement within the Second Great Awakening, that took place in frontier churches in western territories and states in the early nineteenth century.

Fugitive Slave Act (1850) Part of the Compromise of 1850, a provision that authorized federal officials to help capture and then return escaped slaves to their owners without trials.

fundamentalism Anti-modernist Protestant movement started in the early twentieth century that proclaimed the literal truth of the Bible; the name came from *The Fundamentals*, published by conservative leaders.

William Lloyd Garrison (1805–1879) In 1831, he started the anti-slavery newspaper *Liberator* and helped start the New England Anti-Slavery Society. Two years later, he assisted Arthur and Lewis Tappan in the founding of the American Anti-Slavery Society. He and his followers believed that America had been thoroughly corrupted and needed a wide range of reforms, embracing abolition, temperance, pacifism, and women's rights.

Marcus Garvey (1887–1940) He was the leading spokesman for Negro Nationalism, which exalted blackness, black cultural expression, and black exclusiveness. He called upon African Americans to liberate themselves from the surrounding white culture and create their own businesses, cultural centers, and newspapers. He was also the founder of the Universal Negro Improvement Association.

Citizen Genet (1763–1834) As the ambassador to the United States from the new French Republic, he engaged American privateers to attack British ships and conspired with frontiersmen and land speculators to organize an attack on Spanish Florida and Louisiana. His actions and the French radicals' excessive actions against their enemies in the new French Republic caused the French Revolution to lose support among Americans.

Geneva Accords In 1954, the Geneva Accords were signed, which ended French colonial rule in Indochina. The agreement created the independent nations of Laos and Cambodia and divided Vietnam along the 17th parallel until an election in 1956 would reunify the country.

Gettysburg, Battle of (1863) A monumental three-day battle in southern Pennsylvania, widely considered a turning point in the war, in which Union forces successfully countered a second Confederate invasion of the North.

Ghost Dance movement A spiritual and political movement among Native Americans whose followers performed a ceremonial "ghost dance" intended to connect the living with the dead and make the Indians bulletproof in battles intended to restore their homelands.

GI Bill of Rights (1944) Provided unemployment, education, and financial benefits for World War II veterans to ease their transition back to the civilian world.

***Gibbons v. Ogden* (1824)** Supreme Court case that gave the federal government the power to regulate interstate commerce.

Newt Gingrich (1943–) He led the Republican insurgency in Congress in the mid-1990s through mobilizing religious and social conservatives. Along with other Republican congressmen, he created the Contract with America, which was a ten-point anti–big government program. However, the program fizzled out after many of its bills were not passed by Congress.

Gilded Age (1860–1896) An era of dramatic industrial and urban growth characterized by widespread political corruption and loose government oversight over corporations.

The Gilded Age Mark Twain and Charles Dudley Warner's 1873 novel, the title of which became the popular name for the period from the end of the Civil War to the turn of the century.

glasnost Russian term for "openness"; applied to the loosening of censorship in the Soviet Union under Mikhail Gorbachev.

globalization An important, and controversial, transformation of the world economy whereby the Internet helped revolutionize global commerce by creating an international marketplace for goods and services. Led by the growing number of multinational companies and the Americanization of many foreign consumer cultures, with companies like McDonald's and Starbucks appearing in all of the major cities of the world.

Glorious Revolution Successful 1688 coup, instigated by a group of English aristocrats, which overthrew King James II and instated William of Orange and Mary, his English wife, to the British throne.

Barry Goldwater (1909–1998) He was a leader of the Republican right whose book, *The Conscience of a Conservative*, was highly influential to that segment of the party. He proposed eliminating the income tax and overhauling Social Security. In 1964, he ran as the Republican presidential candidate and lost to President Johnson. He campaigned against Johnson's war on poverty, the tradition of New Deal, the nuclear test ban and the Civil Rights Act of 1964. He advocated the wholesale bombing of North Vietnam.

Samuel Gompers (1850–1924) He served as the president of the American Federation of Labor from its inception until his death. He focused on achieving concrete economic gains such as higher wages, shorter hours, and better working conditions.

"good neighbor" policy Proclaimed by President Franklin D. Roosevelt in his first inaugural address in 1933, it sought improved diplomatic relations between the United States and its Latin American neighbors.

Mikhail Gorbachev (1931–) In the late 1980s, Soviet leader Mikhail Gorbachev attempted to reform the Soviet Union through his programs of *perestroika* and *glasnost* and pursued a renewal of détente with America, signing new arms-control agreements with President Reagan. Gorbachev allowed the velvet revolutions of Eastern Europe to occur without outside interference. Eventually the political, social, and economic upheaval he had unleashed would lead to the breakup of the Soviet Union.

Albert Gore Jr. (1948–) He served as a senator of Tennessee and then as President Clinton's vice president. In the 2000 presidential election, he was the Democratic candidate against Governor George W. Bush. The close election came down to Florida's electoral votes. While the votes were being recounted as required by state law, a legal battle was being waged to stop the recount. Finally, the case, *Bush v. Gore*, was presented to the Supreme Court who ruled 5–4 to stop the recount, and Bush was declared the winner.

Jay Gould (1836–1892) As one of the biggest railroad robber barons, he was infamous for buying rundown railroads, making cosmetic improvements, and then reselling them for a profit. He used corporate funds for personal investments and to bribe politicians and judges.

gradualism This strategy for ending slavery involved promoting the banning of slavery in the new western territories and encouraging the release of slaves from slavery. Supporters of this method believed that it would bring about the gradual end of slavery.

Granger Movement Began by offering social and educational activities for isolated farmers and their families and later started to promote "cooperatives" where farmers could join together to buy, store, and sell their crops to avoid the high fees charged by brokers and other middlemen.

Ulysses S. Grant (1822–1885) After distinguishing himself in the western theater of the Civil War, he was appointed general-in-chief of the Union army in 1864. Afterward, he defeated General Robert E. Lee through a policy of aggressive attrition. Lee surrendered to Grant on April 9, 1865 at the Appomattox Court House. His presidential tenure suffered from scandals and fiscal problems, including the debate on whether or not greenbacks, that is, paper money, should be removed from circulation.

Great Awakening Fervent religious revival movement that swept the thirteen colonies from the 1720s through the 1740s.

Great Compromise (Connecticut Compromise) Mediated the differences between the New Jersey and Virginia delegations to the Constitutional Convention by providing for a bicameral legislature, the upper house of which would have equal representation and the lower house of which would be apportioned by population.

Great Depression (1929–1941) Worst economic downturn in American history; it was spurred by the stock market crash in the fall of 1929 and lasted until the Second World War.

Great Migration Mass exodus of African Americans from the rural South to the Northeast and Midwest during and after the First World War.

Great Railroad Strike (1877) A series of demonstrations, some violent, held nationwide in support of striking railroad workers in Martinsburg, West Virginia, who refused to work due to wage cuts.

Great Recession Massive, prolonged economic downturn sparked by the collapse of the housing market and the financial institutions holding unpaid mortgages; it lasted from December 2007 to January 2009 and resulted in 9 million Americans losing their jobs.

Great Sioux War Conflict between Sioux and Cheyenne Indians and federal troops over lands in the Dakotas in the mid-1870s.

Great Society Term coined by President Lyndon B. Johnson in his 1965 State of the Union address, in which he proposed legislation to address problems of voting rights, poverty, diseases, education, immigration, and the environment.

Horace Greeley (1811–1872) In reaction to Radical Reconstruction and corruption in President Ulysses S. Grant's administration, a group of Republicans broke from the party to form the Liberal Republicans. In 1872, the Liberal Republicans chose as their presidential candidate Horace Greeley, who ran on a platform of favoring civil service reform and condemning the Republican's Reconstruction policy.

Greenback party Formed in 1876 in reaction to economic depression, the party favored issuance of unsecured paper money to help farmers repay debts; the movement for free coinage of silver took the place of the greenback movement by the 1880s.

greenbacks Paper money issued during the Civil War. After the war ended, a debate emerged on whether or not to remove the paper currency from circulation and revert back to hard-money currency (gold coins). Opponents of hard money feared that eliminating the greenbacks would shrink the money supply, which would lower crop prices and make it more difficult to repay long-term debts. President Ulysses S. Grant, as well as hard-money currency advocates, believed that gold coins were morally preferable to paper currency.

General Nathanael Greene (1742–1786) He was appointed by Congress to command the American army fighting in the South during the Revolutionary War. Using his patience and his skills of managing men, saving supplies, and avoiding needless risks, he waged a successful war of attrition against the British.

Sarah Grimké (1792–1873) and **Angelina Grimké (1805–1879)** These two sisters gave anti-slavery speeches to crowds of mixed gender that caused some people to condemn them for engaging in unfeminine activities. In 1840, William Lloyd Garrison convinced the Anti-Slavery Society to allow women equal participation in the organization.

Alexander Hamilton (1755–1804) His belief in a strong federal government led him to become a leader of the Federalists. As the first secretary of the Treasury, he laid the foundation for American capitalism through his creation of a federal budget, funded debt, a federal tax system, a national bank, a customs service, and a coast guard. His "Reports on Public Credit" and "Reports on Manufactures" outlined his vision for economic development and government finances. He died in a duel against Aaron Burr.

Alexander Hamilton's economic reforms Various measures designed to strengthen the nation's economy and generate federal revenue through the promotion of new industries, the adoption of new tax policies, the payment of war debts, and the establishment of a national bank.

Warren G. Harding (1865–1923) In the 1920 presidential election, he was the Republican nominee who promised Americans a "return to normalcy." Once in office, Harding's administration dismantled many of the social and economic components of progressivism and pursued a pro-business agenda. Harding appointed four pro-business Supreme Court Justices, cut taxes, increased tariffs, and promoted a lenient attitude toward regulation of corporations. However, he did speak out against racism and ended the exclusion of African Americans from federal positions.

Harlem Renaissance The nation's first self-conscious black literary and artistic movement; it was centered in New York City's Harlem district, which had a largely black population in the wake of the Great Migration from the South.

Hartford Convention A series of secret meetings in December 1814 and January 1815 at which New England Federalists protested American involvement in the War of 1812 and discussed several constitutional amendments, including limiting each president to one term, designed to weaken the dominant Republican Party.

Haymarket Riot (1886) Violent uprising in Haymarket Square, Chicago, where police clashed with labor demonstrators in the aftermath of a bombing.

headright A land-grant policy that promised fifty acres to any colonist who could afford passage to Virginia, as well as fifty more for any accompanying servants. The headright policy was eventually expanded to include any colonists—and was also adopted in other colonies.

Patrick Henry (1736–1799) He inspired the Virginia Resolves, which declared that Englishmen could only be taxed by their elected representatives. In March of 1775, he met with other colonial leaders to discuss the goals of the upcoming Continental Congress and famously declared "Give me liberty or give me death." During the ratification process of the U.S. Constitution, he became one of the leaders of the anti-federalists.

Hessians German mercenary soldiers who were paid by the royal government to fight alongside the British army.

Hiroshima Japanese port city that was the first target of the newly developed atomic bomb on August 6, 1945. Most of the city was destroyed.

Alger Hiss (1904–1996) During the second Red Scare, he served in several government departments and was accused of being a spy for the Soviet Union. He was convicted of lying about espionage. The case was politically damaging to the Truman administration because the president called the charges against Hiss a "red herring."

Adolf Hitler, or *"Führer"* **(1889–1945)** The leader of the Nazis who advocated a violent anti-Semitic, anti-Marxist, pan-German ideology. He started World War II in Europe and orchestrated the systematic murder of some 6 million Jews along with more than a million others.

HIV/AIDS Human immunodeficiency virus (HIV) transmitted via the bodily fluids of infected persons to cause acquired immunodeficiency syndrome (AIDS), an often-fatal disease of the immune system when it appeared in the 1980s.

holding company A corporation established to own and manage other companies' stock rather than to produce goods and services itself.

Holocaust Systematic racist attempt by the Nazis to exterminate the Jews of Europe, resulting in the murder of over 6 million Jews and more than a million other "undesirables."

Homestead Act (1862) Legislation granting "homesteads" of 160 acres of government-owned land to settlers who agreed to work the land for at least five years.

Homestead Steel strike (1892) Labor conflict at the Homestead steel mill near Pittsburgh, Pennsylvania, culminating in a battle between strikers and private security agents hired by the factory's management.

Herbert Hoover (1874–1964) Prior to becoming president, Hoover served as the secretary of commerce in both the Harding and Coolidge administrations. As president during the Great Depression, he believed that the nation's business structure was sound and sought to revive the economy through boosting the nation's confidence. He also tried to restart the economy with government constructions projects, lower taxes, and new federal loan programs, but nothing worked.

horizontal integration The process by which a corporation acquires or merges with its competitors.

horse A tall, four-legged mammal (*Equus caballus*), domesticated and bred since prehistoric times for carrying riders and pulling heavy loads. The Spanish introduced horses to the Americas, eventually transforming many Native American cultures.

House Committee on Un-American Activities (HUAC) Committee of the U.S. House of Representatives formed in 1938; it was originally tasked with investigating Nazi subversion during the Second World War and later shifted its focus to rooting out Communists in the government and the motion-picture industry.

Sam Houston (1793–1863) During Texas's fight for independence from Mexico, Sam Houston was the commander in chief of the Texas forces, and he led the attack that captured General Antonio López de Santa Anna. After Texas gained its independence, he was named its first president.

Jacob Riis' *How the Other Half Lives* Jacob Riis was an early muckraking journalist who exposed the slum conditions in New York City in his book *How the Other Half Lives*.

General William Howe (1729–1814) As the commander of the British army in the Revolutionary War, he seized New York City from Washington's army, but failed to capture it. He missed several more opportunities to quickly end the rebellion, and he resigned his command after the British defeat at Saratoga.

Saddam Hussein (1937–2006) The former dictator of Iraq who became the head of state in 1979. In 1980, he invaded Iran and started the eight-year-long Iran-Iraq War. In 1990, he invaded Kuwait, which caused the Gulf War of 1991. In 2003, he was overthrown and captured when the United States invaded. He was sentenced to death by hanging in 2006.

Anne Hutchinson (1591–1643) The articulate, strong-willed, and intelligent wife of a prominent Boston merchant, who espoused her belief in direct divine revelation. She quarreled with Puritan leaders over her beliefs, and they banished her from the colony.

Immigration Act of 1924 Federal legislation intended to favor northern and western European immigrants over those from southern and eastern Europe by restricting the number of immigrants from any one European country to 2 percent of the total number of immigrants per year, with an overall limit of slightly over 150,000 new arrivals per year.

Immigration and Nationality Services Act of 1965 Legislation that abolished discriminatory quotas based upon immigrants' national origin and treated all nationalities and races equally.

imperialism The use of diplomatic or military force to extend a nation's power and enhance its economic interests, often by acquiring territory or colonies and justifying such behavior with assumptions of racial superiority.

impressment The British navy used press-gangs to kidnap men in British and colonial ports who were then forced to serve in the British navy.

indentured servants Settlers who consented to a defined period of labor (often four to seven years) in exchange for having their passage to the New World paid by their "master."

Independent Treasury Act (1840) System created by President Martin Van Buren and approved by Congress in 1840 whereby the federal government moved its funds from favored state banks to the U.S. Treasury, whose financial transactions could only be in gold or silver coins of paper currency backed by gold or silver.

"Indian New Deal" This phrase refers to the reforms implemented for Native Americans during the New Deal era. John Collier, the commissioner of the Bureau of Indian Affairs (BIA), increased the access Native Americans had to relief programs and employed more Native Americans at the BIA. He worked to pass the Indian Reorganization Act. However, the version of the act passed by Congress was a much-diluted version of Collier's original proposal and did not greatly improve the lives of Native Americans.

Indian Removal Act (1830) Law permitting the forced relocation of Indians to federal lands west of the Mississippi River in exchange for the land they occupied in the East and South.

Indian wars Bloody conflicts between U.S. soldiers and Native Americans that raged in the West from the early 1860s to the late 1870s, sparked by American settlers moving into ancestral Indian lands.

Indochina This area of Southeast Asian consists of Laos, Cambodia, and Vietnam and was once controlled by France as a colony. After the Viet Minh defeated the French, the Geneva Accords were signed, which ended French colonial rule. The agreement created the independent nations of Laos and Cambodia and divided Vietnam along the 17th parallel until an election would reunify the country. Fearing a communist takeover, the U.S. government began intervening in the region during the Truman administration, which led to President Johnson's full-scale military involvement in Vietnam.

industrial war A new concept of war enabled by industrialization that developed from the early 1800s through the Atomic Age. New technologies, including automatic weaponry, forms of transportation like the railroad and airplane, and communication technologies such as the telegraph and telephone, enabled nations to equip large, mass-conscripted armies with chemical and automatic weapons to decimate opposing armies in a "total war."

industrialization Major shift in the nineteenth century from hand-made manufacturing to mass production in mills and factories using water-, coal-, and steam-powered machinery.

infectious diseases Also called contagious diseases, illnesses that can pass from one person to another by way of invasive biological organisms able to reproduce in the bodily tissues of their hosts. Europeans unwittingly brought many such diseases to the Americas, devastating the Native American peoples.

Alfred Thayer Mahan's *The Influence of Sea Power upon History, 1660–1783* **(1890)** Historical work in which Rear Admiral Alfred Thayer Mahan argues that a nation's greatness and prosperity comes from the power of its navy; the book helped bolster imperialist sentiment in the United States in the late nineteenth century.

Intermediate-Range Nuclear Forces (INF) Treaty (1987) Agreement signed by U.S. president Ronald Reagan and Soviet premier Mikhail Gorbachev to eliminate the deployment of intermediate-range missiles with nuclear warheads.

internal improvements Construction of roads, bridges, canals, harbors, and other infrastructure projects intended to facilitate the flow of goods and people.

Interstate Commerce Commission (ICC) An independent federal agency established in 1887 to oversee businesses engaged in interstate trade, especially railroads, but whose regulatory power was limited when tested in the courts.

interstate highway system In the late 1950s, construction began on a national network of interstate superhighways for the purpose of commerce and defense. The interstate highways would enable the rapid movement of military convoys and the evacuation of cities after a nuclear attack.

Iran-Contra affair Reagan administration scandal in 1987 over the secret, unlawful U.S. sale of arms to Iran in partial exchange for the release of hostages in Lebanon; the arms money in turn was used illegally to aid Nicaraguan right-wing insurgents, the Contras.

Iranian hostage crisis Storming of the U.S. embassy in Tehran in 1979 by Iranian revolutionaries, who held fifty-two Americans hostage for 444 days, despite President Carter's appeals for their release as well as a botched rescue attempt.

Irish Potato Famine In 1845, an epidemic of potato rot brought a famine to rural Ireland that killed over 1 million peasants and instigated a huge increase in the number of Irish immigrating to America. By 1850, the Irish made up 43 percent of the foreign-born population in the United States; in the 1850s, they made up over half the population of New York City and Boston.

iron curtain Term coined by Winston Churchill to describe the cold war divide between western Europe and the Soviet Union's Eastern European satellites.

Iroquois League An alliance of the Iroquois tribes, originally formed sometime between 1450 and 1600, that used their combined strength to pressure Europeans to work with them in the fur trade and to wage war across what is today eastern North America.

Andrew Jackson (1767–1837) As a major general in the Tennessee militia, he had a number of military successes. As president, he worked to enable the "common man" to play a greater role in the political arena. He vetoed the rechartering of the Second National Bank and reduced federal spending. When South Carolina nullified the Tariffs of 1828 and 1832, Jackson requested that Congress pass a "force bill" that would authorize him to use the army to compel the state to comply with the tariffs. He forced eastern Indians to move west of the Mississippi River so their lands could be used by white settlers. Groups of those who opposed Jackson came together to form a new political party called the Whigs.

Thomas "Stonewall" Jackson (1824–1863) He was a Confederate general who was known for his fearlessness in leading rapid marches, bold flanking movements, and furious assaults. He earned his nickname at the Battle of the First Bull Run for standing courageously against Union fire. During the battle of Chancellorsville, his own men accidently mortally wounded him.

William James (1842–1910) He was the founder of Pragmatism and one of the fathers of modern psychology. He believed that ideas gained their validity not from their inherent truth, but from their social consequences and practical application.

Jay's Treaty (1794) Agreement between Britain and the United States, negotiated by Chief Justice John Jay, that settled disputes over trade, prewar debts owed to British merchants, British-occupied forts in American territory, and the seizure of American ships and cargo.

"Jazz Age" Term coined by writer F. Scott Fitzgerald to characterize the spirit of rebellion and spontaneity among young Americans in the 1920s, a spirit epitomized by the hugely popular jazz music of the era.

Thomas Jefferson (1743–1826) He was a plantation owner, author, the drafter of the Declaration Independence, ambassador to France, leader of the Republican party, secretary of state, and the third president of the United States. As president, he purchased the Louisiana territory from France, withheld appointments made by President Adams leading to *Marbury v. Madison*, outlawed foreign slave trade, and was committed to a "wise and frugal" government.

Jeffersonian Republicans Political party founded by Thomas Jefferson in opposition to the Federalist Party led by Alexander Hamilton and John Adams; also known as the Democratic-Republican Party.

Jesuits A religious order founded in 1540 by Ignatius Loyola. They sought to counter the spread of Protestantism during the Protestant Reformation and spread the Catholic faith through work as missionaries. Roughly 3,500 served in New Spain and New France.

"Jim Crow" laws In the New South, these laws mandated the separation of races in various public places that served as a way for the ruling whites to impose their will on all areas of black life.

Andrew Johnson (1808–1875) He was elevated to the presidency after Abraham Lincoln's assassination. In order to restore the Union after the Civil War, he issued an amnesty proclamation and required former Confederate states to ratify the Thirteenth Amendment. After disagreements over the power to restore states' rights, the Radical Republicans attempted to impeach Johnson but fell short on the required number of votes needed to remove him from office.

Lyndon B. Johnson (1908–1973) Former member of the House of Representatives and the former Majority Leader of the Senate, Vice President Lyndon B. Johnson assumed the presidency after President Kennedy's assassination. During his presidency, he passed the Civil Rights Act of 1964, declared a "war on poverty" promoting his own social program called the Great Society, and signed the Immigration and Nationality Service Act of 1965. Johnson greatly increased America's role in Vietnam.

Johnson's Restoration Plan President Andrew Johnson's post–Civil War plan to readmit Confederate states into the Union; requirements included the appointment of a Unionist as a provisional governor in each southern state, ratification of the Thirteenth Amendment, and the extension of voting rights to "educated" blacks.

joint-stock companies Businesses owned by investors, who purchase shares of companies' stocks and share all the profits and losses.

Kansas-Nebraska Act (1854) Controversial legislation that created two new territories taken from Native Americans, Kansas and Nebraska, where residents would vote to decide whether slavery would be allowed (popular sovereignty).

Florence Kelley (1859–1932) As the head of the National Consumer's League, she led the crusade to promote state laws to regulate the number of working hours imposed on women who were wives and mothers.

George F. Kennan (1904–2005) While working as an American diplomat, he devised the strategy of containment, which called for the halting of Soviet expansion. It became America's choice strategy throughout the cold war.

John F. Kennedy (1917–1963) He was elected president in 1960. Despite the difficulties he had in getting his legislation through Congress, he established the Alliance for Progress programs to help Latin America, the Peace Corps, the Trade Expansion Act of 1962, and funding for urban renewal projects and the space program. His foreign political involvement included the failed Bay of Pigs invasion and the missile crisis in Cuba, as well as support of local governments in Indochina. In 1963, he was assassinated by Lee Harvey Oswald in Dallas, Texas.

Kent State During the spring of 1970, students on college campuses across the country protested the expansion of the Vietnam War into Cambodia. At Kent State University, the National Guard attempted to quell the rioting students. The guardsmen panicked and shot at rock-throwing demonstrators. Four student bystanders were killed.

Kentucky and Virginia Resolutions (1798–1799) Passed in response to the Alien and Sedition Acts, the resolutions advanced the state-compact theory that held states could nullify an act of Congress if they deemed it unconstitutional.

Francis Scott Key (1779–1843) During the War of 1812, he watched British forces bombard Fort McHenry, but fail to take it. Seeing the American flag still flying over the fort at dawn inspired him to write "The Star-Spangled Banner," which became the American national anthem.

Martin Luther King Jr. (1929–1968) A central leader of the civil rights movement, he urged people to use nonviolent civil disobedience to demand their rights and bring about change. He successfully led the Montgomery Bus Boycott. While in jail for his role in the demonstrations, he wrote his famous "Letter from Birmingham City Jail," in which he defended his strategy of nonviolent protest. In 1963, he delivered his famous "I Have a Dream" speech from the steps of the Lincoln Memorial as a part of the March on Washington. A year later, he was awarded the Nobel Peace Prize. In 1968, he was assassinated.

King Philip's War A bloody, three-year war in New England (1675–1678), resulting from the escalation of tensions between Indians and English settlers; the defeat of the Indians led to broadened freedoms for the settlers and their dispossessing the region's Indians of most of their land.

King William's War (War of the League of Augsburg) First (1689–1697) of four colonial wars between England and France.

Henry Kissinger (1923–) He served as the secretary of state and national security adviser in the Nixon administration. He negotiated with North Vietnam for an end to the Vietnam War, but the cease-fire did not last; South Vietnam fell to North Vietnam. He helped organize Nixon's historic trips to China and the Soviet Union. In the Middle East, he negotiated a cease-fire between Israel and its neighbors following the Yom

Kippur War and solidified Israel's promise to return to Egypt most of the land it had taken during the 1967 war.

Knights of Labor A national labor organization with a broad reform platform; reached peak membership in the 1880s.

Know-Nothings Nativist, anti-Catholic third party organized in 1854 in reaction to large-scale German and Irish immigration.

Ku Klux Klan (KKK) Organized in Pulaski, Tennessee, in 1866 to terrorize former slaves who voted and held political offices during Reconstruction; a revived organization in the 1910s and 1920s stressed white, Anglo-Saxon, fundamentalist Protestant supremacy; the Klan revived a third time to fight the civil rights movement of the 1950s and 1960s in the South.

Marquis de Lafayette (1757–1834) A wealthy French idealist excited by the American cause, he offered to serve in Washington's army for free in exchange for being named a major general. He overcame Washington's initial skepticism to become one of his most trusted aides.

laissez-faire (**"leave things alone"**) An economic doctrine holding that businesses and individuals should be able to pursue their economic interests without government interference.

Land Ordinance of 1785 Directed surveying of the Northwest Territory into townships of thirty-six sections (square miles) each, the sale of the sixteenth section of which was to be used to finance public education.

Bartolomé de Las Casas (1484–1566) A Catholic missionary who renounced the Spanish practice of coercively converting Indians and advocated their better treatment. In 1552, he wrote *A Brief Relation of the Destruction of the Indies*, which described the Spanish's cruel treatment of the Indians.

League of Nations Organization of nations formed in the aftermath of the First World War to mediate disputes and maintain international peace; despite President Wilson's intense lobbying for the League of Nations, Congress did not ratify the treaty and the United States failed to join.

Mary Elizabeth Lease (1850–1933) She was a leader of the farm protest movement who advocated violence if change could not be obtained at the ballot box. She believed that the urban-industrial East was the enemy of the working class.

Robert E. Lee (1807–1870) Even though he had served in the U.S. Army for thirty years, he chose to fight on the side of the Confederacy. Lee was excellent at using his field commanders and his soldiers respected him. However, General Ulysses S. Grant eventually wore down his army, and Lee surrendered to Grant at the Appomattox Court House on April 9, 1865.

Lend-Lease Act (1941) Legislation that allowed the president to lend or lease military equipment to any country whose own defense was deemed vital to the defense of the United States.

Levittown First low-cost, mass-produced development of suburban tract housing built by William Levitt on Long Island, New York, in 1947.

Lewis and Clark expedition (1804) Led by Meriwether Lewis and William Clark, a mission to the Pacific coast commissioned for the purposes of scientific and geographical exploration.

Lexington and Concord, Battle of The first shots fired in the Revolutionary War, on April 19, 1775, near Boston; approximately 100 Minutemen and 250 British soldiers were killed.

Liberator William Lloyd Garrison started this anti-slavery newspaper in 1831 in which he renounced gradualism and called for abolition.

Queen Liliuokalani (1838–1917) In 1891, she ascended to the throne of the Hawaiian royal family and tried to eliminate white control of the Hawaiian government. Two years later, Hawaii's white population revolted and seized power with the support of American marines.

Abraham Lincoln (1809–1865) Shortly after he was elected president in 1860, southern states began seceding from the Union, and in April 1861, he declared war on the seceding states. On January 1, 1863, Lincoln signed the Emancipation Proclamation. At the end of the war, he favored a reconstruction strategy for the former Confederate states that did not radically alter southern social and economic life. He was assassinated by John Wilkes Booth at Ford's Theater on April 14, 1865.

Lincoln-Douglas debates (1858) In the Illinois race between Republican Abraham Lincoln and Democrat Stephen A. Douglas for a seat in the U.S. Senate, a series of seven dramatic debates focusing on the issue of slavery in the territories.

John Locke (1632–1704) An English philosopher whose ideas were influential during the Enlightenment. He argued in his *Essay on Human Understanding* (1690) that humanity is largely the product of the environment, the mind being a blank tablet, *tabula rasa*, on which experience is written.

Henry Cabot Lodge (1850–1924) He was the chairman of the Senate Foreign Relations Committee who favored limiting America's involvement in the League of Nations' covenant and sought to amend the Treaty of Versailles.

de Lôme letter Private correspondence written in 1898 by the Spanish ambassador to the U.S., Depuy de Lôme, that described President McKinley as "weak"; the letter was stolen by Cuban revolutionaries and published in the *New York Journal*, deepening American resentment of Spain and moving the two countries closer to war in Cuba.

Lone Star Republic After winning independence from Mexico, Texas became its own nation and was called the Lone Star Republic. In 1836, Texans drafted themselves a constitution, legalized slavery, banned free blacks, named Sam Houston president, and voted for the annexation to the United States. However, quarrels over adding a slave state and fears of instigating a war with Mexico delayed Texas's entrance into the Union until December 29, 1845.

Huey P. Long (1893–1935) He began his political career in Louisiana where he developed a reputation for being an unscrupulous reformer. As a U.S. senator, he became a critic of President Roosevelt's New Deal Plan and offered his alternative: the Share-the-Wealth program. He was assassinated in 1935.

Lost Generation Label given to modernist writers and authors, such as F. Scott Fitzgerland and Ernest Hemingway, who had lost faith in the values and institutions of Western civilization in the aftermath of the Great War.

Louisiana Purchase (1803) President Thomas Jefferson's purchase of the Louisiana Territory from France for $15 million, doubling the size of U.S. territory.

Lowell girls Young female factory workers at the textile mills in Lowell, Massachusetts, which in the early 1820s provided its employees with prepared meals, dormitories, moral discipline, and educational opportunities.

Lowell system Model New England factory communities that during the first half of the nineteenth century provided employees, mostly young women, with meals, a boardinghouse, and moral discipline, as well as educational and cultural opportunities.

Loyalists Colonists who remained loyal to Great Britain before and during the Revolutionary War.

Lusitania British ocean liner torpedoed and sunk by a German U-boat; the deaths of nearly 1,200 of its civilian passengers, including many Americans, caused international outrage.

Martin Luther (1483–1546) A German monk who founded the Lutheran church. He protested abuses in the Catholic Church by posting his Ninety-five Theses, which began the Protestant Reformation.

General Douglas MacArthur (1880–1964) During World War II, he and Admiral Chester Nimitz dislodged the Japanese military from the Pacific Islands they had occupied. Following the war, he was in charge of the occupation of Japan. After North Korea invaded South Korea, Truman sent the U.S. military to defend South Korea under the command of MacArthur. Later in the war, Truman expressed his willingness to negotiate the restoration of prewar boundaries, which MacArthur attempted to undermine. Truman fired MacArthur for his open insubordination.

James Madison (1751–1836) He participated in the Constitutional Convention during which he proposed the Virginia Plan. He believed in a strong federal government and was a leader of the Federalists. However, he also presented to Congress the Bill of Rights and drafted the Virginia Resolutions. As secretary of state, he withheld a commission for William Marbury, which led to the landmark *Marbury v. Madison* decision. During his presidency, he declared war on Britain in response to violations of American shipping rights, which started the War of 1812.

maize (corn) The primary grain crop in Mesoamerica yielding small kernels often ground into cornmeal. Easy to grow in a broad range of conditions, it enabled a global population explosion after being brought to Europe, Africa, and Asia.

Malcolm X (1925–1964) The most articulate spokesman for black power. Originally the chief disciple of Elijah Muhammad, the black Muslim leader in the United States, Malcolm X broke away and founded his own organization committed to establishing relations between African Americans and the nonwhite peoples of the world. Near the end of his life, he began to preach a biracial message of social change. In 1964, he was assassinated by members of a rival group of black Muslims.

manifest destiny The widespread belief that America was "destined" by God to expand westward across the continent into lands claimed by Native Americans as well as European nations.

Horace Mann (1796–1859) He believed the public school system was the best way to achieve social stability and equal opportunity. As a reformer of education, he sponsored a state board of education, the first state-supported "normal" school for training teachers, a state association for teachers, and the minimum school year of six months. He led the drive for a statewide school system.

Marbury v. Madison **(1803)** First Supreme Court decision to declare a federal law—the Judiciary Act of 1801—unconstitutional.

March on Washington Civil rights demonstration on August 28, 1963, on the National Mall, where Martin Luther King Jr. gave his famous "I Have a Dream" speech.

"March to the Sea" The Union army's devastating march through Georgia from Atlanta to Savannah, led by General William T. Sherman, intended to demoralize civilians and destroy the resources the Confederate army needed to fight.

market-based economy Large-scale manufacturing and commercial agriculture that emerged in America during the first half of the nineteenth century, displacing much of the premarket subsistence and barter-based economy and producing boom-and-bust cycles while raising the American standard of living.

George C. Marshall (1880–1959) As the chairman of the Joint Chiefs of Staff, he orchestrated the Allied victories over Germany and Japan in the Second World War. In 1947, he became President Truman's secretary of state and proposed the massive reconstruction program for western Europe called the Marshall Plan.

Chief Justice John Marshall (1755–1835) During his long tenure as chief justice of the Supreme Court (1801–1835), he established the foundations for American jurisprudence, the authority of the Supreme Court, and the constitutional supremacy of the national government over states.

Marshall Plan (1948) Secretary of State George C. Marshall's post–World War II program providing massive U.S. financial and technical assistance to war-torn European countries.

Massachusetts Bay Colony English colony founded by English Puritans in 1630 as a haven for persecuted Congregationalists.

massive resistance White rallying cry disrupting federal efforts to enforce racial integration in the South.

massive retaliation Strategy that used the threat of nuclear warfare as a means of combating the global spread of communism.

Mayflower Compact A formal agreement signed by the Separatist colonists aboard the *Mayflower* in 1620 to abide by laws made by leaders of their own choosing.

Senator Joseph R. McCarthy (1908–1957) In 1950, this senator became the shrewdest and most ruthless exploiter of America's anxiety of communism. He claimed that the U.S. government was full of Communists and led a witch hunt to find them, but he was never able to uncover a single communist agent.

McCarthyism Anti-Communist hysteria led by Senator Joseph McCarthy's "witch hunts" attacking the loyalty of politicians, federal employees, and public figures, despite a lack of evidence.

George B. McClellan (1826–1885) In 1861, President Abraham Lincoln appointed him head of the Army of the Potomac and, later, general-in-chief of the U.S. Army. He built his army into a well-trained and powerful force. After failing to achieve a decisive victory against the Confederacy, he was removed from command in 1862.

Cyrus Hall McCormick (1809–1884) In 1831, he invented a mechanical reaper to harvest wheat, which transformed the scale of agriculture. By hand, a farmer could only harvest half an acre a day, while the McCormick reaper allowed two people to harvest twelve acres of wheat a day.

McCormick reapers Mechanical reapers invented by Cyrus Hall McCormick in 1831 that dramatically increased the production of wheat.

McCulloch v. Maryland **(1819)** A decision by the Marshall-led Supreme Court that ruled unanimously that Congress had the authority to charter the Bank of the United States and that states did not have the right to tax the national bank.

William McKinley (1843–1901) As a congressman, he was responsible for the McKinley Tariff of 1890, which raised the duties on manufactured products to their highest level ever. Voters disliked the tariff and McKinley, as well as other Republicans, lost his seat in Congress the next election. However, he won the presidential election of 1896 and raised the tariffs again. In 1898, he annexed Hawaii and declared war on Spain. The war concluded with the Treaty of Paris, which gave America control over Puerto Rico, Guam, and the Philippines. Soon America was fighting Filipinos, who were seeking independence for their country. In 1901, McKinley was assassinated.

Robert McNamara (1916–2009) He was the secretary of defense for both President Kennedy and President Johnson and a supporter of America's involvement in Vietnam.

Medicare and **Medicaid** Health care programs designed to aid the elderly and disadvantaged, respectively, as part of President Johnson's Great Society initiative.

Andrew W. Mellon (1855–1937) As President Harding's secretary of the Treasury, he sought to generate economic growth by reducing government spending and lowering taxes. However, he insisted that the tax reductions mainly go to the rich because he believed the wealthy would reinvest their money. In order to bring greater efficiency and nonpartisanship to the government's budget process, he persuaded Congress to created a new Bureau of the Budget and a General Accounting Office.

mercantilism Policy of Great Britain and other imperial powers of regulating the economies of colonies to benefit the mother country.

James Meredith (1933–) In 1962, the governor of Mississippi defied a Supreme Court ruling and refused to allow James Meredith, an African American, to enroll at the University of Mississippi. Federal marshals were sent to enforce the law, which led to clashes between a white mob and the marshals. Federal troops intervened and two people were killed and many others were injured. A few days later, Meredith was able to register at the university.

Metacomet (?–1676) or **King Philip** The chief of the Wampanoages, whom the colonists called King Philip. He resented English efforts to convert Indians to Christianity and waged a war against the English colonists, one in which he was killed.

Mexica Otherwise known as "Aztecs," a Mesoamerican people of northern Mexico who founded the vast Aztec Empire in the fourteenth century, later conquered by the Spanish under Hernán Cortés in 1521.

microprocessor An electronic circuit printed on a small silicon chip; a major technological breakthrough in 1971, it paved the way for the development of the personal computer.

Middle Passage The hellish and often deadly middle leg of the transatlantic "Triangular Trade" in which European ships carried manufactured goods to Africa, then transported enslaved Africans to the Americas and the Caribbean, and finally conveyed American agricultural products back to Europe; from the late sixteenth to the early nineteenth centuries, some 12 million Africans were transported via the Middle Passage, unknown millions more dying en route.

Midway, Battle of A 1942 battle that proved to be a turning point in the Pacific front during World War II; it was the Japanese navy's first major defeat in 350 years.

militant nonviolence After the success of the Montgomery bus boycott, people were inspired by Martin Luther King Jr.'s use of this nonviolent form of protest. Throughout the civil rights movement, demonstrators used this method of protest to challenge racial segregation in the South.

Militia Act (1862) Congressional measure that permitted freed slaves to serve as laborers or soldiers in the United States Army.

Ho Chi Minh (1890–1969) He was the Vietnamese communist resistance leader who drove France and the United States out of Vietnam. After the Geneva Accords divided the region into four countries, he controlled North Vietnam, and ultimately became the leader of all of Vietnam at the conclusion of the Vietnam War.

minstrelsy A form of entertainment that was popular from the 1830s to the 1870s. The performances featured white performers who were made up as African Americans, or blackface. They performed banjo and fiddle music, "shuffle" dances, and lowbrow humor that reinforced racial stereotypes.

Minutemen Special units organized by the militia to be ready for quick mobilization.

Miranda v. Arizona **(1966)** U.S. Supreme Court decision required police to advise persons in custody of their rights to legal counsel and against self-incrimination.

Mississippi Plan Series of state constitutional amendments in 1890 which sought to severely disenfranchise black voters and was quickly adopted by other southern states.

Missouri Compromise (1820) Legislative decision to admit Missouri as a slave state and abolish slavery in the area west of the Mississippi River and north of the parallel 36°30'.

Model T Henry Ford developed this model of car so that it was affordable for everyone. Its success led to an increase in the production of automobiles, which stimulated other related industries such steel, oil, and rubber. The mass use of automobiles increased the speed goods could be transported, encouraged urban sprawl, and sparked real estate booms in California and Florida.

moderate Republicanism Promise to curb federal government and restore state and local government authority, spearheaded by President Eisenhower.

modernism An early-twentieth-century intellectual and artistic movement that rejected traditional notions of reality and adopted radical new forms of artistic expression.

"money question" Late-nineteenth-century national debate over the nature of U.S. currency; supporters of a fixed gold standard were generally money lenders, and thus preferred to keep the value of money high, while supporters of silver (and gold) coinage were debtors, they owed money, so they wanted to keep the value of money low by increasing the currency supply (inflation).

monopoly A corporation so large that it effectively controls the entire market for its products or services.

James Monroe (1758–1831) He served as secretary of state and war under President Madison and was elected president. As the latter, he signed the Transcontinental Treaty with Spain, which gave Florida to the United States and expanded the Louisiana territory's western border to the Pacific coast. In 1823, he established the Monroe Doctrine. This foreign policy proclaimed that the American continents were no longer open to colonization and America would be neutral in European affairs.

Monroe Doctrine (1823) U.S. foreign policy that barred further colonization in the Western Hemisphere by European powers and pledged that there would be no American interference with any existing European colonies.

Montgomery bus boycott Boycott of bus system in Montgomery, Alabama, organized by civil rights activists after the arrest of Rosa Parks.

Moral Majority Televangelist Jerry Falwell's political lobbying organization, the name of which became synonymous with the religious right; conservative evangelical Protestants who helped ensure President Ronald Reagan's 1980 victory.

J. Pierpont Morgan (1837–1913) As a powerful investment banker, he would acquire, reorganize, and consolidate companies into giant trusts. His biggest achievement was the consolidation of the steel industry into the United States Steel Corporation, which was the first billion-dollar corporation.

J. Pierpont Morgan and Company An investment bank under the leadership of J. Pierpont Morgan that bought or merged unrelated American companies, often using capital acquired from European investors.

Mormons Members of the Church of Jesus Christ of Latter-day Saints, which dismissed other Christian denominations, emphasizing universal salvation and a modest lifestyle; Mormons were often persecuted for their secrecy and clannishness.

Morrill Land Grant Act (1862) Federal statute that allowed for the creation of land-grant colleges and universities, which were founded to provide technical education in agriculture, mining, and industry.

Samuel F. B. Morse (1791–1872) In 1832, he invented the telegraph and revolutionized the speed of communication.

mountain men Inspired by the fur trade, these men left civilization to work as trappers and reverted to a primitive existence in the wilderness. They were the first white people to find routes through the Rocky Mountains, and they pioneered trails that settlers later used to reach the Oregon country and California in the 1840s.

muckrakers Writers who exposed corruption and abuses in politics, business, consumer safety, working conditions, and more, spurring public interest in progressive reforms.

Mugwumps Reformers who bolted the Republican party in 1884 to support Democratic Grover Cleveland for president over Republican James G. Blaine, whose secret dealings on behalf of railroad companies had brought charges of corruption.

mulattoes Mixed-race people who constituted most of the South's free black population.

Benito Mussolini, or *"Il Duce"* **(1883–1945)** The Italian founder of the Fascist party who came to power in Italy in 1922 and allied himself with Adolf Hitler and the Axis powers during the Second World War.

National Association for the Advancement of Colored People (NAACP) Organization founded in 1910 by black activists and white progressives that promoted education as a means of combating social problems and focused on legal action to secure the civil rights supposedly guaranteed by the Fourteenth and Fifteenth Amendments.

National Industrial Recovery Act (1933) Passed on the last of the Hundred Days, it created public-works jobs through the Federal Emergency Relief Administration and established a system of self-regulation for industry through the National Recovery Administration, which was ruled unconstitutional in 1935.

National Labor Union (NLU) A federation of labor and reform leaders established in 1866 to advocate for new state and local laws to improve working conditions.

National Recovery Administration (NRA) (1933) Controversial federal agency that brought together business and labor leaders to create "codes of fair competition" and "fair labor" policies, including a national minimum wage.

National Security Act Congressional legislation passed in 1947 that created the Department of Defense, the National Security Council, and the Central Intelligence Agency.

National Socialist German Workers' Party (Nazi) Founded in the 1920s, this party gained control over Germany under the leadership of Adolf Hitler in 1933 and continued in power until Germany's defeat at the end of the Second World War. It advocated a violent anti-Semitic, anti-Marxist, pan-German ideology. The Nazi party perpetrated the Holocaust.

National Trades' Union Formed in 1834 to organize all local trade unions into a stronger national association, only to be dissolved amid the economic depression during the late 1830s.

nativists Members of a reactionary conservative movement characterized by heightened nationalism, anti-immigrant sentiment, and the enactment of laws setting stricter regulations on immigration.

natural rights An individual's basic rights that should not be violated by any government or community.

Navigation Acts Restrictions passed by the British Parliament between 1650 and 1775 to control colonial trade and bolster the mercantile system.

Negro nationalism A cultural and political movement in the 1920s spearheaded by Marcus Garvey which exalted blackness, black cultural expression, and black exclusiveness.

Negrophobia A violent new wave of racism that spread in the late nineteenth century largely spurred by white resentment for African-American financial success and growing political influence.

"neutrality laws" Series of laws passed by Congress aimed at avoiding entering a Second World War; these included the Neutrality Act of 1935, which banned loans to warring nations.

"New Democrats" Centrist ("moderate") Democrats led by President Bill Clinton that emerged in the late 1980s and early 1990s to challenge the "liberal" direction of the party.

"new economy" Period of sustained economic prosperity during the nineties marked by budget surpluses, the explosion of dot.com industries, low inflation, and low unemployment.

New France The name used for the area of North America that was colonized by the French. Unlike Spanish or English colonies, New France had a small number of colonists, which forced them to initially seek good relations with the indigenous people they encountered.

New Freedom Program championed in 1912 by the Woodrow Wilson campaign that aimed to restore competition in the economy by eliminating all trusts rather than simply regulating them.

New Frontier Proposed domestic program championed by the incoming Kennedy administration in 1961 that aimed to jump-start the economy and trigger social progress.

"new immigrants" Wave of newcomers from southern and eastern Europe, including many Jews, who became a majority among immigrants to America after 1890.

New Jersey Plan The delegations to the Constitutional Convention were divided between two plans on how to structure the government: New Jersey wanted one legislative body with equal representation for each state.

New Left Term coined by the Students for a Democratic Society to distinguish their efforts at grassroots democracy from those of the 1930s Old Left, which had embraced orthodox Marxism.

New Mexico A U.S. territory and later a state in the American Southwest, originally established by the Spanish, who settled there in the sixteenth century, founded Catholic missions, and exploited the region's indigenous peoples.

New Nationalism Platform of the Progressive party and slogan of former President Theodore Roosevelt in the presidential campaign of 1912; stressed government activism, including regulation of trusts, conservation, and recall of state court decisions that had nullified progressive programs.

"New Negro" In the 1920s, a slow and steady growth of black political influence occurred in northern cities where African Americans were freer to speak and act. This political activity created a spirit of protest that expressed itself culturally in the Harlem Renaissance and politically in "new Negro" nationalism.

New Netherland Dutch colony conquered by the English in 1667 and out of which four new colonies were created: New York, New Jersey, Pennsylvania, and Delaware.

New Orleans, Battle of (1815) Final major battle in the War of 1812, in which the Americans under General Andrew Jackson unexpectedly and decisively countered the British attempt to seize the port of New Orleans, Louisiana.

New South *Atlanta Constitution* editor Henry W. Grady's 1886 term for the prosperous post–Civil War South: democratic, industrial, urban, and free of nostalgia for the defeated plantation South.

William Randolph Hearst's *New York Journal* In the late 1890s, the *New York Journal* and its rival, the *New York World*, printed sensationalism on the Cuban revolution as part of their heated competition for readership. The *New York Journal* printed a negative letter from the Spanish ambassador about President McKinley and inflammatory coverage of the sinking of the *Maine* in Havana Harbor. These two events roused the American public's outcry against Spain.

Joseph Pulitzer's *New York World* In the late 1890s, the *New York World* and its rival, *New York Journal*, printed sensationalism on the Cuban revolution as part of their heated competition for readership.

Admiral Chester Nimitz (1885–1966) During the Second World War, he was the commander of central Pacific. Along with General Douglas MacArthur, he dislodged the Japanese military from the Pacific Islands they had occupied.

Nineteenth Amendment Constitutional amendment that granted women the right to vote in 1920.

Richard M. Nixon (1913–1994) He first came to national prominence as a congressman involved in the investigation of Alger Hiss, and later served as vice president during the Eisenhower administration. After being elected president in 1968, he slowed the federal enforcement of civil rights and appointed pro-Southern justices to the Supreme Court. He began a program of Vietnamization of the war. In 1973, America, North and South Vietnam, and the Viet Cong agreed to end the war and the United States withdrew. However, the cease-fire was broken, and South Vietnam fell to North Vietnam. In 1970, Nixon declared that the America was no longer the world's policemen and he would seek some partnerships with Communist countries, historically travelling to China and the Soviet Union. In 1972, he was reelected, but the Watergate scandal erupted shortly after his victory. He resigned the presidency under threat of impeachment.

nonviolent civil disobedience Tactic of defying unjust laws through peaceful actions championed by Dr. Martin Luther King Jr.

Lord North (1732–1792) The first minister of King George III's cabinet whose efforts to subdue the colonies only brought them closer to revolution. He helped bring about the Tea Act of 1773, which led to the Boston Tea Party. In an effort to discipline Boston, he wrote, and Parliament passed, four acts that galvanized colonial resistance.

North American Free Trade Agreement (NAFTA) Agreement eliminating trade barriers that was signed in 1994 by the United States, Canada, and Mexico, making North America the largest free-trade zone in the world.

North Atlantic Treaty Organization (NATO) Defensive political and military alliance formed in 1949 by the United States, Canada, and ten Western European nations to deter Soviet expansion in Europe.

Northwest Ordinance (1787) Land policy for new western territories in the Ohio valley that established the terms and conditions for self-government and statehood while also banning slavery from the region.

NSC-68 (1950) Top-secret policy paper approved by President Truman that outlined a militaristic approach to combating the spread of global communism.

nullification The right claimed by some states to veto a federal law deemed unconstitutional.

Barack Obama (1961–) In the 2008 presidential election, Senator Barack Obama mounted an innovative Internet-based and grassroots-oriented campaign. As the nation's economy nosedived in the fall of 2008, Obama linked the Republican economic philosophy with the country's dismal financial state and promoted a message of "change" and "politics of hope," which resonated with voters. He decisively won the presidency and became America's first person of color to be elected president.

Occupy Wall Street A grassroots movement protesting a capitalist system that fostered social and economic inequality. Begun in Zuccotti Park, New York City, during 2011, the movement spread rapidly across the nation, triggering a national conversation about income inequality and protests of the government's "bailouts" of the banks and corporations allegedly responsible for the Great Recession.

Sandra Day O'Connor (1930–) She was the first woman to serve on the Supreme Court of the United States and was appointed by President Reagan. Reagan's critics charged that her appointment was a token gesture and not a sign of any real commitment to gender equality.

Ohio gang In order to escape the pressures of the White House, President Harding met with a group of people, called the "Ohio gang," in a house on K Street in Washington, D.C. Members of this gang were given low-level positions in the American government and they used their White House connection to "line their pockets" by granting government contracts without bidding, which led to a series of scandals, most notably the Teapot Dome Scandal.

Old Southwest Region covering western Georgia, Alabama, Mississippi, Louisiana, Arkansas, and Texas, where low land prices and fertile soil attracted hundreds of thousands of settlers after the American Revolution.

Open Door policy Official U.S. insistence that Chinese trade would be open to all nations; Secretary of State John Hay unilaterally announced the policy in 1899 in hopes of protecting the Chinese market for U.S. exports.

open shop Business policy of not requiring union membership as a condition of employment; such a policy, where legal, has the effect of weakening unions and diminishing workers' rights.

open range Informal system of governing property on the frontier in which small ranchers could graze their cattle anywhere on unfenced lands; brought to an end by the introduction of barbed wire, a low-cost way to fence off one's land.

Operation Desert Shield After Saddam Hussein invaded Kuwait in 1990, President George H. W. Bush sent American military forces to Saudi Arabia on a strictly defensive mission. They were soon joined by a multinational coalition. When the coalition's mission changed to the retaking of Kuwait, the operation was renamed Desert Storm.

Operation Desert Storm (1991) Assault by American-led multinational forces that quickly defeated Iraqi forces under Saddam Hussein in the First Gulf War, ending the Iraqi occupation of Kuwait.

Operation Overlord The Allies' assault on Hitler's "Atlantic Wall," a seemingly impregnable series of fortifications and minefields along the French coastline that German forces had created using captive Europeans for laborers.

J. Robert Oppenheimer (1904–1967) He led the group of physicists at the laboratory in Los Alamos, New Mexico, who constructed the first atomic bomb.

Oregon Country The Convention of 1818 between Britain and the United States established the Oregon Country as being west of the crest of the Rocky Mountains and the two countries were to jointly occupy it. In 1824, the United States and Russia signed a treaty that established the line of 54°40′ as the southern boundary of Russia's territorial claim in North America. A similar agreement between Britain and Russia finally gave the Oregon Country clearly defined borders, but it remained under joint British and American control.

Oregon fever The lure of fertile land and economic opportunities in the Oregon Country that drew thousands of settlers westward, beginning in the late 1830s.

Osceola (1804?–1838) He was the leader of the Seminole nation who resisted the federal Indian removal policy through a protracted guerilla war. In 1837, he was treacherously seized under a flag of truce and imprisoned at Fort Moultrie, where he was left to die.

Overland Trails Trail routes followed by wagon trains bearing settlers and trade goods from Missouri to the Oregon Country, California, and New Mexico, beginning in the 1840s.

A. Mitchell Palmer (1872–1936) As the attorney general, he played an active role in the government's response to the Red Scare. After several bombings across America, including one at Palmer's home, he and other Americans became convinced that there was a well-organized Communist terror campaign at work. The federal government launched a campaign of raids and deportations and collected files on radical individuals.

Panic of 1819 A financial panic that began a three-year-long economic crisis triggered by a reduced demand of American imports, declining land values, and reckless practices by local and state banks.

Panic of 1837 A financial calamity in the United States brought on by a dramatic slowdown in the British economy and exacerbated by falling cotton prices, failed crops, high inflation, and reckless state banks.

Panic of 1873 A major economic collapse caused by President Grant's efforts to remove greenbacks from circulation; the resultant depression, in which thousands of businesses closed and millions lost their jobs, was then the worst in the nation's history.

Panic of 1893 A major collapse in the national economy after several major railroad companies declared bankruptcy, leading to a severe depression and several violent clashes between workers and management.

panning A method of mining that used a large metal pan to sift gold dust and nuggets from riverbeds during the California gold rush of 1849.

Rosa Parks (1913–2005) In 1955, she refused to give up her seat to a white man on a city bus in Montgomery, Alabama, which a local ordinance required of blacks. She was arrested for disobeying the ordinance. In response, black community leaders organized the Montgomery bus boycott.

Parliament Legislature of Great Britain, composed of the House of Commons, whose members are elected, and the House of Lords, whose members are either hereditary or appointed.

party bosses Powerful political leaders who controlled a "machine" of associates and operatives to promote both individual and party interests, often using informal tactics such as intimidation or the patronage system.

paternalism A moral position developed during the first half of the nineteenth century which claimed that slaves were deprived of liberty for their own "good." Such a rationalization was adopted by some slave owners to justify slavery.

Patriots Colonists who rebelled against British authority before and during the Revolutionary War.

patronage An informal system (sometimes called the "spoils system") used by politicians to reward their supporters with government appointments or contracts.

Alice Paul (1885–1977) She was a leader of the women's suffrage movement and head of the Congressional Committee of National Women Suffrage Association. She instructed female suffrage activists to use more militant tactics, such as picketing state legislatures, chaining themselves to public buildings, inciting police to arrest them, and undertaking hunger strikes.

Norman Vincent Peale (1898–1993) He was a champion of the upbeat and feel-good theology that was popular in the 1950s religious revival. He advocated getting rid of any depressing or negative thoughts and replacing them with "faith, enthusiasm and joy," which would make an individual popular and well liked.

Pearl Harbor Surprise Japanese attack on the U.S. fleet at Pearl Harbor on December 7, 1941, which prompted the immediate American entry into the war.

"peculiar institution" A phrase used by whites in the antebellum South to refer to slavery without using the word slavery.

Pennsylvania English colony founded by William Penn in 1681 as a Quaker commonwealth, though it welcomed people of all religions.

Pentagon Papers Informal name for the Defense Department's secret history of the Vietnam conflict; leaked to the press by former official Daniel Ellsberg and published in the *New York Times* in 1971.

People's party (Populists) Political party largely made up of farmers from the South and West that struggled to gain political influence from the East. Populists advocated a variety of reforms, including free coinage of silver, a progressive income tax, postal savings banks, regulation of railroads, and direct election of U.S. senators.

Pequot War Massacre in 1637 and subsequent dissolution of the Pequot Nation by Puritan settlers, who seized the Indians' lands.

perestroika Russian term for "economic restructuring"; applied to Mikhail Gorbachev's series of political and economic reforms that included shifting a centrally planned Commmunist economy to a mixed economy allowing for capitalism.

Commodore Matthew Perry (1794–1858) In 1854, he negotiated the Treaty of Kanagawa, which was the first step in starting a political and commercial relationship between the United States and Japan.

John J. Pershing U.S. general sent by President Wilson to put down attacks on the Mexican border led by Francisco "Pancho" Villa.

Personal Responsibility and Work Opportunity Act of 1996 (PRWOA) Comprehensive welfare-reform measure, passed by a Republican Congress and signed by President Clinton, that aimed to decrease the size of the "welfare state" by limiting the amount of government aid provided to the unemployed so as to encourage recipients to find jobs.

"pet banks" During President Andrew Jackson's fight with the national bank, Jackson resolved to remove all federal deposits from it. To comply with Jackson's demands, Secretary of Treasury Taney continued to draw on government's accounts in the national bank, but deposit all new federal receipts in state banks. The state banks that received these deposits were called "pet banks."

Pilgrims Puritan Separatists who broke completely with the Church of England and sailed to the New World aboard the *Mayflower,* founding Plymouth Colony on Cape Cod in 1620.

Gifford Pinchot (1865–1946) As the head of the Division of Forestry, he implemented a conservation policy that entailed the scientific management of natural resources to serve the public interest. His work helped start the conservation movement.

Elizabeth Lucas Pinckney (1722?–1793) One of the most enterprising horticulturists in colonial America, she began managing her family's three plantations in South Carolina at the age of sixteen. She had tremendous success growing indigo, which led to many other plantations growing the crop as well.

Pinckney's Treaty Treaty with Spain negotiated by Thomas Pinckney in 1795; established United States boundaries at the Mississippi River and the 31st parallel and allowed open transportation on the Mississippi.

Francisco Pizarro (1478?–1541) In 1531, he led his Spanish soldiers to Peru and conquered the Inca Empire.

"plain white folk" Yeoman farmers who lived and worked on their own small farms, growing food and cash crops to trade for necessities.

plantation mistress Matriarch of a planter's household, responsible for supervising the domestic aspects of the estate.

planter Owner of a large farm in the South that was worked by twenty or more slaves and supervised by overseers.

political "machine" A network of political activists and elected officials, usually controlled by a powerful "boss," that attempts to manipulate local politics.

James Knox Polk, or "Young Hickory" (1795–1849) As president, his chief concern was the expansion of the United States. Shortly after taking office, Mexico broke off relations with the United States over the annexation of Texas. Polk declared war on Mexico and sought to subvert Mexican authority in California. The United States defeated Mexico, and the two nations signed the Treaty of Guadalupe Hidalgo, in which Mexico gave up any claims on Texas north of the Rio Grande River and ceded New Mexico and California to the United States.

Pontiac's Rebellion An Indian attack on British forts and settlements after France ceded to the British its territory east of the Mississippi River, as part of the Treaty of Paris in 1763, without consulting France's Indian allies.

popular sovereignty Legal concept by which the white male settlers in a new U.S. territory would vote to decide whether or not to permit slavery.

Pottawatomie Massacre In retaliation for the "sack of Lawrence," John Brown and his abolitionist cohorts hacked five men to death in the pro-slavery settlement of Pottawatomie, Kansas, on May 24, 1856, triggering a guerrilla war in the Kansas Territory that cost 200 settlers' lives.

Powhatan Confederacy An alliance of several powerful Algonquian tribes under the leadership of Chief Powhatan, organized into thirty chiefdoms along much of the Atlantic coast in the late sixteenth and early seventeenth centuries.

Chief Powhatan Wahunsonacock He was called Powhatan by the English after the name of his tribe, and was the powerful, charismatic chief of numerous Algonquian-speaking towns in eastern Virginia representing over 10,000 Indians.

professions Occupations requiring specialized knowledge of some field; the Industrial Revolution and its new organization of labor created an array of professions in the nineteenth century.

Progressive party In the 1912 election, Theodore Roosevelt was unable to secure the Republican nomination for president. He left the Republican party and formed his own party of progressive Republicans, called the "Bull Moose" party (later Progressive Party). Roosevelt and Taft split the Republican vote, which allowed Democrat Woodrow Wilson to win.

Prohibition National ban on the manufacture and sale of alcohol that lasted from 1920 to 1933, though the law was widely violated and proved too difficult to enforce effectively.

proprietary colonies A colony owned by an individual, rather than a joint-stock company.

Protestant Reformation Sixteenth-century religious movement initiated by Martin Luther, a German monk whose public criticism of corruption in the Roman Catholic Church, and whose teaching that Christians can communicate directly with God, gained a wide following and led to the Protestant Reformation.

public schools Elementary and secondary schools funded by the state and free of tuition.

pueblos The Spanish term for the adobe cliff dwellings of the indigenous people of the southwestern United States.

Pullman strike (1894) A national strike by the American Railway Union, whose members shut down major railways in sympathy with striking workers in Pullman, Illinois; ended with intervention of federal troops.

Puritans English religious dissenters who sought to "purify" the Church of England of its Catholic practices.

Quakers George Fox founded the Quaker religion in 1647. They rejected the use of formal sacraments and ministry, refused to take oaths, and embraced pacifism. Fleeing persecution, they settled and established the colony of Pennsylvania.

race-based slavery Institution that uses racial characteristics and myths to justify enslaving a people.

Radical Republicans Senators and congressmen who, strictly identifying the Civil War with the abolitionist cause, sought swift emancipation of the slaves, punishment of the rebels, and tight controls over the former Confederate states after the war.

railroads Steam-powered vehicles that improved passenger transportation, quickened western settlement, and enabled commercial agriculture in the nineteenth century.

Raleigh's Roanoke Island Colony English expedition of 117 settlers, including Virginia Dare, the first English child born in the New World; colony disappeared from Roanoke Island in the Outer Banks sometime between 1587 and 1590.

A. Philip Randolph (1889–1979) He was the head of the Brotherhood of Sleeping Car Porters who planned a march on Washington, D.C., to demand an end to racial discrimination in the defense industries. To stop the march, the Roosevelt administration negotiated an agreement with the Randolph group. The demonstration would be called off and an executive order would be issued that forbade discrimination in defense work and training programs and set up the Fair Employment Practices Committee.

range wars In the late 1800s, conflicting claims over land and water rights triggered violent disputes between farmers and ranchers in parts of the western United States.

Ronald Reagan (1911–2004) In 1980, the former actor and governor of California was elected president. In office, he reduced social spending, cut taxes, and increased defense spending. During his presidency, the federal debt tripled, the federal deficit rose, programs such as housing and school lunches were cut, and the HIV/AIDS crisis grew to prominence in the United States. He signed an arms-control treaty with the Soviet Union in 1987 and authorized covert CIA operations in Central America. In 1986 the Iran-Contra scandal was revealed.

Reaganomics President Reagan's "supply-side" economic philosophy combining tax cuts with the goals of decreased government spending reduced regulation of business, and a balanced budget.

Reconstruction Finance Corporation (RFC) (1932) Federal program established under President Hoover to loan money to banks and other corporations to help them avoid bankruptcy.

Red Power Activism by militant Native American groups to protest living conditions on Indian reservations through demonstrations, legal action, and, at times, violence.

Redeemers Post–Civil War Democratic leaders who supposedly saved the South from Yankee domination and preserved the primarily rural economy.

Dr. Walter Reed (1851–1902) His work on yellow fever in Cuba led to the discovery that the fever was carried by mosquitoes. This understanding helped develop more effective controls of the worldwide disease.

reform Darwinism A social philosophy developed by Lester Frank War that challenged the ruthlessness of social Darwinism by asserting that humans were not passive pawns of evolutionary forces. Instead, people could actively shape the process of evolutionary social development through cooperation, innovation, and planning.

Reformation European religious movement that challenged the Catholic Church and resulted in the beginnings of Protestant Christianity. During this period, Catholics and Protestants persecuted, imprisoned, tortured, and killed each other in large numbers.

religious right Christian conservatives with a faith-based political agenda that includes prohibition of abortion and allowing prayer in public schools.

reparations As a part of the Treaty of Versailles, Germany was required to confess its responsibility for the First World War and make payments to the victors for the entire expense of the war. These two requirements created a deep bitterness among Germans.

Alexander Hamilton's Report on Manufactures First secretary of the Treasury Alexander Hamilton's 1791 analysis that accurately foretold the future of American industry and proposed tariffs and subsidies to promote it.

Republican ideology Political belief in representative democracy in which citizens govern themselves by electing representatives, or legislators, to make key decisions on the citizens' behalf.

republican simplicity Deliberate attitude of humility and frugality, as opposed to monarchial pomp and ceremony, adopted by Thomas Jefferson in his presidency

Republicans First used during the early nineteenth century to describe supporters of a strict interpretation of the Constitution, which they believed would safeguard individual freedoms and states' rights from the threats posed by a strong central government. The idealist Republican vision of sustaining an agrarian-oriented union was developed largely by Thomas Jefferson.

"return to normalcy" Campaign promise of Republican presidential candidate Warren G. Harding in 1920, meant to contrast with Woodrow Wilson's progressivism and internationalism.

Paul Revere (1735–1818) On the night of April 18, 1775, British soldiers marched toward Concord to arrest American Revolutionary leaders and seize their depot of supplies. Paul Revere famously rode through the night and raised the alarm about the approaching British troops.

Roaring Twenties The 1920s, an era of social and intellectual revolution in which young people experimented with new forms of recreation and sexuality. The Eastern, urban cultural shift clashed with conservative and insular Midwestern America, which increased the tensions between the two regions.

Jackie Robinson (1919–1972) In 1947, he became the first African American to play major league baseball. He won over fans and players and stimulated the integration of other professional sports.

rock-and-roll music Alan Freed, a disc jockey, noticed white teenagers were buying rhythm and blues records that had been only purchased by African Americans and Hispanic Americans. Freed began playing these records, but called them rock-and-roll records as a way to overcome the racial barrier. As the popularity of the music genre increased, it helped bridge the gap between "white" and "black" music.

John D. Rockefeller (1839–1937) In 1870, he founded the Standard Oil Company of Ohio, which was his first step in creating his vast oil empire. He perfected the idea of a holding company.

Roe v. Wade (1973) Landmark Supreme Court decision striking down state laws that banned abortions during the first trimester of pregnancy.

Roman Catholicism The Christian faith and religious practices of the Roman Catholic Church, which exerted great political, economic, and social influence on much of Western Europe and, through the Spanish and Portuguese Empires, on the Americas.

Romanticism Philosophical, literary, and artistic movement of the nineteenth century that was largely a reaction to the rationalism of the previous century; Romantics valued emotion, mysticism, and individualism.

Eleanor Roosevelt (1884–1962) She redefined the role of the presidential spouse and was the first woman to address a national political convention, write a nationally syndicated column, and hold regular press conferences. She travelled throughout the nation to promote the New Deal, women's causes, and organized labor, and to meet with African American leaders.

Franklin Delano Roosevelt (1882–1945) Elected during the Great Depression, Roosevelt sought to help struggling Americans through his New Deal programs that created employment and social programs, such as Social Security. After the bombing of Pearl Harbor, he declared war on Japan and Germany and led the country through most of the Second World War before dying of a cerebral hemorrhage.

Theodore Roosevelt (1858–1919) As the assistant secretary of the navy, he supported expansionism, American imperialism, and war with Spain. He led the Rough Riders, in Cuba during the War of 1898 and used the notoriety of this military campaign for political gain. As President McKinley's vice president, he succeeded McKinley after his assassination. His forceful foreign policy became known as "big stick diplomacy." Domestically, his policies on natural resources helped start the conservation movement. Unable to win the Republican nomination for president in 1912, he formed his own party of progressive Republicans: the "Bull Moose" party.

Roosevelt Corollary President Theodore Roosevelt's 1904 revision of the Monroe Doctrine (1823) in which he argued that the United States could use military force in Central and South American nations to prevent European nations from intervening in the Western Hemisphere.

Rough Riders The First U.S. Volunteer Cavalry, led in the War of 1898 by Theodore Roosevelt; they were victorious in their only engagement, the Battle of San Juan Hill near Santiago, Cuba, and Roosevelt was celebrated as a national hero, bolstering his political career.

Royal Proclamation of 1763 Statement issued by King George III in the wake of the Treaty of Paris which prohibited British colonists from settling any lands beyond the Appalachian mountains.

Nicola Sacco (1891–1927) In 1920, he and Bartolomeo Vanzetti were Italian immigrants who were arrested for stealing $16,000 and killing a paymaster and his guard. Their trial took place during a time of numerous bombings by anarchists and their judge was openly prejudicial; many liberals and radicals believe that their conviction was based on their political ideas and ethnic origin rather than the evidence against them.

Sacco and Vanzetti case The 1921 trial of two Italian immigrants that occurred at the height of Italian immigration and against the backdrop of numerous terror attacks by anarchists; despite a lack of clear evidence, the two defendants, both self-professed anarchists, were convicted of murder and were executed in 1927.

saloons Bars or taverns where mostly men would gather to drink, eat, relax, play games, and, often, to discuss politics.

salutary neglect Informal British policy during the first half of the eighteenth century that allowed the American colonies considerable freedom to pursue their economic and political interests in exchange for colonial obedience.

same-sex marriage The legal right for gay and lesbian couples to marry; it became the most divisive issue in the culture wars of the early 2010s as more and more court rulings affirmed this right in states and municipalities across the United States. In a landmark 2015 decision, the Supreme Court ruled in favor of legalizing same-sex marriage nationwide.

Sand Creek Massacre (1864) A brutal slaughter of unarmed Indian men, women, and children who had been promised protection by the territorial governor of Colorado; the massacre ignited warfare between Americans and Indians across the central plains for the next three years.

Sandinista Cuban-sponsored government that came to power in Nicaragua after toppling a corrupt dictator. The State Department believed that the Sandinistas were supplying the leftist Salvadoran rebels with Cuban and Soviet arms. In response, the Reagan administration ordered the CIA to train and supply guerrilla bands of anti-Communist Nicaraguans called Contras. A cease-fire agreement between the Contras and Sandinistas was signed in 1988.

Sandlot Incident Violence occurring during the Great Railroad Strike of 1877, when mobs of frustrated working-class whites in San Francisco attacked Chinese immigrants, blaming them for economic hardship.

General Antonio López de Santa Anna (1794–1876) In 1834, he seized political power in Mexico and became a dictator. In 1835, Texans rebelled against him and he led his army to Texas to crush their rebellion. He captured the missionary called the Alamo and killed all of its defenders, which inspired Texans to continue to resistance and Americans to volunteer to fight for Texas. The Texans captured Santa Anna during a surprise attack and he bought his freedom by signing a treaty recognizing Texas's independence.

Saratoga, Battles of Decisive defeat of 5,000 British troops under General John Burgoyne in several battles near Saratoga, New York, in October 1777; the American victory helped convince France to enter the war on the side of the Patriots.

scalawags White southern Republicans—some former Unionists—who served in Reconstruction governments.

Phyllis Schlafly (1924–) A right-wing Republican activist who spearheaded the anti-feminism movement. She believed feminists were "anti-family, anti-children, and pro-abortion." She worked against the equal rights amendment for women and civil rights protection for gays.

Scopes Trial Highly publicized 1925 trial of a high school teacher in Tennessee for violating a state law that prohibited the teaching of evolution; the trial was seen as the climax of the fundamentalist war on Darwinism.

Winfield Scott (1786–1866) During the Mexican War, he was the American general who captured Mexico City, which ended the war. Using his popularity from his military success, he ran as a Whig party candidate for President.

Sears, Roebuck and Company By the end of the nineteenth century, this company dominated the mail-order industry and helped create a truly national market. Its mail-order catalog and low prices allowed people living in rural areas and small towns to buy products that were previously too expensive or available only to city dwellers.

secession Shortly after President Abraham Lincoln was elected, southern states began dissolving their ties with the United States because they believed Lincoln and the Republican party were a threat to slavery.

Second Bank of the United States (B.U.S.) Established in 1816 after the first national bank's charter expired; it stabilized the economy by creating a sound national currency, by making loans to farmers, small manufacturers, and entrepreneurs, and by regulating the ability of state banks to issue their own paper currency.

Second Great Awakening Religious revival movement that arose in reaction to the growth of secularism and rationalist religion and spurred the growth of the Baptist and Methodist churches.

Second Industrial Revolution Beginning in the late nineteenth century, a wave of technological innovations, especially in iron and steel production, steam and electrical power, and telegraphic communications, all of which spurred industrial development and urban growth.

Second New Deal (1935–1938) Expansive cluster of legislation proposed by President Roosevelt that established new regulatory agencies, strengthened the rights of workers to organize unions, and laid the foundation of a federal social welfare system through the creation of Social Security.

second two-party system Domination of national politics by two major political parties, such as the Whigs and Democrats during the 1830s and 1840s.

Securities and Exchange Commission (1934) Federal agency established to regulate the issuance and trading of stocks and bonds in an effort to avoid financial panics and stock market "crashes."

Seneca Falls Convention (1848) Convention organized by feminists Lucretia Mott and Elizabeth Cady Stanton to promote women's rights and issue the pathbreaking Declaration of Sentiments.

"separate but equal" Principle underlying legal racial segregation, which was upheld in *Plessy v. Ferguson* (1896) and struck down in *Brown v. Board of Education* (1954).

separation of powers Strict division of the powers of government among three separate branches (executive, legislative, and judicial) which, in turn, check and balance each other.

September 11 On September 11, 2001, Islamic terrorists, who were members of the al Qaeda terrorist organization, hijacked four commercial airliners. Two were flown into the World Trade Center, a third into the Pentagon, and a fourth plane was brought down in Pennsylvania. In response, President George W. Bush launched his "war on terrorism." His administration assembled an international coalition to fight terrorism, which invaded Afghanistan after the country's government would not turn over Osama bin Laden. Bush and Congress passed the USA Patriot Act, which allowed government agencies to try suspected terrorists in secret military courts and eavesdrop on confidential conversations.

settlement houses Product of the late nineteenth-century movement to offer a broad array of social services in urban immigrant neighborhoods; Chicago's Hull House was one of hundreds of settlement houses that operated by the early twentieth century.

Seventeenth Amendment (1913) Constitutional amendment that provided for the direct election of senators rather than the traditional practice allowing state legislatures to name them.

Shakers Founded by Mother Ann Lee Stanley in England, the United Society of Believers in Christ's Second Appearing settled in Watervliet, New York, in 1774 and subsequently established eighteen additional communes in the Northeast, Indiana, and Kentucky.

share tenants Poor farmers who rented land to farm in exchange for a substantial share of the crop, though they would often have their own horse or mule, tools, and line of credit with a nearby store.

sharecroppers Poor, mostly black farmers who would work an owner's land in return for shelter, seed, fertilizer, mules, supplies, and food, as well as a substantial share of the crop produced.

Share-the-Wealth program Huey Long offered this program as an alternative to the New Deal. The program proposed to confiscate large personal fortunes, which would be used to guarantee every poor family a cash grant of $5,000 and every worker an annual income of $2,500. This program promised to provide pensions, reduce working hours, pay veterans' bonuses, and ensures a college education to every qualified student.

Shays's Rebellion Storming of the Massachusetts federal arsenal in 1787 by Daniel Shays and 1,200 armed farmers seeking debt relief from the state legislature through issuance of paper currency and lower taxes.

silent majority Term popularized by President Richard Nixon to describe the great majority of American voters who did not express their political opinions publicly—"the non-demonstrators."

Sixteenth Amendment (1913) Constitutional amendment that authorized the federal income tax.

slave codes Ordinances passed by a colony or state to regulate the behavior of slaves, often including brutal punishments for infractions.

Alfred E. Smith (1873–1944) In the 1928 presidential election, he won the Democratic nomination, but failed to win the presidency. Rural voters distrusted him for being Catholic and the son of Irish immigrants as well as for his anti-Prohibition stance.

Captain John Smith (1580–1631) A swashbuckling soldier of fortune with rare powers of leadership and self-promotion, he was appointed to the resident council to manage Jamestown.

Joseph Smith (1805–1844) In 1823, he claimed that the Angel Moroni showed him the location of several gold tablets on which the Book of Mormon was written. Using the Book of Mormon as his gospel, he founded the Church of Jesus Christ of Latter-day Saints, or Mormons. In 1839, they settled in Commerce, Illinois, to avoid persecution. In 1844, Joseph and his brother were arrested and jailed for ordering the destruction of a newspaper that opposed them. While in jail, an anti-Mormon mob stormed the jail and killed both of them.

social Darwinism The application of Charles Darwin's theory of evolutionary natural selection to human society; social Darwinists used the concept of "survival of the fittest" to justify class distinctions, explain poverty, and oppose government intervention in the economy.

social gospel Protestant movement that stressed the Christian obligation to address the mounting social problems caused by urbanization and industrialization.

social justice An important part of the Progressive's agenda, social justice sought to solve social problems through reform and regulation. Methods used to bring about social justice ranged from the founding of charities to the legislation of a ban on child labor.

Social Security Act (1935) Legislation enacted to provide federal assistance to retired workers through tax-funded pension payments and benefit payments to the unemployed and disabled.

Sons of Liberty First organized by Samuel Adams in the 1770s, groups of colonists dedicated to militant resistance against British control of the colonies.

Hernando de Soto (1500?–1542) A conquistador who explored the west coast of Florida, western North Carolina, and along the Arkansas river from 1539 till his death in 1542.

Southern Christian Leadership Conference (SCLC) Civil rights organization formed by Dr. Martin Luther King Jr. that championed nonviolent direct action as a means of ending segregation.

"southern strategy" This strategy was a major reason for Richard Nixon's victory in the 1968 presidential election. To gain support in the South, Nixon assured southern conservatives that he would slow the federal enforcement of civil rights laws and appoint pro-southern justices to the Supreme Court. As president, Nixon fulfilled these promises.

Spanish Armada A massive Spanish fleet of 130 warships that was defeated at Plymouth in 1588 by the English navy during the reign of Queen Elizabeth I.

Spanish flu Unprecedentedly lethal influenza epidemic of 1918 that killed more than 22 million people worldwide.

Herbert Spencer (1820–1903) As the first major proponent of social Darwinism, he argued that human society and institutions are subject to the process of natural selection and that society naturally evolves for the better. He was against any form of government interference with the evolution of society, like business regulations, because it would help the "unfit" to survive.

spirituals Songs with religious messages sung by slaves to help ease the strain of field labor and to voice their suffering at the hands of their masters and overseers.

spoils system The term—meaning the filling of federal government jobs with persons loyal to the party of the president—originated in Andrew Jackson's first term; the system was replaced in the Progressive Era by civil service.

Square Deal Roosevelt's progressive agenda of the "Three C's": control of corporations, conservation of natural resources, and consumer protection.

stagflation Term coined by economists during the Nixon presidency to describe the unprecedented situation of stagnant economic growth and consumer price inflation occurring at the same time.

Joseph Stalin (1879–1953) The Bolshevik leader who succeeded Lenin as the leader of the Soviet Union in 1924 and ruled the country until his death. During his totalitarian rule of the Soviet Union, he used purges and a system of forced labor camps to maintain control over the country, and claimed vast areas of Eastern Europe for Soviet domination.

Stalwarts Conservative Republican party faction during the presidency of Rutherford B. Hayes, 1877–1881; led by Senator Roscoe B. Conkling of New York, Stalwarts opposed civil service reform and favored a third term for President Ulysses S. Grant.

Stamp Act Act of Parliament requiring that all printed materials (e.g., newspapers, bonds, and even playing cards) in the American colonies use paper with an official tax stamp in order to pay for British military protection of the colonies.

Stamp Act Congress Twenty-seven delegates from nine of the colonies met from October 7–25, 1765 and wrote a Declaration of the Rights and Grievances of the Colonies, a petition to the King, and a petition to Parliament for the repeal of the Stamp Act.

Standard Oil Company Corporation under the leadership of John D. Rockefeller that attempted to dominate the entire oil industry through horizontal and vertical integration.

Elizabeth Cady Stanton (1815–1902) She was a prominent reformer and advocate for the rights of women, and she helped organize the Seneca Falls Convention to discuss women's rights. The convention was the first of its kind and produced the Declaration of Sentiments, which proclaimed the equality of men and women.

staple crops Profitable market crops, such as cotton, tobacco, or rice, that predominate in a given region.

state constitutions Charters that define the relationship between the state government and local governments and individuals, also protecting their rights from violation by the national government.

steamboats Ships and boats powered by wood-fired steam engines. First used in the early nineteenth century, they made two-way traffic possible in eastern river systems, creating a transcontinental market and an agricultural empire.

Thaddeus Stevens (1792–1868) As one of the leaders of the Radical Republicans, he argued that the former Confederate states should be viewed as conquered provinces, which were subject to the demands of the conquerors. He believed that all of Southern society needed to be changed, and he supported the abolition of slavery and racial equality.

Adlai E. Stevenson (1900–1965) In the 1952 and 1956 presidential elections, he was the Democratic nominee who lost to Dwight Eisenhower. He was also the U.S. Ambassador to the United Nations and is remembered for his famous speech in 1962 before the UN Security Council that unequivocally demonstrated that the Soviet Union had built nuclear missile bases in Cuba.

Stonewall Riots Violent clashes between police and gay patrons of New York City's Stonewall Inn in 1969; seen as the starting point of the modern gay rights movement.

Stono Rebellion A 1739 slave uprising in South Carolina that was brutally quashed, leading to executions as well as a severe tightening of the slave code.

Strategic Arms Limitation Treaty (SALT I) Agreement signed in 1972 by President Nixon and Secretary Brezhnev prohibiting the development of missile defense systems in the United States and Soviet Union and limiting the quantity of nuclear warheads for both.

Strategic Defense Initiative (SDI) (1983) Ronald Reagan's proposed space-based anti-missile defense system, dubbed "Star Wars" by the media, that aroused great controversy and escalated the arms race between the United States and the Soviet Union.

Levi Strauss (1829–1902) A Jewish tailor who followed miners to California during the gold rush and began making durable work pants that were later dubbed blue jeans or Levi's.

Student Nonviolent Coordinating Committee (SNCC) Interracial organization formed in 1960 with the goal of intensifying the effort to end racial segregation.

Students for a Democratic Society (SDS) Major organization of the New Left, founded at the University of Michigan in 1960 by Tom Hayden and Al Haber.

suburbia Communities formed from mass migration of middle-class whites from urban centers.

Suez crisis British, French, and Israeli attack on Egypt in 1956 after Nasser's seizure of the Suez Canal; President Eisenhower interceded to demand the withdrawal of the British, French, and Israeli forces from the Sinai peninsula and canal.

Sunbelt The label for an arc that stretched from the Carolinas to California. During the postwar era, much of the urban population growth occurred in this area.

the "surge" In early 2007, President Bush decided he would send a "surge" of new troops to Iraq and implement a new strategy. U.S. forces would shift their focus from offensive operations to the protection of Iraqi civilians from attacks by terrorist insurgents and sectarian militias. While the "surge" reduced the violence in Iraq, Iraqi leaders were still unable to develop a self-sustaining democracy.

Taft-Hartley Labor Act (1947) Congressional legislation that banned "unfair labor practices" by labor unions, required union leaders to sign anti-Communist "loyalty oaths," and prohibited federal employees from going on strike.

Taliban A coalition of ultraconservative Islamists who rose to power in Afghanistan after the Soviets withdrew. The Taliban leaders gave Osama bin Laden a safe haven in their country in exchange for aid in fighting the Northern Alliance, who were rebels opposed to the Taliban. After they refused to turn bin Laden over to the United States, America invaded Afghanistan.

Tammany Hall The "city machine" used by "Boss" Tweed to dominate politics in New York City until his arrest in 1871.

tariffs Taxes on goods imported from other nations, typically used to protect home industries from foreign competitors and to generate revenue for the federal government.

Tariff of 1816 A cluster of taxes on imports passed by Congress to protect America's emerging iron and textile industries from British competition.

Tariff of 1832 This tariff act reduced the duties on many items, but the tariffs on cloth and iron remained high. South Carolina nullified it along with the tariff of 1828. President Andrew Jackson sent federal troops to the state and asked Congress to grant him the authority to enforce the tariffs. Henry Clay presented a plan of gradually reducing the tariffs until 1842, which Congress passed and thereby ended the crisis.

Tariff of Abominations (1828) Tax on imported goods, including British cloth and clothing, that strengthened New England textile companies but hurt southern consumers, who experienced a decrease in British demand for raw cotton grown in the South.

tariff reform Effort led by the Democratic party to reduce taxes on imported goods, which Republicans argued were needed to protect American industries from foreign competition.

Zachary Taylor (1784–1850) During the Mexican War, he scored two quick victories against Mexico, which made him very popular in America. He used his popularity from his military victories to be elected the president as a member of the Whig party, but died before he could complete his term.

Taylorism Labor system based on detailed study of work tasks, championed by Frederick Winslow Taylor, intended to maximize efficiency and profits for employers.

Tea Party Right-wing populist movement, largely made up of middle-class, white male conservatives, that emerged as a response to the expansion of the federal government under the Obama administration.

Teapot Dome Affair Harding administration scandal in which Secretary of the Interior Albert B. Fall profited from secret leasing of government oil reserves in Wyoming to private oil companies.

Tecumseh (1768–1813) He was a leader of the Shawnee tribe who tried to unite all Indians into a confederation that could defend their hunting grounds. He believed that no land cessions could be made without the consent of all the tribes because they held the land in common. His beliefs and leadership made him seem dangerous to the American government and they waged war on him and his tribe. He was killed at the Battle of the Thames.

Tecumseh's Indian Confederacy A group of Native Americans under leadership of Shawnee leader Tecumseh and his prophet brother Tenskwatawa; its mission of fighting off American expansion was thwarted in the Battle of Tippecanoe (1811), when the confederacy fell apart.

Tejanos Texas settlers of Spanish or Mexican descent.

telegraph system System of electronic communication invented by Samuel F. B. Morse that could be transmitted instantaneously across great distances (first used in the 1840s).

Teller Amendment Addition to the congressional war resolution of April 20, 1898, which marked the U.S. entry into the war with Spain; the amendment declared that the United States' goal in entering the war was to ensure Cuba's independence, not to annex Cuba as a territory.

temperance A widespread reform movement, led by militant Christians, focused on reducing the use of alcoholic beverages.

tenements Shabby, low-cost inner-city apartment buildings that housed the urban poor in cramped, poorly ventilated apartments.

Tenochtitlán The capital city of the Aztec Empire. The city was built on marshy islands on the western side of Lake Tetzcoco, which is the site of present-day Mexico City.

Tet offensive Surprise attack by Viet Cong guerrillas and the North Vietnamese army on U.S. and South Vietnamese forces in 1968 that shocked the American public and led to widespread sentiment against the war.

Texas Revolution (1835–1836) Conflict between Texas colonists and the Mexican government that resulted in the creation of the separate Republic of Texas in 1836.

textile industry Commercial production of thread, fabric, and clothing from raw cotton in mills in New England during the first half of the nineteenth century, and later in the South in the late nineteenth century.

Thirteenth Amendment (1865) Amendment to the U. S. Constitution that freed all slaves in the United States.

Battle of Tippecanoe (1811) Battle in northern Indiana between U.S. troops and Native American warriors led by Tenskwatawa, the brother of Tecumseh, who had organized an anti-American Indian confederacy to fight American efforts to settle on Indian lands.

tobacco A cash crop grown in the Caribbean as well as the Virginia and Maryland colonies, made increasingly profitable by the rapidly growing popularity of smoking in Europe after the voyages of Columbus.

Gulf of Tonkin incident On August 2 and 4 of 1964, North Vietnamese vessels attacked two American destroyers in Gulf of Tonkin off the coast of North Vietnam. President Johnson described the attacks as unprovoked. In reality, the U.S. ships were monitoring South Vietnamese attacks on North Vietnamese islands that American advisers had planned. The incident spurred the Tonkin Gulf resolution.

Tonkin Gulf Resolution Congressional action that granted the president unlimited authority to defend U.S. forces abroad, passed in August 1964 after an allegedly unprovoked attack on American warships off the coast of North Vietnam.

Tories Term used by Patriots to refer to Loyalists, or colonists who supported the Crown after the Declaration of Independence.

Townshend Acts Parliamentary measures to extract more revenue from the colonies; the Revenue Act of 1767, which taxed tea, paper, and other colonial imports, was one of the most notorious of these policies.

Trail of Tears The Cherokees' eight-hundred mile journey (1838–1839) from the southern Appalachians to Indian Territory (in present-day Oklahoma); four thousand people died along the way.

transcendentalism Philosophy of a small group of New England writers and thinkers who advocated personal spirituality, self-reliance, social reform, and harmony with nature.

Transcontinental railroad First line across the continent from Omaha, Nebraska, to Sacramento, California, established in 1869 with the linkage of the Union Pacific and Central Pacific railroads at Promontory, Utah.

Transcontinental Treaty (Adams-Onís Treaty)(1819) Treaty between Spain and the United States that clarified the boundaries of the Louisiana Purchase and arranged the transfer of Florida to the United States in exchange for cash.

Treaty of Ghent (1814) Agreement between Great Britain and the United States that ended the War of 1812, signed on December 24, 1814.

Treaty of Guadalupe Hidalgo (1848) Treaty between United States and Mexico that ended the Mexican-American War.

Treaty of Paris Settlement between Great Britain and France that ended the French and Indian War.

Treaty of Versailles (1919) Peace treaty that ended the First World War, forcing Germany to dismantle its military, pay immense war reparations, and give up its colonies around the world.

trench warfare A form of prolonged combat between the entrenched positions of opposing armies, often with little tactical movement.

Trenton, Battle of A surprising and pivotal victory for General Washington and American forces in December 1776 that resulted in major British and Hessian losses.

triangular trade A network of trade in which exports from one region were sold to another region, which sent its exports to a third region, which exported its own goods back to the first country or colony.

Troubled Asset Relief Program (TARP) In 2008, President George W. Bush signed into law the bank bailout fund called Troubled Asset Relief Program (TARP), which required the Treasury Department to spend $700 billion to keep banks and other financial institutions from collapsing.

Harry S. Truman (1884–1972) As President Roosevelt's vice president, he succeeded him after his death near the end of the Second World War. After the war, Truman wrestled with the inflation of both prices and wages, worked with Congress to pass the National Security Act, and banned racial discrimination in the hiring of federal employees and ended racial segregation in the armed forces. In foreign affairs, he established the Truman Doctrine to contain communism, developed the Marshall Plan to rebuild Europe, and sent the U.S. military to defend South Korea after North Korea invaded.

Truman Doctrine (1947) President Truman's program of "containing" communism in Eastern Europe and providing economic and military aid to any nations at risk of Communist takeover.

trust A business arrangement that gives a person or corporation (the "trustee") the legal power to manage another person's money or another company without owning those entities outright.

Sojourner Truth (1797?–1883) She was born into slavery, but New York State freed her in 1827. She spent the 1840s and 1850s travelling across the country and speaking to audiences about her experiences as slave and asking them to support abolition and women's rights.

Harriet Tubman (1820–1913) She was born a slave, but escaped to the North. Then she returned to the South nineteen times and guided 300 slaves to freedom.

Frederick Jackson Turner An influential historian who authored the "Frontier Thesis" in 1893, arguing that the existence of an alluring frontier and the experience of persistent westward expansion informed the nation's democratic politics, unfettered economy, and rugged individualism.

Nat Turner (1800–1831) He was the leader of the only slave revolt to get past the planning stages. In August 1831, the revolt began with the slaves killing the members of Turner's master's household. Then they attacked other neighboring farmhouses and recruited more slaves until the militia crushed the revolt. At least fifty-five whites were killed during the uprising and seventeen slaves were hanged afterward.

Nat Turner's Rebellion (1831) Insurrection in rural Virginia led by black overseer Nat Turner, who killed slave owners and their families; in turn, federal troops indiscriminately killed hundreds of slaves in the process of putting down Turner and his rebels.

Tuskegee Airmen U.S. Army Air Corps unit of African American pilots whose combat success spurred military and civilian leaders to desegregate the armed forces after the war.

Mark Twain (1835–1910) Born Samuel Langhorne Clemens in Missouri, he became a popular humorous writer and lecturer and established himself as one of the great American satirists and authors. His two greatest books, *The Adventures of Tom Sawyer* and *The Adventures of Huckleberry Finn*, drew heavily on his childhood in Missouri.

William "Boss" Tweed (1823–1878) An infamous political boss in New York City, Tweed used his "city machine," the Tammany Hall ring, to rule, plunder, and sometimes improve the city's government. His political domination of New York City ended with his arrest in 1871 and conviction in 1873.

Twenty-first Amendment (1933) Repealed prohibition on the manufacture, sale, and transportation of alcoholic beverages, effectively nullifying the Eighteenth Amendment.

U-boats German military submarines (*Unterseeboot*) used during the First World War to attack enemy naval vessels as well as merchant ships of enemy and neutral nations.

Underground Railroad A secret system of routes and safe houses through which runaway slaves were led to freedom in the North.

Unitarians Members of the liberal New England Congregationalist offshoot, often well-educated and wealthy, who profess the oneness of God and the goodness of rational man.

United Farm Workers (UFW) Organization formed in 1962 to represent the interests of Mexican American migrant workers.

United Nations Security Council A major agency within the United Nations which remains in permanent session and has the responsibility of maintaining international peace and security. Originally, it consisted of five permanent members, (United States, Soviet Union, Britain, France, and the Republic of China), and six members elected to two-year terms. After 1965, the number of rotating members was increased to ten. In 1971, the Republic of China was replaced with the People's Republic of China, and the Soviet Union was replaced by the Russian Federation in 1991.

Universalists Members of a New England religious movement, often from the working class, who believed in a merciful God and universal salvation.

USA Patriot Act (2001) Wide-reaching Congressional legislation, triggered by the war on terror, which gave government agencies the right to eavesdrop on confidential conversations between prison inmates and their lawyers and permitted suspected terrorists to be tried in secret military courts.

U.S. battleship *Maine* American warship that exploded in the Cuban port of Havana on January 25, 1898; though later discovered to be the result of an accident, the destruction of the *Maine* was attributed by war-hungry Americans to Spain, contributing to the onset of the War of 1812.

utopian communities Ideal communities that offered innovative social and economic relationships to those who were interested in achieving salvation.

Valley Forge American military encampment near Philadelphia, where more than 3,500 soldiers deserted or died from cold and hunger in the winter of 1777–1778.

Cornelius Vanderbilt (1794–1877) In the 1860s, he consolidated several separate railroad companies into one vast entity, New York Central Railroad.

Bartolomeo Vanzetti (1888–1927) In 1920, he and Nicola Sacco were Italian immigrants who were arrested for stealing $16,000 and killing a paymaster and his guard. Their trial took place during a time of numerous bombings by anarchists and their judge was openly prejudicial. Many liberals and radicals believe that their conviction was based on their political ideas and ethnic origin rather than the evidence against them.

vertical integration The process by which a corporation gains control of all aspects of the resources and processes needed to produce and sell a product.

Amerigo Vespucci (1455–1512) Italian explorer who reached the New World in 1499 and was the first to suggest that South America was a new continent. Afterward, European mapmakers used a variant of his first name, America, to label the New World.

Vicksburg, Battle of (1863) A protracted battle in northern Mississippi in which Union forces under Ulysses Grant besieged the last major Confederate fortress on the Mississippi River, forcing the inhabitants into starvation and then submission.

Viet Cong Communist guerrillas in Vietnam who launched attacks on the Diem government.

Vietnamization Nixon-era policy of equipping and training South Vietnamese forces to take over the burden of combat from U.S. troops.

Francisco Pancho Villa (1877–1923) While the leader of one of the competing factions in the Mexican civil war, he provoked the United States into intervening. He hoped attacking the United States would help him build a reputation as an opponent of the United States, which would increase his popularity and discredit Mexican president Carranza.

Virginia Company A joint-stock enterprise that King James I chartered in 1606. The company was to spread Christianity in the New World as well as find ways to make a profit in it.

Virginia Plan The delegations to the Constitutional Convention were divided between two plans on how to structure the government: Virginia called for a strong central government and a two-house legislature apportioned by population.

Virginia Statute of Religious Freedom A Virginia law, drafted by Thomas Jefferson in 1777 and enacted in 1786, that guarantees freedom of, and from, religion.

virtual representation The idea that the American colonies, although they had no actual representative in Parliament, were "virtually" represented by all members of Parliament.

Voting Rights Act of 1965 Legislation ensuring that all Americans were able to vote; the law ended literacy tests and other means of restricting voting rights.

Wagner Act (1935) Legislation that guaranteed workers the right to organize unions, granted them direct bargaining power, and barred employers from interfering with union activities.

George Wallace (1919–1998) An outspoken defender of segregation. As the governor of Alabama, he once attempted to block African American students from enrolling at the University of Alabama. He ran as the presidential candidate for the American Independent party in 1968, appealing to voters who were concerned about rioting anti-war protesters, the welfare system, and the growth of the federal government.

war hawks In 1811, congressional members from the southern and western districts who clamored for a war to seize Canada and Florida were dubbed "war hawks."

War of 1812 Conflict fought in North America and at sea between Great Britain and the United States, 1812–1815, over American shipping rights and British efforts to spur Indian attacks on American settlements. Canadians and Native Americans also fought in the war.

war on terror Global crusade to root out anti-American, anti-Western Islamist terrorist cells launched by President George W. Bush as a response to the 9/11 attacks.

War Powers Act (1973) Legislation requiring the president to inform Congress within 48 hours of the deployment of U.S. troops abroad and to withdraw them after 60 days unless Congress approves their continued deployment.

War Production Board Federal agency created by President Roosevelt in 1942 that converted America's industrial output to war production.

"war relocation camps" Detention camps housing thousands of Japanese Americans from the West Coast who were forcibly interned from 1942 until the end of the Second World War.

Warren Court The U.S. Supreme Court under Chief Justice Earl Warren, 1953–1969, decided such landmark cases as *Brown v. Board of Education* (school desegregation), *Baker v. Carr* (legislative redistricting), and *Gideon v. Wainwright* and *Miranda v. Arizona* (rights of criminal defendants).

Booker T. Washington (1856–1915) He founded a leading college for African Americans in Tuskegee, Alabama, and become the foremost black educator in America by the 1890s. He believed that the African American community should establish an economic base for its advancement before striving for social equality. His critics charged that his philosophy sacrificed educational and civil rights for dubious social acceptance and economic opportunities.

George Washington (1732–1799) In 1775, the Continental Congress named him the commander in chief of the Continental Army which defeated the British in the American Revolution. He had previously served as an officer in the French and Indian War. In 1787, he was the presiding officer over the Constitutional Convention, but participated little in the debates. In 1789, the Electoral College chose Washington to be the nation's first president. Washington faced the nation's first foreign and domestic crises, maintaining the United States' neutrality in foreign affairs. After two terms in office, Washington chose to step down, and the power of the presidency was peacefully passed to John Adams.

Watergate (1972–1974) Scandal that exposed the criminality and corruption of the Nixon administration and ultimately led to President Nixon's resignation in 1974.

weapons of mass destruction (WMDs) According to the Bush Doctrine, these were in the hands of terrorist groups and rogue nations which required the United States to use preemptive military action in order to disable the threat.

Daniel Webster (1782–1852) As a representative from New Hampshire, he led the New Federalists in opposition to the moving of the second national bank from Boston to Philadelphia. Later, he served as representative and a senator for Massachusetts and emerged as a champion of a stronger national government. He also switched from opposing to supporting tariffs because New England had built up its manufactures with the understanding tariffs would protect them from foreign competitors.

Webster-Ashburton Treaty Settlement in 1842 of U.S.–Canadian border disputes in Maine, New York, Vermont, and in the Wisconsin Territory (now northern Minnesota).

Webster-Hayne debate U.S. Senate debate of January 1830 between Daniel Webster of Massachusetts and Robert Hayne of South Carolina over nullification and states' rights.

Western Front The contested frontier between the Central and Allied Powers that ran along northern France and across Belgium.

Whig party Political party founded in 1834 in opposition to the Jacksonian Democrats; Whigs supported federal funding for internal improvements, a national bank, and high tariffs on imported goods.

Whigs Another name for revolutionary Patriots.

Whiskey Rebellion (1794) Violent protest by western Pennsylvania farmers against the federal excise tax on corn whiskey, put down by a federal army.

Eli Whitney (1765–1825) He invented the cotton gin, which separated cotton from its seeds. One machine operator could separate fifty times more cotton than a worker could by hand, which led to an increase in cotton production and prices. These increases gave planters a new profitable use for slavery and a lucrative slave trade emerged from the coastal South to the Southwest.

Wilderness Road Originally an Indian path through the Cumberland Gap, it was used by over 300,000 settlers who migrated westward to Kentucky in the last quarter of the eighteenth century.

Roger Williams (1603–1683) Puritan who believed that the purity of the church required a complete separation between church and state and freedom from coercion in matters of faith. In 1636, he established the town of Providence, the first permanent settlement in Rhode Island and the first to allow religious freedom in America.

Wendell L. Willkie (1892–1944) In the 1940 presidential election, he was the Republican nominee who ran against President Roosevelt. He supported aid to the Allies and criticized the New Deal programs. Voters looked at the increasingly dangerous world situation and chose to keep President Roosevelt in office for a third term.

Wilmot Proviso (1846) Proposal by Congressman David Wilmot, a Pennsylvania Democrat, to prohibit slavery in any land acquired in the Mexican-American War.

Woodrow Wilson (1856–1924) In the 1912 presidential election, Woodrow Wilson ran under the slogan of New Freedom, which promised to improve of the banking system, lower tariffs, and break up monopolies. At the beginning of the First World War, Wilson kept America neutral, but provided the Allies with credit for purchases of supplies; however, the sinking of U.S. merchant ships and the Zimmermann telegram caused him to ask Congress to declare war on Germany. Wilson supported the entry of America into the League of Nations and the ratification of the Treaty of Versailles, but Congress would not approve the entry or ratification.

John Winthrop Puritan leader and Governor of the Massachusetts Bay Colony who resolved to use the colony as a refuge for persecuted Puritans and as an instrument of building a "wilderness Zion" in America.

woman suffrage Movement to give women the right to vote through a constitutional amendment, spearheaded by Susan B. Anthony and Elizabeth Cady Stanton's National Woman Suffrage Association.

Women Accepted for Voluntary Emergency Services (WAVES) During the Second World War, the increased demand for labor shook up old prejudices about gender roles in workplace and in the military. Nearly 200,000 women served in the Women's Army Corps or its naval equivalent, Women Accepted for Volunteer Emergency Service (WAVES).

Women's Army Corps (WAC) Women's branch of the United States Army; by the end of the Second World War nearly 150,000 women had served in the WAC.

women's movement Wave of activism sparked by Betty Friedan's *The Feminine Mystique* (1963); it argued for equal rights for women and fought against the cult of domesticity of the 1950s that limited women's roles to the home as wife, mother, and housewife.

women's work The traditional term referring to routine tasks in the house, garden, and fields performed by women. The sphere of women's occupations expanded in the colonies to include medicine, shopkeeping, upholstering, and the operation of inns and taverns.

Woodstock In 1969, roughly half a million young people converged on a farm near Bethel, New York, for a three-day music festival that was an expression of the flower children's free spirit.

Works Progress Administration (WPA) (1935) Government agency established to manage several federal job programs created under the New Deal; it became the largest employer in the nation.

Wounded Knee, Battle of Last incident of the Indians Wars took place in 1890 in the Dakota Territory, where the U.S. Cavalry killed over 200 Sioux men, women, and children who were in the process of surrender.

XYZ affair French foreign minister Tallyrand's three anonymous agents demanded payments to stop French plundering of American ships in 1797; refusal to pay the bribe led to two years of sea war with France (1798–1800).

Yalta Conference (1945) Meeting of the "Big Three" Allied leaders, Franklin D. Roosevelt, Winston Churchill, and Joseph Stalin, to discuss how to divide control of postwar Germany and eastern Europe

yellow journalism A type of news reporting, epitomized in the 1890s by the newspaper empires of William Randolph Hearst and Joseph Pulitzer, that intentionally manipulates public opinion through sensational headlines, illustrations, and articles about both real and invented events.

yeomen Small landowners (the majority of white families in the South) who farmed their own land and usually did not own slaves.

Yorktown, Battle of Last major battle of the Revolutionary War; General Cornwallis along with over 7,000 British troops surrendered to George Washington at Yorktown, Virginia, on October 17, 1781.

surrender at Yorktown Last battle of the Revolutionary War; General Lord Charles Cornwallis, along with over 7,000 British troops, surrendered at Yorktown, Virginia, on October 17, 1781.

Brigham Young (1801–1877) Following Joseph Smith's death, he became the leader of the Mormons and promised Illinois officials that the Mormons would leave the state. In 1846, he led the Mormons to Utah and settled near the Salt Lake. After the United States gained Utah as part of the Treaty of Guadalupe Hidalgo, he became the governor of the territory and kept the Mormons virtually independent of federal authority.

youth culture The youth of the 1950s had more money and free time than any previous generation and this allowed a distinct youth culture to emerge. A market emerged for products and activities that were specifically for young people such as transistor radios, rock records, *Seventeen* magazine, and Pat Boone movies.

Zimmermann telegram Message sent by a German official to the Mexican government in 1917 urging an invasion of the United States; the telegram was intercepted by British intelligence agents and angered Americans, many of whom called for war against Germany.

APPENDIX

The Declaration of Independence (1776)

When in the Course of human events, it becomes necessary for one people to dissolve the political bands which have connected them with another, and to assume among the powers of the earth, the separate and equal station to which the Laws of Nature and of Nature's God entitle them, a decent respect to the opinions of mankind requires that they should declare the causes which impel them to the separation.

We hold these truths to be self-evident, that all men are created equal, that they are endowed by their Creator with certain unalienable Rights, that among these are Life, Liberty and the pursuit of Happiness.—That to secure these rights, Governments are instituted among Men, deriving their just powers from the consent of the governed,—That whenever any Form of Government becomes destructive of these ends, it is the Right of the People to alter or to abolish it, and to institute new Government, laying its foundation on such principles and organizing its powers in such form, as to them shall seem most likely to effect their Safety and Happiness. Prudence, indeed, will dictate that Governments long established should not be changed for light and transient causes; and accordingly all experience hath shewn, that mankind are more disposed to suffer, while evils are sufferable, than to right themselves by abolishing the forms to which they are accustomed. But when a long train of abuses and usurpations, pursuing invariably the same Object evinces a design to reduce them under absolute Despotism, it is their right, it is their duty, to throw off such Government, and to provide new Guards for their future security.—Such has been the patient sufferance of these Colonies; and such is now the necessity which constrains them to alter their former

Systems of Government. The history of the present King of Great Britain is a history of repeated injuries and usurpations, all having in direct object the establishment of an absolute Tyranny over these States. To prove this, let Facts be submitted to a candid world.

He has refused his Assent to Laws, the most wholesome and necessary for the public good.

He has forbidden his Governors to pass Laws of immediate and pressing importance, unless suspended in their operation till his Assent should be obtained; and when so suspended, he has utterly neglected to attend to them.

He has refused to pass other Laws for the accommodation of large districts of people, unless those people would relinquish the right of Representation in the Legislature, a right inestimable to them and formidable to tyrants only.

He has called together legislative bodies at places unusual, uncomfortable, and distant from the depository of their public Records, for the sole purpose of fatiguing them into compliance with his measures.

He has dissolved Representative Houses repeatedly, for opposing with manly firmness his invasions on the rights of the people.

He has refused for a long time, after such dissolutions, to cause others to be elected; whereby the Legislative powers, incapable of Annihilation, have returned to the People at large for their exercise; the State remaining in the mean time exposed to all the dangers of invasion from without, and convulsions within.

He has endeavoured to prevent the population of these States; for that purpose obstructing the Laws for Naturalization of Foreigners; refusing to pass others to encourage their migrations hither, and raising the conditions of new Appropriations of Lands.

He has obstructed the Administration of Justice, by refusing his Assent to Laws for establishing Judiciary powers.

He has made Judges dependent on his Will alone, for the tenure of their offices, and the amount and payment of their salaries.

He has erected a multitude of New Offices, and sent hither swarms of Officers to harrass our people, and eat out their substance.

He has kept among us, in times of peace, Standing Armies without the Consent of our legislatures.

He has affected to render the Military independent of and superior to the Civil power.

He has combined with others to subject us to a jurisdiction foreign to our constitution, and unacknowledged by our laws; giving his Assent to their Acts of pretended Legislation:

For Quartering large bodies of armed troops among us:

For protecting them, by a mock Trial, from punishment for any Murders which they should commit on the Inhabitants of these States:

For cutting off our Trade with all parts of the world:

For imposing Taxes on us without our Consent:

For depriving us in many cases, of the benefits of Trial by Jury:

For transporting us beyond Seas to be tried for pretended offences

For abolishing the free System of English Laws in a neighbouring Province, establishing therein an Arbitrary government, and enlarging its Boundaries so as to render it at once an example and fit instrument for introducing the same absolute rule into these Colonies:

For taking away our Charters, abolishing our most valuable Laws, and altering fundamentally the Forms of our Governments:

For suspending our own Legislatures, and declaring themselves invested with power to legislate for us in all cases whatsoever.

He has abdicated Government here, by declaring us out of his Protection and waging War against us.

He has plundered our seas, ravaged our Coasts, burnt our towns, and destroyed the lives of our people.

He is at this time transporting large Armies of foreign Mercenaries to compleat the works of death, desolation and tyranny, already begun with circumstances of Cruelty & perfidy scarcely paralleled in the most barbarous ages, and totally unworthy the Head of a civilized nation.

He has constrained our fellow Citizens taken Captive on the high Seas to bear Arms against their Country, to become the executioners of their friends and Brethren, or to fall themselves by their Hands.

He has excited domestic insurrections amongst us, and has endeavoured to bring on the inhabitants of our frontiers, the merciless Indian Savages, whose known rule of warfare, is an undistinguished destruction of all ages, sexes and conditions.

In every stage of these Oppressions We have Petitioned for Redress in the most humble terms: Our repeated Petitions have been answered only by repeated injury. A Prince whose character is thus marked by every act which may define a Tyrant, is unfit to be the ruler of a free people.

Nor have We been wanting in attentions to our Brittish brethren. We have warned them from time to time of attempts by their legislature to extend an unwarrantable jurisdiction over us. We have reminded them of the circumstances of our emigration and settlement here. We have appealed to their native justice and magnanimity, and we have conjured them by the ties of our common kindred to disavow these usurpations, which, would inevitably interrupt our connections and correspondence. They too have been deaf to the voice of justice and of consanguinity. We must, therefore, acquiesce in the necessity, which denounces our Separation, and hold them, as we hold the rest of mankind, Enemies in War, in Peace Friends.

We, therefore, the Representatives of the united States of America, in General Congress, Assembled, appealing to the Supreme Judge of the world for the rectitude of our intentions, do, in the Name, and by Authority of the good People of these Colonies, solemnly publish and declare, That these United Colonies are, and of Right ought to be Free and Independent States; that they are Absolved from all Allegiance to the British Crown, and that all political connection between them and the State of Great Britain, is and ought to be totally dissolved; and that as Free and Independent States, they have full Power to levy War, conclude Peace, contract Alliances, establish Commerce, and to do all other Acts and Things which Independent States may of right do. And for the support of this Declaration, with a firm reliance on the protection of divine Providence, we mutually pledge to each other our Lives, our Fortunes and our sacred Honor.

Georgia
Button Gwinnett
Lyman Hall
George Walton

North Carolina
William Hooper
Joseph Hewes
John Penn

South Carolina
Edward Rutledge
Thomas Heyward, Jr.
Thomas Lynch, Jr.
Arthur Middleton

Massachusetts
John Hancock

Maryland
Samuel Chase
William Paca
Thomas Stone
Charles Carroll of
   Carrollton

Virginia
George Wythe
Richard Henry Lee
Thomas Jefferson
Benjamin Harrison
Thomas Nelson, Jr.
Francis Lightfoot Lee
Carter Braxton

Pennsylvania
Robert Morris
Benjamin Rush
Benjamin Franklin
John Morton
George Clymer
James Smith
George Taylor
James Wilson
George Ross

Delaware
Caesar Rodney
George Read
Thomas McKean

New York
William Floyd
Philip Livingston
Francis Lewis
Lewis Morris

New Jersey
Richard Stockton
John Witherspoon
Francis Hopkinson
John Hart
Abraham Clark

New Hampshire
Josiah Bartlett
William Whipple

Massachusetts
Samuel Adams
John Adams
Robert Treat Paine
Elbridge Gerry

Rhode Island
Stephen Hopkins
William Ellery

Connecticut
Roger Sherman
Samuel Huntington
William Williams
Oliver Wolcott

New Hampshire
Matthew Thornton

ARTICLES OF CONFEDERATION (1778)

TO ALL TO WHOM these Presents shall come, we the undersigned Delegates of the States affixed to our Names send greeting.

Whereas the Delegates of the United States of America in Congress assembled did on the fifteenth day of November in the Year of our Lord One Thousand Seven Hundred and Seventy-seven, and in the Second Year of the Independence of America agree to certain articles of Confederation and perpetual Union between the States of Newhampshire, Massachusetts-bay, Rhodeisland and Providence Plantations, Connecticut, New York, New Jersey, Pennsylvania, Delaware, Maryland, Virginia, North-Carolina, South-Carolina and Georgia in the Words following, viz.

Articles of Confederation and perpetual Union between the States of Newhampshire, Massachusetts-bay, Rhodeisland and Providence Plantations, Connecticut, New-York, New-Jersey, Pennsylvania, Delaware, Maryland, Virginia, North-Carolina, South-Carolina and Georgia.

ARTICLE I. The stile of this confederacy shall be "The United States of America."

ARTICLE II. Each State retains its sovereignty, freedom and independence, and every power, jurisdiction and right, which is not by this confederation expressly delegated to the United States, in Congress assembled.

ARTICLE III. The said States hereby severally enter into a firm league of friendship with each other, for their common defence, the security of their liberties, and their mutual and general welfare, binding themselves to assist each other, against all force offered to, or attacks made upon them, or any of them, on account of religion, sovereignty, trade or any other pretence whatever.

ARTICLE IV. The better to secure and perpetuate mutual friendship and intercourse among the people of the different States in this Union, the free inhabitants of each of these States, paupers, vagabonds and fugitives from justice excepted, shall be entitled to all privileges and immunities of free citizens in the several States; and the people of each State shall have free ingress and regress to and from any other State, and shall enjoy therein all the privileges of trade and commerce, subject to the same duties, impositions and restrictions as the inhabitants thereof respectively, provided that such restrictions shall not extend so far as to prevent the removal of property imported into any State, to any other State of which the owner is an inhabitant; provided also that no imposition, duties or restriction shall be laid by any State, on the property of the United States, or either of them.

If any person guilty of, or charged with treason, felony, or other high misdemeanor in any State, shall flee from justice, and be found in any of the United States, he shall upon demand of the Governor or Executive power, of the State from which he fled, be delivered up and removed to the State having jurisdiction of his offence.

Full faith and credit shall be given in each of these States to the records, acts and judicial proceedings of the courts and magistrates of every other State.

ARTICLE V. For the more convenient management of the general interests of the United States, delegates shall be annually appointed in such manner as the legislature of each State shall direct, to meet in Congress on the first Monday in November, in every year, with a power reserved to each State, to recall its delegates, or any of them, at any time within the year, and to send others in their stead, for the remainder of the year.

No State shall be represented in Congress by less than two, nor by more than seven members; and no person shall be capable of being a delegate for more than three years in any term of six years; nor shall any person, being a delegate, be capable of holding any office under the United States, for which he, or another for his benefit receives any salary, fees or emolument of any kind.

Each State shall maintain its own delegates in a meeting of the States, and while they act as members of the committee of the States.

In determining questions in the United States, in Congress assembled, each State shall have one vote.

Freedom of speech and debate in Congress shall not be impeached or questioned in any court, or place out of Congress, and the members of Congress shall be protected in their persons from arrests and imprisonments, during the time of their going to and from, and attendance on Congress, except for treason, felony, or breach of the peace.

ARTICLE VI. No State without the consent of the United States in Congress assembled, shall send any embassy to, or receive any embassy from, or enter into any conference, agreement, alliance or treaty with any king, prince or state; nor shall any person holding any office of profit or trust under the United States, or any of them, accept of any present, emolument, office or title of any kind whatever from any king, prince or foreign state; nor shall the United States in Congress assembled, or any of them, grant any title of nobility.

No two or more States shall enter into any treaty, confederation or alliance whatever between them, without the consent of the United States in Congress assembled, specifying accurately the purposes for which the same is to be entered into, and how long it shall continue.

No State shall lay any imposts or duties, which may interfere with any stipulations in treaties, entered into by the United States in Congress assembled, with any king, prince or state, in pursuance of any treaties already proposed by Congress, to the courts of France and Spain.

No vessels of war shall be kept up in time of peace by any State, except such number only, as shall be deemed necessary by the United States in Congress assembled, for the defence of such State, or its trade; nor shall any body of forces be kept up by any State, in time of peace, except such number only, as in the judgment of the United States, in Congress assembled, shall be deemed requisite to garrison the forts necessary for the defence of such State; but every State shall always keep up a well regulated and disciplined militia, sufficiently armed and accoutred, and shall provide and constantly have ready for use, in public stores, a due number of field pieces and tents, and a proper quantity of arms, ammunition and camp equipage.

No State shall engage in any war without the consent of the United States in Congress assembled, unless such State be actually invaded by enemies, or shall have received certain advice of a resolution being formed by some nation of Indians to invade such State, and the danger is so imminent as not to admit of a delay, till the United States in Congress assembled can be consulted: nor shall any State grant commissions to any ships or vessels of war, nor letters of marque or reprisal, except it be after a declaration of war by the United States in Congress assembled, and then only against the kingdom or state and the subjects thereof, against which war has been so declared, and under such regulations as shall be established by the United States in Congress assembled, unless such State be infested by pirates, in which case vessels of war may be fitted out for that occasion, and kept so long as the danger shall continue, or until the United States in Congress assembled shall determine otherwise.

ARTICLE VII. When land-forces are raised by any State of the common defence, all officers of or under the rank of colonel, shall be appointed by the Legislature of each State respectively by whom such forces shall be raised, or in such manner as such State shall direct, and all vacancies shall be filled up by the State which first made the appointment.

ARTICLE VIII. All charges of war, and all other expenses that shall be incurred for the common defence or general welfare, and allowed by the United States in Congress assembled, shall be defrayed out of a common treasury, which shall be supplied by the several States, in proportion to the value of all land within each State, granted to or surveyed for any person, as such land and the buildings and improvements thereon shall be estimated according to such mode as the United States in Congress assembled, shall from time to time direct and appoint.

The taxes for paying that proportion shall be laid and levied by the authority and direction of the Legislatures of the several States within the time agreed upon by the United States in Congress assembled.

ARTICLE IX. The United States in Congress assembled, shall have the sole and exclusive right and power of determining on peace and war, except in the cases mentioned in the sixth article—of sending and receiving ambassadors— entering into treaties and alliances, provided that no treaty of commerce shall be made whereby the legislative power of the respective States shall be restrained from imposing such imposts and duties on foreigners, as their own people are subjected to, or from prohibiting the exportation or importation of and species of goods or commodities whatsoever—of establishing rules for deciding in all cases, what captures on land or water shall be legal, and in what manner prizes taken by land or naval forces in the service of the United States shall be divided or appropriated—of granting letters of marque and reprisal in times of peace—appointing courts for the trial of piracies and felonies committed on the high seas and establishing courts for receiving and determining finally appeals in all cases of captures, provided that no member of Congress shall be appointed a judge of any of the said courts.

The United States in Congress assembled shall also be the last resort on appeal in all disputes and differences now subsisting or that hereafter may arise between two or more States concerning boundary, jurisdiction or any other cause whatever; which authority shall always be exercised in the manner following. Whenever the legislative or executive authority or lawful agent of any State in controversy with another shall present a petition to Congress, stating the matter in question and praying for a hearing, notice thereof shall be given by order of Congress to the legislative or executive authority of the other State in controversy, and a day assigned for the appearance of the parties by their lawful agents, who shall then be directed to appoint by joint consent, commissioners or judges to constitute a court for hearing and determining the matter in question: but if they cannot agree, Congress shall name three persons out of each of the United States, and from the list of such persons each party shall alternately strike out one, the petitioners beginning, until the number shall be reduced to thirteen; and from that number not less than seven, nor more than nine names as Congress shall direct, shall in the presence of Congress be drawn out by lot, and the persons whose names shall be so drawn or any five of them, shall be commissioners or judges, to hear and finally determine the controversy, so always as a major part of the judges who shall hear the cause shall agree in the determination: and if either party shall neglect to attend at the day appointed, without reasons, which Congress shall judge sufficient, or being present shall refuse to strike, the Congress shall proceed to nominate three persons out of each State, and the Secretary of Congress shall strike in behalf of such party absent or refusing; and the judgment and sentence of the court to be appointed, in the manner before prescribed, shall be final and conclusive; and if any of the parties shall refuse to submit to the authority of such court, or to appear or defend their claim or cause, the court shall nevertheless proceed to pronounce sentence, or judgment, which shall in like manner be final and decisive, the judgment or sentence and other proceedings being in either case transmitted to Congress, and lodged among the acts of Congress for the security of the parties concerned: provided that every commissioner, before he sits in judgment, shall take an oath to be administered by one of the judges of the supreme or superior court of the State where the case shall be tried, "well and truly to hear and determine the matter in question, according to the best of his judgment, without favour, affection or hope of reward:" provided also that no State shall be deprived of territory for the benefit of the United States.

All controversies concerning the private right of soil claimed under different grants of two or more States, whose jurisdiction as they may respect such lands, and the states which passed such grants are adjusted, the said grants or either of them being at the same time claimed to have originated antecedent to such settlement of jurisdiction, shall on the petition of either party to the Congress of the United States, be finally determined as near as may be in the same manner as is before prescribed for deciding disputes respecting territorial jurisdiction between different States.

The United States in Congress assembled shall also have the sole and exclusive right and power of regulating the alloy and value of coin struck by their own authority, or by that of the respective States—fixing the standard of weights and measures throughout the United States—regulating the trade and managing all affairs with the Indians, not members of any of the States, provided that the legislative right of any State within its own limits be not infringed or violated—establishing and regulating post-offices from one State to another, throughout all of the United States, and exacting such postage on the papers passing thro' the same as may be requisite to defray the expenses of the said office—appointing all officers of the land forces, in the service of the United States, excepting regimental officers—appointing all the officers of the naval forces, and commissioning all officers whatever in the service of the United States—making rules for the government and regulation of the said land and naval forces, and directing their operations.

The United States in Congress assembled shall have authority to appoint a committee, to sit in the recess of Congress, to be denominated "a Committee of the States," and to consist of one delegate from each State; and to appoint such other committees and civil officers as may be necessary for managing the general affairs of the United States under their direction—to appoint one of their number to preside, provided that no person be allowed to serve in the office of president more than one year in any term of three years; to ascertain the necessary sums of money to be raised for the service of the United States, and to appropriate and apply the same for defraying the public expenses—to borrow money, or emit bills on the credit of the United States, transmitting every half year to the respective States an account of the sums of money so borrowed or emitted,—to build and equip a navy—to agree upon the number of land forces, and to make requisitions from each State for its quota, in proportion to the number of white inhabitants in such State; which requisition shall be binding, and thereupon the Legislature of each State shall appoint the regimental officers, raise the men and cloath, arm and equip them in a soldier like manner, at the expense of the United States; and the officers and men so cloathed, armed and equipped shall march to the place appointed, and within the time agreed on by the United States in Congress assembled: but if the United States in Congress assembled shall, on consideration of circumstances judge proper that any State should not raise men, or should raise a smaller number of men than the quota thereof, such extra number shall be raised, officered, cloathed, armed and equipped in the same manner as the quota of such State, unless the legislature of such State shall judge that such extra number cannot be safely spared out of the same, in which case they shall raise officer, cloath, arm and equip as many of such extra number as they judge can be safely spared. And the officers and men so cloathed, armed and equipped, shall march to the place appointed, and within the time agreed on by the United States in Congress assembled.

The United States in Congress assembled shall never engage in a war, nor grant letters of marque and reprisal in time of peace, nor enter into any treaties or alliances, nor coin money, nor regulate the value thereof, nor ascertain the sums and expenses necessary for the defence and welfare of the United States, or any of them, nor emit bills, nor borrow money on the credit of the

United States, nor appropriate money, nor agree upon the number of vessels to be built or purchased, or the number of land or sea forces to be raised, nor appoint a commander in chief of the army or navy, unless nine States assent to the same: nor shall a question on any other point, except for adjourning from day to day be determined, unless by the votes of a majority of the United States in Congress assembled.

The Congress of the United States shall have power to adjourn to any time within the year, and to any place within the United States, so that no period of adjournment be for a longer duration than the space of six months, and shall publish the journal of their proceedings monthly, except such parts thereof relating to treaties, alliances or military operations, as in their judgment require secrecy; and the yeas and nays of the delegates of each State on any question shall be entered on the Journal, when it is desired by any delegate; and the delegates of a State, or any of them, at his or their request shall be furnished with a transcript of the said journal, except such parts as are above excepted, to lay before the Legislatures of the several States.

ARTICLE X. The committee of the States, or any nine of them, shall be authorized to execute, in the recess of Congress, such of the powers of Congress as the United States in Congress assembled, by the consent of nine States, shall from time to time think expedient to vest them with; provided that no power be delegated to the said committee, for the exercise of which, by the articles of confederation, the voice of nine States in the Congress of the United States assembled is requisite.

ARTICLE XI. Canada acceding to this confederation, and joining in the measures of the United States, shall be admitted into, and entitled to all the advantages of this Union: but no other colony shall be admitted into the same, unless such admission be agreed to by nine States.

ARTICLE XII. All bills of credit emitted, monies borrowed and debts contracted by, or under the authority of Congress, before the assembling of the United States, in pursuance of the present confederation, shall be deemed and considered as a charge against the United States, for payment and satisfaction whereof the said United States, and the public faith are hereby solemnly pledged.

ARTICLE XIII. Every State shall abide by the determinations of the United States in Congress assembled, on all questions which by this confederation are submitted to them. And the articles of this confederation shall be inviolably observed by every State, and the Union shall be perpetual; nor shall any alteration at any time hereafter be made in any of them; unless such alteration be agreed to in a Congress of the United States, and be afterwards confirmed by the Legislatures of every State.

And whereas it has pleased the Great Governor of the world to incline the hearts of the Legislatures we respectively represent in Congress, to approve of, and to authorize us to ratify the said articles of confederation and perpetual union. Know ye that we the undersigned delegates, by virtue of the power and authority to us given for that purpose, do by these presents, in the name and in behalf of our respective constituents, fully and entirely ratify and confirm each and every of the said articles of confederation and perpetual union, and all and singular the matters and things therein contained: and we do further solemnly plight and engage the faith of our respective constituents, that they shall abide by the determinations of the United States in Congress assembled, on all questions, which by the said confederation are submitted to them. And that the articles thereof shall be inviolably observed by the States we respectively represent, and that the Union shall be perpetual.

In witness thereof we have hereunto set our hands in Congress. Done at Philadelphia in the State of Pennsylvania the ninth day of July in the year of our Lord one thousand seven hundred and seventy-eight, and in the third year of the independence of America.

The Constitution of the United States (1787)

We the People of the United States, in Order to form a more perfect Union, establish Justice, insure domestic Tranquility, provide for the common defence, promote the general Welfare, and secure the Blessings of Liberty to ourselves and our Posterity, do ordain and establish this Constitution for the United States of America.

Article. I.

SECTION. 1. All legislative Powers herein granted shall be vested in a Congress of the United States, which shall consist of a Senate and House of Representatives.

SECTION. 2. The House of Representatives shall be composed of Members chosen every second Year by the People of the several States, and the Electors in each State shall have the Qualifications requisite for Electors of the most numerous Branch of the State Legislature.

No Person shall be a Representative who shall not have attained to the Age of twenty five Years, and been seven Years a Citizen of the United States, and who shall not, when elected, be an Inhabitant of that State in which he shall be chosen.

Representatives and direct Taxes shall be apportioned among the several States which may be included within this Union, according to their respective Numbers, which shall be determined by adding to the whole Number of free Persons, including those bound to Service for a Term of Years, and excluding Indians not taxed, three fifths of all other Persons. The actual Enumeration shall be made within three Years after the first Meeting of the Congress of the United States, and within every subsequent Term of ten Years, in such Manner as they shall by Law direct. The Number of Representatives shall not exceed one for every thirty Thousand, but each State shall have at Least one Representative; and until such enumeration shall be made, the State of New Hampshire shall be entitled to chuse three, Massachusetts eight, Rhode-Island and Providence Plantations one, Connecticut five, New-York six, New Jersey four, Pennsylvania eight, Delaware one, Maryland six, Virginia ten, North Carolina five, South Carolina five, and Georgia three.

When vacancies happen in the Representation from any State, the Executive Authority thereof shall issue Writs of Election to fill such Vacancies.

The House of Representatives shall chuse their Speaker and other Officers; and shall have the sole Power of Impeachment.

SECTION. 3. The Senate of the United States shall be composed of two Senators from each State, chosen by the Legislature thereof for six Years; and each Senator shall have one Vote.

Immediately after they shall be assembled in Consequence of the first Election, they shall be divided as equally as may be into three Classes. The Seats of the Senators of the first Class shall be vacated at the Expiration of the second Year, of the second Class at the Expiration of the fourth Year, and of the third Class at the Expiration of the sixth Year, so that one third may be chosen every second Year; and if Vacancies happen by Resignation, or otherwise, during the Recess of the Legislature of any State, the Executive thereof may make temporary Appointments until the next Meeting of the Legislature, which shall then fill such Vacancies.

No Person shall be a Senator who shall not have attained to the Age of thirty Years, and been nine Years a Citizen of the United States, and who shall not, when elected, be an Inhabitant of that State for which he shall be chosen.

The Vice President of the United States shall be President of the Senate, but shall have no Vote, unless they be equally divided.

The Senate shall chuse their other Officers, and also a President pro tempore, in the Absence of the Vice President, or when he shall exercise the Office of President of the United States.

The Senate shall have the sole Power to try all Impeachments. When sitting for that Purpose, they shall be on Oath or Affirmation. When the President of the United States is tried, the Chief Justice shall preside: And no Person shall be convicted without the Concurrence of two thirds of the Members present.

Judgment in Cases of Impeachment shall not extend further than to removal from Office, and disqualification to hold and enjoy any Office of honor, Trust or Profit under the United States: but the Party convicted shall nevertheless be liable and subject to Indictment, Trial, Judgment and Punishment, according to Law.

SECTION. 4. The Times, Places and Manner of holding Elections for Senators and Representatives, shall be prescribed in each State by the Legislature thereof; but the Congress may at any time by Law make or alter such Regulations, except as to the Places of chusing Senators.

The Congress shall assemble at least once in every Year, and such Meeting shall be on the first Monday in December, unless they shall by Law appoint a different Day.

SECTION. 5. Each House shall be the Judge of the Elections, Returns and Qualifications of its own Members, and a Majority of each shall constitute a Quorum to do Business; but a smaller Number may adjourn from day to day, and may be authorized to compel the Attendance of absent Members, in such Manner, and under such Penalties as each House may provide.

Each House may determine the Rules of its Proceedings, punish its Members for disorderly Behaviour, and, with the Concurrence of two thirds, expel a Member.

Each House shall keep a Journal of its Proceedings, and from time to time publish the same, excepting such Parts as may in their Judgment require Secrecy; and the Yeas and Nays of the Members of either House on any question shall, at the Desire of one fifth of those Present, be entered on the Journal.

Neither House, during the Session of Congress, shall, without the Consent of the other, adjourn for more than three days, nor to any other Place than that in which the two Houses shall be sitting.

SECTION. 6. The Senators and Representatives shall receive a Compensation for their Services, to be ascertained by Law, and paid out of the Treasury of the United States. They shall in all Cases, except Treason, Felony and Breach of the Peace, be privileged from Arrest during their Attendance at the Session of their respective Houses, and in going to and returning from the same; and for any Speech or Debate in either House, they shall not be questioned in any other Place.

No Senator or Representative shall, during the Time for which he was elected, be appointed to any civil Office under the Authority of the United States, which shall have been created, or the Emoluments whereof shall have been encreased during such time; and no Person holding any Office under the United States, shall be a Member of either House during his Continuance in Office.

SECTION. 7. All Bills for raising Revenue shall originate in the House of Representatives; but the Senate may propose or concur with Amendments as on other Bills.

Every Bill which shall have passed the House of Representatives and the Senate, shall, before it become a Law, be presented to the President of the United States: If he approve he shall sign it, but if not he shall return it, with his Objections to that House in which it shall have originated, who shall enter the Objections at large on their Journal, and proceed to reconsider it. If after such Reconsideration two thirds of that House shall agree to pass the Bill, it shall be sent, together with the Objections, to the other House, by which it shall likewise be reconsidered, and if approved by two thirds of that House, it shall become a Law. But in all such Cases the Votes of both Houses shall be determined by yeas and Nays, and the Names of the Persons voting for and against the Bill shall be entered on the Journal of each House respectively. If any Bill shall not be returned by the President within ten Days (Sundays excepted) after it shall have been presented to him, the Same shall be a Law, in like Manner as if he had signed it, unless the Congress by their Adjournment prevent its Return, in which Case it shall not be a Law.

Every Order, Resolution, or Vote to which the Concurrence of the Senate and House of Representatives may be necessary (except on a question of Adjournment) shall be presented to the President of the United States; and before the Same shall take Effect, shall be approved by him, or being disapproved by him, shall be repassed by two thirds of the Senate and House of Representatives, according to the Rules and Limitations prescribed in the Case of a Bill.

SECTION. 8. The Congress shall have Power To lay and collect Taxes, Duties, Imposts and Excises, to pay the Debts and provide for the common Defence and general Welfare of the United States; but all Duties, Imposts and Excises shall be uniform throughout the United States;

To borrow Money on the credit of the United States;

To regulate Commerce with foreign Nations, and among the several States, and with the Indian Tribes;

To establish an uniform Rule of Naturalization, and uniform Laws on the subject of Bankruptcies throughout the United States;

To coin Money, regulate the Value thereof, and of foreign Coin, and fix the Standard of Weights and Measures;

To provide for the Punishment of counterfeiting the Securities and current Coin of the United States;

To establish Post Offices and post Roads;

To promote the Progress of Science and useful Arts, by securing for limited Times to Authors and Inventors the exclusive Right to their respective Writings and Discoveries;

To constitute Tribunals inferior to the supreme Court;

To define and punish Piracies and Felonies committed on the high Seas, and Offences against the Law of Nations;

To declare War, grant Letters of Marque and Reprisal, and make Rules concerning Captures on Land and Water;

To raise and support Armies, but no Appropriation of Money to that Use shall be for a longer Term than two Years;

To provide and maintain a Navy;

To make Rules for the Government and Regulation of the land and naval Forces;

To provide for calling forth the Militia to execute the Laws of the Union, suppress Insurrections and repel Invasions;

To provide for organizing, arming, and disciplining, the Militia, and for governing such Part of them as may be employed in the Service of the United States, reserving to the States respectively, the Appointment of the Officers, and the Authority of training the Militia according to the discipline prescribed by Congress;

To exercise exclusive Legislation in all Cases whatsoever, over such District (not exceeding ten Miles square) as may, by Cession of particular States, and the Acceptance of Congress, become the Seat of the Government of the United States, and to exercise like Authority over all Places purchased by the Consent of the Legislature of the State in which the Same shall be, for the Erection of Forts, Magazines, Arsenals, dock-Yards, and other needful Buildings;—And

To make all Laws which shall be necessary and proper for carrying into Execution the foregoing Powers, and all other Powers vested by this Constitution in the Government of the United States, or in any Department or Officer thereof.

SECTION. 9. The Migration or Importation of such Persons as any of the States now existing shall think proper to admit, shall not be prohibited by the Congress prior to the Year one thousand eight hundred and eight, but a Tax or duty may be imposed on such Importation, not exceeding ten dollars for each Person.

The Privilege of the Writ of Habeas Corpus shall not be suspended, unless when in Cases of Rebellion or Invasion the public Safety may require it.

No Bill of Attainder or ex post facto Law shall be passed.

No Capitation, or other direct, Tax shall be laid, unless in Proportion to the Census or enumeration herein before directed to be taken.

No Tax or Duty shall be laid on Articles exported from any State.

No Preference shall be given by any Regulation of Commerce or Revenue to the Ports of one State over those of another; nor shall Vessels bound to, or from, one State, be obliged to enter, clear, or pay Duties in another.

No Money shall be drawn from the Treasury, but in Consequence of Appropriations made by Law; and a regular Statement and Account of the Receipts and Expenditures of all public Money shall be published from time to time.

No Title of Nobility shall be granted by the United States: And no Person holding any Office of Profit or Trust under them, shall, without the Consent of the Congress, accept of any present, Emolument, Office, or Title, of any kind whatever, from any King, Prince, or foreign State.

SECTION. 10. No State shall enter into any Treaty, Alliance, or Confederation; grant Letters of Marque and Reprisal; coin Money; emit Bills of Credit; make any Thing but gold and silver Coin a Tender in Payment of Debts; pass any Bill of Attainder, ex post facto Law, or Law impairing the Obligation of Contracts, or grant any Title of Nobility.

No State shall, without the Consent of the Congress, lay any Imposts or Duties on Imports or Exports, except what may be absolutely necessary for executing it's inspection Laws: and the net Produce of all Duties and Imposts, laid by any State on Imports or Exports, shall be for the Use of the Treasury of the United States; and all such Laws shall be subject to the Revision and Controul of the Congress.

No State shall, without the Consent of Congress, lay any Duty of Tonnage, keep Troops, or Ships of War in time of Peace, enter into any Agreement or Compact with another State, or with a foreign Power, or engage in War, unless actually invaded, or in such imminent Danger as will not admit of delay.

ARTICLE. II.

SECTION. 1. The executive Power shall be vested in a President of the United States of America. He shall hold his Office during the Term of four Years, and, together with the Vice President, chosen for the same Term, be elected, as follows:

Each State shall appoint, in such Manner as the Legislature thereof may direct, a Number of Electors, equal to the whole Number of Senators and Representatives to which the State may be entitled in the Congress: but no Senator or Representative, or Person holding an Office of Trust or Profit under the United States, shall be appointed an Elector.

The Electors shall meet in their respective States, and vote by Ballot for two Persons, of whom one at least shall not be an Inhabitant of the same State with themselves. And they shall make a List of all the Persons voted for, and of the Number of Votes for each; which List they shall sign and certify, and transmit sealed to the Seat of the Government of the United States, directed to the President of the Senate. The President of the Senate shall, in the Presence of the Senate and House of Representatives, open all the Certificates, and the Votes shall then be counted. The Person having the greatest Number of Votes shall be the President, if such Number be a Majority of the whole Number of Electors appointed; and if there be more than one who have such Majority, and have an equal Number of Votes, then the House of Representatives shall immediately chuse by Ballot one of them for President; and if no Person have a Majority, then from the five highest on the List the said House shall in like Manner chuse the President. But in chusing the President, the Votes shall be taken by States, the Representation from each State having one Vote; A quorum for this purpose shall consist of a Member or Members from two thirds of the States, and a Majority of all the States shall be necessary to a Choice. In every Case, after the Choice of the President, the Person having the greatest Number of Votes of the Electors shall be the Vice President. But if there should remain two or more who have equal Votes, the Senate shall chuse from them by Ballot the Vice President.

The Congress may determine the Time of chusing the Electors, and the Day on which they shall give their Votes; which Day shall be the same throughout the United States.

No Person except a natural born Citizen, or a Citizen of the United States, at the time of the Adoption of this Constitution, shall be eligible to the Office of President; neither shall any Person be eligible to that Office who shall not have attained to the Age of thirty five Years, and been fourteen Years a Resident within the United States.

In Case of the Removal of the President from Office, or of his Death, Resignation, or Inability to discharge the Powers and Duties of the said Office, the Same shall devolve on the Vice President, and the Congress may by Law provide for the Case of Removal, Death, Resignation or Inability, both of the President and Vice President, declaring what Officer shall then act as President, and such Officer shall act accordingly, until the Disability be removed, or a President shall be elected.

The President shall, at stated Times, receive for his Services, a Compensation, which shall neither be increased nor diminished during the Period for which he shall have been elected, and he shall not receive within that Period any other Emolument from the United States, or any of them.

Before he enter on the Execution of his Office, he shall take the following Oath or Affirmation:—"I do solemnly swear (or affirm) that I will faithfully execute the Office of President of the United States, and will to the best of my Ability, preserve, protect and defend the Constitution of the United States."

SECTION. 2. The President shall be Commander in Chief of the Army and Navy of the United States, and of the Militia of the several States, when called into the actual Service of the United States; he may require the Opinion, in writing, of the principal Officer in each of the executive Departments, upon any Subject relating to the Duties of their respective Offices, and he shall have Power to grant Reprieves and Pardons for Offences against the United States, except in Cases of Impeachment.

He shall have Power, by and with the Advice and Consent of the Senate, to make Treaties, provided two thirds of the Senators present concur; and he shall nominate, and by and with the Advice and Consent of the Senate, shall appoint Ambassadors, other public Ministers and Consuls, Judges of the supreme Court, and all other Officers of the United States, whose Appointments are not herein otherwise provided for, and which shall be established by Law: but the Congress may by Law vest the Appointment of such inferior Officers, as they think proper, in the President alone, in the Courts of Law, or in the Heads of Departments.

The President shall have Power to fill up all Vacancies that may happen during the Recess of the Senate, by granting Commissions which shall expire at the End of their next Session.

SECTION. 3. He shall from time to time give to the Congress Information of the State of the Union, and recommend to their Consideration such Measures as he shall judge necessary and expedient; he may, on extraordinary Occasions, convene both Houses, or either of them, and in Case of Disagreement between them, with Respect to the Time of Adjournment, he may adjourn them to such Time as he shall think proper; he shall receive Ambassadors and other public Ministers; he shall take Care that the Laws be faithfully executed, and shall Commission all the Officers of the United States.

SECTION. 4. The President, Vice President and all civil Officers of the United States, shall be removed from Office on Impeachment for, and Conviction of, Treason, Bribery, or other high Crimes and Misdemeanors.

ARTICLE III.

SECTION. 1. The judicial Power of the United States shall be vested in one supreme Court, and in such inferior Courts as the Congress may from time to time ordain and establish. The Judges, both of the supreme and inferior Courts, shall hold their Offices during good Behaviour, and shall, at stated Times, receive for their Services a Compensation, which shall not be diminished during their Continuance in Office.

SECTION. 2. The judicial Power shall extend to all Cases, in Law and Equity, arising under this Constitution, the Laws of the United States, and Treaties made, or which shall be made, under their Authority;—to all Cases affecting Ambassadors, other public Ministers and Consuls;—to all Cases of admiralty and maritime Jurisdiction;—to Controversies to which the United States shall be a Party;—to Controversies between two or more States;— between a State and Citizens of another State,—between Citizens of different States,—between Citizens of the same State claiming Lands under Grants of different States, and between a State, or the Citizens thereof, and foreign States, Citizens or Subjects.

In all Cases affecting Ambassadors, other public Ministers and Consuls, and those in which a State shall be Party, the supreme Court shall have original Jurisdiction. In all the other Cases before mentioned, the supreme Court shall have appellate Jurisdiction, both as to Law and Fact, with such Exceptions, and under such Regulations as the Congress shall make.

The Trial of all Crimes, except in Cases of Impeachment, shall be by Jury; and such Trial shall be held in the State where the said Crimes shall have been committed; but when not committed within any State, the Trial shall be at such Place or Places as the Congress may by Law have directed.

SECTION. 3. Treason against the United States, shall consist only in levying War against them, or in adhering to their Enemies, giving them Aid and Comfort. No Person shall be convicted of Treason unless on the Testimony of two Witnesses to the same overt Act, or on Confession in open Court.

The Congress shall have Power to declare the Punishment of Treason, but no Attainder of Treason shall work Corruption of Blood, or Forfeiture except during the Life of the Person attainted.

ARTICLE. IV.

SECTION. 1. Full Faith and Credit shall be given in each State to the public Acts, Records, and judicial Proceedings of every other State. And the Congress may by general Laws prescribe the Manner in which such Acts, Records and Proceedings shall be proved, and the Effect thereof.

SECTION. 2. The Citizens of each State shall be entitled to all Privileges and Immunities of Citizens in the several States.

A Person charged in any State with Treason, Felony, or other Crime, who shall flee from Justice, and be found in another State, shall on Demand of the executive Authority of the State from which he fled, be delivered up, to be removed to the State having Jurisdiction of the Crime.

No Person held to Service or Labour in one State, under the Laws thereof, escaping into another, shall, in Consequence of any Law or Regulation therein, be discharged from such Service or Labour, but shall be delivered up on Claim of the Party to whom such Service or Labour may be due.

SECTION. 3. New States may be admitted by the Congress into this Union; but no new State shall be formed or erected within the Jurisdiction of any other State; nor any State be formed by the Junction of two or more States, or Parts of States, without the Consent of the Legislatures of the States concerned as well as of the Congress.

The Congress shall have Power to dispose of and make all needful Rules and Regulations respecting the Territory or other Property belonging to the United States; and nothing in this Constitution shall be so construed as to Prejudice any Claims of the United States, or of any particular State.

SECTION. 4. The United States shall guarantee to every State in this Union a Republican Form of Government, and shall protect each of them against Invasion; and on Application of the Legislature, or of the Executive (when the Legislature cannot be convened), against domestic Violence.

ARTICLE. V.

The Congress, whenever two thirds of both Houses shall deem it necessary, shall propose Amendments to this Constitution, or, on the Application of the Legislatures of two thirds of the several States, shall call a Convention for proposing Amendments, which, in either Case, shall be valid to all Intents and Purposes, as Part of this Constitution, when ratified by the Legislatures of three fourths of the several States, or by Conventions in three fourths thereof, as the one or the other Mode of Ratification may be proposed by the Congress; Provided that no Amendment which may be made prior to the Year One thousand eight hundred and eight shall in any Manner affect the first and fourth Clauses in the Ninth Section of the first Article; and that no State, without its Consent, shall be deprived of its equal Suffrage in the Senate.

ARTICLE. VI.

All Debts contracted and Engagements entered into, before the Adoption of this Constitution, shall be as valid against the United States under this Constitution, as under the Confederation.

This Constitution, and the Laws of the United States which shall be made in Pursuance thereof; and all Treaties made, or which shall be made, under the Authority of the United States, shall be the supreme Law of the Land; and the Judges in every State shall be bound thereby, any Thing in the Constitution or Laws of any State to the Contrary notwithstanding.

The Senators and Representatives before mentioned, and the Members of the several State Legislatures, and all executive and judicial Officers, both of the United States and of the several States, shall be bound by Oath or Affirmation, to support this Constitution; but no religious Test shall ever be required as a Qualification to any Office or public Trust under the United States.

ARTICLE. VII.

The Ratification of the Conventions of nine States, shall be sufficient for the Establishment of this Constitution between the States so ratifying the Same.

The Word, "the," being interlined between the seventh and eighth Lines of the first Page, the Word "Thirty" being partly written on an Erazure in the fifteenth Line of the first Page, The Words "is tried" being interlined between the thirty second and thirty third Lines of the first Page and the Word "the" being interlined between the forty third and forty fourth Lines of the second Page.

Attest William Jackson Secretary done in Convention by the Unanimous Consent of the States present the Seventeenth Day of September in the Year of our Lord one thousand seven hundred and Eighty seven and of the Independance of the United States of America the Twelfth In witness whereof We have hereunto subscribed our Names,

G°. Washington
Presidt and deputy from Virginia

Delaware	Geo: Read Gunning Bedford jun John Dickinson Richard Bassett Jaco: Broom	Massachusetts	Nathaniel Gorham Rufus King
		Connecticut	Wm. Saml. Johnson Roger Sherman
Maryland	James McHenry Dan of St Thos. Jenifer Danl. Carroll	New York	Alexander Hamilton
Virginia	John Blair James Madison Jr.	New Jersey	Wil: Livingston David Brearley Wm. Paterson Jona: Dayton
North Carolina	Wm. Blount Richd. Dobbs Spaight Hu Williamson	Pennsylvania	B Franklin Thomas Mifflin Robt. Morris Geo. Clymer Thos. FitzSimons Jared Ingersoll James Wilson Gouv Morris
South Carolina	J. Rutledge Charles Cotesworth Pinckney Charles Pinckney Pierce Butler		
Georgia	William Few Abr Baldwin		
New Hampshire	John Langdon Nicholas Gilman		

AMENDMENTS TO THE CONSTITUTION

THE BILL OF RIGHTS: A TRANSCRIPTION

THE PREAMBLE TO THE BILL OF RIGHTS Congress of the United States begun and held at the City of New-York, on Wednesday the fourth of March, one thousand seven hundred and eighty nine.

THE Conventions of a number of the States, having at the time of their adopting the Constitution, expressed a desire, in order to prevent misconstruction or abuse of its powers, that further declaratory and restrictive clauses should be added: And as extending the ground of public confidence in the Government, will best ensure the beneficent ends of its institution.

RESOLVED by the Senate and House of Representatives of the United States of America, in Congress assembled, two thirds of both Houses concurring, that the following Articles be proposed to the Legislatures of the several States, as amendments to the Constitution of the United States, all, or any of which Articles, when ratified by three fourths of the said Legislatures, to be valid to all intents and purposes, as part of the said Constitution; viz.

ARTICLES in addition to, and Amendment of the Constitution of the United States of America, proposed by Congress, and ratified by the Legislatures of the several States, pursuant to the fifth Article of the original Constitution.

Note: The following text is a transcription of the first ten amendments to the Constitution in their original form. These amendments were ratified December 15, 1791, and form what is known as the "Bill of Rights."

AMENDMENT I

Congress shall make no law respecting an establishment of religion, or prohibiting the free exercise thereof; or abridging the freedom of speech, or of the press; or the right of the people peaceably to assemble, and to petition the Government for a redress of grievances.

AMENDMENT II

A well regulated Militia, being necessary to the security of a free State, the right of the people to keep and bear Arms, shall not be infringed.

AMENDMENT III

No Soldier shall, in time of peace be quartered in any house, without the consent of the Owner, nor in time of war, but in a manner to be prescribed by law.

AMENDMENT IV

The right of the people to be secure in their persons, houses, papers, and effects, against unreasonable searches and seizures, shall not be violated, and no Warrants shall issue, but upon probable cause, supported by Oath or affirmation, and particularly describing the place to be searched, and the persons or things to be seized.

AMENDMENT V

No person shall be held to answer for a capital, or otherwise infamous crime, unless on a presentment or indictment of a Grand Jury, except in cases arising in the land or naval forces, or in the Militia, when in actual service in time of War or public danger; nor shall any person be subject for the same offence to be twice put in jeopardy of life or limb; nor shall be compelled in any criminal case to be a witness against himself, nor be deprived of life, liberty, or property, without due process of law; nor shall private property be taken for public use, without just compensation.

AMENDMENT VI

In all criminal prosecutions, the accused shall enjoy the right to a speedy and public trial, by an impartial jury of the State and district wherein the crime shall have been committed, which district shall have been previously ascertained by law, and to be informed of the nature and cause of the accusation; to be confronted with the witnesses against him; to have compulsory process for obtaining witnesses in his favor, and to have the Assistance of Counsel for his defence.

AMENDMENT VII

In Suits at common law, where the value in controversy shall exceed twenty dollars, the right of trial by jury shall be preserved, and no fact tried by a jury, shall be otherwise re-examined in any Court of the United States, than according to the rules of the common law.

Amendment VIII

Excessive bail shall not be required, nor excessive fines imposed, nor cruel and unusual punishments inflicted.

Amendment IX

The enumeration in the Constitution, of certain rights, shall not be construed to deny or disparage others retained by the people.

Amendment X

The powers not delegated to the United States by the Constitution, nor prohibited by it to the States, are reserved to the States respectively, or to the people.

Amendment XI

Passed by Congress March 4, 1794. Ratified February 7, 1795.

Note: Article III, section 2, of the Constitution was modified by amendment 11.

The Judicial power of the United States shall not be construed to extend to any suit in law or equity, commenced or prosecuted against one of the United States by Citizens of another State, or by Citizens or Subjects of any Foreign State.

Amendment XII

Passed by Congress December 9, 1803. Ratified June 15, 1804.

Note: A portion of Article II, section 1 of the Constitution was superseded by the 12th amendment.

The Electors shall meet in their respective states and vote by ballot for President and Vice-President, one of whom, at least, shall not be an inhabitant of the same state with themselves; they shall name in their ballots the person voted for as President, and in distinct ballots the person voted for as Vice-President, and they shall make distinct lists of all persons voted for as President, and of all persons voted for as Vice-President, and of the number of votes for each, which lists they shall sign and certify, and transmit sealed to the seat of the government of the United States, directed to the President of the Senate; — the President of the Senate shall, in the presence of the Senate and House of Representatives, open all the certificates and the votes shall then be counted; — The person having the greatest number of votes for President, shall be the President, if such number be a majority of the whole number of Electors appointed; and if no person have such majority, then from the persons having the highest numbers not exceeding three on the list of those voted for as President, the House of Representatives shall choose immediately, by ballot, the President. But in choosing the President, the votes shall be taken by states, the representation from each state having one vote; a quorum for this purpose shall consist of a member or members from two-thirds of the states, and a majority of all the states shall be necessary to a choice. [And if the House of Representatives shall not choose a President whenever the right of choice shall devolve upon them, before the fourth day of March next following, then the Vice-President shall act as President, as in case of the death or other constitutional disability of the President. —]* The person having the greatest number of votes as Vice-President, shall be the Vice-President, if such number be a majority of the whole number of Electors appointed, and if no person have a majority, then from the two highest numbers on the list, the Senate shall choose the Vice-President; a quorum for the purpose shall consist of two-thirds of the whole number of Senators, and a majority of the whole number shall be necessary to a choice. But no person constitutionally ineligible to the office of President shall be eligible to that of Vice-President of the United States.

AMENDMENT XIII

Passed by Congress January 31, 1865. Ratified December 6, 1865.

Note: A portion of Article IV, section 2, of the Constitution was superseded by the 13th amendment.

SECTION 1. Neither slavery nor involuntary servitude, except as a punishment for crime whereof the party shall have been duly convicted, shall exist within the United States, or any place subject to their jurisdiction.

SECTION 2. Congress shall have power to enforce this article by appropriate legislation.

---

*Superseded by section 3 of the 20th amendment.

AMENDMENT XIV

Passed by Congress June 13, 1866. Ratified July 9, 1868.

Note: Article I, section 2, of the Constitution was modified by section 2 of the 14th amendment.

SECTION 1. All persons born or naturalized in the United States, and subject to the jurisdiction thereof, are citizens of the United States and of the State wherein they reside. No State shall make or enforce any law which shall abridge the privileges or immunities of citizens of the United States; nor shall any State deprive any person of life, liberty, or property, without due process of law; nor deny to any person within its jurisdiction the equal protection of the laws.

SECTION 2. Representatives shall be apportioned among the several States according to their respective numbers, counting the whole number of persons in each State, excluding Indians not taxed. But when the right to vote at any election for the choice of electors for President and Vice-President of the United States, Representatives in Congress, the Executive and Judicial officers of a State, or the members of the Legislature thereof, is denied to any of the male inhabitants of such State, being twenty-one years of age,* and citizens of the United States, or in any way abridged, except for participation in rebellion, or other crime, the basis of representation therein shall be reduced in the proportion which the number of such male citizens shall bear to the whole number of male citizens twenty-one years of age in such State.

SECTION 3. No person shall be a Senator or Representative in Congress, or elector of President and Vice-President, or hold any office, civil or military, under the United States, or under any State, who, having previously taken an oath, as a member of Congress, or as an officer of the United States, or as a member of any State legislature, or as an executive or judicial officer of any State, to support the Constitution of the United States, shall have engaged in insurrection or rebellion against the same, or given aid or comfort to the enemies thereof. But Congress may by a vote of two-thirds of each House, remove such disability.

SECTION 4. The validity of the public debt of the United States, authorized by law, including debts incurred for payment of pensions and bounties for services in suppressing insurrection or rebellion, shall not be

*Changed by section 1 of the 26th amendment.

questioned. But neither the United States nor any State shall assume or pay any debt or obligation incurred in aid of insurrection or rebellion against the United States, or any claim for the loss or emancipation of any slave; but all such debts, obligations and claims shall be held illegal and void.

SECTION 5. The Congress shall have the power to enforce, by appropriate legislation, the provisions of this article.

AMENDMENT XV

Passed by Congress February 26, 1869. Ratified February 3, 1870.

SECTION 1. The right of citizens of the United States to vote shall not be denied or abridged by the United States or by any State on account of race, color, or previous condition of servitude—

SECTION 2. The Congress shall have the power to enforce this article by appropriate legislation.

AMENDMENT XVI

Passed by Congress July 2, 1909. Ratified February 3, 1913.

Note: Article I, section 9, of the Constitution was modified by amendment 16.

The Congress shall have power to lay and collect taxes on incomes, from whatever source derived, without apportionment among the several States, and without regard to any census or enumeration.

AMENDMENT XVII

Passed by Congress May 13, 1912. Ratified April 8, 1913.

Note: Article I, section 3, of the Constitution was modified by the 17th amendment.

The Senate of the United States shall be composed of two Senators from each State, elected by the people thereof, for six years; and each Senator shall have one vote. The electors in each State shall have the qualifications requisite for electors of the most numerous branch of the State legislatures.

When vacancies happen in the representation of any State in the Senate, the executive authority of such State shall issue writs of election to fill such vacancies: *Provided*, That the legislature of any State may empower the executive thereof to make temporary appointments until the people fill the vacancies by election as the legislature may direct.

This amendment shall not be so construed as to affect the election or term of any Senator chosen before it becomes valid as part of the Constitution.

AMENDMENT XVIII

Passed by Congress December 18, 1917. Ratified January 16, 1919. Repealed by amendment 21.

SECTION 1. After one year from the ratification of this article the manufacture, sale, or transportation of intoxicating liquors within, the importation thereof into, or the exportation thereof from the United States and all territory subject to the jurisdiction thereof for beverage purposes is hereby prohibited.

SECTION 2. The Congress and the several States shall have concurrent power to enforce this article by appropriate legislation.

SECTION 3. This article shall be inoperative unless it shall have been ratified as an amendment to the Constitution by the legislatures of the several States, as provided in the Constitution, within seven years from the date of the submission hereof to the States by the Congress.

AMENDMENT XIX

Passed by Congress June 4, 1919. Ratified August 18, 1920.

The right of citizens of the United States to vote shall not be denied or abridged by the United States or by any State on account of sex.

Congress shall have power to enforce this article by appropriate legislation.

AMENDMENT XX

Passed by Congress March 2, 1932. Ratified January 23, 1933.

Note: Article I, section 4, of the Constitution was modified by section 2 of this amendment. In addition, a portion of the 12th amendment was superseded by section 3.

SECTION 1. The terms of the President and the Vice President shall end at noon on the 20th day of January, and the terms of Senators and Representatives at noon on the 3rd day of January, of the years in which such terms would have ended if this article had not been ratified; and the terms of their successors shall then begin.

SECTION 2. The Congress shall assemble at least once in every year, and such meeting shall begin at noon on the 3d day of January, unless they shall by law appoint a different day.

SECTION 3. If, at the time fixed for the beginning of the term of the President, the President elect shall have died, the Vice President elect shall become President. If a President shall not have been chosen before the time fixed for the beginning of his term, or if the President elect shall have failed to qualify, then the Vice President elect shall act as President until a President shall have qualified; and the Congress may by law provide for the case wherein neither a President elect nor a Vice President shall have qualified, declaring who shall then act as President, or the manner in which one who is to act shall be selected, and such person shall act accordingly until a President or Vice President shall have qualified.

SECTION 4. The Congress may by law provide for the case of the death of any of the persons from whom the House of Representatives may choose a President whenever the right of choice shall have devolved upon them, and for the case of the death of any of the persons from whom the Senate may choose a Vice President whenever the right of choice shall have devolved upon them.

SECTION 5. Sections 1 and 2 shall take effect on the 15th day of October following the ratification of this article.

SECTION 6. This article shall be inoperative unless it shall have been ratified as an amendment to the Constitution by the legislatures of three-fourths of the several States within seven years from the date of its submission.

AMENDMENT XXI

Passed by Congress February 20, 1933. Ratified December 5, 1933.

SECTION 1. The eighteenth article of amendment to the Constitution of the United States is hereby repealed.

SECTION 2. The transportation or importation into any State, Territory, or Possession of the United States for delivery or use therein of intoxicating liquors, in violation of the laws thereof, is hereby prohibited.

SECTION 3. This article shall be inoperative unless it shall have been ratified as an amendment to the Constitution by conventions in the several States, as provided in the Constitution, within seven years from the date of the submission hereof to the States by the Congress.

AMENDMENT XXII

Passed by Congress March 21, 1947. Ratified February 27, 1951.

SECTION 1. No person shall be elected to the office of the President more than twice, and no person who has held the office of President, or acted as President, for more than two years of a term to which some other person was elected President shall be elected to the office of President more than once. But this Article shall not apply to any person holding the office of President when this Article was proposed by Congress, and shall not prevent any person who may be holding the office of President, or acting as President, during the term within which this Article becomes operative from holding the office of President or acting as President during the remainder of such term.

SECTION 2. This article shall be inoperative unless it shall have been ratified as an amendment to the Constitution by the legislatures of three-fourths of the several States within seven years from the date of its submission to the States by the Congress.

AMENDMENT XXIII

Passed by Congress June 16, 1960. Ratified March 29, 1961.

SECTION 1. The District constituting the seat of Government of the United States shall appoint in such manner as Congress may direct:

A number of electors of President and Vice President equal to the whole number of Senators and Representatives in Congress to which the District would be entitled if it were a State, but in no event more than the least populous State; they shall be in addition to those appointed by the States, but they shall be considered, for the purposes of the election of President and Vice President, to be electors appointed by a State; and they shall meet in the District and perform such duties as provided by the twelfth article of amendment.

SECTION 2. The Congress shall have power to enforce this article by appropriate legislation.

AMENDMENT XXIV

Passed by Congress August 27, 1962. Ratified January 23, 1964.

SECTION 1. The right of citizens of the United States to vote in any primary or other election for President or Vice President, for electors for President or Vice President, or for Senator or Representative in Congress, shall not be denied or abridged by the United States or any State by reason of failure to pay poll tax or other tax.

SECTION 2. The Congress shall have power to enforce this article by appropriate legislation.

AMENDMENT XXV

Passed by Congress July 6, 1965. Ratified February 10, 1967.

Note: Article II, section 1, of the Constitution was affected by the 25th amendment.

SECTION 1. In case of the removal of the President from office or of his death or resignation, the Vice President shall become President.

SECTION 2. Whenever there is a vacancy in the office of the Vice President, the President shall nominate a Vice President who shall take office upon confirmation by a majority vote of both Houses of Congress.

SECTION 3. Whenever the President transmits to the President pro tempore of the Senate and the Speaker of the House of Representatives his written declaration that he is unable to discharge the powers and duties of his office, and until he transmits to them a written declaration to the contrary, such powers and duties shall be discharged by the Vice President as Acting President.

SECTION 4. Whenever the Vice President and a majority of either the principal officers of the executive departments or of such other body as Congress may by law provide, transmit to the President pro tempore of the Senate and the Speaker of the House of Representatives their written declaration that the President is unable to discharge the powers and duties of his office, the Vice President shall immediately assume the powers and duties of the office as Acting President.

Thereafter, when the President transmits to the President pro tempore of the Senate and the Speaker of the House of Representatives his written declaration that no inability exists, he shall resume the powers and duties of his office unless the Vice President and a majority of either the principal officers of the executive department or of such other body as Congress may by law provide, transmit within four days to the President pro tempore of the Senate and the Speaker of the House of Representatives their written declaration that the President is unable to discharge the powers and duties of his office. Thereupon Congress shall decide the issue, assembling within forty-eight hours for that purpose if not in session. If the Congress, within twenty-one days after receipt of the latter written declaration, or, if Congress is not in session, within twenty-one days after Congress is required to assemble, determines by two-thirds vote of both Houses that the President is unable to discharge the powers and duties of his office, the Vice President shall continue to discharge the same as Acting President; otherwise, the President shall resume the powers and duties of his office.

AMENDMENT XXVI

Passed by Congress March 23, 1971. Ratified July 1, 1971.

Note: Amendment 14, section 2, of the Constitution was modified by section 1 of the 26th amendment.

SECTION 1. The right of citizens of the United States, who are eighteen years of age or older, to vote shall not be denied or abridged by the United States or by any State on account of age.

SECTION 2. The Congress shall have power to enforce this article by appropriate legislation.

AMENDMENT XXVII

Originally proposed Sept. 25, 1789. Ratified May 7, 1992.

No law, varying the compensation for the services of the Senators and Representatives, shall take effect, until an election of representatives shall have intervened.

PRESIDENTIAL ELECTIONS

Year	Number of States	Candidates	Parties	Popular Vote	% of Popular Vote	Electoral Vote	% Voter Participation
1789	11	**GEORGE WASHINGTON**	No party			69	
		John Adams	designations			34	
		Other candidates				35	
1792	15	**GEORGE WASHINGTON**	No party			132	
		John Adams	designations			77	
		George Clinton				50	
		Other candidates				5	
1796	16	**JOHN ADAMS**	Federalist			71	
		Thomas Jefferson	Democratic-Republican			68	
		Thomas Pinckney	Federalist			59	
		Aaron Burr	Democratic-Republican			30	
		Other candidates				48	
1800	16	**THOMAS JEFFERSON**	Democratic-Republican			73	
		Aaron Burr	Democratic-Republican			73	
		John Adams	Federalist			65	
		Charles C. Pinckney	Federalist			64	
		John Jay	Federalist			1	
1804	17	**THOMAS JEFFERSON**	Democratic-Republican			162	
		Charles C. Pinckney	Federalist			14	

Year	Number of States	Candidates	Parties	Popular Vote	% of Popular Vote	Electoral Vote	% Voter Participation
1808	17	**JAMES MADISON**	Democratic-Republican			122	
		Charles C. Pinckney	Federalist			47	
		George Clinton	Democratic-Republican			6	
1812	18	**JAMES MADISON**	Democratic-Republican			128	
		DeWitt Clinton	Federalist			89	
1816	19	**JAMES MONROE**	Democratic-Republican			183	
		Rufus King	Federalist			34	
1820	24	**JAMES MONROE**	Democratic-Republican			231	
		John Quincy Adams	Independent			1	
1824	24	**JOHN QUINCY ADAMS**	Democratic-Republican	108,740	30.5	84	26.9
		Andrew Jackson	Democratic-Republican	153,544	43.1	99	
		Henry Clay	Democratic-Republican	47,136	13.2	37	
		William H. Crawford	Democratic-Republican	46,618	13.1	41	
1828	24	**ANDREW JACKSON**	Democratic	647,286	56.0	178	57.6
		John Quincy Adams	National-Republican	508,064	44.0	83	

Year	Number of States	Candidates	Parties	Popular Vote	% of Popular Vote	Electoral Vote	% Voter Participation
1832	24	**ANDREW JACKSON**	Democratic	688,242	54.5	219	55.4
		Henry Clay	National-Republican	473,462	37.5	49	
		William Wirt	Anti-Masonic	101,051	8.0	7	
		John Floyd	Democratic			11	
1836	26	**MARTIN VAN BUREN**	Democratic	765,483	50.9	170	57.8
		William H. Harrison	Whig			73	
		Hugh L. White	Whig	739,795	49.1	26	
		Daniel Webster	Whig			14	
		W. P. Mangum	Whig			11	
1840	26	**WILLIAM H. HARRISON**	Whig	1,274,624	53.1	234	80.2
		Martin Van Buren	Democratic	1,127,781	46.9	60	
1844	26	**JAMES K. POLK**	Democratic	1,338,464	49.6	170	78.9
		Henry Clay	Whig	1,300,097	48.1	105	
		James G. Birney	Liberty	62,300	2.3		
1848	30	**ZACHARY TAYLOR**	Whig	1,360,967	47.4	163	72.7
		Lewis Cass	Democratic	1,222,342	42.5	127	
		Martin Van Buren	Free Soil	291,263	10.1		
1852	31	**FRANKLIN PIERCE**	Democratic	1,601,117	50.9	254	69.6
		Winfield Scott	Whig	1,385,453	44.1	42	
		John P. Hale	Free Soil	155,825	5.0		
1856	31	**JAMES BUCHANAN**	Democratic	1,832,955	45.3	174	78.9
		John C. Frémont	Republican	1,339,932	33.1	114	
		Millard Fillmore	American	871,731	21.6	8	

Year	Number of States	Candidates	Parties	Popular Vote	% of Popular Vote	Electoral Vote	% Voter Participation
1860	33	**ABRAHAM LINCOLN**	Republican	1,865,593	39.8	180	81.2
		Stephen A. Douglas	Democratic	1,382,713	29.5	12	
		John C. Breckinridge	Democratic	848,356	18.1	72	
		John Bell	Constitutional Union	592,906	12.6	39	
1864	36	**ABRAHAM LINCOLN**	Republican	2,206,938	55.0	212	73.8
		George B. McClellan	Democratic	1,803,787	45.0	21	
1868	37	**ULYSSES S. GRANT**	Republican	3,013,421	52.7	214	78.1
		Horatio Seymour	Democratic	2,706,829	47.3	80	
1872	37	**ULYSSES S. GRANT**	Republican	3,596,745	55.6	286	71.3
		Horace Greeley	Democratic	2,843,446	43.9	66	
1876	38	**Rutherford B. Hayes**	Republican	4,036,572	48.0	185	81.8
		Samuel J. Tilden	Democratic	4,284,020	51.0	184	
1880	38	**JAMES A. GARFIELD**	Republican	4,453,295	48.5	214	79.4
		Winfield S. Hancock	Democratic	4,414,082	48.1	155	
		James B. Weaver	Greenback-Labor	308,578	3.4		
1884	38	**GROVER CLEVELAND**	Democratic	4,879,507	48.5	219	77.5
		James G. Blaine	Republican	4,850,293	48.2	182	
		Benjamin F. Butler	Greenback-Labor	175,370	1.8		
		John P. St. John	Prohibition	150,369	1.5		
1888	38	**BENJAMIN HARRISON**	Republican	5,477,129	47.9	233	79.3
		Grover Cleveland	Democratic	5,537,857	48.6	168	
		Clinton B. Fisk	Prohibition	249,506	2.2		
		Anson J. Streeter	Union Labor	146,935	1.3		

Year	Number of States	Candidates	Parties	Popular Vote	% of Popular Vote	Electoral Vote	% Voter Participation
1892	44	**GROVER CLEVELAND**	Democratic	5,555,426	46.1	277	74.7
		Benjamin Harrison	Republican	5,182,690	43.0	145	
		James B. Weaver	People's	1,029,846	8.5	22	
		John Bidwell	Prohibition	264,133	2.2		
1896	45	**WILLIAM McKINLEY**	Republican	7,102,246	51.1	271	79.3
		William J. Bryan	Democratic	6,492,559	47.7	176	
1900	45	**WILLIAM McKINLEY**	Republican	7,218,491	51.7	292	73.2
		William J. Bryan	Democratic; Populist	6,356,734	45.5	155	
		John C. Wooley	Prohibition	208,914	1.5		
1904	45	**THEODORE ROOSEVELT**	Republican	7,628,461	57.4	336	65.2
		Alton B. Parker	Democratic	5,084,223	37.6	140	
		Eugene V. Debs	Socialist	402,283	3.0		
		Silas C. Swallow	Prohibition	258,536	1.9		
1908	46	**WILLIAM H. TAFT**	Republican	7,675,320	51.6	321	65.4
		William J. Bryan	Democratic	6,412,294	43.1	162	
		Eugene V. Debs	Socialist	420,793	2.8		
		Eugene W. Chafin	Prohibition	253,840	1.7		
1912	48	**WOODROW WILSON**	Democratic	6,296,547	41.9	435	58.8
		Theodore Roosevelt	Progressive	4,118,571	27.4	88	
		William H. Taft	Republican	3,486,720	23.2	8	
		Eugene V. Debs	Socialist	900,672	6.0		
		Eugene W. Chafin	Prohibition	206,275	1.4		

Year	Number of States	Candidates	Parties	Popular Vote	% of Popular Vote	Electoral Vote	% Voter Participation
1916	48	**WOODROW WILSON**	Democratic	9,127,695	49.4	277	61.6
		Charles E. Hughes	Republican	8,533,507	46.2	254	
		A. L. Benson	Socialist	585,113	3.2		
		J. Frank Hanly	Prohibition	220,506	1.2		
1920	48	**WARREN G. HARDING**	Republican	16,143,407	60.4	404	49.2
		James M. Cox	Democratic	9,130,328	34.2	127	
		Eugene V. Debs	Socialist	919,799	3.4		
		P. P. Christensen	Farmer-Labor	265,411	1.0		
1924	48	**CALVIN COOLIDGE**	Republican	15,718,211	54.0	382	48.9
		John W. Davis	Democratic	8,385,283	28.8	136	
		Robert M. La Follette	Progressive	4,831,289	16.6	13	
1928	48	**HERBERT C. HOOVER**	Republican	21,391,993	58.2	444	56.9
		Alfred E. Smith	Democratic	15,016,169	40.9	87	
1932	48	**FRANKLIN D. ROOSEVELT**	Democratic	22,809,638	57.4	472	56.9
		Herbert C. Hoover	Republican	15,758,901	39.7	59	
		Norman Thomas	Socialist	881,951	2.2		
1936	48	**FRANKLIN D. ROOSEVELT**	Democratic	27,752,869	60.8	523	61.0
		Alfred M. Landon	Republican	16,674,665	36.5	8	
		William Lemke	Union	882,479	1.9		
1940	48	**FRANKLIN D. ROOSEVELT**	Democratic	27,307,819	54.8	449	62.5
		Wendell L. Willkie	Republican	22,321,018	44.8	82	
1944	48	**FRANKLIN D. ROOSEVELT**	Democratic	25,606,585	53.5	432	55.9
		Thomas E. Dewey	Republican	22,014,745	46.0	99	

Year	Number of States	Candidates	Parties	Popular Vote	% of Popular Vote	Electoral Vote	% Voter Participation
1948	48	**HARRY S. TRUMAN**	Democratic	24,179,345	49.6	303	53.0
		Thomas E. Dewey	Republican	21,991,291	45.1	189	
		J. Strom Thurmond	States' Rights	1,176,125	2.4	39	
		Henry A. Wallace	Progressive	1,157,326	2.4		
1952	48	**DWIGHT D. EISENHOWER**	Republican	33,936,234	55.1	442	63.3
		Adlai E. Stevenson	Democratic	27,314,992	44.4	89	
1956	48	**DWIGHT D. EISENHOWER**	Republican	35,590,472	57.6	457	60.6
		Adlai E. Stevenson	Democratic	26,022,752	42.1	73	
1960	50	**JOHN F. KENNEDY**	Democratic	34,226,731	49.7	303	62.8
		Richard M. Nixon	Republican	34,108,157	49.5	219	
1964	50	**LYNDON B. JOHNSON**	Democratic	43,129,566	61.1	486	61.9
		Barry M. Goldwater	Republican	27,178,188	38.5	52	
1968	50	**RICHARD M. NIXON**	Republican	31,785,480	43.4	301	60.9
		Hubert H. Humphrey	Democratic	31,275,166	42.7	191	
		George C. Wallace	American Independent	9,906,473	13.5	46	
1972	50	**RICHARD M. NIXON**	Republican	47,169,911	60.7	520	55.2
		George S. McGovern	Democratic	29,170,383	37.5	17	
		John G. Schmitz	American	1,099,482	1.4		
1976	50	**JIMMY CARTER**	Democratic	40,830,763	50.1	297	53.5
		Gerald R. Ford	Republican	39,147,793	48.0	240	

Year	Number of States	Candidate	Party	Popular Vote	% of Popular Vote	Electoral Vote	% Voter Participation
1980	50	**RONALD REAGAN**	Republican	43,901,812	50.7	489	52.6
		Jimmy Carter	Democratic	35,483,820	41.0	49	
		John B. Anderson	Independent	5,719,437	6.6		
		Ed Clark	Libertarian	921,188	1.1		
1984	50	**RONALD REAGAN**	Republican	54,451,521	58.8	525	53.1
		Walter F. Mondale	Democratic	37,565,334	40.6	13	
1988	50	**GEORGE H. W. BUSH**	Republican	47,917,341	53.4	426	50.1
		Michael Dukakis	Democratic	41,013,030	45.6	111	
1992	50	**BILL CLINTON**	Democratic	44,908,254	43.0	370	55.0
		George H. W. Bush	Republican	39,102,343	37.4	168	
		H. Ross Perot	Independent	19,741,065	18.9		
1996	50	**BILL CLINTON**	Democratic	47,401,185	49.0	379	49.0
		Bob Dole	Republican	39,197,469	41.0	159	
		H. Ross Perot	Independent	8,085,295	8.0		
2000	50	**GEORGE W. BUSH**	Republican	50,455,156	47.9	271	50.4
		Al Gore	Democrat	50,997,335	48.4	266	
		Ralph Nader	Green	2,382,897	2.7		
2004	50	**GEORGE W. BUSH**	Republican	62,040,610	50.7	286	60.7
		John F. Kerry	Democrat	59,028,444	48.3	251	
2008	50	**BARACK OBAMA**	Democrat	69,456,897	52.92	365	63.0
		John McCain	Republican	59,934,814	45.66	173	
2012	50	**BARACK OBAMA**	Democrat	65,915,795	51.1	332	54.9
		Mitt Romney	Republican	60,933,504	47.2	206	

Candidates receiving less than 1 percent of the popular vote have been omitted. Thus the percentage of popular vote given for any election year may not total 100 percent.

Before the passage of the Twelfth Amendment in 1804, the electoral college voted for two presidential candidates; the runner-up became vice president.

ADMISSION OF STATES

Order of Admission	State	Date of Admission	Order of Admission	State	Date of Admission
1	Delaware	December 7, 1787	26	Michigan	January 26, 1837
2	Pennsylvania	December 12, 1787	27	Florida	March 3, 1845
3	New Jersey	December 18, 1787	28	Texas	December 29, 1845
4	Georgia	January 2, 1788	29	Iowa	December 28, 1846
5	Connecticut	January 9, 1788	30	Wisconsin	May 29, 1848
6	Massachusetts	February 7, 1788	31	California	September 9, 1850
7	Maryland	April 28, 1788	32	Minnesota	May 11, 1858
8	South Carolina	May 23, 1788	33	Oregon	February 14, 1859
9	New Hampshire	June 21, 1788	34	Kansas	January 29, 1861
10	Virginia	June 25, 1788	35	West Virginia	June 30, 1863
11	New York	July 26, 1788	36	Nevada	October 31, 1864
12	North Carolina	November 21, 1789	37	Nebraska	March 1, 1867
13	Rhode Island	May 29, 1790	38	Colorado	August 1, 1876
14	Vermont	March 4, 1791	39	North Dakota	November 2, 1889
15	Kentucky	June 1, 1792	40	South Dakota	November 2, 1889
16	Tennessee	June 1, 1796	41	Montana	November 8, 1889
17	Ohio	March 1, 1803	42	Washington	November 11, 1889
18	Louisiana	April 30, 1812	43	Idaho	July 3, 1890
19	Indiana	December 11, 1816	44	Wyoming	July 10, 1890
20	Mississippi	December 10, 1817	45	Utah	January 4, 1896
21	Illinois	December 3, 1818	46	Oklahoma	November 16, 1907
22	Alabama	December 14, 1819	47	New Mexico	January 6, 1912
23	Maine	March 15, 1820	48	Arizona	February 14, 1912
24	Missouri	August 10, 1821	49	Alaska	January 3, 1959
25	Arkansas	June 15, 1836	50	Hawaii	August 21, 1959

POPULATION OF THE UNITED STATES

Year	Number of States	Population	% Increase	Population per Square Mile
1790	13	3,929,214		4.5
1800	16	5,308,483	35.1	6.1
1810	17	7,239,881	36.4	4.3
1820	23	9,638,453	33.1	5.5
1830	24	12,866,020	33.5	7.4
1840	26	17,069,453	32.7	9.8
1850	31	23,191,876	35.9	7.9
1860	33	31,443,321	35.6	10.6
1870	37	39,818,449	26.6	13.4
1880	38	50,155,783	26.0	16.9
1890	44	62,947,714	25.5	21.1
1900	45	75,994,575	20.7	25.6
1910	46	91,972,266	21.0	31.0
1920	48	105,710,620	14.9	35.6
1930	48	122,775,046	16.1	41.2
1940	48	131,669,275	7.2	44.2
1950	48	150,697,361	14.5	50.7
1960	50	179,323,175	19.0	50.6
1970	50	203,235,298	13.3	57.5
1980	50	226,504,825	11.4	64.0
1985	50	237,839,000	5.0	67.2
1990	50	250,122,000	5.2	70.6
1995	50	263,411,707	5.3	74.4
2000	50	281,421,906	6.8	77.0
2005	50	296,410,404	5.3	77.9
2010	50	308,745,538	9.7	87.4

IMMIGRATION TO THE UNITED STATES, FISCAL YEARS 1820–2013

Year	Number	Year	Number	Year	Number	Year	Number
1820–1989	**55,457,531**	**1871–80**	**2,812,191**	**1921–30**	**4,107,209**	**1971–80**	**4,493,314**
1820	8,385	1871	321,350	1921	805,228	1971	370,478
1821–30	**143,439**	1872	404,806	1922	309,556	1972	384,685
1821	9,127	1873	459,803	1923	522,919	1973	400,063
1822	6,911	1874	313,339	1924	706,896	1974	394,861
1823	6,354	1875	227,498	1925	294,314	1975	386,914
1824	7,912	1876	169,986	1926	304,488	1976	398,613
1825	10,199	1877	141,857	1927	335,175	1976	103,676
1826	10,837	1878	138,469	1928	307,255	1977	462,315
1827	18,875	1879	177,826	1929	279,678	1978	601,442
1828	27,382	1880	457,257	1930	241,700	1979	460,348
1829	22,520	**1881–90**	**5,246,613**	**1931–40**	**528,431**	1980	530,639
1830	23,322	1881	669,431	1931	97,139	**1981–90**	**7,338,062**
1831–40	**599,125**	1882	788,992	1932	35,576	1981	596,600
1831	22,633	1883	603,322	1933	23,068	1982	594,131
1832	60,482	1884	518,592	1934	29,470	1983	559,763
1833	58,640	1885	395,346	1935	34,956	1984	543,903
1834	65,365	1886	334,203	1936	36,329	1985	570,009
1835	45,374	1887	490,109	1937	50,244	1986	601,708
1836	76,242	1888	546,889	1938	67,895	1987	601,516
1837	79,340	1889	444,427	1939	82,998	1988	643,025
1838	38,914	1890	455,302	1940	70,756	1989	1,090,924
1839	68,069	**1891–1900**	**3,687,564**	**1941–50**	**1,035,039**	1990	1,536,483
1840	84,066	1891	560,319	1941	51,776	**1991–2000**	**9,090,857**
1841–50	**1,713,251**	1892	579,663	1942	28,781	1991	1,827,167
1841	80,289	1893	439,730	1943	23,725	1992	973,977
1842	104,565	1894	285,631	1944	28,551	1993	904,292
		1895	258,536	1945	38,119	1994	804,416
		1896	343,267	1946	108,721		

Year	Number	Year	Number	Year	Number	Year	Number
1843	52,496	1897	230,832	1947	147,292	1995	720,461
1844	78,615	1898	229,299	1948	170,570	1996	915,900
1845	114,371	1899	311,715	1949	188,317	1997	798,378
1846	154,416	1900	448,572	1950	249,187	1998	660,477
1847	234,968					1999	644,787
1848	226,527	1901–10	8,795,386	1951–60	2,515,479	2000	841,002
1849	297,024	1901	437,918	1951	205,717	2001–13	10,501,053
1850	369,980	1902	648,743	1952	265,520	2001	1,058,902
		1903	857,046	1953	170,434	2002	1,059,356
1851–60	2,598,214	1904	812,870	1954	208,177	2003	705,827
1851	379,466	1905	1,026,499	1955	237,790	2004	957,883
1852	371,603	1906	1,100,735	1956	321,625	2005	1,122,373
1853	368,645	1907	1,285,349	1957	326,867	2006	1,266,129
1854	427,833	1908	782,870	1958	253,265	2007	1,052,415
1855	200,877	1909	751,786	1959	260,686	2008	1,107,126
1856	200,436	1910	1,041,570	1960	265,398	2009	1,130,818
1857	251,306					2010	1,042,625
1858	123,126	1911–20	5,735,811	1961–70	3,321,677	2011	1,062,040
1859	121,282	1911	878,587	1961	271,344	2012	1,031,631
1860	153,640	1912	838,172	1962	283,763	2013	990,553
		1913	1,197,892	1963	306,260		
1861–70	2,314,824	1914	1,218,480	1964	292,248		
1861	91,918	1915	326,700	1965	296,697		
1862	91,985	1916	298,826	1966	323,040		
1863	176,282	1917	295,403	1967	361,972		
1864	193,418	1918	110,618	1968	454,448		
1865	248,120	1919	141,132	1969	358,579		
1866	318,568	1920	430,001	1970	373,326		
1867	315,722						
1868	138,840						
1869	352,768						
1870	387,203						

Source: U.S. Department of Homeland Security.

IMMIGRATION BY REGION AND SELECTED COUNTRY OF LAST RESIDENCE, FISCAL YEARS 1820–2013

Region and country of last residence	1820 to 1829	1830 to 1839	1840 to 1849	1850 to 1859	1860 to 1869	1870 to 1879	1880 to 1889	1890 to 1899
Total	128,502	538,381	1,427,337	2,814,554	2,081,261	2,742,137	5,248,568	3,694,294
Europe	99,272	422,771	1,369,259	2,619,680	1,877,726	2,251,878	4,638,677	3,576,411
Austria-Hungary	—	—	—	—	3,375	60,127	314,787	534,059
Austria	—	—	—	—	2,700	54,529	204,805	268,218
Hungary	—	—	—	—	483	5,598	109,982	203,350
Belgium	28	20	3,996	5,765	5,785	6,991	18,738	19,642
Bulgaria	—	—	—	—	—	—	—	52
Czechoslovakia	—	—	—	—	—	—	—	—
Denmark	173	927	671	3,227	13,553	29,278	85,342	56,671
Finland	—	—	—	—	—	—	—	—
France	7,694	39,330	75,300	81,778	35,938	71,901	48,193	35,616
Germany	5,753	124,726	385,434	976,072	723,734	751,769	1,445,181	579,072
Greece	17	49	17	32	51	209	1,807	12,732
Ireland	51,617	170,672	656,145	1,029,486	427,419	422,264	674,061	405,710
Italy	430	2,225	1,476	8,643	9,853	46,296	267,660	603,761
Netherlands	1,105	1,377	7,624	11,122	8,387	14,267	52,715	29,349
Norway-Sweden	91	1,149	12,389	22,202	82,937	178,823	586,441	334,058
Norway	—	—	—	—	16,068	88,644	185,111	96,810
Sweden	—	—	—	—	24,224	90,179	401,330	237,248
Poland	19	366	105	1,087	1,886	11,016	42,910	107,793
Portugal	177	820	196	1,299	2,083	13,971	15,186	25,874
Romania	—	—	—	—	—	—	5,842	6,808
Russia	86	280	520	423	1,670	35,177	182,698	450,101
Spain	2,595	2,010	1,916	8,795	6,966	5,540	3,995	9,189
Switzerland	3,148	4,430	4,819	24,423	21,124	25,212	81,151	37,020
United Kingdom	26,336	74,350	218,572	445,322	532,956	578,447	810,900	328,759
Yugoslavia	—	—	—	—	—	—	—	—
Other Europe	3	40	79	4	9	590	1,070	145

Asia	34	55	121	36,080	54,408	134,128	71,151	61,285
China	3	8	32	35,933	54,028	133,139	65,797	15,268
Hong Kong	—	—	—	42	50	166	247	102
India	9	38	33	—	—	—	—	102
Iran	—	—	—	—	—	—	—	—
Israel	—	—	—	—	138	193	1,583	13,998
Japan	—	—	—	—	—	—	—	—
Jordan	—	—	—	—	—	—	—	—
Korea	—	—	—	—	—	—	—	—
Philippines	—	—	—	—	—	—	—	—
Syria	—	—	—	—	—	—	—	—
Taiwan	—	—	—	—	—	—	—	—
Turkey	19	8	45	94	129	382	2,478	27,510
Vietnam	—	—	—	—	—	—	—	—
Other Asia	3	1	11	11	63	248	1,046	4,407
America	9,655	31,905	50,516	84,145	130,292	345,010	524,826	37,350
Canada and Newfoundland	2,297	11,875	34,285	64,171	117,978	324,310	492,865	3,098
Mexico	3,835	7,187	3,069	3,446	1,957	5,133	2,405	734
Caribbean	3,061	11,792	11,803	12,447	8,751	14,285	27,323	31,480
Cuba	—	—	—	—	—	—	—	—
Dominican Republic	—	—	—	—	—	—	—	—
Haiti	—	—	—	—	—	—	—	—
Jamaica	—	—	—	—	—	—	—	—
Other Caribbean	3,061	11,792	11,803	12,447	8,751	14,285	27,323	31,480
Central America	57	94	297	512	70	173	279	649
Belize	—	—	—	—	—	—	—	—
Costa Rica	—	—	—	—	—	—	—	—
El Salvador	—	—	—	—	—	—	—	—
Guatemala	—	—	—	—	—	—	—	—
Honduras	—	—	—	—	—	—	—	—
Nicaragua	—	—	—	—	—	—	—	—
Panama	—	—	—	—	—	—	—	—
Other Central America	57	94	297	512	70	173	279	649
South America	405	957	1,062	3,569	1,536	1,109	1,954	1,389
Argentina	—	—	—	—	—	—	—	—
Bolivia	—	—	—	—	—	—	—	—

Region and country of last residence	1820 to 1829	1830 to 1839	1840 to 1849	1850 to 1859	1860 to 1869	1870 to 1879	1880 to 1889	1890 to 1899
Brazil	—	—	—	—	—	—	—	—
Chile	—	—	—	—	—	—	—	—
Colombia	—	—	—	—	—	—	—	—
Ecuador	—	—	—	—	—	—	—	—
Guyana	—	—	—	—	—	—	—	—
Paraguay	—	—	—	—	—	—	—	—
Peru	—	—	—	—	—	—	—	—
Suriname	—	—	—	—	—	—	—	—
Uruguay	—	—	—	—	—	—	—	—
Venezuela	—	—	—	—	—	—	—	—
Other South America	405	957	1,062	3,569	1,536	1,109	1,954	1,389
Other America	—	—	—	—	—	—	—	—
Africa	15	50	61	84	407	371	763	432
Egypt	—	—	—	—	4	29	145	51
Ethiopia	—	—	—	—	—	—	—	—
Liberia	1	8	5	7	43	52	21	9
Morocco	—	—	—	—	—	—	—	—
South Africa	14	42	56	77	35	48	23	9
Other Africa	—	—	—	—	325	242	574	363
Oceania	3	7	14	166	187	9,996	12,361	4,704
Australia	2	1	2	15	—	8,930	7,250	3,098
New Zealand	—	—	—	—	—	39	21	12
Other Oceania	1	6	12	151	187	1,027	5,090	1,594
Not Specified	19,523	83,593	7,366	74,399	18,241	754	790	14,112

Total	8,202,388	6,347,380	4,295,510	699,375	856,608	2,499,268	3,213,749	6,244,379
Europe	7,572,569	4,985,411	2,560,340	444,359	472,524	1,404,973	1,133,443	668,866
Austria-Hungary	2,001,376	1,154,727	60,891	12,531	13,574	113,015	27,590	20,437
Austria	532,416	589,174	31,392	5,307	8,393	81,354	17,571	15,374
Hungary	685,567	565,553	29,499	7,224	5,181	31,661	10,019	5,063
Belgium	37,429	32,574	21,511	4,013	12,473	18,885	9,647	7,028
Bulgaria	34,651	27,180	2,824	1,062	449	97	598	1,124
Czechoslovakia	—	—	101,182	17,757	8,475	1,624	2,758	5,678
Denmark	61,227	45,830	34,406	3,471	4,549	10,918	9,797	4,847
Finland	—	—	16,922	2,433	2,230	4,923	4,310	2,569
France	67,735	60,335	54,842	13,761	36,954	50,113	46,975	32,066
Germany	328,722	174,227	386,634	119,107	119,506	576,905	209,616	85,752
Greece	145,402	193,108	60,774	10,599	8,605	45,153	74,173	37,729
Ireland	344,940	166,445	202,854	28,195	15,701	47,189	37,788	22,210
Italy	1,930,475	1,229,916	528,133	85,053	50,509	184,576	200,111	55,562
Netherlands	42,463	46,065	29,397	7,791	13,877	46,703	37,918	11,234
Norway-Sweden	426,981	192,445	170,329	13,452	17,326	44,224	36,150	13,941
Norway	182,542	79,488	70,327	6,901	8,326	22,806	17,371	3,835
Sweden	244,439	112,957	100,002	6,551	9,000	21,418	18,779	10,106
Poland	—	—	223,316	25,555	7,577	6,465	55,742	63,483
Portugal	65,154	82,489	44,829	3,518	6,765	13,928	70,568	42,685
Romania	57,322	13,566	67,810	5,264	1,254	914	2,339	24,753
Russia	1,501,301	1,106,998	61,604	2,463	605	453	2,329	33,311
Spain	24,818	53,262	47,109	3,669	2,774	6,880	40,793	22,783
Switzerland	32,541	22,839	31,772	5,990	9,904	17,577	19,193	8,316
United Kingdom	469,518	371,878	341,552	61,813	131,794	195,709	220,213	153,644
Yugoslavia	—	—	49,215	6,920	2,039	6,966	17,990	16,267
Other Europe	514	6,527	22,434	9,978	5,584	11,756	6,845	3,447
Asia	299,836	269,736	126,740	19,231	34,532	135,844	358,605	2,391,356
China	19,884	20,916	30,648	5,874	16,072	8,836	14,060	170,897
Hong Kong	—	—	—	—	—	13,781	67,047	112,132
India	3,026	3,478	2,076	554	1,692	1,850	18,638	231,649
Iran	—	—	208	198	1,144	3,195	9,059	98,141
Israel	—	—	—	—	98	21,376	30,911	43,669

Region and country of last residence	1820 to 1829	1830 to 1839	1840 to 1849	1850 to 1859	1860 to 1869	1870 to 1879	1880 to 1889	1890 to 1899
Japan	139,712	77,125	42,057	2,683	1,557	40,651	40,956	44,150
Jordan	—	—	—	—	—	4,899	9,230	28,928
Korea	—	—	—	—	83	4,845	27,048	322,708
Philippines	—	—	—	391	4,099	17,245	70,660	502,056
Syria	—	—	5,307	2,188	1,179	1,091	2,432	14,534
Taiwan	—	—	—	—	—	721	15,657	119,051
Turkey	127,999	160,717	40,450	1,327	754	2,980	9,464	19,208
Vietnam	—	—	—	—	—	290	2,949	200,632
Other Asia	9,215	7,500	5,994	6,016	7,854	14,084	40,494	483,601
America	277,809	1,070,539	1,591,278	230,319	328,435	921,610	1,674,172	2,695,329
Canada and Newfoundland	123,067	708,715	949,286	162,703	160,911	353,169	433,128	156,313
Mexico	31,188	185,334	498,945	32,709	56,158	273,847	441,824	1,009,586
Caribbean	100,960	120,860	83,482	18,052	46,194	115,661	427,235	790,109
Cuba	—	—	12,769	10,641	25,976	73,221	202,030	132,552
Dominican Republic	—	—	—	1,026	4,802	10,219	83,552	221,552
Haiti	—	—	—	156	823	3,787	28,992	121,406
Jamaica	—	—	—	—	—	7,397	62,218	193,874
Other Caribbean	100,960	120,860	70,713	6,229	14,593	21,037	50,443	120,725
Central America	7,341	15,692	16,511	6,840	20,135	40,201	98,560	339,376
Belize	77	40	285	193	433	1,133	4,185	14,964
Costa Rica	—	—	—	431	1,965	4,044	17,975	25,017
El Salvador	—	—	—	597	4,885	5,094	14,405	137,418
Guatemala	—	—	—	423	1,303	4,197	14,357	58,847
Honduras	—	—	—	679	1,874	5,320	15,078	39,071
Nicaragua	—	—	—	405	4,393	7,812	10,383	31,102
Panama	—	—	—	1,452	5,282	12,601	22,177	32,957
Other Central America	7,264	15,652	16,226	2,660	—	—	—	—

South America	15,253	39,938	43,025	9,990	19,662	78,418	250,754	399,862
Argentina	—	—	—	1,067	3,108	16,346	49,384	23,442
Bolivia	—	—	—	50	893	2,759	6,205	9,798
Brazil	—	—	4,627	1,468	3,653	11,547	29,238	22,944
Chile	—	—	—	347	1,320	4,669	12,384	19,749
Colombia	—	—	—	1,027	3,454	15,567	68,371	105,494
Ecuador	—	—	—	244	2,207	8,574	34,107	48,015
Guyana	—	—	—	131	596	1,131	4,546	85,886
Paraguay	—	—	—	33	85	576	1,249	3,518
Peru	—	—	—	321	1,273	5,980	19,783	49,958
Suriname	—	—	—	25	130	299	612	1,357
Uruguay	—	—	—	112	754	1,026	4,089	7,235
Venezuela	—	—	—	1,155	2,182	9,927	20,758	22,405
Other South America	15,253	39,938	38,398	4,010	7	17	28	61
Other America	—	—	29	25	25,375	60,314	22,671	83
Africa	6,326	8,867	6,362	2,120	6,720	13,016	23,780	141,990
Egypt	—	—	1,063	781	1,613	1,996	5,581	26,744
Ethiopia	—	—	—	10	28	302	804	12,927
Liberia	—	—	—	35	37	289	841	6,420
Morocco	—	—	—	73	879	2,703	2,880	3,471
South Africa	6,326	8,867	—	312	1,022	2,278	4,360	15,505
Other Africa	—	—	5,299	909	3,141	5,448	9,314	76,923
Oceania	12,355	12,339	9,860	3,306	14,262	11,353	23,630	41,432
Australia	11,191	11,280	8,404	2,260	11,201	8,275	14,986	16,901
New Zealand	—	—	935	790	2,351	1,799	3,775	6,129
Other Oceania	1,164	1,059	521	256	710	1,279	4,869	18,402
Not Specified	33,493	488	930	—	135	12,472	119	305,406

Region and country of last residence	1990 to 1999	2000 to 2009	2010	2011	2012	2013
Total	9,775,398	10,299,430	1,042,625	1,062,040	1,031,631	990,553
Europe	1,348,612	1,349,609	95,429	90,712	86,956	91,095
Austria-Hungary	27,529	33,929	4,325	4,703	3,208	2,061
Austria	18,234	21,151	3,319	3,654	2,199	1,053
Hungary	9,295	12,778	1,006	1,049	1,009	1,008
Belgium	7,077	8,157	732	700	698	803
Bulgaria	16,948	40,003	2,465	2,549	2,322	2,720
Czechoslovakia	8,970	18,691	1,510	1,374	1,316	1,258
Denmark	6,189	6,049	545	473	492	546
Finland	3,970	3,970	414	398	373	360
France	35,945	45,637	4,339	3,967	4,201	4,668
Germany	92,207	122,373	7,929	7,072	6,732	6,880
Greece	25,403	16,841	966	1,196	1,264	1,526
Ireland	65,384	15,642	1,610	1,533	1,694	1,765
Italy	75,992	28,329	2,956	2,670	2,946	3,233
Netherlands	13,345	17,351	1,520	1,258	1,294	1,376
Norway-Sweden	17,825	19,382	1,662	1,530	1,441	1,665
Norway	5,211	4,599	363	405	314	389
Sweden	12,614	14,783	1,299	1,125	1,127	1,276
Poland	172,249	117,921	7,391	6,634	6,024	6,073
Portugal	25,497	11,479	759	878	837	917
Romania	48,136	52,154	3,735	3,679	3,477	3,475
Russia	433,427	167,152	7,502	8,548	10,114	10,154
Spain	18,443	17,695	2,040	2,319	2,316	2,970
Switzerland	11,768	12,173	868	861	916	1,040
United Kingdom	156,182	171,979	14,781	13,443	13,938	15,321
Yugoslavia	57,039	131,831	4,772	4,611	4,488	4,445
Other Europe	29,087	290,871	22,608	20,316	16,865	17,839

Asia	2,859,399	3,470,835	410,209	438,580	416,488	389,301
China	342,058	591,711	67,634	83,603	78,184	68,410
Hong Kong	116,894	57,583	3,263	3,149	2,642	2,614
India	352,528	590,464	66,185	66,331	63,320	65,506
Iran	76,899	76,755	9,078	9,015	8,955	9,658
Israel	41,340	54,081	5,172	4,389	4,640	4,555
Japan	66,582	84,552	7,100	6,751	6,581	6,383
Jordan	42,755	53,550	9,327	8,211	7,014	5,949
Korea	179,770	209,758	22,022	22,748	20,802	22,937
Philippines	534,338	545,463	56,399	55,251	55,441	52,955
Syria	22,906	30,807	7,424	7,983	6,674	3,999
Taiwan	132,647	92,657	6,785	6,206	5,295	5,336
Turkey	38,687	48,394	7,435	9,040	7,362	7,189
Vietnam	275,379	289,616	30,065	33,486	27,578	26,578
Other Asia	637,116	745,444	112,320	122,417	122,000	107,232
America	5,137,743	4,441,529	426,981	423,277	409,664	399,380
Canada and Newfoundland	194,788	236,349	19,491	19,506	20,138	20,489
Mexico	2,757,418	1,704,166	138,717	142,823	145,326	134,198
Caribbean	1,004,687	1,053,357	139,389	133,012	126,615	121,349
Cuba	159,037	271,742	33,372	36,261	32,551	31,343
Dominican Republic	359,818	291,492	53,890	46,036	41,535	41,487
Haiti	177,446	203,827	22,336	21,802	22,446	20,083
Jamaica	177,143	172,523	19,439	19,298	20,300	19,052
Other Caribbean	181,243	113,773	10,352	9,615	9,783	9,384
Central America	610,189	591,130	43,597	43,249	39,837	44,056
Belize	12,600	9,682	997	933	875	969
Costa Rica	17,054	21,571	2,306	2,230	2,152	2,232
El Salvador	273,017	251,237	18,547	18,477	15,874	18,015
Guatemala	126,043	156,992	10,263	10,795	9,857	9,829
Honduras	72,880	63,513	6,381	6,053	6,773	8,795

Region and country of last residence	1990 to 1999	2000 to 2009	2010	2011	2012	2013
Nicaragua	80,446	70,015	3,476	3,314	2,943	2,940
Panama	28,149	18,120	1,627	1,447	1,363	1,276
Other Central America	—				-	-
South America	570,624	856,508	85,783	84,687	77,748	79,287
Argentina	30,065	47,955	4,312	4,335	4,218	4,227
Bolivia	18,111	21,921	2,211	2,113	1,920	2,005
Brazil	50,744	115,404	12,057	11,643	11,248	10,772
Chile	18,200	19,792	1,940	1,854	1,628	1,751
Colombia	137,985	236,570	21,861	22,130	20,272	20,611
Ecuador	81,358	107,977	11,463	11,068	9,284	10,553
Guyana	74,407	70,373	6,441	6,288	5,282	5,564
Paraguay	6,082	4,623	449	501	454	437
Peru	110,117	137,614	14,063	13,836	12,414	12,370
Suriname	2,285	2,363	202	167	216	170
Uruguay	6,062	9,827	1,286	1,521	1,348	1,314
Venezuela	35,180	82,087	9,497	9,229	9,464	9,512
Other South America	28	2	1	2	-	1
Other America	37	19	4	-	-	1
Africa	346,416	759,734	98,246	97,429	103,685	94,589
Egypt	44,604	81,564	9,822	9,096	10,172	10,719
Ethiopia	40,097	87,207	13,853	13,985	15,400	13,484
Liberia	13,587	23,316	2,924	3,117	3,451	3,036
Morocco	15,768	40,844	4,847	4,249	3,534	3,202
South Africa	21,964	32,221	2,705	2,754	2,960	2,693
Other Africa	210,396	494,582	64,095	64,228	68,168	61,455
Oceania	56,800	65,793	5,946	5,825	5,573	6,061
Australia	24,288	32,728	3,077	3,062	3,146	3,529
New Zealand	8,600	12,495	1,046	1,006	980	1,027
Other Oceania	23,912	20,570	1,823	1,757	1,447	1,505
Not Specified	25,928	211,930	5,814	6,217	9,265	10,127

—Represents zero or not available.

PRESIDENTS, VICE PRESIDENTS, AND SECRETARIES OF STATE

President	Vice President	Secretary of State
1. George Washington, Federalist 1789	John Adams, Federalist 1789	Thomas Jefferson 1789 Edmund Randolph 1794 Timothy Pickering 1795
2. John Adams, Federalist 1797	Thomas Jefferson, Dem.-Rep. 1797	Timothy Pickering 1797 John Marshall 1800
3. Thomas Jefferson, Dem.-Rep. 1801	Aaron Burr, Dem.-Rep. 1801 George Clinton, Dem.-Rep. 1805	James Madison 1801
4. James Madison, Dem.-Rep. 1809	George Clinton, Dem.-Rep. 1809 Elbridge Gerry, Dem.-Rep. 1813	Robert Smith 1809 James Monroe 1811
5. James Monroe, Dem.-Rep. 1817	Daniel D. Tompkins, Dem.-Rep. 1817	John Q. Adams 1817
6. John Quincy Adams, Dem.-Rep. 1825	John C. Calhoun, Dem.-Rep. 1825	Henry Clay 1825
7. Andrew Jackson, Democratic 1829	John C. Calhoun, Democratic 1829 Martin Van Buren, Democratic 1833	Martin Van Buren 1829 Edward Livingston 1831 Louis McLane 1833 John Forsyth 1834
8. Martin Van Buren, Democratic 1837	Richard M. Johnson, Democratic 1837	John Forsyth 1837
9. William H. Harrison, Whig 1841	John Tyler, Whig 1841	Daniel Webster 1841

	President	Vice President	Secretary of State
10.	John Tyler, Whig and Democratic 1841	None	Daniel Webster 1841 Hugh S. Legaré 1843 Abel P. Upshur 1843 John C. Calhoun 1844
11.	James K. Polk, Democratic 1845	George M. Dallas, Democratic 1845	James Buchanan 1845
12.	Zachary Taylor, Whig 1849	Millard Fillmore, Whig 1848	John M. Clayton 1849
13.	Millard Fillmore, Whig 1850	None	Daniel Webster 1850 Edward Everett 1852
14.	Franklin Pierce, Democratic 1853	William R. King, Democratic 1853	William L. Marcy 1853
15.	James Buchanan, Democratic 1857	John C. Breckinridge, Democratic 1857	Lewis Cass 1857 Jeremiah S. Black 1860
16.	Abraham Lincoln, Republican 1861	Hannibal Hamlin, Republican 1861 Andrew Johnson, Unionist 1865	William H. Seward 1861
17.	Andrew Johnson, Unionist 1865	None	William H. Seward 1865
18.	Ulysses S. Grant, Republican 1869	Schuyler Colfax, Republican 1869 Henry Wilson, Republican 1873	Elihu B. Washburne 1869 Hamilton Fish 1869
19.	Rutherford B. Hayes, Republican 1877	William A. Wheeler, Republican 1877	William M. Evarts 1877

	President	Vice President	Secretary of State
20.	James A. Garfield, Republican 1881	Chester A. Arthur, Republican 1881	James G. Blaine 1881
21.	Chester A. Arthur, Republican 1881	None	Frederick T. Frelinghuysen 1881
22.	Grover Cleveland, Democratic 1885	Thomas A. Hendricks, Democratic 1885	Thomas F. Bayard 1885
23.	Benjamin Harrison, Republican 1889	Levi P. Morton, Republican 1889	James G. Blaine 1889 John W. Foster 1892
24.	Grover Cleveland, Democratic 1893	Adlai E. Stevenson, Democratic 1893	Walter Q. Gresham 1893 Richard Olney 1895
25.	William McKinley, Republican 1897	Garret A. Hobart, Republican 1897 Theodore Roosevelt, Republican 1901	John Sherman 1897 William R. Day 1898 John Hay 1898
26.	Theodore Roosevelt, Republican 1901	Charles Fairbanks, Republican 1905	John Hay 1901 Elihu Root 1905 Robert Bacon 1909
27.	William H. Taft, Republican 1909	James S. Sherman, Republican 1909	Philander C. Knox 1909
28.	Woodrow Wilson, Democratic 1913	Thomas R. Marshall, Democratic 1913	William J. Bryan 1913 Robert Lansing 1915 Bainbridge Colby 1920
29.	Warren G. Harding, Republican 1921	Calvin Coolidge, Republican 1921	Charles E. Hughes 1921
30.	Calvin Coolidge, Republican 1923	Charles G. Dawes, Republican 1925	Charles E. Hughes 1923 Frank B. Kellogg 1925

	President	Vice President	Secretary of State
31.	Herbert Hoover, Republican 1929	Charles Curtis, Republican 1929	Henry L. Stimson 1929
32.	Franklin D. Roosevelt, Democratic 1933	John Nance Garner, Democratic 1933 Henry A. Wallace, Democratic 1941 Harry S. Truman, Democratic 1945	Cordell Hull 1933 Edward R. Stettinius, Jr. 1944
33.	Harry S. Truman, Democratic 1945	Alben W. Barkley, Democratic 1949	Edward R. Stettinius, Jr. 1945 James F. Byrnes 1945 George C. Marshall 1947 Dean G. Acheson 1949
34.	Dwight D. Eisenhower, Republican 1953	Richard M. Nixon, Republican 1953	John F. Dulles 1953 Christian A. Herter 1959
35.	John F. Kennedy, Democratic 1961	Lyndon B. Johnson, Democratic 1961	Dean Rusk 1961
36.	Lyndon B. Johnson, Democratic 1963	Hubert H. Humphrey, Democratic 1965	Dean Rusk 1963
37.	Richard M. Nixon, Republican 1969	Spiro T. Agnew, Republican 1969 Gerald R. Ford, Republican 1973	William P. Rogers 1969 Henry Kissinger 1973
38.	Gerald R. Ford, Republican 1974	Nelson Rockefeller, Republican 1974	Henry Kissinger 1974
39.	Jimmy Carter, Democratic 1977	Walter Mondale, Democratic 1977	Cyrus Vance 1977 Edmund Muskie 1980

	President	Vice President	Secretary of State
40.	Ronald Reagan, Republican 1981	George H. W. Bush, Republican 1981	Alexander Haig 1981 George Schultz 1982
41.	George H. W. Bush, Republican 1989	J. Danforth Quayle, Republican 1989	James A. Baker 1989 Lawrence Eagleburger 1992
42.	William J. Clinton, Democratic 1993	Albert Gore, Jr., Democratic 1993	Warren Christopher 1993 Madeleine Albright 1997
43.	George W. Bush, Republican 2001	Richard B. Cheney, Republican 2001	Colin L. Powell 2001 Condoleezza Rice 2005
44.	Barack Obama, Democratic 2009	Joseph R. Biden, Democratic 2009	Hillary Rodham Clinton 2009 John Kerry 2013

FURTHER READINGS

CHAPTER 1

A fascinating study of pre-Columbian migration is Brian M. Fagan's *The Great Journey: The Peopling of Ancient America*, rev. ed. (2004). Alice B. Kehoe's *North American Indians: A Comprehensive Account*, 2nd ed. (1992), provides an encyclopedic treatment of Native Americans. See also Charles Mann's *1491: New Revelations of the Americas before Columbus* (2005) and *1493: Uncovering the New World that Columbua Created* (2011), and Daniel K. Richter, *Before the Revolution: America's Ancient Pasts* (2011). On North America's largest Native American city, see Timothy R. Pauketat, *Cahokia* (2010).

The conflict between Native Americans and Europeans is treated well in James Axtell's *The Invasion Within: The Contest of Cultures in Colonial North America* (1986) and *Beyond 1492: Encounters in Colonial North America* (1992). Colin G. Calloway's *New Worlds for All: Indians, Europeans, and the Remaking of Early America* (1997) explores the ecological effects of European settlement.

Laurence Bergreen examines the voyages of Columbus in *Columbus: The Four Voyages* (2011). To learn about the queen who sent Columbus to the New World, see Kristin Downey's *Isabella: The Warrior Queen* (2014). For sweeping overviews of Spain's creation of a global empire, see Hugh Thomas's *Rivers of Gold: The Rise of the Spanish Empire, from Columbus to Magellan* (2004) and Robert Goodwin, *Spain: The Center of the World, 1519–1682* (2015). David J. Weber examines Spanish colonization in *The Spanish Frontier in North America* (1992). For the French experience, see William J. Eccles's *France in America*, rev. ed. (1990). For an insightful comparison of Spanish and English modes of settlement, see J. H. Elliott, *Empires of the Atlantic World: Britain and Spain in America, 1492–1830* (2006).

CHAPTER 2

Two excellent surveys of early American history are Peter C. Hoffer's *The Brave New World: A History of Early America,* 2nd ed. (2006), and William R. Polk's *The Birth of America: From before Columbus to the Revolution* (2006).

Bernard Bailyn's *The Barbarous Years: The Peopling of British North America: The Conflict of Civilizations, 1600–1675* (2013) tells the often brutal story of British settlement in America during the seventeenth century. Jack P. Greene offers a brilliant synthesis of British colonization in *Pursuits of Happiness: The Social Development of Early Modern British Colonies and the Formation of American Culture* (1988). On the impact of the American environment on colonial settlement, see Malcolm Gaskill's *Between Two Worlds: How the English Became Americans* (2015). The best overview of the colonization of North America is Alan Taylor's *American Colonies: The Settling of North America* (2001). On the interactions among Indian, European, and African cultures, see Gary B. Nash's *Red, White, and Black: The Peoples of Early North America,* 5th ed. (2005).

A good overview of the founding of Virginia and Maryland is Jean and Elliott Russo's *The Early Chesapeake in British North America* (2012). For information regarding the Puritan settlement of New England, see David D. Hall's *A Reforming People: Puritanism and the Transformaiton of Public Life in New England* (2013). The best biography of John Winthrop is Francis J. Bremer's *John Winthrop: America's Forgotten Founding Father* (2003). On Roger Williams, see John M. Barry's *Roger Williams and the Creation of the American Soul* (2012).

The pattern of settlement in the middle colonies is illuminated in Barry Levy's *Quakers and the American Family: British Settlement in the Delaware Valley* (1988). On the early history of New York, see Russell Shorto's *The Island at the Center of the World: The Epic Story of Dutch Manhattan and the Forgotten Colony That Shaped America* (2004). Settlement of the areas along the Atlantic in the South is traced in James Horn's *Adapting to a New World: English Society in the Seventeenth-Century Chesapeake* (1994).

On shifting political life in England, see Steve Pincus, *1688: The First Modern Revolution* (2009). For a study of race and the settlement of South Carolina, see Peter H. Wood's *Black Majority: Negroes in Colonial South Carolina from 1670 through the Stono Rebellion* (1974). On the flourishing trade in captive Indians, see Alan Gallay's *The Indian Slave Trade: The Rise of the English Empire in the American South, 1670–1717* (2002). On the Yamasee War, see Steven J. Oatis's *A Colonial Complex: South Carolina's Frontiers in the Era of the Yamasee War, 1680–1730* (2004).

CHAPTER 3

The diversity of colonial societies may be seen in David Hackett Fischer's *Albion's Seed: Four British Folkways in America* (1989). John Frederick Martin's *Profits in the Wilderness: Entrepreneurship and the Founding of New England Towns in the Seventeenth Century* (1991) indicates that economic concerns rather than spiritual motives were driving forces in many New England towns.

Bernard Rosenthal challenges many myths concerning the Salem witch trials in *Salem Story: Reading the Witch Trials of 1692* (1993). Mary Beth Norton's *In the Devil's Snare: The Salem Witchcraft Crisis of 1692* (2002) emphasizes the role of Indian violence.

Discussions of women in the New England colonies can be found in Laurel Thatcher Ulrich's *Good Wives: Image and Reality in the Lives of Women in Northern New England, 1650–1750* (1980), and Mary Beth Norton, *Separated by Their Sex: Women in Public and Private in the Colonial Atlantic World* (2011). On women and religion, see Susan Juster's *Disorderly Women: Sexual Politics and Evangelicalism in Revolutionary New England* (1994). John Demos describes family life in *A Little Commonwealth: Family Life in Plymouth Colony*, new ed. (2000).

For an excellent overview of Indian relations with Europeans, see Colin G. Calloway's *New Worlds for All: Indians, Europeans, and the Remaking of Early America* (1997). For analyses of Indian wars, see Alfred A. Cave's *The Pequot War* (1996) and Jill Lepore's *The Name of War: King Philip's War and the Origins of American Identity* (1998). The story of the Iroquois is told well in Daniel K. Richter's *The Ordeal of the Longhouse: The Peoples of the Iroquois League in the Era of European Colonization* (1992). Indians in the southern colonies are the focus of James Axtell's *The Indians' New South: Cultural Change in the Colonial Southeast* (1997). On the fur trade, see Eric Jay Dolan, *Fur, Fortune, and Empire: The Epic Story of the Fur Trade in America* (2010).

For the social history of the southern colonies, see Allan Kulikoff's *Tobacco and Slaves: The Development of Southern Cultures in the Chesapeake, 1680–1800* (1986). On the interaction of the cultures of blacks and whites, see Mechal Sobel's *The World They Made Together: Black and White Values in Eighteenth-Century Virginia* (1987). On the slave trade, see William St. Clair's *The Door of No Return* (2007). African Americans during colonial settlement are the focus of Timothy H. Breen and Stephen Innes's *"Myne Owne Ground": Race and Freedom on Virginia's Eastern Shore, 1640–1676*, new ed. (2004). David W. Galenson's *White Servitude in Colonial America: An Economic Analysis* (1981) looks at the indentured labor force.

Henry F. May's *The Enlightenment in America* (1976) and Donald H. Meyer's *The Democratic Enlightenment* (1976) examine intellectual trends in eighteenth-century America. On the Great Awakening, see Frank Lambert's *Inventing the "Great Awakening"* (1999), and Thomas S. Kidd's *The Great Awakening: The Roots of Evangelical Christianity in Colonial America* (2007). Excellent biographies of the key revivalists are Phillip F. Gura's *Jonathan Edwards: A Life* (2003) and Thomas S. Kidd's *George Whitefield* (2015).

CHAPTER 4

A good introduction to the imperial phase of the colonial conflicts is Douglas Edward Leach's *Arms for Empire: A Military History of the British Colonies in North America, 1607–1763* (1973). Also useful is Brendan Simms's *Three Victories and a Defeat: The Rise and Fall of the Fiurst British Empire* (2008). Fred Anderson's *Crucible of War: The Seven Years' War and the Fate of Empire in British North America, 1754–1766* (2000) is the best history of the Seven Years' War. For the implications of the British victory in 1763, see Colin G. Calloway's *The Scratch of a Pen: 1763 and the Transformation of North America* (2006). On the French colonies in North America, see Allan Greer's *The People of New France* (1997).

For a narrative survey of the events leading to the Revolution, see Edward Countryman's *The American Revolution,* rev. ed. (2003). For Great Britain's perspective on the imperial conflict, see Ian R. Christie's *Crisis of Empire: Great Britain and the American Colonies, 1754–1783* (1966). Also see Jeremy Black's *George III: America's Last King* (2007) and David Preston's *Braddock's Defeat* (2015). For the British perspective, see Nick Bunker's *An Empire on the Edge: How Britain Came to Fight America* (2015).

The intellectual foundations of revolt are traced in Bernard Bailyn's *The Ideological Origins of the American Revolution* (1992). To understand how these views were connected to organized protest, see Jon Butler's *Becoming America: The Revolution before 1776* (2000) and Kevin Phillips's *1775: A Good Year for a Revolution* (2012). On the first major battle, see Nathaniel Philbrick's *Bunker Hill: A City, A Siege, A Revolution* (2013).

On the efforts of colonists to boycott the purchase of British goods, see T. H. Breen's *The Marketplace of Revolution: How Consumer Politics Shaped American Independence* (2004). For the events during the summer of 1776, see Joseph J. Ellis's *Revolutionary Summer: The Birth of American Independence.* Pauline Maier's *American Scripture: Making the Declaration of Independence* (1997) remains the best analysis of the framing of that document. The best analysis of why Americans supported independence is Thomas Slaughter's *Independence: The Tangled Roots of the American Revolution* (2014).

CHAPTER 5

Military affairs in the early phases of the Revolutionary War are handled in John W. Shy's *Toward Lexington: The Role of the British Army in the Coming of the American Revolution* (1965). The Revolutionary War is the subject of Gordon S. Wood's *The Radicalism of the American Revolution* (1991) and Jeremy Black's *War for America: The Fight for Independence, 1775–1783* (1991). John Ferling's *Setting the World Ablaze: Washington, Adams, Jefferson, and the American Revolution* (2000) highlights the roles played by key leaders. For a splendid account of Washington's generalship, see Robert Middlekauf's *Washington's Revolution: The Making of America's First Great Leader* (2015).

On the social history of the Revolutionary War, see John W. Shy's *A People Numerous and Armed: Reflections on the Military Struggle for American Independence*, rev. ed. (1990). Colin G. Calloway tells the neglected story of the Indian experiences in the Revolution in *The American Revolution in Indian Country: Crisis and Diversity in Native American Communities* (1995).

Why some Americans remained loyal to the Crown is the subject of Thomas B. Allen's *Tories: Fighting for the King in America's First Civil War* (2010) and Maya Jasanoff's *Liberty's Exiles: American Loyalists in the Revolutionary War* (2011). A superb study of African Americans during the Revolutionary era is Douglas R. Egerton's *Death or Liberty: African Americans and Revolutionary America* (2009).

Carol Berkin's *Revolutionary Mothers: Women in the Struggle for America's Independence* (2005) documents the role that women played in securing independence. A superb biography of Revolutionary America's most prominent woman is Woody Holton's *Abigail Adams* (2010). A fine new biography of America's commander in chief is Ron Chernow's *Washington: A Life* (2010). The best analysis of the British side of the war is Andrew Jackson O'Shaughnessy's *The Men Who Lost America: British Leadership, the American Revolution, and the Fate of Empire* (2013).

CHAPTER 6

A good overview of the Confederation period is Richard B. Morris's *The Forging of the Union, 1781–1789* (1987). Another useful analysis of this period is Richard Buel Jr.'s *Securing the Revolution: Ideology in American*

Politics, 1789–1815 (1972). David P. Szatmary's *Shays's Rebellion: The Making of an Agrarian Insurrection* (1980) covers that fateful incident. For a fine account of cultural change during the period, see Joseph J. Ellis's *After the Revolution: Profiles of Early American Culture* (1979).

An excellent overview of post-Revolutionary life is Joyce Appleby's *Inheriting the Revolution: The First Generation of Americans* (2000). On the political philosophies contributing to the drafting of the Constitution, see Ralph Lerner's *The Thinking Revolutionary: Principle and Practice in the New Republic* (1987). For the dramatic story of the framers of the Constitution, see Richard Beeman's *Plain, Honest Men: The Making of the American Constitution* (2009). Woody Holton's *Unruly Americans and the Origins of the Constitution* (2007) emphasizes the role of taxes and monetary policies in the crafting of the Constitution. The complex story of ratification is well told in Pauline Maier's *Ratification: The People Debate the Constitution, 1787–1788* (2010). An excellent study of James Madison's development as a political theorist is Michael Signer's *Becoming Madison* (2015).

The best introduction to the early Federalists remains John C. Miller's *The Federalist Era, 1789–1801* (2011). Other works analyze the ideological debates among the nation's first leaders. Richard Buel Jr.'s *Securing the Revolution: Ideology in American Politics, 1789–1815* (1972), Joyce Appleby's *Capitalism and a New Social Order: The Republican Vision of the 1790s* (1984), and Stanley Elkins and Eric McKitrick's *The Age of Federalism: The Early American Republic, 1788–1800* (1993) trace the persistence and transformation of ideas first fostered during the Revolutionary crisis. The best study of Washington's political career is John Ferling's *The Ascent of George Washington: The Hidden Political Genius of an American Icon* (2009). For compelling portraits of four key leaders, see Joseph J. Ellis's *The Quartet: Orchestrating the Second American Revolution, 1783–1789* (2015).

The 1790s may also be understood through the views and behavior of national leaders. See the following biographies: Richard Brookhiser's *Founding Father: Rediscovering George Washington* (1996), *Alexander Hamilton, American* (1999), and *James Madison* (2013), and Joseph J. Ellis's *Passionate Sage: The Character and Legacy of John Adams* (1993).

On the formation of the federal government and its economic policies, see Thomas K. McCraw's *The Founders and Finance* (2012). Federalist foreign policy is explored in Jerald A. Comb's *The Jay Treaty: Political Battleground of the Founding Fathers* (1970) and William Stinchcombe's *The XYZ Affair* (1980).

CHAPTER 7

Marshall Smelser's *The Democratic Republic, 1801–1815* (1968) presents an overview of the Republican administrations. Even more comprehensive is Gordon S. Wood's *Empire of Liberty: A History of the Early Republic, 1789–1815* (2010). The best treatment of the election of 1800 is Edward J. Larson's *A Magnificent Catastrophe: The Tumultuous Election of 1800* (2008).

The standard biography of Jefferson is Joseph J. Ellis's *American Sphinx: The Character of Thomas Jefferson* (1996). A more recent analysis is Andrew Burstein's *Democracy's Muse* (2015). On the life of Jefferson's friend and successor, see Drew R. McCoy's *The Last of the Fathers: James Madison and the Republican Legacy* (1989). Joyce Appleby's *Capitalism and a New Social Order: The Republican Vision of the 1790s* (1984) minimizes the impact of Republican ideology.

Linda K. Kerber's *Federalists in Dissent: Imagery and Ideology in Jeffersonian American* (1970) explores the Federalists while out of power. The concept of judicial review and the courts can be studied in Cliff Sloan and David McKean's *The Great Decision: Jefferson, Adams, Marshall, and the Battle for the Supreme Court* (2009). Liff Sloan and David McKean's *The Great Decision: Jefferson, Adams, Marshall, and the Battle for the Supreme Court* (2009). Milton Lomask's two volumes, *Aaron Burr: The Years from Princeton to Vice President, 1756–1805* (1979) and *The Conspiracy and the Years of Exile, 1805–1836* (1982), trace the career of that remarkable American.

For the Louisiana Purchase, consult Jon Kukla's *A Wilderness So Immense: The Louisiana Purchase and the Destiny of America* (2003). For a captivating account of the Lewis and Clark expedition, see Stephen Ambrose's *Undaunted Courage: Meriwether Lewis, Thomas Jefferson, and the Opening of the American West* (1996).

Burton Spivak's *Jefferson's English Crisis: Commerce, Embargo, and the Republican Revolution* (1979) discusses Anglo-American relations during Jefferson's administration; Clifford L. Egan's *Neither Peace Nor War: Franco-American Relations, 1803–1812* (1983) covers America's relations with France. An excellent revisionist treatment of the events that brought on war in 1812 is J. C. A. Stagg's *Mr. Madison's War: Politics, Diplomacy, and Warfare in the Early American Republic, 1783–1830* (1983). See also Paul A. Gilje's *Free Trade and Sailors' Rights in the War of 1812* (2013). The war itself is the focus of Donald R. Hickey's *The War of 1812: A Forgotten Conflict* (1989). For the perspective of those who fought in the war, see A. J. Langguth's *Union 1812: The Americans Who Fought the Second War of Independence* (2007). See also Alan Taylor's award-winnning *The Civil War of 1812: American Citizens, British Subjects, Irish Rebels, and Indian Allies* (2011).

CHAPTER 8

The best overview of the second quarter of the nineteenth century is Daniel Walker Howe, *What Hath God Wrought: The Transformation of America, 1815–1845* (2007). The classic study of transportation and economic growth is George Rogers Taylor's *The Transportation Revolution, 1815–1860* (1951). A more recent treatment is Sarah H. Gordon's *Passage to Union: How the Railroads Transformed American Life, 1829–1929* (1996). On the Erie Canal, see Carol Sheriff's *The Artificial River: The Erie Canal and the Paradox of Progress, 1817–1862* (1996). See also John Lauritz Larson's *Internal Improvement: National Public Works and the Promise of Popular Government in the Early United States* (2001).

Several books focus on social issues of the post-Revolutionary period, including *Keepers of the Revolution: New Yorkers at Work in the Early Republic* (1992), edited by Paul A. Gilje and Howard B. Rock; Ronald Schultz's *The Republic of Labor: Philadelphia Artisans and the Politics of Class, 1720–1830* (1993); and Peter Way's *Common Labor: Workers and the Digging of North American Canals, 1780–1860* (1993).

On the industrial revolution, see Charles R. Morris's *The Dawn of Innovation: The First American Industrial Revolution* (2013). The impact of technology is traced in David J. Jeremy's *Transatlantic Industrial Revolution: The Diffusion of Textile Technologies between Britain and America, 1790–1830s* (1981). On the invention of the telegraph, see Kenneth Silverman's *Lightning Man: The Accursed Life of Samuel F. B. Morse* (2003). For the story of steamboats, see Andrea Sutcliffe's *Steam: The Untold Story of America's First Great Invention* (2004).

The outlook of the working class during this time of transition is surveyed in Edward E. Pessen's *Most Uncommon Jacksonians: The Radical Leaders of the Early Labor Movement* (1967). Detailed case studies of working communities include Anthony F. C. Wallace's *Rockdale: The Growth of an American Village in the Early Industrial Revolution* (1978), Thomas Dublin's *Women at Work: The Transformation of Work and Community in Lowell, Massachusetts, 1826–1860* (1979), and Sean Wilentz's *Chants Democratic: New York and the Rise of the American Working Class, 1788–1850* (1984).

For a fine treatment of urbanization, see Charles N. Glaab and A. Theodore Brown's *A History of Urban America* (1967). On immigration, see Jay P.

Dolan's *The Irish Americans* (2008) and John Kelly's *The Graves Are Walking: The Great Famine and the Saga of the Irish People* (2012).

CHAPTER 9

The standard overview of the Era of Good Feelings remains George Danger-field's *The Awakening of American Nationalism, 1815–1828* (1965). A classic summary of the economic trends of the period is Douglass C. North's *The Economic Growth of the United States, 1790–1860* (1961). An excellent synthesis of the era is Charles Sellers's *The Market Revolution: Jacksonian America, 1815–1846* (1991).

On diplomatic relations during James Monroe's presidency, see William Earl Weeks's *John Quincy Adams and American Global Empire* (1992). For relations after 1812, see Ernest R. May's *The Making of the Monroe Doctrine* (1975). The campaign that brought Andrew Jackson to the White House is analyzed in Robert Vincent Remini's *The Election of Andrew Jackson* (1963).

CHAPTER 10

The best comprehensive surveys of politics and culture during the Jacksonian era are Daniel Walker Howe's *What Hath God Wrought: The Transformation of America, 1815–1848* (2007) and David S. Reynolds's *Waking Giant: America in the Age of Jackson* (2008). A more political focus can be found in Harry L. Watson's *Liberty and Power: The Politics of Jacksonian America* (1990). On the rise of urban political machines, see Terry Golway's *Machine Made: Tammany Hall and the Creation of Modern American Politics* (2014).

For an outstanding analysis of women in New York City during the Jacksonian period, see Christine Stansell's *City of Women: Sex and Class in New York, 1789–1860* (1986). In *Chants Democratic: New York City and the Rise of the American Working-Class, 1788–1850* (1984), Sean Wilentz analyzes the social basis of working-class politics. More recently, Wilentz has traced the democratization of politics in *The Rise of American Democracy: Jefferson to Lincoln* (2009).

The best biography of Jackson remains Robert Vincent Remini's three-volume work: *Andrew Jackson: The Course of American Empire, 1767–1821* (1977), *Andrew Jackson: The Course of American Freedom, 1822–1832* (1981), and *Andrew Jackson: The Course of American Democracy, 1833–1845* (1984). A more critical study of the seventh president is Andrew Burstein's *The Passions of Andrew Jackson* (2003).

On Jackson's successor, consult John Niven's *Martin Van Buren: The Romantic Age of American Politics* (1983) and Ted Widmer's *Martin Van Buren* (2005). Studies of other major figures of the period include John Niven's *John C. Calhoun and the Price of Union: A Biography* (1988), Merrill D. Peterson's *The Great Triumvirate: Webster, Clay, and Calhoun* (1987), and Robert Vincent Remini's *Henry Clay: Statesman for the Union* (1991) and *Daniel Webster: The Man and His Time* (1997).

The political philosophies of Jackson's opponents are treated in Michael F. Holt's *The Rise and Fall of the American Whig Party: Jacksonian Politics and the Onset of the Civil War* (1999) and Harry L. Watson's *Andrew Jackson vs. Henry Clay: Democracy and Development in Antebellum America* (1998). The outstanding book on the nullification issue remains William W. Freehling's *Prelude to Civil War: The Nullification Controversy in South Carolina, 1816–1836* (1965). John M. Belohlavek's *"Let the Eagle Soar!": The Foreign Policy of Andrew Jackson* (1985) is a thorough study of Jacksonian diplomacy. A. J. Langguth's *Driven West: Andrew Jackson and the Trail of Tears to the Civil War* (2010) analyzes the controversial relocation policy.

CHAPTER 11

Three efforts to understand the mind of the Old South and its defense of slavery are Eugene D. Genovese's *The Slaveholders' Dilemma: Freedom and Progress in Southern Conservative Thought, 1820–1860* (1992), William W. Freehling's *The Road to Disunion: Secessionists Triumphant, 1854–1861* (2007), and Walter Johnson's *River of Dark Dreams: Slavery and Empire in the Cotton Kingdom* (2013). Stephanie McCurry's *Masters of Small Worlds: Yeoman Households, Gender Relations, and the Political Culture of the Antebellum South Carolina Low Country* (1995) describes southern households, religion, and political culture. The best recent book on the role of slavery in creating the cotton culture is Edward E. Baptist's *The Half Has Never Been Told: Slavery and the Making of American Capitalism* (2014).

Other essential works on southern culture and society include Bertram Wyatt-Brown's *Honor and Violence in the Old South* (1986), Elizabeth Fox-Genovese's *Within the Plantation Household: Black and White Women of the Old South* (1988), Catherine Clinton's *The Plantation Mistress: Woman's World in the Old South* (1982), Joan E. Cashin's *A Family Venture: Men and Women on the Southern Frontier* (1991), and Theodore Rosengarten's *Tombee: Portrait of a Cotton Planter* (1986).

John W. Blassingame's *The Slave Community: Plantation Life in the Antebellum South*, rev. and enlarged ed. (1979), Eugene D. Genovese's *Roll, Jordan,*

Roll: The World the Slaves Made (1974), and Herbert G. Gutman's *The Black Family in Slavery and Freedom, 1750–1925* (1976) all stress the theme of a persisting and identifiable slave culture. On the question of slavery's profitability, see Robert William Fogel and Stanley L. Engerman's *Time on the Cross: The Economics of American Negro Slavery* (1974), and Edward E. Baptist's *The Half Has Never Been Told* (2014). Charles Joyner's *Down by the Riverside: A South Carolina Slave Community* (1984) offers a vivid reconstruction of one community.

CHAPTER 12

Russel Blaine Nye's *Society and Culture in America, 1830–1860* (1974) provides a wide-ranging survey of the Romantic movement. On the reform impulse, consult Ronald G. Walter's *American Reformers, 1815–1860*, rev. ed. (1997). Revivalist religion is treated in Nathan O. Hatch's *The Democratization of American Christianity* (1989), Christine Leigh Heyrman's *Southern Cross: The Beginnings of the Bible Belt* (1997), and Ellen Eslinger's *Citizens of Zion: The Social Origins of Camp Meeting Revivalism* (1999). On the Mormons, see Alex Beam's *American Crucifixion: The Murder of Joseph Smith and the Fate of the Mormon Church* (2014).

The best treatments of transcendentalist thought are Paul F. Boller's *American Transcendentalism, 1830–1860: An Intellectual Inquiry* (1974) and Philip F. Gura's *American Transcendentalism: A History* (2007). On Henry D. Thoreau, see Michael Sims's *The Adventures of Henry Thoreau* (2014). Edgar Allan Poe is the subject of Jerome McGann's *The Poet Edgar Allan Poe: Alien Angel* (2015). For the war against alcohol, see W. J. Rorabaugh's *The Alcoholic Republic: An American Tradition* (1979) and Barbara Leslie Epstein's *The Politics of Domesticity: Women, Evangelism, and Temperance in Nineteenth-Century America* (1981). On prison reform and other humanitarian projects, see David J. Rothman's *The Discovery of the Asylum: Social Order and Disorder in the New Republic*, rev. ed. (2002), and Thomas J. Brown's biography *Dorothea Dix: New England Reformer* (1998).

Useful surveys of abolitionism include Seymour Drescher's *Abolition: A History of Slavery and Antislavery* (2009), James Brewer Stewart's *Holy Warriors: The Abolitionists and American Slavery*, rev. ed. (1997), and Julie Roy Jeffrey's *The Great Silent Army of Abolitionism: Ordinary Women in the Antislavery Movement* (1998). For the pro-slavery argument as it developed in the South, see Larry E. Tise's *Proslavery: A History of the Defense of Slavery in America, 1701–1840* (1987) and James Oakes's *The Ruling Race: A History of American Slaveholders* (1982). The problems southerners had in justifying slavery are explored in Kenneth S. Greenberg's *Masters and Statesmen: The Political Culture of American Slavery* (1985). For the dramatic story of the role of the Underground Railroad in freeing slaves, see Eric Foner's *Gateway to Freedom: The Hidden History of the Underground Railroad* (2015).

CHAPTER 13

For background on Whig programs and ideas, see Michael F. Holt's *The Rise and Fall of the American Whig Party: Jacksonian Politics and the Onset of the Civil War* (1999). On John Tyler, see Edward P. Crapol's *John Tyler: The Accidental President* (2006). On the expansionist impulse westward, see Thomas R. Hietala's *Manifest Design: Anxious Aggrandizement in Late Jacksonian America* (1985), Walter Nugent's *Habits of Empire: A History of American Expansionism* (2008) and Richard White's *"It's Your Misfortune and None of My Own": A New History of the American West* (1991).

For the expansionism of the 1840s, see Steven E. Woodworth's *Manifest Destinies: America's Westward Expansion and the Road to the Civil War* (2010). The movement of settlers to the West is ably documented in John Mack Faragher's *Women and Men on the Overland Trail*, 2nd ed. (2001), David Dary's *The Santa Fe Trail: Its History, Legends, and Lore* (2000), and Rinker Buck's *The Oregon Trail* (2015).

Gene M. Brack's *Mexico Views Manifest Destiny, 1821–1846: An Essay on the Origins of the Mexican War* (1975) takes Mexico's viewpoint on U.S. designs on the West. For the American perspective on Texas, see Joel H. Silbey's *Storm over Texas: The Annexation Controversy and the Road to Civil War* (2005). On the siege of the Alamo, see William C. Davis's *Three Roads to the Alamo: The Lives and Fortunes of David Crockett, James Bowie, and William Barret Travis* (1998) and James Donovan's *The Blood of Heroes* (2012). An excellent biography related to the emergence of Texas is Gregg Cantrell's *Stephen F. Austin: Empresario of Texas* (1999).

On James K. Polk, see Robert W. Merry's *A Country of Vast Designs: James K. Polk, the Mexican War, and the Conquest of the American Continent* (2009). The best survey of the military conflict is John S. D. Eisenhower's *So Far from God: The U.S. War with Mexico, 1846–1848* (1989). The Mexican War as viewed from the perspective of the soldiers is ably described in Richard Bruce Winders's *Mr. Polk's Army: American Military Experience in the Mexican War* (1997). On the diplomatic aspects of Mexican-American relations, see David M. Pletcher's *The Diplomacy of Annexation: Texas, Oregon, and the Mexican War* (1973).

CHAPTER 14

The best surveys of the forces and events leading to the Civil War include James M. McPherson's *Battle Cry of Freedom: The Civil War Era* (1988), Stephen B. Oates's *The Approaching Fury: Voices of the Storm, 1820–1861* (1997), James Oakes's *The Scorpion's Sting: Antislavery and the Coming of the Civil War* (2015), and Bruce Levine's *Half Slave and Half Free: The Roots of Civil War* (1992). The most recent narrative of the political debate leading to secession is Michael A. Morrison's *Slavery and the American West: The Eclipse of Manifest Destiny and the Coming of the Civil War* (1997).

Mark J. Stegmaier's *Texas, New Mexico, and the Compromise of 1850: Boundary Dispute and Sectional Crisis* (1996) probes that crucial dispute, while Michael F. Holt's *The Political Crisis of the 1850s* (1978) traces the demise of the Whigs. See also Fergus M. Bordewich's *America's Great Debate: Henry Clay, Stephen A. Douglas, and the Compromise That Preserved the Union* (2012). Eric Foner, in *Free Soil, Free Labor, Free Men: The Ideology of the Republican Party before the Civil War* (1970), shows how events and ideas combined in the formation of a new political party. The pivotal *Dred Scott* case is ably assessed in Earl M. Maltz's *Dred Scott and the Politics of Slavery* (2007).

On the role of John Brown in the sectional crisis, see Robert E. McGlone's *John Brown's War Against Slavery* (2009). A detailed study of the South's journey to secession is William W. Freehling's *The Road to Disunion*, vol. 1, *Secessionists at Bay, 1776–1854* (1990), and *The Road to Disunion*, vol. 2, *Secessionists Triumphant, 1854–1861* (2007). Robert E. Bonner traces the emergence of southern nationalism in *Mastering America: Southern Slaveholders and the Crisis of American Nationhood* (2009).

On the Buchanan presidency, see Jean H. Baker's *James Buchanan* (2004). Maury Klein's *Days of Defiance: Sumter, Secession, and the Coming of the Civil War* (1997) treats the Fort Sumter controversy. An excellent collection of interpretive essays is *Why the Civil War Came* (1996), edited by Gabor S. Boritt.

CHAPTER 15

On the start of the Civil War, see Adam Goodheart's *1861: The Civil War Awakening* (2011). The best one-volume overview of the Civil War period is James M. McPherson's *Battle Cry of Freedom: The Civil War Era* (1988). A more recent synthesis of the war and its effects is David Goldfield's *America*

Aflame: How the Civil War Created a Nation (2011). A good introduction to the military events is Herman Hattaway's *Shades of Blue and Gray: An Introductory Military History of the Civil War* (1997). The outlook and experiences of the common soldier are explored in James M. McPherson's *For Cause and Comrades: Why Men Fought in the Civil War* (1997. For the global dimensions of the conflict, see Don H. Doyle's *The Cause of All Nations: An International History of the American Civil War* (2015).

The northern war effort is ably assessed in Gary W. Gallagher's *The Union War* (2011). For emphasis on the South, see Gallagher's *The Confederate War* (1997). A sparkling account of the birth of the Rebel nation is William C. Davis's *"A Government of Our Own": The Making of the Confederacy* (1994). On the president of the Confederacy, see James M. McPherson's *Embattled Rebel: Jefferson Davis as Commander in Chief* (2014). . On two of the leading Confederate commanders, see Michael Korda's *Clouds of Glory: The Life and Legend of Robert E. Lee* (2014) and S. C. Gwynne's *Rebel Yell: Stonewall Jackson* (2014). On the key Union generals, see Lee Kennett's *Sherman: A Soldier's Life* (2001) and Josiah Bunting III's *Ulysses S. Grant* (2004). The controversy over Sherman's March to the Sea is the focus of Matthew Carr's *Sherman's Ghosts: Soldiers, Civilians, and the American Way of War* (2015).

The history of the North during the war is surveyed in Philip Shaw Paludan's *A People's Contest: The Union and Civil War, 1861–1865,* 2nd ed. (1996), and J. Matthew Gallman's *The North Fights the Civil War: The Home Front* (1994). See also Jennifer L. Weber's *Copperheads: The Rise and Fall of Lincoln's Opponents in the North* (2006). The central northern political figure, Abraham Lincoln, is the subject of many books. See James McPherson's *Abraham Lincoln* (2009) and Ronald C. White Jr., *A. Lincoln: A Biography* (2009).

The experience of the African American soldier is surveyed in Joseph T. Glatthaar's *Forged in Battle: The Civil War Alliance of Black Soldiers and White Officers* (1990) and Ira Berlin, Joseph P. Reidy, and Leslie S. Rowland's *Freedom's Soldiers: The Black Military Experience in the Civil War* (1998). For the African American woman's experience, see Jacqueline Jones's *Labor of Love, Labor of Sorrow: Black Women, Work and the Family, from Slavery to the Present* (1985). On Lincoln's evolving racial views, see Eric Foner's *The Fiery Trial: Abraham Lincoln and American Slavery* (2010). The war's impact on slavery is the focus of James Oakes's *Freedom National: The Destruction of Slavery in the United States, 1861–1865* (2013) and Bruce Levine's *The Fall of the House of Dixie* (2013). On the emancipation proclamation, see Louis P. Masur's *Lincoln's Hundred Days: The Emancipation Proclamation and the War for the Union* (2012). For a sensory perspective on the fighting, see Mark M. Smith's *The Smell of Battle, the Taste of Siege: A Sensory History of the Civil War* (2014).

Recent gender and ethnic studies include Nina Silber's *Gender and the Sectional Conflict* (2008), Drew Gilpin Faust's *Mothers of Invention: Women of the Slaveholding South in the American Civil War* (1996), George C. Rable's *Civil Wars: Women and the Crisis of Southern Nationalism* (1989), and William L. Burton's *Melting Pot Soldiers: The Union's Ethnic Regiments*, 2nd ed. (1998). What Civil War veterans experienced after the conflict ended is the subject of Brian Matthew Jordan's *Marching Home* (2015) and Gregory P. Downs's *After Appomattox: Military Occupation and the Ends of War* (2015).

CHAPTER 16

The most comprehensive treatment of Reconstruction is Eric Foner's *Reconstruction: America's Unfinished Revolution, 1863–1877* (1988). On Andrew Johnson, see Hans L. Trefousse's *Andrew Johnson: A Biography* (1989) and David D. Stewart's *Impeached: The Trial of Andrew Johnson and the Fight for Lincoln's Legacy* (2009). An excellent brief biography of Grant is Josiah Bunting III's *Ulysses S. Grant* (2004).

Scholars have been sympathetic to the aims and motives of the Radical Republicans. See, for instance, Herman Belz's *Reconstructing the Union: Theory and Policy during the Civil War* (1969) and Richard Nelson Current's *Those Terrible Carpetbaggers: A Reinterpretation* (1988). The ideology of the Radicals is explored in Michael Les Benedict's *A Compromise of Principle: Congressional Republicans and Reconstruction, 1863–1869* (1974). On the black political leaders, see Phillip Dray's *Capitol Men: The Epic Story of Reconstruction through the Lives of the First Black Congressmen* (2008).

The intransigence of southern white attitudes is examined in Michael Perman's *Reunion without Compromise: The South and Reconstruction, 1865–1868* (1973) and Dan T. Carter's *When the War Was Over: The Failure of Self-Reconstruction in the South, 1865–1867* (1985). Allen W. Trelease's *White Terror: The Ku Klux Klan Conspiracy and Southern Reconstruction* (1971) covers the various organizations that practiced vigilante tactics. On the massacre of African Americans, see Charles Lane's *The Day Freedom Died: The Colfax Massacre, the Supreme Court, and the Betrayal of Reconstruction* (2008).

The difficulties former slaves had in adjusting to the new labor system are documented in James L. Roark's *Masters without Slaves: Southern Planters in the Civil War and Reconstruction* (1977). Books on southern politics during Reconstruction include Michael Perman's *The Road to Redemption: Southern*

Politics, 1869–1879 (1984), Terry L. Seip's *The South Returns to Congress: Men, Economic Measures, and Intersectional Relationships, 1868–1879* (1983), and Mark W. Summers's *Railroads, Reconstruction, and the Gospel of Prosperity: Aid under the Radical Republicans, 1865–1877* (1984).

Numerous works study the freed blacks' experience in the South. Start with Leon F. Litwack's *Been in the Storm So Long: The Aftermath of Slavery* (1979). The Freedmen's Bureau is explored in William S. McFeely's *Yankee Stepfather: General O. O. Howard and the Freedmen* (1968). The situation of freed slave women is discussed in Jacqueline Jones's *Labor of Love, Labor of Sorrow: Black Women, Work and the Family, from Slavery to the Present* (1985).

The politics of corruption outside the South is depicted in William S. McFeely's *Grant: A Biography* (1981). The political maneuvers of the election of 1876 and the resultant crisis and compromise are explained in Michael Holt's *By One Vote: The Disputed Presidential Election of 1876* (2008).

CREDITS

PART 1: **p. 1**: Werner Forman/Art Resource, NY; **p. 2**: British Museum/Art Resource.

CHAPTER 1: **p. 4**: bpk, Berlin/Kunstbibliothek, Staatliche Museen/Knud Petersen/Art Resource; **p. 10**: Richard A. Cooke/Corbis; **p. 11**: MPI/Getty Images; **p. 22**: The Benson Latin American Collection, University of Texas; **p. 26**: Atlantide Phototravel/Corbis; **p. 31**: Werner Forman/Art Resource, NY; **p. 36**: Bettmann/Corbis.

CHAPTER 2: **p. 40**: British Library, London, UK/© British Library Board. All Rights Reserved/ Bridgeman Images; **p. 42**: Granger Collection; **p. 49**: Granger Collection; **p. 55**: Granger Collection; **p. 56**: Granger Collection; **p. 62**: The Mariners' Museum/Corbis; **p. 67**: Stapleton Collection/Corbis; **p. 72**: Library of Congress; **p. 76**: Granger Collection; **p. 78**: Granger Collection.

CHAPTER 3: **p. 82**: Granger Collection; **p. 84**: Granger Collection; **p. 87**: Connecticut Historical Society Museum; **p. 89**: Granger Collection; **p. 92**: Granger Collection; **p. 101**: Granger Collection; **p. 104**: Library Company of Philadelphia; **p. 106**: Stock Montage/Getty Images; **p. 109**: Granger Collection; **p. 110**: National Portrait Gallery, London.

CHAPTER 4: **p. 116**: Granger Collection; **p. 119**: Snark/Art Resource, NY; **p. 122**: I.N. Phelps Stokes Collection Miriam and Ira D. Wallach Division of Art, Prints and Photographs, New York Public Library, Astor, Lenox and Tilden Foundations. Art Resource, NY; **p. 128**: Library of Congress; **p. 129**: Granger Collection; **p. 137**: Library of Congress; **p. 140**: Library of Congress; **p. 145**: Granger Collection; **p. 148**: Courtesy of the Historical Society of Pennsylvania Collection, Atwater Kent Museum of Philadelphia; **p. 150** National Archives; **p. 151**: North Wind Picture Archives/Alamy.

PART 2: **p. 157**: Granger Collection; **p. 158**: Granger Collection.

CHAPTER 5: **p. 160**: Francis G. Mayer/Corbis; **p. 163**: US Senate Collection; **p. 167 (left)**: Private Collection/Photo © Christie's Images/The Bridgeman Art Library; **(right)**: Granger Collection; **p. 172**: Anne S.K. Brown Military Collection, Brown University Library **p. 175**: Granger Collection; **p. 191**: Granger Collection.

CHAPTER 6: **p. 198**: Granger Collection; **p. 204**: Print Collection, Miriam and Ira D. Wallach Division of Art, Prints, and Photographs, The New York Public Library; Astor, Lenox, and Tilden Foundations; **p. 206**: Granger Collection; **p. 209**: Granger Collection; **p. 212**: Independence National Historical Park; **p. 214**: Granger Collection; **p. 218**: Library of Congress; **p. 223**: Independence National Historical Park; **p. 228**: Granger Collection; **p. 234**: Granger Collection; **p. 236**: Granger Collection; **p. 238**: Granger Collection; **p. 239**: Granger Collection.

CHAPTER 7: **p. 246**: Photography by Erik Arnesen © Nicholas S. West; **p. 250**: Library of Congress; **p. 253**: Collection of the New-York Historical Society/Bridgeman Art Library; **p. 259**: Photo by EncMstr / Wikimedia Commons; https://creativecommons.org/licenses/by-sa/3.0/deed.en; **p. 261**: Library of Congress; **p. 265**: Library of Congress; **p. 274**: Granger Collection.

PART 3: **p. 283**: Saint Louis Art Museum, Gift of Bank of America; **p. 284**: Yale University Art Gallery/Wikimedia, pd; **p. 285**: The Walters Art Museum, Baltimore.

CHAPTER 8: p. 286: Granger Collection; **p. 294**: © Collection of the New-York Historical Society/ Bridgeman Images; **p. 297**: Fenimore Art Museum; **p. 300**: Granger Collection; **p. 303**: Granger Collection; **p. 308**: Board of Trustees, National Gallery of Art, Washington 1980.62.9. (2794) PA; **p. 309**: Library of Congress; **p. 312**: Library of Congress; **p. 314**: The New York Public Library/Art Resource, NY; **p. 315**: John W. Bennett Labor Collection, Special Collections and University Archives, W. E. B. Du Bois Library, University of Massachusetts Amherst.

CHAPTER 9: p. 320: Photo © Christie's Images/Bridgeman Images; **p. 325**: Image copyright © The Metropolitan Museum of Art. Image source: Art Resource, NY; **p. 327**: Granger Collection; **p. 333**: Granger Collection; **p. 338**: Image copyright © The Metropolitan Museum of Art. Image source: Art Resource, NY.

CHAPTER 10: p. 346: The Museum of the City of New York/Art Resource, NY; **p. 349**: Library of Congress; **p. 352**: Library of Congress; **p. 357**: Granger Collection; **p. 359**: Library of Congress; **p. 362**: Courtesy Boston Art Commission 2014; **p. 366**: Saint Louis Art Museum, Gift of Bank of America; **p. 372**: Corbis; **p. 374**: Library of Congress.

CHAPTER 11: p. 382: Universal History Archive/UIG/Bridgeman Images; **p. 387**: Paul Verkin/ National Geographic Society/Corbis; **p. 394**: Fotosearch/Getty Images; **p. 398**: Courtesy of The Charleston Museum, Charleston, South Carolina; **p. 405**: Private Collection/Peter Newark American Pictures/Bridgeman Art Library; **p. 408**: The Historic New Orleans Collection/Bridgeman Images; **p. 413**: Library of Congress.

CHAPTER 12: p. 418: Munson-Williams-Proctor Arts Institute/Art Resource, NY; **p. 423**: Granger Collection; **p. 425**: Image copyright © The Metropolitan Museum of Art. Image source: Art Resource, NY; **p. 429**: Lordprice Collection/Alamy; **p. 433**: Wikimedia Commons; pd; **p. 434**: Bettmann/Corbis; **p. 439**: The Walters Art Museum, Baltimore; **p. 442 (left)**: Library of Congress; **(right)**: Private Collection/J. T. Vintage/Bridgeman Images; **p. 444**: Granger Collection; **p. 448**: Granger Collection; **p. 451 (left and right)**: Library of Congress; **p. 454 (left)**: Granger Collection; **(right)**: Library of Congress.

PART 4: p. 461: The Stapleton Collection/The Bridgeman Art Library; **p. 462**: Civil War Archive/ The Bridgeman Art Library.

CHAPTER 13: p. 464: The Oregon Trail, 1869 (oil on canvas), Bierstadt, Albert (1830-1902)/Butler Institute of American Art, Youngstown, OH, Gift of Joseph G. Butler III 1946/Bridgeman Images; **p. 468**: Library of Congress. **p. 470:** Image copyright © The Metropolitan Museum of Art. Image source: Art Resource, NY; **p. 475**: Private Collection/Peter Newark American Pictures/Bridgeman Art Library; **p. 478**: MPI/Getty Image; **p. 484**: Granger Collection; **p. 487**: American Antiquarian Society, Worcester, Massachusetts/Bridgeman Images.

CHAPTER 14: p. 496: Granger Collection; **p. 498**: American Antiquarian Society, Worcester, Massachusetts/Bridgeman Art Library; **p. 501**: Art Resource; **p. 504**: Granger Collection; **p. 507**: Granger Collection; **p. 509**: Granger Collection; **p. 513**: akg-images/The Image Works; **p. 519**: Private Collection/ Peter Newark American Pictures/Bridgeman Art Library; **p. 521**: Private Collection/Peter Newark American Pictures/Bridgeman Art Library; **p. 525**: Granger Collection.

CHAPTER 15: p. 530: Chicago Historical Museum; **p. 535**: Buyenlarge/Getty Images; **p. 538**: Bettmann/ Corbis; **p. 540**: Private Collection/The Stapleton Collection/Bridgeman Art Library; **p. 545**: Library of Congress; **p. 546**: Library of Congress; **p. 548**: Library of Congress; **p. 549**: Library of Congress; **p. 553**: Beinecke Rare Book and Manuscript Library, Yale University/Wikimedia Commons; **p. 555**: Library of Congress; **p. 556**: Boston Athenaeum/Bridgeman Art Library; **p. 558**: Library of Congress; **p. 560**: Library of Congress; **p. 562**: Library of Congress; **p. 566**: Library of Congress; **p. 570**: National Archives.

CHAPTER 16: p. 578: Smithsonian American Art Museum, Washington, DC/Art Resource; **p. 581**: Granger Collection; **p. 587**: Library of Congress; **p. 589**: Library of Congress; **p. 595**: Library of Congress; **p. 596**: Bettmann/Corbis; **p. 597**: Granger Collection; **p. 606**: Library of Congress; **p. 608**: Library of Congress.

INDEX

Page numbers in *italics* refer to illustrations.